Fodor's 200

W9-DCA-867

CARIBBEAN
PORTS OF CALL

**Where to Stay and Eat
for All Budgets**

**Must-See Sights
and Local Secrets**

Ratings You Can Trust

Portions of this book appear in Fodor's The Complete Guide to Caribbean Cruises.

Fodor's Travel Publications   New York, Toronto, London, Sydney, Auckland
www.fodors.com

FODOR'S CARIBBEAN PORTS OF CALL

Editor: Douglas Stallings

Editorial Production: Astrid deRidder, Eric Wechter

Editorial Contributors: Diane Bair, Carol M. Bareuther, John Bigley, Cheryl Blackerby, Linda Coffman, Marvette Darien, Lynne Helm, Clint Hill, Michele Joyce, Lynda Lohr, Maribeth Mellin, Elise Meyer, Paris Permenter, Vernon O'Reilly Ramesar, Elise Rosen, Eileen Robinson Smith, Jordan Simon, Lan Sluder, Roberta Sotonoff, Kerry Speckman, Mark Sullivan, Robin Barr Sussman, Jim and Cynthia Tunstall, Jeff Van Fleet, Chelle Koster Walton, CiCi Williamson, Pamela Wright, Jane E. Zarem

Maps: David Lindroth, *cartographer;* Bob Blake and Rebecca Baer, *map editors*

Design: Fabrizio La Rocca, *creative director;* Guido Caroti, *art director;* Melanie Marin, *senior photo editor*

Production/Manufacturing: Angela McLean

Cover Photo: Holland America Line

ISBN 978–1–4000–1802–4

ISSN 1090–7343

SPECIAL SALES

This book is available for special discounts for bulk purchases for sales promotions or premiums. Special editions, including personalized covers, excerpts of existing books, and corporate imprints, can be created in large quantities for special needs. For more information, write to Special Markets/Premium Sales, 1745 Broadway, MD 6-2, New York, New York 10019, or e-mail specialmarkets@randomhouse.com.

AN IMPORTANT TIP & AN INVITATION

Although all prices, opening times, and other details in this book are based on information supplied to us at press time, changes occur all the time in the travel world, and Fodor's cannot accept responsibility for facts that become outdated or for inadvertent errors or omissions. So **always confirm information when it matters,** especially if you're making a detour to visit a specific place. Your experiences—positive and negative—matter to us. If we have missed or misstated something, **please write to us.** We follow up on all suggestions. Contact the Caribbean Ports of Call editor at editors@fodors.com or c/o Fodor's at 1745 Broadway, New York, New York 10019.

PRINTED IN THE UNITED STATES OF AMERICA

10 9 8 7 6 5 4 3 2 1

Be a Fodor's Correspondent

Your opinion matters. It matters to us. It matters to your fellow Fodor's travelers, too. And we'd like to hear it. In fact, we *need* to hear it.

When you share your experiences and opinions, you become an active member of the Fodor's community. That means we'll not only use your feedback to make our books better, but we'll publish your names and comments whenever possible. Throughout our guides, look for "Word of Mouth," excerpts of your unvarnished feedback.

Here's how you can help improve Fodor's for all of us.

Tell us when we're right. We rely on local writers to give you an insider's perspective. But our writers and staff editors—who are the best in the business—depend on you. Your positive feedback is a vote to renew our recommendations for the next edition.

Tell us when we're wrong. We're proud that we update most of our guides every year. But we're not perfect. Things change. Hotels cut services. Museums change hours. Charming cafés lose charm. If our writer didn't quite capture the essence of a place, tell us how you'd do it differently. If any of our descriptions are inaccurate or inadequate, we'll incorporate your changes in the next edition and will correct factual errors at fodors.com *immediately.*

Tell us what to include. You probably have had fantastic travel experiences that aren't yet in Fodor's. Why not share them with a community of like-minded travelers? Maybe you chanced upon a beach or bistro or took a great shore excursion that you don't want to keep to yourself. Tell us why we should include it. And share your discoveries and experiences with everyone directly at fodors.com. Your input may lead us to add a new listing or highlight a place we cover with a "Highly Recommended" star or with our highest rating, "Fodor's Choice."

Give us your opinion instantly at our feedback center at www.fodors.com/feedback. You may also e-mail editors@fodors.com with the subject line "Caribbean Ports of Call Editor." Or send your nominations, comments, and complaints by mail to Caribbean Ports of Call Editor, Fodor's, 1745 Broadway, New York, NY 10019.

You and travelers like you are the heart of the Fodor's community. Make our community richer by sharing your experiences. Be a Fodor's correspondent.

Bon Voyage!

Tim Jarrell, Publisher

CONTENTS

MAPS AND CHARTS

ABOUT THIS BOOK

What's in this Book

Up front you'll find a **Cruise Primer**, with some basic information about cruising and cruise ships.

Cruising the Caribbean gives you the low-down on the cruise lines that regularly ply the waters of the Caribbean. This section will help you understand what to expect on your cruise.

Ports of Embarkation gives you background on the most important U.S. ports for joining a cruise, including suggestions for where to stay and eat, and what you might want to do if you spend an extra day or two there before or after your cruise.

Ports of Call gives you our best advice on what to do in each major Caribbean cruise port if you want to go your own way, as well as a rundown of our favorite shore excursions offered by most ships if you don't.

Disagree with any of our choices? Care to nominate a place or suggest that we rate one more highly? Visit our feedback center at www.fodors.com/feedback.

Budget Well

Hotel and restaurant price categories from ¢ to $$$$ are defined in the opening pages of each chapter. For attractions, we always give standard adult admission fees; reductions are usually available for children, students, and senior citizens. Want to pay with plastic? **AE, D, DC, MC, V** following restaurant and hotel listings indicate if American Express, Discover, Diner's Club, MasterCard, and Visa are accepted.

Restaurants

Unless we state otherwise, restaurants are open for lunch and dinner daily. We mention dress only when there's a specific requirement and reservations only when they're essential or not accepted—it's always best to book ahead.

Hotels

Hotels have private bath, phone, TV, and air-conditioning and operate on the European Plan (a.k.a. EP, meaning without meals), unless we specify that they use the Continental Plan (CP, with a Continental breakfast), Breakfast Plan (BP, with a full breakfast), or Modified American Plan (MAP, with breakfast and dinner) or are all-inclusive (including all meals and most activities). We always list facilities but not whether you'll be charged an extra fee to use them, so when pricing accommodations, find out what's included.

Many Listings

★	Fodor's Choice
★	Highly recommended
⊠	Physical address
♁	Directions
⌑	Mailing address
☎	Telephone
📠	Fax
⊕	On the Web
✉	E-mail
▨	Admission fee
☉	Open/closed times
►	Start of walk/itinerary
Ⓜ	Metro stations
▭	Credit cards

Hotels & Restaurants

⊡	Hotel
↳	Number of rooms
⚲	Facilities
⑩	Meal plans
✕	Restaurant
⚑	Reservations
⌂	Dress code
↘	Smoking
⚎	BYOB
✕⊡	Hotel with restaurant that warrants a visit

Outdoors

⚐	Golf
⚠	Camping

Other

☾	Family-friendly
⊞	Contact information
⇨	See also
⊠	Branch address
☞	Take note

Cruise Primer

"My wife and I (late 60s) went on three different cruises 15 or so years ago . . . We are planning on going on a Caribbean cruise for about 9 days in the next month or two. How has cruising changed over those 15 years? What differences can we expect? Thanks in advance."

–Gerhardt

"We were going crazy trying to decide on which island to vacation. Then, a waitress at a local restaurant suggested a cruise . . . So, here we are, never having considered cruising before and seeing all the choices—wow! Do we ever need help!"

–tabcourt

By Linda
Coffman

IF YOU'VE NEVER BEEN ON A CRUISE BEFORE, it's tempting to ask, "What's so special about a cruise vacation?" It's a good question. Until the age of the airplane, ocean travel was simply a means to get to your far-flung destination—often the only way. But even in the early decades of the 20th century, venerable ocean liners such as the *Normandie* offered the occasional round-trip cruise to an exotic locale.

The passengers on the earliest cruises didn't have a fun-in-the-sun mindset as they sailed to faraway ports. They sailed to broaden their horizons and learn about ports of call that couldn't be reached by overland travel. Perhaps they booked a cruise to Panama to observe the construction of the canal or, like the *Normandie*'s passengers, were bound for Brazil and the daring excitement of Carnival.

Regardless of *why* they were cruising, early cruisers steamed toward the unfamiliar with many fewer comforts than contemporary passengers. On the *Normandie,* air-conditioned comfort was available only in the ship's first-class dining room, though at least passengers could find relief from Rio's heat by taking a dip in one of the era's few outdoor swimming pools at sea. In those days, if an ocean liner had a permanent swimming pool, it was often indoors and deep in the hull.

Carnival Cruise Line executives like to reminisce about the tiny "gyms" on their early ships, which were converted ocean liners, and then point to how far ship designs have evolved. I remember them well. It was even difficult to find the casino on Carnival's first "Fun Ship" *Mardi Gras,* let alone locate the indoor swimming pool. That's hardly the case today. Designed for contemporary travelers and tastes, modern cruise ships carry passengers amid conveniences unheard of in the heyday of the North Atlantic ocean liner or even in the earliest vessels permanently dedicated to cruises. As over 11 million passengers discovered when they went to sea in 2005, there's a lot to like on ships these days.

The allure of a modern sea cruise is its ability to appeal to a wide range of vacationers as a safe and convenient way to travel. Today's cruise ships are lively and luxurious floating resorts that offer something to satisfy the expectations of almost everyone. The first thing you'll find is that although cruise ships differ dramatically in the details and how they craft and deliver the cruise experience, most ships have the same basic features. And although the decisions and considerations in booking one cruise over another can be complex, the more you know about cruise travel in general, the better prepared you will be when it comes to making your choices.

BEFORE YOU GO

To expedite your pre-boarding paperwork, some cruise lines have convenient forms on their Internet Web sites. As long as you have your reservation number, you can provide the required immigration information, pre-reserve shore excursions, and even indicate any special requests from the comfort of your home. Less "wired" cruise lines might mail pre-boarding paperwork to you or your travel agent for completion after you make your final payment and request that you return the forms by mail or fax. No matter how you submit them, be sure to make hard copies of any forms you fill out and bring them with you to the pier to smooth the embarkation process.

Documents

It is every passenger's responsibility to have proper identification. If you arrive at the port without it, you may not be allowed to board, and the line will issue no fare refund. Most travel agents know the requirements and can guide you to the proper agency to obtain what you need if you don't have it.

Everyone must have proof of citizenship and identity to travel abroad. For American citizens on cruises to the Bahamas and the Caribbean, that means a valid passport. As of January 2008, all Americans traveling to the Caribbean and the Bahamas by sea as well as air may be required to carry a valid passport in order to return to the United States. While most cruise-ship passengers have not been required to have a valid passport— even to visit countries such as Barbados and Belize that normally require incoming tourists to have them—that will certainly change in the future, though the date may be pushed off further. And if your cruise begins in a far-flung port such as Barbados or Grenada, you will need your passport for the flight there as well. Moreover, should you miss the ship due to flight delays or other complications (or if you must depart from your cruise early), you will need your passport to fly to the next port to join your ship or to fly home. Additionally, some countries to which cruise ships call, including Brazil, require visas for all passengers.

Children under the age of 18, when they are not traveling with both parents, almost always require a letter of permission from the absent parent(s). Airlines, cruise lines, and immigration agents can deny minor children initial boarding or entry to foreign countries without proper proof of identification and citizenship *and* a notarized permission letter from absent or noncustodial parents. Your travel agent or cruise line can help with the wording of such a letter.

Getting or Renewing a Passport

In the past, cruise lines sailing to the Caribbean rarely asked to see the passports of American passengers. Since that policy is now changing, you should apply for a passport as far in advance of your cruise as possible. The process usually takes at least eight weeks and can take much longer during very busy periods. If your passport is delayed, you can still expedite your passport application if you are traveling within two weeks by paying an additional fee of $60 (in addition to the regular passport fee) and appearing in person at a regional passport office. You can also expedite a passport application that is already in progress if you are traveling within the next two weeks by calling the U.S. Passport Office. Several passport expediting services will handle your entire application for you (for a hefty fee, of course) and can get you a passport in as few as 72 hours.

U.S. Passport Information **U.S. Department of State** ☎877/487-2778 ⊕http://travel. state.gov/passport.

📶 U.S. Passport & Visa Expediters **A. Briggs Passport & Visa Expeditors** ☎ 800/806-0581 or 202/338-0111 ⊕ www.abriggs.com. **American Passport Express** ☎ 800/455-5166 or 800/841-6778 ⊕ www.americanpassport.com. **Passport Express** ☎ 800/362-8196 ⊕ www.passportexpress.com. **Travel Document Systems** ☎ 800/874-5100 or 202/638-3800 ⊕ www.traveldocs.com. **Travel the World Visas** ☎ 866/886-8472 or 301/495-7700 ⊕ www.world-visa.com.

What to Pack

As far as clothing goes, cruise wear falls into three categories: casual, informal, and formal. Cruise documents should include information indicating how many evenings fall into each category. You will know when to wear what by reading your ship's daily newsletter—each evening's dress code will be prominently announced.

For the day, you'll need casual wear. For warm-weather cruises, you'll typically need swimwear, a cover-up, and sandals for pool and beach. Time spent ashore touring and shopping calls for shorts topped with T-shirts or polo shirts and comfy walking shoes. Conservative is a rule to live by, and mix-and-match will save room in your suitcase. Forget denim, which is too hot, and concentrate on lighter fabrics that will breathe in the Caribbean heat. At night, casual means khaki-type slacks and nice polo or sport shirts for men. Ladies' outfits are sundresses, skirts and tops, or pants outfits. By sticking to two or three complementary colors and a few accessories, you can mix up tops and bottoms for a different look every night.

Informal dress is a little trickier. It applies only to evening wear and can mean different things depending on the cruise line. Informal for women is a dressier dress or pants outfit; for men it almost always includes a sport coat and sometimes a tie. Check your documents carefully.

Formal night means dressing up, but these days even that is a relative notion. You will see women in everything from simple cocktail dresses to elaborate glittering gowns. A tuxedo (either all black or with white dinner jacket) or dark suit is required for gentlemen. If you have been a "Mother-of-the-Bride" lately, chances are your outfit for the wedding is just perfect for formal night. For children, Sunday-best is entirely appropriate.

Men can usually rent their formal attire from the cruise line, and if they do so, it will be waiting when they board. Be sure to make these arrangements in advance; your travel agent can get the details from the cruise line. But if you are renting a tux, buy your own studs: a surefire way to spot a rented tuxedo is by the inexpensive studs that come with it. Also, many men with a little "girth" consider a vest more comfortable than a cummerbund.

An absolute essential for women is a shawl or light sweater. Aggressive air-conditioning can make public rooms uncomfortable, particularly if you are sunburned from a day at the beach.

Put things you can't do without—such as prescription medication, spare eyeglasses, toiletries, a swimsuit, and change of clothes for the first day—in your carry-on. Most cruise ships provide soap, shampoo, and conditioner, so you probably won't need those.

And plan carefully. In fact, we'd strongly advise you to make a list so you don't forget anything.

Accessibility Issues

As recently as the early 1990s, "accessibility" on a cruise ship meant little more than a few inside staterooms set aside for passengers with mobility issues. Most public restrooms and nearly all en suite bathrooms had a "step-over" threshold. Newer ships are more sensitive to the needs of passengers with disabilities, but many older ships still have physical barriers in both cabins and public rooms. And once you get off the ship—particularly in some Caribbean ports—your problems will be compounded.

All cruise lines offer a limited number of staterooms designed to be wheelchair- and scooter-accessible. Booking a newer vessel will generally assure more choices. On newer ships, public rooms are generally more accessible, and more facilities have been planned with wheelchair users in mind. Auxiliary aids, such as flashers for the hearing impaired and buzzers for visually impaired passengers, as well as lifts for swimming pools and hot tubs, are available upon request. However, more than the usual amount of preplanning is necessary for smooth sailing if you have special needs.

For example, when a ship is unable to dock—as is the case in Grand Cayman, for instance—passengers are taken ashore on tenders that are sometimes problematic even for the able-bodied to negotiate under adverse conditions. Some people with limited mobility may find it difficult to embark or disembark the ship when docked due to the steep angle of gangways during high or low tide at certain times of day. In some situations, crew members may offer assistance that involves carrying guests, but if the sea is choppy when tendering is a necessity, that might not be an option.

Passengers who require continuous oxygen or have service animals have further hurdles to overcome. You can bring both aboard a cruise ship, but your service animal may not be allowed to go ashore with you if the port has strict laws regarding animal quarantines.

Insurance

We believe that comprehensive trip insurance is especially valuable if you're booking a very expensive or complicated trip (particularly to an isolated region) or if you're booking far in advance. Who knows what could happen six months down the road? But whether or not you get insurance has more to do with how comfortable you are assuming all that risk yourself.

Comprehensive travel policies typically cover trip-cancellation and interruption, letting you cancel or cut your trip short because of a personal emergency, illness, or, in some cases, acts of terrorism in your destination. Such policies also cover evacuation and medical care. Some also cover you for trip delays because of bad weather or mechanical problems as well as for lost or delayed baggage. Another type of coverage to look for is financial default—that is, when your trip is disrupted because a tour operator, airline, or cruise line goes out of business. Generally you must buy this when you book your trip or shortly thereafter, and it's only available to you if your operator isn't on a list of excluded companies.

If you're going abroad, consider buying medical-only coverage at the very least. Neither Medicare nor some private insurers cover medical expenses anywhere outside of the United States (including time aboard a cruise ship, even if it leaves from a U.S. port). Medical-only policies typically reimburse you for medical care (excluding that related to preexisting conditions) and hospitalization abroad, and provide for evacuation. You still have to pay the bills and await reimbursement from the insurer, though.

Expect comprehensive travel insurance policies to cost about 4% to 7% or 8% of the total price of your trip (it's more like 8%–12% if you're over age 70). A medical-only policy may or may not be cheaper than a comprehensive policy. Always read the fine print of your policy to make sure that you are covered for the risks that are of most concern to you. Compare several policies to make sure you're getting the best price and range of coverage available.

🚩 U.S. Travel Insurers **Access America** ☎ 800/729-6021 ⊕ www.accessamerica. com. **CSA Travel Protection** ☎ 800/873-9855 ⊕ www.csatravelprotection.com. **HTH Worldwide** ☎ 610/254-8700 or 888/243-2358 ⊕ www.hthworldwide.com. **Travelex Insurance** ☎ 800/228-9792 ⊕ www.travelex-insurance.com. **Travel Guard International** ☎ 715/345-0505 or 800/826-4919 ⊕ www.travelguard.com. **Travel Insured International** ☎ 800/243-3174 ⊕ www.travelinsured.com.

ARRIVING & EMBARKING

Most cruise-ship passengers fly to the port of embarkation. If you book your cruise far enough in advance, you'll be given the opportunity to purchase an air-and-sea package, which may, or may not, save you money on your flight. You might get a lower fare by booking your flight independently, so it's a good idea to check for the best fare available.

If you buy an air-and-sea package from your cruise line, a uniformed cruise line agent will meet you to smooth your way from airport to pier. You will need to claim your own bags and give them to the transfer driver so they can be loaded on the bus. Upon arrival at the pier, luggage is automatically transferred to the ship for delivery to your cabin. The cruise line ground transfer system can also be available to independent fliers. However, be sure to ask your travel agent how much it costs; you may find that a taxi or shuttle service is less expensive and more convenient.

In addition to the busiest embarkation ports such as Miami, Fort Lauderdale, and New York City, cruises now leave from less-familiar port cities all around the East and Gulf coasts. Galveston and Port Canaveral have become major home ports in recent years and are considered now to be among the nation's top 10 cruise ports. Many people prefer to drive to these ports if they are close enough to home; happily, secure parking is always available, either within the port itself or nearby.

Boarding

1

Once the planning, packing, and anticipation are behind them, veteran cruise passengers sometimes view embarkation day as anticlimactic. However, for first-time cruise travelers, embarking on their first ship can be more than exhilarating—it can be downright intimidating. What exactly can you expect?

Check-In

Once inside the cruise terminal, you'll see a check-in line. Actual boarding time is often scheduled for noon, but some cruise lines will begin processing early arrivals and then direct them to a "holding" area. During check-in, you will be asked to produce your documents and any forms you were sent to complete ahead of time, plus proof of citizenship and a credit card (to cover onboard charges). You are issued a boarding card that often also doubles as your stateroom "key" and shipboard charge card. At some point—either before you enter the check-in area or before proceeding to the ship—you and your hand luggage will pass through a security procedure similar to those at airports.

The lines for check-in can be long, particularly at peak times. If check-in starts at noon but continues to 4 PM, you can expect lines to trail off as the boarding deadline approaches. Everyone is anxious to get on board and begin their vacation, so if you arrive at one of the busy periods, keep in mind that this is not the time to get cranky if you have to wait.

Boarding the Ship

Once boarding begins, you will inevitably have your first experience with the ship's photographer and be asked to pose for an embarkation picture. It only takes a second, so smile. You are under no obligation to purchase any photos taken of you during the cruise, but they are nice souvenirs.

Procedures vary somewhat once you are greeted by staff members lined up just inside the ship's hull; however, you'll have to produce your boarding card and, possibly, a picture ID for the security officer. At some point, either at the check-in desk or when boarding the ship for the first time, you may be photographed for security purposes—your image will display when your boarding card is "swiped" into a computer as you leave and reboard the ship in ports of call. Depending on the cruise line, you will be directed to your cabin, or a steward will relieve you of your carry-on luggage and accompany you. Stewards on high-end cruise lines not only show you the way, but hand you a glass of champagne as a welcome-aboard gesture. However, if you board early, don't be surprised if you are told cabins are not "ready" for occupancy—passageways to accommodations may even be roped off. In that case you can explore the ship, sample the luncheon buffet, or simply relax until an announcement is made that you can go to your cabin.

ON BOARD

Check out your cabin to make sure that everything is in order. Try the plumbing and set the air-conditioning to the temperature you prefer. Your cabin may feel warm while docked but will cool off when the ship is under way. You should find a copy of the ship's daily schedule in the cabin. Take a few moments to look it over—you will want to know what time the muster drill takes place (a placard on the back of your cabin door will indicate directions to your emergency station), as well as meal hours and the schedule for various activities and entertainments.

Rented tuxedoes are either hanging in the closet or will be delivered sometime during the afternoon; Bon Voyage gifts sent by your friends or travel agent usually appear as well. Be patient if you are expecting deliveries, particularly on mega-ships. Cabin stewards participate in the ship's turnaround and are extremely busy, although yours will no doubt introduce himself at the first available opportunity. It will also be a while before your checked luggage arrives, so your initial order of business is usually the buffet, if you haven't already had lunch. Bring along the daily schedule to check over while you eat.

While making your way to the Lido buffet, no doubt you'll notice bar waiters offering trays of colorful and exotic drinks, often in souvenir glasses that you can keep. Beware—they are not complimentary! If you choose one, you will be asked to sign for it. Again, like the photos, you are under no obligation to purchase.

Do your plans for the cruise include booking shore excursions and indulging in spa treatments? The most popular tours sometimes sell out, and spas can be very busy during sea days, so your next stops should be the Shore Excursion Desk to book tours and the spa to make appointments.

Dining room seating arrangements are another matter for consideration. Some people like to check the main dining room to determine where their table is located. If it is not to your liking, or if you requested a large table and find yourself assigned to a small one, you will want to see the head waiter. He will be stationed in a lounge with his charts handy to make changes. The daily schedule will indicate where and when to meet with him. If you plan to dine in the ship's specialty restaurant, make those reservations as soon as possible to avoid disappointment.

Paying for Things on Board

Let's step back a moment and take a look at what happened when you checked in at the pier. Because a cashless society prevails on cruise ships, an imprint was made of your credit card, or you had to place a cash deposit for use against your onboard charges. Then you were issued a charge card that usually doubles as your stateroom "key." Most onboard expenditures are charged to your shipboard account with your signature as verification, with the possible exception of casino gaming—even so, you can often get "cash advances" against your account from the casino cashier.

An itemized bill is provided at the end of the voyage listing your purchases. In order to avoid surprises, it is a good idea to set aside your charge slips and request an interim printout of your bill from the Purser to insure accuracy. Should you change your mind about charging onboard purchases, you can always inform the Purser and pay in cash or traveler's checks instead. If your cash deposit was more than you spent, you will receive a refund.

Tipping

One of the most delicate—yet frequently debated—topics of conversation among cruise passengers involves the matter of tipping. Who do you tip? How much? What's "customary" and "recommended"? Should parents tip the full amount for children or is just half adequate? Why do you have to tip at all?

When transfers to and from your ship are a part of your air-and-sea program, gratuities are generally included for luggage handling. In that case, do not worry about the interim tipping. However, if you take a taxi to the pier and hand over your bags to a stevedore, be sure to tip him. Treat him with respect and pass along at least $5.

During your cruise, room service waiters generally receive a cash tip of $1 to $3 per delivery. A 15% to 18% gratuity will automatically be added to each bar bill during the cruise. If you use salon and spa services, a similar percentage might be added to the bills there as well. If you dine in a specialty restaurant, you may be asked to provide a one-time gratuity for the service staff.

There will be a "Disembarkation Talk" on the last day of the cruise that explains tipping procedures. If you are expected to tip in cash, small white "tip" envelopes will appear in your stateroom that day. If you tip in cash, you usually give the tip envelope directly to each person on the last night of the cruise. Tips generally add up to about $10 to $12 per person per day. You tip the same amount for each person who shares the cabin, including children, unless otherwise indicated.

Most cruise lines now either automatically add gratuities to passengers' onboard charge accounts or offer the option. If that suits you, then do nothing further. However, you are certainly free to adjust the amounts up or down to more appropriate levels or ask that the charge be removed altogether if you prefer distributing cash gratuities.

Dining

All food, all the time? Not quite, but it is possible to literally eat away the day and most of the night on a cruise. A popular cruise directors' joke is, "You came on as passengers, and you will be leaving as cargo." Although it is meant in fun, it does contain a ring of truth. Food—tasty and plentiful—is available 24 hours a day on most cruise ships, and the dining experience at sea has reached almost mythical proportions. Perhaps it has something to do with legendary midnight buffets, the absence of menu prices, or maybe it's the vast selection and availability.

Restaurants

Every ship has at least one main restaurant and a Lido, or casual, buffet alternative. Increasingly important are specialty restaurants. Meals in the primary and buffet restaurants are included in the cruise fare, as are round-the-clock room service, midday tea and snacks, and late-night buffets. Most mainstream cruise lines levy a surcharge for dining in alternative restaurants that may, or may not, also include a gratuity, although there generally is no additional charge on luxury cruise lines.

You may also find a pizzeria or a specialty coffee bar on your ship—increasingly popular favorites cropping up on ships old and new. Although pizza is complimentary, expect an additional charge for specialty coffees at the coffee bar and, quite likely, in the dining room as well. You will also likely be charged for sodas and drinks during meals other than iced tea, regular coffee, tap water, and fruit juice.

There is often a direct relationship between the cost of a cruise and the quality of its cuisine. The food is very sophisticated on some (mostly expensive) lines, among them Crystal, Cunard, Seabourn, and Silversea. In the more moderate price range, Celebrity Cruises gained renown for the culinary stylings of French chef Michel Roux, who acted as a consultant to the line and set the standard for fine dining. The trend toward featuring specialty dishes and even entire menus designed by acclaimed chefs has spread throughout the cruise industy; however, on most mainstream cruise lines, the food is the quality that you would find in any good hotel banquet—perfectly acceptable but certainly not great.

Dinner Seatings

If your cruise ship has traditional seatings for dinner, the one decision that may set the tone for your entire cruise is your dinner seating. Which is best? Early dinner seating is generally scheduled between 6 and 6:30 PM, while late seating can begin from 8:15 to 8:45 PM. So the "best" seating depends on you, your lifestyle, and your personal preference.

Families with young children and older passengers often choose an early seating. Early seating diners are encouraged not to linger too long over dessert and coffee because the dining room has to be readied for late seating. Late seating is viewed by some passengers as more romantic and less rushed.

Cruise lines understand that strict schedules no longer satisfy the desires of all modern cruise passengers. Many cruise lines now include alternatives to the set schedules in the dining room, including casual dinner menus in their buffet facilities where more flexibility is allowed in dress and mealtimes. À la carte restaurants are showing up on more ships and offer yet another choice, though usually for an additional charge.

Open seating is primarily associated with more upscale lines; it allows passengers the flexibility to dine any time during restaurant hours and be seated with whomever they please.

Led by Norwegian Cruise Line and Princess Cruises, more contemporary and premium cruise lines are exploring adaptations of open seating to offer variety and a more personalized experience for their passengers. Carnival Cruise Lines and Holland America Line have added a twist with four seating times instead of the usual two, plus casual evening dining in the Lido buffet.

Drinking on Board

1

IT'S HARD TO AVOID THE SHIP'S BARS since they are social centers, but alcoholic drinks are not usually included in your cruise fare, and bar bills can add up quickly. Drinks at the captain's welcome-aboard cocktail party and at cocktail parties held specifically for past-cruisers are usually free. But if you pick up that boldly colored welcome-aboard cocktail as your ship pulls away from the dock, you may very well be asked to sign for it, and the cost will then be added to your shipboard account.

You should expect to pay about the same for a drink on board a cruise ship that you would pay in a bar at home: $3 to $4 for a domestic beer, $4 to $9 for a cocktail, $5 to $9 for a glass of wine, $1.25 to $2 for a soft drink. On virtually all ships, an automatic 15% gratuity will be added to your tab. What most people don't consider is that specialty coffees are also added to your bar tab, so if you order a cappuccino—and on some ships that applies even if it's in the dining room after dinner—you'll see a charge of $2 to $4 on your bar bill.

To save money on your bar bill, you can follow a few simple strategies. In lounges, request the less-expensive bar brands or the reduced-price drink-of-the-day. On some ships, discounted "beverage cards" for unlimited fountain soft drinks and/or a set number of mixed drinks are available.

In international waters there are, technically, no laws against teenage drinking, but almost all ships now require passengers to be over 21 to purchase alcoholic beverages.

CHANGING TABLES Some cruise lines advise that, although dining preferences may be requested by your travel agent, no requests are guaranteed. Table assignments are generally not confirmed until embarkation; however, every effort is made to satisfy all guests. Should there be a problem, see the maître d' for assistance. Changes after the first evening are generally discouraged, so if you want to change your seating or table, meet with dining room staff and iron out problems on embarkation day. Check the daily program for time and location.

Special Diets

Cruise lines make every possible attempt to insure dining satisfaction. If you have special dietary considerations—such as low-salt, kosher, or food allergies—be sure to indicate them well ahead of time and check to be certain your needs are known by your waiter once on board. In addition to the usual menu items, "spa," low-calorie, low-carbohydrate, or low-fat selections, as well as children's menus are usually available. Requests for dishes not featured on the menu can often be granted if you ask in advance.

Wine

Wine typically costs about what you would expect to pay at a nice lounge or restaurant in a resort or at home (depending on where you live). Wine by the bottle is a more economical choice at dinner than ordering it by the glass. Any wine you don't finish will be kept for you and served the next night. Gifts of wine or champagne ordered from the cruise line (either by you, a friend, or your travel agent) can be taken to the dining room. Wine from any other source will incur a "corkage" fee of approximately $8 to $10 per bottle.

The Captain's Table

Legend has it that a nouveau riche passenger's response to an invitation to dine with the captain during a round-the-world cruise was, "I didn't shell out all those bucks to eat with the help!" Although there are some cruise passengers who decline invitations to dine at the captain's table, there are far more who covet such an experience. You will know you have been included in that exclusive coterie when an embossed invitation arrives in your stateroom on the day of a formal dinner. RSVP as soon as possible—if you are unable to attend, someone else will be invited in your place.

Who is invited? If you are a frequent repeat cruiser, the occupants of an owner's suite, or if you hail from the captain's hometown or speak his native language, you may be considered. Honeymoon couples are sometimes selected at random, as are couples celebrating a golden wedding anniversary. Attractive, unattached female passengers often round out an uneven number of guests. Requests made by travel agents on behalf of their clients sometimes do the trick.

Entertainment

It's hard to imagine, but in the early years of cruise travel, shipboard entertainment consisted of little more than poetry readings and recitals that exhibited the talents of fellow passengers. Those bygone days of sedate amusements in an intimate setting have been replaced by lavish showrooms where sequined and feathered showgirls strut their stuff on stage amid special effects not imagined in the past.

Seven-night Caribbean cruises usually include two original production shows. One of these might be a Las Vegas–style extravaganza and the other a best-of-Broadway show featuring old and new favorites from the Great White Way. Other shows highlight the talents of individual singers, dancers, magicians, comedians, and even acrobats. Don't be surprised if you are plucked from the audience to take the brunt of a comedian's jokes or act as the magician's temporary assistant. Sit in the front row if appearing onstage appeals to you.

Whether it is relegated to a late-afternoon interlude between bingo and dinner, or a featured evening highlight, the Passenger Talent Show is often a "don't miss" production. From pure camp to stylishly slick, what passes for talent is sometimes surprising but seldom boring. Stand-up comedy is generally discouraged; however, passengers who want their performance skills to be considered should answer the call for auditions and plan to rehearse the show at least once.

Enrichment programs have become a popular pastime at sea. It may come as a surprise that port lecturers on many large contemporary cruise ships offer more information on shore tours and shopping than insight into the ports of call. If more cerebral presentations are important to you, consider a cruise on a line that features stimulating enrichment programs and seminars at sea. Speakers can include destination-oriented historians, popular authors, business leaders, radio or television personalities, and even movie stars.

Lounges & Nightclubs

If you find the show lounge stage a bit intimidating and want to perform in a more intimate venue, look for karaoke. Singing along in a lively piano bar is another shipboard favorite for would-be crooners. Some passengers even take the place of the ship's pianist during breaks to demonstrate their skill.

Other lounges might feature easy-listening music, jazz, or combos for pre- and post-dinner social dancing. Later in the evening, lounges pick up the pace with music from the 1950s and '60s; clubs aimed at a younger crowd usually have more contemporary dance music during the late-night hours.

Casinos

A sure sign that your ship is in international waters is the opening of the casino. On most ships, lavish casinos pulsate with activity. The most notable exceptions are the family-oriented ships of Disney Cruise Line, which shun gaming in favor of more wholesome pastimes.

On ships that feature them, the rationale for locating casinos where most passengers must pass either through or alongside them is obvious—the unspoken allure of winning. In addition to slot machines in a variety of denominations, cruise-ship casinos might feature roulette, craps, and a variety of poker games—Caribbean Stud Poker, Let It Ride, Texas Hold 'Em, and blackjack, to name a few. Cruise lines strive to provide fair and professional gambling entertainment and supply gaming guides that set out the rules of play and betting limits for each game.

Casino hours vary based on the itinerary or location of the ship; most are required to close while in port, while others may be able to offer 24-hour slot machines and simply close table games. Every casino has a cashier, and you may be able to charge a cash advance to your onboard account, for a fee.

Other Entertainment

Most vessels have a room for screening movies. On older ships and some newer ones, this is often a genuine cinema-style movie theater, while on other ships it may be just a multipurpose room. Over the course of a weeklong voyage a dozen films may be screened, each repeated several times. Theaters are also used for lectures, religious services, and private meetings. The latest twist in video programming can be found on some Princess, Disney, and Carnival ships—huge outdoor LED screens where movies, music video concerts, news channels, and even the ship's activities are broadcast for passengers lounging poolside.

With a few exceptions, cruise ships equip their cabins with closed-circuit TVs showing movies (continuously on some newer ships), shipboard lectures, news channels, and regular programs (thanks to satellite reception). Ships with in-cabin VCRs or DVDs usually provide a selection of movies at no charge (a deposit is sometimes required).

Most medium and large ships have video arcades, and nearly all ships now have computer centers.

Sports & Fitness

Onboard sports facilities might include a court for basketball, volleyball, tennis—or all three—a jogging track, or even an in-line skating track. Some ships are even offering innovative and unexpected features, such as rock-climbing walls, bungee trampolines, and surfing pools on some Royal Caribbean ships. For the less adventurous, there's always table tennis and shuffleboard.

Naturally, you will find at least one swimming pool and, possibly, several. Cruise-ship pools are generally on the small side—more appropriate for cooling off than doing laps—and the majority contain filtered salt water. But some are elaborate affairs, with waterslides. Princess Grand-class ships have challenging, freshwater "swim against the current" pools for swimming enthusiasts who want to get their low-impact exercise while on board.

Golf is a perennial seagoing favorite of players who want to take their games to the next level and include the Caribbean's most beautiful and challenging courses on their scorecards. Shipboard programs can include clinics, use of full-motion golf cages, and even individual instruction from resident pros using state-of-the-art computer analysis. Once ashore, escorted excursions include everything needed for a satisfying round of play, including equipment and tips from the pro, and the ability to schedule tee times at exclusive courses.

Fitness Centers
Cruise vacations can be hazardous to your waistline if you are not careful. Eating "out" for all meals and sampling different cuisines tend to pile on unaccustomed calories. But shipboard fitness centers have become ever more elaborate, offering state-of-the-art exercise machines, treadmills, and stair steppers, not to mention weights and weight machines. As a bonus, many fitness centers with floor-to-ceiling windows have the world's most inspiring sea views.

For guests who prefer a more social atmosphere as they burn off sinful chocolate desserts, there are specialized fitness classes for all levels of ability. High-impact, energetic aerobics are not for everyone, but any class that raises the heart rate can be toned down and tailored to individual capabilities. Stretching classes help you warm up for a light jog or brisk walk on deck, and there are even sit-for-fitness classes for mature passengers or those with delicate joints. Fees are usually charged for specialty classes, such as Pilates, spinning, and yoga. Personal trainers are usually on board to get you off on the right foot, also for a fee.

Health & Safety at Sea

SAFETY BEGINS WITH YOU, the passenger. Once settled into your cabin, locate life vests and review posted emergency instructions. Make sure vests are in good condition and learn to secure them properly. Make certain the ship's purser knows if you have a physical infirmity that may hamper a speedy exit from your cabin so that in an emergency he or she can quickly dispatch a crew member to assist you. If you're traveling with children, be sure that child-size life jackets are placed in your cabin.

Within 24 hours of embarkation, you'll be asked to attend a mandatory lifeboat drill. Do so and listen carefully. If you're unsure about how to use your vest, now is the time to ask. Only in the most extreme circumstances will you need to abandon ship—but it has happened. The time you spend learning the procedure may serve you well in a mishap.

In actuality, the greatest danger facing cruise-ship passengers is fire. All cruise lines must meet international standards for fire safety, which require sprinkler systems, smoke detectors, and other safety features. Fires on cruise ships are not common, but they do happen, and these rules have made ships much safer. You can do your part by *not* using an iron in your cabin and taking care to properly extiguish smoking materials. Never throw a lit cigarette overboard—it could be blown back into an opening in the ship and start a fire.

All large ships have an infirmary to deal with minor medical emergencies, but these infirmaries are not suitable for dealing with major procedures. The ship's doctor should be able to treat you as well as any general practitioner or clinic ashore for minor problems. For really complicated medical conditions, such as a heart attack or appendicitis, the ship's medical team evacuates passengers to the nearest hospital ashore. While at sea, evacuation expenses can rise as fast as the helicopter that whisks the patient away. You'll need supplementary insurance to cover evacuation costs.

Two of the most prevalent diseases that spread through cruise-ship populations are influenza and noroviruses that cause intestinal and stomach upsets. Annual influenza vaccination is the primary method for preventing influenza and its complications. But to prevent all kinds of infections—including noroviruses—frequent hand-washing is also essential; take advantage of the dispensers of hand-sanitizer, and use it when entering any dining room. Or slip into the restroom to wash your hands with soap and hot water.

Spas

With all the usual pampering and service in luxurious surroundings, simply being on a cruise can be a stress-reducing experience. Add to that the menu of spa and salon services at your fingertips and you have a recipe for total sensory pleasure. Spas have also become among the most popular of shipboard areas.

Some spa offerings sound good enough to eat. A Milk-and-Honey Hydrotherapy Bath, Coconut Rub and Milk Ritual Wrap or Float, and a Javanese Steam Wrap incorporating cinnamon, ginger, coffee, sea salt, and honey are just a few of the tempting items found on spa menus. Not quite as exotic sounding, other treatments and services are nonetheless therapeutic for the body and soul. Steiner Leisure is the largest spa and salon operator at sea (the company also operates the Mandara- and the Greenhouse-brand spas), with facilities on more than 100 cruise ships worldwide.

In addition to facials, manicures, pedicures, massages, and sensual body treatments, other hallmarks of Steiner Leisure are salon services and products for hair and skin. Founded in 1901 by Henry Steiner of London, a single salon prospered when Steiner's son joined the business in 1926 and was granted a Royal Warrant as hairdresser to Her Majesty Queen Mary in 1937. In 1956, Steiner won its first cruise-ship contract to operate the salon on board the ships of the Cunard Line. By the mid-1990s, Steiner Leisure began taking an active role in creating shipboard spas offering a wide variety of wellness therapies and beauty programs for both women and men.

Shipboard Services

Communications

Just because you are out to sea does not mean you have to be out of touch. Ship-to-shore telephone calls can cost $5 to $15 a minute, so it makes more economic sense to use e-mail to remain in contact with your home or office. Most ships have basic computer systems, while some newer vessels offer more high-tech connectivity—even in-cabin hookups or wireless connections for either your own laptop computer or one you can rent on board. Expect charges in the 50¢- to $1-per-minute range for the use of these Internet services. Ships usually offer some kind of package so that you get a reduced per-minute price if you pay a fee up front.

The ability to use your own mobile phone from the high seas is a relatively new alternative that is gaining popularity. It's usually cheaper than using a cabin phone if your ship offers the service, but it can still cost up to $4 or $5 a minute. It's a rather ingenious concept, with the ship acting as a cell "tower" in international waters—you use your own cell phone and your own number when roaming at sea. When in port, depending on the agreements your mobile service-provider has established, you may be able to connect to local networks. Rates for using the maritime service, as well as any roaming charges from Caribbean islands, are established by your mobile service carrier and are worth checking into before you leave home.

Laundry & Dry Cleaning

Most cruise ships offer valet laundry and pressing (and some also offer dry-cleaning) service. Expenses can add up fast, especially for laundry, since charges are per item and the rates are similar to those charged in hotels. If doing laundry is important to you and you do not want to send it out to be done, many cruise ships have a self-service laundry room

Crime on Ships

CLOSE UP

CRIME ABOARD CRUISE SHIPS has occasionally become headline news, thanks in large part to a few well-publicized cases. Most people never have any type of problem, but you should exercise the same precautions aboard ship that you would at home. Keep your valuables out of sight—on big ships virtually every cabin has a small safe. Don't carry too much cash ashore, use your credit card whenever possible, and keep your money in a secure place, such as a front pocket that's harder to pick. Single women traveling with friends should stick together, especially when returning to their cabins late at night. When assaults occur, it often comes to light that excessive drinking of alcohol is a factor. Be careful about whom you befriend, as you would anywhere, whether it's a fellow passenger or a member of the crew. Don't be paranoid, but do be prudent.

Your cruise is a wonderful opportunity to leave everyday responsibilities behind, but don't neglect to pack your common sense. After a few drinks it might seem like a good idea to sit on a railing or lean over the rail to get a better view of the ship's wake. Passengers have been known to fall. "Man overboard" is more likely to be the result of carelessness than criminal intent.

(which usually features an iron and ironing board in addition to washer and dryer). If you book one of the top-dollar suites, laundry service may be included for no additional cost. Upscale ships, such as those in the Radisson Seven Seas Cruises, Silversea Cruises, and Seabourn fleets, have complimentary self-service launderettes. On other cruise lines, such as Princess Cruises, Oceania Cruises, Carnival Cruise Lines, Disney Cruise Line, and Holland America Line (except Vista-class ships), you can do your own laundry for about $3 or less per load. None of the vessels in the Royal Caribbean or Celebrity Cruises fleets has self-service laundry facilities.

Shore Excursion Desk

Manned by a knowledgeable staff, the Shore Excursion Desk can offer not only the sale of ship-sponsored tours, but may also be the place to learn more about ports of call and garner information to tour independently. Although staff members and the focus of their positions vary widely, the least you can expect is basic information and port maps. Happily, some shore excursion staff members possess a wealth of information and share it without reservation. On some ships the port lecturer may emphasize shopping and "recommended" merchants, with little to impart regarding sightseeing or the history and culture of ports.

DISEMBARKATION

All cruises come to an end eventually, and it hardly seems fair that you have to leave when it feels like your vacation has just begun, but leave you must. The disembarkation process actually begins the day before you arrive at your ship's home port. During that day your cabin steward delivers special luggage tags to your stateroom, along with customs forms and instructions.

The night before you disembark, you'll need to set aside clothing to wear the next morning when you leave the ship. Many people dress in whatever casual outfits they wear for the final dinner on board, or change into travel clothes after dinner. Also, do not forget to put your passport or other proof of citizenship, airline tickets, and medications in your hand luggage.

After you finish packing, attach your new luggage tags (they are color- or number-coded according to post-cruise transportation plans and flight schedules). Follow the instructions provided and place the locked luggage outside your stateroom door for pickup during the hours indicated.

A statement itemizing your onboard charges is delivered before you arise on disembarkation morning. Plan to get up early enough to check it over for accuracy, finish packing your personal belongings, and vacate your stateroom by the appointed hour. Any discrepancies in your onboard account should be taken care of before leaving the ship, usually at the Purser's Desk.

Room service is not available on most ships on the last day; however, breakfast is served in the main restaurant as well as the buffet. After breakfast, there is not much to do but wait comfortably in a lounge or on deck for your tag color or number to be called. Disembarkation procedures can sometimes be drawn out by passengers who are unprepared. This is no time to abandon your patience or sense of humor.

Remember that all passengers must meet with customs and immigration officials before disembarkation, either on the ship or in the terminal. Procedures vary and are outlined in your instructions. In some ports, passengers must meet with the officials at a specified hour (usually very early) in an onboard lounge; in other ports, customs forms are collected in the terminal and passports/identification papers are examined there as well.

Once in the terminal, locate your luggage and proceed to your motor coach, taxi, or retrieve your vehicle from the parking lot.

Customs & Duties

U.S. Customs

Before a ship docks, each individual or family must fill out a customs declaration. If your purchases total less than the limit for your destination, you will not need to itemize them. Be prepared to pay whatever duties are owed directly to the customs inspector, with cash or check. Be sure to keep receipts for all purchases; and you may be asked to show officials what you've bought.

U.S. Customs pre-clears ships sailing into and out of some ports—it's done on the ship before you disembark. In other ports you must collect your luggage from the dock, then stand in line to pass through the inspection point. This can take up to an hour.

1

ALLOWANCES You're always allowed to bring goods of a certain value back home without having to pay any duty or import tax. There's also a limit on the amount of tobacco and liquor you can bring back duty-free, and some countries have separate limits for perfumes; for exact figures, check with your customs department. The values of so-called "duty-free" goods are included in these amounts. When you shop abroad—and in the Caribbean, this means all islands except for Puerto Rico, which is considered a part of the U.S. for customs purposes—save all your receipts as customs inspectors may ask to see them as well as the items you purchased. If the total value of your goods is more than the duty-free limit, then you'll have to pay a tax (most often a flat percentage) on the value of everything beyond that limit.

Individuals entering the United States from the Caribbean are allowed to bring in $800 worth of duty-free goods for your personal use ($1,600 from the U.S. Virgin Islands), including 1 liter of alcohol (2 liters if one was produced in the Caribbean and 5 liters from the USVI), two cartons of cigarettes and 100 non-Cuban cigars. Antiques and original artwork are also duty-free.

SENDING Although you probably won't want to spend your time looking for a
PACKAGES HOME post office, you can send packages home duty-free, with a limit of one parcel per addressee per day (except alcohol or tobacco products or perfume worth more than $5). You can mail up to $200 worth of goods for personal use; label the package "personal use" and attach a list of the contents and their retail value. If the package contains your used personal belongings, mark it "personal goods returned" to avoid paying duty on your laundry. You may also send up to $100 worth of goods as a gift with the same limit of one parcel per addressee per day ($200 from the U.S. Virgin Islands); mark the package "unsolicited gift." Items you mailed do not affect your duty-free allowance on your return.

NONCITIZENS Non–U.S. citizens who are returning home within hours of docking may be exempt from all U.S. Customs duties. Everything you bring into the United States must leave with you when you return home, though. When you reach your own country, you will have to pay duties there.

Cruising the Caribbean

WORD OF MOUTH

"Have never been on a cruise before. Looking for some advice on a Caribbean Cruise . . . What is a good cruise line for a beginner cruiser age 28 for activities and night life? Is it best to book flight separate or package together? Any tips I need to be aware of? Thanks."

—Newmarket Cruiser

"For first time cruisers, the variety of cruise lines can be confusing . . . Which cruise line is more appropriate for the 35–55 age group? Which one has the most relaxed atmosphere (no formal nights)? Looking for fun, relaxation, casual elegance, not stuffy and country clubby, some activities and a casino but nothing over the top. Also what's your favorite itinerary on these cruise lines?"

—bosco

By Linda
Coffman

MORE CRUISE SHIPS PLY THE WATERS of the Caribbean than any other spot on Earth. Some are huge ships carrying more than 3,000 passengers; some are "midsize" ships welcoming about 1,500 cruisers; and others are comparatively small ships on which you'll find yourself with 300 or fewer other passengers. There are fancy ships and party ships, ships with sails, ships that pride themselves on the numbers of ports they visit, and ships that provide so much activity right on board that you hardly have time or inclination to go ashore. In peak season, it's not uncommon for thousands of passengers to disembark from several ships into a small island port on the same day—a phenomenon not always enjoyed by locals. With such an abundance of cruise ships in this area, however, you can choose the ship and the itinerary that suit you best.

CHOOSING YOUR CRUISE

Some of the best "islands" in the Caribbean are the ones that float and move—they are called cruise ships. Just as Caribbean islands have distinct histories and cultures, cruise ships also have individual personalities. Determined by their size, the year they were built, and their style, on one hand, they can be bold, brassy, and exciting—totally unlike home, but a great place to visit. Big ships offer stability and a huge variety of activities and facilities. On the other hand, small ships feel intimate, like private clubs or, more appropriately, personal yachts. For every big-ship fan there is someone who would never set foot aboard a "floating resort." Examine your lifestyle—there's sure to be a cruise ship to match your expectations.

After giving some thought to your itinerary and where in the Caribbean you might wish to go, the ship you select is the most vital factor in your Caribbean cruise vacation, since it will not only determine which islands you will visit, but also how you will see them. Big ships visit major ports of call such as St. Thomas, St. Maarten/St. Martin, Nassau, and San Juan; when they call at smaller islands with shallower ports, passengers must disembark aboard shore tenders (small boats that ferry dozens of passengers to shore at a time). Or they may skip these smaller ports entirely. Small and midsize ships can visit smaller islands, such as St. Barths, St. Kitts, or Tortola, more easily; passengers are often able to disembark directly onto the pier without having to wait for tenders to bring them ashore.

Itineraries

You'll want to give some consideration to your ship's Caribbean itinerary when you are choosing your cruise. The length of the cruise will determine the variety and number of ports you visit, but so will the type of itinerary and the point of departure. **Round-trip cruises** start and end at the same point and usually explore ports close to one another; **one-way cruises** start at one point and end at another and range farther afield.

Most cruises to the Bahamas, Mexico's Mayan Riviera, and other points in the Caribbean are loop cruises. On Caribbean itineraries, you often have a choice of U.S. mainland departure points. Ships sailing out of San Juan, Puerto Rico, can visit up to five ports in seven days, while loop cruises out of Florida can reach up to four ports in the same length of time. The Panama Canal can also be combined with a Caribbean cruise: the 50-mi (83-km) canal is a series of locks, which make up for the height difference between the Caribbean and the Pacific. Increasingly popular are partial transit cruises that enter the Panama Canal, anchor in Gatun Lake for a short time, and depart through the same set of locks.

Eastern Caribbean Itineraries

Eastern Caribbean itineraries consist of two or three days at sea as well as stops at some of the Caribbean's busiest cruise ports. A typical cruise will usually take in three or four ports of call, such as St. Thomas in the U.S. Virgin Islands, San Juan, or St. Maarten/St. Martin, along with a visit to the cruise line's "private" island for beach time. Every major cruise line has at least two of those popular islands on its itineraries. Some itineraries might also include others, such as Tortola, Dominica, Barbados, St. Kitts, or Martinique.

Western Caribbean Itineraries

Western Caribbean itineraries embarking from Galveston, Houston, Fort Lauderdale, Miami, Port Canaveral, New Orleans, Mobile, or Tampa might include Belize, Cozumel or the Costa Maya Cruise Port in Mexico, Key West, the Cayman Islands, or Jamaica—all perfect choices for passengers who enjoy scuba diving and snorkeling and look forward to exploring Mayan ruins. Ships often alternate itineraries in the Western Caribbean with itineraries in the Eastern Caribbean on a weekly basis, offering the ability to schedule a 14-night back-to-back cruise without repeating ports.

Southern Caribbean Itineraries

Southern Caribbean cruises tend to be longer in duration with more distant ports of call. They often originate in a port that is not on the U.S. mainland. Embarking in San Juan, for example, allows you to reach the lower Caribbean on a seven-day cruise with as many as four or five ports of call. Southern Caribbean itineraries might leave Puerto Rico for the Virgin Islands, Guadeloupe, Grenada, Curaçao, Barbados, Antigua, St. Lucia, Martinique, or Aruba. Smaller ships leave from embarkation ports as far south as Bridgetown, Barbados, and cruise through the Grenadines. Every major cruise line offers some Southern Caribbean itineraries, but these cruises aren't as popular as Western and Eastern Caribbean cruises.

Other Itineraries

In recent years, shorter itineraries have grown in appeal to time-crunched and budget-constrained travelers. If you are planning your first cruise in the tropics, a short sailing to the Bahamas allows you to test your appetite for cruising before you take a chance on a longer and more expensive cruise. Embarking at Fort Lauderdale, Miami, Port Canaveral, or Jacksonville, you will cruise for three to five days, taking in at least one port of call (usually Nassau or Freeport in the Bahamas) and possibly a visit to a "private" island or Key West. Four- and five-night cruises may also include a day at sea. Cruises also depart from ports farther north on the east coast; you might depart from Charleston, Baltimore, or New York City and cruise to Bermuda or the Bahamas.

When to Go

Average year-round temperatures throughout the Caribbean are 78°F–85°F, with a low of 65°F and a high of 95°F; downtown shopping areas always seem to be unbearably hot. Low season runs from approximately mid-September through mid-April. Many travelers, especially families with school-age children, make reservations months in advance for the most expensive and most crowded summer months and holiday periods; however, with the many new cruise ships that have entered the market, you can often book fairly close to your departure date and still find room, although you may not get exactly the kind of cabin you would prefer. A summer cruise offers certain advantages: temperatures are virtually the same as in winter (cooler on average than in parts of the U.S. mainland), island flora is at its most dramatic, the water is smoother and clearer, and although there is always a breeze, winds are rarely strong enough to rock a ship. Some Caribbean tourist facilities close down in summer, however, and many ships move to Europe, Alaska, or the northeastern United States.

Hurricane season runs a full six months of the year—from June 1 through November 30. Although cruise ships stay well out of the way of these storms, hurricanes and tropical storms—their less-powerful relatives—can affect the weather throughout the Caribbean for days, and damage to ports can force last-minute itinerary changes.

Cruise Costs

The average daily price for Caribbean itineraries varies dramatically depending on several circumstances. The cost of a cruise on a luxury line such as Silversea or Seabourn may be three to four times the cost of a cruise on a mainstream line such as Carnival or even premium lines like Princess. When you sail will also affect your costs: published brochure rates are usually highest during the peak summer season and holidays. When snow blankets the ground and temperatures are in single digits, a Caribbean cruise can be a welcome respite and less expensive than land resorts, which often command top dollar in winter months.

Solo travelers should be aware that single cabins have virtually disappeared from cruise ships. Taking a double cabin can cost twice the advertised per-person rates (which are based on double occupancy). Some cruise lines will find same-sex roommates for singles; each then pays the per-person, double-occupancy rate.

Extras

In addition to the cost of your cruise there are further expenses to consider, such as airfare to the port city. These days, virtually all cruise lines offer air add-ons, which are sometimes, but not always, less expensive than the lowest available airline fare. Shore excursions can also be a substantial expense; the best shore excursions are not cheap. But if you skimp too much on your excursion budget you'll deprive yourself of an important part of the Caribbean cruising experience. Finally, there will be many extras added to your shipboard account during the cruise, includ-

Saving Money on Your Cruise Fare

YOU CAN SAVE ON YOUR CRUISE FARE in several ways. Obviously, you should shop around. Some travel agents will discount cruise prices, though this is becoming a thing of the past. One thing never changes—do not ever, under any circumstances, pay brochure rate. You can do better, often as much as half off published fares. These are a few simple strategies you can follow:

• Book early: Cruise lines discount their cruises if you book early, particularly during the annual "Wave" season between January and March.

• Cruise during the off-season: If you take a cruise during the latter months of hurricane season (especially October and November) or the period between Thanksgiving and Christmas, you'll often find specials.

• Book late: Sometimes you can book a last-minute cruise at substantial savings if the ship hasn't filled all its cabins.

• Choose accommodations with care: Cabins are usually standardized and location determines the fare. Selecting a lower category can result in savings while giving up nothing in terms of cabin size and features.

• Book a "guarantee": You won't be able to select your own cabin because the cruise line will assign you one in the category you book, but a "guarantee" fare can be substantially lower than a regular fare.

• Cruise with friends and family: Book a minimum number of cabins, and your group can generally receive a special discounted fare.

• Reveal your age and affiliations: Fare savings may be available for seniors and members of certain organizations, as well as cruise line stockholders.

• Cruise often: Frequent cruisers usually get discounts from their preferred cruise lines.

ing drinks (both alcoholic and nonalcoholic), activity fees (you pay to use that golf simulator), dining in specialty restaurants, spa services, and even cappuccino and espresso on most ships.

Tipping

Tipping is another add-on. At the end of the cruise, it's customary to tip your room steward, dining-room waiter, and the person who buses your table. You should expect to pay an average of $10 to $12 per person per day in tips. Most major cruise lines are moving away from the traditional method of tipping the service staff in cash at the end of the cruise, instead adding the recommended amount per day to your on-board account to cover tips, which you may adjust upward or downward according to the level of service you receive. Bar bills generally include an automatic 15%–18% gratuity, so the one person you don't need to tip is your bartender. Some cruise lines have gratuities-included policies, though some passengers tip for any extra services received anyway. Each cruise line offers guidelines.

CRUISE LINES

Seated in an airplane after a week of enjoying an exceptionally nice cruise, I overheard the couple behind me discussing their "dreadful" cruise vacation. What a surprise when they mentioned the ship's name. It was the one I'd just spent a glorious week on. I never missed a meal. They hated the food. My cabin was comfortable and cheery, if not large. Their identical accommodations resembled a "cave." One size definitely does not fit all in cruising. What's appealing to one passenger may be unacceptable to another. Ultimately, most cruise complaints arise from passengers whose expectations were not met. The couple I eavesdropped on were on the wrong cruise line and ship for them.

I enjoy cruises. Some have suited me more than others, but I've never sailed on a cruise that was completely without merit. Make no mistake about it: cruise lines have distinct personalities, but not all luxury or mainstream cruise lines are alike, although they will share many basic similarities. The cruise industry is a fluid one—that means that when new features are introduced, they may not be found on all ships, even those within the same cruise line. For instance, you won't find an ice skating rink on any but the biggest Royal Caribbean ships. However, most cruise lines attempt to standardize the overall experience throughout their fleets, which is why you'll find a water slide on every Carnival ship.

Just as trends and fashion evolve over time, cruise lines embrace the ebb and flow of change. To keep pace with today's lifestyles, some cruise lines strive to include something that will appeal to everyone on their ships. Others focus on narrower elements and are more traditional. Today's passengers have higher expectations and they sail on ships that are far superior to their predecessors. And they often do so at a much lower comparable fare than in the past.

So which cruise line is best? Only you can determine which is best for you. You won't find ratings by Fodor's—either quality stars or value scores. Why? Think of those people seated behind me on the airplane. Ratings are personal and heavily weighted to the reviewer's opinion. Your responsibility is to select the right cruise for you—no one knows your expectations better than you do yourself. It's your time, money, and vacation that's at stake. No matter how knowledgeable your travel agent is, how sincere your friends are, or what any expert can tell you, you are the only one who really knows what you like. The short wait for a table might not bother you because you would prefer a casual atmosphere with open seating; however, some people want the security of a set time at an assigned table served by a waiter who gets to know their preferences. You know what you are willing to trade off in order to get what you want.

The following Cruise Line Profiles offer a general idea of what you can expect in terms of overall experience, quality, and service from each major cruise line that operates in the Caribbean, Bermuda, and the Bahamas. You will want to compare the features of several cruise lines to determine which ones come closest to matching your needs. Then narrow them down further to a few that appeal most to you. Keep in mind that not all ships belonging to the cruise lines described in the following profiles are deployed in the Caribbean year-round; some head for Alaska and Europe during summer months and others call port cities on the Pacific coast their home year-round.

LUXURY CRUISE LINES
Comprising only 5% of the market, the exclusive luxury cruise lines, which include Crystal, Cunard, Regent Seven Seas, Seabourn, SeaDream, Silversea, and Windstar, offer high staff-to-guest ratios for personal service, superior cuisine in a single seating (except Crystal, with two assigned seatings and Cunard, with dual-class dining assignments), and a highly inclusive product with few onboard charges. These small and mid-size ships offer much more space per passenger than you will find on the mainstream lines' vessels. Lines differ in what they emphasize, with some touting luxurious accommodations and entertainment and others focusing on exotic destinations and onboard enrichment.

If you consider travel a necessity rather than a luxury and frequent posh resorts, then you will appreciate the extra attention and the higher level of comfort that luxury cruise lines offer.

Itineraries on these ships often include the big casino and most popular island beach resorts, but luxury ships also visit some of the more uncommon Caribbean destinations. With a shallow draft and intimate size, the smaller luxury ships can visit such ports as Anguilla, St. Barths, Tobago, and Jost Van Dyke and Virgin Gorda in the British Virgin Islands.

MAINSTREAM CRUISE LINES
More than 85% of the Caribbean is covered by 10 mainstream cruise lines. They offer the advantage of something for everyone and nearly every available sports facility imaginable. Some ships even have ice-skating rinks, 18-hole miniature golf courses, bowling alleys, and rock-climbing walls.

Generally speaking, the mainstream lines have two basic ship sizes—large cruise ships and mega-ships—in their fleets. These cruise ships have plentiful outdoor deck space, and many have a wraparound outdoor promenade deck that allows you to stroll or jog the ship's perimeter. In the newest vessels, traditional meets trendy. You'll find atrium lobbies and expansive sun and sports decks, picture windows instead of portholes, and cabins that open onto private verandas. For all their resort-style innovations, they still feature cruise-ship classics—afternoon tea, complimentary room service, and lavish pampering. The smallest ships carry 1,000 passengers or fewer, while the largest accommodate more than 3,000 passengers and are filled with diversions.

If you're into big, bold, brassy, and nonstop activity, these huge ships offer it all. The centerpiece of most mega-ships is a 3-, 5-, or even 11-story central atrium. However, these giant vessels are most readily distinguished by their profile: the boxy hull and superstructure rise as many as 14 stories out of the water and are capped by a huge sun or sports deck with a jogging track and one or more swimming pools. Some mega-ships have a traditional wraparound promenade deck. Picture windows are standard equipment, and cabins in the top categories have private verandas. From their casinos and discos to their fitness centers, everything is bigger and more extravagant than on other ships. You may want to rethink a cruise aboard one of these ships if you want a little downtime, since you'll be joined by 1,500 to 3,000 fellow passengers.

OTHER CRUISE LINES A few small cruise lines sail through the Caribbean and offer boutique to nearly bed-and-breakfast experiences. Notably, Cruise West, Star Clippers, Windjammer Barefoot Cruises, and relative newcomer easy-Cruise appeal to passengers who eschew mainstream cruises. Most of these niche vessels accommodate 200 or fewer passengers, and their focus is on soft adventure. Cruising between nearby ports and anchoring out so passengers can swim and snorkel directly from the ship, their itineraries usually leave plenty of time for exploring and other activities on- or offshore. Many of these cruises schedule casual enrichment talks that often continue on decks, at meals, and during trips ashore.

Carnival Cruise Lines

Carnival Cruise Lines has grown to be the largest and most successful cruise line in the world, with a fleet of 23 ships and no sign of slowing down. Today's Carnival is a decidedly different company from the one launched in 1972 by entrepreneur Ted Arison, who made a vacation experience once reserved for only the well-heeled accessible to nearly everyone. From a "fleet" consisting of one refitted transatlantic ocean liner, Carnival became the standard by which moderately priced cruise lines are measured. Not even its critics can deny that the line delivers on its promises. Brash and always fun, Carnival throws a great party. Activities and entertainment are nonstop, beginning just after sunrise and continuing well into the night. Food has been upgraded in recent years with the addition of menu items created by world-renowned French master chef George Blanc; it is plentiful and fairly diverse, better tasting and well presented, with healthful options. Dining in upscale supper clubs on the newest ships in the fleet rivals the best steak houses on land.

Cabins are spacious and comfortable, often as much as 50% larger than on other ships in this price category, and feature the "Carnival Comfort Bed" sleep system consisting of plush mattresses, luxury duvets, high-quality linens, and cushy pillows. Carnival's ships are like floating theme parks, though each one has a distinct personality. The effect is most exaggerated on the newer, bigger ships, including those in the Fantasy, Destiny, Spirit, and Conquest classes. Manned by staff members trained to keep passengers in shipshape form, Carnival's trademark spas and fitness centers are some of the largest and best-equipped at sea. Run year-round by professionals, dedicated "Camp Carnival" facilities include great playrooms and earn high marks for keeping young cruisers happy and content. "Club O2" are spacious teen clubs where kicking back is the order of the day.

Carnival cruises are popular with young single cruisers as well as with those older than 55. The line's offerings also appeal to parents cruising with their children. A choice of flexible dining options and casual family-friendly alternative restaurants is available on Carnival ships. Staggered dining-room schedules, which include a selection of four set evening mealtimes (5:45 or 6:15 PM and 8 or 8:30 PM), means the ships' galleys serve fewer meals at any one time. The result is better service and higher-quality food preparation. All ships offer something for everyone at all hours, including pizza and 24-hour room service.

Gratuities of $10 per passenger, per day are automatically added to onboard accounts and are distributed to stewards and waitstaff. Passengers may adjust the amount based on the level of service experienced. A 15% gratuity is automatically added to bar and beverage tabs.

Carnival Cruise Lines, 3655 N.W. 87th Ave., Miami, FL 33178-2428 305/599–2600 or 800/227–6482 www.carnival.com.

Celebrity Cruises

Celebrity Cruises has based its reputation on sleek ships and superior food. Style and layout vary from ship to ship, lending each a unique personality. In terms of size and amenities, Celebrity's vessels rival almost any in cruising, but with a level of refinement rare on bigger ships. In less than a decade, Celebrity won the admiration of its passengers and its competitors—who have copied its nouvelle cuisine and cigar clubs and hired its personnel (a true compliment). Celebrity rose above typical mass-market cruise cuisine by hiring chef Michel Roux as a consultant. While Roux is no longer affiliated with the line, his legacy remains. Menus are creative; both familiar and exotic dishes have been customized to appeal to American palates. All food is prepared from scratch, using only fresh produce and herbs, aged beef, and fresh fish— even the ice cream on board is homemade. Entertainment choices range from Broadway-style productions, captivating shows, and lively discos to Monte Carlo–style casinos and specialty lounges. Multimillion-dollar art collections grace the entire fleet, which merged with Royal Caribbean International in 1997.

Celebrity attracts everyone from older couples to honeymooners. Summertime children's programs are as good as those on any cruise line. Service is friendly and first class, rapid and accurate in the dining rooms. Waiters, stewards, and bartenders are enthusiastic, take pride in their work, and try to please.

Tip your cabin steward/butlers $3.50 per day; chief housekeeper 50¢ per day; dining-room waiter $3.50 per day; assistant waiter $2 per day; and restaurant manager 75¢ per day, for a total of $10.25 per person, per day. Passengers may adjust the amount based on the level of service experienced. A 15% service charge is added to all beverage checks. For children under 12, or the third or fourth person in the stateroom, half the above amounts is recommended. Gratuities are typically handed out on the last night of the cruise, but they may be charged to your shipboard account as well.

Celebrity Cruises, 1050 Caribbean Way, Miami, FL 33132-2096 305/539–6000 or 800/437–3111 800/437–5111 www. celebritycruises.com.

Costa Cruises

The Genoa-based Costa Crociere, parent company of Costa Cruises, had been in the shipping business for more than 100 years and in the passenger business for almost 50 years when it was bought by Airtours and Carnival Cruises in 1997; Carnival gained sole ownership of the line in 2000, but the ships retain their original flavor. Costa's Italian-inspired vessels bring the Mediterranean vitality of *La Dolce Vita* to far-flung regions of the Caribbean. The ships are a combination of classic and modern design. A new vessel-building program has brought Costa ships into the 21st century with innovative, large-ship designs that reflect their Italian heritage and style without overlooking the amenities expected by modern cruisers. Festive shipboard activities include some of Italy's favorite pastimes, such as games of boccie and a wacky toga party, yet there is also a nod to the traditional cruise-ship entertainment expected by North Americans. Supercharged social staffs work overtime to get everyone in the mood and encourage everyone to be a part of the action.

Passengers tend to be a little older—the average age is 54—and have an interest in all things Italian. You don't find a lot of first-time cruisers on Costa ships.

Suggested tipping guidelines are as follows: cabin steward, $3 per day; waiter, $3 per day; busboy, $1.50 per day; maître d' and head waiter, $1 per day. A 15% gratuity is added to beverage bills (including mineral water in the dining room). Gratuities are charged to your shipboard account for convenience but may be adjusted based on the level of service experienced.

🖅 *Costa Cruises, 200 S. Park Rd., Suite 200, Hollywood, FL 33021-8541* ☎ *954/266–5600 or 800/462–6782* 🖷 *954/266–2100* ⊕ *www.costacruises.com.*

Cruise West

The yachtlike vessels that make up Cruise West's Caribbean fleet are small, American-built and U.S.-registered coastal cruisers. With their shallow drafts and inflatable, motorized landing craft, they are well suited to exploring remote and otherwise inaccessible tropical waters. Cruises are billed as soft adventure and educational, and every sailing features at least one Cruise West Exploration Leader, an expert in the history, culture, and biology of destinations, who leads lectures and field trips. Schedules are flexible enough that captains can stop or make course changes for unexpected encounters with wildlife. Itineraries include a full range of organized shore excursions, one of which is complimentary in each port of call, but there are few other organized activities: there are no discos, casinos, or musical reviews aboard these diminutive vessels, and reading, socializing, and board games are the most popular activities. Sometimes local entertainers perform on board, and there may be movies in the dining room after dinner. These cruises don't sacrifice aesthetics, and such shipboard refinements as fine dining in a single open seating are emphasized, though service by the American staff is not of the white-glove variety. The dress requirements are as relaxed and casual as the onboard ambience—there is no need to pack dress-up finery. Passengers are typically older (often in their mid-sixties).

Gratuities are included in the cruise fare and additional tipping is not required or expected. No service charges are added to wine or bar bills.

Cruise West, 2301 5th Ave., Seattle, WA 98121 ☎ *206/441–8687 or 888/851–8133* ⊕ *www.cruisewest.com.*

Crystal Cruises

Crystal's two midsize ships stand out for their modern design, amenities, and spaciousness. Built to deliver the first-rate service and amenities expected from a luxury line, these vessels have many of the onboard facilities of a big ship. Crystal ships have long set standards for pampering—one reason these vessels often spend several days at sea rather than in port. White-glove service, stellar cuisine, and tasteful, understated surroundings create a comfortable cocoon for passengers. Large spas offer innovative therapies, body wraps, and exotic, Asian-inspired treatments by Steiner Leisure. Feng shui principles were scrupulously adhered to in their creation, so the spa areas are havens of serenity. To the typical panoply of cruise-ship diversions, Crystal adds enrichment opportunities that include destination-oriented lectures and talks by scholars, political figures, and diplomats; hands-on classes in music and art; and deluxe theme cruises that emphasize such topics as food and wine or the fine arts.

The food alone is a good enough reason to book a Crystal cruise. Dining in the main restaurants is an event starring Continental-inspired cuisine served by European-trained waiters. Off-menu item requests are honored when possible, and special dietary considerations are handled with ease. Casual poolside dining from the grills is offered on some evenings in a relaxed, no-reservations-required option. While two assigned dining-room seatings are advertised as an advantage that offers "flexibility," the reality is that open seating is the true mark of choice and the preferred option at this level of luxury cruising. If you haven't done so in advance, on embarkation day you can reserve a table to dine one night in each specialty restaurant, but don't dawdle until the last minute. Most passengers hurry to request reservations during the time allotted and if you wait, you may find a line has developed—one of the few lines you'll encounter on board—and all the choice dining times are already booked.

Crystal's target clientele is affluent and older but still active. On select cruises highly trained and experienced youth counselors are brought in to oversee activities for kids and teens, but this is not a particularly family-friendly cruise line. Baby food, high chairs, and booster seats are available upon request.

Staff are well trained, friendly, highly motivated, and thoroughly professional. However, Crystal's fares do not include tips, so the crew can be noticeably solicitous of gratuities. Suggested tipping guidelines are as follows: stewardess, $4 per passenger, per day (single travelers, $5 per day); senior waiter, $4 per passenger, per day; waiter, $3 per passenger, per day; butler (Penthouse Decks), $4 per passenger, per day. For specialty restaurants, $6 per person, per dinner is suggested. Gratuities for the maître d', headwaiter, assistant stewardess, and room service personnel are at your discretion. A 15% gratuity for bar drinks and wines is automatically added to bar checks. The suggested gratuity for Crystal Spa & Salon services is also 15%. Gratuities may be prepaid or charged to your shipboard account.

    Crystal Cruises, 2049 Century Park E, Suite 1400, Los Angeles, CA 90067 ☎ 310/785–9300 or 888/799–4625 🖷 310/785–9201 ⊕ www. crystalcruises.com.

Cunard Line

One of the world's most distinguished names in ocean travel since 1840, Cunard Line's history of deluxe transatlantic crossings and worldwide cruising is legendary for comfortable accommodations, excellent cuisine, and personal service. Though the line is now owned by Carnival, its high-end ships still carry on with a decidedly British sensibility. The line's newest ship, the *Queen Mary 2,* has a short season of Caribbean cruises, which are highly prized by fans of the line.

Entertainment has a strong English flavor, with nightly production shows or cabaret-style performances and even plays starring Great Britain's Royal Academy of Dramatic Arts alumni. An authentic pub adds to the British ambience, while a wide variety of musical styles can be found for dancing and listening in other bars and lounges. Cunard's fine enrichment programs are presented by expert guest lecturers in their fields. Classes vary by cruise and include a wide assortment of topics taught by top designers, master chefs, and artists. Even seamanship and navigation courses are offered to novice mariners. You can pre-plan your activities prior to departure by consulting the syllabus of courses available online at Cunard Line's Web site.

In the tradition of multiple-class ocean liners, dining-room assignments are made according to the accommodation category booked. The line's ships also have highly regarded specialty restaurants with menus by acclaimed chefs Daniel Boulud and Todd English. Discerning, well-traveled American and British couples from their late-30s to retirees are attracted by Cunard's traditional style and the notion of a cruise aboard an ocean liner. Resort-casual clothing prevails throughout the day, but Cunard vessels are ocean liners at heart and, as expected, are dressier than most cruise ships at night. Although most crew members are international rather than British, service is formal and sophisticated.

Suggested gratuities of $13 per person, per day (for Grill Restaurant accommodations) or $11 per person, per day (all other accommodations) are automatically charged to shipboard accounts for distribution to stewards and waiter staff. A 15% gratuity is added to beverage tabs for bar service. At passengers' discretion, gratuities for special services may be presented directly to individual crew members.

    Cunard Line, 24303 Town Center Dr., Valencia, CA 91355 ☎ 661/ 753–1000 or 800/728–6273 ⊕ www.cunard.com.

Disney Cruise Line

Disney Cruise Line launched its first ship, *Disney Magic,* in 1998, followed by her sister ship, *Disney Wonder,* in 1999. Dozens of the best ship designers, industry veterans, and Disney creative minds planned intensely for three years to produce these vessels, which make a positive impression on adults and children alike. Exteriors are reminiscent of the great ocean liners of the early 20th century, resplendent with two funnels and black hulls, but interiors are technologically up-to-the-minute and full of novel developments in dining, cabin, and entertainment facilities. Three- and four-night *Disney Wonder* cruises to the Bahamas can be coupled with a stay at Walt Disney World, or you can opt for a weeklong Caribbean cruise on *Disney Magic.* Passengers represent a cross-section of North Americans and Europeans of all ages, but there are certainly more kids on board than on many other cruise ships, and plenty of activities to keep them occupied.

Entertainment leans heavily on popular Disney themes and characters. Parents are actively involved in the audience with their children at production shows, movies, "live" character meetings, deck parties, and dancing in the family nightclub. Teens have a supervised, no-adults-allowed club space where they gather for activities and parties. For adults, there are traditional no-kids-allowed bars and lounges with live music, dancing, theme parties, and late-night comedy as well as daytime wine-tasting sessions, game shows, culinary arts and home entertaining demonstrations, and behind-the-scenes lectures on animation and filmmaking. Don't expect top chefs and gourmet food. This is Disney and the fare is all-American for the most part. Naturally, all restaurants have children's menus with an array of their favorite sandwiches and entrées. A bonus is complimentary soft drinks throughout the sailing available at beverage stations that are always open.

Suggested gratuities are calculated on a per-person/per-cruise rather than per-night basis and can be added to onboard accounts for convenience or offered in cash on the last night of the cruise. For the dining-room server, assistant server, head server, and stateroom host/hostess, guidelines are $32.50 for three-night cruises, $43.75 for four-night cruises, and $76.25 for seven-night cruises. Gratuities may be charged to your onboard account. Tips for room service delivery and the dining manager are at your discretion. A 15% gratuity is added to bar service tabs.

Disney Cruise Line, 210 Celebration Pl., Celebration, FL 34747 🕾 *407/566–3500 or 888/325–2500* ⊕ *www.disneycruise.com.*

easyCruise

Introduced in Europe with great fanfare by Stelios (like celebrities, he goes by one name), easyCruise is easily the quirkiest endeavor to hit the cruise industry. Stelios, known as a "serial" entrepreneur and the guiding force behind low-fare air carrier easyJet, has designed a cross between a traditional cruise ship and a ferry. Aimed at youthful travelers interested in island-hopping and sampling the local nightlife, itineraries are scheduled to arrive in port mid-morning, stay until the partying winds down, and then move on to the next destination. Rather than book an entire voyage, independent-minded passengers are offered the flexibility to book as few as two nights onboard the ship, embarking and departing in any scheduled port along the way. Stelios is said to be on the lookout for a south Florida home port, but until he finds an appropriate one, all cruises are confined to the Southern Caribbean, where passengers embark in such ports as Barbados and St. Maarten.

EasyCruise is able to offer rock-bottom pricing by eliminating all onboard frills and nearly all necessities. Be prepared to entertain yourself—there are no shows, no library, no casino. You won't find any formal entertainment at all. The best bet is to pack your own iPod, a good book, and a deck of playing cards. If dancing and karaoke are your thing, you'll find a DJ in action nightly and an occasional passenger participation game.

Passengers are encouraged to dine ashore because no meals are included in the cruise fare; initially, the only onboard meal options were a snack and sports bar, and then only for an extra charge; however, due to passenger demand, a more extensive shipboard dining experience has been developed, and an upgraded restaurant supplements the diner-quality snacks, sandwiches, and dessert items that have always been available. Still, think Starbucks and Ruby Tuesday in terms of dining. The best offerings are often found at breakfast, and you'll still shell out extra cash for all food and beverages. There is even a fee for housekeeping services—you'll pay for all cabin services, including fresh towels and bed linens. Fellow passengers on easyCruise are generally in their 20s, 30s, and 40s and don't seem to mind making their own beds.

Gratuities are up to your discretion.

☞ *easyCruise (UK) Ltd, The Rotunda, 42/43 Gloucester Crescent, London, NW1 7DL, UK ☎ 0906/292–9000 ⊕ www.easycruise.com.*

Holland America Line

Founded in 1873, Holland America Line (HAL) is one of the oldest names in cruising. Steeped in the traditions of the transatlantic crossing, its cruises are classic, conservative affairs renowned for their grace and gentility. Service is taken seriously: the line maintains a school in Indonesia to train staff members. Food is very good by cruise-ship standards, and presentations on Rosenthal china are creative. In response to the challenge presented by its competitors, Holland America has introduced a lighter side to its menus, including many pastas and "heart-healthy" dishes. Holland America passengers tend to be older and less active than those traveling on the ships of its parent line, Carnival; however, despite an infusion of younger adults and families on board, they remain refined without being stuffy or stodgy. As its ships attract a more youthful clientele, Holland America has taken steps to shed its "old folks" image, now offering stops at a private island in the Bahamas, trendier cuisine, a culinary arts center, and an expanded "Club Hal" children's program. Still, these are not party cruises, and Holland America has managed to preserve the refined and relaxing qualities that have always been its hallmark, even on sailings that cater more to younger passengers and families.

In late 2003 HAL initiated the "Signature of Excellence" program to raise product and service standards throughout the fleet; upgrades to all ships were complete by the end of 2006 and add significantly to the onboard experience. Pillow-top mattresses, 250-thread-count cotton bed linens, Egyptian-cotton towels, magnifying makeup mirrors, waffle and terry robes, fresh fruit baskets, flat-screen televisions, and DVD players are features of all accommodations. In addition, all suites have duvets on beds, fully stocked minibars, personalized stationery, and access to the exclusive Neptune Lounge where beverages, breakfast pastries, afternoon snacks, and evening canapés are available. Dining is enhanced by the reservations-only Pinnacle Grill on every ship, one-on-one service in the main dining rooms, and table-side beverage service in the Lido casual dining room. The spas have tranquil relaxation areas and trendy thermal suites furnished with heated tile chaises. Explorations Café, powered by *The New York Times,* combines a coffee bar, computer center, and cozy library–reading room complete with tabletop versions of the *Times'* infamous crossword puzzles.

Gratuities of $10 per passenger, per day are automatically added to onboard accounts to be distributed to stewards and waitstaff. Passengers may adjust the amount based on the level of service experienced. Tips for room service delivery and spa and salon services are at passengers' discretion. A 15% gratuity is added to bar service tabs.

Holland America Line, 300 Elliott Ave. W, Seattle, WA 98119 206/281–3535 or 800/577–1728 206/281–7110 www. hollandamerica.com.

MSC Cruises

With several seasons of Caribbean sailing behind it, MSC Cruises has outgrown its "newcomer" status in the region. More widely known as one of the world's largest cargo shipping companies, parent company Mediterranean Shipping Company has operated cruises with an eclectic fleet since the late 1980s but expanded their cruising reach by introducing graceful, medium-size ships in the Caribbean. Prices are toward the low end of the mainstream premium category.

While sailing Caribbean itineraries, MSC Cruises adopts activities that appeal to American passengers without abandoning those preferred by Europeans—prepare for announcements in Italian as well as in English. In addition to guest lecturers, computer classes, and cooking lessons featured in the onboard enrichment program, a popular option is Italian language classes. Nightly shows accentuate MSC Cruises' Mediterranean heritage—there might be a flamenco show in the main showroom and live music for listening and dancing in the smaller lounges. Dinner on MSC ships is a traditional seven-course event centered around authentic Italian fare. Menus list Mediterranean regional specialties and classic favorites prepared from scratch the old-fashioned way. In a nod to American tastes, broiled chicken breast, grilled salmon, and Caesar salad are always available in addition to the regular dinner menu.

Suggested amounts for gratuities covering services on board are approximately $8 to $12 per passenger, per day. MSC Cruises advises that the amount of a gratuity should naturally reflect the quality of services received. Gratuities are incorporated into all bar purchases.

�腺 *MSC Cruises, 6750 N. Andrews Ave., Fort Lauderdale, FL 33309* ☎ *954/772–6262 or 800/666–9333* ⊕ *www.msccruises.com.*

Norwegian Cruise Line

Norwegian Cruise Line (NCL) was established in 1966, when one of Norway's oldest and most respected shipping companies, Oslo-based Klosters Rederi A/S, acquired the *Sunward* and repositioned the ship from Europe to the then-obscure Port of Miami. With the formation of a company called Norwegian Caribbean Lines, the cruise industry as we know it today was born. NCL launched an entirely new concept with its regularly scheduled cruises to the Caribbean on a single-class ship, with an informal kind of luxury. No longer simply a means of transportation, the ship became a destination unto itself, offering guests an affordable alternative to land-based resorts. The *Sunward*'s popularity prompted other cruise lines to build ships to accommodate the burgeoning market, eventually turning Miami into the world's number one port of embarkation. NCL led the way with its fleet of sleek new ships. In another bold move, NCL purchased the former *France* in 1979 and rebuilt the grand ocean liner in Bremerhaven, Germany, for Caribbean cruising. Rechristened *Norway,* she assumed the honored position as flagship of the fleet and was retired from service in 2003. The late 1980s brought new ships and a new corporate name when Norwegian Caribbean Lines became Norwegian Cruise Line in 1987. NCL continued its expansion by acquiring other cruise lines, stretching and refurbishing older ships, and building new mega-ships, including the line's newest, two 2,400-berth "Freestyle Cruising" ships, *Norwegian Pearl* and *Norwegian Gem.*

Freestyle Cruising created a sensation in the industry when Asian shipping giant Star Cruises acquired NCL early in 2000—the new owners were confounded that Americans meekly conformed to rigid dining schedules and dress codes. All that changed with NCL's introduction of a host of flexible dining options that allow passengers to choose open seating in the main dining rooms or dine in any of a number of à la carte and specialty restaurants at any time and with whom they please. While the Freestyle Cruising concept now applies to the entire NCL fleet, you'll still see fewer options on some of the smaller, older ships. The line has even loosened the dress code to resort casual at all times and eased the disembarkation process by inviting passengers to relax in their cabins until it's time to leave the ship (instead of gathering in a lounge to wait for their numbers to be called). Noted for top-quality, high-energy entertainment and emphasis on fitness facilities and programs, NCL combines action and activities in a casual, free-flowing atmosphere. For children and teens, each NCL vessel offers the "Kid's Crew" program of supervised entertainment for young cruisers ages 2 through 17. An abundance of family-friendly staterooms interconnect in most categories, enabling families of nearly any size to find suitable accommodations. NCL's passenger list usually includes a wide range of ages, including families and couples, mostly from the United States and Canada.

NCL applies a service charge to passengers' shipboard accounts: $10 per passenger, per day for those 13 and older and $5 per day for children ages 3–12. A 15% gratuity is added to bar tabs and spa bills.

Norwegian Cruise Line, 7665 Corporate Center Dr., Miami, FL 33126 *305/436–4000 or 800/327–7030 ⊕ www.ncl.com.*

Oceania Cruises

This distinctive cruise line was founded by Frank Del Rio and Joe Watters, cruise industry veterans with the know-how to satisfy inquisitive passengers by offering interesting ports of call and upscale touches for fares much lower than you would expect. Oceania Cruises set sail in 2003 to carve a unique, almost "boutique" niche in the cruise industry by obtaining midsize "R-class" ships once part of the now-defunct Renaissance Cruises fleet.

Intimate and cozy public spaces reflect the importance of socializing on Oceania ships. Evening entertainment leans toward light cabaret, solo artists, music for dancing, and conversation with fellow passengers; however, you'll find lively karaoke sessions on the schedule as well. The sophisticated adult atmosphere is enhanced on sea days by a combo performing jazz or easy-listening melodies poolside. Several top cruise-industry chefs were lured away from other cruise lines to insure that the artistry of world-renowned master chef Jacques Pépin, who crafted 5-Star menus for Oceania, is properly carried out. The results are sure to please the most discriminating palate. Oceania serves some of the best food at sea, particularly impressive for a cruise line that charges far less than luxury rates. Intimate specialty restaurants require reservations, but there is no additional charge for the Italian restaurant or the steak house. While small, the spa, salon, and well-equipped fitness center are adequate for the number of passengers on board.

Varied, destination-rich itineraries are an important characteristic of Oceania Cruises, and most Caribbean sailings are in the 10- to 12-night range, which means more interesting, less-visited ports. Before arrival in ports of call, lectures are presented on the historical background, culture, and traditions of the islands. Oceania Cruises appeal to singles and couples from their late-30s to well-traveled retirees, who have the time for—and prefer—longer cruises. Most passengers are attracted to the casually sophisticated atmosphere, creative cuisine, and European service. Oceania Cruises are adult-oriented and not a good choice for families, particularly those traveling with infants and toddlers. No dedicated children's facilities are available; however, teenagers with sophisticated tastes (and who don't mind the absence of a video arcade) would enjoy the emphasis on intriguing ports of call.

For convenience, $11.50 per person, per day is added to onboard accounts for distribution to stewards and waitstaff and an additional $3.50 per person, per day is added for suite occupants where butler serv-

Drinking & Gambling Ages

CLOSE UP

MANY UNDERAGE PASSENGERS HAVE LEARNED to their chagrin that the rules that apply on land are also adhered to at sea. On most mainstream cruise ships you must be 21 in order to imbibe alcoholic beverages. There are exceptions—for instance, on cruises departing from countries where the legal drinking age is typically lower than 21. By and large, if you haven't achieved the magic age of 21, your shipboard charge card will be coded as booze-free, and bartenders won't risk their jobs to sell you alcohol.

Gambling is a bit looser, and 18-year-olds can try their luck on cruise lines such as Carnival, Celebrity, Holland America, Silversea, Norwegian, and Royal Caribbean; most other cruise lines adhere to the age-21 minimum. Casinos are trickier to patrol than bars, though, and minors who look "old enough" may get away with dropping a few coins in an out-of-the-way slot machine before being spotted on a hidden security camera. If you hit a big jackpot, you may have a lot of explaining to do to your parents.

ice is provided. Passengers may adjust the amount based on the level of service experienced. Bar bills add an automatic 18% to all beverage tabs for bartenders and servers.

📮 *Oceania Cruises, 8300 N.W. 33rd St., Suite 308, Miami, FL 33122* ☎ *305/514–2300 or 800/531–5658* ⊕ *www.oceaniacruises.com.*

Princess Cruises

Rising from modest beginnings in 1965, when it began offering cruises to Mexico with a single ship, Princess has become one of the world's best-known cruise lines. Its fleet sails to more destinations each year than any other major line, though many cruises depart from the West Coast of the United States and do not sail in the Caribbean. Princess was catapulted to stardom in 1977, when its flagship became the setting for *The Love Boat* television series, which introduced millions of viewers to the still-new concept of a seagoing vacation. The name and famous "seawitch" logo have remained synonymous with cruising ever since. While the recent addition of three medium-size vessels to the fleet offers a welcome smaller-ship choice, Princess more often follows the "big is better" trend when designing new ships. Even so, the line doesn't sacrifice quality for quantity when it comes to building beautiful vessels. Decor and materials are top-notch, and service, especially in the dining rooms, is of a high standard. In short, Princess is refined without being pretentious.

All Princess ships plying the Caribbean feature the line's innovative "Personal Choice Cruising" program, an individualized, unstructured style of cruising that gives passengers choice and flexibility in customizing their cruise experience—multiple dining locations, flexible entertainment, and affordable private balconies are all highlights. For traditionalists, one dining room is reserved for two assigned dinner seatings. Alternative restaurants are a staple throughout the fleet, but vary by ship class. Enrichment programs featuring guest lecturers and opportunities to learn new skills or crafts are welcome additions to a roster of adult activities, which still includes staples such as bingo and art auctions. You can even earn PADI scuba diving certification in just one week by participating in the "Open Water Diver" program during select sailings.

Princess passengers' average age is 45, and you see a mix of younger and older couples on board. For young passengers age 3 to 17, each Princess vessel has a playroom, teen center, and programs of supervised activities designed for different age-specific groups. The ships are some of the most accessible at sea, and passengers with disabilities can select from staterooms in a variety of categories that are tailored for their special needs.

Princess suggests tipping $10 per person, per day. Gratuities are automatically added to onboard accounts, which passengers can adjust at the purser's desk; 15% is added to bar bills.

⌂ *Princess Cruises, 24305 Town Center Dr., Santa Clarita, CA 91355-4999* ☎ *661/753–0000 or 800/774–6237* ⊕ *www.princess.com.*

Regent Seven Seas Cruises

Regent Seven Seas Cruises (RSSC) is part of Carlson Hospitality Worldwide, one of the world's major hotel-and-travel companies. The cruise line was formed in December 1994 with the merger of the one-ship Diamond Cruises and Seven Seas Cruises lines. From these modest beginnings, RSSC has grown into a major luxury player in the cruise industry, adopting the "Regent" label in early 2006. With the launch of the *Seven Seas Mariner* in March 2001, RSSC introduced the world's first all-suite, all-balcony cruise ship. *Seven Seas Voyager,* a second 700-passenger all-suite, all-balcony ship followed in April 2003. Subtle improvements throughout the fleet are ongoing, such as computer service with Wi-Fi capability for your own laptop and cell phone access, even when you are at sea. New bedding with down comforters and Egyptian cotton linens, Regent-branded bath amenities, flat-screen televisions, DVD players, and new clocks will be added to all accommodations. Top suites will also feature iPod music systems and Bose speakers.

The line's spacious ocean-view staterooms have the industry's highest percentage of private balconies; you'll always find open seating at dinner; tips are included in the fare and no additional tipping is expected. With an emphasis on Continental and regional cuisines, dining room menus may appear to be the usual Beef Wellington and Maine lobster, but in the hands of Regent Seven Seas chefs the results are outstanding. Specialty dining varies by ship within the fleet, but casual, Mediterranean-inspired bistro dinners are offered in the venues that serve as daytime casual Lido buffet restaurants. Regent has introduced an all-inclusive beverage policy that offers not only soft drinks and bottled water but also cocktails and select wines at all bars and restaurants throughout the ships. Activities are oriented toward onboard enrichment programs, socializing, and exploring the destinations on the itinerary. Spa and salon services are provided by the high-end Carita of Paris. Avoid disappointment by prearranging your preferred spa appointments and specialty restaurant reservations through the line's Web site. While RSSC's vessels are adult-oriented and do not have dedicated children's facilities, a "Club Mariner" youth program for children is offered on selected sailings. Although passengers tend to be older and affluent, they are quite active. Regent Seven Seas Cruises manages to provide a high level of personal service and sense of intimacy on small-to-midsize ships, which have the stability of larger vessels.

📖 *Regent Seven Seas Cruises, 1000 Corporate Dr., Suite 500, Fort Lauderdale, FL 33334* ☎ *954/776–6123 or 877/505–5370* 🖷 *954/772–3763* 🌐 *www.rssc.com.*

Royal Caribbean International

Imagine if the Mall of America were sent to sea. That's a fair approximation of what the mega-ships of Royal Caribbean International (RCI) are all about. These large-to-giant vessels are indoor-outdoor wonders, with every conceivable activity in a resortlike atmosphere, including atrium lobbies, shopping arcades, large spas, expansive sundecks, and rock-climbing walls. Several ships have such elaborate facilities as 18-hole miniature-golf courses, ice-skating rinks, and in-line skating tracks. Freedom-class ships, RCI's latest additions, and presently the world's largest cruise ships, even have the first surf parks at sea. These mammoth ships are quickly overshadowing the smaller vessels in Royal Caribbean's fleet, although RCI regularly rejuvenates older vessels, adding new facilities to mirror the latest trends, including plush new bedding that has been installed fleetwide. Happily, passengers now have five generations of mega-ships to choose from, including the prototype, the *Sovereign of the Seas,* which was completely renovated in late 2004.

The centerpiece of Royal Caribbean mega-ships is the multi-deck atrium, a hallmark that has been duplicated by many other cruise lines. The brilliance of this design is that all the major public rooms radiate from this central point, so you can learn your way around these huge ships within minutes of boarding. Ships in the Vision series (*Legend, Splendour, Enchantment, Grandeur,* and *Rhapsody of the Seas*) are especially bright and airy, with sea views almost anywhere you happen to be. The main problem with RCI's otherwise well-conceived vessels is that, when booked to over 100% capacity, there are too many people on board, making for an exasperating experience during embarkation, when tendering, and at disembarkation. However, waiting in lines and other small annoyances aside, Royal Caribbean is one of the best-run and most popular cruise lines.

Although the line competes directly with Carnival and NCL for passengers—active couples and singles in their thirties to fifties, as well as a large family contingent—there are distinct differences of ambience and energy. Royal Caribbean is a bit more sophisticated and subdued than the competition, even while delivering a good time on a grand scale.

Royal Caribbean suggests the following tips per passenger: stateroom attendant, $3.50 a day; dining-room waiter, $3.50 a day; assistant waiter, $2 a day. Gratuities for headwaiters and other service personnel are at your discretion. A 15% gratuity is automatically added to beverage and bar bills. All gratuities may be charged to your onboard account.

🕮 *Royal Caribbean International, 1050 Caribbean Way, Miami, FL 33132* ☎ *305/539–6000 or 800/327–6700* ⊕ *www.royalcaribbean.com.*

Seabourn Cruise Line

Ultraluxury pioneer Seabourn was founded on the principle that dedication to personal service in elegant surroundings would appeal to sophisticated, independent-minded passengers whose lifestyles demand the best. Its fleet of three nearly identical, all-suite ships is known simply as the "Yachts of Seabourn." Following extensive makeovers in early 2006, they belie their age. The "yachts" remain favorites with people who can take care of themselves but would rather do so aboard a ship that caters to their individual preferences. Dining and evening socializing are generally more stimulating to Seabourn passengers than splashy song-and-dance reviews; however, proportionately scaled productions and cabaret shows are presented in the main showroom and smaller lounge. The library stocks not only books but also movies for those who prefer to watch them in the privacy of their suites (popcorn will naturally be delivered with a call to room service). Complimentary "Massage Moments" on deck are mini-previews of the relaxing treatments available in the spa, which offers a variety of massages, body wraps, and facials.

These sleek 10,000-ton ships are celebrated for extraordinary levels of personalized service, suites of 277 square feet or more—40% with balconies—and exceptional cuisine designed by famed chef-restaurateur Charlie Palmer. Casual dining alternatives have been introduced, including "Tastings £ 2," serving innovative cuisine in multiple courses nightly in the Veranda Café, where outdoor tables enhance the romantic atmosphere, and a second—even more laid back—"Sky Grill" dinner with sizzling steaks and seafood sometimes offered in the open-air Sky Bar. While both require reservations, there is no additional charge for either. All drinks, including wine and alcohol, are complimentary throughout the voyage, and tipping is neither required nor expected. Shore excursions often include privileged access to historic and cultural sites during hours when they are not open to the public.

Seabourn's yachtlike vessels appeal to affluent couples of all ages who enjoy destination-intense itineraries, a subdued atmosphere, and exclusive service. Passengers tend to be in their 50s and up and retired couples who are accustomed to evening formality. The ships are adult-oriented with no children's programs or facilities. Additionally, Seabourn does not allow children under one year of age.

🕮 *Seabourn Cruise Line, 6100 Blue Lagoon Dr., Suite 400, Miami, FL 33126* ☎ *305/463–3000 or 800/929–9391* 📠 *305/463–3010* ⊕ *www. seabourn.com.*

Past Passengers—An Exclusive Group

YOUR CRUISE IS OVER—pat yourself on the back. Your plans and preparation for an out-of-the-ordinary trip have paid off, and you'll now have lasting memories of a great vacation. Before you even have a chance to fill your scrapbook, the cruise line wants you to consider doing it all over again. And why not? You're a seasoned sailor, so take advantage of your experience. To entice you back on a future cruise, you may find you're automatically a member of an exclusive club—Latitudes (Norwegian Cruise Line), Mariner Society (Holland America Line), Captain's Circle (Princess Cruises), Castaway Club (Disney Cruise Line), Venetian Society (Silversea Cruises)—to name but a few. Members receive the cruise line's magazine for past passengers, exclusive offers, shipboard perks such as a repeaters' party hosted by the captain, and even members-only cruises.

SeaDream Yacht Club

Launched in 1984 as Sea Goddess mega-yachts, these boutique ships have changed hands through the years, evolving into their present incarnations—after a total renovation in 2002—as the pride of SeaDream Yacht Club. Voyages are all about personal choice. Passengers enjoy an unstructured holiday at sea doing whatever pleases them, giving the diminutive vessels the feel of true private yachts with a select guest list. Other than a pianist in the tiny piano bar, a small casino, and movies in the main lounge, there is no roster of activities. The rocking late-night place to be is the Top of the Yacht Bar, where passengers gather to share the day's experiences and kick their shoes off to dance on the teak deck. The Captain hosts welcome aboard and farewell cocktail receptions in the Main Salon each week. Otherwise, you are on your own to do as you please. A well-stocked library has books and movies for those who prefer quiet pursuits in the privacy of their staterooms. SeaDream's unique Asian Spa facilities are on the small side, yet offer a full menu of gentle Asian treatments that includes massages, facials, and body wraps utilizing Eastern techniques.

Every meal is prepared to order using the freshest seafood and U.S. Prime cuts of beef. Menus include vegetarian alternatives and Oriental wellness cuisine for the health-conscious. Wines are chosen to complement each luncheon and dinner menu from onboard cellars that stock 3,500 bottles on each ship.

Ports of call almost seem an intrusion on socializing amid the chic surroundings, although a picnic on a secluded beach adds the element of a private island paradise to each Caribbean cruise. While the ambience is sophisticated, all cruises are "yacht" casual, and you can leave your formal clothing at home. All drinks, including wine and alcohol, are complimentary. SeaDream yachts attract energetic, affluent travelers of all ages, as well as affinity groups. Passengers tend to be couples from their 40s and up who enjoy the unstructured informality, subdued ambience, and utterly exclusive service. There are no facilities or programs for children, and these ships are not recommended for passengers confined to wheelchairs. Although there is one stateroom on each vessel considered "accessible," public facilities have thresholds, and the elevator doesn't reach the uppermost deck. Tide conditions can cause the gangway to be steep when docked, and negotiating shore tenders would be impossible. Tipping is neither required nor expected.

SeaDream Yacht Club, 2601 S. Bayshore Dr., Penthouse 1B, Coconut Grove, FL 33133 ☎ 305/856–5622 or 800/707–4911 ᕫ 305/856–7599 ⊕ www.seadreamyachtclub.com.

Silversea Cruises

High-quality features and personalization are Silversea maxims. Silversea ships have full-size showrooms, domed dining rooms, and a selection of bars and shops, yet all accommodations are spacious outside suites, most with private verandas. Silversea ships have large swimming pools in expansive Lidos—the space- and crew-to-passenger ratios are among the best at sea in the luxury small-ship category. Although their ships schedule more activities than other comparably sized luxury vessels, you can either take part or opt instead for a good book and any number of quiet spots to read or snooze in the shade. South Pacific–inspired Mandara Spa offers numerous treatments, including exotic massages, facials, and body wraps. A plus is that appointments for spa treatments and salon services, as well as shore excursion bookings, can be made online from 60 days until 48 hours prior to sailing.

European-style service is personal—exacting and hospitable, yet discreet. A major selling point is the nearly all-inclusive nature of Silversea voyages, which include gratuities and all beverages. Silversea is so all-inclusive that you'll find your room key/charge card is seldom used for anything but opening your suite door. Perhaps more compelling is the line's flair for originality. The pasta chef's daily special is a passenger favorite, as is the galley brunch, held just once each cruise, when the galley is transformed into a buffet restaurant. Dishes from Silversea's chefs are complemented by those of La Collection du Monde, created by the cruise line's culinary partner Relais & Châteaux. Menus include both hot and cold appetizers, at least four entrée selections, a vegetarian alternative, and "Cruiselite" cuisine that is low in cholesterol, sodium, and fat. Special off-menu orders are prepared whenever possible as long as the ingredients are on board. In the event that they aren't, you may find after a day in port that a trip to the market was made in order to fulfill your request.

Silversea Cruises appeal to sophisticated, affluent couples who enjoy the country club–like atmosphere, exquisite cuisine, and polished service. Adult-oriented, these ships have no dedicated children's facilities, and

Silversea does not allow children less than one year of age and may limit the number of children under three on any particular cruise. Tipping is neither required nor expected.

Silversea Cruises, 110 E. Broward Blvd., Fort Lauderdale, FL 33301 ☎ *954/522–4477 or 800/722–9955* ⊕ *www.silversea.com.*

Star Clippers

In 1991 Star Clippers presented a new tall-ship alternative to sophisticated travelers whose wants included adventure at sea, but not on board a conventional cruise ship. Star Clippers vessels are the world's largest barkentine and full-rigged sailing ships—four- and five-masted sailing beauties filled with modern, high-tech equipment as well as amenities more often found on private yachts. The ships rely on sail power while at sea unless conditions require the assistance of the engines. Old-fashioned sailing is the key to Star Clippers' appeal; minimum heeling, usually less than 6%, is achieved through judicious control of the sails. The day officially begins when the captain holds an informative daily briefing on deck with a bit of sailing lore tossed in. Star Clippers are not cruise ships in the ordinary sense with strict agendas and pages of activities. You can lounge on deck and simply soak in the nautical ambience or join crew members steering the ship, as well as learn about navigational techniques from the captain. Although the line's laid-back philosophy is similar to Windjammer's, Star Clippers vessels are more upscale. Public rooms are larger than those aboard Windjammer ships, as are cabins, which have hair dryers, televisions, and telephones. Star Clippers ships also have swimming pools. Other amenities fall somewhere between those of a true sailing yacht and the high-tech Windstar ships. The differences are more than just in the level of luxury—Star Clippers are true sailing vessels, albeit with motors, while Windstar ships are trim ocean liners with masts and sails. Prices, however, are a bit more affordable and often less than you would pay on a high-end cruise ship.

Passengers are an international group: about half are European (mostly French, German, and Swedish), and nearly all are couples, from honeymooners to well-traveled retirees. This is not a cruise line for the physically challenged; there are no elevators and ramps or staterooms/bathrooms with wheelchair accessibility. Gangways and shore launches can be difficult to navigate. Star Clippers ships are adult-oriented, and while children are welcome and may participate in shipboard activities suited to their ability, there are no dedicated youth facilities.

Star Clippers recommends the following gratuities: room steward, €3 per day; dining-room staff, €5 per day. A 15% gratuity is added to bar bills. Onboard charges are billed in euros, but there's no need to do any currency exchange since gratuities may be charged to your shipboard account, and then you can pay all costs by credit card.

Star Clippers, 4101 Salzedo Ave., Coral Gables, FL 33146 ☎ *305/442–0550 or 800/442–0551* ⊕ *www.starclippers.com.*

Windjammer Barefoot Cruises

The world's largest fleet of tall ships evolved from a modest beginning—a single 19-foot sloop, *The Hangover,* on which Windjammer Barefoot Cruises founder Mike Burke sailed his friends from South Florida to the Bahamas. Or so the legend goes. The resulting fleet consists of four tall ships ranging in size from 327 tons to 1,740 tons, which carry between 64 and 119 passengers. Each vessel has a distinctive and unique heritage, usually as the private yacht of some legendary financial mogul or European royal or in the service of a government for oceanographic and meteorological research. Carefully restored, they sail affordable 7- and 14-day cruises year-round to out-of-the-way islands and anchor in pristine waters where traditional cruise ships can't go.

Windjammer cruises combine the adventure of a traditional sailing voyage with a nod to basic comforts. These are not frou-frou ships (translation: big, white cruise liners) and have no gyms, spas, or hair salons. In fact, you might want to save room in your duffle bag by leaving your blow dryer and curling iron at home—you could use them, but probably won't. Serious exercise is climbing the stairs (there are no elevators) and swimming, either at the beaches or sometimes right from the ship. Buccaneers at heart, many passengers join the crew to work the sails and participate in informal nautical games like crab racing contests and masquerading as pirates. Laid-back days begin with complimentary Bloody Marys and sticky buns; Rum Swizzle time comes late every afternoon, when passengers need no encouragement to show up for their daily ration of complimentary grog. With a relatively small number of passengers, the ships provide a totally casual experience, and there are certainly no "formal" evenings. You might want to save a clean T-shirt for the Captain's Dinner—anyone dressing to impress should be prepared to walk the plank.

Though Windjammer offers singles-only and other specialty cruises, a typical sailing includes a diverse, unpretentious socioeconomic mix of shipmates who love the sea and the tall ships and wouldn't be caught dead on a traditional cruise ship. In summer months, Windjammer offers a supervised children's program called the "Junior Jammers Club," similar to a summer camp, so that parents can relax and enjoy their vacation time.

Windjammer recommends $75 per passenger/per week in optional gratuities, which are shared equally by the entire crew, though not by officers. Tips are usually extended in cash on the last day of the cruise.

⌖ *Windjammer Barefoot Cruises, Box 190120, Miami, FL 33119-0120* ☎ *305/672–6453 or 800/327–2601* 🖷 *305/674–1219* ⊕ *www. windjammer.com.*

Windstar Cruises

Are they cruise ships with sails or sailing ships designed for cruises? Since 1986, the Windstar vessels have presented a conundrum. In actuality they are masted sailing yachts, pioneers in the upscale sailing niche. Although the sails add speed, Windstar ships seldom depend on wind alone to sail—motors are necessary in order to maintain their schedules. However, if you are fortunate and conditions are perfect, you might experience the thrill of pure sailing in total silence. The ships' design may be reminiscent of sailing vessels of yore, but the amenities and shipboard service are among the best at sea. Life on board is unabashedly sybaritic, attracting a sophisticated, relatively young crowd happy to sacrifice bingo and pool games for the attractions of remote islands and water sports; even motorized water sports are included, and passengers pay extra only for scuba diving. A retractable marina at the stern allows water sports directly from the ship at anchor. Service is comprehensive, competent, and designed to create an elite and privileged atmosphere. Expect small, considerate touches such as the offer of an icy, lemon-scented towel or a refreshing sorbet served in an orange half while lounging poolside on a steamy day.

Since 1994, Windstar menus have featured *Signature Cuisine,* a collection of dishes originated by trendy West Coast chef and restaurateur Joachim Splichal and his Patina Group of bistro-style restaurants. In a nod to healthy dining, low-calorie and low-fat Sail Lite spa cuisine alternatives created by chef and cookbook author Jeanne Jones are prepared to American Heart Association guidelines. Additional choices are offered from the vegetarian menu.

Windstar Cruises appeal to upscale professional couples from their late-30s to retirees who enjoy the unpretentious, yet casually sophisticated, atmosphere, creative cuisine, and refined service. These ships are especially popular with honeymooners. Windstar does not discriminate against persons with disabilities, but the ships were not designed for accessibility and are not a good choice for the physically challenged. Although every attempt is made to accommodate passengers with disabilities, *Wind Surf* has only two elevators, and the smaller ships have none. There are no staterooms or bathrooms with wheelchair accessibility, and gangways can be difficult to navigate, depending on the tide and angle of ascent. Windstar's unregimented atmosphere is adult-oriented, and children—especially toddlers—are not encouraged. The line doesn't allow children under 2. Needless to say, there are no dedicated children's facilities.

⌂ *Windstar Cruises, 300 Elliott Ave., Seattle, WA 98119* ☎ *206/281–3535 or 800/258–7245* 🖷 *206/281–7110* ⊕ *www.windstarcruises.com.*

Ports of Embarkation

WORD OF MOUTH

"I want to go on a birthday cruise in Jan. with a friend and another couple. Charleston, S.C. is the best departure port for all of us. Any cruise lines leave from there?" —Minette

"Any ideas for a few hours in the port area—restaurants/walks/shopping? We'll be in [New Orleans] for a few days pre-cruise also, so this will be our last chance to enjoy and say good-bye to the city." —CaliNurse

"We are taking a cruise out of Miami and wanted to stay in Miami for a day or 2 before the cruise. How far is Miami (by the beach) from the Port? Does anybody have any recommendations for hotels?" —AimeeNC

MIAMI IS THE WORLD'S CRUISE CAPITAL, and more cruise ships are based here year-round than anywhere else. Caribbean cruises depart for their itineraries from several ports on either of Florida's coasts, as well as cities on the Gulf Coast and East Coast of the United States. Generally, if your cruise is on an Eastern Caribbean itinerary, you'll likely depart from Miami, Fort Lauderdale, Jacksonville, or Port Canaveral; short 3- and 4-day cruises to the Bahamas also depart from these ports. Most cruises on Western Caribbean itineraries depart from Tampa, Mobile, New Orleans, Galveston, or Houston, though some depart from Miami as well. Cruises from ports farther up the East Coast of the United States, including such ports as Baltimore, Maryland, Charleston, South Carolina, and even New York City, usually go to the Bahamas or Key West and often include a private-island stop or a stop elsewhere in Florida. Cruises to the Southern Caribbean might depart from Miami if they are 10 days or longer, but more likely they will depart from San Juan, Puerto Rico, or some other port deeper in the Caribbean.

Regardless of which port you depart from, air connections may prevent you from leaving home on the morning of your cruise or going home the day you return to port. Or you may wish to arrive early simply to give yourself a bit more peace of mind, or you may just want to spend more time in one of these interesting port cities. Many people choose to depart from New Orleans just to have an excuse to spend a couple of days in the city before or after their cruise.

PORT ESSENTIALS

Car Rental

🔳 Major Agencies **Alamo** 🕾 800/462-5266 ⊕ www.alamo.com. **Avis** 🕾 800/230-4898 ⊕ www.avis.com. **Budget** 🕾 800/527-0700 ⊕ www.budget.com. **Hertz** 🕾 800/654-3131 ⊕ www.hertz.com. **National Car Rental** 🕾 800/227-7368 ⊕ www.nationalcar.com.

SURCHARGES To avoid a hefty refueling fee, fill the tank just before you turn in the car, but be aware that gas stations near the rental outlet may charge more than those farther away. It's almost never a deal to buy the tank of gas that's in the car when you rent it; the understanding is that you'll return it empty, but some fuel usually remains. Surcharges may apply if you are under 25 or over 75 years old, if you want to add an additional driver to the contract, or if you want to drive over state borders or out of a specific radius from your point of rental. You'll pay extra for child seats (about $6 a day), which are compulsory for children under five, and usually for additional drivers (about $10 per day).

Dining

Unless otherwise noted, all prices are given in U.S. dollars. The following price categories are used in this book.

WHAT IT COSTS In US$				
$$$$	**$$$**	**$$**	**$**	**¢**
AT DINNER over $30	$20–$30	$12–$20	$8–$12	under $8

Prices are per person for a main course at dinner and do not include any service charges or taxes.

Lodging

Whether you are driving or flying into your port of embarkation, it is often more convenient to arrive the day before or to stay for a day after your cruise. Thus, we offer lodging suggestions for each port of embarkation.

The lodgings we list are convenient to the cruise port and the cream of the crop in each price category. We always list the facilities that are available, but we don't specify whether they cost extra; when pricing accommodations, always ask what's included. Properties are assigned price categories based on the range between their least expensive standard double room at high season (excluding holidays) and the most expensive. But if you find everything sold out or wish to find a more predictable place to stay, there are chain hotels at almost all ports of embarkation.

Assume that hotels operate on the **European Plan** (EP, with no meals) unless we specify that they use either the **Continental Plan** (CP, with a Continental breakfast), **Breakfast Plan** (BP, with a full breakfast), or the **Modified American Plan** (MAP, with breakfast and dinner). The following price categories are used in this book.

WHAT IT COSTS In US$				
$$$$	**$$$**	**$$**	**$**	**¢**
FOR 2 PEOPLE over $250	$175–$250	$120–$175	$70–$120	under $70

Prices are for a double room, excluding service and taxes.

CHARLESTON, SOUTH CAROLINA

Eileen
Robinson Smith

Charleston looks like a movie set or an 18th-century etching brought to life. The spires and steeples of more than 180 churches punctuate her low skyline, and tourists ride in horse-pulled carriages that pass grandiose, centuries-old mansions and antique gardens brimming with heirloom plants. Preserved through the poverty following the Civil War, and natural disasters like fires, earthquakes, and hurricanes, much of Charleston's earliest public and private architecture still stands. And thanks to a rigorous preservation movement and strict Board of Architectural Review, the city's new structures blend with the old ones. If you're embarking your cruise ship here, it's worth coming a few days early to explore the historic downtown and to eat in one of the many superb restaurants. In late spring, plan in advance for the Spoleto U.S.A. Festival. For 30 memorable years, arts patrons have gathered to enjoy both international and regional concerts, dance performances, operas, improv shows, and plays at creative venues citywide.

Essentials

HOURS Most shops are open from 9 or 10 AM to at least 6 PM, but some are open later. A new city ordinance requires bars to close by 2 AM.

INTERNET While almost all hotels (and even B&Bs) offer some kind of Internet service, Internet cafés are rare in the Charleston historic district; however, many coffee shops, including all the local Starbucks, offer Wi-Fi for a fee.

Charleston, SC

↑
TO MOUNT PLEASANT
AND U.S. 17N

KEY

⛴ *Cruise Ship Terminal*

❶ *What to See*

① *Where to Stay & Eat*

The **Charleston Visitor Center** (✉ *375 Meeting St., Upper King* 🖫 *423 King St., 29403* ☎ *843/853–8000 or 800/868–8118* 🌐 *www.charlestoncvb. com),* which is one of the most handsome in the country, is housed in a marvelous restoration of a 19th-century railroad warehouse with local artwork and multimedia displays of Charleston. It has information on Kiawah Island, Seabrook Island, Mount Pleasant, North Charleston, Edisto Island, Summerville, and the Isle of Palms, too.

The Cruise Port

Cruise ships embarking in Charleston leave from the Union Pier Terminal, which is in Charleston's historic district. If you are driving, however, and need to leave your car parked, take the East Bay Street exit off the new, majestic Arthur Ravenel, Jr. Bridge on I–17 and follow the signs to the Charleston Aquarium.

🚢 **Port of Charleston** ✉ 196 Concord St., Market area, at foot of Market St. ☎ 843/577–8776 for Union Pier 🌐 www.port-of-charleston.com.

AIRPORT
TRANSFERS Several cab companies service the airport, including the new Charleston Black Cab Company, which operates a fleet of genuine London cabs with uniformed drivers and costs no more than calling a regular cab—about $24.50 to downtown. Airport Ground Transportation arranges shuttles, which cost $14 per person to the downtown area, $25 round-trip. CARTA's bus #11, a public bus, now goes to the airport for a mere $1.25; it leaves downtown from the Meeting/Mary St. parking garage every 50 minutes, starting at 5:45 AM until 11:09 PM.

PARKING An outdoor parking lot is near the pier and patrolled 24 hours a day. Parking costs $15 per day ($105 per week) for regular vehicles, $25 per day ($150 per week) for RVs or other vehicles more than 20 feet in length. You pay in advance, but credit cards are not accepted. A free shuttle bus takes you to the cruise-passenger terminal. Be sure to drop your large luggage off at Union Pier before you park your car; only carry-on size luggage is allowed on the shuttle bus. If you have any bags larger than 22 inches by 14 inches, they will have to be checked before you park. You'll need your cruise tickets to board the shuttle bus.

> **CHARLESTON BEST BETS**
>
> ■ **Viewing Art.** The city is home to more than 133 galleries, so you'll never run out of places to see world-class art. The Charleston Museum and dozens of others add to the mix.
>
> ■ **The Battery.** The views from the point–both natural and man-made–are the loveliest in the city. Look west to see the harbor; to the east you'll find elegant Charleston mansions.
>
> ■ **Historic Homes.** Charleston's preserved 19th-century houses, including the Nathaniel Russell House, are highlights.

Exploring Charleston

Numbers in the margin correspond to points of interest on the Charleston map.

The heart of the city is on a peninsula, sometimes just called "downtown" by the nearly 60,000 residents who populate the area. Walking

Charleston's peninsula is the best way to get to know the city. If you don't wish to walk, there are bikes, pedicabs, and trolleys. Street parking is irksome, as meter readers are among the city's most efficient public servants. Parking garages, both privately and publicly owned, charge around $1.50 an hour.

❸ Aiken-Rhett House. This stately 1818 mansion still has its original wallpaper, paint colors, and some of its furnishings. The kitchen, slave quarters, and work yard are much as they were when the original occupants lived here, making this one of the most complete examples of urban slave life of the period. Confederate general P. G. T. Beauregard made his headquarters here during his 1864 Civil War defense of Charleston. ⊠ *48 Elizabeth St., Upper King* ☏ *843/723–1159* ⊕ *www.historiccharleston. org* ≊ *$10, $16 with admission to Nathaniel Russell House* ⊙ *Mon.–Sat. 10–5, Sun. 2–5.*

❻ Avery Research Center for African-American History and Culture. This center, part museum and part archives, was once a school for freed slaves. Collections include slavery artifacts (manacles, bills of sale, slave badges), old manuscripts, and African artifacts with ties to Lowcountry slaves. A riveting mural chronicles the Middle Passage—the journey slaves made from Africa to Charleston's shores. The free tour includes a brief film. Although it's a short five-block walk from the Cistern quad, Avery Research Center is affiliated with the College of Charleston. ⊠ *125 Bull St., College of Charleston Campus* ☏ *843/953–7609* ⊕ *www.cofc.edu* ≊ *Free* ⊙ *Weekdays noon–5, mornings by appointment.*

★ ☾ ❷ Charleston Museum. Founded in 1773, the country's oldest museum is now housed in a contemporary complex. The museum's decorative arts holdings and its permanent Civil War exhibit are extraordinary. There are more than 500,000 items in the collection. In addition to displaying Charleston silver, fashions, toys, snuffboxes, and the like, there are exhibits relating to natural history, archaeology, and ornithology. The 1803, Federal-style **Joseph Manigault House,** owned by the Charleston Museum, is across the street. George Washington once slept at the 1772 **Heyward-Washington House,** which is seven blocks southeast of its parent, the Charleston Museum. ⊠ *360 Meeting St., Upper King* ☏ *843/722–2996* ⊕ *www.charlestonmuseum.org* ≊ *$10* ⊙ *Mon.–Sat. 9–5, Sun. 1–5.*

★ ☾ ❺ Children's Museum of the Lowcountry. Daily art projects and other exhibits promote hands-on science, culture, and creativity for toddlers up to 12-year-olds. Kids can climb on a replica of a local shrimp boat, play in exhibits that show how water evaporates from and returns to the Lowcountry, wander the inner workings of a medieval castle, and more. This kids' museum is both exceptional and fun. ⊠ *25 Ann St., Upper King* ☏ *843/ 853–8962* ⊕ *www.explorecml.org* ≊ *$7* ⊙ *Tues.–Sat. 10–5, Sun. 1–5.*

⓭ Edmonston-Alston House. First built in 1825 in late-Federal style, the Edmondston-Alston House was transformed into the imposing Greek Revival structure you see today during the 1840s. Tours of the home—furnished with antiques, portraits, Piranesi prints, silver, and fine china—are informative and in-depth. The home commands an excellent view of Charleston Harbor. ✉ *21 E. Battery, South of Broad* ☎ *843/722–7171* ⊕ *www.middletonplace.org* 💲 *$10* ☉ *Tues.–Sat. 10–4:30, Mon. 1:30–4:30.*

★ ☾ ⑪ **Ft. Sumter National Monument.** On a man-made island in Charleston Harbor, Confederate forces fired the first shot of the Civil War on April 12, 1861. After a 34-hour bombardment, Union forces surrendered and Confederate troops occupied Sumter, which became a symbol of Southern resistance. The Confederacy held the fort, despite almost continual bombardment, from August 1863 to February 1865; when it was finally evacuated, the place was a heap of rubble. Today, the National Park Service oversees the Ft. Sumter National Monument complex. The **Ft. Sumter Liberty Square Visitor Center,** next to the South Carolina Aquarium, contains exhibits on the Civil War. You reach the island by ferry; there are six ferry crossings daily from mid-March through mid-August, some leaving from Liberty Square, others from Patriots Point. The schedule is abbreviated from mid-August to mid-March. Check the Spirit Line Cruises web site for details. ✉ *340 Concord St., Upper King* ☎ *843/577–0242 for Liberty Square Visitor Center* ⊕ *www.nps.gov/ fosu or www.spiritlinecruises.com* 💲 *Fort free; ferry $14* ☉ *Apr.–early Sept., daily 10–5:30; early Sept.–Mar., daily 10-4.*

❹ **Joseph Manigault House.** A National Historic Landmark and an outstanding example of Federal architecture, this home was designed by Charleston architect Gabriel Manigault in 1803 and is noted for its carved-wood mantels, elaborate plasterwork, and garden "folly." Furnishings are antiques from France, England, and Charleston; the pieces of rare tricolor Wedgwood are noteworthy. ✉ *350 Meeting St., Upper King* ☎ *843/722–2996* ⊕ *www.charlestonmuseum.org* 💲 *$10* ☉ *Mon.–Sat. 10–5, Sun. 1–5.*

❼ **Market Hall.** Built in 1841, this imposing landmark was modeled after the Temple of Nike in Athens. The hall contains the **Confederate Museum,** in which the United Daughters of the Confederacy preserve and display flags, uniforms, swords, and other Civil War memorabilia. ✉ *188 Meeting St., Market area* ☎ *843/723–1541* 💲 *$5* ☉ *Tues.–Sat. 11–3:30.*

⑫ **Nathaniel Russell House.** One of the nation's finest examples of Adam-style architecture, the Nathaniel Russell House was built in 1808. The interior is distinguished by its ornate detailing, its lavish period furnishings, and the "free-flying" circular staircase that spirals three stories with no visible support. The garden is well worth a stroll. ✉ *51 Meeting St., South of Broad* ☎ *843/724–8481* ⊕ *www.historiccharleston.org* 💲 *$7, garden free, combination ticket with Aiken-Rhett House $16* ☉ *Mon.–Sat. 10–5, Sun. 2–5.*

☾ ❽ **Old City Market.** Although often called the Slave Market, slaves were not sold here. Instead, it's where household slaves once shopped for produce and fish. Today, stalls are lined with restaurants and shops selling children's toys, Charleston souvenirs, crafts, praline candies, and more. Local "basket ladies" weave and sell sweetgrass, pine-straw, and palmetto-leaf baskets—a craft passed down through generations from their

West African ancestors. ⊠ *N. and S. Market Sts. between Meeting and E. Bay Sts., Market area* ⊗ *Daily 9–dusk.*

❾ St. Philip's (Episcopal) Church. The namesake of Church Street, this graceful late-Georgian building is the second on its site: the congregation's first building burned down in 1835 and was rebuilt in 1838. During the Civil War, the steeple was a target for shelling; one Sunday a shell exploded in the churchyard—the minister continued his sermon. Afterward, the congregation gathered elsewhere for the duration of the war. Notable Charlestonians (like John C. Calhoun) can be found in the graveyard, which flanks the church. ⊠ *146 Church St., Market area* ☎ *843/ 722–7734* ⊕ *www.stphilipschurchsc.org* ⊗ *Church: weekdays 9–11 and 1–4; cemetery: daily 9–4.*

★ ☉ ❿ South Carolina Aquarium. The 380,000-gallon Great Ocean Tank has the tallest aquarium window in North America. Exhibits display more than 10,000 living organisms. You travel through the five major regions of the Southeast Appalachian Watershed as found in South Carolina, from the mountains to the ocean. Little ones can pet stingrays at one touch tank and horseshoe crabs and conch at another. The adjacent Fountain Walk has fun shops and restaurants, including the Toucan Reef. The views here of the new Arthur Ravenel Bridge (North America's longest cable-stayed bridge) and the harbor's fascinating marine activity, are ideal photo ops. ⊠ *100 Aquarium Wharf, Upper King* ☎ *843/720–1990 or 800/722–6455* ⊕ *www.scaquarium.org* ⊠ *$16* ⊗ *Mid-Apr.–mid-Aug., Mon.–Sat. 9–5, Sun. noon–5; mid-Aug.–mid-Apr., Mon.–Sat. 9–4, Sun. noon–4.*

❶ Charleston Visitors Center. The center's 20-minute film is a fine introduction to the city. The first 30 minutes are free at the parking lot; after that it is $1.50 per hour. Garage parking here is $1.50 per hour, $10 a day. ⊠ *375 Meeting St., Upper King* ☎ *843/853–8000 or 800/868–8118* ⊕ *www.charlestoncvb.com* ⊠ *Free* ⊗ *Apr.–Aug., daily 8:30–5:30; Sept.–Mar., Mon.–Sat. daily 8:30–5.*

Shopping

King Street is the major shopping street in town. Lower King (from Broad to Market streets) is lined with high-end antiques dealers. Middle King (from Market to Calhoun streets) is a mix of national chains like Banana Republic and Pottery Barn. Upper King (*from Calhoun Street to Cannon street*) is the up-and-coming area where fashionistas like the alternative shops like Putumayo. **Shops at Charleston Place** (⊠ *130 Market St., Market Area*) is home to Gucci, Caché, St. John, Godiva, The Limited, Express, Brookstone, and more. The Market area is a cluster of shops and restaurants centered around the **Farmers Market** (⊠ *E. Bay and Market Sts., Market area*). Sweetgrass basket weavers work here, and you can buy the resulting wares.

Where to Eat

For price categories, *see* Dining at the beginning of this chapter.

$–$$ ✕ **A.W. Shucks.** The State Street door opens to a typical Lowcountry oyster bar, as earthy as pluff-mud, with the freshest shellfish outside of water. The South Market Street exit drops down to the deck, a perfect location to people-watch the market activity. A centuries-old warehouse, this family restaurant is where you can still get a root beer float, and local specialties like shrimp and grits, and a steam pot—a bountiful cauldron of shellfish, crab legs, smoked sausage, potatoes, and corn on the cob. T-shirts that read "Big Mussels, Great Legs & Fantastic Tails" could be your funky souvenir gift. ⊠ *70 State St.* ☎ *843/723–1151* ⊟ *AE.*

> **WAITER KNOWS BEST**
>
> If your waiter frowns when you make a menu selection, follow his lead. He knows what's good on the dining room menu and what isn't.

★ $$$–$$$$ ✕ **Slightly North of Broad.** This former warehouse with brick-and-stucco walls has a chef's table that looks directly into the open kitchen. It's a great place to perch, as Chef Frank Lee, who wears a baseball cap instead of a toque, is one of the city's culinary characters. Known for his talent in preparing game, his venison is exceptional. Many of the items come as small plates, which make them perfect for sharing. The braised lamb shank with a ragout of white beans, arugula and a red demi-glace is divine and is an example of a "main" on the $9.95 Express Lunch, a phenomenal value. ⊠ *192 East Bay St.* ☎ *843/723–3424* ⊟ *AE, D, MC, V* ☉ *No lunch Sat., Sun.*

¢–$ ✕ **Fleet Landing.** This is one fun place, smack in the marsh within sight of the cruise-ship dock, so there's little danger of being left behind. A youthful redo of a former Navy depot, there are B&W pics from the 1940s and orange life preservers as art. You can sit out on the deck and—to the envy of the circling seagulls—ingest the freshest of bivalves. On Saturdays, buckets of steamed oysters are $8.95; a guitarist sings southern rock at Sunday brunch. The menu includes classic Charleston dishes like blue crab cakes, fried platters, and *moderne* salads like fried oysters atop warm spinach with a bacon vinaigrette; there's always pecan pie. ⊠ *186 Concord St.* ☎ *843/722–8100* ⊟ *AE, D, MC, V.*

Where to Stay

While the city's best hotels and B&Bs are in the historic district, most of them do not have free parking. If you stay outside of downtown in a chain hotel, you will give up much in charm and convenience but pay significantly less. High-season rates are traditionally March through May and September through November.

★ $$$$ ☷ **Charleston Place Hotel.** Even casual passersby enjoy gazing up at the handblown Moreno glass chandelier in the hotel's open lobby, clicking across the Italian marble floors, and admiring the antiques from Sotheby's. A gallery of upscale shops complete the ground floor offerings. Rooms are furnished with period reproductions. The impeccable service is what you would expect from an Orient-Express property, particularly on the Club Level. A truly deluxe day spa, with an adjacent fitness room, has an inviting indoor pool illuminated by skylights. ⊠ *205 Meeting St., Lower King, 29401* ☎ *843/722–4900 or 800/611–5545* ⊟ *843/722–0728* ⊕ *www.charlestonplacehotel.com* ↵ *400 rooms, 42 suites* ⚲ *In room: safe, dial-up. In hotel: 2 restaurants, room service, bar, gym, spa,* *concierge floor, public Internet, parking (fee), no-smoking rooms* ⊟ *AE, D, DC, MC, V* ⃝ *EP.*

$$$ 🖼 **Hampton Inn–Historic District.** Hardwood floors and a fireplace in the lobby of what was once an 1800s warehouse help elevate this chain hotel a bit above the rest. Spindle posts on the headboards give guest rooms a little personality. Rooms are not large but have little perks like coffeemakers. The location is perfect for exploring downtown. ⊠ *373 Meeting St., Upper King 29403* 📞 *843/723–4000 or 800/426–7866* 📠 *843/722–3725* ⊕ *www.hamptoninn.com* ⃔ *166 rooms, 5 suites* ⛛ *In room: refrigerator (some), dial-up. In hotel: pool, laundry facilities, laundry service, public Internet, parking (fee), no-smoking rooms* ⊟ *AE, D, DC, MC, V* ⃝ *BP.*

$$–$$$ 🖼 **Andrew Pinckney Inn.** The lobby of this boutique inn has a homey ambience that blends South Carolina and the West Indies. The two-story town-house suites, which sleep four, are ideal for longer stays. A heavenly breakfast with fresh-baked pastries and biscuits with sausage gravy is taken on its rooftop, which overlooks the church spires. It's in the bustling market area, so ask for an interior room. ⊠ *40 Pinckney St., 29401* 📞 *843/937–8800 or 800/505–8983* 📠 *843/937–8810* ⊕ *www.andrewpinckneyinn.com* ⃔ *41 rooms, 3 town houses, 1 suite* ⛛ *In hotel: refrigerator (some), dial-up, Wi-Fi. In hotel: public Internet, parking (fee), no-smoking* ⊟ *AE, MC, V* ⃝ *BP.*

FORT LAUDERDALE, FLORIDA

Lynne Helm

In the 1960s, Fort Lauderdale's beachfront was lined with T-shirt shops interspersed with quickie-food outlets, and downtown consisted of a lone office tower, some dilapidated government buildings, and motley other structures waiting to be razed. Today the beach is home to upscale shops and restaurants, while downtown has exploded with new office and luxury residential development. The entertainment and shopping areas—Las Olas Boulevard, Las Olas Riverfront, and Himmarshee Village—are thriving. And Port Everglades is giving Miami a run for its money in passenger cruising, with a dozen cruise-ship terminals hosting more than 20 cruise ships with some 3,000 departures annually. A captivating shoreline with wide ribbons of sand for beachcombing and sunbathing makes Fort Lauderdale and Broward County a major draw for visitors and often tempts cruise-ship passengers to spend an extra day or two in the sun. Fort Lauderdale's 2-mi (3-km) stretch of unobstructed

---

FORT LAUDERDALE BEST BETS

- **The Beach.** With more than 20 mi of ocean shoreline, don't miss soaking up the scene at Greater Fort Lauderdale's best beaches including those along Lauderdale-by-the-Sea and Fort Lauderdale.

- **The Everglades.** Take in the wild reaches in or near the Everglades with an airboat ride. Mosquitos are friendly, so arm yourself accordingly.

- **The Riverwalk.** This is a great place to stroll before and after performances, dinner, libations, and other entertainment.

beachfront has been further enhanced with a sparkling promenade designed more for the pleasure of pedestrians than vehicles.

Essentials

HOURS Many museums close on Monday.

INTERNET If you have your own laptop, Broward County has created a fairly extensive wireless broadband network with numerous Wi-Fi hot spots in downtown Fort Lauderdale, providing free Internet access to anyone using suitably equipped laptops. There's also free Wi-Fi in the airport.

BOAT TOURS **Water Bus** (☎ 954/467–6677 ⊕ *www.watertaxi.com*), also known as Water Bus, provides service along the Intracoastal Waterway in Fort Lauderdale between the 17th Street Causeway and Oakland Park Boulevard daily from 10:30 AM until midnight.

VISITOR **Chamber of Commerce of Greater Fort Lauderdale** (⊠ *512 N.E. 3rd Ave.,*
INFORMATION *Fort Lauderdale 33301* ☎ *954/462–6000* ⊕ *www.ftlchamber.com*).
Greater Fort Lauderdale Convention & Visitors Bureau (⊠ *100 E. Broward Blvd., Suite 200, Fort Lauderdale 33301* ☎*954/765–4466* ⊕*www.sunny. org*). **Hollywood Chamber of Commerce** (⊠ *330 N. Federal Hwy., Hollywood 33020* ☎ *954/923–4000* ⊕ *www.hollywoodchamber.org*).

The Cruise Port

Port Everglades, Fort Lauderdale's cruise port (nowhere near the Everglades, but happily near the beach and less than 2 mi (3 km) from the airport), is among the world's largest, busiest ports. It's also the straightest, deepest port in the southeastern United States, meaning you'll be out to sea in no time flat once your ship sets sail. A few words of caution: Schedule plenty of time to navigate the port from the airport,

> **IT'S A GIRL**
>
> Even as far back as ancient times, mariners have traditionally referred to their ships as "she." To a seaman, a ship is as beautiful and comforting as his mother or sweetheart. You could say a good ship holds a special place in his heart.

your hotel, or wherever else you might be staying, especially if you like to be among the first to embark for your sailing. Increased security combined with increased traffic, larger parking facilities, construction projects, roadway improvements, and other obstacles mean the old days of popping over to Port Everglades and running up a gangplank in the blink of an eye are history.

If you are driving, there are two entrances to the port. One is from 17th Street, west of the 17th Street Causeway Bridge, turning south at the traffic light onto Eisenhower Boulevard. Or to get to the main entrance, take either State Road 84, running east–west, to the intersection of Federal Highway and cross into the port, or take I–595 East straight into the Port (I–595 becomes Eller Drive once inside the Port).

🚩 **Port Everglades** ✉ 1850 Eller Dr. ☎ 954/523-3404 ⊕ www.porteverglades.org.

AIRPORT
TRANSFERS
Fort Lauderdale–Hollywood International Airport is 4 mi (6 km) south of downtown and 2 mi (3 km) (about 5 to 10 minutes) from the docks. If you haven't arranged an airport transfer with your cruise line, you can take a taxi to the cruise-ship terminals. The ride in a metered taxi costs about $12 to $15, depending on your departure terminal. Taxi fares are $4.50 for the first mile and $2.40 for each additional mile, and 40¢ per minute for waiting time. If you are staying over, Airport Express provides limousine service to all parts of Broward County; fares to most Fort Lauderdale beach hotels are in the $25 range.

PARKING
Two covered parking facilities close to the terminals are Northport (with 2,500 spaces, expanding to 4,250) and Midport (for 2,000 cars). Use the Northport garage if your cruise leaves from Piers 1, 2, or 4; use Midport if your cruise leaves from Piers 18, 19, 21, 22/24, 25, 26, 27, or 29. The cost is $2 for the first hour, $5 for one to five hours, or $12 per day for either garage ($15 for oversize vehicles up to 40 feet). To save a few bucks on your parking tab, Park 'N Fly provides remote parking just outside Port Everglades, at the exit off I–595, with shuttle service assistance to all cruise terminals. Rates are $10 per day, $70 per week.

🚩 **Park 'N Fly** ✉ 2200 N.E. 7th Ave., at the Port Everglades exit off I–595 ☎ 954/779-1776 ⊕ www.pnf.com.

Exploring Fort Lauderdale

In a state where gaudy tourist zones often stand aloof from workaday downtowns, Fort Lauderdale is unusual in that the city exhibits consistency at both ends of the 2-mi (3-km) Las Olas corridor. The sparkling look results from efforts to thoroughly improve both beachfront and downtown.

Numbers in the margin refer to points of interest on the Fort Lauderdale map.

Big Cypress Seminole Reservation. Some distance from Fort Lauderdale's tranquil beaches, but worth the hour-plus drive, the reservation has two very different attractions. At the **Billie Swamp Safari,** experience the majesty of the Everglades firsthand. Daily tours of the wetlands and hammocks, where wildlife abounds, yield sightings of deer, water buffalo, bison, wild hogs, hawks, eagles, alligators, and occasionally the rare Florida panther. Animal and reptile shows are also offered. Eco-heritage tours are provided aboard motorized swamp buggies, and airboat rides are available, too. On the property is Swamp Water Café, which serves Seminole foods. ⊠ *19 mi north of I–75 Exit 49* ☎ *863/983–6101 or 800/949–6101* ⊕ *www.seminoletribe.com* ☜ *Free to visit the reservation's Seminole village; swamp buggy tour $25; combined ecotour, show, airboat ride $43* ⊙ *Daily 8:30–5.*

Not far from the Billie Swamp Safari is the **Ah-Tha-Thi-Ki Museum,** whose name means "a place to learn, a place to remember." It is just that. The museum documents and honors the culture and tradition of the Seminole Tribe of Florida through artifacts, exhibits, and reenactments of rituals and ceremonies. The site includes a living-history Seminole village, nature trails, and a boardwalk through a cypress swamp. ⊠ *17 mi north of I–75 Exit 49* ☎ *863/902–1113* ⊕ *www.seminoletribe.com* ☜ *$6* ⊙ *Daily 9–5.*

Bonnet House. A 35-acre oasis in the heart of the beach area, this subtropical estate, having survived a big hit from 2005's Hurricane Wilma, remains as a tribute to the history of Old South Florida. The charming home was the winter residence of the late Frederic and Evelyn Bartlett, artists whose personal touches and small surprises are evident throughout. Whether you're interested in architecture, artwork, or the natural environment, this is a special place. Be on the lookout for playful monkeys swinging from trees, a source of amusement at even some of the most solemn outdoor weddings on the grounds. Hours can vary, so call first. ⊠ *900 N. Birch Rd.* ☎ *954/563–5393* ⊕ *www.bonnethouse.org* ☜ *House tours $15, grounds only $9* ⊙ *Wed.–Fri. 10–3, weekends noon–4.*

Butterfly World. As many as 80 butterfly species from South and Central America, the Philippines, Malaysia, Taiwan, and other Asian nations are typically found within this 3-acre site inside Tradewinds Park. A screened aviary called North American Butterflies is reserved for native species. The Tropical Rain Forest Aviary is a 30-foot-high construction, with observation decks, waterfalls, ponds, and tunnels where thousands of colorful butterflies flutter about. There's also a bug zoo.

✉ *3600 W. Sample Rd., Coconut Creek* ☎ *954/977–4400* ⊕ *www.
butterflyworld.com* 🎫 *$18.95* ◷ *Mon.–Sat. 9–5, Sun. 1–5.*

❺ **Museum of Art.** In an Edward Larrabee Barnes–designed building that's
considered an architectural masterpiece, this museum's impressive permanent collection has 20th-century European and American art, including works by Picasso, Calder, Dalí, Mapplethorpe, Warhol, and Stella,
as well as a notable collection of works by celebrated Ashcan School
artist William Glackens. When its building opened in 1986, the museum
helped launch revitalization of the downtown district and nearby Riverwalk area, and it since has become a magnet for special traveling exhibits (with higher admission fees). ✉ *1 E. Las Olas Blvd.* ☎ *954/
763–6464* ⊕ *www.moafl.org* 🎫 *$7 and up, depending on exhibit*
◷ *Feb–mid-Dec., Fri.–Wed. 11–7, Thurs. 11–9; mid-Dec.–Jan., Fri.–Mon.
and Wed. 11–7, Thurs. 11–9.*

☾ ❸ **Museum of Discovery and Science/Blockbuster IMAX Theater.** The aim here
is to show children—*and* adults—the wonders of science in an entertaining fashion. The 52-foot-tall Great Gravity Clock in the courtyard
entrance lets arrivals know a cool experience awaits. Inside, exhibits include Living in the Everglades, a hands-on exhibit and nature trail
telling about Florida's Everglades restoration; Kidscience, encouraging
youngsters to explore the world around them; and Gizmo City, a look
at how gadgets work. Florida Ecoscapes has a living coral reef as well
as live bees, bats, frogs, turtles, and alligators. An IMAX theater, part
of the complex, shows films (some 3-D) on a five-story-high screen. ✉ *401
S.W. 2nd St.* ☎ *954/467–6637 museum, 954/463–4629 IMAX* ⊕ *www.
mods.org* 🎫 *Exhibits $9, IMAX Show $9, combo ticket $14* ◷ *Mon.–Sat.
10–5, Sun. noon–6.*

❹ **Riverwalk.** Fantastic views and entertainment prevail on this lovely
paved promenade on the New River's north bank, with more strolling
area on the south bank winding past the courthouse. On the first Sunday of every month a jazz brunch attracts visitors. The walk has been
extended 2 mi (3 km) on both sides of the beautiful urban stream, con-
necting the facilities of the Arts and Science District.

Beaches

Fort Lauderdale's **beachfront** offers the best of all possible worlds, with
easy access not only to a wide band of beige sand but also to restaurants and shops. For 2 mi (3 km) heading north, beginning at the Bahia
Mar yacht basin, along Route A1A you'll have clear views, typically across
rows of colorful beach umbrellas, to the sea and ships passing into and
out of nearby Port Everglades. If you're on the beach, gaze back on an
exceptionally graceful promenade.

Pedestrians rank above cars in Fort Lauderdale. Broad walkways line
both sides of the beach road, and traffic has been trimmed to two gently curving northbound lanes, where in-line skaters skim past slow-
moving cars. On the beach side, a low masonry wall doubles as an extended bench, separating sand from the promenade. At night the wall
is accented with ribbons of fiber-optic color, quite pretty when working, although outages are frequent. The most crowded portion of

beach is between Las Olas and Sunrise boulevards. Tackier aspects of this onetime strip—famous for the springtime madness spawned by the film *Where the Boys Are*—are now but a fading memory, with the possible exception of the icon Elbo Room, an ever-popular bar at the corner of Las Olas and A1A.

North of the redesigned beachfront are another 2 mi (3 km) of open and natural coastal landscape. Much of the way parallels the Hugh Taylor Birch State Recreation Area, preserving a patch of primeval Florida.

Shopping

Las Olas Boulevard holds the city's best boutiques, plus top restaurants and art galleries, all along a beautifully landscaped street. When you're downtown, check out the Las Olas Riverfront, a shopping, dining, and entertainment complex.

Where to Eat

For price categories, *see* Dining at the beginning of this chapter.

★ $$$–$$$$ ✕ **Blue Moon Fish Company.** Most tables have stellar views of the Intracoastal Waterway, but Blue Moon's true—if pricey—magic comes from the kitchen, where chefs Baron Skorish and Bryce Statham create moon-and-stars-worthy seafood dishes. Start with the raw bar, a sushi sampler, or the pan-seared fresh shucked oysters. Salads include a hydroponic bibb with hearts of palm, and entrée favorites include shiitake-mushroom-crusted halibut, big-eye tuna, or (for carnivores) veal tenderloin. Always book ahead for the Sunday champagne brunch. ✉ *4405 W. Tradewinds Ave.* ☎ *954/267-9888* ▤ *AE, D, DC, MC, V.*

$–$$ ✕ **Floridian.** This Las Olas landmark with photos of Marilyn Monroe, Richard Nixon, and local notables past and present dishes up some of the best breakfasts around, with oversize omelets that come with biscuits, toast, or English muffins, plus a choice of grits or tomatoes to go with friendly, efficient service. With sausage or bacon on the side, the feast will make you forget about eating again soon. Count on savory sandwiches and hot platters for lunch and dinner. It's open 24 hours every day—even during hurricanes, as long as the power holds out. Feeling flush? Try the Fat Cat Breakfast (New York strip steak, hash browns or grits, toast, and a worthy champagne) or the Not-So-Fat-Cat, with the same grub and a lesser-quality vintage. ✉ *1410 E. Las Olas Blvd.* ☎ *954/463-4041* ▤ *No credit cards.*

$–$$ ✕ **Southport Raw Bar.** If you're lodging near the port and prefer to stick within the area for meals, you can't go wrong at this unpretentious spot where the motto, seen on bumper stickers for miles around, proclaims "Eat fish, live longer, eat oysters, love longer, eat clams, last longer." Raw or steamed clams, raw oysters, and combos, along with peel-and-eat shrimp, are market-priced. Hoagies, subs, and burgers are the ticket for under $10. Sides range from Bimini bread to key lime pie, with conch fritters and beer-battered onion rings in between. Order wine by the bottle or glass and beer by the pitcher, bottle, or can. Eat outside overlooking a canal, or inside at booths, tables, or the bars, in front and back. Limited parking is free, and a shopping center lot is across the street. ✉ *1536 Cordove Rd.* ☎ *954/525-2526* ▤ *MC, V.*

Where to Stay

Fort Lauderdale has a growing and varied roster of lodging options, from beachfront luxury suites to intimate B&Bs to chain hotels along the Intracoastal Waterway. If you want to be on the beach, be sure to mention this when booking your room, since many hotels advertise "waterfront" accommodations that are actually on inland waterways, not the beach.

For price categories, *see* Lodging at the beginning of this chapter.

$$-$$$$
Fodor's Choice
★

Marriott's Harbor Beach Resort. Look down from the upper stories (14 in all) at night, and this 16-acre property, on the secluded south end of Fort Lauderdale Beach, shimmers like a jewel. Spacious guest rooms have rich tropical colors, lively floral art prints, and warm woods. Part of the hotel's big-budget renovation is the addition of a European spa. No other hotel on the beach gives you so many activity options. ☒ *3030 Holiday Dr., 33316* ☎ *954/525–4000 or 800/222–6543* 🖶 *954/766–6152* ⊕ *www.marriottharborbeach.com* 📞 *602 rooms, 35 suites* ⚐ *In-room: dial-up. In-hotel: 3 restaurants, bars, tennis courts, pools, gym, spa, beachfront, water sports, children's programs (ages 5–12)* ▭ *AE, D, DC, MC, V.*

☼ **$$-$$$**
Fodor's Choice
★

Best Western Pelican Beach. On the north end of Fort Lauderdale beach and under new ownership, this already lovely property has been entirely transformed into a nonsmoking resort with a restaurant and lounge, an old-fashioned ice-cream parlor, and Fort Lauderdale's only Lazy River pool, allowing guests to float around a moatlike "river" via circulating current. For small fry, there's also a Funky Fish program. Of 156 rooms and one-bedroom suites in the new building, 117 are oceanfront. With the new building all aglow, the original Sun Tower is getting a makeover. ☒ *2000 N. Atlantic Blvd., 33305* ☎ *954/568–9431 or 800/525–6232* 🖶 *954/565–2622* ⊕ *www.pelicanbeach.com* 📞 *180 rooms* ⚐ *In-hotel: restaurant, bar, pools* ▭ *AE, DC, MC, V.*

GALVESTON, TEXAS

Robin Barr
Sussman

A thin strip of island in the Gulf of Mexico, Galveston is big sister Houston's beach playground—a year-round coastal destination just 50 mi away. Many of the first public buildings in Texas, including a post office, bank, and hotel, were built here, but most were destroyed in the Great Storm of 1900. Those that endured have been well preserved, and the Victorian character of the Strand shopping district and the neighborhood surrounding Broadway is still evident. On the Galveston Bay side of the island (northeast), quaint shops and cafés in old buildings are near the Seaport Museum, harbor-front eateries, and the cruise-ship terminal. On the Gulf of Mexico side (southwest), resorts and restaurants line coastal Seawall Boulevard. The 17-foot-high seawall abuts a long ribbon of sand and provides a place for rollerblading, bicycling, and going on the occasional surrey ride.

Galveston is a port of embarkation for cruises on Western Caribbean itineraries; some Panama Canal cruises leave from here as well. It's an especially popular port of embarkation for people living in the southeastern

Galveston

What to See

Broadway	**1**
Moody Gardens	**2**
Pier 21 Theater	**5**
The Strand	**3**
Texas Seaport Museum	**4**

Where to Eat

Fisherman's Wharf	**4**
Mosquito Café	**5**

Where to Stay

Hotel Galvez	**2**
San Luis Resort	**1**
Tremont House	**3**

KEY

- **1** What to See
- **1** Where to Stay & Eat

Galveston Island Trolley Route

Cruise Ship Terminal

Pelican Island

GALVESTON BAY

Pelican Island Causeway

GULF OF MEXICO

GALVESTON SEAWALL

Moody Mansion

Offatts Bayou

0   1 mile
0   1 km

Boarding Passes

CLOSE UP

SIMPLE PAPER BOARDING passes seem almost as antiquated as the custom of tossing streamers at the sailaway. Environmental awareness nixed the streamers in the 1980s, while modern ID cards and scanning equipment record passenger comings and goings on the majority of cruise ships these days. With a swipe through a machine (it looks much like a credit card swipe at the supermarket), security personnel know who is on board the vessel at all times. On most large ships, passengers' images are recorded digitally at check-in so that when they leave for shore or reboard the ship, security screens display their likeness when their boarding passes are inserted into the scanning machines.

states who don't wish to fly to their cruise. Carnival, Royal Caribbean, and Princess have made Galveston the home port for their ships.

Essentials

HOURS   Shops in the historic district are usually open until at least 7, but some stay open later. This is also the city's nightlife district, and that is hopping until late.

INTERNET   The best place to check your e-mail is at your hotel. Most of the hotels in Galveston offer some kind of Internet service, though usually for a fee. If you have a laptop, the city has a relatively extensive network of free Wi-Fi zones, including several spots on The Strand.

VISITOR   **Strand Visitors Center** (⊠ *2215 Strand* ⊕ *www.galveston.com*) has free
INFORMATION   brochures and maps and is open daily.

The Galveston Cruise Port

The relatively sheltered waters of Galveston Bay are home to the Texas Cruise Ship Terminal. It's only 30 minutes to open water from here. Driving south from Houston on I–45, you cross a long causeway before reaching the island. Take the first exit, Harborside Drive, left after you've crossed the causeway onto Galveston Island. Follow that for a few miles to the port. Turn left on 22nd Street (also called Kemper Street); there is a security checkpoint before you continue down a driveway. The drop-off point is set up much like an airport terminal, with pull-through lanes and curbside check-in.

🚢 **Port of Galveston** ⊠ Harborside Dr. and 22nd St. ☎ 409/765–9321 ⊕ www. portofgalveston.com.

AIRPORT   The closest airports are in Houston, 50 mi from Galveston. Houston has
TRANSFERS   two major airports: Hobby Airport, 9 mi (15 km) southeast of downtown, and George Bush Intercontinental, 15 mi (24 km) northeast of the city.

Unless you have arranged airport transfers through your cruise line, you'll have to make arrangements to navigate the miles between the Houston airport at which you land and the cruise-ship terminal in Galveston. Galveston Limousine Service provides scheduled transportation (return reservations required) between either airport and Galveston hotels or the cruise-ship terminal. Hobby is a shorter ride (1 hour, $35 one-way, $60 round-trip), but Intercontinental (2 hours, $40 one-way, $70 round-trip) is served by more airlines, including international carriers. Taking a taxi allows you to set your own schedule but can cost twice as much (it's also important to note that there aren't always enough taxis to handle the demands of disembarking passengers, so you might have to wait after you leave your ship). Negotiate the price before you get in.

🛈 **Galveston Limousine Service** ☎ 800/640–4826 ⊕ www.galvestonlimousineservice. com.

PARKING Parking is coordinated by the Port Authority. After you drop off your checked luggage and passengers at the terminal, you receive a color-coded parking pass from the attendant, with directions to a parking lot for your cruise departure. The lots are approximately ½ mi (1 km) from the terminal. Check-in, parking, and boarding are generally allowed four hours prior to departure. A shuttle bus (carry-on luggage only) runs back and forth between the lots and the terminal every 7 to 12 minutes on cruise arrival and departure days (be sure to drop off your luggage *before* you park the car). The lot is closed other days. Port Authority security checks the well-lighted, fenced-in lots every two hours; there is also a limited amount of covered parking. Parking for a 5-day cruise is $50 ($60 covered), 7-day is $70 ($80 covered), and 11-day is $85 ($100 covered). Cash, traveler's checks, and credit cards (Visa and MasterCard only) are accepted for payment, which must be made in advance.

Exploring Galveston
Numbers in the margin correspond to points of interest on the Galveston Map.

❶ **Broadway.** The late 1800s were the heyday of Galveston's port (before Houston's was dug out). Victorian splendor is evident in the meticulously restored homes of this historic district, some of which are now museums. If you're in town the first two weekends of May, don't miss the **Galveston Historic Homes Tour.** In addition to visiting the neighborhood's museums, you can walk through privately owned homes dating from the 1800s. For more information about area house museums or the tour, contact the Heritage Visitors Center. **Moody Mansion** (✉ *2618 Broadway* ☎ *409/762–7668*), the residence of generations of one of Texas's most powerful families, was completed in 1895. Tour its interiors of exotic woods and gilded trim filled with family heirlooms and personal effects. **Ashton Villa** (✉ *2328 Broadway* ☎ *409/762–3933*), a formal Italianate villa, was built in 1859 of brick. Look for the curtains that shielded the more modest Victorian guests from the naked Cupids painted on one wall. ✉ *2328 Broadway* ☎ *409/765–7834* ⊕ *www. galvestonhistory.org* 💲 *Visitor center free, museums $6 each, tour $20* 🕙 *Mon.–Sat. 10–4, Sun. noon–4.*

❷ **Moody Gardens** is a multifaceted entertainment and educational complex inside pastel-colored glass pyramid buildings. Attractions include the 13-story **Aquarium Pyramid,** showcasing marine life from four oceans in tanks and touch pools; **Rainforest Pyramid,** a 40,000-square-foot tropical habitat for exotic flora and fauna; **Discovery Pyramid,** a joint venture with

NASA featuring more than 40 inter-active exhibits; and two **IMAX the-aters,** one of which has a space adventure ride. Outside, **Palm Beach** has white-sand beach, landscaped grounds, man-made lagoons, a kid-size waterslide and games, and beach chairs. ⊠ *1 Hope Blvd.* ☎ *409/741–8484 or 800/582–4673* ⊕ *www. moodygardens.com* ⌨ *$8.95–$15.95 per venue, $44.95 day pass* ☉ *Memo-rial Day–Labor Day, daily 10–9; Labor Day–Memorial Day, week-days 10–6, weekends 10–8.*

⑤ Pier 21 Theater. At this theater on the Strand, watch the Great Storm of 1900 come back to life in a multime-dia presentation that includes video clips of archival drawings, still pho-tos, and narrated accounts from survivors' diaries. Also playing is a film about the exploits of pirate Jean Lafitte, who used the island as a base. ⊠ *Pier 21, Harborside Dr. and 21st St.* ☎ *409/763–8808* ⊕ *www. galvestonhistory.org/plc-pier21.htm* ⌨ *Great Storm $5, Pirate Island $4* ☉ *Sun.–Thurs. 11–6, Fri. and Sat. 11–8.*

③ The Strand. This shopping area is defined by the architecture of its 19th- and early-20th-century buildings, many of which survived the storm of 1900 and are on the National Register of Historic Places. When Galve-ston was still a powerful port city—before the Houston Ship Channel was dug, diverting most boat traffic inland—this stretch, formerly the site of stores, offices, and warehouses, was known as the Wall Street of the South. As you stroll up the Strand, you pass dozens of shops and cafés. ⊠ *Between Strand and Postoffice St., 25th and 19th sts.*

④ Texas Seaport Museum. Aboard the restored 1877 tall ship *Elissa,* detailed interpretive signs provide information about the shipping trade in the 1800s, including the routes and cargoes this ship carried into Galveston. Inside the museum building is a replica of the historic wharf and infor-mation about the ethnic groups that immigrated through this U.S. point of entry after 1837. The tall ship *Elissa* was refurbished in 2005. ⊠ *Pier 21* ☎ *409/763–1877* ⊕ *www.tsm-elissa.org* ⌨ *$8* ☉ *Daily 10–5.*

Beaches

The **Seawall** (⊠ *Seawall Blvd. from 61st St. to 25th St.*) on the gulf-side waterfront attracts runners, cyclists, and rollerbladers. Just below it is a long, free beach near many big hotels and resorts. **Stewart Beach Park** (⊠ *6th St. and Seawall Blvd.* ☎ *409/765–5023*) has a bathhouse, amuse-ment park, bumper boats, miniature-golf course, and a water coaster in addition to salt water and sand. It's open weekdays 9 to 5, weekends 8 to 6 from March through May; weekdays 8 to 6 and weekends 8 to 7 from June through September; and weekends 9 to 5 during the first two weekends of October. Admission is $5 per vehicle. **Galveston Island**

GALVESTON BEST BETS

- **Historic Homes.** The island has some lovely historic homes to explore, particularly during early May, when the Historic Homes Tour lets you into many that aren't usually open to the public.

- **Moody Gardens.** There are enough activities at this park to keep any kid happy.

- **The Strand.** Galveston's historic district is a great place to stroll, shop, and eat.

State Park (⊠ *3 Mile Rd., 10 mi (16 km) southwest on Seawall Blvd.* ☎ *409/737–1222*), on the western, unpopulated end of the island, is a 2,000-acre natural beach habitat ideal for birding, walking, and renewing your spirit. It's open daily from 8 AM to 10 PM; admission is $3.

> **CAUTION** ⚠
>
> Do not forget to pack and use your sunscreen. Why take the chance of a nasty sunburn ruining a great cruise vacation? Protect your skin from injury and aging.

Shopping

The **Strand** is the best place to shop in Galveston. Old storefronts are filled with gift shops, antiques stores, and one-of-a-kind boutiques. The area is bounded by Strand and Postoffice Street (running east–west) and 25th and 19th streets (running north–south). More than 50 antiques dealers are represented at **The Emporium at Eibands** (⊠ *2201 Postoffice St.* ☎ *409/763–5495*), an upscale showroom filled with furniture, books, art, and jewelry.

Where to Eat

For price categories, *see* Dining at the beginning of this chapter.

$$–$$$ ✕ **Fisherman's Wharf.** Even though Landry's has taken over this harborside institution along with just about everything else on the Kemah Boardwalk, locals keep coming here for the reliably fresh seafood and reasonable prices. Dine indoors or watch the boat traffic (and waiting cruise ships) from the patio. Start with a cold combo, like boiled shrimp and grilled rare tuna. The fried fish, shrimp, and oysters are hard to beat as an entrée. ⊠ *Pier 22, Harborside Dr. and 22nd St.* ☎ *409/765–5708* ☰ *AE, D, DC, MC, V.*

$$–$$$ ✕ **Mosquito Café.** This chichi eatery in Galveston's historic East End serves fresh, contemporary food—some vegetarian—in a hip, high-ceilinged dining room and on an outdoor patio. Wake up to a fluffy egg frittata or a homemade scone topped with whipped cream, or try a large gourmet salad later on. The grilled snapper with Parmesan grits is a hit in the evening. ⊠ *628 14th St.* ☎ *409/763–1010* ☰ *AE, D, DC, MC, V* ⊗ *No dinner Sun.–Wed.*

Where to Stay

For price categories, *see* Lodging at the beginning of this chapter.

$$–$$$$ ⊡ **San Luis Resort.** A long marble staircase alongside a slender fountain with sculpted dolphins welcomes you to the waterfront elegance of this resort. The upper-floor facade isn't much to look at, but don't let that fool you; inside, the colors of the cool, cream marble and taupe stone in the lobby are echoed in the guest rooms. The sculptural lines of pink granite on the headboards and armchairs say Italian villa. All rooms have balconies facing the gulf, and prices rise with the floor height. Back on ground level, step into the meandering (and heated) grotto pool with a rock waterfall set amid coconut palms and bougainvillea; then have a Balinese massage (or a wildflower compress) at the Spa San Luis. The resort offers free parking for the duration of a cruise as well as transportation to the cruise terminal. ⊠ *5222 Seawall Blvd., 77551* ☎ *409/744–1500 or 800/445–0090* 🖷 *409/744–8452* ⊕ *www.sanluisresort.*

com ➯ *246 rooms* ♿ *In room: dial-up. In hotel: Restaurant, room service, bars, tennis courts, pools, gym, spa, children's programs (ages 4–12), laundry service, executive floor, public Internet, parking (free), no-smoking rooms* ▤ *AE, D, DC, MC, V.*

$$–$$$ 🏨 **Hotel Galvez.** This renovated six-story Spanish colonial hotel, built in 1911, was once called "Queen of the Gulf." Teddy Roosevelt and Howard Hughes are just two of the many well-known guests who have stayed here. Traditional dark wood and plush upholstery pieces furnish both the public and private areas. A pool, swim-up bar, and outdoor grill have been added to the tropical garden facing the sea. ✉ *2024 Seawall Blvd., 77550* 📞*409/765–7721* 📠*409/765–5780* ⊕*www.wyndham. com* ➯ *231 rooms* ♿ *In room: dial-up, Ethernet. In hotel: restaurant, pool, gym, laundry service, public Internet, no-smoking rooms* ▤ *AE, DC, MC, V.*

$–$$ 🏨 **Tremont House.** A four-story atrium lobby, with ironwork balconies and full-size palm trees, showcases an 1872 hand-carved rosewood bar in what was once a busy dry-goods warehouse. It is actually a historic place: Republic of Texas president Sam Houston presented his last speech at this hotel, both Confederate and Union soldiers bunked here, and Great Storm victims took refuge under this roof. Rooms have high ceilings and 11-foot windows. Period reproduction furniture and Victorian-pattern wallpapers add to the authenticity. It's the closest full-service lodging to the port, just a short walk from shopping on the Strand. ✉ *2300 Ship's Mechanic Row, 77550* 📞 *409/763–0300* 📠 *409/763–1539* ⊕ *www.wyndham.com* ➯ *119 rooms* ♿ *In room: dial-up, Ethernet. In hotel: restaurant, room service, bar, laundry service, public Internet, parking (fee), no-smoking rooms* ▤ *AE, D, DC, MC, V.*

HOUSTON, TEXAS

Robin Barr
Sussman

Unbridled energy has always been Houston's trademark. Once a swamp near the junction of the Buffalo and White Oak bayous, Houston is now the nation's fourth-largest city and the energy capital of the United States. Excellent museums, galleries, and performance halls affirm the city's commitment to the arts, and its many ethnic restaurants add to the cosmopolitan flavor. Just a few hours' sailing time from the Gulf of Mexico, the Port of Houston—a vibrant component to the regional economy—comprises the port authority and the 150-plus private industrial companies along the Houston Ship Channel. At this writing, Norwegian Cruise Line bases two ships at Houston's single cruise terminal, operating week-long voyages to the Western Caribbean, including such ports as Roatan Island, Honduras; Belize City; and Cozumel, Mexico. This cruise terminal is convenient for Houstonians and residents of the smaller cities in the bay area.

Essentials

HOURS   Some museums are closed on Monday. Stores in malls tend to be open later, often until 9 PM.

INTERNET Since Houston is so spread out, it's best if you check your e-mail at your hotel rather than go searching for a far-flung Internet café.

VISITOR **Greater Houston Convention & Visitors Bureau** (🏠 *901 Bagby St.*
INFORMATION ☎ *713/437–5200* ⊕ *www.visithoustontexas.com*).

The Port of Houston

The Port of Houston is a 25-mi-long complex of diversified public and private industrial terminal facilities designed to handle general cargo. The facilities of this massive port cover several municipal jurisdictions, including the cities of Houston, Pasadena, Galena Park, LaPorte, Baytown, Deer Park, and Morgan's Point. Within the public terminal facilities is the Barbours Cut Cruise Terminal, which is located in Morgan's Point, near LaPorte, Texas. Norwegian Cruise Line vessels call on the terminal Saturdays and Sundays. To reach the port by car, from downtown Houston, take I–45 south to 610 N, then continue to 225 E. Turn on 146 S to Barbours Cut Boulevard and turn left. Drive 3 mi (5 km) to reach the cruise terminal. The new Bayport Cruise Terminal opened in 2007.

🏴 **Port of Houston** ⊠ Barbours Cut Terminal, 820 North L St., Pier C-7, Morgan's Point ⊠ 111 E. Loop N, Houston ☎ 713/670-2400 ⊕ www.portofhouston.com

AIRPORT There are two major airports in Houston. Bush Intercontinental Airport,
TRANSFERS 15 mi (24 km) northeast of downtown Houston, is 40 mi (64 km) and approximately 45 minutes from the Port of Houston. William P. Hobby

Airport, southeast of downtown, is closer, at 20 mi (32 km) and approximately 25 minutes. You may purchase a transfer option from the cruise line when you book your cruise, or you can arrange your own transfers. A private car transfer from Airport Taxi & Town Car will cost $65–$70 from Houston Hobby and $85 to $90 from Bush Intercontinental; Yellow Cab Houston charges by distance traveled, and their rates will usually be much cheaper than those of a private car service from Hobby and slightly cheaper from Bush Intercontinental (you can estimate your fare on the company's Web site). Visit Houston's official visitor's Web site to research hiring a taxi and current rates.

> **HOUSTON BEST BETS**
>
> ■ Kemah Boardwalk. This bayside entertainment and dining center is a good family destination.
>
> ■ Menil Collection. Art lovers will appreciate this eclectic collection—and it's all free.
>
> ■ NASA Space Center. Though not as extensive in its visitor facilities (or as expensive) as the Kennedy Space Center in Florida, this is still worth a trip.

🚕 **Airport Taxi & Town Car** ☎ 281/630–1137 ⊕ www.24hrairporttaxi.com. **Yellow Cab Houston** ☎ 713/236–1111 ⊕ www.yellowcabhouston.com.

PARKING Outdoor parking facilities operated by the Port of Houston Authority are available at the cruise-ship pier. Twenty-four-hour security is provided, and the facility is secured for the duration of the cruise. Rates are $7 per day. Note that parking fees must be paid with cash or traveler's checks; you can't use credit cards. The parking lot is very close to the terminal. Drive to the front of the terminal, and drop your baggage with the porters; then drive to the parking booth and pay; you'll be able to walk to the terminal.

Exploring Houston

Houston can be divided neatly into three major areas. One is its very modern downtown (including the theater district), which spurred one architecture critic to declare the city "America's future." Another is the area a couple of miles south of downtown, the museum district, where some of the Southwest's leading museums are found along with Rice University and the internationally renowned Texas Medical Center. There is the thriving shopping and business center west of downtown, known as both the Galleria and Uptown. Finally, there are neighborhoods south of downtown Houston that are convenient to the cruise port ripe for exploring.

DOWNTOWN Texas Avenue, downtown's main street, is 100 feet wide, precisely the width needed to accommodate 14 Texas longhorns tip to tip in the days when cattle were driven to market along this route. One good way to start any trip to downtown Houston is to take in the entire urban panorama from the observation deck (weekdays only) of I. M. Pei's 75-story **Chase Tower** (⊠ *600 Travis St.*), built in 1981. **Tranquility Park** (⊠ *between Walker and Rusk Sts. east of Smith St.*), a cool oasis of fountains and walkways, was built to commemorate the first landing on the moon by the *Apollo 11* mission.

Minute Maid Park is a state-of-the-art baseball stadium with a retractable roof to defy Houston's frequently changing weather. The stadium incorporates the 1911 Union Station (designed by Warren and Wetmore of New York's Grand Central Station fame), which houses the ball club offices, retail stores, and eateries.

> **CAUTION**
>
> An endlessly ringing telephone is a hint that you are not home. Before leaving the house, either turn off the telephone ringers or set the answering machine to pick up after two rings.

THE MUSEUM DISTRICT Most museums are clustered within an area bordering the verdant campus of Rice University, one of Texas's finest educational institutions, and Hermann Park, the city's playground. Walking from one institution to the other is possible, but the expanse can be taxing; it's best to segment your visit.

The **Museum of Fine Arts** is remarkable for the completeness of its enormous collection, housed in a complicated series of wings and galleries, many designed by Ludwig Mies van der Rohe. The Audrey Jones Beck Building, the work of famed Spanish architect Rafael Maneo, opened in 2000, doubling the museum's size. Renaissance and 18th-century art is particularly well represented, and there's a nice selection of Impressionist and Post-impressionist works and a museum store. The **Lillie and Hugh Roy Cullen Sculpture Garden** (⊠ *1001 Bissonnet St., at Montrose Ave.*), across the street from the Museum of Fine Arts, displays 19th- and 20th-century sculptures by Rodin, Matisse, Giacometti, and Stella in an outdoor space designed by Isamu Noguchi. It's open daily from 9 AM–10 PM. ⊠ *1001 Bissonnet St., north of Rice University, between Montrose Blvd. and Main St., Museum District* ☎ *713/639–7300* ⊕ *www.mfah.org* 🎫 *Museum $7, free Thurs.; garden free* ◯ *Tues. and Wed. 10–5; Thurs. 10–9, Fri. and Sat. 10–8; Sun. 12:15–7.*

The **Contemporary Arts Museum,** housed in an aluminum-sheathed trapezoid, is the home of avant-garde art in Houston, with many traveling exhibitions and a whimsical gift shop. ⊠ *5216 Montrose Blvd.* ☎ *713/284–8250* ⊕ *www.camh.org* 🎫 *Free* ◯ *Tues. and Wed. 10–5; Thurs. 10–9, Fri. and Sat. 10–5; Sun. 12–5.*

The **Menil Collection** is one of the city's premier cultural treasures. Italian architect Renzo Piano designed the spacious building with airy galleries. John and Dominique de Menil collected the eclectic art, which ranges from tribal African sculptures to Andy Warhol's paintings of Campbell's soup cans. A separate gallery across the street houses the paintings of American artist Cy Twombly. ⊠ *1515 Sul Ross St.* ☎ *713/525–9400* ⊕ *www.menil.org* 🎫 *Free* ◯ *Wed.–Sun. 11–7.*

OTHER NEIGHBORHOODS Kids and adults can learn about space exploration at **Space Center Houston.** Life on the deck of a space shuttle is simulated in the **Space Center Plaza.** In the **Kids Space Place,** children can ride on the lunar rover and try out tasks in the *Apollo* command module. The adjacent **Johnson Space Center** tour includes a visit to Mission Control and laboratories that simulate weightlessness and other space-related concepts. Allow several hours for your visit. ⊠ *1601 NASA Rd. 1, off I–45, 25 mi south of Downtown* ☎ *281/244–2100* ⊕ *www.spacecenter.org* 🕿 *$18.95* 🕙 *Weekdays 10–5, weekends 10–6.*

Take a detour off I–45 between Houston and Galveston to the **Kemah Boardwalk,** a cluster of restaurants, amusement rides, game arcades, and inns on the bustling ship channel. It's a family-oriented destination where you can catch a Gulf breeze, eat seafood, shop, and watch personal and commercial marine craft motor by. ⊠ *Bradford and 2nd St., Kemah* ☎ *877/285–3624* ⊕ *www.kemahboardwalk.com.*

Shopping

You can shop for just about anything in Houston. Shopping centers sprawl across the metropolis from the suburbs at points north (The Woodlands) and south (SugarLand), but the best concentration of fine and specialty stores is inside and just immediately outside Loop–610, commonly referred to as center of the city.

The city's premier shopping area is the **Galleria,** or **Uptown,** area; the business, office towers, and shopping complexes in the area have made it one of the most important business districts in the city. Many of Houston's best restaurants are here, and the River Oaks neighborhood, with its multimillion-dollar mansions and garden parkways, is nearby. The **Galleria Mall** (⊠ *Westheimer Rd. at Post Oak Blvd.*), the region's anchor shopping complex, is famous for high-quality stores like Neiman Marcus, Saks Fifth Avenue, and Tiffany & Co. **Uptown Park** (⊠ *Uptown Park Blvd. at Post Oak Blvd.*) is a charming European-style outdoor shopping center with cafés, upscale restaurants, designer-clothing boutiques, and fine jewelry shops north of the Galleria Mall off Post Oak Boulevard.

For antiques, vintage clothing, and folk art, try the stores in the **Heights,** a re-gentrified neighborhood north of I–10 (19th Street between Heights Boulevard and Yale Street). The **Museum District** is known for art galleries.

Nightlife

There are other hot spots around Houston, but downtown is the main magnet for after-hours activity, with new clubs and restaurants springing up all the time in renovated storefronts and warehouses. **Bayou Place** (⊠ *500 Texas Ave.*), Houston's largest entertainment complex, is a 130,000-square-foot, two-story center of evening activity, with restaurants, clubs, a theater, and the Angelika Film Center, a spinoff of the New York City cinema showing independent and foreign films.

Where to Eat

For price categories, *see* Dining at the beginning of this chapter.

From Vietnamese to Latin American, contemporary American or Indian, the Bayou City is among the more diverse places in Texas. Houston's food culture also mandates barbecue and Tex-Mex, high-end steak houses, and contemporary Italian restaurants as staples. It's a cosmopolitan scene with booming downtown eateries; increasingly, excellent hotel restaurants have become major dining destinations. About 20 mi (32 km) south of downtown Houston, you can experience the Kemah Boardwalk, a waterfront dining park and shopping center that is located near Clear Lake, just south of the port of Houston cruise terminal.

$$–$$$ ✕ **Aquarium Restaurant.** This one-of-a-kind restaurant on the Kemah Boardwalk serves quality seafood and has a sea-themed decor with floor-to-ceiling aquarium tanks. The whole family will be in awe of the myriad sea creatures, fish, sharks, and colorful coral on display. It's a wide-ranging menu that moves easily between fancy seafood entrées and casual, kid-friendly meals. ✉ *11 Kemah Waterfront, Kemah* ☎ *281/334–9010* ▭ *AE, D, DC, MC, V.*

$–$$$ ✕ **Ibiza.** Gutsy, sometimes playful, cuisine prepared by Chef Charles Clark is served in a bustling dining room as seductive as its namesake island off the coast of Spain. Generous portions of seasonal dishes intermingle with delectable Spanish tapas and hearty entrées such as "six-hour" braised lamb shank with Spanish mint oil. Oenophiles will appreciate Ibiza's ever-changing wine list of rare tastes at fair prices. Don't miss the outdoor patio on pretty days, the Sunday paella, or the homemade sangria chock-full of fresh fruit. ✉ *2450 Louisiana St., suite 300* ☎ *713/524–0004* ⚑ *Reservations essential* ▭ *AE, D, DC, MC, V* ⊘ *Closed Mon.*

¢–$ ✕ **Goode Company.** Down-home Texas barbecue is prepared ranch-style—mesquite-smoked and served with tasty red sauce. Patrons line up on the sidewalk to eat at picnic tables on the covered patio. A standard order is the chopped-beef brisket sandwich on jalapeño-cheese bread. Don't skip the celebrated pecan pie for dessert. For hamburgers, tacos, and great weekend breakfasts, visit Goode Company Hamburgers and Taqueria right across the street on Kirby Drive. ✉ *5109 Kirby Dr.* ☎ *713/522–2530* ▭ *AE, D, DC, MC, V.*

Where to Stay

Sprawling Houston has a seemingly endless variety of respectable hotels that are convenient to the port of Houston cruise terminal. However, the revitalized downtown offers both a central location and quick access to I–45 S and the port. Downtown Houston offers world-class hotels, a vibrant nightlife, and varied, if trendy, restaurants. Moderate hotels are even closer to the port of Houston in LaPorte, which is a mostly industrial area, so do not expect the same urban scene. Although rack rates for many Houston hotels seem high, they drop dramatically on weekends or if you make your reservation online or in advance.

$$$ 🏨 **Alden Houston.** Formerly named The Sam Houston Hotel, this small luxury boutique hotel is decidedly modern and well located near bustling Main Street and the ballpark. The guest rooms are stylish, with fine linens, granite bathrooms, high-tech work stations, and suites with plasma TVs. The hotel's award-winning restaurant, 17, is just as modern and attracts a hip international crowd of epicures hungry for contemporary American food. Don't miss it. ✉ *1117 Prairie St., 77002* ☎ *832/200–8800 or 877/348–8800* 🖶 *832/200–8822* ⊕ *www.aldenhotels.com* ↪ *97 rooms* ⚐ *In room: DVD, refrigerator, Wi-Fi. In hotel: Restaurant, room service, bar, gym, concierge, laundry service, public Wi-Fi, some pets allowed* ▭ *AE, D, DC, MC, V* ⦿ *EP.*

$–$$$ 🏨 **Hilton Houston NASA Clear Lake.** On the shores of Clear Lake, this Hilton offers a number of water sports and easy access to NASA, which is across the street. ✉ *3000 NASA Rd. 1, 77058* ☎ *281/333–9300* 🖶 *281/333–*

3750 ⊕ *www.hilton.com* ↩ *243 rooms* ♿ *In hotel: Restaurant, room service, bar, pool, gym, public Internet* ▭ *AE, D, DC, MC, V* ⊙ *EP.*

JACKSONVILLE, FLORIDA

Kerry
Speckman

One of Florida's oldest cities and at 730 square mi (1,891 square km) the largest city in the continental United States, Jacksonville makes for an underrated vacation spot; it's a worthwhile vacation spot for an extra day or two before or after your cruise. It offers appealing downtown riverside areas, handsome residential neighborhoods, the region's only skyscrapers, a thriving arts scene, and, for football fans, the NFL Jaguars and the NCAA Gator Bowl. Remnants of the Old South flavor the city, especially in the Riverside/Avondale historic district, where moss-draped oak trees frame prairie-style bungalows and Tudor Revival mansions; and palm trees, Spanish bayonet, and azaleas populate Jacksonville's landscape.

Essentials

HOURS Many museums close on Monday.

INTERNET Most people access the Internet in their hotel. If you are in town for just the day (or if your hotel has expensive or inadequate Internet access options), there are Internet cafés. **Docking Station** (⊠ *1301-11 Monument Rd.* ☎ *904/722–3625* ⊕ *dstationtech.com*).

VISITOR
INFORMATION
Jacksonville & The Beaches Convention & Visitors Bureau (⊠ *550 Water St., Suite 1000, Jacksonville 32202* ☎ *904/798–9111 or 800/733–2668* ⊕ *www.jaxcvb.com*).

The Cruise Port

Limited in the sizes of ships it can berth, JAXPORT currently serves as home port to the Carnival *Celebration,* which departs weekly on 4- and 5-night cruises to Key West and the Bahamas. Plans are in the works to move the port to a more accessible location within the next several years, but in the meantime, cruises depart from a temporary cruise facility. The facility is fairly sparse, consisting basically of some vending machines and restrooms, but the embarkation staff receives high marks, having won a good-service award from Carnival Cruise Line in 2004 and 2005.

JAXPORT is about 15 minutes from the Jacksonville International Airport. Take I–95 S to S.R. 9-A E. Follow 9-A to Heckscher Drive (S.R. 105) west until you reach August Drive. Head south on August Drive, and follow the signs to the cruise terminal.

🛈 **Jacksonville Port Authority** ⊠ 9810 August Dr., Jacksonville, FL ☎ 904/630–3006 ⊕ www.jaxport.com.

AIRPORT
TRANSFERS
The transfer from Jacksonville airport takes about 15 minutes and costs $20 to $25 for up to four passengers by taxi. Express Shuttle costs $10 per person and departs the airport every 15 minutes.

🛈 **Express Shuttle USA** ☎ 904/353–8880. **Gator City Taxi & Shuttle** ☎ 904/355–8294. **Yellow Cab** ☎ 904/260–1111.

PARKING There is a fenced and guarded parking lot next to the cruise terminal, within walking distance. Parking costs $12 per day for regular vehicles, $20 for RVs. You must pay in advance by cash or major credit card.

Exploring Jacksonville

Because Jacksonville was settled along both sides of the twisting St. Johns River, a number of attractions are on or near a riverbank. Both sides of the river, which is spanned by myriad bridges, have downtown areas and waterfront complexes of shops, restaurants, parks, and museums; some attractions can be reached by water taxi or the Skyway Express monorail system—scenic alternatives to driving back and forth across the bridges—but a car is generally necessary.

Numbers in the margin correspond to points of interest on the Jacksonville map.

7 **Anheuser-Busch Jacksonville Brewery.** Beer lovers will appreciate this behind-the-scenes look at how barley malt, rice, hops, and water form the "King of Beers." Guided tours take guests through the entire brewing and bottling process. Or you can hightail it through the self-guided tour and head straight to the free beer tastings, which is all that true beer lovers really care about anyway. Leave the kids at home, though, since guests must be at least 18 to visit the brewery or shops. ⊠ *111 Busch Dr.* ☎ *904/696–8373* ⊕ *www.budweisertours.com* ☒ *Free* ☽ *Mon.–Sat. 10–4; guided tours Mon.–Sat. 10–3 on the half hr.*

❷ Cummer Museum of Art and Gardens. The world-famous Wark Collection of early-18th-century Meissen porcelain is just one reason to visit this former riverfront estate; it also includes 13 permanent galleries with more than 5,000 items spanning 8,000 years and 3 acres of riverfront gardens reflecting Northeast Florida's blooming seasons and indigenous varieties. For the kids, Art Connections allows them to experience art through hands-on, interactive exhibits. The latest museum's addition, the Thomas H. Jacobsen Gallery of American Art, focuses on works by American artists including Max Weber, N. C. Wyeth, and Paul Manship. ⊠ *829 Riverside Ave.* ☎ *904/356–6857* ⊕ *www.cummer.org* ⊠ *$8* ☉ *Tues. and Thurs. 10–9, Wed., Fri., and Sat. 10–5, Sun. noon–5.*

❹ Jacksonville Landing. During the week, this riverfront festival marketplace caters to locals and tourists alike, with more than 40 specialty shops with home furnishings, apparel, and toys, nine full-service restaurants—including a brew pub, Italian bistro, and steak house—and an internationally flavored food court (though the view is probably the best thing on any of their menus). On the weekends, the Landing hosts more than 250 events each year, ranging from the good clean fun of the American Cancer Society Duck Race to the just plain obnoxious Florida–Georgia game after-party, as well as live music (usually of the local cover band variety) in the courtyard. ⊠ *2 Independent Dr.* ☎ *904/353–1188* ⊕ *www.jacksonvillelanding.com* ⊠ *Free* ☉ *Mon.–Thurs. 10–8, Fri. and Sat. 10–9, Sun. noon–5:30; some restaurants open earlier and close later.*

⟳ **❻ Jacksonville Zoo & Gardens.** Encompassing more than 120 acres on Jacksonville's Northside, this midsize zoo is home to thousands of amphibians, birds, invertebrates, mammals, and reptiles from barking tree frogs and Madagascar hissing cockroaches to dusky pygmy rattlesnakes and giant anteaters. Among the zoo's outstanding exhibits is its collection of rare waterfowl and the Serona Overlook, which showcases some of the world's most venomous snakes. The Florida Wetlands is a 2½-acre area with black bears, bald eagles, white-tailed deer, and other animals native to Florida. The African Veldt has alligators, elephants, and white rhinos, among other species of African birds and mammals. The zoo's newest exhibit, the Range of the Jaguar, includes 4 acres of exotic big cats as well as 20 other species of animals. A new $6.7-million Kids' Zone complete with a splash park, forest play area, maze, and discovery building is expected to be completed by the end of 2006. ⊠ *370 Zoo Pkwy., off Heckscher Dr. E* ☎ *904/757–4463* ⊕ *www.jaxzoo.org* ⊠ *$11* ☉ *Daily 9–5.*

FodorsChoice ★

⟳ **❶ Kids Kampus.** Directly on the St. Johns River adjacent to Metropolitan Park, this 10-acre recreational fa-

> ## JACKSONVILLE BEST BETS
>
> ■ **Jacksonville Zoo.** One of the best mid-size zoos you'll visit.
>
> ■ **Kids Kampus.** If you are traveling with your family, this park may become your favorite place in the city.
>
> ■ **Museum of Contemporary Art Jacksonville.** Though small, this excellent museum is an unexpected treat in Northeast Florida.

cility, developed by local educators, encourages children's natural curiosity with climbing and sliding apparati, engaging playscapes, mini-representations of Jacksonville landmarks, like Bay Street, Kings Road, and the main post office, and a splash park. It's not exactly Disney World, but parents looking for a

way to entertain the kids for a couple of hours, especially in the sweltering Florida heat, report it just might be the happiest place on earth. The "kampus" also has a picnic pavilion and jogging trail. ⊠ *1410 Gator Bowl Blvd.* ☎ *904/630–5437* ⚑ *Free* ⊙ *Mar.–Oct., Mon.–Sat. 8–8, Sun. 10–8; Nov.–Feb., Mon.–Sat. 8–6, Sun. 10–6.*

❺ **Museum of Contemporary Art Jacksonville.** In this loftlike downtown building, the former headquarters of the Western Union Telegraph Company, a permanent collection of 20th-century art shares space with traveling exhibitions. The museum encompasses five galleries and ArtExplorium, a highly interactive educational exhibit for kids. MOCA Jacksonville (previously known as the Jacksonville Museum of Modern Art) also hosts film series, lectures, and workshops throughout the year. ⊠ *Hemming Plaza, 333 N. Laura St.* ☎ *904/366–6911* ⊕ *www.jmoma.org* ⚑ *$6, free Wed. 5–9 and Sun.* ⊙ *Tues. and Fri. 11–5, Wed. and Thurs. 11–9, Sat. 11–4, Sun. noon–4.*

Fodor'sChoice
★

❸ **Museum of Science and History.** You won't find any mad scientists here, but you'll probably find lots of giggling ones. Targeted at the elementary and middle school set, MOSH aims to educate and entertain kids about science and history through a variety of interactive exhibits like the JEA Science Theatre, where they'll participate in live experiments related to electricity and electrical safety; the Florida Naturalist's Center, where they can explore Northeast Florida wildlife (like American alligators, gopher turtles, and various native snakes and birds); and the Universe of Science, where they'll learn about properties of physical science through hands-on demonstrations. Other permanent exhibits include Atlantic Tails, a hands-on exploration of whales, dolphins, and manatees; Currents of Time, chronicling 12,000 years of Northeast Florida history; and Prehistoric Park, featuring a life-size Allosaurus skeleton. The Alexander Brest Planetarium hosts daily shows on astronomy (request your seating pass from the front desk 30 minutes prior to any showing) and, on weekends, Cosmic Concerts, 3-D laser shows set to pop music. ⊠ *1025 Museum Circle* ☎ *904/396–6674* ⊕ *www.themosh.org* ⚑ *$8, Cosmic Concerts $3–$6* ⊙ *Weekdays 10–5, Sat. 10–6, Sun. 1–6.*

Shopping

At **Five Points** (⊠ *Intersection of Park, Margaret, and Lomax Sts.*) you'll find a small but funky shopping district of new and vintage clothing boutiques, shoe stores, and antiques shops, as well as a handful of eateries and bars, not to mention some of the most colorful characters in the city. **San Marco Square** (⊠ *San Marco and Atlantic Blvds.*) has dozens of interesting apparel, home, and jewelry stores and restaurants in

1920s Mediterranean Revival-style buildings. **The Shoppes of Avondale** (⊠ *St. Johns Ave., between Talbot Ave. and Dancy St.*) consist mostly of upscale clothing and accessories boutiques, art galleries, home-furnishing shops, a chocolatier, and trendy restaurants.

Where to Eat

JAXPORT's location on Jacksonville's Westside means there aren't too many nearby restaurants. But by taking a 10- to 15-minute drive south, you'll find a wealth of restaurants for all tastes and price categories.

For price categories, *see* Dining at the beginning of this chapter.

★ **$$–$$$** ✕ **Bistro Aix.** When a Jacksonville restaurant can make Los Angelesians feel like they haven't left home, that's saying a lot. With its slick black leather booths, 1940s brickwork, velvet drapes, and intricate marbled globes, Bistro Aix (pronounced "X") is just that place. Regulars can't get enough of the creamy onion soup, crispy calimari, and house-made potato chips with warm blue cheese appetizers or entrées like oak-fired fish "Aixoise," grilled salmon, and filet mignon, while Aix's on-site pastry chef ensures no sweet tooth leaves unsatisfied. For the most part, waitstaff are knowledgeable and pleasant, though some patrons find their demeanor snooty, except, of course, those patrons from L.A. Call ahead for preferred seating. ⊠ *1440 San Marco Blvd.* ☎ *904/398–1949* ♻ *Reservations not accepted* ☰ *AE, D, DC, MC, V* ⊙ *No lunch weekends.*

$–$$ ✕ **Biscottis.** The local artwork on the redbrick walls is a mild distraction from the jovial crowds (from yuppies to soccer moms to metrosexuals) jockeying for tables in this midsize restaurant. Elbows almost touch, but no one seems to mind. The menu offers the unexpected: wild-mushroom ravioli with a broth of corn, leek, and dried apricot; or curry grilled swordfish with cucumber fig bordelaise. And if you ever have trouble finding the place, just follow the trail of drool down St. Johns Avenue, which leads directly to Biscottis decadent dessert case (we hear the peanut butter ganache is illegal in three states). ⊠ *3556 St. Johns Ave.* ☎ *904/387–2060* ♻ *Reservations not accepted* ☰ *AE, MC, V.*

¢ ✕ **European Street Cafe.** Wicker baskets and lofty shelves brimming with European confections and groceries like Toblerone and Nutella fill practically every inch of space not occupied by café tables. The menu can be similarly overwhelming, with nearly 100 deli sandwiches and salads. This spot is favored by area professionals looking for a quick lunch, as well as the under-forty set doing 23-ounce curls with one of the restaurant's 20-plus beers on tap (plus more than 100 in bottles). 2753 Park St. ☎ *904/384–9999* ♻ *Reservations not accepted* ☰ *AE, D, MC, V.*

Where to Stay

Hotels near the cruise terminals are few and far between, so most cruisers needing a room make the drive to Downtown (15 minutes) or to the Southbank or Riverside (20 minutes).

For price categories, *see* Lodging at the beginning of this chapter.

$$–$$$ ▦ **Hyatt Regency Jacksonville Riverfront.** In Jacksonville, it doesn't get much more convenient than this downtown, waterfront hotel. Perched on the north bank of the St. Johns River, the nine-story property is within walking distance of the Jacksonville Landing, Florida Theatre, and T-U Center, as well as corporate office towers and the county courthouse. The former Adam's Mark Hotel has undergone some significant changes, most notably in its dining options with the addition of the Plaza III Steakhouse, and its guest rooms with a splashier Florida-style decor, triple-sheeted beds, and (gasp!) hotel windows that actually open, while retaining some of its best features, namely the rooftop swimming pool and club-level rooms, where guests enjoy complimentary breakfast every morning and hors d'oeuvres every night. Unfortunately, the heavily mirrored, over-chandeliered, and excessively sconced lobby remains largely intact. ⊠ *225 E. Coastline Dr., 32202* ☎ *904/633–9095 or 800/444–2326* 🖶 *904/633–9988* ⊕ *www.jacksonville.hyatt.com* 🛏 *966 rooms, 21 suites* ⚷ *In-room: refrigerator (some), Ethernet. In-hotel: 3 restaurants, room service, bar, pool, gym, concierge, laundry facilities, laundry service, concierge, executive floor, public Wi-Fi, parking (fee), no-smoking rooms* 🖃 *AE, D, DC, MC, V.*

★ **$–$$$** 🏨 **Omni Jacksonville Hotel.** Further cementing its reputation as Jacksonville's most luxurious hotel, the 16-story Omni underwent a multi-million-dollar renovation enhancing practically every area of the property. Guest rooms are done in a "downtown urban style" with neutral colors (creams and grays), dark wood, stainless steel, and flat-screen TVs and feature complimentary Wi-Fi. The splashy marble-floor lobby leads to the reception area, an upscale lounge—J Bar—and Juliette's Bistro with cozy banquettes and tables that look up to a soaring atrium. It also scores high marks for its family-oriented atmosphere, including Nintendo in every room, no adult films, and the Omni Kids Rule program. Bell service is also exemplary: with most porters having 10-plus years on the job, they can, and will, help you find just about anything. Parking, however, can be a bear when there's a show at the Times-Union Center for the Performing Arts across the street. ⊠ *245 Water St., 32202* ☎ *904/355–6664 or 800/843–6664* 🖶 *904/791–4812* ⊕ *www.omnijacksonville.com* 🛏 *354 rooms, 4 suites* ⚷ *In-room: kitchen (some), Wi-Fi. In-hotel: restaurant, room service, bar, pool, gym, children's programs (ages 3–10), laundry service, concierge, public Wi-Fi, parking (fee), some pets allowed, no-smoking rooms* 🖃 *AE, D, DC, MC, V.*

MIAMI, FLORIDA

Miami is the busiest of Florida's very busy cruise ports. Because there's so much going on here, you might want to schedule an extra day or two before and/or after your cruise to explore North America's most Latin city. Downtown is a convenient place to stay if you are meeting up with a cruise ship, but at night, except for Bayside Marketplace, the AmericanAirlines Arena, and a few ever-changing clubs in warehouses, the area is deserted. Travelers spend little time here, since most tourist attractions are in other neighborhoods. Miami Beach, particularly the 1-square-mi Art Deco District in South Beach—the section south of 24th to 28th streets—is the heart of Miami's vibrant nightlife and restaurant scene. But you may also want to explore beyond the beach, including the Little Havana, Coral Gables, and Coconut Grove sections of the city.

Miami

South Beach (inset map)

Lincoln Rd. — 2
E. Española Way
Lincoln Rd. Mall
16th St.
14th Pl.
14th St.
Flamingo Park
11th St.
10th St.
9th St.
8th St.
5th St.
4th St.
3rd St.
2nd St.
1st St.
Washington Ave.
Pennsylvania Ave.
Euclid Ave.
Meridian Ave.
Jefferson Ave.
Michigan Ave.
Lenox Ave.
West Ave.
Alton Rd.
Collins Ave.
Ocean Dr.
Lummus Park
Atlantic Ocean

ATLANTIC OCEAN

Cruise Ship Terminal

See Inset

Fisher Island

Virginia Key

KEY BISCAYNE

Marine Stadium

Rickenbacker Causeway

Biscayne Bay

Grove Isle

COCONUT GROVE

MIAMI

CORAL GABLES

Miami International Airport

0   2 mile
0   2 kilometer

KEY
1 What to See
① Where to Stay & Eat

What to See

Art Deco District Welcome Center	...3
Bass Museum of Art	...1
Brickell Village	...5
Fairchild Tropical Garden	...8
Lincoln Road Mall	...2
Little Havana	...6
Parrot Jungle Island	...4
Vizcaya Museum & Gardens	...7

Where to Eat

Azul	...4
Crystal Café	...1
Tony Chan's Water Club	...2

Where to Stay

Hyatt Regency Miami	...3
Mandarin Oriental, Miami	...4
Townhouse	...5

The Cruise Port

The Port of Miami, in downtown Miami near Bayside Marketplace and the MacArthur Causeway, justifiably bills itself as the Cruise Capital of the World. Home to 18 ships and the largest year-round cruise fleet in the world, the port accommodates more than 3 million passengers a year. It has 12 air-conditioned terminals, duty-free shopping, and limousine service. You can get taxis at all the terminals, and car-rental agencies offer shuttles to off-site lots.

> **CAUTION**
>
> Airline carry-on restrictions are being updated continuously. Check with your airline before packing, and be aware that large purses will sometimes be counted as a carry-on item!

If you are driving, take I–95 north or south to I–395. Follow the directional signs to the Biscayne Boulevard exit. When you get to Biscayne Boulevard, make a right. Go to 5th Street, which becomes Port Boulevard (look for the AmericanAirlines Arena); then make a left and go over the Port Bridge. Follow the directional signs to your terminal.

Port of Miami ⊠ 1015 North American Way ☎ 305/371–7678 ⊕ www.co.miami-dade.fl.us/portofmiami.

AIRPORT TRANSFERS
If you have not arranged an airport transfer through your cruise line, you have a couple of options to get to the cruise port. The first is a taxi, and the fares are reasonable. The fare between MIA and the Port of Miami is a flat fare of $24. This fare is per trip, not per passenger, and includes tolls and $1 airport surcharge but not tip. SuperShuttle vans transport passengers between MIA and local hotels, as well as the Port of Miami. At MIA the vans pick up at the ground level of each concourse (look for clerks with yellow shirts, who will flag one down). Service from MIA is available on demand; for the return it's best to make reservations 24 hours in advance. The cost from MIA to the cruise port is $15 per person, or $55 if you want the entire van to yourselves.

SuperShuttle ☎ 305/871–2000 from MIA, 954/764–1700 from Broward [Fort Lauderdale], 800/874–8885 from elsewhere.

PARKING
Street-level lots are right in front of each of the cruise terminals. The cost is $12 per day ($24 for RVs), payable in advance. You can pay with a credit card at most terminals (except for numbers 2 and 10), though it's MasterCard and Visa only.

VISITOR INFORMATION
Greater Miami Convention & Visitors Bureau ⊠ 701 Brickell Ave., Suite 2700, Downtown, 33131 ☎ 305/539–3000 or 800/933–8448 ⊕ www.gmcvb.com ⊠ Bayside Marketplace tourist information center, 401 Biscayne Blvd., Bayside Marketplace, 33132 ☎ 305/539–2980.

Exploring Miami

In the 1950s, Miami was best known for alligator wrestlers and you-pick strawberry fields or citrus groves. Well, things have changed. Miami on the mainland is South Florida's commercial hub, while its sultry sister, Miami Beach (America's Riviera), encompasses 17 islands in Biscayne Bay. Seducing winter refugees with its sunshine, beaches, palms, and nightlife, this is what most people envision when planning a trip to what they think of as Miami. If you want to do any exploring, you'll have to drive.

Numbers in the margin correspond to points of interest on the Miami map.

PACK IT, POST IT

Pack a pad of Post-It notes when you take a cruise. They come in handy when you need to leave messages for your cabin steward, family, and shipboard friends.

❸ **Art Deco District Welcome Center.** Run by the Miami Design Preservation League, the center provides information about the buildings in the district. A gift shop sells 1930s–1950s art deco memorabilia, posters, and books on Miami's history. Several tours—covering Lincoln Road, Espanola Way, North Beach, the entire Art Deco District, among others— start here. You can rent audiotapes for a self-guided tour, join one of the regular morning (Wed. & Fri.-Sun.) or Thursday-evening walking tours, or take a bicycle tour. ✉ *1001 Ocean Dr., at Barbara Capitman Way (10th St.), South Beach* 🕿 *305/531–3484 or 305/672–2014* 🖅 *Tours $20* ☉ *Sun.-Thurs. 10–7, Fri.-Sat. 10–6.*

❶ **Bass Museum of Art.** European art is the focus of this impressive museum in historic Collins Park, a short drive north of SoBe's key sights. Works on display include *The Holy Family,* a painting by Peter Paul Rubens; *The Tournament,* one of several 16th-century Flemish tapestries; and works by Albrecht Dürer and Henri de Toulouse-Lautrec. An $8 million, three-phase expansion by architect Arata Isozaki added another wing, cafeteria, and theater, doubling the museum's size to nearly 40,000 square feet. ✉ *2121 Park Ave., South Beach* 🕿 *305/673–7530* ⊕ *www. bassmuseum.org* 🖅 *$8* ☉ *Tues.–Sat. 10–5, Thurs. 10–9, Sun. 11–5.*

❺ **Brickell Village.** Brickell (rhymes with "fickle") is an up-and-coming downtown area with new low- and high-rise condos, a shopping area, Brickell Park, and plenty of popular restaurants. **Perricone's Marketplace and Café** (✉ *15 S.E. 10th St., Brickell Village*) is the biggest and most popular of the area's many Italian restaurants, in a 120-year-old Vermont barn. The cooking is simple and good. Buy your wine from the on-premises deli and bring it to your table for a small corking fee. ✉ *Between Miami River and S.W. 15th St., Brickell Village.*

❽ **Fairchild Tropical Garden.** Comprising 83 acres, this is the largest tropical botanical garden in the continental United States. Eleven lakes, a rain forest, and lots of palm trees, cycads, and flowers, including orchids, mountain roses, bellflowers, coral trees, and bougainvillea make it a garden for the senses—and there's special assistance for the hearing impaired. Take the free guided tram tour, which leaves on the hour. Spicing up the social calendar are garden sales (don't miss the Ramble in November or the International Mango Festival in July), moonlight strolls, and symphony concerts. A gift shop in the visitor center is a popular source for books on gardening and horticulture, ordered by botanists the world over. ✉ *10901 Old Cutler Rd., Coral Gables* 🕿 *305/667–1651* ⊕ *www. fairchildgarden.org* 🖅 *$20* ☉ *Daily 9:30–4:30.*

Fodor'sChoice
★

2 Lincoln Road Mall. The Morris Lapidus–renovated Lincoln Road, just a few blocks from the beach and convention center, is fun, lively, and friendly for people old, young, gay, and straight—and their dogs. Folks skate, scoot, bike, or jog here past the electronics stores at the Collins Avenue end toward the chichi boutiques and outdoor cafés heading west. An 18-screen movie theater anchors the west end of the street. The best times to hit the road are during Sunday-morning farmers' markets and on weekend evenings when cafés are bustling; art galleries, like Romero Britto's Britto Central, schedule openings; street performers take the stage; and bookstores, import shops, and clothing stores are open late. ⊠ *Lincoln Rd. between Collins Ave. and Alton Rd., South Beach.*

FodorśChoice ★

6 Little Havana. More than 40 years ago the tidal wave of Cubans fleeing the Castro regime flooded into an older neighborhood west of downtown Miami. Don't expect a sparkling and lively reflection of 1950s Havana, however. What you will find are ramshackle motels and cluttered storefronts. With a million Cubans and other Latinos—who make up more than half the metropolitan population—dispersed throughout Greater Miami, Little Havana and neighboring East Little Havana remain magnets for Hispanics and Anglos alike, who come to experience the flavor of traditional Cuban culture. That culture, of course, functions in Spanish. Many Little Havana residents and shopkeepers speak little or no English. In Little Havana's commercial heart, **Calle Ocho** (⊠ *S.W. 8th St., Little Havana*), experience such Cuban favorites as hand-rolled cigars or sandwiches piled with meats and cheeses. Although the entire area deserves exploring, if time is limited, try the stretch from Southwest 14th to 11th avenues. In **Plaza de la Cubanidad** (⊠ *W. Flagler St. and S.W. 17th Ave., Little Havana*) redbrick sidewalks surround a fountain and monument with the words of José Martí, a leader in Cuba's struggle for independence from Spain and a hero to Cuban refugees and immigrants in Miami. The quotation, LAS PALMAS SON NOVIAS QUE ESPERAN (The palm trees are waiting brides), counsels hope and fortitude to the Cubans.

4 Parrot Jungle Island. One of South Florida's original tourist attractions, Parrot Jungle opened in 1936 and has relocated to Watson Island, linked by the MacArthur Causeway (I–395) to Miami and Miami Beach. In addition to a thousand exotic birds, the attraction includes a 17-foot Asian crocodile, a 9-foot albino alligator, a serpentarium filled with venomous snakes, a petting zoo, and a two-story-high aviary with more than 100 free-flying macaws. A restaurant with indoor and outdoor seating overlooks a lake where 60 postcard-perfect Caribbean flamingos hang out. Orchids and ferns and even trees from the original site were transplanted along a Disneyesque jungle river that meanders through the park. ⊠ *980 MacArthur Causeway, Watson Island* 🕾 *305/258–6453* ⊕ *www. parrotjungle.com* ⊠ *$27.95 plus $7 parking* ☉ *Daily 10–6; last admission 4:30.*

7 Vizcaya Museum & Gardens. Of the 10,000 people living in Miami between 1912 and 1916, about 1,000 of them were gainfully employed by Chicago industrialist James Deering to build the $20-million Italian Renaissance–style winter residence. Once comprising 180 acres, the grounds now cover a still-substantial 30-acre tract, including a native hammock

FodorśChoice ★

and more than 10 acres of formal gardens and fountains overlooking Biscayne Bay. The house, open to the public, contains 70 rooms, 34 of which are filled with paintings, sculpture, antique furniture, and other decorative arts dating from the 15th through the 19th century and representing the Renaissance, baroque, rococo, and neoclassical styles. ⊠ *3251 S. Miami Ave., Coconut Grove* ☎*305/250–9133* ⊕*www.vizcayamuseum. com* 🖙 *$12* ☉ *House daily 9:30–4:30, garden daily 9:30–5:30.*

Beaches

The **beach on Ocean Drive from 1st to 22nd Street**—primarily the 10-block stretch from 5th to 15th Street—is one of the most talked-about beachfronts in America. The beach is wide, white, and bathed by warm aquamarine waves. Separating the sand from the traffic of Ocean Drive is palm-fringed Lummus Park, with its volleyball nets and chickee huts for shade. The beach also has some of the funkiest lifeguard stands you'll ever see, pop stars shooting music videos, and visitors from all over the world. Popular with gays is the beach at **12th Street.** Because much of South Beach has an adult flavor—women are often casually topless—many families prefer the beach's quieter southern reaches, especially **3rd Street Beach** (⊠ *Ocean Dr. and 3rd St., South Beach*). Unless you're parking south of 3rd Street, metered spaces near the waterfront are rarely empty. Instead, opt for a public garage and walk; you'll have lots of fun people-watching, too. ☎ *305/673–7714.*

Shopping

In Greater Miami you're never more than 15 minutes from a major commercial area that serves as both a shopping and entertainment venue for tourists and locals. The shopping is great on a two-block stretch of **Collins Avenue** between 6th and 8th streets. The busy **Lincoln Road Mall** is just a few blocks from the beach and convention center, making it popular with locals and tourists. There's an energy to shopping here, especially on weekends, when the pedestrian mall is filled with locals. Creative merchandise, galleries, and a Sunday-morning antiques market can be found among the art galleries and cool cafés. An 18-screen movie theater anchors the west end of the street. **Bayside Marketplace** (⊠ *401 Biscayne Blvd., Downtown*), the 16-acre shopping complex on Biscayne Bay, has more than 100 specialty shops, live entertainment, tourboat docks, and a food court. It's open late (until 10 during the week, 11 on Friday and Saturday), but its restaurants stay open even later. Browse, buy, or simply relax by the bay with a tropical drink.

Nightlife

Most of the city's nightlife scene is concentrated in South Beach. The best, most complete source is the *New Times,* a free weekly distributed throughout Miami–Dade County each Thursday. Greater Miami's English-language daily newspaper, the *Miami Herald,* publishes reliable reviews and comprehensive listings in its "Weekend" section on Friday and in the "IN South Florida" section on Sunday. Various tabloids reporting on South Beach entertainment and the Miami social scene come and go but *Ocean Drive Magazine* remains the most reliable glossy monthly publication for what's new and hot in the city's fashion, nightlife, and dining scenes. Buy it on the newsstands at Publix or Books

& Books, or pick it up for free in South Beach's high-end hotels, salons, and boutiques. *Wire* covers the gay scene.

Where to Eat

At many of the hottest spots, you'll need a reservation to avoid a long wait for a table. And when you get your check, note whether a gratuity is included; most restaurants add 15% (ostensibly for the convenience of—and protection from—Latin-American and European tourists who are used to this practice in their homelands and would not normally tip), but you can reduce or supplement it depending on your opinion of the service.

For price categories, *see* Dining at the beginning of this chapter.

$$–$$$$ ✕ **Azul.** This sumptuous eatery has truly conquered the devil in the details. In addition to chef Clay Conley's exquisite French–Caribbean cuisine, the thoughtful touches in service graciously anticipate your needs. Does your sleeveless top mean your shoulders are too cold to properly appreciate the Swiss chard–stuffed pompano with caramelized pears? Ask for one of the house pashminas. Need somewhere to properly place your Birken bag? Ask for a purse stand. Forgot your reading glasses and can't decipher the hanger steak with foie gras sauce? Request a pair from the host. Want to see how the other half lives? Descend the staircase to Café Sambal, the all-day casual restaurant overlooking the shimmering waters and luxurious high-rise buildings of Biscayne Bay. ⊠ *Mandarin Oriental, Miami, 500 Brickell Key Dr., Brickell Key* ☎ *305/913–8288* ⌂ *Reservations essential* ▤ *AE, MC, V* ⊘ *No lunch weekends.*

$–$$$$ ✕ **Tony Chan's Water Club.** Off the lobby of the Doubletree Grand Hotel, this spot overlooks a bayside marina. On the menu of more than 200 appetizers and entrées are minced quail tossed with bamboo shoots and mushrooms wrapped in lettuce leaves. Indulge in a seafood spectacular of shrimp, conch, scallops, fish cakes, and crabmeat tossed with broccoli in a bird's nest, or go for pork chops sprinkled with green pepper in a black bean–garlic sauce. A lighter favorite is steamed sea bass with ginger and garlic. ⊠ *1717 N. Bayshore Dr., Downtown* ☎ *305/374–8888* ▤ *AE, D, DC, MC, V* ⊘ *No lunch weekends.*

$$–$$$ ✕ **Crystal Café.** Classic dishes like beef Stroganoff and chicken *paprikash* are updated and lightened up here; osso buco falls off the bone (there's also a seafood version with salmon). More contemporary items include chicken Kiev, stuffed with goat cheese and topped with a tricolor salad, and pan-seared duck breast with raspberry sauce. Multiple Golden Spoon award–winning Macedonian chef-proprietor Klime Kovaceski takes pride in serving more food than you can possibly manage, including home-baked rhubarb pie. ⊠ *726 41st St., Miami Beach* ☎ *305/673–8266* ▤ *AE, D, DC, MC, V* ⊘ *Closed Mon. No lunch.*

Where to Stay

Staying in downtown Miami will put you close to the cruise terminals, but there is little to do at night. South Beach is the center of the action in Miami Beach, but it's fairly distant from the port. Staying in Miami Beach, but north of South Beach's Art Deco District, will put you on the beach but nominally closer to the port.

For price categories, *see* Lodging at the beginning of this chapter.

$$$$ 🏨 **Mandarin Oriental, Miami.** If you can afford to stay here, do. The lo-
Fodor'sChoice cation, at the tip of Brickell Key in Biscayne Bay, is superb. Rooms fac-
★ ing west overlook the downtown skyline; to the east are Miami Beach
and the blue Atlantic. There's also beauty in the details: sliding screens
that close off the baths, dark wood, crisp linens, and room numbers hand-
painted on rice paper at check-in. The Azul restaurant, with an eye-catching waterfall and private dining area at the end of a catwalk, serves a
mix of Asian, Latin, Caribbean, and French cuisine. The hotel has a
20,000-square-foot private beach and an on-site spa. ⊠ *500 Brickell
Key Dr., Brickell Key, 33131* ☎ *305/913–8288 or 866/888–6780* 🖷 *305/
913–8300* ⊕ *www.mandarinoriental.com* ↝ *327 rooms, 31 suites*
⌂ *In-room: safe, dial-up. In-hotel: 2 restaurants, bars, pool, spa,
concierge, laundry service, parking (fee)* ▭ *AE, D, DC, MC, V* ⏀ *EP.*

$$$ 🏨 **Hyatt Regency Miami.** If your vacation is based on boats, basketball,
business, or bargains, you can't do much better than the Hyatt Regency,
thanks to its adjacent convention facilities and prime location near the
Brickell Avenue business district, Bayside Marketplace, AmericanAir-
lines Arena, the Port of Miami, and downtown shopping. Distinctive
public spaces are more colorful than businesslike, and guest rooms are
a blend of avocado, beige, and blond. The James L. Knight International
Center is accessible without stepping outside, as is the downtown Metro-
mover and its Metrorail connection. The hotel is situated at the mouth
of the Miami River. ⊠ *400 S.E. 2nd Ave., Downtown, 33131* ☎ *305/
358–1234 or 800/233–1234* 🖷 *305/358–0529* ⊕ *www.miamiregency.
hyatt.com* ↝ *561 rooms, 51 suites* ⌂ *In-room: safe, refrigerator, Wi-
Fi. In-hotel: restaurant, room service, bar, pool, gym, concierge, public
Wi-Fi, parking (fee)* ▭ *AE, D, DC, MC, V* ⏀ *EP.*

$$–$$$ 🏨 **Townhouse.** The Townhouse looks like a big adult playhouse and fits
Fodor'sChoice the bill as the most lighthearted hotel on South Beach. A red plastic beach
★ ball welcomes you to spotless rooms bleached white. The rooftop ter-
race has red water beds and a signature water tower. It's no wonder you
find loud parties here on weekend nights. The hotel was designed by
India Madhavi; thank him for the bright, inviting lobby with two, big,
red (of course) bikes, kickstands down, for rent. Off to one side, a de-
lightful sunroom is a great place to read the paper over a generous Con-
tinental breakfast. Just outside, a porch deck has swings and comfortable
chairs. A hip sushi restaurant, Bond St. Lounge, is downstairs. ⊠ *150
20th St., South Beach, 33139* ☎ *305/534–3800 or 877/534–3800*
🖷 *305/534–3811* ⊕ *www.townhousehotel.com* ↝ *69 rooms, 3 suites*
⌂ *In-room: safe, Ethernet, Wi-Fi. In-hotel: restaurant, room service, bar,
bicycles, laundry facilities, laundry service, public Wi-Fi, parking (fee),
no-smoking rooms.* ▭ *AE, D, MC, V.*

MOBILE, ALABAMA

Clint Hill

Fort Condé was the name given by the French in 1711 to the site known
today as Mobile; around it blossomed the first white settlement in what
is now Alabama. For eight years it was the capital of the French colo-
nial empire, and it remained under French control until 1763, long after

the capital had moved to New Orleans. Mobile, known as the "Port City"—not to mention the birthplace of Mardi Gras—is noted for its tree-lined boulevards fanning westward from the riverfront. In the heart of busy downtown is Bienville Square, a park with an ornate cast-iron fountain and shaded by centuries-old live oaks. One of the city's main thoroughfares, Dauphin Street, has many thriving restaurants, bars, and shops.

MOBILE BEST BETS

- Bellingrath Gardens. One of the finest gardens in the South is just outside Mobile.

- Battleship Memorial Park. Many people come to Mobile just to tour the USS *Alabama*.

- Oakleigh. This well-preserved antebellum home is furnished with period antiques; it's a great experience if you like history.

Essentials

HOURS Most stores are open from 10 or 11 until 7 or 8.

INTERNET Your best bet for Internet service in Mobile is your hotel since Internet cafés are few and far between. You can get online at the **Mobile Public Library** (⊠ *704 Government St.* ☎ *251-208-7076*); at this writing, it was operating from a temporary branch, but the main library just across the street was expected to reopen in 2007.

VISITOR INFORMATION **Mobile Bay Convention & Visitor's Bureau** (⊠ *1 S. Water St., Mobile, AL* ☎ *251/208–2000 or 800/566–2453* ⊕ *www.mobilebay.org*).

The Cruise Port

Only one ship is based in Mobile at this writing, and it does shorter (four- and five-day) Western Caribbean itineraries. The cruise terminal is near the downtown area. Free shuttles from Mobile's public transit system, Moda, are provided to the cruise terminal from throughout downtown Mobile on days when ships are in port. It's a good home port to consider if you want to drive to your cruise embarkation point, but it's less convenient by air, with just a few airlines flying to the Mobile Regional Airport; however, the Biloxi and Pensacola airports are a relatively short drive away.

Mobile Alabama Cruise Terminal ⊠ 201 S. Water St., Mobile, AL ☎ 251/338-7447 ⊕ www.shipmobile.com.

AIRPORT TRANSFERS Taxis are available to the cruise terminal, or you can call the Mobile Regional Airport Shuttle, which will transport you for $20 ($30 round-trip). Mobile Bay Transportation Company also operates airport transfers for $13 one-way and $25 round-trip.

Mobile Bay Transportation Company ☎ 251/633-5693 or 800/272-6234 ⊕ www.mobilebaytransportation.com.

Mobile Regional Airport Shuttle ☎ 251/633-0313 or 800/357-5373 ⊕ www.mobairport.com.

PARKING Parking is available in a garage next to the cruise terminal. It costs $50 to park for a 4-day cruise, $60 for a 5-day cruise; RVs cost double. You can pay by cash or credit card.

Exploring Mobile

Numbers in the margin refer to points of interest on the Mobile map.

❸ **Battleship Memorial Park.** On Mobile Bay, east of downtown, is the site of the 155-acre park where the battleship USS *Alabama* is anchored. A self-guided tour gives a fascinating glimpse into the World War II vessel, which had a crew of 2,500. Dry-docked next to it is the USS *Drum*, a World War II submarine. Other exhibits include the B-52 bomber *Calamity Jane*. ⊠ *2703 Battleship Pkwy., Mobile* ☎ *251/433–2703 or 800/426–4929* ⊕ *www.ussalabama.com* 🎫 *$12* ☉ *Apr.–Sept., daily 8–6; Oct.–Mar., daily 8–4.*

❻ **Bellingrath Gardens & Home.** One of the most popular gardens in the South
Fodor'sChoice is Bellingrath, famous for its magnificent azaleas, which are part of 65
★ acres of gardens set amid a 905-acre semitropical landscape. Showtime for the azaleas is mid- to late-March, when some 250,000 plantings of 200 different species are ablaze with color. But Bellingrath is a year-round wonder, with more than 75 varieties of roses blooming in summer, 60,000 chrysanthemum plants cascading in fall, and red fields of poinsettias brightening winter. Countless species and flowering plants spring up along the Fowl River, surround streams, and a lake populated by ducks and swans. A free map lets you plan your own strolls along flagstone paths across charming bridges. In April and October, large numbers of

migratory birds drop by. You can also visit the home of Coca-Cola bottling pioneer Walter D. Bellingrath. Forty-five-minute boat cruises on the Fowl River aboard the *Southern Belle* leave from the dock next to the home daily at 10, noon, and 2 from mid-February through Thanksgiving. Take I–10

> **CAUTION** ⚠
>
> Notify the cruise line of any special dietary restrictions when booking your cruise and follow up on the arrangements a couple of months before embarking.

West to Exit 15, then follow CR 59 South to Theodore. ⊠ *12401 Bellingrath Gardens Rd., Theodore* ☎ *251/973–2217, 800/247–8420, 251/973–1244 for boat cruises* ⊕ *www.bellingrath.org* ⊠ *Gardens $10; gardens and home $18; gardens, home, and cruise $26* ⊙ *Gardens daily 8–5, home daily 9–4.*

❹ **Ft. Condé.** In 1711, France built this fort that would one day expand and become Mobile. The city's French origins endure in its creole cuisine. Now, 150 years after the fort was destroyed, its remains were discovered during construction of the I–10 interchange. A reconstructed portion houses the city's **visitor center,** as well as a museum. Costumed guides conduct tours. ⊠ *150 S. Royal St., Mobile* ☎ *251/208–7304* ⊠ *Free* ⊙ *Daily 8–5.*

🐾 ❷ **Gulf Coast Exploreum Science Center.** Near Ft. Condé, Mobile's science museum for children hosts traveling exhibits and an IMAX dome theater. ⊠ *65 Government St., Mobile* ☎ *251/208–6883 or 877/625–4386* ⊕ *www. exploreum.net* ⊠ *$18.25* ⊙ *Weekdays 9–5, Sat. 10–5, Sun. noon–5.*

❺ **Mobile Carnival Museum.** Mobile celebrates its heritage in this converted 1870 town house dedicated to all things Mardi Gras. The pre-Lenten festival was first celebrated in the New World here in Mobile in 1703, and the museum allows the party to continue 365 days a year. Displays include regal costumes of past kings and queens, traditional Mardi Gras "throws" (items that are thrown from the floats during parades), and even full-size floats. ⊠ *355 Government St.* ☎ *251/432–3324* ⊕ *www. carnivalmuseum.com* ⊠ *$5* ⊙ *Mon., Wed., Fri., Sat. 9–5.*

❶ **Museum of Mobile.** The museum opened in 2001 in the renovated circa-1857 Southern Market/Old City Hall building next to the Exploreum. Interactive exhibits and special collections of antique silver, weapons, and more tell the 300-year history of Mobile. ⊠ *111 S. Royal St., Mobile* ☎ *251/208–7569* ⊕ *www.museumofmobile.com* ⊠ *$5* ⊙ *Mon.–Sat. 9–5, Sun. 1–5.*

★ ❼ **Oakleigh.** About 1½ mi (2½ km) from Ft. Condé, in the heart of the historic Oakleigh Garden District, is an antebellum Greek Revival–style mansion, built between 1833 and 1838. Costumed guides give tours of the home, which has fine period furniture, portraits, silver, jewelry, kitchen implements, toys, and more. Tickets include a tour of neighboring **Cox-Deasy House,** an 1850s cottage furnished with simple 19th-century pieces. ⊠ *350 Oakleigh Pl., Mobile* ☎ *251/432–1281* ⊕ *www. historicmobile.org* ⊠ *$7* ⊙ *Oakleigh: Tues.–Sat. 9–3.*

Shopping

Most shopping in Mobile is in malls and shopping centers in the suburbs. Stores are generally open Monday to Saturday 10–9, Sunday 12–6. Antiques buffs may be interested in Mobile's many antiques stores that are in the Loop area of midtown (where Government Street, Airport Boulevard, and Dauphin Island Parkway converge); several shops are within walking distance of each other.

> ### FRESH, WRINKLE-FREE
>
> You can tuck fabric softener sheets between garments as you pack to keep your clothing smelling fresh during travels. Dry cleaning bags are good to keep out wrinkles.

Nightlife

Most of Mobile's nightlife centers around the downtown's former commercial district, Dauphin Street, which today has a number of restaurants and nightspots spread out over several blocks. Mobilians have taken to calling the area LoDa, short for Lower Dauphin.

Where to Eat

For price categories, *see* Dining at the beginning of this chapter.

$–$$$ ✕ **Loretta's.** At a colorful corner a block off Dauphin Street, this place has its own dramatic flair. It's hidden behind a wall of glass covered in creeping fig, with a unique style—gleaming silver palm trees and whimsical, mismatched salt and pepper shakers. In the kitchen, owner-chef Christopher Hunter adds creative nuances to Southern favorites, such as sausage-stuffed pork loin and pan-seared sashimi tuna steak. ⊠ *19 S. Conception St.* ☎ *251/432–2200* ▤ *AE, D, DC, MC, V* ☉ *Closed Sun. and Mon. No lunch Sat. No dinner Tues.*

$–$$$ ✕ **Wintzell's Oyster House.** "Oysters—fried, steamed, or nude" is the motto for this downtown Mobile institution. Founded in 1938 by Oliver Wintzell, the restaurant is in the same location and with few cosmetic changes since it was founded, the walls still covered by Oliver's homespun sayings. You can get your oysters by the dozen or half-dozen, but won't go wrong sampling any of the seafood on the menu or simply enjoying a cup of homemade gumbo. ⊠ *605 Dauphin St.* ☎ *251/432–4605* ▤ *AE, D, DC, MC, V.*

¢–$ ✕ **Brick Pit.** It's "the best damn barbecue in the state of Alabama," owner Bill Armbrecht insists. Chicken, ribs, and pork are smoked for hours over a blend of hickory and pecan to achieve a distinct flavor. Barbecue sauce comes spicy or sweet, with soft white bread for dipping. Be sure to add your name to the graffiti scrawled in red marker all over the walls and ceiling. Try the smoked pulled-pork plate. ⊠ *5456 Old Shell Rd.* ☎ *251/343–0001* ▤ *AE, DC, MC, V* ☉ *Closed Sun. and Mon.*

Where to Stay

Several local hotels offer cruise packages that include lodging, parking for the duration of your cruise, and a shuttle to the cruise terminal.

For price categories, *see* Lodging at the beginning of this chapter.

$$ ⊡ **Radisson Admiral Semmes Hotel.** This restored 1940 hotel in the historic district is a favorite with local politicians. It's also popular with partygoers, particularly during Mardi Gras, because of its excellent location directly on the parade route. The spacious, high-ceiling rooms have a burgundy-and-green color scheme and are furnished in Queen Anne and Chippendale styles. ✉ *251 Government St., 36602* ☎ *251/432–8000 or 800/333–3333* 🖷*251/405–5942* ⊕*www.radisson.com* 🛏*148 rooms, 22 suites* ⚒ *In room: Ethernet. In hotel: Restaurant, room service, bar, pool, laundry service, public Wi-Fi, no-smoking rooms* ⊟*AE, D, DC, MC, V.*

$–$$ 🏨 **Malaga Inn.** A delightful, romantic getaway, this place comprises two town houses built by a wealthy landowner in 1862. The lobby is furnished with 19th-century antiques and opens onto a landscaped central courtyard with a fountain. The rooms are large, airy, and furnished with antiques. The Malaga is on a quiet street downtown, within walking distance of the Museum of Mobile and the Gulf Coast Exploreum, and offers a cruise package. ✉ *359 Church St., 36602* ☎ *251/438–4701 or 800/235–1586* 🖷 *251/438–4701 Ext. 123* ⊕ *www.malagainn.com* 🛏 *35 rooms, 3 suites* ⚒ *In room: Wi-Fi. In hotel: pool, public Wi-Fi* ⊟ *AE, D, MC, V.*

NEW ORLEANS, LOUISIANA

Tucked between the Mississippi River and Lake Ponchartrain, New Orleans is mostly below sea level, and when Hurricane Katrina struck in August 2005, the city's levees strained under the force of the strong storm's wind and rain, finally breaking. The resulting floods covered 80% of New Orleans. Fortunately, much of the Big Easy that is well known to tourists was relatively untouched by the floods, including most of the French Quarter, the River Walk, the Garden District, and most of Uptown. Within months, these areas rebounded. Although the city is still recovering, all the aforementioned areas are up and running and eager to welcome visitors.

NEW ORLEANS BEST BETS

- **Aquarium of the Americas.** Especially good for families is this fantastic aquarium near the city's convention center.

- **Eating Well.** A highlight in New Orleans is dining. If you ever wanted to splurge on a great restaurant meal, this is the place to do it. At the very least, have a beignet at Café du Monde.

- **Hermann-Grima House.** This is one of the best-preserved historic homes in the French Quarter.

Essentials

HOURS Shops in the French Quarter tend to be open late, but stores in most of the malls close by 9. Restaurants tend to be open late as well.

INTERNET **French Quarter Postal Emporium** (✉ *1000 Bourbon St.* ☎ *504/525–6651* ⊕ *www.frenchquarterpostal.com*) offers Internet service and is also a mailing center.

VISITOR INFORMATION You can get information about visiting New Orleans from the Louisiana Office of Tourism and the New Orleans Convention & Visitors Bureau. 🏛 **Louisiana Office of Tourism** 🖃 Box 94291, Baton Rouge, LA 70804-9291 ☎ 800/633-6970 🖷 225/342-8390 ⊕ www.louisianatravel.com. **New Orleans Convention & Visitors Bureau** ✉ 2020 St. Charles Ave., 70130 ☎ 800/672-6124 or 504/566-5011 🖷 504/

566–5021 ⊕ www.neworleanscvb.com ✉ in the U.K.: ✉ 33 Market Pl., Hitchin, Hertfordshire SG5 1DY ☏ 01462–455323 🖶 01462–455391.

The Cruise Port

The Julia Street Cruise Terminal is at the end of Julia Street on the Mississippi River; the Erato Street Terminal is just to the north. Both terminals are behind the Ernest M. Morial Convention Center. You can walk to the French Quarter from here in about 10 minutes; it's a short taxi ride to the Quarter or nearby hotels. Carnival and Norwegian base ships here at least part of the year, and the *Delta Queen, Mississippi Queen,* and *American Queen* river steamboats leave from the Robin Street Wharf, just south of the Julia Street terminals.

If you are driving, you'll probably approach New Orleans on I–10. Take the Business 90 West/Westbank exit, locally known as Pontchartrain Expressway, and proceed to the Tchoupitoulas Street/South Peters Street exit. Continue to Convention Center Boulevard, where you will take a right turn. Continue to Henderson Street, where you will turn left, and then continue to Port of New Orleans Place. Take a left on Port of New Orleans Place to Julia Street Terminals and to the Erato Street Cruise Terminal 1.

🏢 **Port of New Orleans** ✉ Port of New Orleans Pl. at foot of Julia St. ☏ 504/522–2551 ⊕ www.portno.com.

AIRPORT TRANSFERS Shuttle-bus service to and from the airport and the cruise port is available through Airport Shuttle New Orleans. Buses leave regularly from the ground level near the baggage claim. Return trips to the airport need to be booked in advance. The cost one-way is $13 per person, and the trip takes about 45 minutes.

A cab ride to or from the airport from uptown or downtown New Orleans costs $28 for the first two passengers and $12 for each additional passenger. At the airport, pickup is on the lower level, outside the baggage claim area. There may be an additional charge for extra baggage.

🏢 **New Orleans Tours Airport Shuttle** ☏ 504/522–3500 or 866/596–2699.

PARKING If you are spending some time in the city before or after your cruise, finding a parking space is fairly easy in most of the city, except for the French Quarter, where meter maids are plentiful and tow trucks eager. If in doubt about a space, pass it up and pay to use a parking lot. Avoid parking spaces at corners and curbs: less than 15 feet between your car and the corner will result in a ticket. Watch for temporary NO PARKING signs, which pop up along parade routes and film shoots. Long-term and overnight parking are extremely expensive at hotels and garages. Parking for the duration of your cruise is available for $14 per night and is on Erato Street; if you want, SeaCaps will take your bags directly to the ship so you just have to deal with your hand luggage.

Exploring New Orleans
Numbers in the margin refer to points of interest on the New Orleans map.

The **French Quarter,** the oldest part of the city, lives up to all you've heard: it's alive with the sights, sounds, odors, and experiences of a

New Orleans

KEY
1 What to See
1 Where to Stay & Eat

CBD/Warehouse District

TO FRENCH QUARTER

Canal Street Ferry Terminal

Poydras Street Wharf

Riverwalk Marketplace

Cruise Ship Terminal

Girod Street Wharf

Julia Street Wharf

St. Joseph Street Wharf

Mississippi River

0   1/4 mile
0   1/4 kilometer

Café du Monde

Canal St. Ferry Terminal

SEE INSET

What to See ▶
Aquarium of the Americas **8**
Beauregard-Keyes House **3**
Garden District **7**
Hermann-Grima House **5**
Jackson Square **1**
Jean Lafitte National Park Visitor Center **4**
Lafayette Cemetery No. 1 ....**6**
St. Louis Cathedral ...**2**

Where to Eat ▶
Bayona **6**
Central Grocery **7**
Commander's Palace **1**
Herbsaint **2**

Where to Stay ▶
Ambassador Hotel **3**
New Orleans Hilton Riverside **5**
Omni Royal **4**
Crescent **4**

0   1/2 mile
0   1/2 kilometer

major entertainment hub. At some point, ignore your better judgment and take a stroll down **Bourbon Street,** past the bars, restaurants, music clubs, and novelty shops that have given this strip its reputation as the playground of the South. Be sure to find time to stop at Café du Monde for chicory-laced coffee and beignets. With its beautifully landscaped gardens surrounding elegant antebellum homes, the **Garden District** is mostly residential, but most home owners do not mind your enjoying the sights from outside the cast-iron fences surrounding their magnificent properties.

> ### YOUR CARD, PLEASE
>
> Print cards with your name, address, phone number, and e-mail address to share with new friends. Stiff, business card–style paper can be purchased at nearly any office supply store, and you can make the cards on your computer at home. Having your cards handy sure beats hunting for pens and scribbling on scraps of paper to swap addresses.

🕙 ❽ **Aquarium of the Americas.** Each of the four major exhibit areas—the Amazon Rain Forest, the Caribbean Reef, the Mississippi River, and the Gulf Coast—has fish and animals native to that environment. A fun exhibit called Beyond Green houses more than 25 frog species and includes informative displays. The aquarium's spectacular design allows you to feel part of the watery worlds by providing close-up encounters with the inhabitants. A gift shop and café are on the premises. You can get a combined ticket for the aquarium and the Audubon Zoo, including a round-trip cruise down the river. ✉ *1 Canal St., French Quarter* ☎ *504/581–4629 or 800/774–7394* ⊕ *www.auduboninstitute.org* ✉ *Aquarium $17; combination ticket for aquarium, zoo, and IMAX theater $28* ⊙ *Aquarium Sun.–Thurs. 9:30–6 (last ticket sold at 5), Fri. and Sat. 9:30–7 (last ticket sold at 6).*

FodorsChoice
★

❸ **Beauregard-Keyes House.** This stately 19th-century mansion with period furnishings was the temporary home of Confederate general P. G. T. Beauregard. The house and grounds had severely deteriorated by the 1940s, when the well-known novelist Frances Parkinson Keyes moved in and helped restore it. Her studio at the back of the large courtyard remains intact, complete with family photos, original manuscripts, and her doll and teapot collections. If you do not have time to tour the house, take a peek through the gates at the beautiful walled garden at the corner of Chartres and Ursulines streets. Landscaped in the same sun pattern as Jackson Square, the garden is in bloom throughout the year. ✉ *1113 Chartres St., French Quarter* ☎ *504/523–7257* ✉ *$5* ⊙ *Mon.–Sat. 10–3, tours on the hr.*

❼ **Garden District.** The Garden District is divided into two sections by Jackson Avenue. Upriver from Jackson is the wealthy **Upper Garden District,** where the homes are meticulously kept. Below Jackson, the **Lower Garden District** is considerably rougher. Though the homes here are often just as structurally beautiful, most of them lack the recent restorations of those of the Upper Garden District. The streets are also less well patrolled; wander cautiously. **Magazine Street,** lined with antiques shops and coffeehouses (ritzier along the Upper Garden District, hipper along the Lower Garden District), serves as a southern border to the Garden District, and St. Charles Avenue forms the northern border.

☾ ❺ Hermann-Grima House. One of the largest and best-preserved examples of
Fodor'sChoice American architecture in the Quarter, this Georgian-style house has the only
★ restored private stable and the only working 1830s Creole kitchen in the Quarter. American architect William Brand built the house in 1831. You'll want to check the gift shop, which has many local crafts and books. ⊠ *820 St. Louis St., French Quarter* ☎ *504/525–5661* ✉ *$6, combination ticket with the Gallier House $10* ⊙ *Tours weekdays 10, 11, noon, 2, 3.*

❶ Jackson Square. Surrounded by historic buildings and filled with plenty of the city's atmospheric street life, the heart of the French Quarter is today a beautifully landscaped park. Originally called the Place d'Armes, the square was founded in 1718 as a military parade ground. It was also the site of public executions carried out in various styles, including burning at the stake, beheading, breaking on the wheel, and hanging. A **statue of Andrew Jackson,** victorious leader of the Battle of New Orleans in the War of 1812, commands the center of the square; the park was renamed for him in the 1850s. Among the notable buildings around the square are **St. Louis Cathedral** and **Faulkner House.** Two Spanish colonial–style buildings, the **Cabildo** and the **Presbytère,** flank the cathedral. The handsome rows of brick apartments on each side of the square are the **Pontalba Buildings.** The park is landscaped in a sun pattern, with walkways set like rays streaming out from the center, a popular garden design in the royal court of King Louis XIV, the Sun King. ⊠ *French Quarter* ⊙ *Park daily 8–dusk; flagstone paths on park's periphery open 24 hrs.*

★ ❹ Jean Lafitte National Park Visitor Center. This center has free visual and sound exhibits on the customs of various communities throughout the state, as well as information-rich daily history tours of the French Quarter. The one-hour daily tour leaves at 9:30 AM; tickets are handed out one per person (you must be present to get a ticket), beginning at 9 AM, for that day's tours only. Arrive at least 15 minutes before tour time to be sure of a spot. The office also supervises and provides information on Jean Lafitte National Park Barataria Unit across the river from New Orleans, and the Chalmette Battlefield, where the Battle of New Orleans was fought in the War of 1812. ⊠ *419 Decatur St., French Quarter* ☎ *504/589–2636* ⊙ *Daily 9–5.*

★ ❻ Lafayette Cemetery No. 1. Begun around 1833, this was the first planned cemetery in the city, with symmetrical rows, roadways for funeral vehicles, and lavish aboveground vaults and tombs for the wealthy families who built the surrounding mansions. In 1852, 2,000 yellow fever victims were buried here. The cemetery and environs figure in Anne Rice's popular series *The Vampire Chronicles,* and movies such as *Interview with the Vampire* have used this walled cemetery for its eerie beauty. The cemetery remained intact following Hurricane Katrina, and you can wander the grounds on your own or take an organized tour. One guided tour is arranged by **Save Our Cemeteries** (☎ *504/525–3377*). ⊠ *1400 block of Washington Ave., Garden District* ✉ *Cemetery free,* *tour $6 ☉ Weekdays 7–2:30, Sat. 7–noon; tours Mon., Wed., Fri., and Sat. at 10:30.*

❷ **St. Louis Cathedral.** The oldest active cathedral in the United States, this church at the heart of the Old City is named for the 13th-century French king who led two crusades. The current building, which replaced two structures destroyed by fire, dates from 1794, although it was remodeled and enlarged in 1851. The austere interior is brightened by murals covering the ceiling and stained-glass windows along the first floor. While staff shortages post-Katrina have suspended the tour schedule, new tour guides are currently being trained, and tours of the cathedral should resume in 2006. The statue of the Sacred Heart of Jesus dominates **St. Anthony's Garden,** which extends behind the rectory to Royal Street. This statue was damaged during the storm, losing the thumb and forefinger of one hand. The pieces have been recovered, but the statue's injuries have yet to be repaired. ⊠ *615 Père Antoine Alley, French Quarter* ☎ *504/525–9585* ⊡ *Free* ☉ *Tours Mon.–Sat. 9–4:30, Sun. 1–4:30.*

Shopping

The fun of shopping in New Orleans is in the regional items available throughout the city, in the smallest shops or the biggest department stores. You can take home some of the flavor of the city: its pralines (pecan candies), seafood (packaged to go), Louisiana red beans and rice, coffee (pure or with chicory), and creole and Cajun spices (cayenne pepper, chili, and garlic). The French Quarter is well known for its fine antiques shops, located mainly on Royal and Chartres streets. The main shopping areas in the city are the French Quarter, with narrow, picturesque streets lined with specialty, gift, fashion, and antiques shops and art galleries; the Central Business District (CBD), populated mostly with jewelry, specialty and department stores; and the Warehouse District, best known for contemporary arts galleries and cultural museums. **Jax Brewery** (⊠ *600 Decatur St., French Quarter* ☎ *504/566–7245* ⊕ *www.jacksonbrewery. com*), a historic building that once was a factory for Jax beer, now holds a Jax Beer museum and an upscale mall filled with both local shops and national chains. **Riverwalk Marketplace** (⊠ *1 Poydras St.* ☎ *504/522–1555* ⊕ *www.riverwalkmarketplace.com*), along the riverfront, has a ½-mi-long (1-km-long) marketplace with 180 local and nationally known shops and restaurants, including Café du Monde.

Nightlife

No American city places such a premium on pleasure as New Orleans. From swank hotel lounges to sweaty dance clubs, refined jazz clubs and raucous Bourbon Street bars, this city is serious about frivolity. And famous for it. Partying is more than an occasional indulgence in this city—it's a lifestyle. Bars tend to open in the early afternoon and stay open into the morning hours; live music, though, follows a more restrained schedule. Some jazz spots and clubs in the French Quarter stage evening sets around 6 PM or 9 PM; at a few clubs, such as the Palm Court, the bands actually finish by 11 PM. But this is the exception: for the most part, gigs begin between 10 and 11 PM, and locals rarely emerge for an evening out before 10. Keep in mind that the lack of legal closing time means that shows advertised for 11 may not start until after midnight.

★ **Preservation Hall** (✉ *726 St. Peter St., French Quarter* ☎ *504/522–2841 or 504/523–8939*), the jazz tradition that flowered in the 1920s, is enshrined in this cultural landmark. A bust of legendary New Orleans pianist Professor Longhair, or "Fess," greets visitors at the door of **Tipitina's**
★ (✉ *501 Napoleon Ave., Uptown* ☎ *504/895–8477*), which takes its name from one of his most popular songs. As the concert posters pinned to the walls attest, Tip's hosts a wide variety of touring bands and local acts. The long-running Sunday afternoon Cajun dance still packs the floor. The Tipitina's Foundation has an office and workshop upstairs, where local musicians affected by Hurricane Katrina can network, gain access to resources, and search for gigs.

Sightseeing Tours

Several local tour companies give two- to four-hour city tours by bus that include the French Quarter, the Garden District, uptown New Orleans, and the lakefront. Prices range from $25 to $125 per person, depending on the kind of experience. Both Gray Line and New Orleans Tours offer a longer tour that combines a two-hour city tour by bus with a two-hour steamboat ride on the Mississippi River. Gray Line and Tours by Isabelle both offer tours of Hurricane Katrina devastation as well.

Gray Line ☎ 800/535-7786 or 504/569-1401 ⊕ www.graylineneworleans.com. **New Orleans Tours** ☎ 888/486-8687 or 504/529-4567 ⊕ www.notours.com. **Tours by Isabelle** ☎ 877/665-8687 or 504/391-3544 ⊕ www.toursbyisabelle.com.

Where to Eat

For price categories, *see* Dining at the beginning of this chapter. Don't miss beignets and rich, chicory-laced coffee at **Café du Monde** (✉ *800 Decatur St.*), in the French Quarter, though there's also an outlet in the Riverwalk.

$$$–$$$$ ✕ **Commander's Palace.** No restaurant captures New Orleans's gastro-
Fodor'sChoice nomic heritage and celebratory spirit as well as this one, long consid-
★ ered the Grande Dame of New Orleans fine dining. The post-Katrina renovation has added new life, especially upstairs, where the Garden Room's glass walls have marvelous views of the giant oak trees on the patio below; other rooms promote conviviality with their bright pastels. The menu's classics include foie-gras-and-rabbit pie; a spicy and meaty turtle soup; terrific grilled veal chops with grits; and a wonderful sautéed Gulf fish coated with crunchy pecans. Among the addictive desserts is the bread-pudding soufflé. ✉ *1403 Washington Ave., Garden District* ☎ *504/899–8221* ⌖ *Reservations essential* ▤ *AE, D, DC, MC, V.*

$–$$ ✕ **Herbsaint.** Upscale food and mod-
Fodor'sChoice erate prices are among Herbsaint's
★ assets. Chef Donald Link turns out food that sparkles with robust flavors and top-grade ingredients. "Small plates" and side dishes such as charcuterie, a knock-'em-dead shrimp

---

GET MUGGED

Take along an insulated mug with a lid that you can fill at the beverage station in the buffet area. Your drinks will stay hot or cold, and you won't have to worry about spills. Most bartenders will fill the mug with ice and water or a soft drink. With a straw, your ice will not melt instantly while you lounge at the pool.

bisque, house-made pasta, and cheese- or nut-studded salads are mainstays. Don't overlook the rich and flavorful shrimp and green chile grits cakes with tasso cream sauce. More substantial appetites are courted with duck and dirty rice, and chili-glazed pork belly. For dessert, the warm chocolate beignets filled with molten chocolate

CAUTION

Items confiscated by airport security will not be returned to you. If you are uncertain whether something will pass the security test, pack it in your checked luggage.

are deserving of love poems. The plates provide most of the color in the lighthearted, often noisy, rooms. The wine list is expertly compiled and reasonably priced. ⊠ *701 St. Charles Ave., CBD* ☎ *504/524–4114* ⌂ *Reservations essential* ⊟ *AE, D, DC, MC, V* ⊘ *Closed Sun. No lunch Sat.*

$–$$$
Fodor'sChoice
★
✕ **Bayona.** "New World" is the label Louisiana native Susan Spicer applies to her cooking style, which results in such signature dishes as the goat cheese crouton with mushrooms in Madeira cream, and crispy-fried smoked quail on a salad with bourbon-molasses vinaigrette. Vegetarian options include a farmers' market medley with cheddar spoon bread. These and other imaginative dishes are served in an early-19th-century Creole cottage that fairly glows with flower arrangements, elegant photographs, and trompe l'oeil murals suggesting Mediterranean landscapes. Don't skimp on pastry chef Megan Roen's sweets, such as churros with chocolate mousse, and mint julep ice cream. ⊠ *430 Dauphine St., French Quarter* ☎ *504/525–4455* ⌂ *Reservations essential* ⊟ *AE, DC, MC, V* ⊘ *Closed Sun. No lunch Sat.*

¢–$$
Fodor'sChoice
★
✕ **Central Grocery.** This old-fashioned Italian grocery store produces authentic muffulettas, one of the gastronomic gifts of the city's Italian immigrants. Good enough to challenge the po'boy as the local sandwich champs, they're made by filling round loaves of seeded bread with ham, salami, mozzarella, and a salad of marinated green olives. Each sandwich, about 10 inches in diameter, is sold in wholes and halves. You can eat your muffuletta at a counter, but some prefer to take theirs out to a bench on Jackson Square or the Moon Walk along the Mississippi riverfront. The Grocery closes at 5:30 PM. ⊠ *923 Decatur St., French Quarter* ☎ *504/523–1620* ⊟ *D, MC, V.*

Where to Stay

You can stay in a large hotel near the cruise-ship terminal, in the Warehouse District, or in the French Quarter. Hotel rates in New Orleans tend to be on the high end, though deals abound.

For price categories, *see* Lodging at the beginning of this chapter.

$$$$
⊞ **New Orleans Hilton Riverside.** This sprawling multilevel complex is smack on the Mississippi with superb river views. Guest rooms have French-provincial furnishings; the 180 rooms that share a concierge have fax machines. On Sunday the hotel's Kabby's Restaurant hosts a jazz brunch. The Riverfront streetcar stops out front. Adjacent to Riverwalk Shopping Center and directly across the street from Harrah's New Orleans casino, the hotel has a resident golf pro and a four-hole putting green. The health club is among the best in town. ⊠ *Poydras St. at the Mississippi River, CBD, 70140* ☎ *504/561–0500 or 800/445–8667* ☐ *504/*

568–1721 ⊕ *www.hilton.com* ⟿ *1,600 rooms, 67 suites* ♿ *In-room: Wi-Fi. In-hotel: 3 restaurants, tennis courts, pools, gym, parking (fee), no-smoking rooms* ▤ *AE, D, DC, MC, V.*

\$\$–\$\$\$\$ 🖼 **Omni Royal Crescent.** This elegant white-marble hotel built in 1960 is
Fodor'sChoice a replica of the grand St. Louis Hotel of the 1800s. Sconce-enhanced
★ columns, gilt mirrors, fan windows, and three magnificent chandeliers re-create the atmosphere of old New Orleans. Some rooms have marble baths and marble-top dressers and tables; others have balconies. The recently renovated Rib Room, on the lobby level, has been one of the city's culinary showpieces for more than 40 years. The rooftop pool has the city's best overhead view of the French Quarter. ⊠*621 St. Louis St., French Quarter, 70140* ☎ *504/529–5333 or 800/843–6664* 🖷 *504/529–7089* ⊕ *www.omnihotels.com* ⟿ *346 rooms, 16 suites* ♿ *In-room: Wi-Fi. In-hotel: restaurant, pool, gym, parking (fee)* ▤ *AE, D, DC, MC, V.*

\$\$–\$\$\$ 🖼 **Ambassador Hotel.** Guest rooms at this hotel conveniently bordering the CBD and Warehouse District have real character. Four-poster iron beds, armoires, and local jazz prints are among the furnishings. Exposed brick walls, ceiling fans, and wood floors add to the ambience of the pre–Civil War building. This is a good alternative to huge convention hotels, but it's still just steps from all the major downtown attractions and the Convention Center. The hotel is a five-minute walk from Harrah's New Orleans Casino. ⊠ *535 Tchoupitoulas St., CBD, 70130* ☎ *504/527–5271 or 800/ 455–3417* 🖷*504/599–2107* ⊕*www.ahno.com* ⟿*165 rooms* ♿ *In-room: Wi-Fi. In-hotel: restaurant, bar, parking (fee)* ▤ *AE, D, DC, MC, V.*

NEW YORK, NEW YORK

A few cruise lines now base Caribbean-bound ships in New York City year-round, though most of the market is made up of ships doing seasonal cruises to New England and Bermuda. If you're coming to the city from the immediate area, you can easily arrive the day before and do a bit of sightseeing and perhaps take in a Broadway show. The cruise port in Manhattan is fairly close to Times Square and Midtown hotels and theaters. But the New York City region now has three major cruise ports. You can also leave from Cape Liberty Terminal in Bayonne, New Jersey, on both Celebrity and Royal Caribbean ships. In 2006, a new cruise-ship terminal opened in Red Hook, Brooklyn, and this terminal serves Carnival and Princess ships as well as Cunard's *Queen Mary 2*.

Essentials

HOURS They say that New York never sleeps, and that's particularly true around Times Square, where some stores are open until 11 PM or later

---

**NEW YORK CITY
BEST BETS**

■ **An Art Museum.** Take your pick: the Met, MOMA, or the Frick, but this is a true highlight of New York.

■ **A Broadway Show.** The theater experience in New York is better than almost anywhere else in the world.

■ **Statue of Liberty.** Just the sight of Lady Liberty will melt the coldest heart, though the highlight of the trip is actually the Ellis Island museum, not the statue itself.

even during the week. But most stores outside of the immediate Times Square area are open from 9 or 10 until 6 or 7. Many museums close on Monday.

INTERNET   Internet service is offered by most New York hotels, and there are independent Internet cafés all over town. You might even see cheap Internet service in pizzerias and delis. Starbucks offers wireless service for a fee, but if you have your own laptop, you can use the free outdoor Wi-Fi network in Bryant Park (6th Ave., between 42nd and 41st streets).

VISITOR   **NYC & Company Convention & Visitors Center** (✉ *810 7th Ave., be-*
INFORMATION   *tween W. 52nd and W. 53rd Sts., 3rd fl., Midtown West* ☎ *212/484–1222* ⊕ *www.nycvisit.com*). **Times Square Information Center** (✉ *1560 Broadway, between 46th and 47th Sts., Midtown West* ☎ *212/768–1560* ⊕ *www.timessquarenyc.org*).

The Cruise Port

The **New York Passenger Ship Terminal** is on the far west side of Manhattan, five very long blocks from the Times Square area, between 48th and 52nd streets; the vehicle entrance is at 55th Street. Traffic can be backed up in the area on days that cruise ships arrive and depart, so allow yourself enough time to check in and go through security. There are no nearby subway stops, though city buses do cross midtown at 50th and 42nd streets. If you don't have too much luggage, it is usually faster and more convenient to have a taxi drop you off at the intersection across the street from the entrance to the lower-level of the terminal area between 48th and 49th streets; then you can walk right in and take the elevators up to the embarkation level.

Cape Liberty Terminal in Bayonne is off Route 440. From the New Jersey Turnpike, take Exit 14A, then follow the signs for 440 South, and make a left turn into the Cape Liberty Terminal area (on Port Terminal Boulevard). If you are coming from Long Island, you cross Staten Island, and after crossing the Bayonne Bridge take 440 North, making a right into the terminal area. If you are coming from Manhattan, you can also reach the terminal by public transit. Take the New Jersey Transit light-rail line that connects to the PATH trains in Hoboken; get off at the Bayonne stop, and from there you can take a taxi to the terminal (about 2 mi away); sometimes there is a free shuttle bus on cruise sailing dates, but confirm that with your cruise line.

The new **Brooklyn Cruise Terminal** at Pier 12 in Red Hook, which opened in April 2006, is not convenient to public transportation, so you should plan to take a taxi, drive, or take the bus transfers offered by the cruise lines (the cost for this is about $40 per person from either LaGuardia or JFK). There is a secure, 500-car outdoor parking lot on site. To reach the terminal from LaGuardia Airport, take I–278 W (the Brooklyn-Queens Expressway), Exit 26-Hamilton Avenue; the terminal entrance is actually off Browne Street. From JFK, take I–278 E (again, the Brooklyn-Queens Expressway), and then the same exit. If you arrive early, there's not much in the neighborhood, but there are a few neighborhood delis and restaurants within a 10- to 15-minute walk; the area is a safe place

What to See ▼

American Museum of Natural History 1

Central Park ...2

Frick Collection 3

Grand Central Terminal 7

Metropolitan Museum of Art 4

Museum of Jewish Heritage 9

Museum of Modern Art 5

Staten Island Ferry 8

Statue of Liberty & Ellis Island ...10

Top of the Rock 6

Where to Eat ▼

Becco 4

Burger Joint 2

Marseille 3

Virgil's Real BBQ 5

Where to Stay ▼

Hotel Edison 6

Warwick 1

Westin New York at Times Square ..7

New York City (Midtown)

E. 60th St.
Central Park S.
Columbus Circle   W. 58th St.   E. 58th St.
W. 57th St.   Four Seasons Hotel →
N,R   B,Q   E. 57th St.
W. 56th St.   Dahesh Museum ◆
Fifth Avenue Presbyterian Church   E. 56th St.
W. 55th St.   E. 55th St.
W. 54th St.   E. 54th St.
New York Hilton ◆
W. 53rd St.   Sheraton New York   E,F   E. 53rd St.
W. 52nd St.   E. 52nd St.
Equitable Center   Paine Webber Art Gallery   Raquet & Tennis Club →
W. 51st St.   E. 51st St.
Time & Life Building ◆
C,E   W. 50th St.   Rockefeller   Waldorf-Astoria →
THEATER DISTRICT   N,R   W. 49th St.   B,D,F,Q   Center   E. 49th St.
Christie's ◆
Cruise Ship Terminal   W. 48th St.   E. 48th St.
W. 47th St.   DIAMOND DISTRICT   E. 47th St.
TKTS Ticket Booth   E. 46th St.
W. 46th St.
W. 45th St.   E. 45th St.
W. 44th St.   E. 44th St.
W. 43rd St.   Times Square   E. 43rd St.
A,C,E   Theatre Row   W. 42nd St.   7
42nd & 8th   N,R,S, 1,2,3,7   B,D,F,Q   E. 42nd St.
W. 41st St.   Bryant Park   New York Public Library   E. 41st St.
Port Authority Bus Terminal
W. 40th St.   E. 40th St.
W. 39th St.   E. 39th St.
GARMENT DISTRICT   W. 38th St.   E. 38th St.
W. 37th St.   E. 37th St.
W. 36th St.   E. 36th St.
W. 35th St.   Herald Square   E. 35th St.
W. 34th St.   Empire State Building ◆   E. 34th St.
A,C,E   1,2,3   B,D,F,N,Q,R
W. 33rd St.   0   1/4 mile   E. 33rd St.
Madison Square Garden   Penn Station   0   1/4 kilometer   E. 32nd St.
W. 32nd St.

Eighth Ave.   Broadway   Seventh Ave.   Avenue of the Americas   (Sixth Ave.)   Fifth Ave.   Madison Ave.

3

to walk around during daylight hours. Red Hook is the home of ships from the Carnival, Princess, and Cunard cruise lines.
🚢 **Cape Liberty Terminal** ⊠ 14 Port Terminal Blvd., Bayonne, NJ ☎ 201/823-3737 ⊕ www.cruiseliberty.com. **New York Passenger Ship Terminal** ⊠ 711 12th Ave., Midtown West, New York, NY ☎ 212/246-5450 ⊕ www.nycruiseterminal.com ⊠ Pier 12, Building 112, Red Hook Brooklyn, NY ☎ 718/858-3450.

> **CAUTION**
>
> Do not pack photo film in checked luggage since the newest airport screening equipment will ruin it. Put it in your carry-on instead.

AIRPORT TRANSFERS A cab from JFK to the passenger-ship terminal in **Manhattan** will cost $45 (a flat fare) plus toll and tip; expect to pay at least $35 on the meter if you are coming from LaGuardia and at least $45 or $50 from Newark.

From Newark Airport, it's approximately $30 to **Cape Liberty**, $75 from JFK (plus toll and tip), and $80 from LaGuardia (plus toll and tip). Royal Caribbean offers bus service from several Mid-Atlantic and Northeast cities on sailing dates, but confirm that with the cruise line.

If your cruise is leaving from **Red Hook,** the taxi fare will be much cheaper if you fly into either LaGuardia (about $30) or JFK (about $40); you'll pay at least $60 from Newark Airport. Cruise lines provide bus transfers from all three of the area's airports, but it may be cheaper to take a taxi if you are traveling with more than one other person.

PARKING You can park at the New York Passenger Ship Terminal for $24 a day; the fee is payable in advance in cash or traveler's checks (no credit cards).

Parking at Cape Liberty Terminal in Bayonne is $15 per day, payable only in cash, traveler's checks, and major credit cards.

Parking at Red Hook, Brooklyn, costs $18 per day.

Top Attractions

There's no way to do justice to even the most popular tourist stops in New York. If you have only a day in the city, choose one or two attractions and buy a daily unlimited subway pass to get around. There's a moving series of panels about the World Trade Center at the so-called Ground Zero site across from the Millennium Hotel (take the 1 train to Cortlandt Street or the E to World Trade Center); there's another series of memorial panels underneath at the World Trade Center PATH station, which is accessible from the main, streetside memorial area.

Numbers in the margin refer to points of interest on the New York City (Midtown) map.

❶ **American Museum of Natural History.** With 45 exhibition halls and more than 32 million artifacts and specimens, the world's largest and most important museum of natural history can easily occupy you for half a day. The dioramas might seem dated but are fun. The dinosaur exhibits are probably the highlight. Attached to the museum is the **Rose Center for Earth and Space** with various exhibits and housing the **Hayden Planetarium** and an **IMAX Theater.** ⊠ *Central Park W at W. 79th St., Upper West Side* ☎ *212/769-5200* ⊕ *www.amnh.org* ⊠ *$14 sug-*

gested donation, includes admission to Rose Center; museum and planetarium show combination ticket $30. Prices may vary for special exhibitions ☉ *Daily 10–5:45* Ⓜ *Subway: B, C to 81st St.*

② Central Park. Without the Central Park's 843 acres of meandering paths, tranquil lakes, ponds, and open meadows, New Yorkers might be a lot less sane. You can drop by the zoo (near 64th Street, on the east side) or the famous Bethesda Fountain (mid-park, at around 72nd Street), but the main draw is just to wander the lanes. Central Park has one of the lowest crime rates in the city. Still, use common sense and stay within sight of other park visitors, and don't go into the park after dark. Directions, park maps, and event calendars can be obtained from volunteers at two 5th Avenue **information booths,** at East 60th Street and East 72nd Street. ☎ *212/408–0266 for schedule of park events, 212/360–2727 for schedule of walking tours* ⊕ *www.nycgovparks.org* Ⓜ *Subway: A, C, or 1 to Columbus Circle.*

③ Frick Collection. Coke-and-steel baron Henry Clay Frick (1849–1919) amassed this superb art collection far from the soot and smoke of Pittsburgh, where he made his fortune. The mansion was designed by Thomas Hastings and built in 1913–14. It opened in 1935, but still resembles a gracious private home, albeit one with bona fide masterpieces in almost every room. This is the best small museum in town by a mile. ⊠ *1 E. 70th St., at 5th Ave., Upper East Side* ☎ *212/288–0700* ⊕ *www.frick. org* 🎫 *$15* ☞ *Children under 10 not admitted; those under 16 must be accompanied by an adult* ☉ *Tues.–Sat. 10–6, Sun. 11–5* Ⓜ *Subway: 6 to 68th St./Hunter College.*

⑦ Grand Central Terminal. Grand Central is not only the world's largest railway station (76 acres) and the nation's busiest (500,000 commuters and subway riders use it daily), but also one of the world's greatest public spaces, "justly famous," as critic Tony Hiss has said, "as a crossroads, a noble building . . . and an ingenious piece of engineering." A massive four-year renovation completed in October 1998 restored the 1913 landmark to its original splendor—and then some. *Main entrance* ⊠ *E. 42nd St. at Park Ave., Midtown East* ☎ *212/935–3960* ⊕ *www.grandcentralterminal.com* Ⓜ *Subway: 4, 5, 6, 7, S to 42nd St./Grand Central.*

④ Metropolitan Museum of Art. One of the world's greatest museums, the Met is also the largest art museum in the Western Hemisphere—spanning four blocks and encompassing 2 million square feet. Its permanent collection of nearly 3 million works of art from all over the world includes objects from the Paleolithic era to modern times. There's something for everyone here, but it's a bit overwhelming, so don't even try to see it all. ⊠ *5th Ave. at 82nd St., Upper East Side* ☎ *212/535–7710* ⊕ *www.metmuseum.org* 🎫 *$20 suggested donation* ☉ *Tues.–Thurs. and Sun. 9:30–5:30, Fri. and Sat. 9:30–9* Ⓜ *Subway: 4, 5, 6 to 86th St.*

⑨ Museum of Jewish Heritage—A Living Memorial to the Holocaust. In a granite hexagon rising 85 feet above Robert F. Wagner Jr. Park at the southern end of Battery Park City, this museum pays tribute to the 6 million Jews who perished in the Holocaust. It's one of the best such museums in the country. ✉ *36 Battery Pl., Battery Park City, Lower Manhattan* ☎ *646/437–4200* ⊕ *www.mjhnyc.org* ☜ *$10* ☉ *Thurs. and Sun.–Tues. 10–5:45; Wed. 10–8; Fri. and eve. of Jewish holidays 10–3 (until 5 during Daylight Saving Time)* Ⓜ *Subway: 4, 5 to Bowling Green.*

❺ **Museum of Modern Art (MoMA).** The masterpieces—Monet's *Water Lilies,* Picasso's *Les Demoiselles d'Avignon,* Van Gogh's *Starry Night*—are still here, but for now the main draw at MoMA is, well, MoMA. A "modernist dream world" is how critics described the museum after its $425 million face-lift. Unfortunately, the museum was an instant success, which means lines are sometimes down the block. For the shortest wait, get here before the museum opens; you can avoid some of the crowding by entering through the 54th Street side. Be prepared for sticker shock when you buy your ticket. ✉ *11 W. 53rd St., between 5th and 6th Aves., Midtown East* ☎ *212/708–9400* ⊕ *www.moma.org* ☜ *$20* ☉ *Sat.–Mon., Wed., and Thurs. 10:30–5:30; Fri. 10:30–8* Ⓜ *Subway: E, V to 5th Ave./53rd St.; B, D, E to 7th Ave.; B, D, F, V to 47th–50th Sts./Rockefeller Center.*

❽ **Staten Island Ferry.** The best transit deal in town is the Staten Island Ferry, a free 20- to 30-minute ride across New York Harbor providing great views of the Manhattan skyline, the Statue of Liberty, the Verrazano-Narrows Bridge, and the New Jersey coast. Ferries embark on various schedules: every 15 minutes during rush hours, every 20–30 minutes most other times, and every hour on weekend nights and mornings. If you can manage it, catch one of the older blue-and-orange ferries, which have outside decks. ✉ *State and South Sts., Lower Manhattan* ☎ *718/390–5253* Ⓜ *Subway: 4, 5 to Bowling Green; 1, 9 to South Ferry.*

❿ **Statue of Liberty & Ellis Island.** Though you must endure a long wait and onerous security, it's worth the trouble to see one of the iconic images of New York. But the truth is there's not much to see in the statue itself. You can no longer climb up to the crown, just view the inside from the base. There's a small museum on-site. Much more interesting—and well worth exploring—is the Ellis Island museum, which traces the story of immigration in New York City with moving exhibits throughout the restored processing building. Other parts of the island are still ruins. Make reservations and go early if you want to see everything. The ferry stops first at the statue and then continues to Ellis Island. ✉ *Castle Clinton, Battery Park, Lower Manhattan* ☎ *212/363–3200 for park service, 212/269–5755 for ferry information, 866/782–8834 for ticket reservations, 212/363–3200 for Ellis Island, 212/883–1986 for Wall of Honor information* ⊕ *www.nps.gov/stli/, www.statuereservations.com for reservations* ☜ *Statue and museums free, ferry $11.50 round-trip* ☉ *Daily 9:30–5; extended hrs in summer* Ⓜ *Subway: 5 to Bowling Green; 1, 9 to South Ferry; or W to Whitehall.*

★ ❻ **Top of the Rock.** Rockefeller Center's multifloor observation deck, first opened in 1933, and closed in the early 1980s, reopened in 2005. The experience is infinitely better than that at the Empire State Building, where interminable lines spoil most of the fun. Arrive just before sunset for the best views (which include the Empire State Building). ✉ *Entrance on 50th St., between 5th and 6th Aves., Midtown West* ☎ *877/692–*

7625 or 212/698–2000 ⊕ *www.topoftherocknyc.com* ✉ *$17.50* ☼ *Daily 8–midnight; last elevator at 11:30* PM.

3

> **CAUTION** ⚠
>
> Store any irreplaceable valuables in the ship purser's safe rather than the one in your cabin. Some insurance policies will not cover the loss of items left in your cabin.

Shopping

You can find almost any major store from virtually any designer or chain in Manhattan. High-end designers tend to be along **Madison Avenue**, between 55th and 86th streets. Some are along **57th Street**, between Madison and 7th avenues. **Fifth Avenue,** starting at Saks Fifth Avenue (at 50th Street) and going up to 59th Street, is a hodgepodge of high-end stores and more accessible options, including the high-end department store Bergdorf-Goodman, at 58th Street. More interesting and individual stores can be found in **SoHo** (between Houston and Canal, West Broadway and Lafayette), and the **East Village** (between 14th Street and Houston, Broadway and Avenue A). **Chinatown** is chock-full of designer knockoffs, crowded streets, and dim sum palaces; though frenetic during the day, it's a fun stop. The newest group of stores in Manhattan is at the **Time-Warner Center,** at Columbus Circle (at 8th Avenue and 59th Street); the high-rise mall has upscale stores and some of the city's best-reviewed and most expensive new restaurants.

Broadway Shows

Scoring tickets to Broadway shows is fairly easy except for the very top draws. For the most part, the top ticket price for Broadway musicals is about $110; the best seats for Broadway plays can run as high as $95. **Telecharge** (☎ 212/239–6200 ⊕ www.telecharge.com) sells tickets to most Broadway shows. **Ticketmaster** (☎ 212/307–4100 ⊕ www.ticketmaster.com) sells a lot of Broadway tickets, but probably runs second to Telecharge.

For tickets at 25% to 50% off the usual price, head to **TKTS** (✉ *Duffy Sq., W. 47th St. and Broadway, Midtown West* Ⓜ *Subway: N, R, W to 49th St.; 1, 9 to 50th St.* ✉ *South St. Seaport at Front and John Sts., Lower Manhattan* Ⓜ *Subway: 2, 3 to Fulton St.*). The kiosks accept cash and traveler's checks—no credit cards.

Where to Eat

The restaurants we recommend below are all in Midtown West, near Broadway theaters and hotels. Make reservations at all but the most casual places or face a numbing wait.

For price categories, *see* Dining at the beginning of this chapter.

$$ ✕**Marseille.** With great food and a convenient location near several Broadway theaters, Marseille is perpetually packed. Chef Andy d'Amico's Mediterranean creations are continually impressive. Grilled sardines are served with shards of black pepper brittle and tiny cubes of lemon gelée. The daube is classic: a hunk of beef is slowly braised into submission in red wine, then plated on a crispy square of fried polenta with diced sautéed root vegetables. Leave room for the spongy beignets with chocolate and raspberry dipping sauces. ✉ *630 9th Ave., at W. 44th St., Midtown West* ☏ *212/333–3410* ⌕ *Reservations essential* ▭ *AE, DC, MC, V* Ⓜ *Subway: 6 to 51st St./Lexington Ave.*

$$ ✕ **Becco.** An ingenious concept makes Becco a prime Restaurant Row choice for time-constrained theatergoers. There are two pricing scenarios: one includes an all-you-can-eat selection of antipasti and three pastas served hot out of pans that waiters circulate around the dining room; the other adds a generous entrée to the mix. The pasta selection changes daily but often includes gnocchi, fresh ravioli, and something in a cream sauce. The entrées include braised veal shank, grilled double-cut pork chop, and rack of lamb, among other selections. ✉ *355 W. 46th St., between 8th and 9th Aves., Midtown West* ☏ *212/397–7597* ⌕ *Reservations essential* ▭ *AE, DC, MC, V* Ⓜ *Subway: A, C, E to 42nd St.*

♻ **$$** ✕ **Virgil's Real BBQ.** Neon, wood, and Formica set the scene at this massive roadhouse in the theater district. Start with stuffed jalapeños or—especially—unbelievably succulent barbecued chicken wings. Then, what the hell: go for the "Pig Out"—a rack of pork ribs, Texas hot links, pulled pork, rack of lamb, chicken, and, of course, more. It's that kind of place. There are also five domestic microbrews on tap and a good list of top beers from around the world. The place is absolutely mobbed pretheater, so if that's when you're going, arrive by 6 PM or you'll miss your curtain. ✉ *152 W. 44th St., between 6th Ave. and Broadway, Midtown West* ☏ *212/921–9494* ⌕ *Reservations essential* ▭ *AE, MC, V* Ⓜ *Subway: N, Q, R, S, W, 1, 2, 3, 7 to 42nd St./Times Sq.*

¢ ✕ **Burger Joint.** What's a college burger bar, done up in particleboard and rec room decor, doing hidden inside of a five-star Midtown hotel? This tongue-in-cheek lunch spot buried in the Parker Meridien does such boisterous midweek business that lines often snake through the lobby. Stepping behind the beige curtain you can find baseball cap–wearing grease-spattered cooks dispensing paper-wrapped cheeseburgers and crisp thin fries. The burgers—featuring no Kobe beef or foie gras—are straightforward, cheap, and delicious. ✉ *118 W. 57th St, between 6th and 7th Aves., Midtown West* ☏ *212/245–5000* ▭ *No credit cards* Ⓜ *Subway: F to 57th St.*

Where to Stay

There are no real bargains in the Manhattan hotel world, and you'll find it difficult to get a decent room for under $250. However, occasional weekend deals can be found. All the hotels we recommend for cruise passengers are in Midtown, on the west side, due to the area's relatively easy proximity to the cruise ship terminal.

For price categories, *see* Lodging at the beginning of this chapter.

$–$$$$ 🏨 **Warwick.** Astonishingly, this palatial hotel was built by William Randolph Hearst in 1927 as a private hotel for his friends and family. The Midtown favorite is well placed for the theater district. The marble-floor lobby buzzes with activity; the Randolph Bar is on one side and Murals on 54, a Continental restaurant, is on the other. Handsome, Regency-style rooms have soft pastel color schemes, mahogany armoires, and marble bathrooms. The Cary Grant suite was the actor's New York residence for 12 years, and encapsulates a more refined moment in New York glamour. ⊠ *65 W. 54th St., at 6th Ave., Midtown West 10019* ☎ *212/247–2700 or 800/223–4099* 🖷 *212/713–1751* ⊕ *www. warwickhotels.com* ⤴ *359 rooms, 66 suites* ◊ *In-room: safe, refrigerator, dial-up, Wi-Fi. In-hotel: 2 restaurants, room service, bar, gym, laundry service, concierge, parking (fee), no-smoking rooms* ▤ *AE, DC, MC, V* Ⓜ *Subway: E, V to 53rd St., N, Q, R, W to 57th St.*

$ 🖼 **Hotel Edison.** This offbeat old hotel is a popular budget stop for tour groups from both the United States and abroad. The simple, serviceable guest rooms are clean and fresh. The loan-shark murder scene in *The Godfather* was shot in what is now Sofia's restaurant, and the pink-and-blue plaster Edison Café, known half jokingly as the Polish Tea Room, is a theater-crowd landmark consistently recognized as New York City's best coffee shop. ⊠ *228 W. 47th St., between Broadway and 8th Ave., Midtown West 10036* ☎ *212/840–5000 or 800/637–7070* 🖷 *212/596–6850* ⊕ *www.edisonhotelnyc.com* ⤴ *770 rooms, 30 suites* ◊ *In-room: Wi-Fi. In-hotel: restaurant, bars, gym, laundry service, airport shuttle, parking (fee), no-smoking rooms* ▤ *AE, D, DC, MC, V* Ⓜ *Subway: C, E to 50th St., R to 49th St.*

$ 🖼 **The Westin New York at Times Square.** The Westin changed the skyline of Midtown with this soaring skyscraper that subtly mimics the flow of the city—look for subway patterns in the carpets and the city reflected on the building's exterior. A thoughtful staff helps make the cavernous lobby and throngs of guests tolerable. Exceptionally large rooms are blissfully quiet and built to give you optimal views—especially the light-filled corner rooms. The much-noted Heavenly Bed and double showerheads are indeed praiseworthy, but for even more comfort, spa-floor rooms come with massage chairs, aromatherapy candles, and other pampering pleasures. ⊠ *270 W. 43rd St., at 8th Ave., Midtown West 10036* ☎ *212/201–2700 or 866/837–4183* 🖷 *212/201–2701* ⊕ *www.westinny. com* ⤴ *737 rooms, 126 suites* ◊ *In-room: safe, refrigerator, dial-up, Wi-Fi. In-hotel: restaurant, room service, bars, gym, spa, laundry service, concierge, parking (fee), some pets allowed, no-smoking rooms* ▤ *AE, D, DC, MC, V* Ⓜ *Subway: A, C, E to 42nd St./Times Sq.*

NORFOLK, VIRGINIA

CiCi
Williamson

Founded in 1680, Norfolk is no newcomer to the cruise business. One famous passenger, Thomas Jefferson, arrived here in November 1789 after a two-month crossing of the Atlantic. Over 200 years later, this historic seaport welcomes more than 300,000 cruise passengers annually. Situated at the heart of nautical Hampton Roads, Norfolk is home to the largest naval base in the world and is also a major commercial port.

Essentials

HOURS Most stores are open Monday through Friday from 10 to 9. Some museums close on Monday and/or Tuesday.

INTERNET Most of the hotels offer free Wi-Fi service if you have your own laptop. If not, you may be able to find an Internet café, but the local Norfolk Public Library has free Internet access, so why pay? **Norfolk Public Library** (⊠ *301 E. City Hall Ave.* ☎ *757/664–7337* ⊕ *www.npl.lib.va.us*).

VISITOR
INFORMATION **Hampton Roads Transit kiosk** (⊠ *Waterfront, 333 Waterside Dr.* ☎ *757/ 623–3222* ⊕ *www.watersidemarketplace.com*) is the launching point for tours of the city. **Norfolk Convention & Visitors Bureau** (⊠ *End of 4th View St.* ☎ *757/441–1852 or 800/368–3097* ⊕ *www.norfolkcvb. com*).

Norfolk Cruise Terminal

The new, state-of-the-art Half Moone Cruise Terminal opened in April 2007. Attached to Celebration Center, a large meeting and event space, it's within walking distance to several attractions and amenities in the downtown area.

Parking is off-site at the Ceder Grove parking lot, which is about 14 blocks from the waterfront and the cruise terminal. From I–264, take the City Hall exit (Exit 10). At the light, turn right on St. Paul's Boulevard, and follow the signs to the Cedar Grove parking lot.

🚢 **Half Moone Cruise Terminal & Celebration Center** ⊠ 1 Waterside Dr. ☎ 757/664–1000 for cruise hotline ⊕ www.cruisenorfolk.org.

AIRPORT
TRANSFERS **Norfolk International Airport** (ORF) is 9 mi (15 km) and 20 minutes away from the cruise terminal. One-way, shared shuttle costs range from $6.25 to $20 per person, and a taxi costs about $18 to $25.

🚢 **Norfolk Airport Express** ☎ 800/643–2197 ⊕ www.norfolkairportexpress.com. **Norfolk International Airport (ORF)** ⊠ 200 Norview Ave. ☎ 757/857–3200 ⊕ www.norfolkairport.com.

PARKING Before parking, drop your luggage at Nauticus, where you'll also find the cruise terminal. Depending upon the cruise line you're sailing, park your car in one of two lots, both patrolled by roving security officers. The West Plume Street Garage serves Radisson and accepts cash and traveler's checks only ($10 daily), to be paid when entering. The garage is located directly across the street from Nauticus.

Cedar Grove Parking serves Holland America, Celebrity, and Carnival. The parking fee ($10 daily) is paid upon entering the lot; Visa, MasterCard, American Express, cash, and traveler's checks are accepted. Less than 1 mi (1½ km) from I–264, this lot is located on Monticello Avenue between Virginia Beach Boulevard and Princess Anne Road in Downtown Norfolk. Complimentary shuttles run regularly to Nauticus.

Exploring Norfolk

History meets high-tech in this waterfront city. From 18th-century historic homes and a major art museum to 20th-century battleships and nuclear-powered aircraft carriers, Norfolk has many interesting sites to explore, several of them free and most within walking distance of the cruise terminal.

Numbers in the margin refer to points of interest on the Norfolk map.

★ ❶ **Chrysler Museum of Art.** By any standard this downtown museum qualifies as one of America's major art museums. The permanent collection includes works by Rubens, Gainsborough, Renoir, Picasso, Cézanne, Matisse, Warhol, and Pollock, a list that suggests the breadth available here.

Norfolk

3

Scope Arena

KEY
1 What to See
① Where to Stay & Eat

Portsmouth

Berkley

Elizabeth River

Eastern Branch
Elizabeth River

Southern Branch
Elizabeth River

Crawford Pkwy.

Town Point Park

0 — 1/4 mile
0 — 1/4 kilometer

What to See ▼

Chrysler Museum of Art . . . **1**

Douglas MacArthur
Memorial **3**

Moses Myers House **2**

Nauticus **4**

Norfolk Naval Station **5**

Where to Eat ▼

Freemason Abbey
Restaurant and Tavern **1**

La Galleria **3**

No Frill Bar and Grill **5**

Where to Stay ▼

Holiday Inn Select Airport . **7**

Marriott Courtyard
Downtown **2**

Norfolk Waterside
Marriott **4**

Sheraton Norfolk
Waterside Hotel **6**

Classical and pre-Columbian civiliza-
tions are also represented. The dec-
orative-arts collection includes
exquisite English porcelain and art
nouveau furnishings. The Chrysler
is home to one of the most important glass collections in America,
which includes glass objects from
the 6th century BC to the present,
with particularly strong holdings in
Tiffany, French art glass, and English cameo, as well as artifacts from
ancient Rome and the Near and Far
East. ⊠ *245 W. Olney Rd.* ☏ *757/
664–6200* ⊕ *www.chrysler.org*
⊠ *$7; Wed. by voluntary contri-
bution* ☉ *Wed. 10–9, Thurs.–Sat.
10–5, Sun. 1–5.*

NORFOLK BEST BETS
■ **Chrysler Museum of Art.** Though far from New York, Chicago, or Los Angeles, this is one of the major art museums in the U.S.
■ **Nauticus.** The National Maritime Center is one of the region's most popular attractions and especially good for families.
■ **Norfolk Naval Station.** This giant naval station, the home of the Atlantic Fleet, is an impressive site in itself.

❸ **Douglas MacArthur Memorial.** The memorial is the burial place of one of
America's most distinguished military officers. General Douglas
MacArthur (1880–1964) agreed to this Navy town as the site for his
monument because it was his mother's birthplace. In the rotunda of the
old City Hall, converted according to MacArthur's design, is the mausoleum; 11 adjoining galleries house mementos of MacArthur's career,
including his signature corncob pipe and the Japanese instruments of
surrender that concluded World War II. However, this is a monument
not only to General MacArthur but to all those who served in wars from
the Civil to the Korean War. Its Historical Center holds 2½ million documents and more than 100,000 photographs, and assists scholars, students, and researchers from around the world. The general's staff car
is on display in the gift shop, where a 24-minute biography is shown.
⊠ *Bank St. and City Hall Ave.* ☏ *757/441–2965* ⊕ *www.
macarthurmemorial.org* ⊠ *By donation* ☉ *Mon.–Sat. 10–5, Sun. 11–5.*

❷ **Moses Myers House.** The federal-style redbrick home built by its namesake in 1792 is exceptional, and not just for its elegance. In the long
dining room, a wood writing desk holds a collection of fine china—and
a set of silver kiddush cups (Moses Myers was Norfolk's first permanent Jewish resident). A transplanted New Yorker, Myers made his fortune in Norfolk in shipping, then served as a diplomat and a customhouse
officer. His grandson married James Madison's grandniece, his great-
grandson served as mayor, and the family kept the house for five generations. The furnishings, 70% of them original, include family portraits
by Gilbert Stuart and Thomas Sully. ⊠ *331 Bank St.* ☏ *757/333–1085*
⊕ *www.chrysler.org/houses.asp* ⊠ *Free* ☉ *Wed.–Sat. 10–4, Sun. 1–4.*

★ ☾ ❹ **Nauticus.** A popular attraction on Norfolk's redeveloped waterfront
is the National Maritime Center. With more than 70 high-tech exhibits
on three "decks," the site places ancient shipbuilding exhibits next
to interactive displays depicting the modern naval world. Weather
satellites, underwater archaeology, and the Loch Ness Monster all

come together here. The battleship USS *Wisconsin,* still maintained in a state of reduced readiness to allow reactivation, has found a home here. Most of its interior is off-limits, but its enormous gun turrets and conning tower are impressive up close. The *Wisconsin,* tied up just outside the museum, and the Hamp-

> **BEACH AND BUY**
>
> A nylon tote bag that folds compactly into its own pocket can be used as a beach bag during your cruise and as an extra carry-on for your return home.

ton Roads Naval Museum, within Nauticus, are both operated by the U.S. Navy and can be toured without paying Nauticus's admission price. There are additional fees for the AEGIS Theater and Virtual Adventures. ⊠ *1 Waterside Dr.* ☏ *757/664–1000* ⊕ *www.nauticus.org, www.thenmc.org, www.hrnm.navy.mil* ⛴ *$10* ⊙ *Memorial Day–Labor Day, daily 9–5; Labor Day–Memorial Day, Tues.–Sat. 10–5, Sun. noon–5.*

❺ Norfolk Naval Station. On the northern edge of the city, this naval base is an impressive sight, home to more than 100 ships of the Atlantic Fleet. The base was built on the site of the Jamestown Exposition of 1907: many of the original buildings survive and are still in use. Several large aircraft carriers, built at nearby Newport News, call Norfolk home port and can be seen from miles away, especially at the bridge-tunnel end of the base. You may see four or even more, each with a crew of up to 6,300, beside slightly smaller amphibious carriers that discharge marines in both helicopters and amphibious assault craft. The submarine piers, floating drydocks, supply center, and air station are all worth seeing. *The Victory Rover* and *Carrie B.* provide boat tours from downtown Norfolk to the naval station, and Hampton Roads Transit operates tour trolleys most of the year, departing from the naval-base tour office. Visitor access is by tour only, and photo ID is required to enter the base. ⊠ *9079 Hampton Blvd.* ☏ *757/444–7955* ⊕ *www.navstanorva.navy.mil/tour* ⛴ *Tour $7.50* ⊙ *Tours Oct. 29–Mar. 18, Tues.–Sun. 1:30; Mar. 19–May 20, Tues.–Sun. 11–2 on the hr; May 21–Sept. 2, Tues.–Sun. 10–2 every ½ hr.*

FodorsChoice ★

Shopping

If you forget to pack an item for your cruise, you'll find stores galore within walking distance of the cruise terminal at the handsome MacArthur Center Mall. A car is helpful if you want to visit **Ghent,** where you'll find an eclectic mix of shops, including antiques stores and restaurants. It's a turn-of-the-20th-century neighborhood that runs from the Elizabeth River to York Street, to West Olney Road and Llewellyn Avenue. Colley Avenue and 21st Street is the hub.

The center of Norfolk's downtown, the **MacArthur Center** (⊠ 300 Monticello Ave. ☏ 757/627–6000) has more than 100 stores, including anchors Nordstrom and Dillard's. There are restaurants downstairs and numerous fast-food outlets upstairs offering a variety of reasonably tolerable food.

Where to Eat

In addition to hotel restaurants, downtown Norfolk has many fine-dining restaurants and casual eateries in Waterside Festival Marketplace, which offers a versatile food court. In the MacArthur Center Mall, you'll find Johnny Rockets and Castaldi's—promising good value.

★ **$$–$$$$** ✕ **La Galleria.** This restaurant has a favorable reputation in Norfolk. The interior is classic Mediterannean and includes Ionic columns and large urns imported from Italy. There's entertainment Friday and Saturday nights. Among the menu choices are *vongole al forno* (baked clams sprinkled with herbs, garlic, and bread crumbs) as an appetizer, and many excellent pastas and main courses, such as veal, chicken, steaks, and fish (for example, salmon sautéed in herbs, garlic, and white wine). ⊠ *120 College Pl.* ☎ *757/623–3939* ▭ *AE, DC, MC, V.*

$–$$$ ✕ **Freemason Abbey Restaurant and Tavern.** This former church near the historic business district has been drawing customers for a long time, and not without reason. It has 40-foot-high cathedral ceilings and large windows, making for an airy, and dramatic, dining experience. You can sit upstairs, in the large choir loft, or in the main part of the church downstairs. Beside the bar just inside the entrance is an informal sort of "diner" area, but with the whole menu to choose from. Regular appetizers include artichoke dip and Santa Fe shrimp. There's a dinner special every weeknight, such as lobster, prime rib, and wild game (wild boar or alligator, for example). ⊠ *209 W. Freemason St.* ☎ *757/622–3966* ▭ *AE, D, DC, MC, V.*

★ **¢–$$** ✕ **No Frill Bar and Grill.** This expansive café is in an antique building in the heart of Ghent. Beneath a tin ceiling and exposed ductwork, a central bar is surrounded by several dining spaces with cream-and-mustard walls and wooden tables. Signature items include its ribs; the Funky Chicken Sandwich, a grilled chicken breast with bacon, tomato, melted Swiss cheese, and Parmesan pepper dressing on rye; and the Spotswood Salad of baby spinach, Granny Smith apples, and blue cheese. ⊠ *806 Spotswood Ave., at Colley Ave.* ☎ *757/627–4262* ▭ *AE, MC, V.*

Where to Stay

Within walking distance of the cruise terminal are three handsome hotels, two modern and one century-old boutique hostelry. You can also take the water taxi from Waterside ($1 per person, leaving half-hourly) across the Elizabeth River to Portsmouth to a lower-priced hotel. If you have a car, there are numerous chain motels on the outskirts of town.

$$–$$$$ ▥ **Norfolk Waterside Marriott.** This hotel in the redeveloped downtown area is connected to the Waterside Festival Marketplace shopping area by a ramp and is close to Town Point Park, site of many festivals. The handsome lobby, with wood paneling, a central staircase, silk tapestries, and Federal-style furniture, sets a high standard that continues throughout the hotel. Rooms are somewhat small, but each has most everything the business traveler could ask for—including two telephones, voice mail, and Internet access. ⊠ *235 E. Main St., 23510* ☎ *757/627–4200 or 800/228–9290* ▤ *757/628–6452* ⊕ *www.marriott.com* ↪ *396 rooms, 8 suites* ⌂ *In room: dial-up. In hotel: 2 restaurants, bar, pool* ▭ *AE, D, DC, MC, V* ⦿ *EP.*

$–$$$ ⊞ **Sheraton Norfolk Waterside Hotel.** Modern is the word for this hotel's furnishings, from the bright, spacious lobby to the ample rooms and large suites. A ground-floor bar with dramatic 30-foot windows overlooks the Elizabeth—many rooms also have a beautiful view over the water. This property is convenient to the Waterside Festival Marketplace shopping area. ⊠ *777 Waterside Dr., 23510* ☎ *757/622–6664* 🖷 *757/625–8271* ⊕ *www.sheraton.com* ⤺ *426 rooms, 20 suites* ⟨⟩ *In hotel: Restaurant, bar, pool* ⊟ *AE, D, DC, MC, V* ⋈ *EP.*

$$ ⊞ **Marriott Courtyard Downtown.** Built in 2005, this eight-story hotel is near everything visitors want to see and where business travelers need to be. It's next door to the MacArthur Memorial and near the MacArthur Center and Nauticus. A handsome, inviting lobby has a tailored look; the modern guest rooms have a large desk, comforters, hair dryers, coffeemakers, irons, ironing boards, and a free daily newspaper. ⊠ *520 Plume St., 23510* ☎ *757/963–6000 or 800/321–2211* 🖷 *757/963–6001* ⊕ *www.marriott.com* ⤺ *137 rooms, 3 suites* ⟨⟩ *Restaurant, room service, in-room data ports, refrigerators, cable TV with movies, in-room broadband, indoor pool, wading pool, exercise equipment, shop, dry cleaning, laundry facilities, laundry service, business services, meeting rooms, parking (fee), no-smoking rooms* ⊟ *AE, D, DC, MC, V.*

$–$$ ⊞ **Holiday Inn Select Airport.** Surprisingly plush for a Holiday Inn property, this airport location welcomes business travelers with an elegant lobby bar and fireplace. Rooms are outfitted with two phone lines, high-speed DSL Internet access, and voice mail; the lobby has free Wi-Fi. Behind the hotel is Lake Wright where guests may stroll or relax. ⊠ *Lake Wright Executive Center, 1570 N. Military Hwy., 23502* ☎ *757/213–2231* 🖷 *757/213–2232* ⊕ *www.hiselect.com/norfolkva* ⤺ *147 rooms* ⟨⟩ *Restaurant, microwaves, refrigerators, indoor pool, gym, hot tub, lobby lounge, laundry facilities, business services, meeting rooms, airport shuttle* ⊟ *AE, D, DC, MC, V.*

PORT CANAVERAL, FLORIDA

Kerry Speckman

This once-bustling commercial fishing area is still home to a small shrimping fleet, charter boats, and party fishing boats, but its main business these days is as a cruise-ship port. Cocoa Beach itself isn't the spiffiest place around, but what is becoming quite clean and neat is the north end of the port where the Carnival, Disney, and Royal Caribbean cruise lines set sail, as well as Sun Cruz and Sterling casino boats. Port Canaveral is now Florida's second-busiest cruise port. Because of Port Canaveral's proximity to Orlando theme parks (about an hour away), many cruisers combine a short cruise with a stay in the area. The port is also convenient to popular Space Coast attractions such as the Kennedy Space Center and United States Astronaut Hall of Fame in Titusville.

Essentials

HOURS Most of the area's attractions are open every day.

INTERNET Most people choose to go online at their hotel.

VISITOR INFORMATION **Cocoa Beach Area Chamber of Commerce** (⊠ *400 Fortenberry Rd., Merritt Island 32952* ☎ *321/459–2200* ⊕ *www.visitcocoabeach.com*).

The Cruise Port

Port Canaveral is the second-busiest cruise port in the world, with more than 4.6 million passengers passing through its terminals annually. The port has six cruise terminals and is home to Carnival Cruise Lines, Disney Cruise Line, and Royal Caribbean International. Other cruise lines, such as Holland America and Norwegian Cruise Line, operate seasonally. The port serves as the embarkation point for three-, four-, and seven-day cruises to the Bahamas, Key West, Mexico, Jamaica, and the Virgin Islands.

In Brevard County, Port Canaveral is on State Road (S.R.) 528, also known as the Beeline Expressway, which runs straight to Orlando, which has the nearest airport. To drive to Port Canaveral from there, take the north exit out of the airport, staying to the right, to S.R. 528 (Beeline Expressway) East. Take S.R. 528 directly to Port Canaveral; it's about a 45-minute drive.

🚩 **Canaveral Port Authority** ✉ 9150 Christopher Columbus Dr., Cape Canaveral ☎ 321/783-7831 or 888/767-8226 ⊕ www.portcanaveral.org.

AIRPORT   If you are flying into the area, most visitors choose to fly into Orlando;
TRANSFERS   the Orlando airport is 45 minutes away from the docks. If you have not arranged airport transfers with your cruise line, then you will need to make your own arrangements. Taxis are expensive, but many compa-

nies offer minivan and bus shuttles to Port Canaveral. They are all listed on the Canaveral Port Authority Web site. Some shuttles charge for the entire van, which is a good deal for groups but not for individuals or couples; some will charge a per-person rate. Expect to pay at least $25 per person each way. But you will need to make a reservation in advance regardless of which service you use. Some cruisers who want to do some exploring before the cruise rent a car at the airport and drop it off at the port, which houses several major rental-car agencies.

> **PORT CANAVERAL BEST BETS**
>
> ■ **Kennedy Space Center.** Kennedy Space Center in Titusville is the region's biggest attraction.
>
> ■ **Merritt Island.** If you want to get out and commune with nature, this is the place, especially for bird-watchers.
>
> ■ **Orlando Theme Parks.** With Orlando just an hour away, many cruisers combine a theme-park visit with their cruise.

AAA Cruise Line Connection ☎ 407/908-5566 ⊕ www.aaasuperride.com. **Art's Shuttle** ☎ 371/783-2112 or 800/567-5099 ⊕ www.artsshuttle.com. **Busy Traveler Transport Service** ☎ 321/453-5278 or 800/496-7433 ⊕ www.abusytraveler.com.

PARKING   Outdoor, gated lots and a six-story parking garage are near the terminals and cost $12 per day for vehicles up to 20 feet in length and $24 per day for vehicles over 20 feet, which must be paid in advance, either in cash, traveler's checks, or by major credit card (MasterCard and Visa only).

Exploring the Cape Canaveral Area

With the Kennedy Space Center just 20 minutes away, there is plenty to do in and around Cape Canaveral, though many folks opt to travel the extra hour into Orlando to visit the popular theme parks.

Numbers in the margin refer to points of interest on the Cape Canaveral map.

⑤ **Brevard Museum of History & Science.** To see what the local lay of the land looked like in other eras, check out this local science museum. Hands-on activities for children are the draw here. Not to be missed is the Windover Archaeological Exhibit of 7,000-year-old artifacts indigenous to the region. The museum's nature center has 22 acres of trails encompassing three distinct ecosystems—sand pine hills, lake lands, and marshlands. ⊠ *2201 Michigan Ave., Cocoa* ☎ *321/632-1830* ⊕ *www.brevardmuseum.com* ☞ *$6* ☉ *Mon.–Sat. 10–4, Sun. noon–4.*

④ **Brevard Zoo.** It took 20,000 volunteers two weeks to turn 56 acres of forest and wetlands into the only American Zoo and Aquarium Association–accredited zoo built by a community. Stroll along the shaded boardwalks and get a close-up look at alligators, crocodiles, giant anteaters, marmosets, jaguars, eagles, river otters, kangaroos, exotic birds, and kookaburras. Alligator, crocodile, and river otter feedings are held on alternate afternoons—although the alligators do not dine on the otters. You can also paddle kayaks and keep an eye open for the 4,000 species of wildlife that live in 22 acres of water and woods. ⊠ *8225 N. Wickham Rd., Melbourne* ☎ *321/254-9453* ⊕ *www.brevardzoo.org* ☞ *$10.50; train ride $3* ☉ *Daily 9:30–5.*

Fodor'sChoice ★

① Kennedy Space Center Visitor Complex. This "must-see" sight is just
FodorśChoice   southeast of Titusville. Following the lead of the theme parks, they've
★   switched to a one-price-covers-all admission. To get the most out of your
visit to the space center, take the basic bus tour (included with admission), which makes stops at several facilities. Buses depart every 15 minutes, and you can get on and off any bus whenever you like. If you want
a more special experience, you can pay for many different add-ons. As
you approach the Kennedy Space Center grounds, tune your car radio
to AM1320 for attraction information. New for 2007, the $60-million
Shuttle Launch Experience uses a sophisticated motion-based platform,
special effects seats, and high-fidelity visual and audio components to
simulate the sensations experienced in an actual Space Shuttle launch.
It's included in the basic admission price, which also includes whatever
film is showing in the IMAX theater. ⊠ *Rte. 405, Kennedy Space Center, Titusville* ☎ *321/449–4444* ⊕ *www.kennedyspacecenter.com* ✉ *General admission (includes bus tour, IMAX movies, Visitor Complex shows
and exhibits, and the Astronaut Hall of Fame) $38* ☉ *Space Center daily
9 AM–5:30, last regular tour 3 hrs before closing; closed certain launch
dates; IMAX I and II Theaters daily 10–5:40.*

③ Merritt Island National Wildlife Refuge. If you prefer wading birds over wait-
FodorśChoice   ing in line, don't miss the 140,000-acre wildlife refuge that adjoins the
★   Canaveral National Seashore. It's an immense area dotted by brackish
estuaries and marshes and patches of land consisting of coastal dunes,
scrub oaks, pine forests and flat woods, and palm and oak hammocks.
You can borrow field guides and binoculars at the visitor center to track
down various types of falcons, osprey, eagles, turkeys, doves, cuckoos,
loons, geese, skimmers, terns, warblers, wrens, thrushes, sparrows, owls,
and woodpeckers. A 20-minute video about refuge wildlife and accessibility—only 10,000 acres are developed—can help orient you. Several
well-marked trails help you explore. ⊠ *Rte. 402 across Titusville Causeway, Titusville* ☎ *321/861–0667* ⊕ *merrittisland.fws.gov* ✉ *Free* ☉ *Daily
sunrise–sunset; visitor center open weekdays 8–4:30, Sat. 9–5.*

② United States Astronaut Hall of Fame. The original *Mercury 7* team and the
later Gemini, Apollo, Skylab, and shuttle astronauts contributed to make
this the world's premium archive of astronauts' personal stories. Authentic memorabilia and equipment from their collections tell the story of human
space exploration. You'll watch videotapes of historic moments in the space
program and see one-of-a-kind items like Wally Schirra's relatively archaic
Sigma 7 Mercury space capsule, Gus Grissom's spacesuit (colored silver
only because NASA thought silver looked more "spacey"), and a flag that
made it to the moon. Definitely don't miss the **Astronaut Adventure**, a
hands-on discovery center with interactive exhibits that help you learn
about space travel. ⊠ *Rte. 405, Kennedy Space Center, Titusville, before
the Causeway* ☎ *321/449–4444* ⊕ *www.kennedyspacecenter.com* ✉ *$17
(included in Kennedy Space Center admission price)* ☉ *Daily 10–6:30.*

Beaches

After crossing a long and high bridge just east of Cocoa Village, you'll
be dropped down upon a barrier island. A few miles farther and you'll
reach the Atlantic Ocean and picture-perfect **Cocoa Beach** at Route A1A.

This is one of the Space Coast's nicest beaches, with many wide stretches that are excellent for biking, jogging, power walking, or strolling. In some places there are dressing rooms, showers, playgrounds, picnic areas with grills, snack shops, and surf-side parking lots. Beach vendors offer necessities, and guards are on duty in summer. Cocoa Beach is considered

> ### WRITE EASY
>
> Address a page of stick-on labels before you leave home; use them for postcards to the folks back home and you will not have to carry along a bulky address book.

the capital of Florida's surfing community. North of Cocoa, **Playalinda Beach** (⊠ *Rte. 402, Titusville* ☎ *321/267–1110*), part of the **Canaveral National Seashore,** is the longest undeveloped stretch on Florida's Atlantic coast—hundreds of giant sea turtles come ashore here between May and August to lay their eggs. The park's extreme northern area is favored by nude sunbathers. There are no lifeguards, but park rangers patrol. Take Exit 80 from I–95 and follow Route 406 east across the Indian River, then Route 402 east for another 12 mi (19 km). It's open daily from 6 to 8 (Apr.–Oct.) and 8 to 6 (Nov.–Mar.), and admission is $5 per vehicle. **Sidney Fischer Park** (⊠ *2100 block of Rte. A1A, Cocoa Beach* ☎ *321/ 868–3252*) has showers, playgrounds, changing areas, picnic areas with grills, snack shops, and plenty of well-maintained, inexpensive, surf-side parking lots. Beach vendors carry necessities for sunning and swimming. The parking fee is $5 for cars and RVs.

Shopping

In downtown Cocoa, cobblestone walkways wend through **Cocoa Village,** along Brevard Avenue and Harrison Street, a cluster of restored turn-of-the-20th-century buildings now occupied by restaurants and specialty shops purveying crafts, fine art, and clothing. It's impossible to miss the **Ron Jon Surf Shop** (⊠ *4151 N. Atlantic Ave., Rte. A1A* ☎ *321/ 799–8888* ⊕ *www.ronjons.com*). With a giant surfboard and an aqua, teal, and pink art-deco facade, Ron Jon takes up nearly two blocks along Route A1A.

FodorsChoice
★

Where to Eat

For price categories, *see* Dining at the beginning of this chapter.

★ $$–$$$$ ✕ **Mango Tree Restaurant.** Adult sufferers of attention deficit disorder may want to steer clear of this overstimulating restaurant that resembles an exotic garage sale. Hanging orchids, live swans, climbing vines, ornate planters, palmetto bushes, tropical birds, and a koi pond are just a few of the colorful distractions you'll encounter—and that's just on the way in. Once inside the restaurant, the blur of colors, sounds, and smells only intensifies. The *lobsterocki* appetizer (Maine lobster wrapped in bacon with teriyaki cream sauce) is a favorite with regulars, as are the Indian River crab cakes, coq au vin, or veal Française (scaloppine with mushroom sauce), none of which, unfortunately, comes with a side of Ritalin. ⊠ *118 N. Atlantic Ave., Cocoa Beach* ☎ *321/799–0513* ▱ *AE, MC, V* ☻ *Closed Mon. No lunch.*

¢–$$$ ✕ **Rusty's Seafood & Oyster Bar.** Oysters, prepared raw, steamed, or casino style, are just one of the draws at this casual eatery. Waitresses sporting nylon short-shorts and daily happy hour specials (dollar drafts and 2-for-1 cocktails) are undoubtedly the others. Rusty's quick service and proximity to the cruise ships make it a favorite for those about to hit the high seas. Other menu items include seafood gumbo, spicy wings,

> **BATTERY ALERT**
>
> Even if you don't think you'll need them, bring along extra camera batteries and change them before you think the old ones are "dead."

steamed crab legs, burgers, and baskets of fish-and-chips, clam strips, or fried calamari. ⊠ *628 Glen Cheek Dr., Port Canaveral* ☎ *321/783–2033* ▤ *AE, D, MC, V.*

¢–$$ ✕ **Fischer's Bar & Grill.** This casual eatery, owned by the same family that runs the more upscale Bernard's Surf, is a perfect spot for winding down after a tough day at the beach. Although complete dinners are available, people tend to come for the salads, pasta, burgers, and platters of tasty fried shrimp. The family's fleet of fishing boats brings in fresh seafood daily. Happy hour is from 4 to 7. ⊠ *2 S. Atlantic Ave., Cocoa Beach* ☎ *321/783–2401* ▤ *AE, D, MC, V.*

Where to Stay

Many local hotels offer cruise packages that include one night's lodging, parking for the duration of your cruise, and transportation to the cruise port.

For price categories, *see* Lodging at the beginning of this chapter.

$$–$$$ ▦ **Holiday Inn Cocoa Beach Oceanfront Resort.** When two adjacent beach hotels were redesigned and a promenade park landscaped between them, the Holiday Inn Cocoa Beach Resort was born. Hit hard by the 2004 hurricanes, the oceanfront property underwent a multimillion-dollar renovation with a complete exterior makeover and updates to guest rooms and meeting rooms. Standard rooms are plush, modern, and designed in bright tropical colors; suites and villas have a Key West feel with louvered doors and rattan ceiling fans. Lodging options include standard and king rooms; oceanfront suites, which have a living room with sleeper sofa; villas; or bi-level lofts. Kids are given the royal treatment with specially designed KidsSuites that feature bunk beds and video games and a pirate ship pool with water-blasting cannons. ⊠ *1300 N. Atlantic Ave., Cocoa Beach, 32931* ☎ *321/783–2271 or 800/206–2747* ☎ *321/784–8878* ⊕ *www.hicentralflorida.com/cocoa.html* ⇨ *500 rooms, 119 suites* ♨ *In-room: safe, kitchen (some), refrigerator (some), Wi-Fi. In-hotel: restaurant, bars, tennis courts, pool, gym, beachfront, laundry facilities, laundry service, executive floor, parking (no fee)* ▤ *AE, DC, MC, V.*

$$–$$$ ▦ **Radisson Resort at the Port.** For cruise-ship passengers who can't wait to get underway, this splashy resort, done up in pink and turquoise, already feels like the Caribbean. Guest rooms have wicker furniture, hand-painted wallpaper, tropical-themed decor, and ceiling fans. The pool is lushly landscaped and features a cascading 95-foot mountain waterfall. This resort, directly across the bay from Port Canaveral, is not on the ocean, but it does provide complimentary transportation to the beach, Ron Jon Surf Shop, and the cruise-ship terminals at Port Canaveral. ⊠ *8701 Astronaut Blvd., Cape Canaveral, 32920* ☎ *321/784–0000*

🖺 *321/784–3737* ⊕ *www.radisson.com/capecanaveralfl* 🖙 *284 rooms, 72 suites* ⚬ *In-room: refrigerator (some), kitchen (some), Ethernet. In-hotel: restaurant, bar, tennis court, pool, gym, laundry facilities, laundry service* 🖃 *AE, DC, MC, V.*

★ **$$** 🖺 **Inn at Cocoa Beach.** One of the area's best, this charming oceanfront inn has spacious, individually decorated rooms with four-poster beds, upholstered chairs, and balconies or patios; most have ocean views. Deluxe rooms are much larger, with a king-size bed, sofa, and sitting area; most also have a dining table. Jacuzzi rooms are different sizes; several have fireplaces, and all have beautiful ocean views. Included in the rate are afternoon socials in the breezeway, evening wine and cheese, and a sumptuous Continental breakfast. ⊠ *4300 Ocean Beach Blvd., Cocoa Beach, 32931* 🖺 *321/799–3460, 800/343–5307 outside Florida* 🖺 *321/784–8632* ⊕ *www.theinnatcocoabeach.com* 🖙 *50 rooms* ⚬ *In-room: safe, VCR (some) Wi-Fi. In-hotel: pool, beachfront, public Wi-Fi, parking (no fee), no smoking rooms* 🖃 *AE, D, MC, V* ❧ *BP.*

SAN JUAN, PUERTO RICO

Mark Sullivan   In addition to being a major port of call, San Juan is also a common port of embarkation for cruises on Southern Caribbean itineraries. For information on dining, shopping, nightlife, and sightseeing *see* San Juan, Puerto Rico *in* Chapter 4.

The Cruise Port

Cruise ships dock within a couple of blocks of Old San Juan. The Paseo de la Princesa, a tree-lined promenade beneath the city wall, is a nice place for a stroll—you can admire the local crafts and stop at the refreshment kiosks. A tourist information booth is in the cruise terminal area. Major sights in the Old San Juan area are mere blocks from the piers, but be aware that the streets are narrow and steeply inclined in places. Even if you have only a few hours before your cruise, you'll have time to do a little sightseeing.

AIRPORT The ride from the Luis Muñoz Marín International Airport, east of down-
TRANSFERS town San Juan, to the docks in Old San Juan takes about 20 minutes. The white "taxi turistico" cabs, marked by a logo on the door, have a fixed rate of $19 to the cruise ship piers; there is a 50¢ charge for luggage. Other taxi companies charge by the mile, which can cost a little more. Be sure the driver starts the meter, or agree on a fare beforehand.

VISITOR 🖪 **Puerto Rico Tourism Company** ⊕ www.gotopuertorico.com 🕿 787/721–
INFORMATION 2400 or 800/866–7827.

Where to Stay

If you are planning to spend one night in San Juan before your cruise departs, you'll probably find it easier to stay in Old San Juan, where the cruise ship terminals are. But if you want to spend a few extra days in the city, there are other possibilities near good beaches a bit farther out. We make some nightlife suggestions in the San Juan port of call section (see ⇨ San Juan *in* Chapter 4).

For price categories, *see* Lodging at the beginning of this chapter.

$$ ▣ **Sheraton Old San Juan.** This hotel's triangular shape subtly echoes the cruise ships docked nearby. Rooms facing the water have dazzling views of these behemoths as they sail in and out of the harbor. Others have views over the rooftops of Old San Juan. The rooms have been plushly renovated and have nice touches like custom-designed beds. On the top floor you'll find a sunny patio with a pool and whirlpool bath, as well as a spacious gym with the latest equipment; the concierge level provides hassle-free check-ins, Continental breakfasts, and evening hors d'oeuvres. ⊠ *100 Calle Brumbaugh, Old San Juan 00901* ☎ *787/721–5100 or 866/376–7577* 🖷 *787/289–1910* ⊕ *www.sheratonoldsanjuan.com* ⤳ *200 rooms, 40 suites* ⚲ *In-room: safe, Ethernet. In-hotel: restaurant, room service, bar, pool, gym, laundry service, executive floor, public Internet, public Wi-Fi, parking (fee), no-smoking rooms* ▤ *AE, D, DC, MC, V* ¶◎¶ *EP.*

$$$–$$$$ ▣ **Normandie Hotel.** One of the Caribbean's finest examples of art-deco
Fodor's Choice architecture, this ship-shaped hotel hosted high-society types back in the
★ 1940s. After a stem-to-stern renovation, it's ready to sail again. Egyptian motifs in the grand ballroom and other period details have been meticulously restored. Guest rooms, many of them as big as suites, are decorated in sensuous shades of cream and oatmeal. Business travelers will appreciate the huge desks outfitted with broadband access. Relaxation-seekers need look no farther than the sparkling pool or the compact spa with its massage area overlooking the ocean. N Bar, on the second floor, has quickly become a see-and-be-seen place for the city's trendy crowd. ⊠ *499 Av. Muñoz Rivera, Puerta de Tierra 00901* ☎ *787/729–2929* 🖷 *787/729–3083* ⊕ *www.normandiepr.com* ⤳ *58 rooms, 117 suites* ⚲ *In-room: safe, refrigerator, Wi-Fi. In-hotel: Restaurant, room service, bars, pool, gym, spa, beachfront, laundry service, public Internet, parking (fee), no-smoking rooms* ▤ *AE, MC, V* ¶◎¶ *EP.*

$–$$ ▣ **Numero Uno.** The name refers to the address, but Numero Uno is also how this small hotel rates with its guests. It's not unusual to hear people trading stories about how many times they've returned to this relaxing retreat. Behind a whitewashed wall is a patio where you can catch some rays beside the pool, dine in the restaurant, or enjoy a cocktail at the bar. A few steps away, a sandy beach beckons; guests are provided with beach chairs and umbrellas. Rooms are decorated in sophisticated shades of cream and taupe; several have ocean views. ⊠ *1 Calle Santa Ana, Ocean Park 00911* ☎ *787/726–5010* 🖷 *787/727–5482* ⊕ *www.numero1guesthouse.com* ⤳ *11 rooms, 2 apartments* ⚲ *In-room: kitchen (some), refrigerator, Ethernet. In-hotel: restaurant, bar, pool, beachfront, no elevator* ▤ *AE, MC, V* ¶◎¶ *CP.*

TAMPA, FLORIDA

Jim and
Cynthia Tunstall

Although glitzy Miami seems to hold the trendiness trump card and Orlando is the place your kids want to visit annually until they hit middle school, the Tampa Bay area has that elusive quality that many attribute to the "real Florida." The state's second-largest metro area is less fast-lane than its biggest (Miami), or even Orlando, but its strengths are just as varied, from broad cultural diversity to a sun-worshiping beach culture. Florida's third-busiest airport, a vibrant business community, world-class beaches, and superior hotels and resorts—many of them historic—make this an excellent place to spend a week or a lifetime. Carnival and Royal Caribbean base several ships in Tampa for cruises to the Western Caribbean, Holland America bases one ship, and several other lines base ships here seasonally.

Essentials

HOURS Some museums are closed on Mondays.

INTERNET Most people choose to access the Internet through their hotels. Most Starbucks outlets offer Internet service for a fee if you have your own laptop.

VISITOR INFORMATION **St. Petersburg/Clearwater Area Convention & Visitors Bureau** (✉ 13850 58th St. N, Suite 2200, Clearwater 33760 ☎ 727/464–7200 or 877/352–3224 ⊕ www.floridasbeach.com). **Tampa Bay Convention and Visitors Bureau** (✉ 400 N. Tampa St., Suite 2800, Tampa 33602 ☎ 813/223–1111 or 800/368–2672 ⊕ www.visittampabay.com).

The Cruise Port

Tampa is the largest shipping port in the state of Florida, and it's becoming ever more important to the cruise industry, now with three passenger terminals. In Tampa's downtown area, the port is linked to nearby Ybor City and the rest of the Tampa Bay Area by the TECO street-car line.

To reach the port by car, take I–4 West to Exit 1 (Ybor City), and go south on 21st Street. To get to Terminals 2 and 6, turn right on Adamo Drive (Highway 60), then left on Channelside Drive.

▪ **Tampa Port Authority** ✉ 1101 Channelside Dr. ☎ 813/905-7678, 813/905-5045, or 800/741-2297 ⊕ www.tampaport.com.

AIRPORT TRANSFERS
Bay Shuttle provides van-shuttle service from Tampa International Airport to the cruise-ship terminals for a fee of $11 for each passenger. Make a reservation when you arrive at the airport at their booth in ground transportation. Super Shuttle will take passengers from the Tampa airport to the cruise terminal for $19 for the first passenger and $10 for each additional passenger.

▪ **Bay Shuttle** ☎ 813/259-9998 ⊕ www.tampabayshuttle.com. **Super Shuttle** ☎ 800/258-3826 ⊕ www.supershuttle.com.

PARKING
Parking is available at the port directly across from the terminals. For Terminals 2 and 3 (Carnival and Royal Caribbean), parking is in a garage across the street. For Terminal 6 (Holland America), parking is outdoors in a guarded, enclosed lot. The cost is $12 a day, payable by credit card (MasterCard or Visa) or in cash.

Exploring the Tampa Bay Area

Florida's west coast crown jewel as well as its business and commercial hub, Tampa has high-rises and heavy traffic. Amid the bustle is the region's greatest concentration of restaurants, nightlife, stores, and cultural events.

Numbers in the margin refer to points of interest on the Tampa Bay Area map.

☝ ➏ **Adventure Island.** Waterslides, pools, and artificial-wave pools create a 30-acre wonderland at this water park, a corporate cousin of Busch Gardens. The park's newest thrill ride, Riptide, is a competitive adventure for racing three other riders through twisting tubes and hairpin turns. Rides such as the Key West Rapids and Tampa Typhoon are creative, if geographically incorrect. (There are no rapids in Key West and *typhoon* is a term used only in Pacific regions—Tampa Hurricane just wouldn't have had the same alliterative allure.) The park's planners took the younger kids into account, with offerings such as Fabian's Funport, which has a scaled-down wave pool and interactive water gym. Along with a championship volleyball complex and a surf pool, you'll find cafés, snack bars, picnic and sunbathing areas, and changing rooms. ✉ *1001 Malcolm McKinley Dr., less than 1 mi (1½ km) north of Busch Gardens, Tampa* ☎ *813/987-5660 or 888/800-5447* ⊕ *www.adventureisland. com* ☞ *$34.95* ☉ *Mid-Mar.–late Oct., daily 10–5.*

☝ ➎ **Busch Gardens.** More than 2,000 animals and dazzling live entertainment are just part of the attractions at this sprawling, carefully manicured theme park. The 335-acre adventure park's habitats offer views of some of the world's most endangered and exotic animals.

Fodor'sChoice
★

SheiKra, North America's first dive coaster, opened in mid-2005. On the wings of an African hawk, riders fly through a three-minute journey 200 feet up, then 90 degrees straight down at 70 mi per hour. The park's coaster lineup also includes steel giants **Kumba** and **Montu,** a double wooden roller coaster called **Gwazi,** and **Cheetah Chase**—a five-story family coaster full of hairpin turns and breathtaking dips. The off-road safari **Rhino Rally** brings you face to face with elephants, white rhinos, and Nile crocodiles. **Land of the Dragons** is a 4-acre playland for children that has rides, special shows, play areas, and a three-story tree house

TAMPA BEST BETS

■ Busch Gardens. The area's best theme park is a good family destination.

■ Florida Aquarium. The aquarium is next to the cruise-port, so you can just walk, making it a good option even if you have a couple of hours to kill before boarding (they'll even store your luggage if you want to visit after disembarking).

■ Ybor City. For nightlife and restaurants, this historic district is Tampa's hot spot.

with towers and stairways. You can also take a beer-tasting class—after all, Anheuser-Busch owns the park. ⊠ *3000 E. Busch Blvd., 8 mi (13 km) northeast of downtown Tampa and 2 mi (3 km) east of I–275 Exit 50, Tampa* ☎ *813/987–5082 or 888/800–5447* ⊕ *www. buschgardens.com* ⊠ *$61.95* ☉ *Daily 9–6; later in summer during special events.*

★ ☺ ❶ **Florida Aquarium.** The $84-million aquarium is no overpriced fishbowl; it's a dazzling architectural landmark with an 83-foot-high multitiered glass dome and 200,000 square feet of air-conditioned exhibit space. It has more than 10,000 aquatic plants and animals representing species native to Florida and the rest of the world. The aquarium's most impressive single exhibit is the Coral Reef, in a 500,000-gallon tank ringed with viewing windows, including an awesome 43-foot-wide panoramic opening. Part of the tank is a walkable tunnel, almost giving the illusion of venturing into underwater depths. The outdoor Explore-a-Shore exhibit, which packs appeal for younger kids, is an aquatic playground with a water slide, water jet sprays, and a climbable replica pirate ship. ⊠ *701 Channelside Dr., Tampa* ☎ *813/273–4000* ⊕ *www.flaquarium. org* ⊠ *Aquarium $17.95; Bay Spirit, Wild Dolphin Ecotour $19.95* ☉ *Daily 9:30–5.*

☺ ❹ **Lowry Park Zoo.** In Tampa's 56-acre zoo, exotic creatures live in their lush, natural habitats. Visit the zoo's newest exhibit area, Safari Africa, with a baby African elephant (born in October 2005) and four adult elephants. Feed a giraffe, ride a camel, see the zebra play, and experience a "white rhino encounter." Check out the Asian Domain, with tigers and Indian rhinos, and Primate World, including chimpanzees and colobus monkeys. Spot some fancy flying in the free-flight bird aviary, and come face to face with alligators, panthers, bears, and red wolves at the Florida Wildlife Center. Gentle goats and kangaroos populate the Wallaroo Station children's zoo, and gentle creatures of another kind headline at the Manatee Amphitheater and Aquatic Center. ✉ *1101 W. Sligh Ave., Tampa* ☎ *813/935–8552* ⊕ *www.lowryparkzoo.com* 🎫 *$14.95* ⊘ *Daily 9:30–5.*

⑨ Museum of Fine Arts. Outstanding examples of European, American, pre-Columbian, and Far Eastern art are at St. Petersburg's major art museum. There are also photographic exhibits. Staff members give narrated gallery tours two to five times a day. ✉ *255 Beach Dr. NE, St. Petersburg* ☎ *727/896–2667* ⊕ *www.fine-arts.org* 🎫 *$8* ⊘ *Tues.–Sat. 10–5, Sun. 1–5.*

☾ ⑦ Museum of Science & Industry (MOSI). This fun and stimulating scientific playground is a place where you learn about Florida weather, anatomy, flight, and space by seeing *and* by doing. At the Gulf Coast Hurricane Exhibit you can experience what a hurricane and its 74-mph winds feel like (and live to write home about it). The Bank of America BioWorks Butterfly Garden is a 6,400-square-foot engineered ecosystem project that not only serves as a home for free-flying butterflies but also demonstrates how wetlands can clean water. The 100-seat Saunders Planetarium—Tampa Bay's only planetarium—has afternoon and evening shows, one of them a trek through the universe. There's also an IMAX theater, where films are projected onto a hemispherical 82-foot dome. Kids in Charge, a 40,000-square-foot science center with interactive exhibits aimed at the 12-and-under set, opened in 2005, complete with a flight simulator. ✉ *4801 E. Fowler Ave., 1 mi (1½ km) north of Busch Gardens, Tampa* ☎ *813/987–6300 or 800/995–6674* ⊕ *www.mosi.org* 🎫 *$19.95* ⊘ *Weekdays 9–5, weekends 9–7.*

⑩ Salvador Dalí Museum. The world's most extensive collection of originals by the Spanish surrealist Salvador Dalí is found here. The collection includes 95 oils, more than 100 watercolors and drawings, and 1,300 graphics, sculptures, photographs, and objets d'art, including floor-to-ceiling murals. Frequent tours are led by well-informed docents. How did the collection end up here? A rich northern industrialist and friend of Dalí, Ohio magnate A. Reynolds Morse, was looking for a museum site after his huge personal Dalí collection began to overflow his mansion. The people of St. Petersburg vied admirably for the collection, and the museum was established here as a result. ✉ *1000 3rd St. S, St. Petersburg* ☎ *727/823–3767 or 800/442–3254* ⊕ *www.salvadordalimuseum.org* 🎫 *$15* ⊘ *Mon.–Wed., Fri., and Sat. 9:30–5:30; Thurs. 9:30–8; Sun. noon–5:30.*

FodorśChoice
★

⑧ Seminole Hard Rock Hotel & Casino. If you've brought your body to Tampa but your heart's in Vegas, you can satisfy that urge to hang around a poker table at 4 AM here. The casino has poker tables and gaming machines, and Las Vegas–style level-three slot machines are slated to open in mid-2006. The casino lounge serves drinks 24 hours a day. Floyd's restaurant has dinner and nightlife. ✉ *5223 N. Orient Rd., off I–4 at N. Orient Rd. Exit* ☎ *813/627–7625 or 866/762–5463* ⊕ *www. seminolehardrock.com* 🎫 *Free* ⊘ *Daily 24 hrs.*

③ Tampa Museum of Art. The 35,000-square-foot museum has an impressive permanent collection of Greek and Roman antiquities and 20th–21st-century sculpture, along with five galleries that host traveling exhibits, which range from contemporary to classical. ✉ *600 N. Ashley Dr., Downtown* ☎ *813/274–8130* ⊕ *www.tampamuseum.com* ☞ *$8* ⊙ *Tues.–Sat. 10–5, Sun. 11–5; 3rd Thurs. of month open until midnight.*

☾ ❷ **Ybor City.** One of only three National Historic Landmark districts in
Fodor'sChoice Florida, Tampa's lively Cuban enclave has brick streets and wrought-
★ iron balconies. Cubans brought their cigar-making industry to Ybor
(pronounced *ee*-bore) City in 1866, and the smell of cigars—hand-rolled
by Cuban immigrants—still wafts through the heart of this east Tampa
area, along with the strong aroma of roasting coffee. These days the
neighborhood is emerging as Tampa's hot spot as empty cigar factories and social clubs are transformed into boutiques, galleries, restaurants, and nightclubs that rival those in Miami's sizzling South Beach.
Take a stroll past the ornately tiled **Columbia** restaurant and the stores
lining 7th Avenue. Guided walking tours of the area ($5) enable you
to see artisans hand-roll cigars following time-honored methods. Step
back into the past at **Centennial Park** (✉ *8th Ave. and 18th St.*), which
re-creates a period streetscape and hosts the Fresh Market every Saturday. Ybor City's destination within a destination is the dining and
entertainment palace **Centro Ybor** (✉ *1600 E. 7th Ave.*). It has shops,
trendy bars and restaurants, a 20-screen movie theater, and GameWorks,
an interactive playground developed by Steven Spielberg. The **Ybor City
Museum State Park** provides a look at the history of the cigar industry. Admission includes a tour of La Casita, one of the shotgun houses
occupied by cigar workers and their families in the late 1890s. ✉ *1818
E. 9th Ave., between Nuccio Pkwy. and 22nd St., from 7th to 9th Aves.*
☎ *813/247–6323* ⊕ *www.ybormuseum.org* ☞ *$3* ⊙ *Daily 9–5; walk-
ing tours Sat. 10:30.*

Beaches

Spread over six small islands, or keys, 900-acre **Fort De Soto Park** (✉ 3500
Pinellas Bayway S, Tierra Verde ☎ 727/582–2267) lies at the mouth of
Tampa Bay. It has 7 mi (11 km) of beaches, two fishing piers, picnic and
camping grounds, and a historic fort. The fort was built on the southern end of **Mullet Key** to protect sea lanes in the gulf during the Spanish-
American War. Roam the fort or wander the beaches and the islands.
Pass-A-Grille Beach (✉ *Off Gulf Blvd. [Rte. 699], St. Petersburg Beach*),
at the southern end of St. Pete Beach, has parking meters, a snack bar,
restrooms, and showers. **St. Pete Beach** (✉ *11260 Gulf Blvd., St. Petersburg Beach*) is a free beach on Treasure Island. There are dressing
rooms, metered parking, and a snack bar.

Shopping

The **Channelside shopping and entertainment complex** (✉ 615 Channelside
Dr., Downtown) offers movie theaters, shops, restaurants, and clubs;
the official Tampa Bay visitors center is also here. **Old Hyde Park Village**
(✉ *Swan Ave. near Bayshore Blvd., Hyde Park*) is a gentrified shopping
district like the ones you find in every major American city. Williams-
Sonoma and Brooks Brothers are mixed in with bistros and sidewalk cafés.
If you are shopping for hand-rolled cigars, head for 7th Avenue in **Ybor
City,** where a few hand-rollers practice their craft in small shops.

Nightlife

The biggest concentration of nightclubs, as well as the widest variety, is found along 7th Avenue in Ybor City. It becomes a little like Bourbon Street in New Orleans after the sun goes down.

Where to Eat in the Tampa Bay Area

For price categories, *see* Dining at the beginning of this chapter.

$$$–$$$$ ✕ **Bern's Steak House.** Fine mahogany paneling and ornate chandeliers
Fodor'sChoice define the elegance at legendary Bern's, which many feel is Tampa's best
★ restaurant. Owner David Laxer ages his own beef, grows his own organic vegetables, roasts his own coffee, and maintains his own saltwater fish tanks. Cuts of topmost beef are sold by weight and thickness. The wine list includes some 6,500 selections (with 1,800 dessert wines). After dinner, tour the kitchen and wine cellar before having dessert upstairs in a cozy booth. ✉ *1208 S. Howard Ave., Hyde Park, Tampa* ☎ *813/251–2421, 800/282–1547 in Florida* ⌂ *Reservations essential* ⊟ *AE, D, MC, V* ⊙ *No lunch.*

$$–$$$ ✕ **Columbia.** A fixture since 1905, this magnificent structure with spacious dining rooms and a sunny courtyard takes up an entire city block. The paella is possibly the best in Florida, and the 1905 salad—with ham, olives, cheese, and garlic—is legendary. The menu has Cuban classics such as *ropa vieja* (shredded beef with onions, peppers, and tomatoes) and *arroz con pollo* (chicken with yellow rice). There's flamenco dancing most nights. Buy hand-rolled cigars in the bar. ✉ *2117 E. 7th Ave., Ybor City, Tampa* ☎ *813/248–4961* ⊟ *AE, D, DC, MC, V.*

¢–$ ✕ **Kojak's House of Ribs.** Family-run since its doors opened in 1978, this casual eatery has been voted a Tampa favorite year after year in local polls. Day and night the three indoor dining rooms and outdoor dining terrace are crowded with hungry patrons digging into tender barbecued ribs. There's chicken on the menu, too, and heaping sides of coleslaw, potato salad, parsley potatoes, and corn on the cob. ✉ *2808 Gandy Blvd., South Tampa, Tampa* ☎ *813/837–3774* ⊟ *AE, D, DC, MC, V* ⊙ *Closed Mon.*

Where to Stay in the Tampa Bay Area

If you want to be close to the cruise-ship terminal, then you'll have to stay in Tampa, but if you want to spend more time in the area and perhaps stay on the beach, St. Petersburg and the beaches are close by.

For price categories, *see* Lodging at the beginning of this chapter.

$$$$ 🏨 **Tampa Marriott Waterside.** Across from the Tampa Convention Center, this downtown hotel was built for conventioneers but is also convenient to popular tourist spots such as the Florida Aquarium, the St. Pete Times Forum hockey arena, and shopping and entertainment districts Channelside, Hyde Park, and Ybor City. At least half of the rooms and most of the suites overlook the channel to Tampa Bay; the bay itself is visible from the higher floors of the 27-story hotel. The lobby coffee bar overlooks the water. Il Terrazzo is the hotel's formal, Italian dining room. ✉ *700 S. Florida Ave., Downtown, 33602* ☎ *813/221–4900* 🖷 *813/221–0923* ⊕ *www.tampawaterside.com* 🛏 *681 rooms, 36 suites* ⌂ *In-room: safe, kitchen (some), high-speed Internet, Wi-Fi in lobby. In-hotel: 3 restaurants, room service, bars, pool, gym, spa,* *concierge, laundry facilities, laundry service, executive floor, parking (fee), no-smoking rooms* ☰ *AE, D, DC, MC, V.*

★ **$$–$$$** 🏨 **Don Vicente de Ybor Historic Inn.** This boutique hotel is in a restored building constructed in 1895 by Vicente Martinez Ybor, the founder of Ybor City. From the beige stucco exterior to the white marble staircase in the main lobby, the hotel is an architectural tour de force. Rooms have antique furnishings, Persian rugs, and four-poster canopied beds. Most rooms have wrought-iron balconies. The clubs and shops of Ybor City are within a short walk. ✉ *1915 Republica de Cuba, Ybor City, 33605* ☎ *813/241–4545* 📠 *813/241–6104* ⊕ *www.donvicenteinn.com* ⇨ *13 rooms, 3 suites* ⚐ *In-room: Ethernet. In-hotel: restaurant, bar, laundry service, Wi-Fi* ☰ *AE, D, DC, MC, V* ⧉ *BP.*

$$–$$$ 🏨 **Hilton Garden Inn Tampa Ybor Historic District.** Architecturally, this property pales when compared to the century-old classic structures around it in Ybor City. But it is convenient: it's across the street from the Centro Ybor complex, 3 mi (5 km) from downtown Tampa, and 7 mi (11 km) from Tampa International Airport. The hotel restaurant has a full breakfast buffet and doesn't try to compete with the culinary heavyweights in a six-block radius. Rooms are business traveler–friendly, with high-speed Internet access, dual phone lines, large desks, and ergonomic chairs. ✉ *1700 E. 9th Ave., Ybor City, 33605* ☎ *813/769–9267* 📠 *813/769–3299* ⊕ *www.tampayborhistoricdistrict.gardeninn.com* ⇨ *84 rooms, 11 suites* ⚐ *In-room: refrigerator, Ethernet. In-hotel: restaurant, pool, laundry facilities, laundry service, Wi-Fi* ☰ *AE, D, DC, MC, V* ⧉ *EP.*

Ports of Call

WORD OF MOUTH

"I love planning a trip and seeing the island on my own terms . . . and not with hordes of other people . . . It takes a little more work to research and make arrangements, but it is always worth it to me."
—Cathy

"[T]hese excursion companies depend on the cruise industry for their living, and they are all very much aware of the sailing times. Don't be scared off from arranging your own tours because of the threat of [the ship] leaving without you."

—PumpkinEater

"There are times when it is a good idea to book with the ship. Last year we did a tour that let us swim with the dolphins then it took us to the ship's private beach." —toontown

NOWHERE IN THE WORLD are conditions better suited to cruising than in the Caribbean Sea. Tiny island nations, within easy sailing distance of one another, form a chain of tropical enchantment that curves from Cuba in the north all the way down to the coast of Venezuela. There's far more to life here than sand and coconuts, however. The islands are vastly different, with a variety of cultures, topographies, and languages represented. Colonialism has left its mark, and the presence of the Spanish, French, Dutch, Danish, and British is still felt. Slavery, too, has left its cultural legacy, blending African overtones into the colonial/Indian amalgam. The one constant, however, is the weather. Despite the islands' southerly latitude, the climate is surprisingly gentle, due in large part to the cooling influence of the trade winds.

The Caribbean is made up of the Greater Antilles and the Lesser Antilles. The former consist of those islands closest to the United States: Cuba, Jamaica, Hispaniola (Haiti and the Dominican Republic), and Puerto Rico. (The Cayman Islands lie south of Cuba.) The Lesser Antilles, including the Virgin, Windward, and Leeward islands and others, are greater in number but smaller in size, and constitute the southern half of the Caribbean chain.

GOING ASHORE

Traveling by cruise ship presents an opportunity to visit many places in a short time. The flip side is that your stay in each port of call will be brief. For this reason cruise lines offer shore excursions, which maximize passengers' time. There are a number of advantages to shore excursions arranged by your ship: in some destinations, transportation may be unreliable, and a ship-packaged tour is the best way to see distant sights. Also, you don't have to worry about missing the ship. The disadvantage of a shore excursion is the cost—you usually pay more for the convenience of having the ship do the legwork for you, but it's not always a lot more. Of course, you can always book a tour independently, hire a taxi, or use foot power to explore on your own. For each port of call included in this guide, we've provided some suggestions for the best ship-sponsored excursions—in terms of both quality of experience and price—as well as some suggestions for what to do if you want to explore on your own.

Arriving in Port

When your ship arrives in a port, it will tie up alongside a dock or anchor out in a harbor. If the ship is docked, passengers walk down the gangway to go ashore. Docking makes it easy to move between the shore and the ship.

Tendering

If your ship anchors in the harbor, you will have to take a small boat—called a launch or tender—to get ashore. Tendering is a nuisance. Passengers wishing to disembark may be required to gather in a public room, get sequenced boarding passes, and wait until their numbers are called. The ride to shore may take as long as 20 minutes. If you don't like waiting, plan to go ashore an hour or so after the ship drops its anchor. On a very large ship, the wait for a tender can be quite long and frustrating.

Because tenders can be difficult to board, passengers with mobility problems may not be able to visit certain ports. The larger ships are more likely to use tenders. It is usually possible to learn before booking a cruise whether the ship will dock or anchor at its ports of call.

Before anyone is allowed to walk down the gangway or board a tender, the ship must be cleared for landing. Immigration and customs officials board the vessel to examine passports and sort through red tape. It may be more than an hour before you're allowed ashore. You will be issued a boarding pass, which you'll need to get back on board.

Returning to the Ship

Cruise lines are strict about sailing times, which are posted at the gangway and elsewhere and announced in the daily schedule of activities. Be sure to be back on board (not on the dock waiting to get a tender back to the ship) at least a half hour before the announced sailing time or you may be stranded. If you are on a shore excursion that was sold by the cruise line, however, the captain will wait for your group before casting off. That is one reason many passengers prefer ship-packaged tours.

If you're not on one of the ship's tours and the ship sails without you, immediately contact the cruise line's port representative, whose phone number is often listed on the daily schedule of activities. You may be able to hitch a ride on a pilot boat, although that is unlikely. Passengers who miss the boat must pay their own way to the next port.

CARIBBEAN ESSENTIALS

Currency

The U.S. dollar is the official currency on Puerto Rico, the U.S. Virgin Islands, and the British Virgin Islands. On Grand Cayman you will usually have a choice of Cayman or U.S. dollars when you take money out of an ATM, and you may even be able to get change in U.S. dollars. In most other Caribbean ports, U.S. paper currency (not coins) is accepted readily, but you may need to change a few dollars into local currency for phone calls, tips, and taxis. When you pay in dollars you'll almost always get change in local currency, so it's best to carry bills in small denominations. If you need local currency (say, for a trip to one of the French islands that uses the euro), change money at a local bank or use an ATM for the best rate. Most major credit cards are accepted all over the Caribbean, except at local market stalls and small establishments.

Keeping in Touch

Internet cafés are now fairly common on most islands, and you'll sometimes find Internet cafés in the cruise-ship terminal itself—or perhaps in an attached or nearby shopping center. If you want to call home, most cruise-ship facilities have phones that accept credit cards or local phone

Caribbean

Turks
and
Caicos
Islands

ATLANTIC OCEAN

DOMINICAN
REPUBLIC

Hispaniola

LEEWARD ISLANDS

St. John
St. Thomas — Tortola
Virgin Gorda
San Juan — Anguilla
St. Barthélemy
Santo — St. Maarten/
Domingo — St. Martin — Saba — Barbuda
Puerto — St. St. Eustatius — Antigua
Rico — Croix — St. Kitts
Nevis
Montserrat — Marie
Galante
Guadeloupe

ANTILLES

Dominica

WINDWARD

Martinique
Fort-de-France

Sea

St. Lucia
Barbados

St. Vincent

Bridgetown

Bequia
The
Grenadines
Carriacou
St. George's

LESSER ANTILLES

Aruba
Willemstad
Bonaire
Islas Los
Roques
Curaçao

Grenada
Tobago

Port of Spain
Trinidad

La Guaira

Caracas

VENEZUELA

| 0 | 200 miles |
| 0 | 300 km |

The Mayan Riviera

cards (local phone cards are almost always the cheapest option). And on most islands, GSM multi-band mobile phones will work, though roaming charges may be steep (some plans include Puerto Rico and the U.S. Virgin Islands in their nationwide calling regions).

Where to Eat

Cuisine on the Caribbean's islands is as varied as the islands themselves. The region's history as a colonial battleground and ethnic melting pot creates plenty of variety and adds

> ### BUYING LIQUOR & PERFUME
>
> If you buy duty-free liquor or perfume while in a Caribbean port, don't forget that you may not bring it aboard your flight home. You will have to put it in your checked bags. Many liquor stores will pack your bottles in bubble wrap and pack them in a good cardboard box. Take advantage of this service.

lots of unusual tropical fruit and spices. In fact, the one quality that defines most Caribbean cooking is its spiciness, acquired from nutmeg, mace, allspice, peppers, saffron, and many other seasonings grown in the islands. Dress is generally casual, although throughout the islands, beachwear is inappropriate most anywhere except on the beach. Unless otherwise noted, prices are given in U.S. dollars. The following price categories are used in this book.

WHAT IT COSTS In US$				
$$$$	**$$$**	**$$**	**$**	**¢**
AT DINNER over $30	$20–$30	$12–$20	$8–$12	under $8

Prices are per person for a main course at dinner and do not include any service charges.

Shore Excursions

Typical excursions include an island or town bus tour, a visit to a beach or rum factory, a boat trip, a snorkeling or diving trip, and charter fishing. In recent years, however, shore excursions have gotten more adventurous with mild river rafting, parasailing, jet skiing, hiking, and biking added to the mix. It's often easier to take a ship-arranged excursion, but it's almost never the cheapest option.

If you prefer to break away from the pack, find a knowledgeable taxi driver or tour operator—they're usually within a stone's throw of the pier—or wander around on your own. A group of four to six people will usually find this option more economical and practical than will a single person or a couple.

Renting a car is also a good option on many islands—again, the more people, the better the deal. But get a good island map before you set off, and be sure to find out how long it will take you to get around.

Conditions are ideal for water sports of all kinds—scuba diving, snorkeling, windsurfing, sailing, waterskiing, and fishing excursions abound. Your shore-excursion director can usually arrange these activities for you if the ship offers no formal excursion.

PRIVATE ISLANDS

Linda Coffman   When evaluating the "best" Caribbean ports of call, many repeat cruise passengers often add the cruise lines' own private island to their lists of preferred destinations.

The cruise lines established "private" islands to provide a beach break on an island (or part of one) reserved for their exclusive use. While most passengers don't select an itinerary based solely upon calling at a private island, they usually consider them a highlight of their cruise vacation. The very least you can expect of your private island is lush foliage and a wide swath of beach surrounded by azure water. Facilities vary, but a beach barbecue, water-sports equipment rental, lounge chairs, hammocks, and restrooms are standard. Youth counselors come ashore to conduct sand castle building competitions and lead junior pirates on swashbuckling island treasure hunts.

The use of strollers and wheelchairs equipped with all-terrain wheels may be offered on a complimentary first-come, first-served basis. However, with the exception of some participation sports on the beach, plan to pay for most water toys and activities. Costs associated with private island fun and recreation can range from $6 for use of a snorkel vest (you may use your own snorkel equipment; however, in the event a floatation vest is required for safety, you must rent one) to $30 for rental of an entire snorkeling outfit for the day (mask, fins, snorkel vest, a mesh bag, fish identification card, and fish food). You can often take a banana boat ride for $16 to $19 (15-minute ride), sail a small boat or catamaran for $30 to $50 (one hour), paddle a kayak for $18 to $30 (half hour), ride a jet ski for $59 to $95 (45 minutes to one hour), or parasail for a hefty $69 to $79 (10 minutes or less). Floating mats are a relative bargain at $10 for all-day lounging in the water. You might also find open-air massage cabanas with pricing comparable to the spa charges on board.

There is generally no charge for food or basic beverages, such as those served on board ship. While soft drinks and tropical cocktails can be charged to your shipboard account, you might want to bring a small amount of cash ashore for souvenir shopping, which is usually possible from vendors set up on or near the beach. You will also want to bring beach towels ashore and return them to the ship at the end of the day because, as Princess Cruises reminds passengers, "Although the locals may offer to do this for you, unfortunately we seldom see the towels again!"

Even if you do nothing more than lie in a shaded hammock and sip fruity tropical concoctions, the day can be one of the most fun and relaxing of your entire cruise.

Islands by Cruise Line

Carnival Cruise Lines is currently the only major cruise line without an extensive private island experience available to the entire fleet. However, select Carnival itineraries include calls at Half Moon Cay, Holland

America Line's private paradise. Similarly, certain Regent Seven Seas cruises include beach party days at Princess Cays and Cayo Leventado.

Not a "private island" destination in the strictest sense, the yachts of Seabourn and SeaDream offer passengers a day ashore on secluded private beaches where they can enjoy lavish barbecues and take a break from swimming and snorkeling to indulge in champagne and caviar served in the surf.

COSTA CRUISES An unspoiled island paradise, Costa's **Catalina Island** is located just off the coast of the Dominican Republic. Passengers can participate in Costa's "Beach Olympics," schedule a seaside massage, or just kick back on a chaise lounge or a complimentary water float. Water toy rentals, banana boat rides, and sailing tours are available from independent concessionaires. Local vendors set up souvenir shops offering crafts and T-shirts. The ship provides the food for a lunch barbecue and tropical beverages at the beach bar.

Activities: Snorkeling, sailing, jet skiing, waterskiing, hiking, volleyball, organized games, massages, shopping.

DISNEY CRUISE LINE Unique among private islands, Disney's **Castaway Cay** has a dock, so passengers simply step ashore (rather than tendering, as is required to reach all other private islands). Like everything associated with Disney, the line's private island is almost too good to be true. Located in the Abacos, a chain in the Bahamas, only 10% of Castaway Cay is developed, leaving plenty of unspoiled area to explore in Robinson Crusoe fashion. Trams are provided to reach separate beaches designated for children, teens, families, and adults, and Disney is the only line to offer age-specific activities and extensive, well-planned children's activities. Biking and hiking are so popular that a second nature trail, complete with an observation tower, has been added. Excursions range from as passive as a glass-bottom boat tour to the soaring excitement of parasailing. An interactive experience with stingrays is educational and safe—the gentle creatures' barbs are blunted for safety. In addition to barbecue fare and several beverage stations, beach games, island-style music, and a shaded game pavilion, there are shops, massage cabanas by the sea, and even a post office.

Activities: Snorkeling, kayaking, parasailing, sailing, jet skiing, paddleboats, water cycles, fishing, bicycles, basketball, billiards, hiking, Ping-Pong, shuffleboard, soccer, volleyball, organized games, massages, shopping.

HOLLAND AMERICA LINE Little San Salvador, one of the Bahamian out-islands, was renamed **Half Moon Cay** by Holland America Line to honor Henry Hudson's ship (depicted on the cruise line's logo) as well as to reflect the beach's crescent shape. Even after development, the island is still so unspoiled that it has been named a Wild Bird Preserve by the Bahamian National Trust. Passengers, who are welcomed ashore at a West Indies Village complete with shops and straw market, find Half Moon Cay easily accessible—all facilities are connected by hard-surfaced and packed-sand pathways and meet and exceed ADA requirements. An accessible tram also connects the welcome center with the food pavilion; wheelchairs with balloon tires are available. In addition to the beach area for lazing in the sun or shade, the island has a post office, Bahamian-style chapel, a lagoon where you can interact with stingrays, and, for family fun, you'll find a beach-front water park with water slides and fanciful sea creatures tethered to the sandy bottom of the shallow water. Massage services are available as are fitness activities. Air-conditioned cabanas can be rented for the day, with or without the services of your own butler.

Activities: Scuba diving, snorkeling, windsurfing, kayaking, parasailing, sailing, jet skiing, Aqua Bikes, fishing, bicycles, basketball, hiking, horseback riding, shuffleboard, volleyball, massages, shopping.

MSC CRUISES **Cayo Leventado,** roughly translated as "Floating Island," is located off the Samaná Peninsula on the northeast coast of the Dominican Republic. The unspoiled cay is leased by Bahia Cruises, a development company that has installed beach chairs, umbrellas, bars, a dining facility, and acres of walking paths through the topical rain forest. Not owned outright by MSC Cruises, the private island is available to other cruise lines. In addition to lazing in the sun, swimming in the warm surf, and participating in spirited beach games, you can choose from several tours. Tours offered are a Jeep safari, hiking to a mountain waterfall with horseback riding, a speedboat excursion to a bird sanctuary, a sail-and-snorkel adventure, and even seasonal whale-watching boat trips.

Activities: Snorkeling, sailing, hiking, volleyball, organized games.

Many ships now tender passengers ashore in the town of Samaná; for more information on this port, see ⇨ Samaná, Dominican Republic, *below.*

NORWEGIAN CRUISE LINE Only 120 miles east of Fort Lauderdale in the Berry Island chain of the Bahamas, much of **Great Stirrup Cay** looks as it did when it was acquired by Norwegian Cruise Line in 1977. The first uninhabited island purchased to offer cruise-ship passengers a private beach day, Great Stirrup Cay's white sand beaches are fringed by coral and ideal for snorkeling. Permanent facilities have been added to and improved in the intervening years, but bougainvillea, sea grape, and coconut palms are still as abundant as the colorful tropical fish that inhabit the reef. To reduce beach erosion and preserve the environment, a seawall was erected. A straw market, water sports centers, bars, volleyball courts, beachside massage stations, and food pavilion round out the facilities.

Activities: Snorkeling, kayaking, parasailing, sailing, paddleboats, Ping-Pong, hiking, volleyball, organized games, massages, shopping.

PRINCESS CRUISES **Princess Cays** is a 40-acre haven on the southern tip of Eleuthera Island in the Bahamas. Not quite an uninhabited island, it nevertheless offers a wide ribbon of beach, long enough for passengers to splash in the surf, relax in a hammock, or limbo to the beat of local music and never feel crowded. In a similar fashion to booking shore excursions, water-sports equipment can be reserved ahead of time, either on board the ship or through the Princess Web site. Nestled in a picturesque palm grove, private bungalows with air-conditioning and ceiling fans and a deck for lounging can be rented for parties of up to six. In addition to three tropical bars and the area where a Bahamian barbecue is served, permanent facilities include small shops that sell island crafts and trinkets, but if you head around the back and through the fence, independent vendors sell similar goods for lower prices.

Activities: Snorkeling, kayaking, parasailing, sailing, paddleboats, Aqua Bikes, hiking, organized games, shopping.

ROYAL CARIBBEAN & CELEBRITY CRUISES Royal Caribbean and Celebrity Cruises passengers have twice as many opportunities to visit a private island. The lines share two, and many Caribbean itineraries include one or the other.

Coco Cay is a 140-acre island in the Berry Island chain between Nassau and Freeport. Originally known as Little Stirrup Cay, it's within view of Great Stirrup Cay (NCL's private island) and the snorkeling is just as good, especially around a sunken airplane and a replica of Blackbeard's flagship, *Queen Anne's Revenge*. In addition to activities and games ashore, Coco Cay boasts the largest Aqua Park in the Caribbean, where children and adults alike can jump on an in-water trampoline or climb a floating sand castle before they dig into a beach barbecue or explore a nature trail. The newest attractions include an inflatable 40-foot water slide (fun for adults and kids alike) and a Power Wheels track where youngsters age 3 to 8 can take a miniature car for a spin at a sedate 3 mph.

Activities: Scuba diving, snorkeling, jet skiing, kayaking, parasailing, hiking, volleyball, organized games, shopping.

Labadee is a 260-acre peninsula approximately 6 mi (10 km) from Cap Haitien on the secluded north coast of Haiti (the port of call will often be called "Hispaniola"). In addition to swimming, water sports, an Aqua Park with floating trampolines and water slides, and nature trails to explore, bonuses on Labadee are an authentic folkloric show presented by island performers and a market featuring work of local artists and crafters, where you might find an interesting painting or unique wood carving. Due to the proximity of Labadee to mainland Haiti, it is sometimes necessary to cancel calls there due to political unrest. In that event, an alternate port is usually scheduled.

Activities: Snorkeling, jet skiing, kayaking, parasailing, hiking, volleyball, organized games, shopping.

ANTIGUA

Jordan Simon

Some say Antigua has so many beaches that you could visit a different one every day for a year. Most have snow-white sand, and many are backed by lavish resorts that offer sailing, diving, windsurfing, and snorkeling. The largest of the British Leeward islands, Antigua was the headquarters from which Lord Horatio Nelson (then a mere captain) made his forays against the French and pirates in the late 18th century. You may wish to explore English Harbour and its carefully restored Nelson's Dockyard, as well as tour old forts, historic churches, and tiny villages. Appealing aspects of the island's interior include a small tropical rain forest ideal for hiking, ancient Native American archaeological digs, and restored sugar mills. Due to time constraints, it's best to make trips this far from port with an experienced tour operator. But you can easily take a taxi to any number of fine beaches on your own and escape from the hordes descending from the ship.

Essentials

CURRENCY Eastern Caribbean (E.C.) dollar (EC$2.70 to US$1). U.S. dollars are generally accepted, but change is given in E.C. dollars.

HOURS Banks are generally open weekdays from 8 to 1 and 3 to 5. Although some stores still close for lunch, most are open Monday through Saturday from 9 to 5; if a cruise ship is in port, shops in Heritage and Redcliffe Quays are likely to open Sunday.

INTERNET There are some small Internet cafés in St. John's and English Harbour; ask at the tourist information booth at the cruise-ship pier.

TELEPHONES A GSM tri-band mobile phone will usually work in Antigua. You can use the Caribbean Phone Card (available in $5, $10, and $20 denominations in most hotels and post offices) for local and long-distance calls. To call the United States and Canada, dial 1 + the area code + the seven-digit number, or use the phone card or one of the "CALL USA" phones, which are available at several locations, including the cruise terminal at St. John's and the English Harbour Marina.

Coming Ashore

Though some ships dock at the deep-water harbor in downtown St. John's, most use Heritage Quay, a multimillion-dollar complex with shops, condominiums, a casino, and a food court. Most St. John's attractions are an easy walk from Heritage Quay; the older part of the city is eight blocks away. A tourist information booth is in the main docking building.

If you intend to explore beyond St. John's, consider hiring a taxi driver-guide. Taxis meet every cruise ship. They're unmetered; fares are fixed, and drivers are required to carry a rate card. Agree on the fare before setting off, and plan to tip drivers 10%. Some cabbies may take you from St. John's to English Harbour and wait for a "reasonable" amount of time (about a half hour) while you look around, for about $50; you can usually arrange an island tour for around $25 per hour. Renting your own car isn't usually practical, since you must purchase a $20 temporary driving permit in addition to the car-rental fee, which is usually about $50 per day in the high season.

Shore Excursions

We consider these to be among the better shore excursions for Antigua. They may not be offered by all lines, and tour names may differ as well. Times and prices are approximate.

Highlights Tour. Most highlights tours stop at Nelson's Dockyard and Shirley Heights. Longer versions usually include a beach stop, often at Pigeon Point Beach. Tours usually include a break for refreshments. ⏱ *3–4½ hrs* 🎟 *$48.*

4x4 Off-Road Historical Adventure. By taking a four-wheel-drive vehicle, you'll get to explore some of the quieter, off-the-beaten-track areas of the island, including Betty's Hope. Most of these tours include at least a short beach stop and refreshments. ⏱ *3 hrs* 🎟 *$59–$66.*

Helicopter to Montserrat. If you'd like an up close look at the island's smoldering active volcano, book this expensive but worthwhile aerial tour. ⏱ *2 hrs* 🎟 *$250.*

Kayak & Snorkel Tour. These guided snorkeling tours usually visit one of the uninhabited islands off Antigua's east coast. After the kayaking trip, there's always time to relax on the beach. ⏱ *4½ hrs* 🎟 *$69.*

Zip Line Tour. Antigua's first zip-line tour opened in 2006. It's sometimes hard to get a spot if you don't book through the ship. ⏱ *4½ hrs* 🎟 *$69.*

Exploring Antigua

Numbers in the margin correspond to points of interest on the Antigua map.

❸ Falmouth. This town sits on a lovely bay backed by former sugar plantations and sugar mills. The most important historic site here is St. Paul's Church, which was rebuilt on the site of a church once used by troops during the Nelson period.

❷ Fort George. East of Liberta—one of the first settlements founded by freed slaves—on Monk's Hill, this fort was built from 1689 to 1720. Among the ruins are the sites for 32 cannons, water cisterns, the base of the old flagstaff, and some of the original buildings.

4 Nelson's Dockyard. Antigua's most famous attraction is the world's only Georgian-era dockyard still in use, a treasure trove for history buffs and nautical nuts alike. In 1671 the governor of the Leeward Islands wrote to the Council for Foreign Plantations in London, pointing out the advantages of this landlocked harbor. By 1704 English Harbour was in regular use as a garrisoned station.

In 1784 26-year-old Horatio Nelson sailed in on the HMS *Boreas* to serve as captain and second-in-command of the Leeward Island Station. Under him was the captain of the HMS *Pegasus,* Prince William Henry, duke of Clarence, who was later crowned King William IV. The prince acted as best man when Nelson married Fannie Nisbet on Nevis in 1787.

> **ANTIGUA BEST BETS**
>
> ■ **Dickenson Bay Beach.** One of Antigua's best beaches is just north of St. John's, and it has myriad water-sports outfitters and many beach bars where you can rent chairs and get refreshments.
>
> ■ **Nelson's Dockyard.** This is one of the Caribbean's best historic sights, and if you tire of history, it has abundant stores, restaurants, and bars.
>
> ■ **Eco-Tourism.** Some of the most interesting tours on Antigua explore the island's forested interior on foot or surrounding coves by kayak. Since some areas are far from St. John's, it's usually best to book these tours with your ship.

When the Royal Navy abandoned the station at English Harbour in 1889, it fell into a state of decay, though adventuresome yachties still lived there in near-primitive conditions. The Society of the Friends of English Harbour began restoring it in 1951; it reopened with great fanfare in 1961. Within the compound are crafts shops, restaurants, and two splendidly restored 18th-century hotels, the Admiral's Inn and the Copper & Lumber Store Hotel, which are worth peeking into. (The latter, occupying a supply store for Nelson's Caribbean fleet, is a particularly fine example of Georgian architecture and has an interior courtyard evoking Old England.) The Dockyard National Park also includes serene nature trails accessing beaches, rock pools, and crumbling plantation ruins and hilltop forts.

The **Dockyard Museum,** in the original Naval Officer's House, presents ship models, mock-ups of English Harbour, displays on the people who worked there and typical ships that docked, silver regatta trophies, maps, prints, antique navigational instruments, and Nelson's very own telescope and tea caddy. ⊠ *English Harbour* ☎ *268/481–5022, 268/463–1060, 268/481–5028 for the National Parks Department* ⊕ *www.antiguamuseums.org* ⊡ *$2 suggested donation* ⊙ *Daily 8–5.*

1 St. John's. Antigua's capital, with some 45,000 inhabitants (approximately half the island's population), lies at sea level at the inland end of a sheltered northwestern bay. Although it has seen better days, a couple of notable historic sights and some good waterfront shopping areas and restaurants make it worth a visit. Signs at the **Museum of Antigua & Barbuda** say PLEASE TOUCH, encouraging you to explore Antigua's past. Try your hand at the educational video games or squeeze a cassava through a *matapi* (grass sieve). Exhibits interpret the nation's history, from its geological birth to its political independence in 1981. The museum occupies the former courthouse, which dates from 1750. The superlative gift shop carries such unusual items as calabash purses, seed earrings, and lignum vitae pipes, as well as historic maps and local books. ⊠ *Church and Market Sts.* ☎ *268/462–1469* ⊕ *www.antiguamuseums.org* 🖃 *$2 suggested donation* ☉ *Sun.–Thurs. 8:30–4, Fri. 8:30–3, Sat. 10–2.*

At the south gate of the **Anglican Cathedral of St. John the Divine** are figures of St. John the Baptist and St. John the Divine said to have been taken from one of Napoléon's ships and brought to Antigua. The original church was built in 1681, replaced by a stone building in 1745, and destroyed by an earthquake in 1843. The present neo-baroque building dates from 1845; the parishioners had the interior completely encased in pitch pine, hoping to forestall future earthquake damage. The church attained cathedral status in 1848. Tombstones bear eerily eloquent testament to the colonial days. ⊠ *Between Long and Newgate Sts.* ☎ *268/461–0082.*

Redcliffe Quay, at the water's edge just south of Heritage Quay, is the most appealing part of St. John's. Attractively restored (and superbly re-created) buildings in a riot of cotton-candy colors house shops, restaurants, and boutiques and are linked by courtyards and landscaped walkways.

❺ Shirley Heights. This bluff affords a spectacular view of English Harbour. The heights are named for Sir Thomas Shirley, the governor who fortified the harbor in 1787. At the top is Shirley Heights Lookout, a restaurant built into the remnants of the 18th-century fortifications. Most notable for its boisterous Sunday barbecues that continue into the night with live music and dancing, it serves dependable burgers, pumpkin soup, grilled meats, and rum punches. Not far from Shirley Heights is the **Dows Hill Interpretation Centre,** where observation platforms provide still more sensational vistas of the English Harbour area. A multimedia sound-and-light presentation on island history and culture, spotlighting lifelike figures and colorful tableaux accompanied by running commentary and music, results in a cheery, if bland, portrait of Antiguan life from Amerindian times to the present. ☎ *268/460–2777 for National Parks Authority* 🖃 *EC$15* ☉ *Daily 9–5.*

☺ ❻ Stingray City Antigua. A carefully reproduced "natural" environment has been nicknamed by staffers the "retirement home," though the 30-plus stingrays, ranging from infants to seniors, are frisky. You can stroke, feed, even hold the striking gliders, as well as snorkel in deeper, protected waters. The tour guides do a marvelous job of explaining the animals' habits—from feeding to breeding—and their predators (including man). ⊠ *Seaton's Village* ☎ *268/562–7297 or 268/463–1944.*

Shopping

Redcliffe Quay, on the waterfront at the south edge of St. John's, is by far the most appealing shopping area. Several restaurants and more than 30 boutiques, many with one-of-a-kind wares, are set around landscaped courtyards shaded by colorful trees. **Heritage Quay,** in St. John's, has 35 shops—including many that are duty-free. There are also shops along **St. John's, St. Mary's, High,** and **Long streets.** The tangerine-and-lilac-hue four-story **Vendor's Mall** at the intersection of Redcliffe and Thames streets gathers the pushy, pesky vendors that once clogged the narrow streets. It's jammed with stalls; air-conditioned indoor shops sell some higher-price, if not higher-quality, merchandise.

★ The **Goldsmitty** (⊠ *Redcliffe Quay, St. John's* 🕾 *268/462–4601*) is Hans Smit, an expert goldsmith who turns gold, black coral, and precious and semiprecious stones into one-of-a-kind works of art.

Isis (⊠ *Redcliffe Quay, St. John's* 🕾 *268/462–4602*) sells island and in- ternational bric-a-brac, such as antique jewelry, hand-carved walking sticks, and glazed pottery. **Jacaranda** (⊠ *Redcliffe Quay, St. John's* 🕾 *268/ 462–1888*) sells batik, sarongs, and swimwear as well as Caribbean food, perfumes, soaps, and artwork. **Map Shop** (⊠ *St. Mary's St., St. John's* 🕾 *268/462–3993*) offers a fine assortment of books on Caribbean cui- sine, flora, fauna, and history, as well as maps. **Noreen Phillips** (⊠ *Red- cliffe Quay, St. John's* 🕾 *268/462–3127*) creates glitzy appliquéd and beaded evening wear—inspired by the colors of the sea and sunset—in sensuous fabrics ranging from chiffon and silk to Italian lace and Indian brocade.

★ At **Galley Boutique** (⊠ *Nelson's Dockyard, English Harbour* 🕾 *268/460– 1525*), Janey Easton personally seeks out exclusive creations from both international (Calvin Klein, Adrienne Vittadini) and local Caribbean de- signers, ranging from swimwear to evening garb. She also sells handi- crafts and lovely hammocks.

Activities

ADVENTURE TOURS
Adventure Antigua (🕾 *268/727–3261* ⊕ *www.adventureantigua.com*) is run by enthusiastic Eli Fuller, who is knowledgeable not only about the ecosystem and geography of Antigua but also about its history and pol- itics. The company offers an exceptional daylong boat tour of the is- land. An "Xtreme Tour" takes you on a circumnavigation of the island on a racing speedboat. **"Paddles" Kayak Eco Adventure** (⊠ *Seaton's Vil- lage* 🕾 *268/463–1944 or 268/560–3782* ⊕ *www.antiguapaddles.com*) takes you on a 3½-hour tour of serene mangroves and inlets with in- formative narrative about the fragile ecosystem of the swamp and reefs and the rich diversity of flora and fauna. The tour ends with a hike to sunken caves and snorkeling in the North Sound Marine Park. Experi- enced guides double as kayaking and snorkeling instructors, making this an excellent opportunity for novices.

DIVING
With all the wrecks and reefs, there are lots of undersea sights to ex- plore, from coral canyons to sea caves. The most accessible wreck is the schooner *Andes,* not far out in Deep Bay, off the Five Islands Peninsula. Among the favorite sites are **Green Island, Cades Reef,** and **Bird Island** (a national park). **Dockyard Divers** (⊠ *Nelson's Dockyard, English Harbour* 🕾 *268/460–1178*), owned by British ex-merchant seaman Captain A. G. "Tony" Fincham, is one of the island's most established outfits

and offers diving and snorkeling trips, PADI courses, and dive packages with accommodations. They're geared to seasoned divers, but work patiently with novices.

> **CAUTION** ⚠
>
> Do not bother packing beach towels; they will be provided for your use on board the cruise ship and will be given out when you go ashore.

Beaches

Antigua's beaches are public, and many are dotted with resorts that have water-sports outfitters and beach bars. Most hotels have taxi stands, so getting back to the ship isn't usually a problem. Sunbathing topless or in the buff is strictly illegal except on one of the small beaches at Hawksbill Beach Hotel on the Five Islands Peninsula. Most cruise-ship beach excursions go to the beaches on the west coast.

Dickenson Bay, the closest accessible beach to St. John's, is a lengthy stretch of powder-soft white sand and exceptionally calm water, where you'll find small and large hotels, water sports, concessions, and beachfront restaurants. **Half Moon Bay**, a ¾-mi (1-km) crescent, is a prime snorkeling and windsurfing area. On the Atlantic side of the island the water can be quite rough (the eastern end is calmer). **Johnson's Point/Crab Hill** is a series of connected, deliciously deserted beaches of bleached white sand on the southwest coast overlooking Montserrat. You can explore a ruined fort at one end; notable beach bars are OJ's (try the snapper) and Turner's. **Pigeon Point**, near Falmouth Harbour, has two fine white-sand beaches; the leeward side is calmer, while the windward side is rockier, with sensational views and snorkeling around the point. Several restaurants and bars are nearby, though Billy's satisfies most on-site needs. **Runaway Beach**, a stretch of glittering sand, is still rebuilding after years of hurricane erosion. Both the water and the scene are relatively calm, and beach bars such as the raucous Bikini's offer cool shade and cold beer.

Where to Eat

In restaurants, a 10% service charge and 7% tax are usually added to the bill.

★ $$–$$$$ ✕ **Coconut Grove.** Coconut palms grow through the roof of this open-air thatched restaurant, waves lap the white sand, and the warm waitstaff provides just the right level of service. Jean-François Bellanger's superbly presented dishes fuse French culinary preparations with island ingredients. Top choices include pan-seared snapper medallions served with roasted sweet potato in a saffron white-wine curry; tuna tartare accented by tapenade with molasses drizzle and guacamole; and chicken stuffed with creole vegetables in mango-kiwi sauce. The kitchen can be uneven, and the wine list is merely serviceable. Nonetheless, Coconut Grove straddles the line between casual beachfront boîte and elegant eatery with aplomb. ⊠ *Siboney Beach Club, Dickenson Bay* ☎ *268/462–1538* ▭ *AE, D, MC, V.*

$$–$$$$ ✕ **george.** This downtown eatery is a loving evocation of the building owner's original Georgian family home. The contemporary colonial de-

sign is stunning: beamed ceilings, teal-and-aqua walls, high-back hard-wood chairs, and jalousie shutters that close off to form a second-floor gallery overlooking the busy street scene. The menu updates West Indian classics, from jerk burgers to slow-roasted spareribs with a caramelized passion fruit–pineapple glaze to pepper-seared tuna marinated in sesame-ginger oil. The congenial new British managers plan to add children's and vegetarian menus. Indulge in the bartenders' extensive "Naughty List" of cocktails. ⊠ *Market and Redcliffe Sts., St. John's* ☎ *268/562–4866* ▭ *AE, D, MC, V.*

ARUBA

Vernon O'Reilly Ramesar

Few islands can boast the overt dedication to tourism and the quality of service that Aruba offers. The arid lansdcsape is full of attractions to keep visitors occupied, and the island offers some of the most dazzling beaches in the Caribbean. Casinos and novelty nightclubs abound in Oranjestad, giving the capital an almost Las Vegas appeal. To keep tourists coming back year after year, the island boasts a tremendous variety of restaurants ranging from upscale French eateries to toes-in-the-sand casual dining. Aruba may not be an unexplored paradise, but hundreds of thousands of tourists make it a point to beat a path here every year. Because it's not a very large island, cruise-ship visitors can expect to see a large part of the island on their day ashore. Or they can simply see a lot of the beautiful beaches. Whether you're planning to be active or to simply relax, this is an ideal cruise port.

Essentials

CURRENCY The Aruban florin (AFl1.79 to US$1). Arubans accept U.S. dollars readily, so you need only acquire local currency for pocket change. Note that the Netherlands Antilles florin used on Bonaire and Curaçao is not accepted on Aruba.

HOURS Stores are open Monday through Saturday from 8:30 or 9 to 6. Some stores stay open through the lunch hour (noon to 2), and many open when cruise ships are in port on Sunday and holidays. Most of the larger supermarkets are open on Sunday from 8 to noon.

INTERNET **Café Internet** (⊠ *8 Royal Plaza Mall, Oranjestad* ☎ *297/582–4609*).

TELEPHONES When making calls to anywhere in Aruba, simply dial the seven-digit number. AT&T customers can dial 800–8000 from special phones at the cruise dock and in the airport's arrival and departure halls. Otherwise dial 121 to contact the international operator to place an international call.

Coming Ashore

The Port of Oranjestad is a busy place and is generally full of eager tourists looking for souvenirs or a bite to eat. The port can accommodate up to five ships at a time (and frequently does). The Renaissance Mall is located right on the port, as are a number of souvenir shops and some decent and inexpensive eating places. The main shopping areas of Oranjestad are all within 10 minutes' walk from the port.

Caribbean Sea

4 miles
6 km
0

KEY
Beaches
Dive Sites

Californian Wreck
California Pt.
Malmok Beach
Anilla Shipwreck
Debbie II
Tierra del Sol Golf Course
Fisherman's Hut
Pedernalis Wreck
Palm Beach
Eagle Beach
Manchebo Beach
Mt. Altovista
Noord
Tanki Leendert
Blv. 9
4 A/B
2 A/B
1 A/B
J.E. Irausquin Blvd.
L.G. Smith Blvd.
Druif Bay
Cruise Ship Terminal
Jane Sea Wreck
Bushiribona
Andicouri
Santa Cruz
Paradera
Reina Beatrix International Airport
7 A/B
Mt. Arikok
Miralamar
Mt. Yamanota
Savaneta
Ntunisa Laguua
Mangel Halto Reef (Pos Chiquito Reef)
1 A/B
Boca Prins (sand dunes)
Fontein Cave
Guadikin Cave
Baranca Sunu
Boca Grandi
Bachelor's Beach
Colorado Pt.
Captain Wreck
Seroe Colorado
Grapefield Beach
Coco's Beach
Baby Beach

Aruba

Alto Vista Chapel **6**
Aruba Ostrich Farm **4**
Butterfly Farm **5**
California Lighthouse . . . **7**
Hooiberg **2**
Oranjestad **1**
Rock Formations **3**

Taxis can be flagged down on the street that runs alongside the port (look for license plates with a "TX" tag). Rates are fixed (i.e., there are no meters; the rates are set by the government and displayed on a chart), though you and the driver should agree on the fare before your ride begins. Rides to Eagle Beach run about $5; to Palm Beach, about $8. If you want to rent a car, you can do that for a reasonable price; driving is on the left, just as in the U.S., and it's pretty easy to get around, though a 4-wheel-drive vehicle does help in reaching some of the more out-of-the-way places.

Shore Excursions

We consider these to be among the better shore excursions for Aruba. They may not be offered by all lines, and tour names may differ as well. Times and prices are approximate.

Aruba Sea and See Island Tour. Start by boarding the *Seaworld Explorer*, which lets you sit 5 feet under the water (though the vesssel never actually submerges) to see some spectacular views of marine life. Then it's back to the shore for an exploration of some of Aruba's best-loved attractions such as the California Lighthouse and the rock formations. ⏲ 4 *hrs* 💳 $60.

Cruise & Beach Tour. Board a catamaran at the dock for a music-filled, open-bar tour of the coast with a stop at Palm Beach for some relaxation in the sun. The return trip offers the chance to see the California Lighthouse. ⏲ 3 *hrs* 💳 $45.

De Palm Island Snorkeling Adventure. After an air-conditioned bus ride and a short ferry hop to De Palm Island, it's time to do some snorkeling. Snorkeling equipment is provided as are unlimited complimentary snacks and beverages while on De Palm Island ⏲ 3 ½ *hrs* ⏲ $55.

***Kukoo Kunuku* Bar Hop & Dinner Tour.** Board this Aruba institution, the psychedelically painted 1957 Chevy bus called the *Kukoo Kunuku,* for a champagne toast followed by dinner and an evening of bar-hopping. Included is a so-so dinner, your first drink at each bar stop, and transportation. The price is a $15 premium over what you'd pay otherwise. ⏲ 4–5 *hrs* 💳 $69.

Exploring Aruba

Numbers in the margin correspond to points of interest on the Aruba map.

❻ Alto Vista Chapel. Alone near the island's northwest corner sits the scenic little Alto Vista Chapel. The wind whistles through the simple mustard-colored walls, eerie boulders, and looming cacti. Along the side of the road back to civilization are miniature crosses with depictions of the stations of the cross and hand-lettered signs exhorting PRAY FOR US, SINNERS and the like—a simple yet powerful evocation of faith. To get here, follow the rough, winding dirt road that loops around the island's northern tip, or, from the hotel strip, take Palm Beach Road through three intersections and watch for the asphalt road to the left just past the Alto Vista Rum Shop.

★ ❹ **Aruba Ostrich Farm.** Everything you ever wanted to know about the world's largest living birds can be found at this farm. A large palapa houses a gift shop and restaurant (popular with large bus tours), and tours of the farm are available every half hour. This operation is virtually identical to the facility in Curaçao; it's owned by the same company. ⊠ *Makividiri Rd.* ☎ *297/585–9630* 🖃 *$10* ⊙ *Daily 9–5.*

5 **Butterfly Farm.** Hundreds of butterflies from around the world flutter about this spectacular garden. Guided 20- to 30-minute tours (included in the price of admission) provide an entertaining look into the life cycle of these insects, from egg to caterpillar to chrysalis to butterfly. ⊠ *J. E. Irausquin Blvd., Palm Beach* ☎ *297/586–3656* ⊕ *www. thebutterflyfarm.com* 🖃 *$12* ⊙ *Daily 9–4:30; last tour at 4.*

ARUBA BEST BETS

■ **Beaches.** With few interesting historical sights and not-so-great desert scenery, Aruba's real pleasures are on its dazzling west coast. Palm Beach is as beautiful a stretch of sand as you are likely to find anywhere. You might even learn to windsurf.

■ **Nightlife.** If your ship stays in port late (and in Aruba, many do), take advantage of the island's great bar scene and also its many casinos.

■ **Snorkeling.** Though you can't dive here, you can snorkel to get a glimpse of what's under the sea.

---

7 **California Lighthouse.** The lighthouse, built by a French architect in 1910, stands at the island's far northern end. Although you can't go inside, you can ascend the hill to the lighthouse base for some great views. In this stark landscape, you might feel as though you've just landed on the moon. The lighthouse is surrounded by huge boulders that look like extraterrestrial monsters and sand dunes embroidered with scrub that resemble undulating sea serpents.

2 **Hooiberg.** Named for its shape (*hooiberg* means "haystack" in Dutch), this 541-foot peak lies inland just past the airport. If you have the energy, climb the 562 steps to the top for an impressive view of Oranjestad.

1 **Oranjestad.** Aruba's charming capital is best explored on foot. The palm-lined thoroughfare in the center of town runs between pastel-painted buildings, old and new, of typical Dutch design. You'll find many malls with boutiques and shops here.

The **Archaeological Museum of Aruba** has two rooms chock-full of fascinating artifacts from the indigenous Arawak people, including farm and domestic utensils dating back hundreds of years. ⊠ *J. E. Irausquin Blvd. 2A, Oranjestad* ☎ *297/582–8979* 🖃 *Free* ⊙ *Weekdays 8–noon and 1–4.*

The **Experience Aruba Panorama** brings the island's history and culture to life in a 22-minute cinematic extravaganza that fills five massive screens measuring a total of 13 feet high and 66 feet wide. The breathtaking shows begin in the Crystal Theater at the Renaissance Aruba Beach Resort every hour from 11 to 5. ⊠ *L. G. Smith Blvd. 82, Oranjestad* ☎ *297/583–6000* 🖃 *$12* ⊙ *Mon.–Sat. 11–5.*

One of the island's oldest edifices, **Fort Zoutman** was built in 1796 and played an important role in skirmishes between British and Curaçao troops in 1803. The Willem III Tower, named for the Dutch monarch of that time, was added in 1868 to serve as a lighthouse. Over time, the fort has been a government office building, a police station, and a prison; now its historical museum displays Aruban artifacts in an 18th-century house. ⊠ *Zoutmanstraat* ☎ *297/582–6099* 🎫 *Free* ⊙ *Weekdays 8–noon and 1–4.*

★ The **Numismatic Museum** displays more than 40,000 historic coins and paper money from around the world. A few pieces were salvaged from shipwrecks in the region. Some of the coins circulated during the Roman Empire, the Byzantine Empire, and the ancient Chinese dynasties; the oldest dates to the 3rd century BC. The museum—which is next to the central bus station—had its start as the private collection of an Aruban who dug up some old coins in his garden. It's now run by his granddaughter. ⊠ *Westraat* ☎ *297/582–8831* 🎫 *$5* ⊙ *Mon.–Thurs. 9–4, Fri. 9–1, Sat. 9–noon.*

❸ **Rock Formations.** The massive boulders at Ayo and Casibari are a mystery, as they don't match the island's geological makeup. You can climb to the top for fine views of the arid countryside. On the way you'll doubtless pass Aruba whip-tail lizards—the males are cobalt blue, the females blue with dots. The main path to Casibari has steps and handrails (except on one side), and you must move through tunnels and along narrow steps and ledges to reach the top. At Ayo you can find ancient pictographs in a small cave (the entrance has iron bars to protect the drawings from vandalism). You may also encounter a boulder climber, one of many who are increasingly drawn to Ayo's smooth surfaces. Access to Casibari is via Tanki Highway 4A to Ayo via Route 6A; watch carefully for the turnoff signs near the center of the island on the way to the windward side.

Shopping

Caya G. F. Betico Croes in Oranjestad is Aruba's chief shopping street. Several malls—gabled, pastel-hued re-creations of traditional Dutch colonial architecture—house branches of such top names as Tommy Hilfiger, Little Switzerland, Nautica, and Benetton; the ritziest are the **Royal Plaza** and **Renaissance Mall,** both right near the cruise-ship pier. There are excellent deals to be found on jewelry, watches, liquor, and clothing.

★ If you're in the mood to splurge, **Agatha Boutique** (⊠ *Renaissance Mall, L. G. Smith Blvd. 82, Oranjestad* ☎ *297/583–7965*) has high-style clothing and accessories by Aruba-based New York fashion designer Agatha
★ Brown. **Art & Tradition Handicrafts** (⊠ *Caya G. F. Betico Croes 30, Oranjestad* ☎ *297/583–6534* ⊠ *Royal Plaza Mall, L. G. Smith Blvd. 94, Oranjestad* ☎ *297/582–7862*) sells intriguing souvenirs, most locally made. Filling 6,000 square feet of space, **Boolchand's** (⊠ *Renaissance Mall, L. G. Smith Blvd. 82, Oranjestad* ☎ *297/583–0147*) sells jewelry and watches. It also stocks leather goods, cameras, and electronics. **Confetti** (⊠ *Renaissance Mall, L. G. Smith Blvd. 82, Oranjestad* ☎ *297/583–8614*) has the hottest European and American swimsuits, coverups, and beach essentials. A venerated name in Aruba, **J. L. Penha & Sons** (⊠ *Caya G. F. Betico Croes 11/13, Oranjestad* ☎ *297/582–4160*

or 297/582–4161) sells high-end perfumes and cosmetics. It stocks such brands as Boucheron, Cartier, Dior, and Givenchy.

Activities

BIKING Pedal pushing is a great way to get around the island; the climate is perfect, and the trade winds help to keep you cool. **Melchor Cycle Rental**

> **CAUTION** ⚠
>
> Pack and wear a hat to protect your scalp, ears, and face from sun damage and premature aging. Excessive sun exposure contributes to wrinkles and dark spots.

(⊠ *Bubali 106B, Noord* ☏ *297/587–1787)* rents ATVs and bikes. **Rancho Notorious** (⊠ *Boroncana, Noord* ☏ *297/586–0508* ⊕ *www. ranchonotorious.com)* organizes mountain-biking tours.

DIVING & SNORKELING With visibility of up to 90 feet, the waters around Aruba are excellent for snorkeling and diving. Both advanced and novice divers will find plenty to occupy their time, as many of the most popular sites, including some interesting shipwrecks, are found in shallow waters ranging from 30 feet to 60 feet. **De Palm Watersports** (⊠ *L. G. Smith Blvd. 142, Oranjestad* ☏ *297/582–4400 or 800/766–6016* ⊕ *www.depalm.com)* is one of the best choices for your undersea experience, and the options go beyond basic diving. You can don a helmet and walk along the ocean floor near De Palm Island, home of huge blue parrot fish. You can even do Snuba—which is like scuba diving but without the heavy air tanks—from either a boat or from an island; it costs $56.

GOLF The **Links at Divi Aruba** (⊠ *J. E. Irausquin Blvd. 93, Oranjestad* ☏ *297/581–4653)* is a 9-hole course designed by Karl Litten and Lorie Viola. The par-36 paspalum grass course (best for seaside courses) takes you past beautiful lagoons. Amenities include a golf school with professional instruction, a swing analysis station, a driving range, and a two-story golf clubhouse with a pro shop. Two restaurants are available: Windows on Aruba for fine dining and Mulligan's for a casual and quick lunch. Greens fees are $75 for 9 holes, $110 for 18 (high season); guests of the Divi Village Golf & Beach Resort pay a reduced rate.

KAYAKING Kayaking is a popular sport on Aruba, especially along the south coast, where the waters are calm. It's a great way to explore the coastline. **Aruba Kayak Adventure** (⊠ *Ponton 90, Oranjestad* ☏ *297/587–7722* ⊕ *www. arubakayak.com)* has excellent half-day kayak trips, which start with a quick lesson before you paddle through caves and mangroves and along the scenic coast. The tour makes a lunch stop at De Palm Island, where snorkeling is included as part of the $77 package.

Beaches

Beaches in Aruba are beautiful and clean and easily reachable from the cruise-ship terminal in Oranjestad. On the north side of the island the water is too choppy for swimming, but the views are great. **Eagle Beach** (⊠ *J. E. Irausquin Blvd., north of Manchebo Beach),* on the southwestern coast, across the highway from what is quickly becoming known as Time-Share Lane, is one of the Caribbean's—if not the world's—best beaches. **Fisherman's Huts** (⊠ *1 A/B, at the Holiday Inn SunSpree Aruba)* is a windsurfer's haven with good swimming conditions. Take a picnic

Fodor'sChoice ★

lunch (tables are available) and watch the elegant purple, aqua, and orange sails struggle in the wind. **Manchebo Beach** (⊠ *J. E. Irausquin Blvd., at the Manchebo Beach Resort*) is impressively wide, and this is the spot where officials turn a blind eye to the occasional topless sunbather. This beach merges with Druif Beach, and most locals use the name Manchebo to refer to both. **Palm Beach** (⊠ *J. E. Irausquin Blvd., between the Westin Aruba Beach Resort and the Marriott Aruba Ocean Club*) is the center of Aruban tourism, offering good opportunities for swimming, sailing, and other water sports. In some spots you might find a variety of shells that are great to collect, but not as much fun to step on barefoot—bring sandals just in case.

Where to Eat

Restaurants usually add a 10% to 15% service charge.

$$–$$$ ✕ **Qué Pasa?** This funky eatery recently moved into new digs down the street from its former address; it now serves as something of an art gallery–restaurant. The colors of both the interior and exterior make quite an artistic statement themselves. Despite the name, there isn't a Mexican dish on the menu, which includes everything from sashimi to ribs, but everything is done with Aruban flair and is served by a helpful and friendly staff; the fish dishes are especially good. The bar area is lively and friendly. ⊠ *Wilheminastraat 18, Oranjestad* ☎ 297/583–4888 ▭ *MC, V.*

$–$$$ ✕ **Rumba Bar & Grill.** In the heart of Oranjestad, this lively bistro has an open kitchen where you can watch the chef prepare tasty international fare over a charcoal grill (mostly grilled seafood and beef). The presentations are fanciful, with entrées forming towering shapes over beds of colorful vegetables and sauces. You can dine on the terrace and soak up the local color, or inside amid wicker and warm pink hues; the crowd is always worth watching. It's an AGA Dine-Around member. ⊠ *Havenstraat 4, Oranjestad* ☎ 297/588–7900 ▭ *AE, D, MC, V.*

BARBADOS

Jane Zarem

Barbadians (Bajans) are a warm, friendly, and hospitable people, who are genuinely proud of their country and culture. Although tourism is the island's number one industry, the island has a sophisticated business community and stable government, so life here doesn't skip a beat after passengers return to the ship. Barbados is the most "British" island in the Caribbean. Afternoon tea is a ritual, and cricket is the national sport. The atmosphere, though, is hardly stuffy. This is still the Caribbean, after all. Beaches along the island's south and west coasts are picture-perfect, and all are available to cruise passengers. On the rugged east coast, the Atlantic Ocean attracts world-class surfers. The northeast is dominated by rolling hills and valleys; the interior of the island is covered by acres of sugarcane and dotted with small villages. Historic plantations, a stalactite-studded cave, a wildlife preserve, rum distilleries, and tropical gardens are among the island's attractions. Bridgetown, the capital, is a bustling city with more traffic than charm.

Essentials

CURRENCY Barbados dollar (BDS$), with BDS$1.99 to US$1 at this writing. U.S. dollars are generally accepted, but change is given in Barbados dollars.

HOURS Banks are open Monday through Thursday from 8 to 3, Friday from 8 to 5 (some branches in supermarkets are open Saturday morning from 9 to noon). The General Post Office in Cheapside, Bridgetown, is open weekdays from 7:30 to 5, and branches in each parish are open weekdays from 8 to 3:15. Most stores in Bridgetown are open weekdays from 8:30 or 9 to 4:30 or 5, Saturday from 8:30 to 1 or 2. Stores in shopping malls outside of Bridgetown may stay open later.

INTERNET You'll find Internet cafés in and around Bridgetown and at St. Lawrence Gap on the south coast. Rates range from $2 for 15 minutes to $8 or $9 per hour. **Bean-n-Bagel Internet Cafe** (✉ *St. Lawrence Gap, Dover*). **Connect Internet Cafe** (✉ *Shop #9, 27 Broad St., Bridgetown*).

TELEPHONES A multiband GSM phone will usually work in Barbados. You can purchase phone cards at the cruise-ship terminal. Direct-dialing to the United States, Canada, and other countries is efficient and reasonable. Some toll-free numbers cannot be accessed in Barbados. To charge your overseas call on a major credit card without incurring a surcharge, dial 800/744–2000 from any phone.

Coming Ashore

Up to eight ships at a time can dock at Bridgetown's Deep Water Harbour, on the northwest side of Carlisle Bay. The cruise-ship terminal has duty-free shops, handicraft vendors, a post office, a telephone station, a tourist information desk, and a taxi stand. To get downtown, follow the shoreline to the Careenage. It's a 15-minute walk or a $3 to $5 cab ride.

Taxis await ships at the pier. Drivers accept U.S. dollars and expect a 10% tip. Taxis are unmetered and operate at a fixed hourly rate of $25 per carload (up to three passengers). Most drivers will cheerfully narrate an island tour. You can rent a car with a valid driver's license, but rates are steep—during the high season, up to $85 per day.

Shore Excursions

We consider these to be among the better shore excursions for Barbados. They may not be offered by all lines, and tour names may differ as well. Times and prices are approximate.

Barbados Highlights Tour. This affordable tour takes in the historical highlights of the island, including Gun Hill Signal Station and Sunbury Plantation. ⊙ *4 hrs* ✇ *$38*.

Barbados Rainforest Hike & Cave Adventure. This excursion combines a trip to a small slice of remaining rain forest as well as the island's top attraction, Harrison's Cave. ⊙ *4 hrs* ✇ *$74*.

Kayak and Turtle Encounter. This trip involves 45 minutes of kayaking fol-

> **TIP**
>
> If you don't want to rely on shipboard wake-up calls, be sure to bring your own travel alarm clock; most staterooms do not have them.

Barbados

North Pt.

Crabhill

Cuckold Pt.

1B

ST. LUCY

Gay's Cove

Fairfield

Maycock's
Bay ◣

8 Cherry Tree Hill

Boscobelle

Shermans

Rose
Hill   1

■ Farley Hill

Six Men's Bay

Pamir ◣

St. James Rd.

ST.
PETER

Barclays Park
Beach ☂

Speightstown

Belleplaine   1

7

Barclays Park

Mullins Beach ☂

ST.
ANDREW

Mullins
Bay

Mt. Hillaby

ST.
JOSEPH

ST. JAMES

◆ Flower Forest

Holetown

Blackmans

Dottins Reef ◣

5

ST. THOMAS

Groves

Paynes
Bay ☂   1

Gun Hill

Stavronikita ◣

Warrens   3

ST.
GEORGE

Fresh Water Bay

ST. MICHAEL

4

Bell Buoy ◣   ☂ Brighton
Beach

4

Silver Bank ◣

Bridgetown
1 2
see inset

Deep Water Harbour ⚓

Carlisle Bay ◣   3

Carlisle Bay
Beach   Hastings   Worthing   St. Lawrence
Gap

Accra
Beach   Sandy
Beach   7   Oistins
Bay

Casuarina
Beach ☂

KEY

☂ Beaches

⚓ Cruise Ship Terminal

◣ Dive Sites

4

lowed by snorkeling in an area frequented by turtles; the guides feed the turtles while guests snorkel among them; snorkeling equipment is provided. You'll get drinks on the boat ride back. ☉ 3½ hrs ▣ $76.

Mount Gay Rum Distillery/Banks Beer Tour. Exactly what the title describes, a rum distillery and brewery tour. Beer and rum lovers will enjoy this tour best; samples are provided. ☉ 4 hrs ▣ $39.

Exploring Barbados

Numbers in the margin correspond to points of interest on the Barbados map.

BRIDGETOWN This bustling capital city is a major duty-free port with a compact shopping area. The principal thoroughfare is Broad Street, which leads west from National Heroes Square.

② **Jewish Synagogue.** Providing for the spiritual needs of one of the oldest Jewish congregations in the Western Hemisphere, this synagogue was formed by Jews who left Brazil in the 1620s and introduced sugarcane to Barbados. The adjoining cemetery has tombstones dating from the 1630s. The original house of worship, built in 1654, was destroyed in an 1831 hurricane, rebuilt in 1833, and restored by the Barbados National Trust in 1992. The building is open to the public year-round. ✉ Synagogue La., St. Michael ☎ 246/426–5792 ▣ Donation requested ☉ Weekdays 9–4.

① **Parliament Buildings.** Overlooking National Heroes Square in the center of town, these Victorian buildings were built around 1870 to house the British Commonwealth's third-oldest parliament. A series of stained-glass windows depicts British monarchs from James I to Victoria. ✉ Broad St., St. Michael ☎ 246/427–2019 ▣ Donations welcome ☉ Tours weekdays at 11 and 2, when parliament isn't in session.

CENTRAL & WEST **Gun Hill Signal Station.** The 360-degree view from Gun Hill, 700 feet above sea level, was what made this location of strategic importance to the 18th-century British army. Using lanterns and semaphore, soldiers based here could communicate with their counterparts at The Garrison, on the south coast, and at Grenade Hill in the north. Time moved slowly in 1868, and Captain Henry Wilkinson whiled away his off-duty hours by carving a huge lion from a single rock—which is on the hillside just below the tower. Come for a short history lesson but mainly for the view; it's so gorgeous, military invalids were once sent here to convalesce. ✉ Gun Hill, St. George ☎ 246/429–1358 ▣ $4.60 ☉ Weekdays 9–5.

⑤ **Harrison's Cave.** This limestone cavern, complete with stalactites, stalagmites, subterranean streams, and a 40-foot waterfall, is a rare find in the Caribbean—and one of Barbados's most popular attractions. The one-hour tours are conducted via electric trams, which fill up fast; reserve ahead of time. Hard hats are required and provided, but all that may fall on you is a little dripping water. ✉ Hwy. 2, Welchman Hall, St. Thomas ☎ 246/438–6640 ▣ $13 ☉ Daily 9–6; last tour at 4.

FodorsChoice ★

NORTH & EAST **Andromeda Gardens.** Beautiful and unusual plant specimens from around the world are cultivated in 6 acres of gardens that are nestled among streams, ponds, and rocky outcroppings overlooking the sea above the

Bathsheba coastline. The gardens were created in 1954 with flowering plants collected by the late horticulturist Iris Bannochie. They're now administered by the Barbados National Trust. The Hibiscus Café serves snacks and drinks. ✉ *Bathsheba, St. Joseph* ☎ *246/433–9261* 🎟 *$6* ⏱ *Daily 9–5.*

❽ St. Nicholas Abbey. There's no religious connection here at all. The island's oldest great house (circa 1650) was named after the British owner's hometown, St. Nicholas parish near Bristol, and Bath Abbey nearby. Its stone-and-wood architecture makes it one of only three original Jacobean-style houses still standing in the Western Hemisphere. It has Dutch gables, finials of coral stone, and beautiful grounds. The first floor, fully furnished with period furniture and portraits of family members, is open to the public. Fascinating home movies, shot by the last owner's father, record Bajan life in the 1930s. The Calabash Café, in the rear, serves snacks, lunch, and afternoon tea. ✉ *Cherry Tree Hill, St. Peter* ☎ *246/422–5357* 🎟 *$12.50* ⏱ *Weekdays 10–3:30.*

> ### BARBADOS BEST BETS
>
> ■ **The East Coast.** The island's windward coast, with its crashing surf, is one of the Caribbean's most beautiful sights. It may remind you of California's Big Sur.
>
> ■ **Harrison's Cave.** The island's most popular attraction is an extensive cave system in the limestone deep beneath Barbados.
>
> ■ **St. Nicholas Abbey.** Not an abbey at all, this is the island's oldest great house; it's one of the oldest Jacobean-era houses still standing in the Western Hemisphere.

SOUTH **Barbados Museum.** This intriguing museum, in the former British Military ❸ tary Prison (1815) in the historic Garrison area, has artifacts from Arawak days (around 400 BC) and galleries that depict 19th-century military history and everyday life. You can see cane-harvesting tools, wedding dresses, ancient (and frightening) dentistry instruments, and slave sale accounts kept in a spidery copperplate handwriting. The museum's Harewood Gallery showcases the island's flora and fauna; its Cunard Gallery has a permanent collection of 20th-century Barbadian and Caribbean paintings and engravings; and its Connell Gallery features European decorative arts. Additional galleries include one for children; the museum also has a gift shop and a café. ✉ *Hwy. 7, Garrison Savannah, St. Michael* ☎ *246/427–0201 or 246/436–1956* ⊕ *www.barbmuse.org.bb* 🎟 *$4* ⏱ *Mon.–Sat. 9–5, Sun. 2–6.*

❹ **Tyrol Cot Heritage Village.** This interesting coral-stone cottage just south of Bridgetown was constructed in 1854 and has been preserved as an example of period architecture. In 1929 it became the home of Sir Grantley Adams, the first premier of Barbados and the namesake of its international airport. Part of the Barbados National Trust, the cottage is now filled with antiques and memorabilia of the late Sir Grantley and Lady Adams. It's also the centerpiece of an outdoor "living museum," where artisans and craftsmen have their workshops in a cluster of traditional chattel houses. The crafts are for sale, and refreshments are available at the "rum shop." ✉ *Rte. 2, Codrington Hill, St. Michael* ☎ *246/424–2074 or 246/436–9033* 🎫 *$6* 🕙 *Weekdays 9–5.*

Shopping

Duty-free shopping is found in Bridgetown's Broad Street department stores and their branches in Holetown and at the cruise-ship terminal. (Note that to purchase items duty-free, you must show your passport and cabin key card). Stores are generally open weekdays 8:30–4:30 and Saturdays 8:30–1. **Best of Barbados** (✉ *Worthing, Christ Church* ☎ *246/421–6900*), which has a total of seven locations, offers high-quality artwork and crafts in both "native" style and modern designs; everything is made or designed on Barbados. **Earthworks Pottery** (✉ *No. 2, Edgehill Heights, St. Thomas* ☎ *246/425–0223*) is a family-owned and -operated pottery where you can purchase anything from a dish or knickknack to a complete dinner service or one-of-a-kind art piece. You can find the characteristically blue or green pottery for sale in gift shops throughout the island, but the biggest selection (including some "seconds") is at the pottery, where you also can watch the potters work. **Pelican Craft Centre** (✉ *Princess Alice Hwy., Bridgetown, St. Michael* ☎ *246/427–5350*) is a cluster of workshops halfway between the cruise-ship terminal and downtown Bridgetown, where craftspeople create and sell locally made leather goods, batik, basketry, carvings, jewelry, glass art, paintings, pottery, and other items. It's open weekdays 9 to 5 and Saturday 9 to 2, with extended hours during holidays or to accommodate cruise-ship arrivals.

Sports & Activities

FISHING   *Billfisher II* (☎ *246/431–0741*), a 40-foot Pacemaker, accommodates up to six passengers with three fishing chairs and five rods. Captain Winston ("The Colonel") White has been fishing these waters since 1975. His full-day charters include a full lunch and guaranteed fish (or a 25% refund); all trips include drinks and transportation to and from the boat. *Blue Jay* (☎ *246/429–2326* ⊕ *www.bluemarlinbarbados.com*) is a spacious, fully equipped, 45-foot Sport Fisherman with a crew that knows the denizens of blue marlin, sailfish, barracuda, and kingfish. Four to six people can be accommodated—it's the only charter boat on the island with four chairs. Most fishing is done by trolling. Drinks, snacks, bait, tackle, and transfers are provided.

GOLF   **Barbados Golf Club** (✉ *Hwy. 7, Durants, Christ Church* ☎ *246/428–8463* ⊕ *www.barbadosgolfclub.com*), the first public golf course on Barbados, is an 18-hole championship course (6,805 yards, par 72) redesigned in 2000 by golf course architect Ron Kirby. Greens fees are $119 for 18 holes, plus a $13 per person cart fee. Unlimited three-day and seven-day golf passes are available. Several hotels offer preferential tee-time reservations and reduced rates. Club and shoe rentals are available. At the prestigious **Country Club at Sandy Lane** (✉ *Hwy. 1, Paynes Bay, St. James* ☎ *246/432–2829* ⊕ *www.sandylane.com/golf*), golfers can play on the Old Nine or on either of two 18-hole championship courses: the Tom Fazio–designed Country Club Course or the spectacular Green Monkey Course, which opened in October 2004 and is reserved for hotel guests and club members only. Greens fees in high season are $85 for

9 holes or $200 for 18 holes. Golf carts are equipped with GPS, which alerts you to upcoming traps and hazards, provides tips on how to play the hole, and allows you to order refreshments!

Beaches

All beaches on Barbados are open to cruise-ship passengers. The west coast has the stunning coves and white-sand beaches dear to the hearts of postcard publishers, plus calm, clear water for snorkeling, scuba diving, and swimming. Waterskiing, snorkeling, and parasailing are available on most beaches along the west and south coasts. Windsurfing is best on the south coast. Popular **Accra Beach,** in Rockley, has gentle surf and a lifeguard. There are plenty of places to eat and drink and to rent water-sports equipment. Calm as a lake and just north of Bridgetown, **Brighton Beach** is also the home to the Malibu Beach Club. At **Carlisle Bay,** at Needham's Point, just south of Bridgetown, a broad half-circle of white sand is one of the island's best beaches. At the Boatyard, on Bay Street, you can rent umbrellas and beach chairs and buy refreshments. Picturesque **Mullins Beach,** just south of Speightstown, is a perfect place to spend the day. The water is safe for swimming and snorkeling and Suga Suga Restaurant serves snacks, meals, and drinks—and rents chairs and umbrellas. South of Holetown, **Paynes Bay** is lined with luxury hotels. It's a very pretty area, with plenty of beach to go around and good snorkeling. Public access is available opposite the Coach House. You can grab a bite to eat or a cold drink at Bomba's Beach Bar.

Where to Eat

A 15% V.A.T. (value-added tax) is in effect on Barbados. Most restaurant prices are V.A.T.-inclusive. A 10% service charge is added to most restaurant bills; if no service charge is added, tip waiters 10% to 15%.

$$–$$$ ✕ **Atlantis Hotel Restaurant.** People have been stopping by for lunch with a view here since 1945, when Mrs. Enid Maxwell bought this property, a quaint, 19th-century seaside hotel. New owners have kept up Mrs. Maxwell's tradition—all Bajan cuisine that complements the natural environment. Each Wednesday and Sunday the enormous buffet includes pumpkin fritters, rice and peas, breadfruit casserole, steamed fish creole, oven-barbecued chicken, pepper pot, macaroni pie, ratatouille, and more. Homemade coconut pie tops the dessert list. The Atlantis is a lunch stop for organized day tours, so it sometimes get crowded. ⊠ *Atlantis Hotel, Tent Bay, Bathsheba, St. Joseph* ☎ *246/ 433–9445* ☐ *AE, MC, V.*

$$ ✕ **Waterfront Cafe.** This friendly bistro alongside the Careenage is the perfect place to enjoy a drink, snack, or meal—and to people-watch. Locals and tourists alike gather for all-day alfresco dining on sandwiches, salads, fish, pasta, pepper pot stew, and tasty Bajan snacks such as buljol, fish cakes, or plantation pork (plantains stuffed with spicy minced pork). The panfried flying fish sandwich is especially popular. In the evening you can gaze through the arched windows while savoring nouvelle Caribbean cuisine, enjoying cool trade winds, and listening to live jazz. There's a special Caribbean buffet and steel-pan music on Tuesday night from 7 to 9. ⊠ *The Careenage, Bridgetown, St. Michael* ☎ *246/427–0093* ☐ *AE, DC, MC, V* ☯ *Closed Sun.*

BELIZE

Lan Sluder

Belize probably has the greatest variety of flora and fauna of any country of its size in the world. Here, you'll often find more iguanas or howler monkeys than humans. A few miles off the mainland is the Belize Barrier Reef, a great wall of coral stretching the entire 333 km (200 mi) length of the coast. Over 200 cayes (pronounced keys) dot the reef like punctuation marks, and three coral atolls lie farther out to sea. All are superb for diving and snorkeling. Many, like Ambergris Caye (pronounced Ambur-griss Key) and Caye Caulker, are jolly resort islands with ample supplies of bars and restaurants, easily reachable on day trips from Belize City. The main choice you'll have to make is whether to stay in Belize City for a little shopping, a little walking, and perhaps lunch or a dram at one of the Fort George hotels or restaurants, or alternatively to head out by boat, rental car, taxi, or tour on a more active adventure.

Essentials

CURRENCY The Belize dollar (BD$2 to US$1). Since the U.S. dollar is universally accepted, there's no need to acquire Belize currency.

FLIGHTS Especially if you are going to Ambergris Caye, you may prefer to fly, or you can water taxi over and fly back. There are hourly flights on two airlines. The flight to Caulker takes about 15 minutes and that to San Pedro about 25 minutes. The cost is BZ$115 round-trip to either island. Be sure you fly out of Belize City's Municipal, not out of the international airport north of the city. **Maya Island Airways** (☎ *501/223–1140, 800/225–6732 in the U.S.* ⊕ *www.mayaairways.com*) has hourly flights, and you can make a reservation on the company Web site. **Tropic Air** (☎ *501/226–2012 or 800/422–3435 in the U.S.* ⊕ *www.tropicair.com*) also has frequent flights.

HOURS Banks are open Monday through Thursday from 8 to 1, and Friday from 8 to 1 and 3 to 6. Shops are open from 8 to 12 and from 2 to 8 (although some shops in Belize City do not close for lunch). Few shops are open on Sunday. Most sights and museums close by 4 or 4:30 and have abbreviated hours on weekends.

INTERNET **Click & Sip Internet Café** (✉ *Fort St. in Tourist Village, Belize City* ☎ *223/1305*). **M-Business Solutions** (✉ *13 Cork St., in Great House, Belize City* ☎ *223/6766* ⊕ *www.officeservices.bz*).

TELEPHONES Calling locally or internationally is easy, but rates are high; around 75¢ a minute for calls to the U.S. To call the United States, dial 001 or 10–10–199 plus the area code and number. Pay phones, which are located in the Tourist Village where you are tendered, and elsewhere downtown, accept only pre-paid Belize Telecommunications Ltd. phone cards, available in shops in denominations from $2.50 to $25. Special "USA Connect" prepaid cards, for sale at some stores in Belize City, in denominations of $2.50 to $10, claim discounts of as much as 57% for calls to the U.S. only. Your U.S.-based GSM phone will probably work on Belize's GSM 1900 system. Foreign calling cards are blocked in Belize. Call 113 for local directory assistance, and 115 for an operator.

Coming Ashore

Because Belize City's harbor is shallow, passengers are tendered in. If you're going the independent route, try to get in line early for the tenders, as it sometimes takes 90 minutes or more for all the passengers to be brought ashore. You arrive at the Fort Pointe Tourist Village, which opened in 2002. It has an antiseptic collection of gift shops, restaurants, and tour operators nicely situated along the harbor. Bathrooms are spic-n-span, too. At this writing, Carnival Cruise Lines still plans to build a much-delayed $50-million cruise terminal in another part of the city, but it is unlikely to come online until at least 2008.

> ### BELIZE BEST BETS
>
> ■ **Belize Zoo.** Though small, this collection of native Belize wildlife is excellent.
>
> ■ **Cave Tubing.** If you are not claustrophic, this is an unforgettable excursion.
>
> ■ **Diving.** Belize is becoming known as one of the world's best dive destinations. For the certified, this is a must.
>
> ■ **Snorkeling in Hol Chan.** The water is teeming with fish, and you don't need to be certified to enjoy the underwater world here.

Taxis, tour guides, and car rental desks are readily available. Taxi trips—official taxis have green license plates—within Belize City's small downtown area are supposed to be set at $3.50 plus 50¢ for each additional passenger, although some drivers meeting the cruise ships try to charge whatever the traffic will bear. Taxis don't have meters, so settle on the fare in advance; you shouldn't have to pay more than $6 or $7 to go anywhere in the city. Hourly rates are negotiable, but expect to pay around $25 or $30, or $150 for the day. There's no need to tip cab drivers. Horse and buggy tours of Belize City are available at the Tourist Village. You'll pay around $20 per person for a one-hour city tour. You can also rent a car. Crystal, a local company, has a branch at the Tourist Village, and Hertz and Budget will also arrange cars for cruise passengers, but rates can be high (at least $75 per day), and gas is about $5 per gallon. Green directional signs point you to nearby destinations such as the Belize Zoo.

Shore Excursions

If you don't want to rent a car or arrange your own private tours, then do a ship-sponsored excursion. We consider these to be among the better shore excursions for Belize. They may not be offered by all lines, and tour names may differ as well. Times and prices are approximate.

Altun Ha. If you have never seen Mayan ruins before, then consider this tour. ⊘ *4 hrs* 🖃 *$59.*

Belize Zoo & Belize City. After a trip to the Belize Zoo, you get a short city tour. ⊘ *4 hrs* 🖃 *$49.*

Cave Tubing and Jungle Walk. This popular cave-tubing excursion requires a 45-minute walk through the jungle to the cave entrance after a one-hour ride. The tubing itself takes about an hour, then you have lunch and can either rest or explore further. ⊘ *7 hrs* 🖃 *$79.*

Shark Ray Alley & San Pedro. This excursion takes you to Hol Chan Marine Reserve, where you swim among stingrays and baby nurse sharks and then on to a good snorkeling spot at Horseshoe Reef. Then it's lunch in San Pedro. 🖀 *7 hrs* 🖃 *$79.*

Exploring Belize

Numbers in the margin correspond to points of interest on the Belize map.

Belize City. Many Belize hands will tell you the best way to see Belize City is through a rear view window. But, with an open mind to its peculiarities, and with a little caution (the city has a crime problem, but the tourist police keep a close watch on cruise-ship passengers), you may decide Belize City has a raffish, atmospheric charm rarely found in other Caribbean ports of call. You might even see the ghost of Graham Greene at a hotel bar. A 5- to 10-minute stroll from the perky Tourist Village brings you into the other worlds of Belize City. On the north side of Haulover Creek is the colonial-style world of the Fort George section, where large old homes, stately but sometimes down at the heels, take the breezes off the sea and share their space with hotels and restaurants. On the south side is the bustling world of Albert Street, the main commercial thoroughfare. But don't stroll too far. Parts of Belize City are unsafe by night or day. During the daylight hours, as long as you stay within the main commercial district and the Fort George area—and ignore the street hustlers—you should have no problem.

❷ Fort George Lighthouse towers over the entrance to Belize Harbor at the tip of Fort George Point. ✉ *Marine Parade.*

4 The city's finest colonial structure, the **House of Culture** is said to have been designed by the illustrious British architect Sir Christopher Wren. Built in 1814 it was once the residence of the governor general, the queen's representative in Belize. ⊠ *Regent St. at Southern Foreshore* ☎ *227/3050* 🖅 *BZ$10* ☼ *Weekdays 9–4.*

5 From the **Marine Terminal** you can catch a boat to Ambergris Caye, Caye Caulker, St. George's Caye, and Caye Chapel, from this white clapboard building, which was a firehouse in the 1920s. The **Coastal Zone Museum** is on the main floor and has information about the reef and the creatures that live there. On the second floor is the **Marine Museum,** where you can wander among models of boats that have sailed these waters and tools used by shipwrights. One ticket gets you into both museums. ⊠ *10 N. Front St., at Queen St.* ☎ *223/1969* 🖅 *BZ$8* ☼ *Mon.–Sat. 8–5:30.* Debuting in 2002, the **Museum of Belize,** located

3 in the Central Bank of Belize building complex, has displays on Belize history and culture ranging from ancient Maya artifacts to a cell from the old jail built in 1853. ⊠ *Gabourel La.* ☎ *223/4524* 🖅 *BZ$10* ☼ *Weekdays 9–5.*

1 **St. John's Cathedral,** at the south end of Albert Street, is the oldest Anglican church in Central America and the only one outside England where kings were crowned. From 1815 to 1845 four kings of the Mosquito Coast (a British protectorate along the coast of Honduras and Nicaragua) were crowned here. ⊠ *Albert St.* ☎ *227/2137.*

6 **Altun Ha.** If you've never visited an ancient Maya site, make a trip to Altun Ha, 45 km (28 mi) north of Belize City. ⊹ *From Belize City, take the Northern Hwy. north to Mile 18.9. Turn right (east) on the Old Northern Hwy., which is only partly paved, and go 10½ mi (17 km) to the signed entrance road to Altun Ha on the left. Follow this paved road 2 mi (3 km) to the visitor center* ☎ *609/3540* 🖅 *BZ$10* ☼ *Daily 9–5.*

8 **Belize Zoo.** One of the smallest, but arguably one of the best, zoos in the world, this park houses only animals native to Belize. Highlights include spotted and rare black jaguars, the puma, margay, ocelot, jaguarondi, and the Bairdís tapir, the national animal of Belize. ⊠ *Western Hwy., 30 mi (49 km) west of Belize City* ☎ *220/8004* ⊕ *www.belizezoo.org* 🖅 *BZ$15* ☼ *Daily 9–5.*

7 **Community Baboon Sanctuary.** This interesting wildlife conservation project is a haven for nearly 1,000 black howler monkeys and numerous other species of birds and mammals. ⊠ *Community Baboon Sanctuary, 31 mi (50 km) northwest of Belize City* ☎ *220/2181* 🖅 *BZ$10* ☼ *Daily 8–5.*

9 **Crooked Tree Wildlife Sanctuary.** This interesting wildlife conservation project is a haven for nearly 1,000 black howler monkeys and numerous other species of birds and mammals. ⊠ *Turn west off Northern Hwy. at Mile 30.8, then drive 2 mi (3 km)* ☎ *223/4987 for Belize Audubon Society* ⊕ *www.belizeaudubon.org/html/parks/ctws.htm* 🖅 *BZ$8.*

10 **Hummingbird Highway.** This 78-km (49-mi) paved two-lane, which turns south off the Western Highway, is the country's most scenic route. As you go south toward Dangriga Town, on your right rise the jungle-covered Maya Mountains. Less than half an hour south of Belmopan on the Hummingbird is the **St. Herman's Blue Hole Natural Park,** a natural turquoise pool surrounded by mosses and lush vegetation, excellent for a cool dip. ☉ *Daily 8–4:30* ⊠ *Mile 42.5, Hummingbird Hwy.* ⌨ *BZ$8.*

⑫ **Ambergris Caye.** Ambergris is the queen of the cayes. With a population around 5,000, the island's only town, San Pedro, remains a small, friendly, and prosperous village. It has one of the highest literacy rates in the country and an admirable level of awareness about the fragility of the reef. The large number of substantial private houses being built on the edges of town is proof of how much tourism has enriched San Pedro. A water taxi from the Marine Terminal takes about 75 minutes and costs $27.50 round-trip. You can also fly.

Hol Chan Marine Reserve (Maya for "little channel"), is 6 km (4 mi) from San Pedro at the southern tip of Ambergris. Because fishing is forbidden here, snorkelers and divers can see teeming marine life. You can also snorkel with nurse sharks and rays (which gather here to be fed) at Shark-Ray Alley, a sandbar that is part of the reserve. You need above-average swimming skills, as the current is often strong. ⊠ *Southern tip, Ambergris Caye* ⌨ *BZ$20 plus cost of snorkel tour.*

⑬ **Caye Caulker.** On Caye Caulker, where the one village is home to around 800 people, brightly painted houses on stilts line the coral sand streets. Although the island is being developed more each year, flowers still outnumber cars 10 to 1 (golf carts, bicycles, and bare feet are the preferred means of transportation). The living is easy, as you might guess from all the NO SHIRT, NO SHOES, NO PROBLEM signs at the bars. This is the kind of place where most of the listings in the telephone directory give addresses like "near football field." A water taxi from the Marine Terminal costs about $10 each way and takes about 45 minutes.

Shopping

Belize does not have the crafts tradition of its neighbors Guatemala and Mexico, and imported goods are expensive due to high duties, but hand-carved items of Zircote or other local woods make good souvenirs. Near the Swing Bridge at Market Square is the **Commercial Center,** which has some food and craft vendors on the first floor, and a restaurant and shops on the second. The **Fort Pointe Tourist Village,** where the ship tenders come in, is a collection of bright and clean gift shops selling T-shirts and Belizean and Guatemalan crafts. Beside the Tourist Village is an informal **Street Vendor Market,** with funkier goods and performances by a "Brukdown" band or a group of Garifuna drummers.

Opened in 2004, **Fine Arts Gallery** (⊠ *1 Fort St., next to the Tourist Village* ☎ *501/223–7773*) quickly became one of Belize's top spots to shop for art. It has original paintings by many of Belize's best-known artists, including Pen Cayetano, Walter Castillo, and Patrick Chevailler, along with prints by Carolyn Carr and other artists. The **Image Factory** (⊠ *91 N. Front St.* ☎ *501/223–4151*) is run by a nonprofit foundation. Its exhibitions change monthly and its store sells works by more than 20 Belizean artists. **National Handicraft Center** (⊠ *2 S. Park St.* ☎ *501/*

223–3636) has Belizean souvenir items, including hand-carved figurines, hand-made furniture, pottery, and woven baskets.

Activities

CANOPY TOURS You may feel a little like Tarzan as you dangle 80 feet above the jungle floor, suspended by a harness, moving from one suspended platform to another. **Jaguar Paw Lodge** (✉ *Off Mile 37 of the Western Hwy.* ☎ *501/820–2023*) opened the first zip-line aerial canopy tour in Belize in 2004. It has eight platforms set 100 to 250 feet apart. At the last platform you have to rappel to the ground. The cost is around $60 to $80. There is a 240-pound weight limit.

CAVE TUBING Very popular with cruise passengers are river-tubing trips that go through a cave, where you'll turn off your headlamp for a minute of absolute darkness, but these are not for the claustrophobic or those afraid of the dark. **Cave-Tubing in Belize** (☎ *605/1573* ⊕ *www.cave-tubing.com*) specializes in cave-tubing trips. Tour guide Reginald Tripp, of **Reggie's Tours** (✉ *29 Clinic Rd., Ladyville* ☎ *501/225–2195* ⊕ *www.regtour.com*), has carved out a profitable niche running independent cave-tubing trips for cruise passengers ($45), to Altun Ha ($45), and other tours.

DIVING & SNORKELING Most companies on Ambergris Caye offer morning and afternoon single-tank dives; snorkel trips begin mid-morning or early afternoon. Dive and snorkeling trips that originate in Caye Caulker are a bit cheaper. **Amigos del Mar** (✉ *Off Barrier Reef Dr., near Mayan Princess Hotel, Ambergris Caye* ☎ *501/226–2706* ⊕ *amigosdive.com*) is probably the most consistently recommended dive operation on the island. It offers a range of local dives and snorkel trips. For trips to the Blue Hole and local dives, **Paradise Down** (✉ *Front St. north of the public pier, Caye Caulker* ☎ *501/226–0437*) has three well-equipped dive boats.

GOLF **Caye Chapel Island Resort** (✉ *Caye Chapel, 16 mi (25 km) northeast of Belize City* ☎ *501/226–8250*) has a beautiful 18-hole seaside course occupying much of Caye Chapel. Water taxis to Caye Caulker will drop you here ($10), or you can fly the 12 minutes to the island's private airstrip, by prior arrangement with the resort, for $100 round-trip. Unlimited golf, with clubs and cart rental and a poolside lunch, costs $200. Reservations are required.

INDEPENDENT TOURS Several Belize City–based tour guides and operators offer custom trips for ship passengers; companies will usually meet you at the Tourist Village. Katie Valk of **Belize Trips** (☎ *223/0376* ⊕ *www.belize-trips.com*), a New Yorker with attitude (softened by some 15 years' residency in Belize), can organize a custom trip to just about anywhere in the country. **Coral Breeze Ltd.** (⊕ *www.coralbreezelimited.com*) has a variety of trips for cruise-ship passengers, including cave tubing ($59, with lunch), scuba diving ($139 for two-tank dive), Altun Ha and Belize City tour ($39), and a snorkel tour with lunch ($69).

Beaches

Although the barrier reef just offshore limits the wave action, which, over eons, builds classic wide sandy beaches, and there is a good deal of seagrass on the shore bottom, Ambergris Caye's beaches are among the best in Belize. All beaches in Belize are public. **Mar de Tumbo,** 1½ mi (3 km) south of town near Tropica Hotel, is the best beach on the south end of the island. **North Ambergris,** accessible by water taxi from San Pedro or by golf cart over the new bridge to the north, has miles of narrow beaches and fewer people. **Ramon's Village's beach,** right across from the airstrip, is the best in the town area. The beaches on Caulker are not as good as those on Ambergris. Along the front side of the island is a narrow strip of sand, but the water is shallow and swimming conditions are poor. **The Split,** on the north end of the village (turn to your right from the main public pier), is the best place on Caye Caulker for swimming.

Where to Eat

★ **$$$–$$$$** ✕ **Harbour View.** For the most romantic setting in the city, ask for a table on the wraparound balcony overlooking the harbor. The friendly staff and consistently excellent food also make the Harbour View a favorite of Belize's power brokers. The seafood is especially good; try the snapper with mango chutney, cooked in a banana leaf. Pork dishes, especially Pork Picasso with a hot pepper relish, also are delicious. ✉ *Fort St. near Tourist Village* ☎ *223/6420* ▤ *AE, D, MC, V.*

$–$$ ✕ **Wet Lizard.** Right next to the Tourist Village, overlooking cruise-ship terminals 3 and 4, there's no question of the target market of the Wet Lizard. Even so, it's become a popular bar and a place to grab a sandwich or hamburger, even for those not on a cruise ship. An expansion added a gift shop and upper deck with bright green roof trim. ✉ *1 Fort St.* ☎ *223/2664* ▤ *MC, V.*

BEQUIA, ST. VINCENT & THE GRENADINES

Jane Zarem　　Bequia (pronounced *beck*-way) is the Carib word for "island of the cloud." Part of St. Vincent and the Grenadines, hilly and green Bequia is 9 mi (14½ km) south of St. Vincent's southwestern shore and the largest and most populous of the 32 islands and cays that make up the Grenadines. The capital is Port Elizabeth, a tiny town with waterfront bars, restaurants, and shops where you can buy handmade souvenirs, including the exquisitely detailed model sailboats for which Bequia is famous. Although boatbuilding, whaling, and fishing have been the predominant industries here for generations, sailing and Bequia have now become almost synonymous. Bequia's picturesque Admiralty Bay is one of the prettiest anchorages in the Caribbean and a favored anchorage for private and chartered yachts. With superb views, snorkeling, hiking, and swimming at several gold-sand beaches, the island has much to offer the international mix of visitors who frequent its shores.

Essentials

CURRENCY　Eastern Caribbean (E.C.) dollar (EC$2.70 to US$1). U.S. dollars are generally accepted, but change is given in E.C. dollars.

HOURS　Shops are open weekdays from 8 to 5, Saturday 8 to noon. Most are closed Sunday. Banks on Bequia are open Monday through Thursday from 8 to 1 and Friday 8 to 5.

Hamilton
Battery **2**

Mount
Pleasant **3**

Oldhegg
Turtle
Sanctuary **4**

Port Elizabeth . . **1**

Bequia

TO
ST. VINCENT

KEY

Beaches

Dive Sites

Ferry

Caribbean
Sea

The
Bullet

Devil's
Table

Spring

Industry
Bay

Bequia

Admiralty
Bay

Lower
Bay

Moonhole

Airport

The Wall

Friendship
Bay

Petit
Nevis

ATLANTIC
OCEAN

Pigeon
Island

Isle a Quatre

INTERNET You'll find several Internet cafés in Port Elizabeth, including the following. **Lenroc Internet Cafe** (✉ *Back St., Port Elizabeth, Bequia*). **Sunset Internet Cafe** (✉ *Front St., Port Elizabeth, Bequia*). **Surf 'n' Send Internet Cafe** (✉ *Belmont Walkway, Port Elizabeth, Bequia*).

TELEPHONES Public telephones are located on the jetty and at the Bayshore Mall in Port Elizabeth. Prepaid phone cards, which can be used throughout St. Vincent and many other Caribbean islands, are sold at shops in Port Elizabeth. The phone cards can be used for local or international calls.

Coming Ashore

Cruise ships that call on Bequia anchor offshore in Admiralty Bay and tender passengers to the jetty in Port Elizabeth or to nearby beaches. Although it's the capital of Bequia, Port Elizabeth is a tiny waterfront town that is only a few blocks long and one block deep. A tourist information booth is located on the jetty, shops and restaurants face the bay, and taxis are always lined up under the almond trees to meet cruise-ship passengers and the St. Vincent-Bequia ferry, which docks alongside the jetty. Water taxis are available for transportation between the jetty and nearby beaches for a couple of dollars per person each way, but keep in mind that most of these operators are not insured: ride at your own risk.

To see the views, villages, beaches, and other places of interest in Bequia, the best bet is to hire a taxi. Most taxis are pickup trucks, with a covered bed that is fitted with seating for four or six people. The driver will show you the sights in a couple of hours, point out a place for lunch, and drop you (if you wish) at a beach for swimming and snorkeling and pick you up later on. Negotiate the fare in advance, but expect to pay about $17 per person per hour for the tour. A rental car will cost about $55 per day and, unless you already have an international driver's license, requires a temporary local permit—available for EC$50 (US$20) at the Revenue Office in Port Elizabeth.

> ## BEQUIA BEST BETS
>
> ■ Island Tour. Taxi drivers are always available at the jetty in Port Elizabeth (2 hours, about $40). If you wish, the driver will stop for lunch or for a swim at the beach and pick you up after.
>
> ■ Ferry to St. Vincent. Ferries (EC$25 round-trip) make the 60-minute trip to St. Vincent several times each day. Once in St. Vincent, you can easily explore Kingstown and visit Fort Charlotte and the Botanical Garden before heading back to Bequia. Ferries dock at the jetty in Port Elizabeth.

Shore Excursions

We consider these to be among the better shore excursions for Bequia. They may not be offered by all lines, and tour names may differ as well. Times and prices are approximate.

Island Tour. Island tours by safari van will show you most of the highlights, including some of the beautiful views; almost all tours include a stop at the Oldhegg Turtle Sanctuary. ⊘ *2½ hrs* 🖼 *$28–$35.*

Mustique. You sail to Mustique and have a short island tour, then there is time to relax on the beautiful beaches or go to Basil's Bar. Tours by speedboat tend to be cheaper (almost half as much) but also less relaxing. ⊘ *6–7 hrs* 🖼 *$85–$170.*

Snorkeling Trip. You can get a glimpse of the sea life in the Grenadines on a snorkeling excursion. ⊘ *2½ hrs* 🖼 *$40.*

Exploring Bequia

Numbers in the margin correspond to points of interest on the Bequia map.

② **Hamilton Battery.** Just north of Port Elizabeth, high above Admiralty Bay, the 18th-century battery was built to protect the harbor from marauders. Today it's a place to enjoy a magnificent view.

❸ **Mt. Pleasant.** Bequia's highest point (an elevation of 881 feet) is a reasonable goal for a hiking trek. Alternatively, it's a pleasant drive. The reward is a stunning view of the island and surrounding Grenadines.

★ ⓒ **❹** **Oldhegg Turtle Sanctuary.** In the far northeast of the island, Orton "Brother" King, a retired skin-diving fisherman, tends to endangered hawksbill turtles. He'll be glad to show you around and tell you how his project is increasing the turtle population in Bequia. ⊠ *Park Beach, Industry* ☎ *784/458-3245* 🖼 *$5 donation requested* ⊘ *By appointment only.*

★ ❶ **Port Elizabeth.** Bequia's capital is on the northeast side of Admiralty Bay. The ferry from St. Vincent docks at the jetty, in the center of the tiny town, which is only a few blocks long and a couple of blocks deep. Walk north along Front Street, which faces the water, to the open-air market, where you can buy local fruits and vegetables and some handicrafts; farther along, you can find the model-boat builders' workshops for which Bequia is renowned. Walk south along Belmont Walkway, which meanders along the bay front past shops, cafés, restaurants, bars, and hotels.

Shopping

Long renowned for their boatbuilding skills, Bequians have translated that craftsmanship to model-boat building. In their workshops in Port Elizabeth you can watch as hair-thin lines are attached to delicate sails or individual strips of wood are glued together for decking. Other Bequian artisans create scrimshaw, carve wood, crochet, or work with fabric—designing or hand-painting it first, then creating clothing and gift items for sale.

Most of Bequia's shops are located just steps from the jetty in Port Elizabeth, along Front Street and Belmont Walkway. North of the jetty there's an open-air market, and farther along the road are the model-boat builders' shops. Opposite the jetty, at Bayshore Mall, shops sell ice cream, baked goods, stationery, gifts, and clothing; there's also a grocery, liquor store, pharmacy, travel agent, and bank. On Belmont Walkway, south of the jetty, shops and studios showcase gifts and handmade articles.

Bequia Bookshop (✉ *Belmont Walkway, Port Elizabeth* ☎ *784/458–3905*) has Caribbean literature, plus cruising guides and charts, Caribbean flags, beach novels, souvenir maps, and exquisite scrimshaw and whalebone penknives hand-carved by Bequian scrimshander Sam McDowell.

Local Color (✉ *Belmont Walkway, Port Elizabeth* ☎ *784/458–3202*), above the Porthole restaurant—near the jetty—has an excellent and unusual selection of handmade jewelry, wood carvings, scrimshaw, and resort clothing.

★ **Mauvin's Model Boat Shop** (✉ Front St., Port Elizabeth ☎ *784/458–3344*) is where you can purchase the handmade model boats for which Bequia is known. You can even special-order a replica of your own yacht. They're incredibly detailed and quite expensive—from a few hundred to several thousand dollars. The simplest models take about a week to make.

★ **Sargeant Brothers Model Boat Shop** (✉ *Front St., Port Elizabeth* ☎ *758/ 458–3344*) sells handmade model boats and will build special requests on commission.

Housed in the ruins of an old sugar mill, **Spring Pottery & Studios** (✉ *Spring* ☎ *784/457–3757*) is the working pottery of Mike Goddard and Maggie Overal, with gallery exhibits of ceramics, paintings, and crafts—their own and those of other local artists. All works are for sale.

Activities

BOATING &
SAILING
★
With regular trade winds, visibility for 30 mi (48 km), and generally calm seas, Bequia is a center for some of the best blue-water sailing you can find anywhere in the world, with all kinds of options: day sails or weekly charters, bareboat or fully crewed, monohulls or catamarans—whatever your pleasure. Prices for day trips run $50 to $75 per person, depending on the destination.

Friendship Rose (✉ *Port Elizabeth* ☎☎ *784/458–3373*), an 80-foot schooner that spent its first 25 years as a mail boat, was subsequently refitted to take passengers on day trips from Bequia to Mustique and the Tobago Cays. The 65-foot catamaran **Passion** (✉ *Belmont* ☎ *784/458–3884*), custom-built for day sailing, offers all-inclusive daylong snorkeling and/or sportfishing trips from Bequia to Mustique, the Tobago Cays, and St. Vincent's Falls of Baleine. It's also available for private charter. The Frangipani Hotel owns the **S. Y. Pelangi** (✉ *Port Elizabeth* ☎ *784/458–3255* ⊕ *www.frangipanibequia.com*), a 44-foot CSY cutter, for day sails or longer charters; four people can be accommodated comfortably, and the cost is $200 per day.

DIVING &
SNORKELING
About 35 dive sites around Bequia and nearby islands are accessible within 15 minutes by boat. The leeward side of the 7-mi (11-km) reef that fringes Bequia has been designated a marine park. The **Bullet,** off Bequia's northeast point, has limited access because of rough seas but is a good spot for spotting rays, barracuda, and the occasional nurse shark. **Devil's Table** is a shallow dive at the northern end of Admiralty Bay that's rich in fish and coral and has a sailboat wreck nearby at 90 feet. **Moonhole** is shallow enough in places for snorkelers to enjoy. The **Wall** is a 90-foot drop, off West Cay. Expect to pay dive operators $50 for a one-tank and $85 for a two-tank dive, including equipment. Dive boats welcome snorkelers for about $10 per person, but for the best snorkeling in Bequia, take a water taxi to the bay at Moonhole and arrange a pickup time.

Bequia Dive Adventures (✉ *Belmont Walkway, Admiralty Bay, Port Elizabeth* ☎ *784/458–3826* ⊕ *www.bequiadiveadventures.com*) offers PADI instruction courses and takes small groups on three dives daily; harbor pickup and return is included for customers staying on yachts. **Dive Bequia** (✉ *Belmont Walkway, Admiralty Bay, Port Elizabeth* ☎ *784/458–3504* ⊕ *www.dive-bequia.com*), at the Gingerbread Hotel, offers dive and snorkel tours, night dives, and full equipment rental. Resort and certification courses are available.

Beaches

Bequia has clean, uncrowded white-sand beaches. Some are a healthy trek or water taxi ride from the jetty at Port Elizabeth; others require land transportation.

Friendship Bay. This horseshoe-shape, protected beach on Bequia's mid-south coast can be reached by land taxi. It's a great beach for swimming, snorkeling, and windsurfing; you can rent any equipment you need at Friendship Bay Resort and also grab a bite to eat or a cool drink at the hotel's Moskito Bar & Restaurant.

Hope Bay. Getting to this beach facing Bequia's Atlantic side involves a long taxi ride (about $7.50) and a mile-long (1½-km-long) walk downhill on a semi-paved path. Your reward is a magnificent crescent of white sand, total seclusion, and—if you prefer—nude bathing. Be sure to ask your taxi driver to return at a prearranged time. Bring your own lunch and drinks; there are no facilities. Even though the surf is fairly shallow, swimming may be dangerous because of the undertow.

Industry Bay. This nearly secluded beach is fringed with towering palms on the northeast (windward) side of the island; getting here requires transportation from Port Elizabeth. This is a good beach for snorkelers, but there could be a strong undertow. Bring a picnic; the nearest facilities are at Spring on Bequia resort, a 10- to 15-minute walk from the beach.

★ **Lower Bay.** This broad, palm-fringed beach south of Port Elizabeth and Princess Margaret Beach is reachable by land or water taxi or a healthy hike. It's an excellent beach for swimming and snorkeling. There are restaurants here, as well as facilities to rent water-sports equipment.

Princess Margaret Beach. Quiet and wide, with a natural stone arch at one end, the beach is a half-hour hike over rocky bluffs from Port Elizabeth's Belmont Walkway—or you can take a water or land taxi. Though it has no facilities, it's a popular spot for swimming, snorkeling, or snoozing under the palm and sea grape trees.

Where to Eat

☼ $$–$$$ ✕ **Gingerbread.** The airy dining-room veranda at the Gingerbread Hotel offers a panoramic view of Admiralty Bay and the waterfront activity. The lunch crowd can enjoy barbecued beef kebabs or chicken with fried potatoes or onions, grilled fish, homemade soups, salads, and sandwiches. In the evening, steaks, seafood, and curries are specialties of the house. Save room for warm, fresh gingerbread—served here with lemon sauce. In season, dinner is often accompanied by live music. ⊠ *Gingerbread Hotel, Belmont Walkway, Admiralty Bay, Port Elizabeth* ☎ *784/458–3800* ⌕ *Reservations essential* ▭ *AE, D, MC, V.*

☼ $–$$ ✕ **Mac's Pizzeria.** Overheard at the dock in Mustique: "We're sailing over to Bequia for pizza." The two-hour sunset sail to Admiralty Bay is worth the trip to Mac's, which has been serving pizza in Bequia since 1980. Choose from 17 mouthwatering toppings (including lobster), or select homemade quiche, conch fritters, pita sandwiches, lasagna, or soups and salads. Mac's home-baked cookies, muffins, and banana bread (by the slice or the loaf) are great for dessert or a snack. Or top off your meal with a scoop or two of Maranne's homemade ice cream in tropical flavors. The outdoor terrace offers fuchsia bougainvillea and water views. ⊠ *Belmont Walkway, Admiralty Bay, Port Elizabeth* ☎ *784/458–3474* ⌕ *Reservations essential* ▭ *AE, D, MC, V.*

BERMUDA

Basking in the Atlantic, 508 mi (817 km) due east of Cape Hatteras, North Carolina, restrained, polite Bermuda is a departure from other sunny, beach-strewn isles. You won't find laid-back locals wandering around barefoot proffering piña coladas. Bermuda is somewhat formal, and despite the gorgeous weather, residents wearing stockings and heels or jackets, ties, Bermuda shorts, and knee socks are a common sight, whether on the street by day or restaurants at night. On Bermuda's 22 square miles (57 square km) you will discover that pastel cottages, quaint shops, and manicured gardens betray a more staid, suburban way of life. A self-governing British colony since 1968, Bermuda has maintained some of its English character even as it is increasingly influenced by American culture. Most cruise ships make seven-night loops from U.S. embarkation ports, with four nights at sea and three tied up in port. Increasingly popular are round-trip itineraries originating in northeastern embarkation ports that include a single day or overnight port call in Bermuda before continuing south to the Bahamas or Caribbean.

> **BERMUDA BEST BETS**
>
> ■ **Gibb's Lighthouse.** Make the climb to the top, where the reward is an expansive view of the inlets and harbors.
>
> ■ **Bermuda Maritime Museum.** Absorb Bermuda's nautical and military history in this Royal Navy Dockyard museum.
>
> ■ **St. George's.** Attend the pierside show hosted by the town crier, where gossips and nagging wives are drenched in a dunking stool.

Essentials

CURRENCY The Bermuda dollar (B$) is on par with the U.S. dollar. You can use American money anywhere, but change is often given in Bermudian currency. ATMs are common.

HOURS Banks are usually open on weekdays from 9 or 9:30 to 3:30 or 4:30. Shops are generally open Monday through Saturday from 9 to 5 and closed on Sunday. Some sights close on Sunday.

INTERNET Expect to pay as much as $12 per hour to check the Internet on Bermuda. **Internet Lane** (⊠ *The Walkway, 22 Reid St., Hamilton* ☎ 441/296–9972).

TELEPHONES To make a local call, simply dial the seven-digit number. You'll find specially marked AT&T USADirect phones at the airport, the cruise-ship dock in Hamilton, and King's Square and Ordnance Island in St. George's. You can also make international calls with a calling card from the main post office. You can make prepaid international calls from the Cable & Wireless Office, which also has international telex, cable, and fax services Monday through Saturday from 9 to 5.

Coming Ashore

Three Bermuda harbors serve cruise ships: Hamilton (the capital), St. George's, and King's Wharf at the Royal Naval Dockyard.

In Hamilton, cruise ships tie up right on the city's main street, Front Street. A Visitors Service Bureau is next to the ferry terminal, also on Front Street and nearby; maps and brochures are displayed in the cruise terminal itself.

St. George's actually has two piers that accommodate cruise ships. One is on Ordnance Island, which is in the heart of the city; another pier is nearby. Visitors Service Bureau offices are at each pier.

King's Wharf, in the Royal Naval Dockyard at the westernmost end of the island, is the most isolated of the three cruise-ship berthing areas, and it is where the largest vessels dock. But it is well-connected to the rest of the island by taxi, bus, and ferry. The nearby Cooperage has a Visitors Service Bureau office, and bus stops and the ferry pier are clearly marked.

Taxis are the fastest and easiest way to get around the island, but they are also quite expensive. Four-seaters charge $5.35 for the first mile and $2 for each subsequent mile. You can hire taxis for around $30 per hour (3-hour minimum) if you want to do some exploring, and if you can round up a group of people, this is often cheaper than an island tour offered by your ship. Tip drivers 15%. Rental cars are prohibited, but the island has a good bus and ferry system. You can also rent scooters, but this can be dangerous and is not recommended.

Shore Excursions

We consider these to be among the better shore excursions for Bermuda. They may not be offered by all lines, and tour names may differ as well. Times and prices are approximate.

Dockyard Segway Tour. See the Royal Naval Dockyard by Segway. It's an expensive but unique experience. ⊙ *2 hrs* ⊠ *$78.*

Horseback Riding. Between South Road and the Warwick beaches, sandy trails, most of which are open only to walkers or horseback riders, wind through strands of dune grass and oleander, and over coral bluffs to the beach. ⊙ *1½ hrs* ⊠ *$65–$130.*

Kayaking. Paddle in protected coves or the open ocean, depending on your skill level, accompanied by a skilled guide and trainer. ⊙ *3 hrs* ⊠ *$68.*

Railway Trail Tour. Tour the Bermuda Railway Trail by 21-speed bike with time for a swim. ⊙ *3½ hrs* ⊠ *$72.*

Exploring Bermuda

Numbers in the margin correspond to points of interest on the Bermuda map.

Hamilton. Bermuda's capital since 1815, the City of Hamilton is a small, bustling harbor town. It's the economic and social center of Bermuda, with busy streets lined with shops and offices. International influences, from both business and tourism, have brought a degree of sophistication unusual in so small a city. There are several museums and galleries to explore, but the favorite pastimes are shopping in Hamilton's numerous boutiques and dining in its many upscale restaurants.

★ ❶ The **Museum of the Bermuda Historical Society/Bermuda Public Library** was once the home of Hamilton's first postmaster, William Bennet Perot, and his family. Mark Twain once lamented that the rubber tree in the front yard didn't bear fruit in the form of hot-water bottles and rubber overshoes. The library was founded in 1839, and its reference

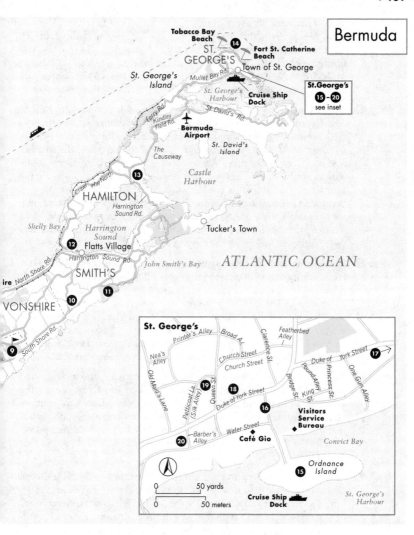

Bermuda

Tobacco Bay Beach
ST. GEORGE'S 14 Fort St. Catherine Beach
Town of St. George
St. George's Island
Mullet Bay Rd.
St. George's Harbour
Cruise Ship Dock
St.George's 15 – 20 see inset
Ferry Rd.
Kindley Field Rd.
St. David's Rd.
Bermuda Airport
The Causeway
St. David's Island
Crow Hill North
13
HAMILTON
Harrington Sound Rd.
Castle Harbour
Shelly Bay
Harrington Sound
12 Flatts Village
Tucker's Town
Harrington Sound Rd.
John Smith's Bay
SMITH'S
ATLANTIC OCEAN
ire North Shore Rd.
10
11
VONSHIRE
9
South Shore Rd.

St. George's

Printer's Alley
Broad A
Clarence St.
Featherbed Alley
Nea's Alley
Church Street
Church Street
Duke of York Street
17
Old Maid's Lane
Pound Alley
Princess St.
One Gun Alley
Petticoat La. (Silk Alley)
Queen St.
19
18
Duke of York Street
Bridge St.
King St.
16
Visitors Service Bureau
Barber's Alley
20
Water Street
Café Gio
Convict Bay
Ordnance Island
15
0 50 yards
0 50 meters
Cruise Ship Dock
St. George's Harbour

section has virtually every book ever written about Bermuda. The museum depicts Bermuda history with household goods and other artifacts, including an 18th-century sedan chair. ⊠ *13 Queen St.* ☏ *441/295–2905 library, 441/295–2487 museum* ⊠ *Donations accepted* ☉ *Library Mon.–Thurs. 8:30–7, Fri. 10–5, Sat. 9–5, Sun. 1–5; closed Sun. in July and Aug.; museum Mon.–Sat. 9:30–3:30* ☞ *Tours by appointment.*

★ ☾ ❷ Set back from the street behind a fountain and lily pond, **City Hall & Arts Centre,** built in 1960, houses Hamilton's administrative offices as well as two art galleries and a performance hall. Rather than a clock, its tower has a wind vane—not surprising in a land where the weather is as important as the time. Massive cedar doors open into a large lobby with beautiful chandeliers and high ceilings. On the first landing, in the East Exhibition Room, is the Bermuda National Gallery, the home of Bermuda's national art collection. Farther up the stairs, in the West Wing, the Bermuda Society of Arts Gallery displays work by its members. ⊠ *17 Church St.* ☏ *441/292–1234* ⊠ *Galleries free* ☉ *City Hall weekdays 9–5; National Gallery and Society of the Arts Mon.–Sat. 10–4.*

★ ❸ Designed in early Greek-revival flourishes, the **Cathedral of the Most Holy Trinity** was constructed out of Bermuda limestone and materials imported from France, Nova Scotia, and Scotland. The cathedral was completed in 1911. It has a copper roof, unusual in Bermuda's sea of whitetopped buildings. After exploring the interior, you can purchase tickets to climb the 150-odd steps (143 feet) of the tower. ⊠ *Church St.* ☏ *441/292–4033* ⊕ *www.anglican.bm* ⊠ *Cathedral free; Tower $3* ☉ *Church daily 7:30–5 and for Sun. services, tower weekdays 10–4.*

★ ☾ ❹ The imposing **Fort Hamilton** has a moat, 18-ton guns, and underground passageways that were cut through solid rock by Royal Engineers in the 1860s. Built to defend the West End's Royal Naval Dockyard from an attack by land, it was outdated even before its completion, though it remains one of the finest surviving examples of a mid-Victorian polygonal fort in Bermuda. ⊠ *Happy Valley Rd.* ☏ *441/292–1234* ⊠ *Free* ☉ *Daily 9:30–5.*

★ ☾ ❺ The Bermuda Underwater Exploration Institute's harborside **Ocean Discovery Centre** has numerous multimedia and interactive displays designed to acquaint you with the deep sea and its inhabitants. Never heard of a bathysphere? See a replica of this deep-sea diving vehicle, which allowed oceanographers William Beebe and Otis Barton to venture 1/2 mi down into the deep in 1934. ⊠ *40 Crow La., off E. Broadway* ☏ *441/292–7219* ⊕ *www.buei.org* ⊠ *$12.50* ☉ *Weekdays 9–5, weekends 10–5, last admission at 4.*

❻ **Paget Marsh.** This small, easily walkable slice of unspoiled native Bermuda
Fodor's Choice is just minutes from bustling Hamilton. Listen for the cries of the na-
★ tive and migratory birds who visit this natural wetland, jointly owned and preserved by the Bermuda National Trust and the Bermuda Audubon Society. ⊠ *Lover's La., Paget Parish* ☏ *441/236–6483* ⊕ *www.bnt.bm* ⊠ *Free* ☉ *Daily dawn–dusk.*

★ ☾ ❼ **Gibb's Hill Lighthouse.** The second cast-iron lighthouse ever built soars above Southampton Parish. Designed in London and opened in 1846, the tower stands 117 feet high and 362 feet above the sea. It's a long haul up the 185 spiral stairs, but you can stop to catch your breath at platforms along the way, where photographs and drawings of the lighthouse divert your attention. ⊠ *68 St. Anne's Rd., Southampton Parish* ☎ *441/238–8069* ⊕ *www.bermudalighthouse.com* ⊠ *$2.50* ⊙ *Daily 9–5; Closed Jan.*

⑥ Bermuda Maritime Museum and Dolphin Quest. Inside Bermuda's largest fort, built between 1837 and 1852, the Maritime Museum exhibits its collections in six old stone munitions warehouses, which surround the parade grounds and the Keep Pond. On top of the hill is the Commissioner's House, an unusual cast-iron building constructed from 1823 to 1828 in England and shipped to Bermuda for the chief administrator of the Dockyard. The Maritime Museum's most popular attraction is **Dolphin Quest**, within the fortress's historic Keep. ⊠ *Maritime Museum, Dockyard* ☎ *441/234–1418 for Museum, 441/234–4464 for Dolphin Quest* ⊕ *www.bmm.bm* ⊠ *$10; Dolphin Quest programs $125–$275* ⊙ *Daily 9:30–5, last admission 4.*

⑨ Botanical Gardens. A fragrant haven for the island's exotic subtropical plants, flowers, and trees, the 36-acre Botanical Gardens encompass a miniature forest, an aviary, a hibiscus garden with more than 150 species, and other plant collections, such as orchids and cacti. The pretty white house within the Gardens is **Camden,** the official residence of Bermuda's premier. Camden is open for tours Monday through Saturday noon to 2, except when official functions are scheduled. Behind Camden is the old Arrowroot Factory, home to the Masterworks Arts Centre. ⊠ *169 South Rd., Paget Parish* ☎ *441/236–5902 for Gardens, 441/236–5732 for Camden* ⊠ *Free* ⊙ *Daily dawn–dusk; Camden tours Tues. & Fri. noon–2.*

★ ⑩ Verdmont. Though it was used as a home until the mid-20th century, the house has had virtually no structural changes since it was built in about 1710. Verdmont holds a notable collection of historic furnishings. Some are imported from England—such as the early-19th-century piano—but most of the furniture is 18th-century cedar, crafted by Bermudian cabinetmakers. ⊠ *6 Verdmont La., off Collector's Hill, Smith's Parish* ☎ *441/236–7369* ⊕ *www.bnt.bm* ⊠ *$5; $10 combination ticket with Bermuda National Trust Museum in the Globe Hotel and Tucker House* ⊙ *Tues.–Sat. 10–4.*

★ ⑪ Spittal Pond Nature Reserve. A showpiece of the Bermuda National Trust, this nature park has 60 acres for carefree roaming, although you're asked to keep to the walkways. On a high bluff overlooking the ocean, Spanish Rock stands out as an oddity. It's now believed that a Portuguese ship was wrecked on the island in 1543 and that her sailors built a new ship on which they departed. The carvings on Spanish Rock are thought to be carved by the sailors, though the original has been removed. ⊠ *South Shore Rd., Smith's Parish* ☎ *441/236–6483* ⊕ *www.bnt.bm* ⊠ *Free* ⊙ *Daily dawn–dusk.*

⑫ Bermuda Aquarium, Museum & Zoo. The aquarium has always been a pleasant diversion, but thanks to an ambitious expansion project it has become truly great. The 145,000-gallon tank holding the North Rock

Exhibit, in the main gallery, gives you a diver's view of Bermuda's famed living coral reefs and colorful marine life. ⊠ *40 North Shore Rd., Flatts Village, Hamilton Parish* ☎ *441/293–2727* ⊕ *www.bamz.org* ⊠ *$10* ☉ *Daily 9–5, last admission at 4; free interpretive tours 1:10 daily Apr.–Dec. (call for winter tour schedule).*

Crystal Caves. This fantastic cavern 120 feet underground, which was discovered in 1907, has spectacular stalactite formations. ⊠ *8 Crystal Caves Rd., off Wilkinson Ave., Bailey's Bay, Hamilton Parish* ☎ *441/293–0640* ⊕ *www.bermudacaves.com* ⊠ *One cave $15; combination ticket $21* ☉ *Daily 9:30–4:30, last combination tour at 4.*

Fort St. Catherine. This restored fortress is one of the most impressive on the island. The original fort was built around 1613, but it was remodeled and enlarged at least five times. As you travel through the tunnels, you'll come across some startlingly lifelike figures tucked into niches. ⊠ *15 Coot Pond Rd., St. George's Parish* ☎ *441/297–1920* ⊠ *$5* ☉ *Daily 10–4.*

St. George's. The settlement of Bermuda began in what is now the **Town of St. George** nearly 400 years ago, when the *Sea Venture* was shipwrecked on Bermuda's treacherous reefs on its way to the colony of Jamestown, Virginia. No trip to Bermuda is complete without a visit to this historic town and UNESCO World Heritage Site.

The **Bermuda National Trust Museum at the Globe Hotel** was built in 1700. During the American Civil War, Confederate Major Norman Walker was stationed in the building, where he coordinated the flow of guns, ammunition, and war supplies through Union blockades in American ports. The house saw service as the Globe Hotel during the mid-19th century and became a National Trust property in 1951. ⊠ *32 Duke of York St.* ☎ *441/297–1423* ⊕ *www.bnt.bm* ⊠ *$5; $10 combination ticket includes admission to Tucker House and Verdmont* ☉ *Mon.–Sat. 10–4.*

In early 2005, **Bermuda Perfumery & Gardens** moved from Bailey's Bay (Smith's Parish) to Stewart Hall, one of the oldest buildings in St. George's. The Lili Perfume Factory has been in existence since 1929, when it began extracting natural fragrances from the island's flowers. Visitors may browse the showroom and walk through the lovely garden behind the building to the old cottage, where the perfumes are actually made. ⊠ *5 Queen St.* ☎ *441/293–0627* ⊕ *www.bermuda-perfumery.com* ⊠ *Free* ☉ *Mon.–Sat. 9–5.*

The history, trials, and accomplishments of black Bermudians are highlighted in **Bermudian Heritage Museum.** A model of the slave ship *Enterprise* is part of a display that describes how the ship, with its load of human "cargo," was blown off its course from Virginia to South Carolina in 1835; it landed in Bermuda, where slavery had already been abolished, so most of the slaves accepted freedom in Bermuda. ⊠ *Water and Duke of York Sts.* ☎ *441/297–4126* ⊠ *$3* ☉ *Tues.–Sat. 10–3.*

A splendid bronze statue of Sir George Somers dominates **Ordnance Island.** The dunking stool is a replica of the one used to dunk gossips, nagging wives, and suspected witches. Demonstrations are sometimes given, although volunteers report that getting dunked is no picnic. Also on the island is the *Deliverance II,* a replica of one of two ships—the other was the *Patience*—built by the survivors of the 1609 wreck of the *Sea Venture* to carry them to Jamestown, Virginia, their original destination. ⊠ *Across from King's Sq.* ☎ *441/297–1459* ◪ *$3* ☉ *Apr.–Oct., weekdays 9:30–5.*

★ ⑱ Because parts of **St. Peter's Church** date to its construction in 1620, it holds the distinction of being the oldest continuously operating Anglican church in the Western Hemisphere. It was not the first church to stand on this site, however. It replaced a 1612 structure of posts and palmetto leaves that was destroyed in a storm. The present church was extended in 1713, and the galleries on either side were added in 1833. ⊠ *33 Duke of York St.* ☎ *441/297–2459* ⊕ *www.anglican.bm* ◪ *Donations accepted* ☉ *Daily 10–4:30; Sun. service at 11:15.*

★ ⑳ Constructed out of native limestone, **Tucker House** is typical of many early Bermudian houses. It was built in 1711 for a merchant who used the basement as storage space for his wares, and it was originally close to the shore—though landfill has since moved the water back. The house is at the corner of Barber's Alley, named for Joseph Haine Rainey, a freed slave from South Carolina who fled to Bermuda at the outbreak of the American Civil War and made his living here as a barber. After the war, Rainey returned home and, in 1870, became the first black man to be elected to the U.S. House of Representatives. ⊠ *5 Water St.* ☎ *441/297–0545* ⊕ *www.bnt.bm* ◪ *$5; $10 combination ticket includes admission to the National Trust Museum in the Globe Hotel and Verdmont* ☉ *Mon.–Sat. 10–4.*

Shopping

Hamilton has the greatest concentration of shops in Bermuda, and Front Street is its pièce de résistance. Lined with small, pastel-color buildings, this most fashionable of Bermuda's streets houses sedate department stores and snazzy boutiques, with several small arcades and shopping alleys spinning away from it. A smart canopy shades the entrance to the 55 Front Street Group, which houses Crisson Jewellers. Modern Butterfield Place has galleries and boutiques selling, among other things, Louis Vuitton leather goods. The Emporium, a renovated building with an atrium, has a range of shops, from antiques to souvenirs.

In **St. George's,** Water Street, Duke of York Street, Hunters Wharf, Penno's Wharf, and Somers Wharf are the sites of numerous renovated buildings that house branches of Front Street stores, as well as artisans' studios. Historic King's Square offers little more than a couple of T-shirt and souvenir shops.

In the West End, **Somerset Village** has a few shops, but they hardly merit a special shopping trip. However, the **Clocktower Mall,** in a historic building at the Royal Naval Dockyard, has a few more shopping opportunities, including branches of Front Street shops and specialty boutiques. The **Dockyard** is also home to the Craft Market, the Bermuda Arts Centre, and Bermuda Clayworks.

Activities

BICYCLING The best (and sometimes only) way to explore Bermuda's nooks and crannies—its little hidden coves and 18th-century tribe roads—is by bicycle or motor scooter. A popular option for biking in Bermuda is the **Railway Trail**, a dedicated cycle path blissfully free of cars. Running intermittently the length of the old Bermuda Railway (old "Rattle 'n' Shake"), this trail is scenic, paved, and restricted to pedestrian and bicycle traffic. You can ask the staff at any bike-rental shop for advice on where to access the trail. **Eve's Cycle Livery** (☒ *Water St., St. George's* ☎ *441/236–0839* ☒ *Reid St., Hamilton* ☎ *441/236–4491*) has two locations convenient for cruise-ship passengers. Eve's rents standard-size mountain bikes, as well as motor scooters, including your mandatory helmet. The staff readily supplies advice on where to ride, and there is no charge for a repair waiver. **Wheels Cycles** (☒ *Front St., near the docks, Hamilton* ☎ *441/292–2245*) has 13 branches all over the island, including one near the cruise-ship pier in Hamilton. You can rent mountain bikes for children and adults.

KAYAKING Good sea-kayaking areas can be found in protected coves and the open
★ ocean. Calm Mangrove Bay in Somerset is an especially popular spot. **SurfShack** (☒ *9 Beaches Resort, Daniel's Head, Somerset* ☎ *441/239–2995* ⊕ *www.surfshack.bm*), based out of the 9 Beaches resort in Somerset, is the newest water-sports center in Bermuda and is fast becoming the place to go for all things aquatic. You can rent kayaks for $15 for an hour. Snorkel safaris, for groups up to 12 people, take you to some of the most secluded and beautiful locations around the island on one- or two-hour jet-ski tours.

GOLF Golf courses make up nearly 17 percent of the island's 21.6 square miles. The scenery on the courses is usually spectacular, with flowering trees and shrubs decked out in multicolored blossoms against a backdrop of brilliant blue sea and sky. The layouts are remarkably challenging, thanks to capriciousocean breezes, daunting natural terrain, and the clever work of world-class golf architects.

Fairmont Southampton Golf Club is known for its steep terrain. ☒ *Fairmont Southampton, South Rd., Southampton Parish* ☎ *441/239–6952* ⊕ *www.fairmont.com/Southampton* ☒ *Greens fees $70 with mandatory cart, $30 sunset walking. Pull-cart rental $7.50. Shoe rentals $10. Titleist-club rentals $25. Lessons $40 per half hour, $80 per hour.*

Mid Ocean Club, a classic 1921 Charles Blair Macdonald design revamped by Robert Trent Jones Sr. in 1953, is ranked as one of the top 50 courses outside the U.S. by *Golf Digest.* ☒ *Mid Ocean Dr., off South Shore Rd., Tucker's Town* ☎ *441/293–0330* 🖷 *441/293–8837* ⊕ *www.themidoceanclubbermuda.com* ☒ *Greens fees $210 ($70 when playing with a member). Nonmembers must be introduced by a club member (your hotelier can arrange this); nonmember starting times available Mon., Wed., and Fri. until noon, except holidays. After noon, every second tee time is available to nonmembers. Caddies $40 per bag, single, or $35 per bag, double (tip not included). Cart rental $25 per person.*

Port Royal Golf Course was once called one of the world's best public courses by Jack Nicklaus. ⊠ *Off Middle Rd., Southampton Parish* ☎ *441/234–0974, 441/234–4653 for automated tee-time reservations up to 7 days in advance* 🖷 *441/234–3562* ⊕ *www.portroyalgolf.bm* 🖅 *Greens fees: $139 including cart. Sunset rates are $85 with cart, $70 walking in summer; and $60 with cart, $50 walking in winter. Club rentals $37. Pull-cart rentals $10. Shoe rentals $15. Lessons $50 for half hour.*

St. George's Golf Club, short but daunting, dominates a secluded head-land at the island's northeastern end. In 2005 the course revamped its greens, which are small and were perpetually thin from constant buf-feting by salty air. ⊠ *1 Park Rd., St. George's Parish* ☎ *441/297–8353 pro shop, 441/234–4653 tee times* 🖷 *441/297–2273* ⊕ *www.stgeorgesgolf.bm* 🖅 *Greens fees $65. Cart rental $28 per person. Pull-cart rental $10. Club rentals $35. Shoe rental $15. Lessons $50 for half hour.*

Beaches

★ **Elbow Beach.** Swimming and body surfing are great at this beach, which is a pleasant setting for a late-evening stroll, with the lights from nearby hotels dancing on the water, but the romance dissipates in daylight, when the beach is noisy and crowded. Protective coral reefs make the waters the safest on the island, and a good choice for families. ⊠ *Off South Rd., Paget Parish* Ⓜ *Bus 2 or 7 from Hamilton.*

Fodor'sChoice
★

Horseshoe Bay Beach. When locals say they're going to "the beach," they are generally referring to Horseshoe Bay Beach, the island's most popu-lar. With clear water, a ⅓-mi crescent of pink sand, a vibrant social scene, and the uncluttered backdrop of South Shore Park, Horseshoe Bay has everything you could ask of a Bermudian beach. The undertow can be strong, especially on the main beach. ⊠ *Off South Rd., Southamp-ton Parish* ☎ *441/238–2651* Ⓜ *Bus 7 from Hamilton.*

Tobacco Bay Beach. The most popular beach near St. George's—about 15 minutes northwest of the town on foot—this small north-shore strand is huddled in a coral cove. It's a 10-minute hike from the bus stop in the town of St. George's, or you can flag down a St. George's Minibus Service van and ask for a lift here ($2 per person). ⊠ *Coot Pond Rd., St. George's Parish* ☎ *441/297–8199* Ⓜ *Bus 1, 3, 10, or 11 from Hamilton.*

Where to Eat

¢–$ ✕ **Docksider.** Locals come to mingle at this sprawling Front Street sports bar. It's generally more popular as a drinking venue, but standard pub fare is available. Go for the English beef pie, fish-and-chips, or a fish sand-wich and sip your dessert—a Dark 'n Stormy—out on the porch as you watch Bermuda stroll by. The pub has a good jukebox and there is often a DJ or a band on summer weekends, when it can become a lively night-spot. ⊠ *121 Front St., Hamilton* ☎ *441/296–3333* ▭ *MC, V.*

$–$$ ✕ **Cafe Gió.** With a waterside terrace on the harbor, Cafe Gió offers tasty Italian cuisine in a pleasant, romantic setting. The fettuccine is good and the Caesar salad is great. ⊠ *36 Water St., St. George's* ☎ *441/297–1307* ▭ *MC, V.*

BONAIRE (KRALENDIJK)

Vernon O'Reilly
Ramesar

Starkly beautiful Bonaire is the consummate desert island. Surrounded by pristine waters, it is a haven for divers and snorkelers who flock here from around the world to take advantage of the excellent visibility, easily accessed reefs and bountiful marine life. Bonaire is the most rustic of the three ABC islands and despite its dependence on tourism it manages to maintain its identity and simple way of life. There are many very good restaurants, most of which are located within walking distance of the port. Most of the island's 11,000 inhabitants live in and around the Kralendijk which must certainly qualify as one of the cutest and most compact capitals in the Caribbean. The best shopping is to be found along the very short stretch of road that constitutes "downtown." Bonaire's beaches tend to be small and rocky, but there is a nice stretch of sandy beach at Lac Bay. It is entirely possible to see almost all of the sights and sounds of the island in one day by taking one of the island tours on offer.

CURRENCY
The NAF guilder (NAF 1.78 to US$1); U.S. currency is accepted almost everywhere on the island, and the island has several ATMs, particularly in Kralendijk.

HOURS
Banks are generally open weekdays from 8:30 to 3:30. Stores in the Kralendijk area are generally open Monday through Saturday from 8 to noon and 2 to 6 but may open earlier or stay open later depending on the season.

INTERNET
Bonaire Access (⊠ *Harbourside Mall, Kralendijk* ☎ *No phone*). *Cyber City* (⊠ *City Café, Kaya Grandi 7, Kralendijk* ☎ *599/717–8286*).

TELEPHONES
You can make international calls from the Telbo central phone company office (next to the tourism office in Kralendijk), which is open 24 hours a day. The country code for Bonaire is 599; 717 is the exchange for every four-digit telephone number on the island. When making interisland calls, dial 717 plus the local four-digit number.

Coming Ashore

One of the great benefits of Bonaire to cruise passengers is that the port is right in downtown Kralendijk. Ships usually tender passengers ashore. A 4-minute walk gives access to most of the best shopping and restaurants on the island.

Bonaire lives for tourism, so upon the arrival of a cruise, the locals are ready. Taxis wait right at the port and operate on fixed government rates. All of the sights of Kralendikj are within easy walking distance, and a taxi ride to one of the larger resorts on the island will run between $5 and $8. A half-day island tour by taxi costs about $30 for up to 4 passengers.

Shore Excursions

We consider these to be among the better shore excursions for Bonaire. They may not be offered by all lines, and tour names may differ as well. Times and prices are approximate.

Best of Bonaire Island Tour. Few roads, small size, and absolutely no traffic means you can take in all of the island's major sights with ease. Explore Kralendijk, the salt pans and flamingoes, the slave huts and the rugged Northern coast in just a few hours with time left for shopping. ⊙ *3 hrs* ▭ *$50.*

Mangrove Kayaking. A quick presentation on the fascinating world of mangroves is followed by a brief kayaking lesson and then a relaxing and scenic tour of the mangrove. These excursions also include refreshments. ⊙ *3 hrs* ▭ *$90.*

Shore Snorkel. It would almost be a sin to visit Bonaire without exploring the underwater wonders of the Bonaire Marine Park. Instructions, transportation, and snorkeling equipment are included. ⊙ *2–4 hrs* ▭ *$50.*

Exploring Bonaire

Numbers in the margin correspond to points of interest on the Bonaire map.

❶ **Kralendijk.** Bonaire's small, tidy capital city (population 3,000) is five minutes from the airport. The main drag, J. A. Abraham Boulevard, turns into **Kaya Grandi** in the center of town. Along it are most of the island's major stores, boutiques, and restaurants. Across Kaya Grandi, opposite the Littman jewelry store, is Kaya L. D. Gerharts, with several small supermarkets, a handful of snack shops, and some of the better restaurants. Walk down the narrow waterfront avenue called Kaya C. E. B. Hellmund, which leads straight to the **North and South piers.** In the center of town, the Harborside Mall has chic boutiques. Along this route is **Fort Oranje**, with its cannons. From December through April, cruise ships dock in the harbor once or twice a week. The diminutive ochre-and-white structure that looks like a tiny Greek temple is the **fish**

> ## BONAIRE BEST BETS
>
> ■ **Diving.** Bonaire is one of the world's top diving destinations. Certified divers shouldn't miss out.
>
> ■ **Snorkeling.** With reefs close to shore, snorkeling is good even from the beach in many spots.
>
> ■ **Washington-Slagbaai National Park.** Bonaire's best land-based sight is this well-preserved national park.

market; local anglers no longer bring their catches here (they sell out of their homes these days), but you can find plenty of fresh produce brought over from Colombia and Venezuela. Pick up the brochure *Walking and Shopping in Kralendijk* from the tourist office to get a map and full listing of all the monuments and sights in the town.

❸ Salt Flats. You can't miss the salt flats—voluptuous white drifts that look something like mountains of snow. Harvested once a year, the "ponds" are owned by Cargill, Inc., which has reactivated the 19th-century salt industry with great success (one reason for that success is that the ocean on this part of the island is higher than the land—which makes irrigation a snap). Keep a lookout for the three 30-foot obelisks—white, blue, and red—that were used to guide the trade boats coming to pick up the salt. Look also in the distance across the pans to the abandoned solar saltworks that's now a designated **flamingo sanctuary.** With the naked eye you might be able to make out a pink-orange haze just on the horizon; with binoculars you will see a sea of bobbing pink bodies. The sanctuary is completely protected, and no entrance is allowed (flamingos are extremely sensitive to disturbances of any kind).

❷ Slave Huts. The salt industry's gritty history is revealed in Rode Pan, the site of two groups of tiny slave huts. The white grouping is on the right side of the road, opposite the salt flats; the second grouping, called the red slave huts (though they appear yellow), stretches across the road toward the island's southern tip. During the 19th century, slaves working the salt pans by day crawled into these huts to rest. Each Friday afternoon they walked seven hours to Rincon to weekend with their families, returning each Sunday. Only very small people will be able to enter, but walk around and poke your head in for a look.

❹ Willemstoren Lighthouse. Bonaire's first lighthouse was built in 1837 and is now automated (but closed to visitors). Take some time to explore the beach and notice how the waves, driven by the trade winds, play a crashing symphony against the rocks. Locals stop here to collect pieces of driftwood in spectacular shapes and to build fanciful pyramids from objects that have washed ashore.

ⓑ ❺ **Washington–Slagbaai National Park.** Once a plantation producing divi-divi trees (the pods were used for tanning animal skins), aloe (used for medicinal lotions), charcoal, and goats, the park is now a model of conservation. It's easy to tour the 13,500-acre tropical desert terrain on the dirt roads. As befits a wilderness sanctuary, the well-marked, rugged routes force you to drive slowly enough to appreciate the animal life and the terrain. If you're planning to hike, bring a picnic lunch, camera, sunscreen, and plenty of water. The short one (15 mi [24 km]) is marked by green arrows. Goats and donkeys may dart across the road, and if you keep your eyes peeled, you may catch sight of large iguanas camouflaged in the shrubbery. A useful guide to the park is available at the entrance for about $6. To get here, take the secondary road north from the town of Rincon. ☎ *599/717–8444* ⊕ *www.bonairenature.com/ washingtonpark* 🎫 *Free* ☉ *Daily 8–5; you must enter before 3.*

Shopping

Though it is a relatively small town, Kralendijk offers a good range of high-end items like watches and jewelry at attractive prices. There are a number of souvenir shops offering T-shirts and trinkets lining the main stretch of Kaya Grandi.

Bon Tiki (⊠ *Kaya C. E. B. Hellmund 3, Kralendijk* ☎ *599/717–6877*) sells unique works from Bonaire's finest artists. **JanArt Gallery** (⊠ *Kaya Gloria 7, Kralendijk* ☎ *599/717–5246*), on the outskirts of town, sells unique watercolor paintings, prints, and art supplies; artist Janice Huckaby also hosts art classes. Whatever you do, make a point of visiting ★ **Jenny's Art** (⊠ *Kaya Betico Croes 6, near post office, Kralendijk* ☎ *599/ 717–5004*). Lots of fun (and sometimes kitschy) souvenirs made out of driftwood, clay, and shells are all handmade by Jenny.

★ **Atlantis** (⊠ *Kaya Grandi 32B, Kralendijk* ☎ *599/717–7730*) carries a large range of precious and semiprecious gems. The tanzanite collection is especially beautiful. Since gold jewelry is sold by weight here, it's an especially good buy. **Littman's** (⊠ *Kaya Grandi 33, Kralendijk* ☎ *599/ 717–8160* ⊠ *Harborside Mall, Kaya Grandi 31, Kralendijk* ☎ *599/717– 2130*) is an upscale jewelry and gift shop where many items are hand-picked by owner Steven Littman on his regular trips to Europe.

Activities

DIVING & **Diving and snorkeling** are almost a religion on Bonaire and are by far
SNORKELING the most popular activities for even cruise visitors. Bonaire has some of the best reef diving this side of Australia's Great Barrier Reef. It takes only 5 to 25 minutes to reach many sites, the current is usually mild, and although some reefs have sudden, steep drops, most begin just offshore and slope gently downward at a 45-degree angle. General visibility runs 60 to 100 feet, except during surges in October and November. You can see several varieties of coral: knobby-brain, giant-brain, elkhorn, staghorn, mountainous star, gorgonian, and black. **Wanna Dive** (⊠ *Hotel Rochaline, Kaya Grandi 7, next to City Café, Kralendijk* ☎ *599/790– 8880* ⊕ *www.wannadivebonaire.com*).

BICYCLING Bonaire is generally flat, so bicycles are an easy way to get around. Because of the heat it's essential to carry water if you're planning to cycle for any distance and especially if your plans involve exploring the deserted interior. There are more than 180 mi (290 km) of unpaved routes (as well as the many paved roads) on the island. **Cycle Bonaire** (✉ *Kaya Gobernador N. Debrot 77A, Kralendijk* ☎ *599/717–2229*) rents mountain bikes and gear (trail maps, water bottles, helmets, locks, repair and first-aid kits) for $15 a day.

Beaches

Don't expect long stretches of glorious powdery sand. Bonaire's beaches are small, and though the water is blue (several shades of it, in fact), the sand isn't always white. In 2005, Bonaire's National Parks Foundation introduced a new "nature fee" that basically requires all nondivers to pay a $10 annual fee in order to enter the water anywhere around the island.

Lac Bay Beach. Known for its festive music on Sunday nights, this open bay area with pink-tinted sand is equally dazzling by day. It's a bumpy drive (10 to 15 minutes on a dirt road) to get here, but you'll be glad when you arrive. It's a good spot for diving, snorkeling, and kayaking (as long as you bring your own), and there are public restrooms and a restaurant for your convenience. ✉ *Off Kaminda Sorobon, Cai.*

★ **Pink Beach.** As the name suggests, the sand here has a pinkish hue that takes on a magical shimmer in the late-afternoon sun. The water is suitable for swimming, snorkeling, and scuba diving. Take the Southern Scenic Route (E. E. G. Boulevard) on the island's western side; the beach is close to the slave huts. It's a favorite Bonairean hangout on the weekend, but it's almost deserted during the week. Because of the coral that is thrown up on the beach, sandals are recommended. ✉ *Southern Scenic Hwy., south of airport.*

Windsock Beach. Near the airport (just off E. E. G. Boulevard), this pretty little spot, also known as Mangrove Beach, looks out toward the north side of the island and has about 200 yards of white sand along a rocky shoreline. It's a popular dive site, and swimming conditions are also good. ✉ *Off E. E. G. Blvd., near airport.*

Where to Eat

$$–$$$ ✕ **City Café/City Restaurant.** This busy waterfront eatery is also one of the most reliable nightspots on the island, so it's always hopping day or night. Breakfast, lunch, and dinner are served daily for reasonable prices. Seafood is always featured, as are a variety of sandwiches and salads. The pita sandwich platters are a good lunchtime choice for the budget challenged. Weekends, there's always live entertainment and dancing. ✉ *Hotel Rochaline, Kaya Grandi 7, Kralendijk* ☎ *599/717–8286* ▭ *AE, MC, V.*

★ $–$$ ✕ **Le Flamboyant.** This intimate restaurant offers good food at affordable prices. The cozy historic house—conveniently downtown—also has a small gourmet food shop, espresso bar, and lovely cocktail bar. The main attraction is the tree-covered courtyard at the back. Lunch offers a selection of ample sandwiches and salads; dinner is mostly seafood and pastas. Vegetarians will not have to pick and hunt for suitable items, as there's a comprehensive vegetarian menu. ✉ *Kaya Grandi 12, Kralendijk* ☎ *599/717–3919* ▭ *AE, MC, V* ☉ *Closed Sun.*

CALICA, MEXICO

Michele Joyce   Just minutes away from Calica, Playa del Carmen has become one of Latin America's fastest-growing communities, with a pace almost as hectic as Cancún's. Hotels, restaurants, and shops multiply here faster than you can say "Kukulcán." Some are branches of Cancún establishments whose owners have taken up permanent residence in Playa—or who commute daily between the two places; others are owned by American and European expats who came here years ago, as early adopters. It makes for a varied, international community. Avenida 5, the first street in town parallel to the beach, is a long, colorfully tiled pedestrian walkway with shops, cafés, and street performers; small hotels and stores stretch north from this avenue. Avenida Juárez, running east–west from the highway to the beach, is the main commercial zone for the Riviera Maya corridor. Here, locals visit the food shops, pharmacies, auto-parts and hardware stores, and banks that line the curbs. People traveling the coast by car usually stop here to stock up on supplies—its banks, grocery stores, and gas stations are the last ones until Tulum.

Essentials

CURRENCY   The Mexican peso (MX$11.13 to US$1). U.S. dollars and credit cards are widely accepted in the area, from the port to Playa del Carmen, but it's best to have pesos—and small bills—when you visit ruins where cashiers often run out of change. There is no advantage to paying in dollars, but there may be an advantage to paying in cash.

HOURS   Many Playa del Carmen restaurants are open for breakfast, lunch, and dinner, operating from around 10 in the morning until 10 at night. On weekends, especially around the busy Avenida 5 area, restaurants and bars stay open later, often until around midnight. Banks are generally open weekdays 9 to 5.

INTERNET   There are several Internet cafes on Avenida 5 in Playa del Carmen. **24 Com Center** (✉ *Av. 24, between Calle 1 and Calle 8, Playa del Carmen* ☎ *984/803–5778*).

TELEPHONES   Most pay phones accept prepaid Ladatel cards, sold in 30-, 50-, or 100-peso denominations. To use the card, insert it in the pay phone's slot, dial 001 (for calls to the U.S.) or 01 (for calls within Mexico), followed by the area code and number. Credit is deleted from the card as you use it, and the balance is displayed on the small screen on the phone.

Coming Ashore

The port at Calica, about 3 mi south of the town of Playa del Carmen (between Playa del Carmen and Xcarat), is small. Sometimes ships actually dock, and other times passengers are tendered to shore. There is a makeshift market at the port, where locals sell crafts. Beyond that, there is not much to do, and you'll need to head into Playa del Carmen proper to find restaurants and even tour operators. If you really want to shop, skip the vendors at the port and head to Playa del Carmen's Avenida 5, where you can easily spend an afternoon browsing shops and enjoying restaurants.

Taxis and tour buses are available at the port to take you to Playa del Carmen and other destinations, but lines often form as passengers wait for taxis, so hurry to the front of the line if you really want to pack a lot of activity into your day. Your taxi will have you in Playa del Carmen or in Xcaret in under 10 minutes, but you'll pay a whopping $10 for the short trip.

Shore Excursions

We consider these to be among the better shore excursions for Calica. They may not be offered by all lines, and tour names may differ as well. Times and prices are approximate.

ATV Tour. The tours in the Calica area usually include some driving both inland and on the beach. Lunch (or at least snacks) are usually provided. ⊗ *6 hrs* 🚲 *$84.*

Catamaran Snorkeling Cruise. Because of the exceptionally clear water, non-divers may wish to do this trip to see some of the wonderful sights below the sea and to visit undiscovered beaches. ⊗ *6 hrs* 🚲 *$84–$97.*

Diving. Certified divers who don't feel like making their own arrangements may wish to opt for ship-arranged diving trip to the excellent reefs around Cozumel. ⊗ *3 hrs* 🚲 *$90.*

Tulum. Because of the distance and crowds, it's sometimes better to take a ship-sponsored tour to Tulum rather than trying to go it alone. You'll go by bus. ⊗ *6 ½ hrs* 🚲 *$97.*

Exploring Calica

Numbers in the margin correspond to points of interest on the Playa del Carmen map.

❶ **Playa del Carmen.** Once upon a time, Playa del Carmen was a fishing village with a ravishing deserted beach. The villagers fished and raised co-conut palms to produce copra (the roasted coconut that is pressed to render coconut oil), and the only foreigners who ventured here were beach bums. That was a long time ago, however. These days, although the beach is still delightful—alabaster-white sand, turquoise-blue waters—it's far from deserted. In fact, Playa has become one of Latin America's fastest-growing commu-

CALICA BEST BETS

A Day at Xcaret. Particularly for families, this ecological theme park is a great way to spend the day.

Beaches. The beaches in the Riviera Maya are some of the best along the Yucatan's Caribbean coast.

Diving. From Playa del Carmen, you're a short hop from some of the Yucatan's best dive sites.

Shopping. Playa del Carmen's Avenida 5 can easily keep you occupied for your day in port if you are a shopaholic.

nities, with a population of more than 135,000 and a pace almost as hectic as Cancún's. The ferry pier, where the hourly boats arrive from and depart for Cozumel, is another busy part of town. The streets leading from the dock have shops, restaurants, cafés, a hotel, a basketball court, and food stands. If you take a stroll north from the pier along the beach, you'll find the serious sun worshippers. On the pier's south side is the edge of the sprawling Playacar complex. The development is a labyrinth of residences and all-inclusive resorts bordered by an 18-hole championship golf course. ⊠ *3 mi (5 km) north of Calica.*

The excellent 32-acre **Xaman Ha Aviary** (⊠ *Paseo Xaman-Ha, Playacar* ☎ *984/873–0235*), in the middle of the Playacar development, is home to more than 30 species of native birds. It's open daily 9–5, and admission is $15.

Tres Rios Eco Park (⊠ *Carretera Cancún–Tulum, Km 54* ☎ *998/850–4849* ⊕ *www.tresrios.com*), located just 7 mi north of Playa, is a great place to get a sense of this region's ecology and natural wonders. Three rivers converge in the expansive 800-acre property (a lush rarity in the dry Yucatán landscape), and you can explore them by kayaking, canoeing, or snorkeling along them. You can also take horseback rides along the beach or bike rides along jungle paths, keeping an eye out for birds and animals; if you're lucky, you might spot a white-fronted parrot, or even a coatimundi. Admission is $18, including lunch; $35 includes lunch and a choice of one activity. The park is open daily from 9 to 5.

❷ **Xcaret.** Once a sacred Maya city and port, Xcaret (pronounced *ish*-car-et) is now a 250-acre ecological theme park on a gorgeous stretch of coastline. A Mexican version of Epcot Center, the park has done a good job to showcase, celebrate, and help preserve the natural environment of the Caribbean coast. ■ TIP→ You can easily spend at least a full day here; there's tons to see and do. Among the most popular attractions are the Paradise River raft tour that takes you on a winding, watery journey through the jungle; the Butterfly Pavillion, where thousands of butterflies float dreamily through a botanical garden while New Age music plays in the background; and an ocean-fed aquarium where you can see local sea life drifting through coral heads and sea fans without getting wet. The list of Xcaret's attractions goes on and on. ⊠ *11 km (6½ mi) south of Playa del Carmen* ☎ *998/881–2451 in Cancún* ⊕ *www.xcaret. net* ⊠ *$53, including show* ☉ *Daily 8:30 AM–9 PM.*

❸ **Tulum.** Tulum (pronounced tool-*lum*) is the Yucatán Peninsula's most-visited Maya ruin, attracting more than 2 million people annually. Though most of the architecture is of unremarkable Postclassic (1000–1521) style, the amount of attention that Tulum receives is not entirely undeserved. Its location by the blue-green Caribbean is breathtaking. Tulum is one of the few Maya cities known to have been inhabited when the conquistadores arrived in 1518. In the 16th century, it functioned as a safe harbor for trade goods from rival Maya factions; it was considered neutral territory where merchandise could be stored and traded in peace. The city reached its height when traders, made wealthy through the exchange of goods, for the first time outranked Maya priests in authority and power. When the Spaniards arrived, they forbade the Maya traders to sail the seas, and commerce among the Maya died. Tulum has long held special significance for the Maya. A key city in the League of Mayapán (AD 987–1194), it was never conquered by the Spaniards, although it was abandoned about 75 years after the conquest. For 300 years thereafter, it symbolized the defiance of an otherwise subjugated people; it was one of the last outposts of the Maya during their insurrection against Mexican rule in the War of the Castes, which began in 1846. Uprisings continued intermittently until 1935, when the Maya ceded Tulum to the government. ⊠ *2 km (1 mi) south of Tankah, 62 km (38 mi) south of Playa del Carmen* ⊠ *$9, use of video camera extra* ☉ *Daily 8–5.*

❹ **Muyil.** This photogenic archaeological site at the northern end of the Reserva de la Biosfera Sian Ka'an is underrated. Once known as Chunyaxché, it's now called by its ancient name, Muyil (pronounced mool-*hill*). It dates from the Late Preclassic era, when it was connected by road to the sea and served as a port between Cobá and the Maya centers in Belize and Guatemala. The most notable site at Muyil today is the remains of the 56-foot **Castillo**—one of the tallest on the Quintana Roo coast—at the center of a large acropolis. During excavations of the Castillo, jade figurines representing the moon and fertility goddess Ixchel were found. Recent excavations at Muyil have uncovered some smaller structures. The ruins stand near the edge of a deep-blue lagoon and are surrounded by almost impenetrable jungle—so be sure to bring bug repellent. You can drive down a dirt road on the side of the ruins to swim or fish in the lagoon. The bird-watching is also exceptional here. ⊠ *24 km (15 mi) south of Tulum, 86 km (53 mi) south of Playa del Carmen* ⊠ *$4, free Sun.* ☉ *Daily 8–5.*

Shopping

Playa del Carmen's Avenida 5 between Calles 4 and 10 is the best place to shop along the coast. Boutiques sell folk art and textiles from around

Mexico, and clothing stores carry lots of sarongs and beachwear made from Indonesian batiks. A shopping area called Calle Corazon, between Calles 12 and 14, has a pedestrian street, art galleries, restaurants, and boutiques. **La Calaca** (⊠ *Av. 5 between Calles 12 and 14* ☎ *984/ 873–0174*) has an eclectic collection of wooden masks, whimsically carved angels and devils, and other crafts. **Maya Arts Gallery** (⊠ *Av. 5 between Calles 6 and 8* ☎ *984/879–3389*) has an extensive collection of hand-carved Maya masks and *huipiles* (the traditional, white, embroidered cotton dresses worn by Maya women) from Mexico and Guatemala.

Activities

DIVING   The PADI-affiliated **Abyss** (⊠ *Calle 12* ☎ *984/873–2164*) offers training ($80 for an introductory course) in addition to dive trips ($50 for one tank, $70 for two tanks) and packages. The oldest shop in town, **Tank-Ha Dive Shop** (⊠ *Av. 5 between Calles 8 and 10* ☎☎ *984/873–5037* ⊕ *www.tankha.com*), has PADI-certified teachers and runs diving and snorkeling trips to the reefs and caverns. A one-tank dive costs $35; for a two-tank trip it's $55; and for a cenote two-tank trip it's $90. Dive packages are also available.

GOLF   Playa's golf course is an 18-hole, par-72 championship course designed by Robert Von Hagge. The greens fee is $180; there's also a special twilight fee of $120. Information is available from the **Casa Club de Golf** (☎ *984/873–0624 or 998/881–6088*).

Where to Eat

¢–$ **Babe's Noodles & Bar.** Photos and paintings of old Hollywood pinup models decorate the walls and are even laminated onto the bar of this Swedish-owned, Asian restaurant, known for its fresh and interesting fare. Everything is cooked to order—no prefab dishes here. Try the spring rolls with peanut sauce, or the sesame noodles, made with chicken or pork, veggies, lime, green curry, and ginger. In the Buddha Garden, you can sip a *mojito*, or sit at the bar and watch the crowds on nearby 5th Avenue. ⊠ *Calle 10 between Avs. 5 and 10* ☎ *984/804–2592* ⊕ *www. babesnoodlesandbar.com* ⊟ *No credit cards* ⊠ *Av. 5, between Calle 28 and 30* ☎ *984/803–0056.*

$–$$$$ **La Parrilla.** Reliably tasty Mexican fare is the draw at this boisterous, touristy restaurant. The smell of sizzling *parrilla mixta* (a grilled, marinated mixture of lobster, shrimp, chicken, and steak) can make it difficult to resist grabbing one of the few available tables. The margaritas here are strong, and there's often live music. ⊠ *Av. 5 and Calle 8* ☎ *984/873–0687* ⊟ *AE, D, MC, V.*

CARTAGENA, COLOMBIA

Jeff Van Fleet   Ever wondered what the "Spanish Main" refers to? This is it. Colombia's Caribbean coast invokes ghosts of conquistadores, pirates, and missionaries journeying to the New World in search of wealth, whether material or spiritual. Anchoring this shore is Cartagena—poetically, officially *Cartagena de Indias* (Cartagena of the Indies)—founded in 1533 and one of Latin America's magnificent colonial cities. Gold and silver passed through here en route to Spain, making the city an obvious target for pirates, hence the construction of Cartagena's trademark walls and fortresses. Outside the *Ciudad Amurallada* (walled city) lie less historic (but no less interesting) beaches and water excursions. If Colombia conjures up images of drug lords and paramilitary guerillas, think again; security is quite visible (without being oppressive) here in the country's top tourist destination. Take the same precautions you'd follow visiting any city of 800,000 people, and you should have a grand time.

Essentials

CURRENCY The Colombian peso (COP 2,203 to US$1). In Colombia, peso prices are denoted with the "$" sign too. If they carry a lot of zeroes, they likely are not dollar prices, but always ask. ATMs are ubiquitous around town.

HOURS Many tourist sights close by 6 PM, meaning you should do your touring early in the day. (It's cooler before noon, as well.) Tourist-oriented shops keep hours from 9 to 9, although many close from 12:30 to 2, and little is open on Sunday. (Truly entrepreneurial store owners don't close when cruise ships are in port.)

INTERNET Upon arrival or before departure, you can check your e-mail at the bank of computers in the Terminal de Cruceros. In town, the computers at **Micronet** (⊠ *Calle de la Estrella No. 4–47*) are quite zippy and will set you back only 2,000 pesos per hour.)

PRECAUTIONS Security is tighter in Cartagena than elsewhere in Colombia, so you certainly can navigate the city on your own. (Knowing some Spanish helps.) However, the scarcity of English speakers or English signage at the city's tourist attractions and the persistence of vendors, street touts and the periodic con artist—they *do* speak English—mean that many cruise passengers opt for the reassurance of an organized shore excursion. If you set out on your own, under no circumstances should you deal with anyone who approaches you on the street offering to change money; rip-offs are guaranteed.

TELEPHONES The Terminal de Cruceros has ample phones for your use. Local numbers in Cartagena have seven digits. For international calls, dial 009 followed by country and area codes and local number. The U.S. mobile carrier Cingular offers roaming options in this region of Colombia for calls back to the United States. **AT&T** (☎*01-800/911–0010*). **MCI** (☎*01-800/916–0001*). **Sprint** (☎ *01-800/913–0010*).

Coming Ashore

Cruise ships dock at the modern Terminal de Cruceros (cruise terminal) on Isla de Manga, an island connected by a bridge to the historic city center, about 3 km (2 mi) northwest of the docks. You'll find telephones, Internet computers, and a duty-free shop in the terminal.

A small army of taxis waits in front of the terminal. Expect to pay 5,000 pesos for the 10-minute drive to the walled city; about 8,000 pesos will get you to the nearby beaches at Bocagrande. Drivers are all too happy to take you on your own do-it-yourself guided tour. Most charge around 10,000 to 15,000 pesos for an hour of waiting time. There's little need to rent a car here. Cartagena, at least that of tourist interest, is so compact, and walking its labyrinth of cobblestone streets in the old city is far more enjoyable than driving them.

Shore Excursions

We consider these to be among the better shore excursions for Cartagena. They may not be offered by all lines, and tour names may differ as well. Times and prices are approximate.

Cruise the Harbor. Approach Cartagena as did everyone in colonial times, from newly arriving residents, to pirates wishing to plunder the city. A boat trip around the city's inner bay allows you to appreciate the city's formidable walls and fortresses, without which, there would likely be no Cartagena today. Some cruise lines allow you to do it aboard a replica Spanish Galleon. ⊙ *2 hrs* 🎫 *$42–$50.*

Mangrove & Swamp Eco-Tour. Better for birdwatchers than anyone else, these kayak tours take you into an extensive mangrove swamp to see the flora and fauna. ⊙ *4 hrs* 🎫 *$56.*

Swim at Isla Barú. Cartagena is history, but nature beckons about 30 minutes away by boat. The beaches of nearby Isla Barú make a far more picturesque alternative to those closer to the city and offer ample swimming and snorkeling opportunities. ⊙ *4 hrs* 🎫 *$60.*

Exploring Cartagena

Numbers in the margin correspond to points of interest on the Cartagena map.

Nothing says Cartagena quite like a ride in a horse-drawn carriage, or *coche,* as it is known locally. Drivers are a wealth of information about Cartagena, and many do speak English. The downside for you is that the rides begin near dusk—it's a far cooler time of the day, after all—and your need to be back on ship may not coincide with that schedule. Do check. You can pick up carriages many places around, including the Plaza de los Coches, near the Puerta del Reloj in the walled city, or the Hotel Caribe in Bocagrande. Expect to pay around $170 to $200 for a 2-hour tour (this kind of excursion is best when the cost is split among a group of four).

⑤ Castillo de San Felipe de Barajas. Designed by Antonio de Arévalo in 1639, the Fort of St. Philip's steep-angled brick and concrete battlements were arranged so that if part of the castle were conquered the rest could still be defended. A maze of tunnels, minimally lighted today to allow for spooky exploration, still connects vital points of the fort. Acoustics were perfect in the tunnels, allowing occupants of the fort to hear the footsteps of the approaching enemy. You can walk here from the walled city in about 30 minutes; an 8,000-peso taxi ride is an easier option. ⊠ *Avenida Pedro de Heredia at Carrera 17* ☎ *666–4790* ☞ *10,000 pesos* ☉ *Daily 8–6.*

② Catedral. Any Latin American city centers on its cathedral and main square. Cartagena's Plaza de Bolívar is a shady place from which to admire Cartagena's 16th-century cathedral, with its colorful bell tower and 20th-century dome. Inside is a massive gilded altar. A statue of South American liberator Simón Bolívar stands watch over his namesake plaza. ⊠ *Plaza de Bolívar.*

⑥ Cerro de la Popa. For spectacular views of Cartagena, ascend this hill,
Fodor'sChoice the highest ground around. Because of its strategic location, the 17th-
★ century hilltop convent did double duty as a fortress during the colonial era. It now houses a museum and a chapel dedicated to the Virgin de la Candelaria, Cartagena's patron saint. No public transport exists to get up here; taxis charge about 6,000 pesos. ✛ *3 km (2 mi) southeast of Ciudad Amurallada* ☎ *666-2331* ☞ *5,000 pesos* ☉ *Daily 9–5.*

❶ Las Murallas. Cartagena survived only because of its walls, and its *murallas* remain today the city's most distinctive feature. Repeated sacking by pirates and foreign invaders convinced the Spaniards of the need to enclose the region's most important port. Construction began about 1600 and was completed in 1796. Walking along the thick walls remains one of Cartagena's time-honored tourist pastimes. The **Puerta del Reloj** is the principal gate to the innermost sector of the Ciudad Amurallada. Its four-sided clock tower was a relatively late addition (1888), and has become the best known symbol of the city. ⊠ *Area bounded by Bahía de las Ánimas, Caribbean Sea, and Laguna de San Lázaro* ☉ *24 hours.*

❸ Museo del Oro y Arqueología. The Gold and Archaeological Museum, a project of Colombia's Central Bank, displays an assortment of artifacts culled from the Sinús, an indigenous group that lived in the region 2,000 years ago. ⊠ *Carrera 4 No. 33–26* ☎ *660–0778* ☒ *Free* ☉ *Tues.–Fri. 10–1 and 3–6, Sat. 10–1 and 2–5.*

Fodor'sChoice
★
❹ Palacio de la Inquisición. Arguably Cartagena's most visited tourist attraction documents the darkest period in the city's history. The 1770 Palace of the Inquisition served as the second headquarters of the repressive arbiters of political and spiritual orthodoxy who once exercised jurisdiction over northern South America. Although the museum also displays benign colonial and pre-Columbian artifacts, everyone heads to the ground floor to "Eeeewww" over the implements of torture—racks and thumbscrews, to name but two. ⊠ *Carrera 4 No. 33–26* ☎ *664–4113* ☒ *3,000 pesos* ☉ *Daily 9–5.*

Shopping

Think "Juan Valdez" if you're looking for something to take the folks back home. Small bags of fine Colombian coffee, the country's signature souvenir, are available in most tourist-oriented shops. Colombia also means emeralds, and you'll find plenty in the jewelry shops on or near Calle Pantaleón, beside the cathedral. Don't forget the duty-free shop in the Terminal de Cruceros for those last-minute purchases. On the high end of Cartagena's shopping spectrum lies **Galería Cano** (⊠ *Plaza de Bolívar* ☎ *664–7078*), which has assembled an exquisite selection of indigenous artisan work from around Colombia. The hats, hammocks, and jewelry here are admittedly pricey, but they do make a lovely souvenir of your day in Cartagena. The name of **Las Bóvedas** (⊠ *North of Plaza Fernández de Madrid* ☎ *No phone*) translates as "the vaults," and the city's best crafts shops occupy this row of storerooms built in the 18th century to hold gunpowder and other military essentials. Your stockpile here will consist of hats, hammocks, and leather goods.

Activities

DIVING   Coral reefs line the coast south of Cartagena, although warm-water currents have begun to erode them in recent years. There is still good diving to be had in the Islas del Rosario, an archipelago of 27 coral islands about 35 km (21 mi) southwest of the city. The **Caribe Dive Shop** (⊠ *Carrera 1A, No. 2–87, Bocagrande* ☎ *665–0155*) at the Hotel Caribe organizes snorkeling trips to the Islas del Rosario and scuba diving at underwater wrecks.

Beaches

Bocagrande. For most people, "beach" plus "Cartagena" equals "Bocagrande," the resort area on a 5 km- (3 mi-) long peninsula south of the walled city. High-rise hotels and condos front the gray-sand beach. It gets quite crowded and is very lively, but Bocagrande is probably not the Caribbean beach of which you've always dreamed. ⊠ *2 km (1 mi) south of Cartagena Bocagrande.*

Playa Blanca. The area's quintessential postcard-perfect white-sand beach lies at Playa Blanca on Isla Barú southeast of Cartagena, a far nicer option than Bocagrande if you have the time. Barú is an island in name only—a canal separates this long peninsula from the mainland—but boat is realistically the only way to get there from Cartagena. Many private boats leave from the Muelle de los Pegasos (the tourist dock) just south of the walled city on the way to Bocagrande, yet their speed frequently translates into recklessness. An organized shore excursion through your ship offers the most reliable trip. ⊠ *35 km (21 mi) southwest of Cartagena, Isla de Barú.*

Where to Eat

$–$$ ✕ **Café de la Plaza.** One of seven cafés spilling out onto the Plaza Santo Domingo, this popular eatery serves tasty food in generous portions and is one of those perfect places to watch the world go by. The menu is predominantly Italian, with a good selection of pastas, salads, and sandwiches. It's also a good place to stop for breakfast. ⊠ *Plaza Santo Domingo* ☎ *664–0920* 🖃 *AE, DC, MC, V.*

$–$$ ✕ **Café San Pedro.** Although it serves primarily Colombian fare, this restaurant's eclectic menu includes dishes from Thailand, Italy, and Japan. You can also drop by to nurse a drink for as long as you like and to watch the activity on the plaza from one of the outdoor tables. ⊠ *Plaza San Pedro* ☎ *664–5121* 🖃 *AE, DC, MC, V.*

COLÓN, PANAMA

Linda Coffman   When you consider the decades it took to build the canal, not to mention the lives lost and government failures and triumphs involved during its construction, it comes as no surprise that the Panama Canal is often called the 8th Wonder of the Modern World. Best described as an aquatic bridge, the Panama Canal connects the Caribbean Sea with the Pacific Ocean by raising ships up and over Central America, through artificially created Gatún Lake, the highest point at 85 feet above sea level, and then lowering them back to sea level by using a series of locks, or water steps. A masterful engineering feat, three pairs of locks—Gatún, Pedro Miguel, and Miraflores—utilize gravity to fill and drain as ships pass through chambers 1,000 feet long by 110 feet wide that are "locked" by doors weighing 80 tons apiece, yet actually float into position. Most cruise ships pass through the canal seasonally, when repositioning from one coast to the other; however, partial transits have become an increasingly popular "destination" on regularly scheduled 10- and 11-night Caribbean itineraries. These loop cruises enter the canal from the Caribbean Sea and sail into Gatún Lake, where they remain for a few hours as passengers are tendered ashore for excursions. Ships then pass back through the locks, returning to the Caribbean and stopping at either Cristobal Pier or Colón 2000 Pier to retrieve passengers at the conclusion of their tours.

A day transiting the canal's Gatún Locks begins before dawn as your passenger ship passes through *Bahia Limon* and lines up with dozens of other vessels to await its turn to enter. Before your ship can proceed, two pilots and a narrator will board. The sight of a massive cruise ship being raised dozens of feet into the air by water is so mesmerizing that passengers eagerly crowd all forward decks at the first lock. If you don't find a good viewing spot, head for the rear decks, where there is usually more room and the view is just as intriguing. If you remain aboard, as many passengers do, you'll find plenty of room up front later in the day as your ship retraces its path down to the sea. Due to the tight scheduling of the day's activities—it takes at least 90 minutes for a ship to pass through Gatún Locks—passengers who wish to go ashore early in the day are advised to sign up for one of the many available shore excursions.

Essentials

CURRENCY The balboa is permanently at par with the U.S. dollar. Panama does not print paper money, and U.S. dollars are used regularly. There is no need to acquire Panamanian money.

HOURS It's all about the cruise ships here. If your ship is docked at the Colón 2000 Pier, the stores will be open.

INTERNET There's an internet café at the Colón 2000 Pier.

TELEPHONES You'll find telephones inside Colón's cruise terminals, where you can purchase phone cards, which are a handy and inexpensive way to make calls.

Coming Ashore

Colón, Panama's second-largest city, has little to offer of historic interest and is simply a jumping-off point to the rain forest and a wide variety of organized tours. Once in a while, a cruise's itinerary may include a day docked in Colón, rather than a partial canal transit. However, no matter how much time your ship spends in Colón, we strongly recommend that you leave the ship on an organized shore excursion, either arranged with the cruise line or through independent tour operators. Taxi drivers await ship arrivals, and some can be acceptable private guides; however, as in any foreign port, before setting out with any unofficial car and driver, you should set a firm price and agree upon an itinerary as well as look over the vehicle carefully.

Although entry time into the canal is always approximate, passenger ships have priority and most pass through Gatún Locks early in the morning. Passengers booked on shore excursions begin the tendering process soon after the ship sets anchor, which can be as early as 8:30 AM. Alternatives to excursions offered by your cruise ship are available from independent tour operators that can be arranged in advance through Web sites or, possibly, travel agents. You will likely be informed that Panamanian regulations restrict passengers going ashore in Gatún Lake to only those who have booked the cruise line's excursions; however, anyone who has a shore excursion reservation with a local company should be able to leave the vessel. Before making independent tour arrangements, confirm with your cruise line that you will be allowed to go ashore after presenting your private tour confirmation to the shore-excursion staff on board the ship.

Upon completion of either full or partial canal transits, cruise ships generally dock at either Cristobal Pier or Colón 2000 Pier late in the afternoon, where they may remain for several hours. Passengers who remained on board throughout the canal passage have the opportunity to go ashore and those who set out on land tours end at the terminals, where they rejoin the ship. All of Colón is considered a high crime area, and pickpockets have been known to strike even in the seemingly secure areas of the cruise-ship terminals. If you go ashore, you are well advised to leave jewelry and other valuables aboard your ship and carry only the cash you need.

Shore Excursions

If you wish to see a bit of Panama during your canal transit, you'll almost certainly need to book a shore excursion. This is one of the few cruise destinations where that is the case. The following shore excursions are offered by major cruise lines in Panama. They may not be offered by all lines, and tour names may differ as well. Times and prices are approximate.

Authentic Embera Indian Village. You travel by dugout canoe to an Embera village in the Chagres National Park. The village chief greets you with a traditional welcome, and his people perform native song, dance, and music and display their crafts. ☉ 3½ hrs 🖃 $99.

Caribbean Rain Forest Nature & Wildlife Hike. Explore remote jungle trails on the western shore of the canal during your guided nature hike through Fort Sherman, site of the former United States Army elite jungle-training school. You may see toucans, sloths, anteaters, and howler monkeys in the intricate jungle ecosystem. ☉ 4½–5 hrs 🖃 $59.

Gatún Lake Kayak & Eco Adventure. After a short bus ride, you arrive at the kayak staging area where you will set out on your ecological tour through the islands that surround Gatún Lake. Afterward, you will trade in your kayak for a bus and stop at the Gatún Locks Observation Area to watch ships traverse the locks. The observation platform has 80 steps; an alternate viewing site is available at ground level. Beverages and snacks are included. ☉ *4 hrs* ⌨ *$62.*

Panama Canal Railway Journey. Travel Panama's transcontinental railroad from Colón to Panama City, where you will then take a scenic drive and stop at Amador Causeway before returning to Colón by air-conditioned bus. Snacks and beverages are served on the train. The more expensive trip is in a dome car. ☉ *5½ hrs* ⌨ *$139–$199.*

Panama City Tour. Drive from the Atlantic to the Pacific through the rain forest from Colón to Panama City, where you will tour the city's highlights. Depending on when you leave, you'll get lunch or dinner. ☉ *8 hrs* ⌨ *$99.*

Panama's Rain Forest Aerial Tram. Transfer by bus from Colón to Gamboa Rain Forest Resort, where the aerial tram ride begins. After your narrated ascent through the forest canopy, you can walk to the observation platform before stopping for a picnic lunch on the way back to Colón. ☉ *4½ hrs* ⌨ *$99.*

SHOPPING   While the Colón Free Zone is the world's second-largest tax-free zone—and is within walking distance of Colón 2000—it is situated amid uninviting squalor sure to intimidate even the boldest shopper; further, merchants here are supposed to do only wholesale sales. We can't recommend that you shop here, though some merchants will sell to tourists.

Better bets are within the large terminals adjacent to both Cristobal Pier and Colón 2000 Pier, where you will find Internet access, telephones, refreshments, and duty-free souvenir shopping in relatively secure environments. Stores in both locations feature local crafts such as baskets, wood carvings, and toys, as well as liquor, jewelry, and the ubiquitous souvenir T-shirts. In addition to shops and cafés, Cristobal Pier features an open-air arts and crafts market; Colón 2000 Pier has a well-stocked supermarket. The most unique locally made souvenirs are colorful appliquéd *molas,* the whimsical textile artwork created by native Kuna women, who come from the San Blas Islands; they are likely to be hand stitching new designs while they sell the ones they just completed. The Kuna ladies drive a hard bargain and, considering the intricate nature of their handiwork, prices are quite fair. This is not a particularly authentic experience, but prices can be good.

Watch for local folkloric dancers who often perform for tips in the terminal areas or pierside at sailaway.

COSTA MAYA, MEXICO

Michele Joyce   The newest cruise-ship destination on Mexico's Caribbean Coast, Puerto Costa Maya is an anomaly. Unlike other tourist attractions in the area (the island of Cozumel being the primary Yucatán cruise port), this port of call near Majahual has been created exclusively for cruise-ship passengers. The shops, restaurants, activities, and entertainment you'll find here aren't open to the general public. At first glance, the port complex itself may seem to be little more than an outdoor mall. The docking pier (which can accommodate three ships at once) leads to a 70,000 square-foot bazaar-type compound, where shops selling local crafts—jewelry, pottery, woven straw hats and bags, and embroidered dresses—are interspersed with duty-free stores and souvenir shops. There are two alfresco restaurants, which serve seafood, American-friendly Mexican dishes like tacos and quesadillas, and cocktails at shaded tables. An outdoor amphitheater stages eight daily performances of traditional music and dance. The strip of beach edging the complex has been outfitted with colorful lounge chairs and *hamacas* (hammocks), and may tempt you to linger and sunbathe. If you want to have a truly authentic Mexican experience, though, you'll take advantage of the day tours offered to outlying areas. These give you a chance to see some of the really spectacular sights in this part of Mexico, many of which are rarely visited. This is one port where the shore excursion is the point, and there are no options except to purchase what your ship offers. You can preview what excursions may be offered on the Puerto Costa Maya's own Web site. Among the best tours are those that let you explore the gorgeous (and usually deserted) Mayan ruin sites of Kohunlich, Dzibanche, and Chacchoben. The ancient pyramids and temples at these sites, surrounded by jungle that's protected them for thousands of years, are still dazzling to behold. Since the sites are some distance from the port complex—and require some road travel in one of the port's air-conditioned vans—these tours are all-day affairs.

Essentials

CURRENCY   The Mexican peso (MX$11.13 to US$1). U.S. dollars and credit cards are accepted by everyone at the port. There is no advantage to paying in dollars, but there may be an advantage to paying in cash. Ten pesos are worth a little bit less than $1.

INFORMATION   **Puerto Costa Maya** (⊕ *www.puertocostamaya.com*).

TELEPHONES   Most pay phones accept prepaid Ladatel cards, which are sold in 30-, 50-, or 100-peso denominations. To use the card, insert it in the pay phone's slot, dial 001 (for calls to the U.S.) or 01 (for calls within Mexico), followed by the area code and number. Credit is deleted from the card as you use it, and the balance is displayed on a small screen on the phone.

Shore Excursions

We consider these to be among the better shore excursions for Costa Maya. They may not be offered by all lines, and tour names may differ as well. Times and prices are approximate. This is one place where your choice of a shore excursion can be crucial. You can reach some less-visited Maya sites that aren't easily reached from other parts of the country.

Catamaran and Snorkel. If you prefer your adventures on—or under—the water, an excellent tour choice is the catamaran and snorkeling trips to the nearby reef at Banco Chinchorro. ⊗ *3 hrs* 🖃 *$48.*

Chacchoben. An air-conditioned bus transports you to a secluded jungle setting near the border with Belize. Your guide will explain the significance of the excavated portion of the 10-acre site, which includes detailed Maya temples and the remains of the Maya village. Afterward, you have time for more exploration or to shop for crafts. Walking and climbing is over uneven surfaces. ☉ *4 hrs* ✈ *$72.*

Jungle Beach Break. If you just want to relax, take a shuttle to nearby Uvero Beach. Included are an open bar and use of beach chairs, hammocks, and nonmotorized water sports. Stay as long as you like. Freshwater showers, restrooms, and changing rooms are available. There's a restaurant, but you must pay for the food here. ☉ *At your discretion* ✈ *$40.*

Kohunlich. An air-conditioned bus takes you to an isolated site near the Belize border where, spread over a wide area, the ruins include a variety of architectural styles, from the wide lawns of the ball courts and public plazas to the great temples with sculpted masks. Considerable walking and climbing is over uneven surfaces. A snack is included. Some tours (usually called "Mayan Explorer") also include Dzibanche and last eight hours. ☉ *7–8 hrs* ✈ *$82–$98.*

Speed Boat Trip. If you enjoy the power of a speedboat, then this tour will appeal to you. These are among the fastest speedboats you'll find, and you'll be able to reach some less visited beaches for downtime before returning to the ship. ☉ *3½ hrs* ✈ *$96.*

COZUMEL, MEXICO

Maribeth
Mellin

Cozumel, with its sun-drenched ivory beaches fringed with coral reefs, fulfills the tourist's vision of a tropical Caribbean island. It's a heady mix of the natural and the commercial. Despite a mini-construction boom in the island's sole city, San Miguel, there are still wild pockets scattered throughout the island where flora and fauna flourish. Smaller than Cancún, Cozumel surpasses its fancier neighbor in many ways. It has more history and ruins, superior diving and snorkeling, more authentic cuisine, and a greater diversity of handicrafts at better prices. The numerous coral reefs, particularly the world-renowned Palancar Reef, attract divers from around the world. On a busy cruise-ship day, the island can seem completely overrun, but it's still possible to get away, and some good Maya sights are within reach on long (and expensive) shore excursions.

Essentials

CURRENCY The Mexican peso (MX$11.13 to US$1). U.S. dollars and credit cards are widely accepted in the area, from the port to Playa del Carmen, but it's best to have pesos—and small bills—when you visit ruins where cashiers often run out of change. There is no advantage to paying in dollars, but there may be an advantage to paying in cash.

HOURS Many Cozumel restaurants are open for breakfast, lunch, and dinner, operating from around 10 in the morning until 10 at night. Banks are generally open weekdays 9 to 5.

INTERNET **Calling Station** (✉ *Av. Rafael E. Melgar 27, at Calle 3 Sur* ☎ *987/872–1417*). **The Crew Office** (✉ *Av. 5, No. 201, between Calle 3 Sur and Av. Rosada Salas* ☎ *987/869–1485*). **CreWorld Internet** (✉ *Av. Rafael E. Melgar and Calle 11 Sur* ☎ *987/872–6509*).

TELEPHONES Most pay phones accept prepaid Ladatel cards, sold in 30-, 50-, or 100-peso denominations. To use the card, insert it in the pay phone's slot, dial 001 (for calls to the U.S.) or 01 (for calls within Mexico), followed by the area code and number. Credit is deleted from the card as you use it, and the balance is displayed on a small screen on the phone.

Coming Ashore

As many as six ships call at Cozumel on a busy day, tendering passengers to the downtown pier in the center of San Miguel or docking at the two international piers 4 mi (6 km) away. From the downtown pier you can walk into town or catch the ferry to Playa del Carmen. Taxi tours are also available. An island tour, including the ruins and other sights, costs about $50 to $70, but negotiate the price before you get in the cab. The international pier is close to many beaches, but you'll need a taxi to get into town. There's rarely a wait for a taxi, but prices are high, and drivers are often aggressive, asking double or triple the reasonable fare. Expect to pay $10 for the ride into San Miguel from the pier. Tipping is not necessary.

> ### COZUMEL BEST BETS
>
> ■ **Diving & Snorkeling.** Excellent reefs close to shore make either diving or snorkeling a must-do activity.
>
> ■ **Maya Ruins.** Some of the most famous and dazzling ruins are reachable from Cozumel, and if you have never seen a Maya pyramid, this is your chance.
>
> ■ **Shopping.** Because the dollar is still worth something in Mexico, you can get very good buys, and Cozumel is a major shopping destination.

Passenger ferries to Playa del Carmen leave Cozumel's main pier approximately every other hour from 5 AM to 10 PM. They also leave Playa del Carmen's dock about every other hour on the hour, from 6 AM to 11 PM (but note that service sometimes varies according to demand). The trip takes 45 minutes. Verify the times: bad weather and changing schedules can prompt cancellations.

Shore Excursions

Cozumel offers more worthwhile shore excursions than most Caribbean ports. If you want to see Maya sites, then you should take a ship-sponsored tour because of the travel distances (often ships stop briefly off Playa del Carmen to discharge passengers going on these tours, a real time-saver). The following shore excursions are offered by major cruise lines in Cozumel. They may not be offered by all lines, and tour names may differ as well. Times and prices are approximate.

Atlantis Submarine Trip. Since the reefs here are so amazing, it's worth the money to take this submarine trip if you're not an accredited diver. You'll go 100 feet below the surface without getting wet. ⊙ 2¼ hrs ⌦ $98.
Diving. If you're an accredited diver, it can be worth taking a ship-sponsored excursion to maximize your time and minimize the arrangements you have to make. ⊙ 4½ hrs ⌦ $98.
Jungle ATV Tour. This off-road tour is good if you want to release some of your adrenaline. ⊙ 3½ hrs ⌦ $89.

Cozumel

Punta Molas

Punta Norte

Isla de
Pasión

Sea

Playa
Santa
Pilar

**Cozumel
Country Club**

Playa
San
Juan

Airport

TO PUERTO MORELOS

Playa
Bonita

Caribbean Sea

TO PLAYA
DEL CARMEN

*Plaza
Central*

Av. Benito Juárez

Playa
Los Cocos

Punta
Este

Punta
Morena

Caribbean

Av. Rafael Melgar

La Ceiba

Playa
Corona

Playa San
Clemente

Playa San
Francisco

Playa
Sol

Nachi-
Cocom

Punta Francesca

Playa del
Palancar

*Laguna
Colombia*

*Laguna
Chunchacaab*

El Caracol

Playa
Paradiso

Playa de
San Martin

Punta
Chiqueros

El Trono

El Mirador

R E E F S

Faro de Punta Celerain

KEY	
🏖	*Beaches*
🚢	*Cruise Ship*
⛴	*Ferry*
🔺	*Ruins*

0 ——— 6 miles

0 ——— 9 km

Snorkel Tours. Popularized by Jacques Cousteau, Cozumel's coral reefs are considered to be some of the world's finest. Most ships offer snorkeling excursions, some with lessons and equipment provided. Locales and tour lengths vary by cruise line; the more expensive tours take you closer to the reefs; the cheaper tours include snorkeling from the beach only. ☉ *Approx. 4 hrs* ▣ *$44.*

Tequila Tasting Seminar. With the popularity of high-end tequilas has come this chance to learn more about the spirit and how to tell good from bad. This is a popular trip. ☉ *Approx. 3 hrs* ▣ *$82.*

Tulum Mayan Ruins. The only Maya settlement built on a cliff overlooking the sea was dedicated to the setting sun. After taking the public ferry to Playa del Carmen, you travel by bus to the site and tour the ruins. A stop at Xel-ha for snorkeling and swimming is usually an option; otherwise, you go back to Cozumel for shopping rather than to the ship. ☉ *6½–8 hrs* ▣ *$109.*

Exploring Cozumel

Numbers in the margin correspond to points of interest on the Cozumel map.

San Miguel is tiny—you cannot get lost—and is best explored on foot. The main attractions are the small eateries and shops that line the streets, and the activity centers at the main square, where the locals congregate in the evenings.

⑤ Castillo Real. A Maya site on the coast near the island's northern end, the "royal castle" includes a lookout tower, the base of a pyramid, and a temple with two chambers capped by a false arch. The waters here harbor several shipwrecks, and it's a fine spot for snorkeling because there are few visitors to disturb the fish. Note, however, that you can't get here by rental car; plan to explore the area on a guided tour.

③ El Cedral. Spanish explorers discovered this site, once the hub of Maya life on Cozumel, in 1518. Later, it became the island's first official city, founded in 1847. Today it's a farming community with small well-tended houses and gardens. Conquistadores tore down much of the Maya temple and, during World War II, the U.S. Army Corps of Engineers destroyed the rest to make way for the island's first airport. All that remains of the Maya ruins is one small structure with an arch. Nearby is a green-and-white cinder-block church, decorated inside with crosses shrouded in embroidered lace; legend has it that Mexico's first Mass was held here. Each May there's a fair here with dancing and bullfights. More small ruins are hidden in the surrounding jungle, but you need a guide to find them. Check with horseback riding companies for specialized tours. ✉ *Turn at Km 17.5 off Carretera Sur or Av. Rafael E. Melgar, then drive 3 km (2 mi) inland to the site* ☏ *No phone* ▣ *Free* ☉ *Daily dawn–dusk.*

★ ☾ ② Parque Chankanaab. Chankanaab (which means "small sea") is a national park with a saltwater lagoon, an archaeological park, and a botanical garden. Scattered throughout are reproductions of a Maya village, and of Olmec, Toltec, Aztec, and Maya stone carvings. The gardens were severely damaged by Hurricane Wilma in 2005 and are slowly recovering. You can enjoy a cool walk through pathways leading to the sea, where parrot fish and sergeant majors swarm around snorkelers. You can swim, scuba dive, or snorkel at the beach. There's plenty to see: underwater caverns, a sunken ship, crusty old cannons and anchors, and a sculpture of la Virgen del Mar (Virgin of the Sea). To preserve the ecosystem, park rules forbid touching the reef or feeding the fish. Dive shops, restaurants, gift shops, a snack stand, and dressing rooms with lockers and showers are right on the sand. A small museum has exhibits on coral, shells, and the park's history, as well as some sculptures. ⊠ *Carretera Sur, Km 9* ☎ *987/872–2940* ▭ *$10* ۞ *Daily 7–5.*

🐣 ❹ **Parque Punta Sur.** This 247-acre national preserve at Cozumel's southernmost tip is a protected habitat for numerous birds and animals, including crocodiles, flamingos, egrets, and herons. Cars aren't allowed, so you'll need to use park transportation (rented bicycles or public buses) to get around here. From observation towers you can spot crocodiles and birds in **Laguna Colombia** or **Laguna Chunchacaab.** Or visit the ancient Maya lighthouse, **El Caracol,** constructed to whistle when the wind blows in a certain direction. At the park's (and the island's) southernmost point is the **Faro de Celarain,** a lighthouse that is now a museum of navigation. Climb the 134 steps to the top; it's a steamy effort, but the views are incredible. Beaches here are wide and deserted, and there's great snorkeling offshore. Snorkeling equipment is available for rent, as are kayaks. The park also has an excellent restaurant (it's prohibited to bring food and drinks to the park), an information center, a small souvenir shop, and restrooms. Without a rental car, expect to pay about $40 for a round-trip taxi ride from San Miguel. ⊠ *Southernmost point in Punta Sur Park and the coastal rd.* ☎ *987/872–2940 or 987/872–8462* ▭ *$10* ۞ *Daily 9–5.*

❻ **San Gervasio.** Surrounded by a forest, these temples comprise Cozumel's largest remaining Maya and Toltec site. San Gervasio was once the island's capital and ceremonial center, dedicated to the fertility goddess Ixchel. The Classic- and Postclassic-style buildings were continuously occupied from AD 300 to 1500. Typical architectural features include limestone plazas and arches atop stepped platforms, as well as stelae and bas-reliefs. Be sure to see the "Las Manitas" temple with red handprints all over its altar. Plaques clearly describe each structure in Maya, Spanish, and English. ⊠ *From San Miguel, take the cross-island road (follow signs to the airport) east to San Gervasio access road; turn left and follow road for 4½ mi (7 km)* ▭ *$5.50* ۞ *Daily 7–4.*

★ ❶ **San Miguel.** Cozumel's only town feels more traditional the farther you walk away from the water; the waterfront has been taken over by large shops selling jewelry, imported rugs, leather boots, and souvenirs to cruise-ship passengers. Head inland to the pedestrian streets around the plaza, where family-owned restaurants and shops cater to locals and savvy travelers.

Shopping

San Miguel's biggest industry—even bigger than diving—is selling souvenirs to cruise-ship passengers. The primary items are ceramics, onyx, brass, wood carvings, colorful blankets and hammocks, reproductions of Maya artifacts, shells, silver, gold, sportswear, T-shirts, perfume, and liquor. Look for Mexican pewter; it's unusual, affordable, and attractive. Almost all stores take U.S. dollars. If your ship docks at International Pier, you can shop dockside for T-shirts, crafts, and more.

Before you spend any serious cash, though, keep in mind the following tips. Don't pay attention to written

SHIP SALES
If you find prices on board too much to bear, shop the ship's boutiques on the last day of your cruise, when they are likely to run special sales.

or verbal offers of "20% discount, today only" or "only for cruise-ship passengers"—they're nothing but bait to get you inside. Similarly, many of the larger stores advertise "duty-free" wares, but prices tend to be higher than retail prices in the United States. Avoid buying from street vendors, as the quality of their merchandise can be questionable, which may not be apparent until it's too late. Don't buy anything from the black coral "factories." The items are overpriced, and black coral is an endangered species.

The center of the shopping district is the main square off Avenida Melgar, across from the ferry terminal, where you'll find some upscale malls geared toward cruise-ship shoppers. The district extends north along Avenida Melgar and Calles 5 Sur and Norte. As a general rule, the newer, trendier shops line the waterfront, and the better crafts shops can be found around Avenida 5a. Other plazas include Plaza del Sol (on the east side of the main plaza), Villa Mar (on the north side of the main plaza), and the Plaza Confetti (on the south side of the main plaza).

Los Cinco Soles (⊠ *Av. Rafael E. Melgar and Calle 8 Norte* ☎ *987/872–0132*) is the best one-stop shop for crafts from around Mexico. Several display rooms, covering almost an entire block, are filled with clothing, furnishings, home decor items, and jewelry. **Diamond Creations** (⊠ *Av. Rafael E. Melgar Sur 131* ☎ *987/872–5330*) lets you custom-design pieces of jewelry from a collection of loose diamonds, emeralds, rubies, sapphires, or tanzanite. The shop and its affiliates, Tanzanite International, Diamond Creations, and Silver International, have multiple locations along the waterfront and in the shopping malls—in fact, you can't avoid them. At Cozumel's best art gallery, **Galeria Azul** (⊠ *Calle 10 Sur between Av. Salas and Calle 1* ☎ *987/869–0963*), artist Greg Deitrich displays his engraved blown glass along with paintings, jewelry, and other works by local artists. **Mr. Buho** (⊠ *Av. Rafael E. Melgar between Calles 6 and 8* ☎ *987/869–1601*) specializes in white and black clothes and has well-made guayabera shirts and cotton dresses. **Viva Mexico** (⊠ *Av. Rafael E. Melgar and Calle Adolfo Rosada Salas* ☎ *987/872–0791*) sells souvenirs and handicrafts from all over Mexico; it's a great place to find T-shirts, blankets, and trinkets.

Activities

DIVING &
SNORKELING

Cozumel is famous for its reefs. In addition to Chankanaab Nature Park, a great dive site is La Ceiba Reef, in the waters off La Ceiba and Sol Caribe hotels. Here lies the wreckage of a sunken airplane blown up for a Mexican disaster movie. Cozumel has plenty of dive shops to choose from. **Aqua Safari** (⊠ *Av. Rafael E. Melgar 429, between Calles 5 and*

7 Sur ☎ *987/872–0101*) is one of the oldest and most professional shops and offers PADI certification. **Blue Angel** (✉ *Caribe Blu Hotel, Carretera Sur, Km 2.3* ☎ *987/872–1631*) has an ideal location for both boat and shore dives. **Dive Cozumel-Yellow Rose** (✉ *Calle Adolfo Rosado Salas 85, between Avs. Rafael E. Melgar and 5 Sur* ☎ *987/872–4567*) specializes in cave diving for experienced divers.

Eagle Ray Divers (✉ *La Caleta Marina, near the Presidente Inter-Continental hotel* ☎ *987/872–5735*) offers snorkeling trips. The company also tracks the eagle rays that appear off Cozumel from December to February and runs trips for advanced divers to walls where the rays congregate.

FISHING   Regulations forbid commercial fishing, sportfishing, spear fishing, and collecting any marine life in certain areas around Cozumel. It's illegal to kill some species within marine reserves, including billfish, so be prepared to return prize catches to the sea. You can charter high-speed fishing boats for about $420 per half day or $600 per day (with a maximum of six people). **Albatross Deep Sea Fishing** (☎ *987/872–7904 or 888/333–4643*) offers full-day rates that include boat and crew, tackle and bait, and lunch with beer and soda. **3 Hermanos** (☎ *987/872–6417 or 987/876–8931*) specializes in deep-sea and fly-fishing trips. Their rates for a half-day deep-sea fishing trip start at $350.

Beaches

Cozumel's beaches vary from sandy treeless stretches to isolated coves to rocky shores. Most of the development is on the leeward (western) side. Beach clubs have sprung up on the southwest coast; admission, however, is usually free, as long as you buy food and drinks. Clubs offer typical tourist fare: souvenir shops, *palapa* (thatch-roofed) restaurants, kayaks, and cold beer. A cab ride from San Miguel to most clubs costs about $15 each way. Reaching beaches on the windward (eastern) side is more difficult, but the solitude is worth it. A small parking lot on the side of Carretera Sur just south of town marks the entrance to **Playa Caletita**. A few palapas are up for grabs, and the small restaurant has restrooms and beach chairs. South of the resorts lies the mostly ignored (and therefore serene) **Playa Palancar** (✉ *Carretera Sur* ☎ *987/878–5238*). Offshore is the famous Palancar Reef, easily accessed by the on-site dive shop. There's also a water-sports center, a bar-café, and a long beach with hammocks hanging under coconut palms. The aroma of grilled fish with garlic butter is tantalizing. Playa del Palancar keeps prices low and rarely feels crowded. If it weren't for the pretentious stone arch at the entrance, **Playa San Francisco** would look much like it did a decade ago. The inviting 3-mi (5-km) stretch of sandy beach, which extends along Carretera Sur, south of Parque Chankanaab at about Km 10, is among the longest and finest on Cozumel. Encompassing beaches known as Playa Maya and Santa Rosa, it's typically packed with cruise-ship passengers in high season. On Sunday, locals flock here to eat fresh fish and hear live music. Amenities include two outdoor restaurants, a bar, dressing rooms, gift shops, volleyball nets, beach chairs, and water-sports equipment rentals. Divers use this beach as a jumping-off point for the San Francisco reef and Santa Rosa wall. The abundance of turtle grass in the water, however, makes this a less-than-ideal spot for swimming. **Punta Chiqueros,** a half-moon-shaped cove sheltered by an offshore reef, is the first popular swimming area on the windward side as you drive north on the coastal road (it's about 8 mi [12 km] north of Parque Punta Sur). Part of a longer beach that some locals call **Playa Bonita,** it has fine sand, clear water, and moderate waves. This is a great place to swim, watch the sunset, and eat fresh fish at the restaurant, also called Playa Bonita.

Where to Eat

Some restaurants serving large groups may add a 10% to 15% service charge to the bill. Otherwise, a 15% to 20% tip is customary.

★ **$–$$$** ✕ **Guido's.** Chef Ivonne Villiger works wonders with fresh fish—if the wahoo with spinach is on the menu, don't miss it. But Guido's is best known for its pizzas baked in a wood-burning oven, which makes sections of the indoor dining room rather warm. Sit in the pleasantly overgrown courtyard instead, and order a pitcher of sangria to go with the puffy garlic bread. ⊠ *Av. Rafael E. Melgar 23, between Calles 6 and 8 Norte* ☎ *987/872–0946* ▭ *AE, D, MC, V.*

¢–$ ✕ **El Foco.** Locals fuel up before and after partying at this traditional *taquería* (it's open until midnight, or until the last customer leaves). The soft tacos stuffed with pork, chorizo, cheese, or beef are cheap and filling. ⊠ *Av. 5 Sur 13B, between Calles Adolfo Rosado Salas and 3 Sur* ☎ *987/ 872–5980* ▭ *No credit cards.*

CURAÇAO

Elise Rosen   Try to be on deck as your ship sails into Curaçao. The tiny Queen Emma Floating Bridge swings aside to allow ships to pass through the narrow channel. Pastel gingerbread buildings on shore look like dollhouses, especially from a large cruise ship. Although the gabled roofs and red tiles show a Dutch influence, the gleeful colors of the facades are peculiar to Curaçao. It's said that an early governor of the island suffered from migraines that were aggravated by the color white, so all the houses were painted in hues from magenta to mauve. Thirty-five mi (56 km) north of Venezuela and 42 mi (67 km) east of Aruba, Curaçao is, at 38 mi (61 km) long and 3 to 7½ mi (5 to 12 km) wide, the largest of the Netherlands Antilles. Although always sunny, it's never stiflingly hot here because of the constant trade winds. Water sports attract enthusiasts from all over the world, and the reef diving is excellent.

Essentials

CURRENCY   The NAf guilder (NAF1.78 to US$1); U.S. currency is accepted almost everywhere on the island, and ATMs are plentiful.

HOURS   Banks are open weekdays from 8 to 3:30. Post office hours are from 7:30 to 5 weekdays. Most shops are open Monday through Saturday from 8 to 6. Some are open on Sunday mornings and holidays when cruise ships are in port.

INTERNET   **Café Internet** (⊠ *Handelskade 3B, Punda, Willemstad* ☎ *5999/465– 5088).* **Dot Com** (⊠ *Saliña Galleries, Saliña* ☎ *5999/461–9702).* **Suya-**

Curaçao

Christoffel National Park ... **11**
Curaçao Aloe Plantation &
Factory **10**
Curaçao Sea Aquarium **9**
Floating Market **4**
Fort Amsterdam **1**
Hato Caves **8**

Kurá Hulanda Museum **7**
Maritime Museum **6**
Mikveh Israel-Emanuel
Synagogue **2**
Queen Emma Bridge **3**
Scharloo **5**

KEY

≈ Beaches

Cruise Ship Terminal

◼ Dive Sites

Spot Internet C@fe (✉ *Pietermaaiplein 13, Punda, Willemstad* ☎ *5999/461–5388*). **Wireless Internet Café** (✉ *Hanchi Snoa 4, Punda, Willemstad* ☎ *5999/461–0590*).

TELEPHONES   The telephone system is reliable. To place a local call, dial the seven-digit number. A local call costs NAf.50 from a pay phone. You can use the AT&T calling center at the cruise-ship terminal and at the mega pier in Otrobanda to call the U.S. From other public phones, use phones marked "Lenso." You can also call direct from the air-conditioned Curaçao Telecom (CT) center using a prepaid phone card (open 8 AM to 5:30 PM Monday through Saturday; the center also offers Internet access).

Coming Ashore

Ships dock at the terminal just beyond the Queen Emma Bridge, which leads to the floating market and the shopping district. The walk to downtown takes less than 10 minutes. Easy-to-read maps are posted dockside and in the shopping area. The terminal has a duty-free shop, telephones, and a taxi stand. Taxis, which meet every ship, now have meters, although rates are still fixed from point to point of your journey. The government-approved rates, which do not include waiting time, can be found in a brochure called "Taxi Tariff Guide," available at the cruise-ship terminal and at the Tourist Board. Rates are for up to four passengers. There's a 25% surcharge after 11 PM. It's easy to see the sights on Curaçao without going on an organized shore excursion. Downtown can be done on foot, and a taxi for up to four people will cost about $30 an hour. Taxi fares to places in and around the city range from $5 to $15. Car rentals are available but are not cheap (about $60 per day, plus $10 compulsory insurance).

> **CURAÇAO BEST BETS**
>
> ■ **Diving.** After Bonaire, Curaçao has probably the best diving in the region.
>
> ■ **The Floating Market.** This unique market is a fun destination, even though it's mostly fruits and vegetables; go as early as you can.
>
> ■ **Kurá Hulanda Museum.** History is one of Curaçao's best offerings, and this museum gathers it all in one place.

Shore Excursions

The following shore excursions are offered by major cruise lines in Curaçao. They may not be offered by all lines, and tour names may differ as well. Times and prices are approximate.

Curaçao Mountain Bike Adventure. Because it's not too mountainous, this is a good island to try out mountain-biking, which is mostly off-road. And the excursion ends with a swim. ⊘ *3½ hrs* 🖼 *$58.*

Curaçao Snorkeling Tour. This snorkeling trip goes to Caracas Bay Island, in the Underwater Park, a worthwhile destination even if you don't dive. ⊘ *2½ hrs* 🖼 *$34.*

Discover Curaçao. This is a good tour if you'd like to see Westpunt and Mt. Christoffel but don't want to drive an hour there yourself. Other stops are made at a land house, Hato Caves, and some historic sights. ⊙ *3½ hrs* ⊠ *$40.*

Scuba Dive with Equipment. Many of the best sites in Curaçao are under the sea. If you're a certified diver, this is a good place to do some underwater exploring. ⊙ *4 hrs* ⊠ *$95.*

Exploring Curaçao

Numbers in the margin correspond to points of interest on the Curaçao map.

Willemstad. Willemstad is small and navigable on foot. You needn't spend more than two or three hours wandering around here, although the narrow alleys and various architectural styles are enchanting. English, Spanish, and Dutch are widely spoken. Narrow Santa Anna Bay divides the city into two sides: Punda, where you'll find the main shopping district, and Otrabanda (literally, the "other side"), where the cruise ships dock. Punda is crammed with shops, restaurants, monuments, and markets. Otrabanda has narrow, winding streets full of colonial homes notable for their gables and Dutch-influenced designs.

You can cross from Otrabanda to Punda in one of three ways: walk over the Queen Emma Bridge; ride the free ferry, which runs when the bridge swings open to let seagoing vessels pass; or take a cab across the Juliana Bridge (about $7). On the Punda side of the city, Handelskade is where you'll find Willemstad's most famous sights—the colorful colonial buildings that line the waterfront. The original red roof tiles came from Europe on trade ships as ballast.

★ ❹ Each morning dozens of Venezuelan schooners laden with tropical fruits and vegetables arrive at the bustling **Floating Market** on the Punda side of the city. Mangoes, papayas, and exotic vegetables vie for space with freshly caught fish and herbs and spices. The buying is best at 6:30 AM— too early for most cruise-ship visitors—but there's plenty of action throughout the afternoon. Any produce bought here, however, should be thoroughly washed or peeled before being eaten. ⊠ *Sha Caprileskade, Punda.*

❶ Step through the archway of **Fort Amsterdam** and enter another century. The entire structure dates from the 1700s, when it was the center of the city and the island's most important fort. Now it houses the governor's residence, the Fort Church, the Council of Ministers, and government offices. Outside the entrance, a series of majestic gnarled wayaka trees are fancifully carved with human forms—the work of local artist Mac Alberto. ⊠ *Foot of Queen Emma Bridge, Punda* ☎ *5999/ 461–1139* ⊠ *Free; $1.75 for church museum* ⊙ *Weekdays 9–noon and 2–5, Sun. service at 10.*

❼ Opened in 1999, the **Kurá Hulanda Museum** features exhibits on African history and is the largest of its kind in the Caribbean. Displays include a full-size reconstruction of a slave ship's hold and gut-wrenching firsthand accounts of the slave-trade era. ⊠ *Klipstraat 9, Otrobanda* ☎ *5999/ 462–1400* ⊕ *www.kurahulanda.com* ⊠ *$6* ⊙ *Daily 10–5.*

FodorśChoice
★

❻ The 40-odd chronological exhibits at the **Maritime Museum** truly give you a sense of Curaçao's maritime history, using ship models, maps, nautical charts, navigational equipment, and audiovisual displays. The third floor hosts temporary exhibits, and the museum also offers a two-hour guided tour on its "water bus" through Curaçao's harbor—a route familiar to traders, smugglers, and pirates. When you're ready for a break, drop anchor at the Harbor Café or browse through the souvenir shop. ⊠ *Van der Brandhofstraat 7, Scharloo* ☎ *5999/465–2327* ⊕ *www. curacaomaritime.com* ✉ *Museum $6; museum and harbor tour $12* ⊙ *Tues.–Sat. 10–4.*

★ ❷ The **Mikveh Israel-Emanuel Synagogue** was founded in 1651 and is the oldest temple still in use in the Western Hemisphere. It draws 20,000 visitors a year. Enter through the gates around the corner on Hanchi Di Snoa. The Jewish Cultural Museum in the back displays antiques and fine Judaica. ⊠ *Hanchi Snoa 29, Punda* ☎ *5999/461–1067* ⊕ *www. snoa.com* ✉ *$5; donations also accepted* ⊙ *Weekdays 9–4:30.*

❸ The **Queen Emma Bridge** is affectionately called the Swinging Old Lady by the locals, and connects the two sides of Willemstad—Punda and Otrobanda—across the Santa Anna Bay. The bridge swings open at least 30 times a day to allow passage of ships to and from sea. The original bridge, built in 1888, was the brainchild of the American consul Leonard Burlington Smith, who made a mint off the tolls he charged for using it: 2¢ per person for those wearing shoes, free to those crossing barefoot. Today it's free to everyone.

❺ The **Wilhelmina Drawbridge** connects Punda with the once-flourishing district of **Scharloo**, where the early Jewish merchants built stately homes. The end of the district closest to Kleine Werf is now a run-down red-light district, but the rest of the area is well worth a visit. The architecture along Scharlooweg (much of it from the 17th century) is intriguing, and many of the structures that had become dilapidated have been meticulously renovated.

⑪ **Christoffel National Park** is a good hour from Willemstad but worth a visit. This 4,450-acre garden and wildlife preserve with Mt. Christoffel at its center consists of three former plantations. As you drive through the park, watch for deer, goats, and smaller wildlife that might suddenly dart in front of your car. If you skip everything else on the island, it's possible to drive to the park and climb 1,239-foot Mt. Christoffel, which takes two to three strenuous hours. On a clear day you can then see the mountain ranges of Venezuela, Bonaire, and Aruba. ⊠ *Savonet* ☎ *5999/864–0363 for information and tour reservations, 5999/462–6262 for jeep tours, 5999/864–0535 for horseback tours* ✉ *$10* ⊙ *Mon.–Sat. 8–4, Sun. 6–3; last admission 1 hr before closing.*

⑩ Drop in at the **Curaçao Aloe Plantation & Factory** for a fascinating tour that takes you through the various stages of production of the aloe vera plant, renowned for its healing powers. You'll get a look at everything from the aloe fields to the final products. At the gift shop, you can buy CurAloe products including homemade goodies like aloe wine, soap, pure aloe gel, and pure aloe juice, as well as sunscreen and other skin care products made off-site. The plantation is right on the way to the Ostrich Farm, which is run by the same owner. Tours begin every hour.

✉ *Weg Naar Groot St. Joris z/n, Groot St. Joris* ☎ *5999/767–5577* ⊕ *www.aloecuracao.com* ☒ *$4* ☉ *Mon.–Sat. 9–4; last tour at 3.*

❾ At the **Curaçao Sea Aquarium** more than 400 varieties of exotic fish and vegetation are displayed. Outside is a 1,623-foot-long artificial beach of white sand, well suited to novice swimmers and children. There's also a platform overlooking the wreck of the steamship SS *Oranje Nassau* and an underwater observatory where you can watch divers and snorkelers swimming with stingrays and feeding sharks.

At the **Dolphin Academy** (☎ *5999/465–8900* ⊕ *www.dolphin-academy. com*), you can watch a fanciful dolphin show (included in the price of Sea Aquarium admission). For more up-close interaction, you may choose from several special programs (extra charges apply and reservations are essential) to encounter the dolphins in shallow water, or to swim, snorkel, or dive with them. ✉ *Bapor Kibra z/n, Sea Aquarium Beach* ☎ *5999/461–6666* ⊕ *www.curacao-sea-aquarium.com* ☒ *$15; animal encounters $54 for divers, $34 for snorkelers; sea lion programs $39–$149; Dolphin Academy $69–$300* ☉ *Sea aquarium daily 8:30–5:30; Dolphin Academy daily 8:30–4:30.*

❽ Hour-long guided tours of the **Hato Caves** wind down into various chambers to the water pools, a "voodoo" chamber, a wishing well, fruit bats' sleeping quarters, and Curaçao Falls, guarded by a limestone "dragon." Hidden lights illuminate the limestone formations and gravel walkways. This is one of the better Caribbean caves open to the public, but keep in mind that there are 49 steep steps to reach the entrance, and the cave itself is dank and hot (though they've put electric fans in some areas to provide relief). To reach the caves, head northwest toward the airport, take a right onto Gosieweg, follow the loop right onto Schottegatweg, take another right onto Jan Norduynweg, a final right onto Rooseveltweg, and follow signs. ✉ *Rooseveltweg z/n, Hato* ☎ *5999/868–0379* ☒ *$7* ☉ *Daily 10–5.*

Shopping

Curaçao has some of the best shops in the Caribbean, but in many cases the prices are no lower than in U.S. discount stores. Hours are usually Monday through Saturday, from 8 to noon and 2 to 6. Most shops are within the six-block area of Willemstad described above. The main shopping streets are Heerenstraat, Breedestraat, and Madurostraat. **Bamali** (✉ *Breedestraat, Punda, Willemstad* ☎ *5999/461–2258*) sells funky, fabulous women's apparel, including Indonesian batik clothing; charming jewelry made of beads, shells, gemstones, and silver; handbags of leather and other fabrics; and lots of other unique accessories. Custom-made clothing is available here, too. **Boolchand's** (✉ *Heerenstraat 4B, Punda, Willemstad* ☎ *5999/461–6233*) sells electronics, jewelry, Swarovski crystal, Swiss watches, and cameras behind a facade of red-and-white checkered tiles. A sweet aroma permeates **Cigar Emporium** (✉ *Gomezplein, Punda, Willemstad* ☎ *5999/465–3955*), where you can find the largest selection of Cuban cigars on the island, including H. Upmann, Romeo & Julieta, and Montecristo. Visit the climate-controlled cedar cigar room. However, remember that Cuban cigars cannot be taken back to the United States legally. **Julius L. Penha & Sons** (✉ *Heerenstraat 1, Punda, Willemstad* ☎ *5999/461–2266*), near the Pontoon Bridge, sells French perfumes and cosmetics, clothing, and accessories, in a baroque-style building dating from 1708. **New Amsterdam** (✉ *Gomezplein 14, Punda, Willemstad* ☎ *5999/461–2437* ✉ *Breedestraat 29, Punda, Willemstad* ☎ *5999/461–3239*) is the place to price hand-embroidered tablecloths, napkins, and pillowcases, as well as blue delft.

SUNGLASSES

When selecting sunglasses, the most important considerations are the amount of UV light that is blocked by the lenses and a proper fit. The lenses should shield your eyes from most angles. Darker lenses do not necessarily offer better UV protection. Look for sunglasses that block 99% of harmful UV rays.

Activities

BIKING
So you wanna bike Curaçao? **Wanna Bike Curaçao** (☎ *5999/527–3720* ⊕ *www.wannabike.net*) has the fix: kick into gear and head out for a guided mountain-bike tour through the Caracas Bay peninsula and the salt ponds at the Jan Thiel Lagoon. Although you should be fit to take on the challenge, mountain-bike experience is not required. A two-hour tour runs about $29 and covers the bike, helmet, water, refreshments, park entrance fee, and the guide, but don't forget to bring a camera.

DIVING &
SNORKELING
★ ☾
★
The **Curaçao Underwater Marine Park** is about 12½ mi (21 km) of untouched coral reef that has national park status. Mooring buoys mark the most interesting dive sites. **Ocean Encounters** (✉ *Lions Dive & Beach Resort, Bapor Kibra z/n, Sea Aquarium Beach* ☎ *5999/461–8131* ⊕ *www.oceanencounters.com*) is the largest dive operator on the island and also operates Toucan Diving at Kontiki Beach, which caters to walk-ins. **Sunset Divers** (✉ *Sunset Waters Beach Resort, Santa Marta Bay* ☎ *5999/864–1708* ⊕ *www.sunsetdiver.com*), the closest full-service PADI operation to the famous Mushroom Forest, offers daily one- and two-tank dives, 24-hour shore diving, and custom dives. The friendly, expert staff takes you to dive sites along the west-side reef system, which has gently sloping walls with lots of coral growth, soft and hard. Lesser known but no less spectacular sites the company often visits include Harry's Hole and Boca Hulu.

Beaches

Curaçao doesn't have long, powdery stretches of sand. Instead you'll discover the joy of inlets: tiny bays marked by craggy cliffs, exotic trees, and scads of interesting pebbles, and coral that has washed up on the beaches. **Cas Abou** is a white-sand gem with the brightest blue water in Curaçao. Divers and snorkelers will appreciate the on-site dive shop, and sunbathers can make use of the small snack bar. The restrooms and showers are immaculate. Entry is $3. You'll pay a fee ($3 per person) to enter **Sea Aquarium Beach,** but the amenities (restrooms, showers, boutiques, water-sports center, snack bar, restaurants with beach bars, thatched shelters and palm trees for shade, security patrols) on this 1,600-foot (490-m) man-made sandy beach and the calm waters protected by a carefully placed breakwater are well worth it. Two protected coves offer crystal-clear, turquoise water at **Playa Knip,** an expanse of alluring white sand, perfect for swimming and snorkeling. You can rent beach chairs and hang out under the palapas, or cool off with ice cream at the snack bar. There are restrooms here, but no showers. Best of all, there's no fee, but that means it's popular with locals and particularly crowded on Sunday.

Where to Eat

Restaurants usually add a 10% to 15% service charge.

Ⓒ **$–$$** ✕ **Mambo Beach.** Spread over the sand, this open-air bar and grill serves hearty sandwiches and burgers for lunch. Steaks, fresh seafood, and pasta fill the dinner menu. There's an excellent fish buffet on Friday. ✉ *Bapor Kibra z/n, Sea Aquarium Beach* ☎ *5999/461–8999* ▤ *MC, V.*

¢–$$ ✕ **Time Out Café.** In the shopping heartland of Punda, this outdoor spot serves up light bites like tuna sandwiches and grilled cheese, as well as heartier fare, including chicken shwarma. From Breedestraat facing Little Switzerland, take the alley to the left of the store (Kaya A. M. Prince) and walk about 20 yards, or look for the sign in Gomezplein Square and follow the arrow. ✉ *Keukenplein 8, Punda, Willemstad* ☎ *5999/524–5071* ▤ No credit cards ☉ *Closed Sun.*

DOMINICA (ROSEAU)

Roberta
Sotonoff

In the center of the Caribbean archipelago, wedged between the two French islands of Guadeloupe, to the north, and Martinique, to the south, Dominica is a wild place. So unyielding is the terrain that colonists surrendered efforts at colonization, and the last survivors of the Caribbean's original people, the Carib Indians, have made her rugged northeast their home. Dominica—just 29 mi (47 km) long and 16 mi (26 km) wide—is an English-speaking island, though family and place names are a mélange of French, English, and Carib. The capital is Roseau (pronounced rose-*oh*). If you've had enough of casinos, crowds, and swim-up bars and want to take leave of everyday life—to hike, bike, trek, spot birds and butterflies in the rain forest; explore waterfalls; discover a boiling lake; kayak, dive, snorkel, or sail in marine reserves; or go out in search of the many resident whale and dolphin species—this is the place to do it.

Essentials

CURRENCY Eastern Caribbean dollar (EC$2.70 to the US$1). U.S. currency is readily accepted, but you will get change in E.C. dollars. Most major credit cards are accepted, as are traveler's checks.

HOURS Banks are open Monday through Thursday from 8 to 2, until 5 on Friday. Most stores are open Monday from 8 to 5, until 4 Tuesday through Friday, and until 1 on Saturday. Some stores have longer hours, especially if a cruise ship is in port on a Saturday.

INTERNET You'll find two cyber cafés in Roseau. **Cornerhouse Café** (✉ *Old and King George V Sts., Roseau* ☎ *767/449–9000*). **Cyber Land Internet Café** (✉ *George St., Roseau* ✉ *Woodstone Shopping Mall, Roseau*).

TELEPHONES   The island has direct-dial international service. All pay phones are equipped for local and overseas dialing, accepting either EC coins, credit cards, or phone cards, which you can buy at many island stores and at the airports. To call Dominica from the United States, dial the area code (767) and the local access code (44), followed by the five-digit local number. On the island, dial only the seven-digit number that follows the area code.

Coming Ashore

In Roseau, most ships dock along the Bayfront. Across the street from the pier, in the Old Post Office, is a visitor information center. Taxis, minibuses, and tour operators are available at the berths. If you do decide to tour with one of them, choose one who is certified, and be explicit when discussing where you will go and how much you will pay—don't be afraid to ask questions. The drivers usually quote a fixed fare, which is regulated by the Division of Tourism and the National Taxi Association. Drivers also offer their services for tours anywhere on the island beginning at $25 to $30 an hour for up to four people; a 4- to 5-hour island tour for up to four people will cost approximately $150. You can rent a car in Roseau for about $40, not including insurance and a mandatory EC30 driving permit, but it can be difficult to find things, so you might do better on a guided tour here.

DOMINICA BEST BETS

■ **Rain Forest Trips.** Dominica has some of the Caribbean's best undeveloped rain forest. Hiking is the best way, but try to get out and see the scenery, even if you only view it from the comfort of a car.

■ **Snorkeling in Champagne.** You can snorkel near a bubbling volcanic vent near the island's southern tip that puffs steam into the sea, which makes you feel as if you are swimming in warm champagne.

■ **Whale-Watching.** If you're there in season, the island has the best whale-watching in the Caribbean.

Shore Excursions

We consider these to be among the better shore excursions for Dominica. They may not be offered by all lines, and tour names may differ as well. Times and prices are approximate.

Dominica Favorites. This excursion normally hits two very popular natural sites: Emerald Pool, in Morne Trois Pitons World Heritage Site, and Trafalgar Falls. The visit to Trafalgar Falls requires a 10-minute hike. ⏱ *5 hrs* 🎫 *$49.*

Kayak & Snorkel. Done at the southern tip of the island, the kayaking trip hits some hard-to-reach areas and allows time for snorkeling. ⏱ *3½ hrs* 🎫 *$59.*

Layou River Tubing. Travel down the Layou River by inner tube, passing unspoiled vegetation and the soaring cliffs above. Many tours also visit the Emerald Pool on the way back to the ship. ⏱ *4 ½ hrs* 🎫 *$69.*

Whale & Dolphin Watching. Dominica is one of the best whale-watching destinations in the Caribbean, so if you are there during the season and

Dominica

4

Roseau

Botanical Gardens
Independence St.
Great George St.
Old St.
Roseau River
King George V St.
J. W. Edwards Building
Post Office
Bay St.
Bath Rd.
Tropicrafts
Dominica Museum/Old Market Plaza
Fort Young

Dominica Passage

Capucin Pt.
Toucari Beach and Reef
Morne Aux Diables
Vieille Case
Hampstead
Hodges
L'Anse Tortue
Douglas Bay
Cabrits Drop-Off
Purple Beach
Calibishie
Woodford Hill Bay
Fort Shirley
Portsmouth
Indian Rd.
Bense
Indian R.
Melville Hall Airport
Marigot
Prince Rupert Bay
Picard Beach
Picard R.
ATLANTIC OCEAN
Londonderry Bay
Pt. Ronde
Morne Diablotin
Dublanc
Colihaut
Nose Reef
Brain Coral Garden
Salisbury Falls
Salisbury
Castle Bruce
Mero
Layon River
Castaways
Macoucherie River
Petit Soufrière Bay
Rosalie
Rodney's Rock
Mahaut
Pont Casse
Bout Sable Bay
Pringles Bay
Cochrane
Laudat
Trafalgar
Pt. Giraud
Canefield Airport
Woodbridge Bay
Watten Waven Rd.
La Plaine
Caribbean Sea
Roseau
see inset
Petit Savanne/Delices Rd.
Pointe Michel
Champagne
Soufrière Bay
Soufriere Marine Reserve
Scotts Head Village
Grand Bay
Scotts Head
Martinique Passage

KEY

Beaches

Cruise Ship Terminal

Dive Sites

0   4 miles
0   6 km

have the opportunity to do this excursion, take it. Most tours include a stop for snorkeling. ⊙ *4 hrs* ⊠ *$79.*

Exploring Dominica

Most of Dominica's roads are narrow and winding, so you'll need a few hours to take in the sights. Be adventurous, whether you prefer sightseeing or hiking—you'll be amply rewarded.

Numbers in the margin correspond to points of interest on the Dominica map.

❺ Cabrits National Park. The Cabrits National Park's Ft. Shirley ruins are among the most significant historic sites in the Caribbean. Just north of the town of Portsmouth, this 1,300-acre park includes a marine park and herbaceous swamps, which are an important environment for several species of rare birds and plants. At the heart of the park is the Ft. Shirley military complex. Built by the British between 1770 and 1815, it once comprised 50 major structures, including storehouses that were also quarters for 700 men. With the help of the Royal Navy (which sends sailors ashore to work on the site each time a ship is in port) and local volunteers, historian Dr. Lennox Honychurch restored the fort and its surroundings, incorporating a small museum that highlights the natural and historic aspects of the park and an open canteen-style restaurant. ⊠ *Portsmouth* ☎ *No phone* ⊠ *$2* ⊙ *Museum daily 8–4.*

★ ❹ Carib Indian Territory. In 1903, after centuries of conflict, the Caribbean's first settlers, the Kalinago (more popularly known as the Caribs), were granted a portion of land (approximately 3,700 acres) on the island's northeast coast, on which to establish a reservation with their own chief. Today it's known as Carib Territory, clinging to the northeasterly corner of Dominica, where a group of just over 3,000 Caribs live and try to maintain their cultural heritage. **Kalinago Barana Auté** (⊠ *Crayfish River* ☎ *767/445–7979* ⊕ *www.kalinagobaranaaute.com*) is Carib Territory's place to learn about Carib customs, history, and culture. A guided, 45-minute tour explores the village, stopping along the way to learn about plants, dugout canoes, basket weaving, and *kasava* bread making. The path offers wonderful viewpoints of the Atlantic and a chance to witness Isukati Falls. Admission is $8; the site is closed on Monday from October 15–April 15 and on Wednesday and Sunday the rest of the year.

❸ Emerald Pool. Quite possibly the most-visited nature attraction on the island, this emerald-green pool fed by a 50-foot waterfall is an easy trip to make. To reach this spot in the vast Morne Trois Pitons National Park, you follow a trail that starts at the side of the road near the reception center (it's an easy 20-minute walk). Along the way you can pass lookout points with views of the windward (Atlantic) coast and the forested interior. If you don't want a crowd, check whether there are cruise ships in port before going out, as this spot is popular with cruise-ship tour groups.

❷ Morne Trois Pitons National Park. A UNESCO World Heritage Site, this 17,000-acre swath of lush, mountainous land in the south-central interior (covering 9% of Dominica) is the island's crown jewel. Named after one of the highest (4,600 feet) mountains on the island, it contains the island's famous "boiling lake," majestic waterfalls, and cool mountain lakes. Access to the park is possible from most points of the compass, though the easiest approaches are via the small mountaintop villages of Laudat (pronounced low-*dah*) and Cochrane.

About 5 mi (8 km) out of Roseau, the Wotton Waven Road branches off

> ### BIBS
>
> With limited and expensive laundry facilities on ships, you may not want to spend your free time cleaning up after your child. It's convenient to bring along a pack of disposable bibs for mealtimes to keep baby's clothing cleaner and stain-free, avoiding messy garments after meals and a lot of laundry time on board the ship.

toward Sulphur Springs, where you can see the belching, sputtering, and gurgling releases of volcanic hot springs. At the base of Morne Micotrin you can find two crater lakes: the first, at 2,500 feet above sea level, is **Freshwater Lake.** According to a local legend, it's haunted by a vindictive mermaid and a monstrous serpent. Farther on is **Boeri Lake,** fringed with greenery and with purple hyacinths floating on its surface. The undisputed highlight of the park is **Boiling Lake.** Reputedly the world's largest such lake, it's a cauldron of gurgling gray-blue water, 70 yards wide and of unknown depth, with water temperatures from 180°F to 197°F. The lake is actually a flooded fumarole, a crack through which gases escape from the molten lava below. As many visitors discovered in late 2004, the "lake" can sometimes dry up, though it fills again within a few months and, shortly after that, once more starts to boil. The two- to four-hour (one-way) hike up to the lake is challenging (on a very rainy day, be prepared to slip and slide the whole way up and back). You'll need attire appropriate for a strenuous hike, and a guide is a must. Most guided trips start early (no later than 8:30 AM) for this all-day, 7-mi (11-km) round-trip trek, which passes through the Valley of Desolation and offers some opportunities for swimming in cold mountain streams along the way.

FodorśChoice
★

Just beyond the village of Trafalgar and up a short hill, there's the reception facility, where you can purchase passes to the national park and find guides to take you on a rain-forest trek to the twin **Trafalgar Falls;** the 125-foot-high waterfall is called the Father, and the wider, 95-foot-high one, the Mother. If you like a little challenge, let your guide take you up the riverbed to the cool pools at the base of the falls. Guides for this hike are available at the trailheads; still, it's best to arrange a tour before even setting out.

❶ **Roseau.** Although it's one of the smallest capitals in the Caribbean, Roseau has the highest concentration of inhabitants of any town in the Eastern Caribbean. Caribbean vernacular architecture and a bustling marketplace transport visitors back in time. Although you can walk the entire town in about an hour, you'll get a much better feel for the place on a leisurely stroll. **Lilac House,** on Kennedy Avenue, has three types of gingerbread fretwork, latticed veranda railings, and heavy hurricane shutters. The **J. W. Edwards Building,** at the corner of Old and King

George V streets, has a stone base and a wooden second-floor gallery. **The old market plaza** is the center of Roseau's historic district, which was laid out by the French on a radial plan rather than a grid, so streets such as Hanover, King George V, and Old radiate from this area. South of the marketplace is the Fort Young Hotel, built as a British fort in the 18th century; the nearby state house, public library, and Anglican cathedral are also worth a visit.

☺ The 40-acre **Botanical Gardens**, founded in 1891 as an annex of London's Kew Gardens, is a great place to relax, stroll, or watch a cricket match. In addition to the extensive collection of tropical plants and trees, there's also a parrot aviary. At the Forestry Division office, which is also on the garden grounds, you can find numerous publications on the island's flora, fauna, and national parks. The forestry officers are particularly knowledgeable on these subjects and can also recommend good hiking guides. ⊠ *Between Bath Rd. and Valley Rd.* ☎ *767/448–2401 Ext. 3417* ☜ *$2* ☉ *Mon. 8–1 and 2–5, Tues.–Fri. 8–1 and 2–4.*

The old post office now houses the **Dominica Museum.** This labor of love by local writer and historian Dr. Lennox Honychurch contains furnishings, documents, prints, and maps that date back hundreds of years; you can also find an entire Carib hut as well as Carib canoes, baskets, and other artifacts. ⊠ *Dame M. E. Charles Blvd., opposite cruise-ship berth* ☎ *767/448–8923* ☜ *$3* ☉ *Weekdays 9–4:30 and Sat. 9–1, closed Sun. except when a cruise ship is in port.*

Shopping

Dominicans produce distinctive handicrafts, with communities specializing in materials-at-hand: *vertivert* straw rugs, screwpine tableware, *larouma* basketware, and wood carvings are just some. Also notable are local herbs, spices, condiments, and herb teas.

One of the easiest places to pick up a souvenir is the Old Market Plaza. Slaves were once sold here, but today it's the scene of happier trading: key rings, magnets, dolls, baskets, handcrafted jewelry, T-shirts, spices, souvenirs, and batiks are available from a select group of entrepreneurs in open-air booths set up on the cobblestones. **Baroon International** (⊠ *Kennedy Ave., Roseau* ☎ *767/449–2888*) sells unusual jewelry from Asia, the United States, and other Caribbean islands; there are also pieces that are assembled in the store, as well as personal accessories, souvenirs, and special gifts. **Dominica Pottery** (⊠ *Bayfront St. and Kennedy Ave., Roseau* ☎ *No phone*) carries products made from various local clays and glazes. **Tropicrafts** (⊠ *Independence St. and Turkey La., Roseau* ☎ *767/ 448–2747*) has a back room where you can watch local ladies weave grass mats. You can also find arts and crafts from around the Caribbean, local wood carvings, rum, hot sauces, perfumes, and traditional Carib baskets, hats, and woven mats.

Activities

ADVENTURE PARKS The **Rainforest Aerial Tram** (⊠ *Laudat* ☎ *767/448–8775, 767/440–3266, 866/759–8726 in U.S.* ⊕ *www.rfat.com*) gives you a bird's-eye view of a pristine forest aboard an open, eight-person gondola. For 90 minutes to two hours, you slowly skim the treetop canopy while a guide provides scientific information about the flora and fauna. At the top, there is an optional walking tour, which is worth the steps. The price is $65; with transportation and lunch, $85. It's popular with cruise-ship passengers, so try to reserve ahead.

Wacky Rollers (✉ *Front St., Roseau* ⌂ *Box 900, Roseau* ☎ *767/440–4386* ⊕ *www.wackyrollers.com*) will make you feel as if you are training for the Marines as you swing on a Tarzan-style rope and grab on to a vertical rope ladder, rappel across zip lines and traverse suspended log bridges, a net bridge, and four monkey bridges (rope loops). It costs $60 and should take from 1½ to 3½ hours to conquer the 28 "games." There is also an abbreviated kids' course. Wacky Rollers also organizes adventure tours around the island. Although the office is in Roseau, the park itself is in Hillsborough Estate, about 20 to 25 minutes north of Roseau.

DIVING &
SNORKELING
Dominica's dive sites are awesome. The best are those in the southwest—within and around **Soufrière/Scotts Head Marine Reserve.** This bay is the site of a submerged volcanic crater. Within a ½ mi (1 km) of the shore, there are vertical drops of 800 feet (240 m) to more than 1,500 feet (450 m), with visibility frequently extending to 100 feet (30 m). Shoals of boga fish, creole wrasse, and blue cromis are common, and you might even see a spotted moray eel or a honeycomb cowfish. Crinoids (rare elsewhere) are also abundant here, as are giant barrel sponges. The going rate is about $65–$85 for a two-tank dive. All scuba-diving operators also offer snorkeling; equipment rents for $10 to $20 a day; trips with gear begin at about $15. The **Anchorage Dive & Whale Watch Center** (✉ *Anchorage Hotel, Castle Comfort* ☎ *767/448–2638* ⊕ *www.anchoragehotel. dm*) has two dive boats that can take you out day or night. It also offers PADI instruction (all skill levels), snorkeling and whale-watching trips, and shore diving. One of the island's first dive operations, it offers many of the same trips as Dive Dominica. **Dive Dominica** (✉ *Castle Comfort Lodge, Castle Comfort* ☎ *767/448—2188 or 888/414-7626* ⊕ *www.divedominica.com*), one of the island's dive pioneers, conducts NAUI, PADI, and SSI courses as well as Nitrox certification. With four boats, it offers diving, snorkeling, and whale-watching trips and packages including accommodation at the Castle Comfort Lodge. Its trips are similar to Anchorage's.

HIKING
The island is crisscrossed by ancient footpaths of the Arawak and Carib Indians and the Nègres Maroons, escaped slaves who established camps in the mountains. Existing trails range from easygoing to arduous. To make the most of your excursion, you'll need sturdy hiking boots, insect repellent, a change of clothes (kept dry), and a guide. Hikes and tours run $25 to $50 per person, depending on destinations and duration. Some of the natural attractions within the island's national parks require visitors to purchase a site pass. These are sold for varying numbers of visits. A single-entry site pass costs $2, a day pass $5, and a week pass $10. Local bird and forestry expert **Bertrand Jno Baptiste** (☎ *767/446–6358*) leads hikes up Morne Diablotin and along the Syndicate Nature Trail; if he's not available, ask him to recommend another guide. Hiking guides can be arranged through the **National Development Corporation** (NDC or Dominica Tourist Office) (✉ *Valley Rd., Roseau* ☎ *767/448–2045* ⊕ *www.dominica.dm*).

Beaches

★ On the west coast, just south of the village of Pointe Michel, **Champagne,** a stony beach, is one of the island's best spots for swimming, snorkeling, and diving. It gets its name from volcanic vents that constantly puff steam into the sea, which makes you feel as if you are swimming in warm champagne. **Pointe Baptiste.** Extravagantly shaped, red-sandstone boulders surround this beautiful golden-sand beach. Access is a 15-minute walk, entering through private property, so the beach is quiet and unpopulated. Come here to relax, tan, take dips in the ocean, and climb these incredible rock formations. There are no facilities, but this is one of the nicest beaches on the island. It's near the Pointe Baptiste Guest House. ⊠ *Calibishie.*

Where to Eat

There is a 5% sales tax added to all bills. Some restaurants include a 10% service charge in the final tab; otherwise tip 10% for good service.

¢ ✕ **Cornerhouse Café.** Just off the Old Market Plaza in a historic, three-story stone-and-wood town house, this is Dominica's only true Internet café. An eclectic menu of meals and other treats is on offer to sustain you during your surfing: bagels with an assortment of toppings, delicious soups, fish, sandwiches, salads, cakes, and coffee. Computers are rented by the half hour; relax on soft chairs and flip through books and magazines while you wait. ⊠ *Old and King George V Sts., Roseau* ☎ *767/449-9000* ⊕ *www.avirtualdominica.com/cornerhouse* ⊟ *No credit cards* ⊘ *Closed Sun.*

$–$$$$ ✕ **Guiyave.** This popular restaurant in a quaint Caribbean town house also has a shop downstairs serving a scrumptious selection of sweet and savory pastries, tarts, and cakes. These can also be ordered upstairs, along with more elaborate fare such as garlic shrimp and spicy crab backs, when in season. Choose to dine either in the airy dining room or on the sunny, narrow balcony perched above Roseau's colorful streets—the perfect spot to indulge in one of the fresh-squeezed tropical juices. ⊠ *15 Cork St., Roseau* ☎ *767/448-2930* ⊟ *AE, D, MC, V* ⊘ *Closed Tues. and Wed.*

FREEPORT-LUCAYA, BAHAMAS

Chelle Koster
Walton

Grand Bahama Island, the fourth-largest island in the Bahamas, lies only 52 mi (84 km) off Palm Beach, Florida. In 1492, when Columbus first set foot in the Bahamas, Grand Bahama was already populated. Skulls found in caves attest to the existence of the peaceable Lucayans, who were constantly fleeing the more bellicose Caribs. But it was not until the 1950s, when the harvesting of Caribbean yellow pine trees (now protected by Bahamian environmental law) was the island's major industry, that American financier Wallace Groves envisioned Grand Bahama's grandiose future as a tax-free port for the shipment of goods to the United States. It was in that era that the city of Freeport and later Lucaya evolved. They are separated by a 4-mi (6-km) stretch of East Sunrise Highway, although few can tell you where one community ends and the other begins. Most of Grand Bahama's commercial activity is concentrated in

Freeport, the Bahamas' second-largest city. Lucaya, with its sprawling shopping complex and water-sports reputation, stepped up to the role of island tourism capital. Resorts, beaches, a casino, and golf courses make both cities popular with visitors.

Essentials

CURRENCY   The Bahamian dollar, which trades one-to-one with the U.S. dollar, which is universally accepted. There's no need to acquire any Bahamian currency.

HOURS   Banks are generally open Monday–Thursday 9:30 to 3 and Friday 9:30 to 4:30. Hours for attractions vary; most open by 9 or 10 and close by 5. Most shops are open from 10 to 6.

INTERNET   Port Lucaya Marina has free Wi-Fi service if you have your own laptop.

TELEPHONES   Calling locally or internationally is easy in the Bahamas. To place a local call, dial the seven-digit phone number. To call the United States, dial 1 plus the area code. Pay phones cost 25¢ per call; Bahamian and U.S. quarters are accepted, as are BATELCO phone cards. To place a call using a calling card, use your long-distance carrier's access code or dial 0 for the operator. Be aware that when placing a toll-free call from your hotel, you are charged as if for a regular long-distance call.

Coming Ashore

Cruise-ship passengers arrive at Lucayan Harbour, which has a clever Bahamian-style look, extensive cruise-passenger terminal facilities, and an entertainment-shopping village. The harbor lies about 10 minutes west of Freeport. Taxis and limos meet all cruise ships. Two passengers are charged $16 and $24 for trips to Freeport and Lucaya, respectively. Fare to Xanadu Beach is $17; it's $24 to Taino Beach. The price per person drops with larger groups. It's customary to tip taxi drivers 15%. A three-hour sightseeing tour of the Freeport-Lucaya area costs $25 to $35. Four-hour West End trips cost about $40.

Grand Bahama's flat terrain and straight, well-paved roads make for good scooter riding. Rentals run $35 a day (about $15 an hour). Helmets are required and provided. Look for small rental stands in parking lots and along the road in Freeport and Lucaya and at the larger resorts. It's usually cheaper to rent a car than to hire a taxi. Automobiles, jeeps, and vans can be rented at the Grand Bahama International Airport. Some agencies provide free pickup and delivery service to the cruise-ship port and Freeport and Lucaya, but prices are still not cheap; cars begin at $50 per day, but insurance of up to $17 per day is also required by law.

FREEPORT-LUCAYA BEST BETS

- **Diving with UNEXSO.** Simply one of the world's most respected diving facilities.

- **Lucayan National Park.** The highest peak in the Virgin Islands has breathtaking views and is a great hiking destination.

- **Shopping.** Duty-free shopping in the Port Lucaya Marketplace is still good; be sure to haggle if you shop at the straw markets.

Freeport-Lucaya, Bahamas

Bahamas National Trust
Rand Nature Centre **3**
The Dolphin Experience **6**
International Bazaar **1**
Lucayan National Park **7**

Perfume Factory **2**
Port Lucaya Marketplace **4**
Underwater Explorers
Society (UNEXSO) **5**

KEY
↗ Beaches
▬ Cruise Ship Terminal
◪ Dive Sites

Shore Excursions

We consider these to be among the better shore excursions for Freeport-Lucaya. They may not be offered by all lines, and tour names may differ as well. Times and prices are approximate.

Jeep safari. Part of this trip goes off-road to explore the island's interior, but there's always time for a stop by the beach. ☉ *5½ hrs* ⌦ *$89.*

> ### PLASTIC BAGS
>
> Use Ziploc bags for all toiletries and anything that might spill. Toss a few extras into your suitcase. You may need them later to pack dirty or damp clothes.

Kayaking Tour. A kayaking trip in Lucayan National Park is combined with a stop for lunch and swimming on a nice beach. ☉ *6 hrs* ⌦ *$83–$89.*

Snorkeling Tour. Board a 72-foot catamaran with a slide and rock-climbing wall and sail to Lucaya Beach, where you anchor near an offshore reef and snorkel among the colorful fish. Refreshments and (sometimes) lunch are served on the return sail to the dock; if lunch is included, the cost may be higher. ☉ *3 hrs* ⌦ *$40.*

Exploring Freeport-Lucaya

Numbers in the margin correspond to points of interest on the Freeport-Lucaya map.

Grand Bahama is the only planned island in the Bahamas. Its towns, villages, and sights are well laid out but far apart. Downtown Freeport and Lucaya are both best appreciated on foot. Buses and taxis can transport you the 4-mi (6-km) distance between the two. In Freeport, shopping is the main attraction. Bolstered by the Westin & Sheraton Grand Bahama Island resort complex, Lucaya has its beautiful beach and water-sports scene, plus more shopping and a big, beautiful new casino. Outside of town, isolated fishing villages, beaches, natural attractions, and the once-rowdy town of West End make it worthwhile to hire a tour or rent a car. The island stretches 96 mi (154 km) from one end to the other. The island is still recovering from hurricanes in 2004 and 2005.

EXPLORING FREEPORT **❸** **Bahamas National Trust Rand Nature Centre.** On 100 acres just minutes from downtown Freeport, ½ mi (1 km) of self-guided botanical trails shows off 130 types of native plants, including many orchid species. The center is the island's birding hot spot, where you might spy a red-tailed hawk or a Cuban emerald hummingbird sipping hibiscus nectar. The center's flamingo flock was killed off by raccoons and is in the process of being replaced. The new visitors center hosts changing local art exhibits and some resident live animals such as the Bahama boa. Outside, you can visit a caged one-eyed Bahama parrot the center has adopted. The reserve is named for philanthropist James H. Rand, the former president of Remington Rand, who donated a hospital and library to the island. ✉ *E. Settlers Way, Freeport* ☎ *242/352–5438* ⌦ *$5* ☉ *Weekdays 9–4.*

❶ **International Bazaar.** The effect of recent hurricanes on the now-closed Royal Oasis Resort & Casino results in a down-at-the-heels look for this once-vibrant shopping arena. Some restaurants and shops remain open, along with the straw market. At the entrance stands a 35-foot *torii* arch, a red-lacquered gate that is a traditional symbol of welcome in Japan. ✉ *W. Sunrise Hwy. and Mall Dr.* ☎ *242/352–2828* 🎟 *Free* ☉ *Mon.–Sat. 10–6.*

★ ❷ **Perfume Factory.** The quiet and elegant Perfume Factory is in a replica 19th-century Bahamian mansion— the kind built by Loyalists who settled in the Bahamas after the

> **HANGERS**
>
> Folding or inflatable travel hangers are useful if you need to dry out hand laundry or a bathing suit in your cabin. The ones in your cabin's closet may not be removable.

American Revolution. The interior resembles a tasteful drawing room. This is the home of Fragrance of the Bahamas, a company that produces perfumes, colognes, and lotions using the scents of jasmine, cinnamon, gardenia, spice, and ginger. Take a free five-minute tour of the mixology laboratory. For $30 an ounce, you can blend your own perfume using any of the 35 scents ($15 for 1.5 ounces of blend-it-yourself body lotion). Sniff mixtures until they hit the right combination, then bottle, name, and take home the personalized potion. ✉ *Behind International Bazaar, on access rd.* ☎ *242/352–9391* ⊕ *www.perfumefactory.com* 🎟 *Free* ☉ *Weekdays 9–5, Sat. 11–3.*

EXPLORING Lucaya, on Grand Bahama's southern coast and just east of Freeport, LUCAYA was developed as the island's resort center. These days, it's booming with the megaresort complex called the Westin & Sheraton Grand Bahama Island resort, a fine sandy beach, championship golf courses, a casino, a first-class dive operation, and Port Lucaya's shopping and marina facilities.

❻ **The Dolphin Experience.** Encounter Atlantic bottle-nosed dolphins in Sanc-
Fodor'sChoice tuary Bay at one of the world's first and largest dolphin facilities,
★ about 2 mi (3 km) east of Port Lucaya. A ferry takes you from Port Lucaya to the bay to observe and photograph the animals. If you don't mind getting wet, you can sit on a partially submerged dock or stand waist deep in the water, and one of these friendly creatures will swim up and touch you. You can also engage in one of two swim-with-the-dolphins programs (children must be 55 inches or taller). The Dolphin Experience began in 1987, when it trained five dolphins to interact with people. Later, the animals learned to head out to sea and swim with scuba divers on the open reef. A two-hour dive program is available. Buy tickets for The Dolphin Experience at the Underwater Explorers Society (UNEXSO) in Port Lucaya. Make reservations as early as possible. ✉ *The Dolphin Experience, Port Lucaya* ☎ *242/373–1244 or 800/992–3483* 🖷 *242/373–8956* ⊕ *www.unexso.com* 🎟 *2-hr interaction program $75, 2-hr swim program $169, dolphin dive $159, open-ocean experience $199* ☉ *Daily 9–5.*

★ ❹ **Port Lucaya Marketplace.** Lucaya's capacious and lively shopping complex—a dozen low-rise, pastel-painted colonial buildings whose style was influenced by traditional island homes—is on the waterfront 4 mi (6 km) east of Freeport and across the street from a massive resort compound. The shopping center, whose walkways are lined with hibiscus, bougainvillea, and croton, has about 100 well-kept establishments, among them waterfront restaurants and bars, and shops that sell clothes, crystal and china, watches, jewelry, perfumes, and local arts and crafts. A straw market embraces the complex at both ends. ⊠ *Sea Horse Rd., Port Lucaya* ☎ *242/373–8446* ⊕ *www.portlucaya.com* ⊘ *Mon.–Sat. 10–6.*

⑤ Underwater Explorers Society (UNEXSO). One of the world's most respected diving facilities, UNEXSO welcomes more than 50,000 individuals each year and trains hundreds of them in scuba diving. Their newest program, Mini-B Shallow Water Scuba Diving, uses a lightweight and compact scuba kit for three levels of short training and dive sessions. UNEXSO's facilities include an 18-foot-deep training pool with windows that look out on the harbor, changing rooms and showers, docks, equipment rental, and an air-tank filling station. ⊠ *On the wharf at Port Lucaya MarketPl.* ☎ *242/373–1244 or 800/992–3483* ⊕ *www.unexso. com* ⊠ *Resort dives $85, dives from $35, dolphin dives $159, shark dives $89* ⊘ *Daily 8–5.*

FodorśChoice ★

BEYOND FREEPORT-LUCAYA

Grand Bahama Island narrows at picturesque West End, once Grand Bahama's capital and still home to descendants of the island's first settlers. Seaside villages, with concrete block houses painted in bright blue and pastel yellow, fill in the landscape between Freeport and West End. The East End is Grand Bahama's "back-to-nature" side. The road east from Lucaya is long, flat, and mostly straight. It cuts through a vast pine forest to reach McLean's Town, the end of the road.

⑦ Lucayan National Park. In this 40-acre seaside land preserve, trails and elevated walkways wind through a natural forest of wild tamarind and gumbo-limbo trees, past an observation platform, a mangrove swamp, sheltered pools containing rare marine species, and what is believed to be the largest explored underwater cave system in the world (7 mi long). You can enter the caves at two access points. One is closed during bat nursing season (June and July). Just 20 mi (32 km) east of Lucaya, the park contains examples of the island's five ecosystems: beach, sandy or whiteland coppice (hardwood forest), mangroves, rocky coppice, and pine forest. Across the road, trails and boardwalks lead through pine forest and mangrove swamp to Gold Rock Beach, a beautiful, lightly populated strand of white sand, aquamarine sea, and coral reef. Signs along the trail detail the park's distinctive features. ⊠ *Grand Bahama Hwy.* ☎ *242/352–5438* ⊠ *$3 (tickets must be purchased in advance at Rand Nature Centre)* ⊘ *Daily 8:30–4:30.*

FodorśChoice ★

Shopping
In the stores, shops, and boutiques in Freeport's International Bazaar and at the Port Lucaya Marketplace, you can find duty-free goods costing up to 40% less than what you might pay back home. At the numerous perfume shops, fragrances are often sold at a sweet-smelling 25% below U.S. prices. Be sure to limit your haggling to the straw markets.

Activities
FISHING Fishing charters for up to four people cost $250 to $500 for a half-day and $350 and up for a full-day trip; many fishing outfitters charge by the person—often about $100. In deep waters, anglers pull up dolphin-

fish, kingfish, or wahoo. Along the flats, the elusive bonefish is the catch of fishing aficionados. **Reef Tours Ltd.** (⊠ *Port Lucaya Market Pl.* ☎ *242/373–5880*) offers sportfishing for four to six people on custom boats. Equipment and bait are provided free.

GOLF Because Grand Bahama is such a large island, it can afford long fairways puddled with lots of water and fraught with challenge. Two championship golf courses at the Westin & Sheraton and one 9-hole course keep duffers busy. **Fortune Hills Golf & Country Club** (⊠ *E. Sunrise Hwy., Lucaya* ☎ *242/373–2222*) is a 3,453-yard, 9-hole, par-36 course designed by Dick Wilson and Joe Lee. **Lucayan Course** (⊠ *The Westin & Sheraton Grand Bahama Island Resort, Lucaya* ☎ *242/373–1066, 242/373–1333*)—6,824 yards, par 72—is a dramatic 18-hole course. The course features tree-lined holes and fast, well-bunkered greens. The 18th hole has a double lake, and a new clubhouse is being built nearby. The property is home to the Jim McLean School of Golf, the school's first international location. The state-of-the-art instruction facilities include a practice putting green with bunker and chipping areas, covered teaching bays, and a teaching seminar area. **Reef Course** (⊠ *Westin & Sheraton Grand Bahama Island Resort, Lucaya* ☎ *242/373–2002*), a 6,930-yard, par-72 course, was designed by Robert Trent Jones Jr. It has lots of water, wide fairways flanked by strategically placed bunkers, and a tricky dog-leg left on the 18th hole.

HORSEBACK
RIDING **Pinetree Stables** (⊠ *Beachway Dr., Freeport* ☎ *242/373–3600*) runs trail and beach rides twice-daily for $75; it's closed on Monday. All two-hour trail rides are accompanied by an experienced guide. Rides for expert equestrians are also available. Reservations are essential.

Beaches

Some 60 miles of magnificent, pristine stretches of sand extend between Freeport-Lucaya and the island's eastern end. Most are used only by people who live in adjacent settlements. The beaches have no public facilities, so beachgoers often headquarter at one of the local beach bars, which often provide free transportation. **Lucayan Beach** is readily accessible from the town's main drag and is always lively and lovely. **Taíno Beach**, near Freeport, is fun for families, water-sports enthusiasts, and partyers. Near Freeport, **Xanadu Beach** provides a mile of white sand.

Where to Eat

¢–$ ✕ **Becky's Restaurant & Lounge.** This popular eatery opens at 7 AM and may be the best place in town to fuel up before a full day of gambling or shopping. Its diner-style booths provide a comfortable backdrop for the inexpensive menu of traditional Bahamian and American food, from conch salad and curried mutton to seafood or a BLT. Pancakes, eggs, and special Bahamian breakfasts—"stew" fish, "boil" fish, or chicken souse (the latter two are both lime-seasoned soups), with johnnycake or grits—are served all day. ⊠ *E. Beach Dr. and E. Sunrise Hwy., Freeport* ☎ *242/352–5247* ▭ *D, MC, V.*

¢–$$ ✕ **Pub at Lucaya.** On the Port Lucaya waterfront, this amiable pub has a reputation for dependable English fare, such as bangers 'n' mash and shepherd's and steak-and-ale pies. You also can't go wrong with the frenched lamb chops, Bahamian lobster tail, or strip sirloin. Lunchtime brings burgers, pasta, and deli sandwiches. The nautical decor incorporates antiques, heavy rustic tables, and ersatz Tiffany lamps suspended from a wood-beam ceiling. Ask for a table on the outside terrace. ✉ *Port Lucaya MarketPl.* ☎ *242/373–8450* ▱ *AE, DC, MC, V.*

GRAND CAYMAN, CAYMAN ISLANDS

Marvette Darien

The largest and most populous of the Cayman Islands, Grand Cayman is also one of the most popular cruise destinations in the Western Caribbean, largely because it doesn't suffer from the ailments afflicting many larger ports: panhandlers, hasslers, and crime. Instead, the Cayman economy is a study in stability and the environment is healthy and prosperous. Though the island is rather featureless, Grand Cayman is a diver's paradise, with pristine waters and a colorful variety of marine life. Compared with other Caribbean ports, there are few things to see on land here; instead, the island's most impressive sights are underwater. Snorkeling, diving, and glass-bottom boat and submarine rides top every ship's shore-excursion list and can also be arranged at major aquatic shops if you don't go on a ship-sponsored excursion. Grand Cayman is also famous for the 554 offshore banks in George Town; not surprisingly, the standard of living is high, and nothing is cheap.

Essentials

CURRENCY The Cayman Island dollar (CI$1 to US$1.25). The U.S. dollar is accepted everywhere, and ATMs often dispense cash in both currencies, though you may receive change in Cayman dollars. Prices are often quoted in Cayman dollars, so make sure you know which currency you're dealing with so you don't end up paying 25% more than you expected.

HOURS Banks are open Monday through Friday from 9 to 4. Post offices are open weekdays from 8:30 to 3:30 and Saturday from 9:00 to 12:30. Shops are open weekdays from 9 to 5 and Saturday in George Town from 10 to 2.

INTERNET **Caybiz** (✉ *The Village, 7 Dr. Roy's Dr., George Town*) is an Internet café within walking distance of the cruise-ship pier.

TELEPHONES To dial the United States, dial 1 followed by the area code and telephone number. To place a credit-card call, dial 1–800/744–7777; credit-card and calling-card calls can be made from any public phone.

Coming Ashore

Ships anchor in George Town Harbour and tender passengers onto Harbour Drive, the center of the shopping district. If you just want to walk around town and shop or visit Seven Mile Beach, you're probably better off on your own, but the Stingray Sandbar snorkeling trip is a highlight of many Caribbean vacations and fills up quickly on cruise-ship days, so it's often better to order that excursion from your ship even though it will be more crowded than if you took an independent trip.

A tourist information booth is on the pier, as is the taxis queue for disembarking passengers. Taxi fares are determined by an elaborate structure set by the government, and although rates may seem high, cabbies rarely try to rip off tourists. Ask to see the chart if you want to check a quoted fare. Taxi drivers won't usually do hourly rates for small-group tours; you must arrange a sightseeing tour with a company. Car rentals are not terribly expensive, beginning at about $50 a day (plus a $7.50 driving permit), so they are a good option if you want to do some independent exploring. You can easily see the entire island and have time to stop at a beach in a single day.

Shore Excursions

We consider these to be among the better shore excursions for Grand Cayman. They may not be offered by all lines, and tour names may differ as well. Times and prices are approximate.

Atlantis Submarine. Your real submarine dives beneath the waters off Grand Cayman to reveal marine life and an underwater vista usually only visible to scuba divers. ⊘ 2 hrs ⊠ $94.

Reef and Wreck Snorkel. Trips will show you several good snorkeling sites, including the wreck of the *Cali.* ⊘ 2 hrs ⊠ $44.

***Seaworld Explorer* Cruise.** A semi-submersible boat with seating five feet below the water's surface takes you on an air-conditioned, narrated voyage around George Town Harbour to view sunken ships, tropical fish, and coral reefs. Some ships offer a longer (and more expensive) tour that involves snorkeling. ⊘ 1 hr ⊠ $37.

Stingray City Snorkel Tour. A boat brings you offshore to a shallow sandbar inside the North Sound reef where guides feed the waiting stingrays as you swim and play with the gentle creatures; you follow up with a snorkeling stop. This is by far the most popular water excursion for non-divers, and while the area is overrun for most of these cruise-ship visits, it's still a thrilling experience. ⊘ 3 hrs ⊠ $45; *an additional land tour increases price to $69.*

Exploring Grand Cayman

Numbers in the margin correspond to points of interest on the Grand Cayman map.

❼ Blowholes. When the trade winds blow hard, crashing waves force water into caverns and send geysers shooting up through the ironshore. The blowholes were partially filled during Hurricane Ivan in 2004, so the water has to be pretty rough before they are as dramatic as they once were. ⊠ *Frank Sound Rd., near East End.*

❷ Boatswain's Beach. What was Cayman's premier attraction, the Turtle Farm, has been transformed into a marine theme park and rebranded as Boatswain's Beach. The expanded complex now has several shops for souvenirs, jewelry, and cigars as well as restaurants, a nature trail, butterfly garden, and small zoo. A snorkel lagoon provides the adven-

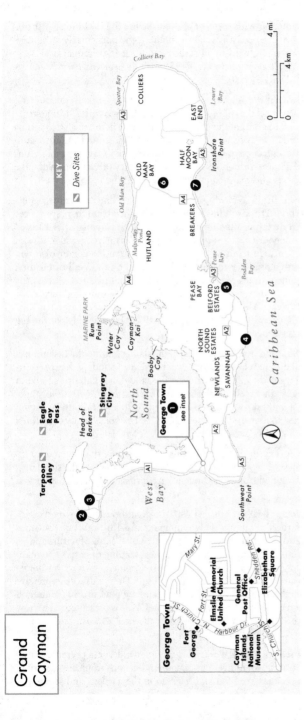

Grand Cayman

KEY

Dive Sites

George Town

ture of swimming with some of the marine life that are found just off-shore the Cayman coastline. Unfortunately, the particularly steep new admission price may give you some serious second thoughts. ⊠ *West Bay Rd., West Bay* ☎ *345/949–3893* ⊕ *www.boatswainsbeach.ky* ⬚ *$60* ⊙ *Daily 8–4:30.*

❺ Bodden Town. In the island's original south-shore capital you can find an old cemetery on the shore side of the road. Graves with A-frame structures are said to contain the remains of pirates. There are also the ruins of a fort and a wall erected by slaves in the 19th century. A curio shop serves as the entrance to what's called the Pirate's Caves, partially underground natural formations that are more hokey (decked out with fake treasure chests and mannequins in pirate garb) than spooky.

❶ George Town. Begin exploring the capital by strolling along the waterfront, Harbour Drive to **Elmslie Memorial United Church,** named after the first Presbyterian missionary to serve in the Caymans. Its vaulted ceiling, wooden arches, and sedate nave reflect the religious nature of island residents. In front of the court building, in the center of town, names of influential Caymanians are inscribed on the **Wall of History,** which commemorates the islands' quincentennial in 2003. Across the street is the Cayman Islands Legislative Assembly Building, next door to the 1919 Peace Memorial Building. In the middle of the financial district is the **General Post Office,** built in 1939. Let the kids pet the big blue iguana statues.

☾ Built in 1833, the home of the **Cayman Islands National Museum** has had several different incarnations over the years, including that of courthouse, jail (now the gift shop), post office, and dance hall. It's small but fascinating, with excellent displays and videos that illustrate local geology, flora and fauna, and island history. At this writing, the museum was expected to reopen sometime in 2007. ⊠ *Harbour Dr., George Town* ☎ *345/949–8368* ⬚ *$5* ⊙ *Weekdays 9–5, Sat. 10–2.*

❸ Hell. The touristy stopover in West Bay is little more than a patch of incredibly jagged black rock formations. The attractions are the small post office and a gift shop, where you can get cards and letters postmarked from Hell.

☾ **❹ Pedro St. James Castle.** Built in 1780, the great house is Cayman's oldest stone structure and the only remaining late-18th-century residence on the island. The buildings are surrounded by 8 acres of natural parks and woodlands. You can stroll through landscaping of native Caymanian flora and experience one of the most spectacular views on the island from atop the dramatic Great Pedro Bluff. Don't miss the impressive multimedia theater show complete with smoking pots, misting rains, and two film screens where the story of Pedro's Castle is presented. The show plays on the hour; see it before you tour the site. ⊠ *Savannah* ☎ *345/947–3329* ⬚ *$8* ⊙ *Daily 8:30–5.*

❻ Queen Elizabeth II Botanic Park. This 65-acre wilderness preserve showcases a wide range of indigenous and nonindigenous tropical vegetation. Rare blue iguanas are bred and released in the gardens and seen regularly. If you're lucky, you'll see the brilliant green Cayman parrot—not just here but virtually anywhere in Cayman. ⊠ *Frank Sound Rd., Frank Sound* ☏ *345/947–9462, 345/947–3558 info line* ✉ *$3* ⊗ *Daily 9–6:30; last admission at 5:30.*

Shopping

The **Anchorage Centre** across from the cruise-ship North Terminal has 10 of the most affordable stores and boutiques selling duty-free goods from such great brand names as John Hardy, Movado, and Concord,

as well as designer ammolite jewelry. Downtown is the **Kirk Freeport Plaza,** known for its boutiques selling fine watches, duty-free china, Gucci goods, perfumes, and cosmetics. Just keep walking—there's plenty of shopping in all directions. Stores in the **Landmark** sell perfumes, treasure coins, and upscale beachwear; Breezes by the Bay restaurant is upstairs.

★ The **Camera Store** (⊠ *Waterfront Centre, N. Church St., George Town* ☏ *345/949–4551*) has friendly and knowledgeable service, lots of duty-free digital cameras, accessories, and fast photo printing from self-serv-
★ ice kiosks. **Cathy Church's Underwater Photo Centre & Gallery** (⊠ *S. Church St., George Town* ☏ *345/949–7415*) has a collection of Cathy's spectacular color and limited-edition black-and-white underwater photos. Framed prints are shipped to the United States at no extra charge. Have her autograph her latest coffee-table book. One of many local artists,
★ Horacio Esteban, from Cayman Brac, sculpts Caymanite at **Esteban Gallery** (⊠ *AALL Trust Bank Bldg., ground floor, Waterfront, George Town* ☏ *345/946–2787*). His work is beautiful, uniquely Cayman, and
★ worth a look. The **Heritage Crafts Shop** (⊠ *Harbour Dr., George Town* ☏ *345/945–6041*), near the harbor, sells local crafts and gifts. **Pure Art** (⊠ *S. Church St., George Town* ☏ *345/949–9133*) sells watercolors, wood carvings, lacework, and much more by local artists. It is about 1½ mi (2½ km) south of George Town. This is a great place to browse even if you aren't planning a purchase.

Activities

DIVING & SNORKELING Pristine water (visibility often exceeding 100 feet [30 m]), breathtaking coral formations, and plentiful and exotic marine life mark the **Great Wall**—a world-renowned dive site just off the north side of Grand Cayman. A must-see for adventurous souls is **Stingray City** in the North Sound, noted as the best 12-foot (3½-m) dive in the world, where dozens of stingrays congregate, tame enough to suction squid from your outstretched palm. Nondivers gravitate to **Stingray Sandbar,** a shallower part of the North Sound, which has become a popular snorkeling spot; it is also a popular spot for the stingrays. **Don Foster's Dive Cayman Islands** (⊠ *218 S. Church St., George Town* ☏ *345/949–5679 or 800/833–4837* ⊕ *www.donfosters.com*) has a pool with a shower and also snorkeling along the ironshore. The shore diving includes a few interesting swimthroughs, or you can book a boat dive. **Eden Rock Diving Center** (✉ *124 S. Church St., George Town* ☎ *345/949–7243* ⊕ *www.edenrockdive. com*), south of George Town, provides easy access to Eden Rock and Devil's Grotto. It has full equipment rental, lockers, and shower facilities. **Red Sail Sports** (☎ *345/949–8745 or 877/733–7245* ⊕ *www. redsailcayman.com*) offers daily trips from most of the major hotels. Dives are often run as guided tours, a perfect option for beginners. If you're experienced and if your air lasts a long time, discuss this with the boat captain to see if he requires that you come up with the group as determined by the first person who runs low on air. There is a full range of kids' dive options for ages 5 to 15. The company also operates dinner and sunset sails.

FISHING   Cayman waters are abundant with blue and white marlin, yellowfin tuna, sailfish, dolphinfish, bonefish, and wahoo. Two dozen boats are available for charter. **Sea Star Charters** (☎ *345/949–1016, 345/916–5234 after 8 AM*) is run by Clinton Ebanks, a fine and very friendly Caymanian, who will do whatever it takes to make sure that you have a wonderful time on his small, 28-foot cabin cruiser, enjoying light-tackle, bone-, and bottom-fishing. He's a good choice for beginners and offers a nice cultural experience, as well as sailing charters. Only cash and traveler's checks are accepted.

HIKING   The National Trust's **Mastic Trail** (✉ *Frank Sound Rd., entrance by fire station at botanic park, Breakers* ☎ *345/949–0121 for guide reservations*) is a rugged 2-mi (3-km) slash through woodlands, mangrove swamps, and ancient rock formations. In the 1800s this woodland trail was used as a direct path to and from the North Side. A comfortable walk depends on weather, winter being better because it is drier. Call the National Trust to determine suitability and to book a guide for $45; tours are run daily from 9 to 5 by appointment only. Or walk on your own with a $5 guidebook. The trip takes about three hours.

Beaches

The west coast, the island's most developed area, is where you'll find the famous **Seven Mile Beach.** This white, powdery, 5½-mi-long (9-km-long) strand is Grand Cayman's busiest vacation center, and most of the island's resorts, restaurants, and shopping centers are along this strip. At the public beach toward the north end you can find chairs for rent ($10 for the day, including a beverage) and plenty of water toys, two beach bars, restrooms, and showers.

Where to Eat

Many restaurants add a 10% to 15% service charge. If a service charge is not added, tip 15% of the total bill.

$–$$$ ✕ **Breezes by the Bay.** This cheerful restaurant overlooks the busy George Town harbor from across Harbor Drive, so go to the second floor to avoid traffic noise. Prices are a bargain, especially for peel-and-eat shrimp. The desserts are huge. The bar mixes great specialty drinks. Inside is no-smoking. ✉*Harbor Dr., George Town* ☎*345/943–8469* ▭*AE, MC, V.*

★ ¢–$$ ✕ **Full of Beans Cafe.** If you want freshly squeezed juices, homegrown herbs, lots of vegetarian options, low prices, and three meals a day, seek out this strip-mall café. You can get takeout, delivery, and even catering if you're planning a party. A surprisingly large, eclectic menu includes everything from fresh banana bread and mango smoothies to cranberry-Brie salad, a Thai chicken wrap, and steak au poivre, not to mention choice salads. Plus you get to feast your eyes on the interesting collection of art, some from local artists, that adorns the walls. ⊠ *Pasadora Place, Smith Rd., George Town* ☎ *345/943–2326* ▭ *No credit cards* ⊘ *Closed Sun.*

GRAND TURK, TURKS & CAICOS ISLANDS

Ramona Settle   Just 7 mi (11 km) long and a little over 1 mi (2½ km) wide, Grand Turk, the political capital of the Turks & Caicos Islands, has been a longtime favorite destination for divers eager to explore the 7,000-foot-deep pristine coral walls that drop down only 300 yards out to sea. On shore, the tiny, quiet island is home to white-sand beaches, the National Museum, and a small population of wild horses and donkeys, which leisurely meander past the white-walled courtyards, pretty churches, and bougainvillea-covered colonial inns on their daily commute into town. The main settlement on the island is tranquil Cockburn Town, and that's where most of the small hotels, not to mention Pillory Beach, can be found. Although it has the second-largest number of inhabitants of all the Turks & Caicos Islands, Grand Turk's permanent population has still not reached 4,000. Grand Turk is new to the cruise-ship scene, welcoming its first ships in 2006, but estimates place the number of likely cruise-ship visitors at 300,000 in relatively short order.

Essentials

CURRENCY   The U.S. dollar. You'll find branches of Scotiabank and FirstCaribbean on Grand Turk, with ATMs; all of these are in tiny Cockburn Town.

HOURS   Banks are open Monday through Thursday from 9 to 3, Friday 9 to 5. Post offices are open weekdays from 8 to 4. Shops are generally open weekdays from 8 or 8:30 to 5.

INTERNET   There's no Internet café at the cruise center, but if you have a laptop, you might take it to the restaurant at the Osprey Beach Hotel, where you can take advantage of the hotel's free Wi-Fi.

TELEPHONES   To make local calls, dial the seven-digit number. To make calls from the Turks & Caicos, dial 0, then 1, the area code, and the number. All telephone service is provided by Cable & Wireless, and your U.S. cell phone may work on Grand Turk. Calling cards are available, or you can make a call using AT&T's USADirect by dialing 800/872–2881 to charge the call to your credit card or an AT&T prepaid calling card.

Coming Ashore

Cruise ships dock at the southern end of the island, near the former U.S. Air Force base south of the airport. The purpose-built, $40-million cruise center, which opened in February 2006, is about 3 mi (5 km) from the tranquil Cockburn Town, Pillory beach, and the Ridge, and far from most of the western shore dive-sites. The center has many facilities, including shopping, a large, free-form pool, car-rental booths, and even a dock from which many sea-bound excursions depart. Gover-

WATER
Tap water on your ship is perfectly safe to drink; purchasing bottled water is only necessary if you prefer the taste.

nor's Beach is adjacent to the cruise-ship complex and one of the island's best beaches, but others are right in and around Cockburn Town.

If you want to come into Cockburn Town, it's reachable by taxi. You can also rent a car. However, all cruise-ship passengers can purchase a pass for the Guana "Hop On, Hop Off" Bus Tour of the island, which includes admission to several attractions, including the lighthouse and the old prison in Cockburn Town. This is usually cheaper than renting a car and drops you near the good beaches in town.

Shore Excursions

If you want to do more than just enjoy the cruise center or the beach, you'll need to sign up for one of the many shore excursions offered on the island, most geared exclusively for cruise-ship visitors. We consider these to be among the better shore excursions for Grand Turk. They may not be offered by all lines, and tour names may differ as well. Times and prices are approximate.

Certified Diving. Grand Turk lies in close proximity to amazing reefs; if you are a certified diver, that's the activity you should consider. Most cruise lines also offer programs for noncertified divers (these programs will be slightly more expensive and not as long). ☉ 4 hrs 🖾 $109.

4 X 4 Excursion. A multi-passenger 4x4 tour of the island takes you to some off-the-beaten-track places in the north. The tour includes a short stop and walk-around in Cockburn Town. ☉ 2 hrs 🖾 $90.

Dune Buggy Safari. This excursion is good for thrill-seekers, and these dune buggies are inspired by those used in the Peruvian desert. ☉ 2 hrs 🖾 $99.

Gibbs Cay with Stingrays. Gibbs Cay is a beautiful deserted island with a lovely beach and playful stingrays who are used to people. ☉ 2 hrs 🖾 $59.

Ultimate Snorkeling. With amazing reefs just offshore, Grand Turk has a wealth of sea life to visit and see close up. These trips go to Horseshoe Reef, where the water is 6 to 12 feet deep. There's a second stop at Round Cay. ☉ 2½ hrs 🖾 $49.

Exploring Grand Turk

Numbers in the margin correspond to points of interest on the Grand Turk map.

Pristine beaches with vistas of turquoise waters, small local settlements, historic ruins, and native flora and fauna are among the sights on Grand Turk. Fewer than 5,000 people live on this 7½-square-mi (19-square-km) island, and it's hard to get lost, as there aren't many roads.

Grand Turk

Northwest
Point

NORTH
WELLS

North Creek

Corktree
Beach

CORK-
TREE

RIDGE

Flamingo Cove
Marina

North Salina

BREEZY
BRAE

Victoria Library

St. Mary's Church

Town Pond

Red Salina

ATLANTIC OCEAN

Red Salina

Grand Turk
International
Airport

South Creek

Gibbs
Cay

Hawks
Pond

WATERLOO

Hawks Nest
Plantation

Round
Cay

Former U.S.
A.F.B.

Cruise
Ship
Port

Hawk's
Nest
Salina

White Sands
Beach

Columbus'
Landfall

0   1/2 mi

0   1/2 km

❶ Cockburn Town. The buildings in the colony's capital and seat of government reflect a 19th-century Bermudian style. Narrow streets are lined with low stone walls and old street lamps, which are now powered by electricity. The once-vital salinas have been restored, and covered benches along the sluices offer shady spots for observing wading birds, including flamingos that frequent the shallows. Be sure to pick up a copy of the Tourist Board's Heritage Walk guide to discover Grand Turk's rich architecture.

> **GRAND TURK BEST BETS**
>
> ■ **Beaches.** Powdery soft sand is prevalent on the island's beaches, and you'll have a wide variety.
>
> ■ **Diving.** If you're certified, there are several world-class dive sights within reach.
>
> ■ **Gibb's Cay.** If you're not a diver, this might be the best offshore day-trip; tours include a picnic on the beach and swimming with stingrays, but you'll have to take a ship-sponsored trip.

In one of the oldest stone buildings on the islands, the **Turks & Caicos National Museum** houses the Molasses Reef wreck, the earliest shipwreck—dating to the early 1500s—discovered in the Americas. The natural-history exhibits include artifacts left by Taíno, African, North American, Bermudian, French, and Latin American settlers. The museum has a 3-D coral reef exhibit, a walk-in Lucayan cave with wooden artifacts, and a gallery dedicated to Grand Turk's little-known involvement in the Space Race (Grand Turk was John Glenn's first earthside landfall after his moon walk). An interactive children's gallery keeps knee-high visitors even more "edutained." The museum also claims that Grand Turk was Columbus's first landfall in the New World. ⊠ *Duke St., Cockburn Town* ☎ *649/946–2160* ⊕ *www.tcmuseum.org* 🖅 *$5* ⊙ *Mon., Tues., Thurs., and Fri. 9–4, Wed. 9–5, Sat. 9–1.*

❷ Grand Turk Lighthouse. More than 150 years old, the lighthouse, built in the United Kingdom and transported piece by piece to the island, used to protect ships in danger of wrecking on the northern reefs. Use this panoramic landmark as a starting point for a breezy clifftop walk following the donkey trails to the deserted eastern beach. ⊠ *Lighthouse Rd., North Ridge.*

Shopping

There's not much to buy in Grand Turk, and shopping isn't a major activity here. However, a duty-free mall is located right at the cruise-ship center, where you'll find the usual array of upscale shops, which were just beginning to open at this writing. There are also shops in Cockburn Town itself.

Activities

CYCLING The island's mostly flat terrain isn't very taxing, and most roads have hard surfaces. Take water with you: there are few places to stop for refreshment. Most hotels have bicycles available, but you can also rent them for $10 to $15 a day from **Oasis Divers** (⊠ *Duke St., Cockburn Town* ☎☎ *649/946–1128* ⊕ *www.oasisdivers.com*).

DIVING &
SNORKELING
★

In these waters you can find undersea cathedrals, coral gardens, and count-less tunnels, but note that you must carry and present a valid certificate card before you'll be allowed to dive. As its name suggests, the **Black Forest** offers staggering black-coral formations as well as the occasional black-tip shark. In the **Library** you can study fish galore, including large numbers of yellowtail snapper. At the Columbus Passage separating South Caicos from Grand Turk, each side of a 22-mi-wide (35-km-wide) chan-nel drops more than 7,000 feet. From January through March, thou-sands of Atlantic humpback whales swim through en route to their winter breeding grounds. **Gibb's Cay,** a small cay a couple of miles off of Grand Turk, makes a great excursion swimming with stingrays.

Dive outfitters can all be found in Cockburn Town. Two-tank boat dives generally cost $60 to $80. **Blue Water Divers** (⊠ *Duke St., Cockburn Town* 🖼 *649/946–2432* ⊕ *www.grandturkscuba.com*) has been in opera-tion on Grand Turk since 1983 and is the only PADI Gold Palm five-star dive center on the island. Owner Mitch will doubtless put some of your underwater adventures to music in the evenings when he plays at the Osprey Beach Hotel or Salt Raker Inn. **Oasis Divers** (⊠ *Duke St., Cockburn Town* 🖼 *649/946–1128* ⊕ *www.oasisdivers.com*) special-izes in complete gear handling and pampering treatment. It also sup-plies Nitrox and rebreathers. Besides daily dive trips to the Wall, **Sea Eye Diving** (⊠ *Duke St., Cockburn Town* 🖼 *649/946–1407* ⊕ *www. seaeyediving.com*) offers encounters with friendly stingrays on a popu-lar snorkeling trip to nearby Gibbs Cay.

Beaches

Grand Turk is spoiled for choices when it comes to beach options: sun-set strolls along miles of deserted beaches, picnics in secluded coves, beach-combing on the coralline sands, snorkeling around shallow coral heads close to shore, and always the impossibly turquoise-blue waters to ad-mire. **Pillory Beach** is at the north end of Cockburn Town, **Osprey Beach** is at the south end. **Governor's Beach** is a crescent of powder-soft sand and shallow, calm turquoise waters that fronts the official British gov-ernor's residence, called Waterloo, framed by tall casuarina trees that provide plenty of natural shade. It's close to the cruise-ship center and is fairly crowded when there is a ship in port. For more of a beachcomb-ing experience, **Little Bluff Point Beach,** just west of the Grand Turk Light-house, is a low, limestone cliff-edged, shell-covered beach that looks out onto shallow waters, mangroves, and often flamingos, especially in spring and summer.

Where to Eat

There's a Margaritaville restaurant right at the cruise-ship center, so many people won't even want to leave to dine.

$–$$ ✗ **Sand Bar.** Run by two Canadian sisters, this popular beachside bar is a good value, though the menu is limited to fish-and-chips, quesadillas, and similarly basic bar fare. The tented wooden terrace jutting out on to the beach provides shade during the day, making it an ideal lunch spot. The service is friendly, and the local crowd often spills into the street. ⊠ *Duke St., Cockburn Town* 🖃 *MC, V.*

¢–$ ✕ **Courtyard Café.** A great spot for people-watching, this café offers omelets, wraps, and giant subs, as well as cakes for those with sweeter tastes. Daily specials range from lasagna and quiche to island-style beef patties. ⊠ *Duke St., Cockburn Town* ☎ *649/946–1453* ▭ *AE, MC, V.*

GRENADA

Jane Zarem

Nutmeg, cinnamon, cloves, cocoa . . . those heady aromas fill the air in Grenada (pronounced gruh-*nay*-da). Only 21 mi (33½ km) long and 12 mi (19½ km) wide, the Isle of Spice is a tropical gem of lush rain forests, white-sand beaches, secluded coves, exotic flowers, and enough locally grown spices to fill anyone's kitchen cabinet. St. George's is one of the most picturesque capital cities in the Caribbean—and St. George's Harbour is one of the most picturesque harbors. Grenada's Grand Anse Beach is one of the region's finest beaches. The island has friendly, hospitable people and enough good shopping, restaurants, historic sites, and natural wonders to make it a popular port of call. About one-third of Grenada's visitors arrive by cruise ship, and that number continues to grow each year.

Essentials

CURRENCY   Eastern Caribbean (E.C.) dollar (EC$2.70 to US$1). U.S. dollars are generally accepted, but change is given in E.C. dollars.

HOURS   Banks are open Monday through Thursday from 8 to 2, Friday from 8 to 4. The main post office, at Burns Point by the port in St. George's, is open weekdays from 8 to 3:30. Stores are generally open weekdays from 8 to 4 or 4:30 and Saturday from 8 to 1; some close from noon to 1 during the week.

INTERNET   **Java-Kool Internet Cafe** (⊠ *The Carenage, St. George's* ☎ *473/435–3506*) is open Monday through Saturday from 9 AM to 9 PM.

TELEPHONES   Prepaid phone cards, which can be used in special card phones throughout the Caribbean for local or international calls, are sold in various denominations at shops, attractions, transportation centers, and other convenient outlets. For international calls using a major credit card, dial 111; to place a collect call or use a calling card, dial 800/225–5872 from any telephone. Pay phones are available at the cruise-ship welcome center, or at the Cable & Wireless office on the Carenage in St. George's, shopping centers, and other convenient locations.

Coming Ashore

A new cruise-ship terminal opened in 2005 near Market Square on the north side of St. George's, allowing larger ships to dock rather than anchor outside the harbor. Passenger facilities are available at the terminal, and more are being added. You can easily tour the capital on foot, but be prepared to climb up and down steep hills. If you don't want to walk up and down through town, you can find a taxi ($3 or $4 each way) or a water taxi ($2 per person each way) right at the terminal to take you around The Carenage. To explore areas outside St. George's, hiring a taxi or arranging a guided tour is more sensible than renting a car. Taxis are plentiful, and fixed rates to popular island destinations are posted at the terminal's welcome center.

A taxi ride from the terminal to the beach will cost $13, but water taxis are a less expensive and more picturesque way to get there; the one-way fare is $6 to Grand Anse. Minibuses are the least expensive way to travel between St. George's and Grand Anse; pay EC$1.50 (55¢), but hold on to your hat. They're crowded with local people getting from here to there and often take turns at quite a clip! Still, it's an inexpensive, fun, and safe way to travel around the island. If you want to rent a car and explore on your own, be prepared to pay $12 for a temporary driving permit and about $55 to $75 for a day's car rental.

GRENADA BEST BETS

- **Fishing.** Deep-sea fishing is excellent in these waters, and if you can get a group together a half-day trip is not too expensive.

- **Grand Anse Beach.** Grenada has one of the Caribbean's most beautiful beaches, and the market here is also one of the island's best.

- **Spice Tours.** It's not known as the island of spice for nothing; touring one of the fragrant processing facilities is a highlight.

Shore Excursions

We consider these to be among the better shore excursions for Grenada. They may not be offered by all lines, and tour names may differ as well. Times and prices are approximate.

4 X 4 Adventure. After driving through St. George Parish, travel north, stopping at a sulphur spring and pond, then pass through Grenada's central mountain range to the rain forest, Crater Lake, and Grand Étang National Park. ⊘ *4 hrs* 🖾 *$74.*

Island Tours. Tours of Grenada usually focus on either the island's natural beauty, which includes Concord Falls and Grand Étang, or the historical sights, which include Dougaldston Estate, the Gouyave Nutmeg Cooperative, and a rum distillery. Some include a bit of both. Daylong tours usually include lunch and cover a lot of ground. ⊘ *4–8 hrs* 🖾 *$49–$95.*

Nature Walk & Swim. You travel to an undisturbed rain forest, which is an important island watershed. There, you'll climb to the summit of the hill (1,420 feet) and get a panoramic view from Port Salines in the south all the way to Grand Étang forest. Most tours end at Grande Anse Beach for a swim and refreshments. ⊘ *4 hrs* 🖾 *$54.*

Rhum Runner Cruise. The cruise on this 60-foot catamaran is a favorite of island visitors. You normally stop at a deserted beach for a swim on half-day cruises. ⊘ *3 hrs* 🖾 *$42.*

Exploring Grenada

Numbers in the margin correspond to points of interest on the Grenada map.

❸ Concord Falls. About 8 mi (13 km) north of St. George's, a turnoff from the West Coast Road leads to Concord Falls—actually three separate waterfalls. The first is at the end of the road; when the currents aren't

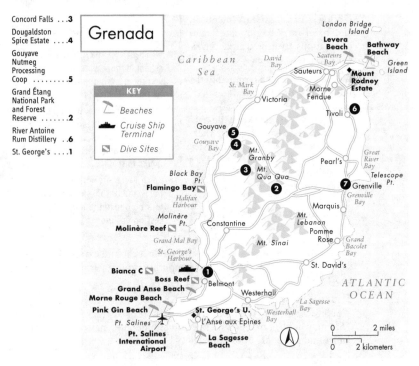

too strong, you can take a dip under the cascade. Reaching the two other waterfalls requires an hour's hike into the forest reserve. The third and most spectacular waterfall, at Fountainbleu, thunders 65 feet over huge boulders and creates a small pool. It's smart to hire a guide. The path is clear, but slippery boulders toward the end can be treacherous without assistance. ⊠ *Main interior road, 15 mins northeast of St. George's, St. George* ☎ *473/440–2452* ⬜ *$1* ⊗ *Daily 9–5.*

🖑 ❹ **Dougaldston Spice Estate.** Just south of Gouyave, this historic plantation, now primarily a living museum, still grows and processes spices the old-fashioned way. You can see cocoa, nutmeg, mace, cloves, and other spices laid out on giant racks to dry in the sun. A worker will be glad to explain the process (and will appreciate a small donation). You can buy spices for about $2 a bag. ⊠ *Gouyave, St. John* ☎ *No phone* ⬜ *Free* ⊗ *Weekdays 9–4.*

🖑 ❺ **Gouyave Nutmeg Processing Cooperative.** Touring the nutmeg processing co-op, in the center of the west coast fishing village of Gouyave (pronounced *gwahve*), is a fragrant, fascinating way to spend half an hour. You can learn all about nutmeg and its uses, see the nutmegs laid out in bins, and watch the workers sort them by hand and pack them into burlap bags for shipping worldwide. The three-story plant turned out 3 million pounds of Grenada's most famous export each year prior to Hurricane

Ivan's devastating effect on the crop in 2004. It will take a few more years for the nutmeg industry to get back to that level. ⊠ *Gouyave, St. John* ☎ *473/444–8337* 🖾 *$1* ☾ *Weekdays 10–1 and 2–4.*

★ ☾ ❷ **Grand Étang National Park and Forest Reserve.** Deep in the mountainous interior of Grenada is a bird sanctuary and forest reserve with miles of hiking trails, lookouts, and fishing streams. **Grand Étang Lake** is a 36-acre expanse of cobalt-blue water that fills the crater of an extinct volcano 1,740 feet above sea level. Although legend has it the lake is bottomless, maximum soundings are recorded at 18 feet. The informative **Grand Étang Forest Center** has displays on the local wildlife and vegetation. A forest manager is on hand to answer questions. A small snack bar and souvenir stands are nearby. ⊠ *Main interior road, between Grenville and St. George's, St. Andrew* ☎ *473/440–6160* 🖾 *$1* ☾ *Daily 8:30–4.*

❻ **River Antoine Rum Distillery.** At this rustic operation, kept open primarily as a tourist attraction, a limited quantity of Rivers rum is produced by the same methods used since the distillery opened in 1785. The process begins with the crushing of sugarcane from adjacent fields in the River Antoine (pronounced an-*twine*) Estate. The result is a potent overproof rum, sold only in Grenada, that will knock your socks off. ⊠ *River Antoine Estate, St. Patrick* ☎ *473/442–7109* 🖾 *$2* ☾ *Guided tours daily 9–4.*

❶ **St. George's.** Grenada's capital is a busy West Indian city, most of which remains unchanged from colonial days. Narrow streets lined with shops wind up, down, and across steep hills. Pastel-painted warehouses cling to the waterfront, while small rainbow-hue houses rise from the waterfront and disappear into steep green hills.

St. George's Harbour is the center of town. Schooners, ferries, and tour boats tie up along the seawall or at the small dinghy dock. On weekends a tall ship is likely to be anchored in the middle of the harbor, giving the scene a 19th-century flavor. **The Carenage** (pronounced car-a-*nahzh*), which surrounds horseshoe-shape St. George's Harbour, is the capital's main thoroughfare. Warehouses, shops, and restaurants line the waterfront. At the south end of the Carenage, the Grenada Board of Tourism has its offices. At the center of the Carenage, on the pedestrian plaza, sits the *Christ of the Deep* statue. It was presented to Grenada by Costa Cruise Line in remembrance of its ship *Bianca C,* which burned and sank in the harbor in 1961 and is now a favorite dive site.

☾ The **Grenada National Museum** (⊠ *Young and Monckton Sts.* ☎ *473/440–3725* 🖾 *$1* ☾ *Weekdays 9–4:30, Sat. 10–1*), a block from the Carenage, is built on the foundation of a French army barracks and prison that was originally

> ## ID CASES
>
> You can keep track of your boarding pass, shipboard charge/key card, and picture ID when you go ashore by slipping them into a bi-fold business-card carrying case. Cases with a sueded finish are less likely to fall out of your pocket. With security as tight as it is these days, you don't want to lose your ID.

built in 1704. The small museum has exhibitions of news items, photos, and proclamations relating to the 1983 intervention, along with Empress Josephine's childhood bathtub and other memorabilia from earlier historical periods.

Ft. George (✉ *Church St.*) is high on the hill at the entrance to St. George's Harbour. It's Grenada's oldest fort—built by the French in 1705 to protect the harbor. No shots were ever fired here until October 1983, when Prime Minister Maurice Bishop and some of his followers were assassinated in the courtyard. The fort now houses police headquarters, but is open to the public daily; admission is free. The 360-degree view of the capital city, St. George's Harbour, and the open sea is spectacular. An engineering feat for its time, the 340-foot-long **Sendall Tunnel** was built in 1895 and named for an early governor. It separates the harborside of St. George's from the Esplanade on the bay side of town, where you can find the markets (produce, meat, and fish), the cruise-ship terminal, and the public bus station.

Don't miss St. George's picturesque **Market Square** (✉ *Granby St.*), a block from the cruise-ship terminal. It's open every weekday morning, but really comes alive on Saturday from 8 to noon. Vendors sell baskets, spices, brooms, clothing, knickknacks, coconut water, and heaps of fresh produce. Market Square is historically where parades and political rallies take place—and the beginning of the minibus routes to all areas of the island.

Built in 1825, the beautiful **St. George's Anglican Church** (✉ *Church St.*) is filled with statues and plaques depicting Grenada in the 18th and 19th centuries. **St. George's Methodist Church** (✉ *Green St., near Herbert Blaize St.*) was built in 1820 and is the oldest original church in the city. The Gothic tower of **St. George's Roman Catholic Church** (✉ *Church St.*) dates from 1818, but the current structure was built in 1884; the tower is the city's most visible landmark. **York House** (✉ *Church St.*), dating from 1801, is home to Grenada's Houses of Parliament and Supreme Court. It, the neighboring Registry Building (1780), and Government House (1802) are fine examples of early Georgian architecture.

Overlooking the city of St. George's and the inland side of the harbor, historic **Fort Frederick** (✉ *Richmond Hill*) provides a panoramic view of two-thirds of Grenada. The fort was started by the French and completed in 1791 by the British; it was also the headquarters of the People's Revolutionary Government during the 1983 coup. Today you can get a bird's-eye view of much of Grenada from here.

Shopping

Grenada's best souvenirs or gifts for friends back home are spice baskets filled with cinnamon, nutmeg, mace, bay leaves, cloves, turmeric, and ginger. You can buy them for as little as $2 in practically every shop, at the open-air produce market at **Market Square** in St. George's, at the vendor stalls near the pier, and at the **Vendor's Craft & Spice Market** on Grand Anse Beach. Vendors also sell handmade fabric dolls, coral jewelry, seashells, and hats and baskets handwoven from green palm fronds. Bargaining is not appropriate in the shops, and it isn't customary with vendors—although most will offer you "a good price." **Art Fabrik** (⊠ *9 Young St., St. George's, St. George* ☎ *473/440–0568*) is a studio where you can watch artisans create batik before turning it into clothing or accessories. In the shop you can find fabric by the yard or fashioned into dresses, shirts, shorts, hats, and scarves. **Art Grenada** (⊠ *Grand Anse Shopping Centre, Suite 7, Grand Anse, St. George* ☎ *473/444–2317*) displays and sells paintings, drawings, and watercolors exclusively by Grenadian artists, among them Canute Caliste, Lyndon Bedeau, and Susan Mains. Exhibitions change monthly, and you can have your purchases shipped. **Tikal** (⊠ *Young St., St. George's, St. George* ☎ *473/440–2310*) is known for its exquisite baskets, artwork, jewelry, batik items, and fashions, both locally made and imported from Africa and Latin America.

Activities

DIVING You can see hundreds of varieties of fish and some 40 species of coral at more than a dozen sites off Grenada's southwest coast—only 15 to 20 minutes by boat. Depths vary from 20 to 120 feet, and visibility varies from 30 to 100 feet.

A spectacular dive is **Bianca C**, a 600-foot cruise ship that caught fire in 1961, sank to 100 feet, and is now encrusted with coral and a habitat for giant turtles, spotted eagle rays, barracuda, and jacks. **Boss Reef** extends 5 mi (8 km) from St. George's Harbour to Point Salines, with a depth ranging from 20 to 90 feet. **Flamingo Bay** has a wall that drops to 90 feet and is teeming with fish, sponges, sea horses, sea fans, and coral. **Molinère Reef** slopes from about 20 feet below the surface to a wall that drops to 65 feet. It's a good dive for beginners, and advanced divers can continue farther out to view the wreck of the **Buccaneer**, a 42-foot sloop.

Aquanauts Grenada (⊠ *Grand Anse Beach, Grand Anse* ☎ *473/444–1126* ⊕ *www.aquanautgrenada.com* ⊠ *True Blue Bay Resort, True Blue* ☎ *473/439–2500*) has a multilingual staff, so instruction is available in English, German, Dutch, French, and Spanish. Two-tank dive trips, accommodating no more than eight divers, are offered each morning to both the Caribbean and Atlantic sides of Grenada. **Dive Grenada** (⊠ *Flamboyant Hotel, Morne Rouge, St. George* ☎ *473/444–1092* ⊕ *www. divegrenada.net*) offers dive trips twice daily (at 10 AM and 2 PM), specializing in diving the *Bianca C.* **EcoDive** (⊠ *Grenada Grand Beach Resort, Grand Anse, St. George* ☎ *473/444–7777* ⊕ *www.ecodiveandtrek. com*) offers two dive trips daily, both drift and wreck dives. The company also runs Grenada's marine conservation and education center, which conducts coral-reef monitoring and turtle projects.

FISHING Deep-sea fishing around Grenada is excellent, with marlin, sailfish, yellowfin tuna, and dolphinfish topping the list of good catches. You can arrange a half-day sportfishing trip for $375 or so, depending on the number of people. **True Blue Sportfishing** (☎ *473/444–2048*) offers big-game charters on its "purpose-built" 31-foot Sport Fisherman, *Yes Aye.* It has an enclosed cabin, fighting chair, and professional tackle. British-born Capt. Gary Clifford, who has been fishing since the age of six, has operated True Blue Sportfishing since 1998. Refreshments and courtesy transport are included.

Beaches

Bathway Beach, a broad strip of sand with a natural reef that protects swimmers from the rough Atlantic surf on Grenada's far northern shore, has changing rooms at the Levera National Park headquarters.

Grand Anse Beach, in the southwest about 3 mi (5 km) south of St. George's, is Grenada's loveliest and most popular beach. It's a gleaming 2-mi (3-km) semicircle of white sand lapped by clear, gentle surf. Sea grape trees and coconut palms provide shady escapes from the sun. Brilliant rainbows frequently spill into the sea from the high green mountains that frame St. George's Harbour to the north. A public entrance is at Camerhogne Park, just a few steps from the main road. Beachfront hotels have water-sports centers where you can rent small sailboats, Windsurfers, and Sunfish (as well as beach chairs). The Grand Anse Craft & Spice Market is at the midpoint of the beach.

Where to Eat

Restaurants add an 8% government tax to your bill and usually add a 10% service charge; if not, tip 10% to 15% for a job well done.

★ **$–$$$** ✕ **Coconut Beach Restaurant.** Take local seafood, add butter, wine, and Grenadian spices, and you have excellent French creole cuisine. Throw in a beautiful location on Grand Anse Beach, and this West Indian cottage—rebuilt by owner Dennot "Scratch" McIntyre after Hurricane Ivan ripped it to shreds—becomes a perfect spot for an alfresco lunch or oceanfront dinner. Lobster is a specialty, perhaps wrapped in a crepe, dipped in garlic butter, or added to pasta. Or try the Caribbean chicken, seafood platter, lambi, or even grilled steak. Homemade coconut pie is a winner for dessert. On Wednesday and Sunday nights in season, dinner is a beach barbecue with live music. ⊠ *Grand Anse, St. George* ☎ *473/444–4644* ▭ *AE, D, MC, V* ⊘ *Closed Tues.*

¢–$ ✕ **The Nutmeg.** West Indian specialties, fresh seafood, great hamburgers, and a waterfront view make this a favorite with locals and visitors alike. It's upstairs on the Carenage (above Sea Change bookstore), with large, open windows from which you can watch the harbor activity as you eat. Try the callaloo soup, curried lambi, fresh seafood, or a steak—or just stop by for a rum punch and a roti, a fish sandwich and a Carib beer, or a hamburger and a Coke. ⊠ *The Carenage, St. George's, St. George* ☎ *473/440–2539* ▭ *AE, D, MC, V.*

GUADELOUPE (POINT-À-PITRE)

Eileen
Robinson Smith

On a map, Guadeloupe looks like a giant butterfly resting on the sea between Antigua and Dominica. Its two wings—Basse-Terre and Grande-Terre—are the two largest islands in the 1,054-square-km (659-square-mi) Guadeloupe archipelago. The Rivière Salée, a 6-km (4-mi) channel between the Caribbean and the Atlantic, forms the "spine" of the butterfly. A drawbridge near Pointe-à-Pitre, the main city, connects the two islands. Guadeloupe is one of the most physically endowed islands in the Caribbean. If you're seeking a resort atmosphere, casinos, and white sandy beaches, your target is Grande-Terre. On the other hand, Basse-Terre's Parc National de la Guadeloupe, laced with mountain trails and washed by waterfalls and rivers, is a 74,100-acre haven for hikers, nature lovers, and anyone brave enough to peer into the steaming crater of an active volcano. The tropical beauty you will see equates to the mythical Garden of Eden.

Essentials

CURRENCY The euro (€1 to US$1.31). Some of the larger liquor and jewelry stores may accept dollars, but don't count on that. You cannot cash traveler's checks or dollars at the bank, only at a bureau de change, so ATMs are your best bet if you need euros; there is one right outside the tourist office.

HOURS Banks are open weekdays from 8 to noon and 2 to 4. Most shops stay open all day, but some still close from noon to 2 or 2:30.

INTERNET Pointe-à-Pitre has several Internet cafés; the tourist office can point you in their direction.

TELEPHONES To call the United States from Guadeloupe, dial 001, the area code, and the local number. For calls within Guadeloupe, you now have to put 0590 before the six-digit number. You'll need to purchase a *télécarte* at the post office or at tobacco and grocery shops in order to use the phone booths.

Coming Ashore

Ships dock at the Maritime Terminal of Centre St-John Perse in downtown Pointe-à-Pitre, about a five-minute walk from the shopping district. Passengers are greeted by local musicians and hostesses, usually dressed in the traditional madras costumes—and often dispensing samplings of local rum and creole specialties. These multilingual staffers operate the information booth and can pair you up with an English-speaking taxi driver for a customized island tour. To get to the main tourist office, walk along the quay to the Place de la Victoire.

Taxi fares (more expensive here than on most other islands) are regulated by the government and posted at taxi stands. Renting a car is a good way to see Guadeloupe even though rentals can be expensive. Just be aware that traffic around Pointe-à-Pitre can be dreadful during rush hour, so allow plenty of time to drop off your car rental and get back to the ship. There are several rental agencies at the airport near Pointe-à-Pitre.

Shore Excursions

We consider these to be among the better shore excursions for Guadeloupe. They may not be offered by all lines, and tour names may differ as well. Times and prices are approximate.

Botanical Garden & Distillery. This is a good tour if you want to see a little of Basse-Terre but aren't feeling too adventurous. It starts at the beautiful Deshaies Botanical Garden; after, you visit the Domaine de Séverin distillery for some rum tasting. ☺ *4 hrs* 🚌 *$69.*

Cousteau Reserve. This trip to Pigeon Island, which was dubbed one of the world's best dive sites by Jacques Cousteau, won't give you time to do any diving, but there is a stop for snorkeling. ☺ *4 hrs* 🚌 *$86.*

Plantation Tour. You get a glimpse of the life of the plantocracy on this visit to Bel Air Plantation, which includes a stop at a rum distillery on the way back. ☉ 4 hrs ▨ $69.

Rainforest Excursion. If you want to see what makes Guadeloupe so amazing, take this tour to the rain forest on wild Basse-Terre, where you do a canopy walk and stop at the Cascade aux Ecrevisses, one of the island's grandest waterfalls. ☉ 4 hrs ▨ $89.

Exploring Guadeloupe

Numbers in the margin correspond to points of interest on the Guadeloupe map.

➊ **Pointe-à-Pitre,** a city of some 100,000 people, lies almost on the "backbone" of the butterfly, near the bridge that crosses the Salée River. This is not a postcard-pretty destination, but the Place de la Victoire, surrounded by wood buildings with balconies and shutters and lined with sidewalk cafés, has charm. The large, white Victorian building, with the wraparound veranda, is the tourist bureau. The square was named in honor of Victor Hugues's 1794 victory over the British. During the French Revolution a guillotine here lopped off the heads of many an aristocratic planter.

Anyone with an interest in French literature and culture won't want to miss the **Musée St-John Perse,** which is dedicated to Guadeloupe's most famous son and one of the giants of world literature, Alexis Léger, better known as St-John Perse, winner of the Nobel Prize for literature in 1960. Some of his finest poems are inspired by the history and landscape—particularly the sea—of his beloved Guadeloupe. The museum contains a collection of his poetry and some of his personal belongings. Before you go, look for his birthplace at 54 rue Achille René-Boisneuf. ⊠ *At rues Noizières and Achille René-Boisneuf* ☎ *0590/90–01–92* 🖅 *€2* ⊗ *Thurs.–Tues. 8:30–12:30 and 2:30–5:30.*

Musée Schoelcher celebrates Victor Schoelcher, a high-minded abolitionist from Alsace who fought against

> ### GUADELOUPE BEST BETS
>
> ■ **Diving.** Jacques Cousteau called the reef off Pigeon Island one of the world's top dive sites.
>
> ■ **Hiking.** The Parc National de la Guadeloupe is one of the Caribbean's most spectacular scenic destinations.
>
> ■ **Shopping.** Though Point-à-Pitre itself can be frenetic, it does have a good choice of European wares, though you may not be so excited about the prices.

slavery in the French West Indies in the 19th century. The museum contains many of his personal effects, and exhibits trace his life and work. Come for the architecture, the works of art, and the music history. ⊠ *24 rue Peynier* ☎ *0590/82–08–04* 🖅 *€3* ⊗ *Weekdays 9–5.*

For fans of French ecclesiastical architecture, there's the imposing **Cathédrale de St-Pierre et St-Paul** (⊠ *Rue Alexandre Isaac at rue de l'Eglise*), built in 1807. Although battered by hurricanes, it has fine stained-glass windows and creole-style balconies and is reinforced with pillars and ribs that look like leftovers from the Eiffel Tower.

❷ **Aquarium de la Guadeloupe.** Unique in the Antilles, this aquarium in the marina near Pointe-à-Pitre is a good place to spend an hour. The well-planned facility has an assortment of tropical fish, crabs, lobsters, moray eels, puffy coffers, a shark or two, and some live coral. It's also a turtle rescue center. The retail shop has sea-related gifts, toys, and jewelry. ⊠ *Pl. Créole, off Rte. N4, Pointe-à-Pitre* ☎ *0590/90–92–38* 🖅 *€7.50* ⊗ *Daily 9–7.*

❸ **Fort Fleur d'Épée.** The main attraction in Bas-du-Fort is this 18th-century fortress, which hunkers down on a hillside behind a deep moat. It was the scene of hard-fought battles between the French and the English in 1794. You can explore its well-preserved dungeons and battlements and take in a sweeping view of Iles des Saintes and Marie-Galante. ⊠ *Bas-du-Fort* ☎ *0590/90–94–61* 🖅 *€6* ⊗ *Mon. 10–5, Tues.–Sun. 9–5.*

★ ❹ **Parc National de la Guadeloupe.** This 74,100-acre park has been recognized by UNESCO as a Biosphere Reserve. Before going, pick up a *Guide to the National Park* from the tourist office; it rates the hiking trails according to difficulty, and most are quite difficult indeed. Most mountain trails are in the southern half of the park. The park is bisected by the Route de la Traversée, a 16-mi (26-km) paved road lined with masses of tree ferns, shrubs, flowers, tall trees, and green plantains. It's the ideal point of entry to the park. Wear rubber-sole shoes and take along a swimsuit, a sweater, and perhaps food for a picnic. Try to get an early start to stay ahead of the hordes of cruise-ship passengers making a day of it. Check on the weather; if Basse-Terre has had a lot of rain, give it up. In the past, after intense rainfall, rockslides have closed the road for months. ⊠ *Administrative Headquarters, Rte. de la Traversée, St-Claude* ☎ *0590/80–86–00* ⊕ *www.guadeloupe-parcnational.com* ✉ *Free* ☉ *Weekdays 8–5:30.*

❺ Cascade aux Ecrevisses. Part of the Parc National de la Guadeloupe, Crayfish Falls is one of the island's loveliest (and most popular) spots. There's a marked trail (walk carefully—the rocks can be slippery) leading to this splendid waterfall, which dashes down into the Corossol River—a good place for a dip. Come early, though; otherwise you definitely won't have it to yourself.

Shopping

For serious shopping in Pointe-à-Pitre, browse the boutiques and stores along rue Schoelcher, rue Frébault, and rue Noizières. The multicolored market square and stalls of La Darse are filled mostly with vegetables, fruits, delicious homemade rum liqueurs, and housewares. The air is filled with the fragrance of spices and they have lovely gift baskets of spices and vanilla lined with madras fabric.

Au Bonheur des Dames (⊠ *49 rue Frébault, Pointe-à-Pitre, Grande-Terre* ☎ *0590/82–00–30*) sells several different lines of cosmetics and skin-care products in addition to its perfumes. **Délice Shop** (⊠ *45 rue Achille René-Boisneuf, Pointe-à-Pitre, Grande-Terre* ☎ *0590/82–98–24*) is the spot for island rum and edibles from France—from cheese to chocolate. **DODY** (⊠ *31 rue Frébault, Pointe-a-Pitre, Grande-Terre* ☎ *0590/82–18–59*) is the place if you have wanted to purchase white eyelet—blouses, skirts, dresses, or even bustiers—the shop has a high-quality designer line, but you will pay. There's lots of madras, too, which is especially cute in children's clothing. **Rosebleu** (⊠ *5 rue Frébault, Pointe-à-Pitre, Grande-Terre* ☎ *0590/82–93–43*) sells china, crystal, and silver by top manufacturers, including Christofle. **Vendôme** (⊠ *8–10 rue Frébault, Pointe-à-Pitre, Grande-Terre* ☎ *0590/83–42–84*) is Guadeloupe's exclusive purveyor of Stendhal and Germaine Monteil cosmetics.

Activities

DIVING The main diving area at the **Cousteau Underwater Park,** just off Basse-Terre near Pigeon Island, offers routine dives to 60 feet. But the numerous glass-bottom boats and day-trippers make the site feel like a crowded marine parking lot. The underwater wonders, however, are spectacular. Guides and instructors here are certified under the French CMAS (some also have PADI). Most operators offer two-hour dives for about €45–€50 per dive; three-dive packages are €120–€145. **Les Heures Saines** (⊠ *Rocher de Malendure, Plage de Malendure, Bouillante, Basse-Terre* ☎ *0590/98–86–63 or 0690/55–40–47* ⊕ *www.plongee-guadeloupe.com*) is the premier operator for dives in the Cousteau Reserve. Trips to Les Saintes offer one or two dives, for medium and advanced cardholders, with time for lunch and sightseeing. The instructors, many English-speaking, are excellent with children. The company also offers sea kayaking and winter whale- and dolphin-watching trips with marine biologists as guides, all aboard a 60-foot catamaran equipped with hydrophones.

HIKING With hundreds of trails and countless rivers and waterfalls, the Parc National de la Guadeloupe on Basse-Terre is the main draw for hikers. Some of the trails should be attempted only with an experienced guide. All tend to be muddy, so wear a good pair of boots. Know that even the young and fit can find these outings arduous; the unfit may find them painful. Start off slowly, with a shorter hike, then go for the gusto. **Vert Intense** (☒ *Basse-Terre* ☎ *0590/99–34–73 or 0690/55–40–47* ⊕ *www. ecotourisme-guadeloupe.net*) organizes fascinating hikes in the Parc National de la Guadeloupe. You will move from steaming hot springs to an icy waterfall in the same hike. The French-speaking guides, who also know some English and Spanish, can also take you to other tropical forests and rivers, but hikes must be booked in advance.

Beaches

Plage Caravelle. Just southwest of Ste-Anne is one of Grande-Terre's longest and prettiest stretches of sand, the occasional dilapidated shack notwithstanding. Protected by reefs, it's also a fine snorkeling spot. Club Med occupies one end of this beach, where nude bathing is no longer permitted. Nonguests can enjoy its beach and water sports, as well as lunch and drinks by buying a day-pass (approximately €90). ☒ *Rte. N4, southwest of Ste-Anne, Grande-Terre.*

Pointe des Châteaux. This is one of the island's most dramatic, wild seascapes; looming above are rugged cliffs topped by a huge crucifix. **Pointe Tarare,** a secluded, sandy strip just before the tip, is the island's only nude beach. If you don't feel comfortable with that, just keep walking and find your own white, sandy spot. Makeshift bars and snack stands crowd the parking area, but it's still best to bring some water and food. ☒ *Rte. N4, southeast of St-François, Grande-Terre.*

La Grande-Anse. One of Guadeloupe's widest beaches, La Grande-Anse has soft, beige sand sheltered by palms. To the west is a round, verdant mountain. There's a large parking area and some food concessionaires, but no other facilities. The beach can be crowded, not to mention littered, on Sunday. Beyond the parking lot you can see signs for the creole restaurant Le Karacoli; if you have lunch there (it's not inexpensive), you can take a nap on the chaise lounges. ☒ *Rte. N6, north of Deshaies, Basse-Terre.*

Where to Eat

Restaurants are required to include a 15% service charge in the menu price. Extra gratuities make Americans popular.

★ $$–$$$$ ✕ **Le Rocher de Malendure.** Guests climb the yellow stairs for the panoramic sea views but return for the food. If you arrive before noon, when the divers pull in, you might snag one of the primo tables in a gazebo, which literally hang over the Caribbean. Begin with a perfectly executed mojito. With such fresh fish, don't hesitate to try the sushi *antilliaise,* a mixed-fish ceviche. The housemade, golden raisin rolls are perfect with the warm goat cheese salad with honey sauce perfumed by *herbes du Provence.* Grilled crayfish and lobster; octopus fricasse, shellfish bouillabaisse, and *dorade* (mahimahi) with a vanilla cream sauce have contemporary presentations and classic good flavor. Stone and steam cooking at the table are so guilt-free. UAC member. ⊠ *Bord de Mer, Malendure de Pigeon, Bouillante* ☎ *0590/98–70-84* ⊟ *AE, MC, V* ⊘ *Closed Wed. and Sept.*

¢–$ ✕ **Caraïbes Café.** This sidewalk café straight out of Paris is the *in* place for lunch and also a spot for a quick breakfast, a fresh juice cocktail (try *corossel/mangue*), a cappuccino, a sundae (*un coupe*), or a Pernod while you watch the people and listen to French crooners and "Desperado." The *formule* (fixed-price menu) is always the best deal. Then there are crepes, both main course and dessert crepes, sandwiches and grilled sirloin steak (*entrecote*) with perfect *pommes frites*. Service is fast, friendly and can even be in English. ⊠ *Place de la Victoire, Pointe-à-Pitre* ☎ *0590/82–92–23* ⊟ *MC, V* ⊘ *Closed Sun. No dinner.*

ISLA MARGARITA, VENEZUELA

Venezuelans are enormously fond of the island they call the "pearl in the Caribbean." Margarita's status as a duty-free port and its proximity to the mainland make it the top vacation spot for Venezuelans. Miles of white sandy beaches, glittering hotels and restaurants, and vibrant nightlife, as well as 16th-century forts and national parks, have transformed Isla Margarita into a newly popular destination for cruise-ship visitors as well. Isla Margarita is split into two sections linked by an 11-mi (18-km) spit of sand. Most of the island's 350,000 residents occupy the more developed eastern half, especially the bustling city of Porlamar and the adjoining Pampatar. Others are found in the much smaller city of La Asunción, the capital of the region that also encompasses the neighboring islands of Coche and Cubagua. Roads on Isla Margarita are good, which means a car is the easiest way to venture out on your own. Taxis and vans serve as public transportation throughout the island.

Essentials

CURRENCY The Honduran bolívar (Bs2,147 to US$1). Italcambio, the largest of the *casas de cambio* (exchange houses), is permitted to exchange dollars and American Express traveler's checks denominated in dollars for bolívars, but not vice-versa. (Most banks will not exchange currency, and none will accept traveler's checks.) Given Venezuela's currency restrictions at this writing, there will be no shortage of black market dealers approaching you quietly about changing money in public places, but the so-called *mercado negro* is officially illegal and a dangerous risk for robbery.

HOURS Stores and attractions will be open if there is a cruise ship in port.

INTERNET **Tucupita Expeditions** (⊠ *Boulevard Playa El Agua, Playa El Agua, in front of Playa El Agua Beach Hotel* ☎ *0295/249–1864*) is an Internet café and travel agency in the most popular beach area on the island.

TELEPHONES All telephone numbers have seven digits. Area codes begin with a "0" followed by a three-digit number, the first of which is a 2. International calls are extremely expensive; the average international rate per minute is $3.50 to the United States and $10 to Europe. You can reach an English-speaking long-distance operator by dialing 122. To use a calling card or credit card, or to place a collect call, use the various international access numbers from your home country.

Coming Ashore

Ships dock at El Guamache, which is in an isolated area about 45 minutes by taxi from the main city of Porlamar. Outside the dock, you'll find both indoor and outdoor shopping ranging from arts and crafts to high-end duty-free items. There is also a lively bar in the complex.

Margarita is a largely desert island, but it is easy enough to rent a car at the port and take a scenic drive around. Roads are well paved, and the driving conditions are quite good. If you plan to do any serious off-road exploring, then a 4x4 is essential. Taxis are clearly marked and are readily available at the port and in the major towns. Fares are posted on the taxi windows, but be sure to agree on a price to your destination beforehand, as some taxis will try to tack on a little extra to the fare. The fare to Porlamar from the port is about $50 for the round-trip; fares in and around Porlamar usually do not exceed $5.

> ### ISLA MARGARITA BEST BETS
>
> ■ **Beaches.** This is a great place to simply relax on the beach. Try the busy strand at Playa El Agua.
>
> ■ **Kayaking.** Good mangrove forests mean good kayaking, particularly in the Parque Nacional Laguna de la Restinga.
>
> ■ **Snorkeling.** There's enough sea life in these waters to make a snorkeling trip a worthwhile endeavor.

Shore Excursions

The following shore excursions are offered by major cruise lines in Isla Margarita. They may not be offered by all lines, and tour names may differ as well. Times and prices are approximate.

Caribbean Kayaking Tour. After 90 minutes of kayaking, you have time to relax on the beach. ☉ *5 hrs* 🖃 *$65.*

Land Cruiser Nature Adventure. You'll take off in a four-wheel-drive vehicle to explore some of the island's natural beauty. ☉ *4 hrs* 🖃 *$74.*

Margarita Splash. It's hard to resist the opportunity to drive your own speedboat around the island. ☉ *4½ hrs* 🖃 *$98.*

Round the Island Tour. This full-day tour takes in basically every sight on the island and includes detailed explanations of points of interest. Culture-seekers will be pleased by the inclusion of the museum, and fun-seekers will enjoy the beach stop in *Playa El Agua.* The tour also includes refreshments and a chance to shop for local handicrafts. ☉ *5 hrs* 🖃 *$28.*

Exploring Margarita Island

Numbers in the margin correspond to points of interest on the Margarita map.

❸ La Asunción. From the mountains in the center of the island there are striking views as the road slowly descends to La Asunción, the small capital of the region. The sleepy little town, ignored by the bargain-hunting throngs, is the opposite of the bustling Porlamar. A handful of pretty colonial buildings are found around La Asunción's tree-covered Plaza Bolívar. ⊠ *3 mi (5 km) north of El Valle.*

On Bolivar Square in the capital city of Asuncion the **Catedral de Nuestra Señora of La Asunción** built in 1617 is one of the oldest churches in Venezuela. Built of lime and local stone the small structure features beautiful statuary of various saints that date back many centuries.

2 **Diverland.** A giant Ferris wheel leads you to the island's largest amusement park. There are 16 attractions, including a roller coaster and water slide. ⊠ *Av. Jóvito Villalba Pampatar* ☎ *0295/262–0813* 🎫 *$5* ☉ *Dec.–Apr. daily, 10 AM–11 PM; May–Nov., most weekends only (call for hours).*

5 **Museo Marino de Margarita.** This museum's eight exhibit halls serve as a repository for Venezuela's astounding variety of marine life. As aquariums go, this is a small facility, but you can find everything from barracudas to flying fish. Many of the exhibits focus on the history of sea exploration in northern South America. ⊠ *Boulevar El Paseo, Boca del Rio, Macanao Peninsula* ☎ *0295/291–3231* 🎫 *Bs 6,000* ☉ *Daily 8–4:30.*

4 **Parque Nacional Laguna de la Restinga.** The mangrove forests of this national reserve cover the 12-mi (20-km) thread of sand that makes up the tenuous link between the main part of the island and the Península de Macanao. Here you'll find a variety of colorful birds, such as the scarlet ibis. The park has an unspoiled beach and a sprinkling of fishermen's huts where you can buy the catch of the day.

❶ **Porlamar.** Porlamar, with about a third of Isla Margarita's population, is the island's center of commerce. Since it was granted free-port status in 1973, its boutique-lined avenues have been mobbed with tourists in search of tax-free bargains. Many of the goods found here are no cheaper than on the mainland, however. Porlamar is also the most cosmopolitan city on Isla Margarita, boasting countless restaurants, bars, clubs, and casinos.

> ### PACK AHEAD
>
> When you put your summer wardrobe away for the winter, set aside the casual outfits, sandals, swimwear, and sleepwear you want to wear on your cruise and store them in the suitcase you plan to use. You will already be half-packed and will not be hunting down an outfit or a pair of shoes later.

Museo de Arte Contemporáneo Francisco Narvá is named after the native Margariteño sculptor whose works also can be viewed on the grounds of the Bella Vista Hotel. Here you'll find a permanent collection of Narváez's works, plus a rotating exhibit of national and international artworks. ✉ *Calle Igualdad at Calle Diaz* ☎ *0295/261–8668* 💳 *Bs 1,000* ☉ *Tues.–Fri. 9–5, Sat.–Sun. 10–4.*

Shopping

Although Isla Margarita is a major destination for Venezuelan day-trippers taking advantage of the duty-free prices, real bargains are hard to find. Your best bets are liquor and jewelry. Aside from the less expensive shops along Bulevar Guevara and Bulevar Gómez, shoppers are attracted to boutiques along Avenidas Santiago Mariño and 4 de Mayo, all in Porlamar. More and more shoppers are heading to the ubiquitous malls that are taking over the island. One of the most popular is the massive **Jumbo Mall** on 4 de Mayo. The stadium-size **Centro Sambil** has 137 stores and is the offspring of its mammoth parent shopping center in Caracas.

Activities

GOLF **Hesperia Playa El Agua** (✉ *Av. 31 de Julio, Pedro González* ☎ *0295/249–0433*), is a hotel that has the island's only 18-hole golf course. It is also handy that there is a lovely deserted beach located nearby for an after-game cooldown.

HORSEBACK RIDING **Walter's Tours** (✉ *C.C. La Redoma, Local #05, Los Robles* ☎ *0295/174–1265* ⊕ *www.margaritaislandguide.com*) offers two-hour horseback riding tours in either the morning or afternoon. The route begins at the Cabatucan Ranch.

Beaches

Easily the most famous and crowded beach on the island, palm-lined **Playa El Agua** is a remarkable stretch of fine white sand that runs along the coast just north of Pampatar. For much of its 2-mi (3-km) length, restaurants and bars lure sunbathers with blaring salsa music and ice-cold beers. **Playa Guacuco** sits just outside Porlamar and is comparatively quiet compared to many other beaches on the island. The beach is lined with palm trees and there are gentle waves that allow for excellent body surfing. **Playa Parguito** is popular with surfers and offers excellent restaurants and shower facilities. It is located on the north of the island. It is also an excellent beach for people watching.

Where to Eat

There are many excellent restaurants on Isla Margarita and seafood is a favorite theme. On popular Playa El Agua, there are many casual beachside restaurants.

$$-$$$ ✕ **Bahi.** With large bay windows overlooking the beach, this place has a long-standing reputation for serving fine Spanish-style seafood dishes. Expect strolling musicians while you struggle to decide between the tasty paella and the succulent crab. Best of all, the prices are quite reasonable. ✉ *Av. Raúl Leoni, Porlamar* ☎ *0295/261–4156* ▤ *AE, D, MC, V.*

$$-$$$ ✕ **Poseidón.** The god of the sea serves top-quality seafood artfully presented with a local touch, and is among the most exclusive—and best— in Isla Margarita. The restaurant has a tropical fish aquarium. ✉ *Centro Comercial Jumbo, Av. 4 de Mayo, Porlamar* ▤ *AE, MC, V.*

KEY WEST, FLORIDA

Diane Bair and Pamela Wright

Along with the rest of Florida, Key West—the southernmost city in the continental United States—became part of American territory in 1821. In the late 19th century, it was Florida's wealthiest city per capita. The locals made their fortunes from "wrecking"—rescuing people and salvaging cargo from ships that foundered on nearby reefs. Cigar making, fishing, shrimping, and sponge gathering also became important industries. Capital of the self-proclaimed "Conch Republic," Key West today makes for a unique port of call. A genuinely American town, it nevertheless exudes the relaxed atmosphere and pace of a typical Caribbean island. Major attractions include the home of the Conch Republic's most famous residents, Ernest Hemingway and Harry Truman; the imposing Key West Museum of Art & History, a former U.S. Customs House and site of the military inquest of the USS *Maine*; and the island's renowned sunset celebrations.

Essentials

CURRENCY The U.S. dollar.

HOURS Many museums are closed on Mondays. Otherwise, regular 9–5 hours apply for most businesses.

INTERNET **Crossroads Internet Cafe** (✉ *500 Truman Ave. #7* ☎ *305/294–9118*).

TELEPHONES Public phones are found at or near all three cruise docks: Mallory Square, Pier B at the Hilton, and Outer Mall (where the Conch Train drops passengers at Duval and Front streets). They're also along the major tourist thoroughfares.

Coming Ashore

Cruise ships dock at three different locations. Mallory Square and Pier B are within walking distance of Duval and Whitehead streets, the two main tourist thoroughfares. Passengers on ships that dock at Outer Mall are shuttled via Conch Train to Duval and Front streets. Because Key West is so easily explored on foot, there is rarely a need to hire a cab. If you plan to venture beyond the main tourist district, a fun way to get around is by bicycle or scooter. Key West is a cycling town. In fact, there are so many bikes around that cyclists must watch out for one another as much as for cars. You can get tourist information from the Greater Key West Chamber of Commerce, which is just off Mallory Square.

The Conch Tour Train can be boarded at Mallory Square or Flagler Station every half hour; it costs $25 for the 90-minute tour. The Old Town Trolley operates trolley-style buses starting from Mallory Square every 30 minutes for the same price, but the smaller trolleys go places the train won't fit. Scooters can be easily rented. **Keys Moped & Scooter** (⊠ *523 Truman Ave.* ☎ *305/294–0399*) rents beach cruisers with large baskets as well as scooters. Rates for scooters start at $30 for three hours. Look for the huge American flag on the roof. **Moped Hospital** (⊠ *601 Truman Ave.* ☎ *305/ 296–3344*) supplies balloon-tire bikes ($18 a day) with yellow safety baskets, as well as mopeds ($40) and double-seater scooters ($65).

> ## KEY WEST BEST BETS
>
> - **Boat Cruise.** Whether you take a catamaran out to do some snorkeling or just do a sunset booze cruise, being out on the water is what Key West is all about.
>
> - **Kayaking.** Kayaking, either around Florida Bay or in the Great Heron National Wildlife Refuge, is a great way to spend a few hours.
>
> - **Sunset in Mallory Square.** The nightly street party is the quintessential Key West experience, and no one should miss it.

Shore Excursions

The following shore excursions are offered by major cruise lines in Key West. They may not be offered by all lines, and tour names may differ as well. Times and prices are approximate.

Fury Catamaran Reef Snorkeling. You sail out to the only living coral reef in the continental U.S., where the catamaran drops anchor and gives you the chance to snorkel. Refreshments are served on the way back. ⊘ *3 hrs* ▭ *$49.*

Harley Poker Run. This tour is scandalously expensive, but how often do you get a chance to ride on the overseas highway on a Harley? ⊘ *3½ hrs* ▭ *$375.*

Lloyd's Original Tropical Bike Tour. This leisurely tour takes you around Key West by bike. ⊘ *2½ hrs* ▭ *$45.*

Exploring Key West
Numbers in the margin correspond to points of interest on the Key West map.

❺ Audubon House & Gardens. If you've ever seen an engraving by ornithologist John James Audubon, you'll understand why his name is synonymous with birds. (OK, he shot a lot of them so they would lie still enough for his art, but we consider him to be part of our environmental conscience.) See his work in this three-story house, which was built in the

1840s for Captain John Geiger but now commemorates Audubon's 1832 stop in Key West. Several rooms of period antiques and a children's room are also of interest. Admission includes an audiotape (in English, French, German, or Spanish) for a self-guided tour of the house and tropical gardens, complemented by an informational booklet and signs that identify the rare indigenous plants and trees. ✉ *205 Whitehead St.* ☎ *305/294–2116 or 877/294–2470* ⊕ *www.audubonhouse.com* 🖭 *$10* ☉ *Daily 9:30–5; last tour starts at 4.*

★ ⑩ **Eco-Discovery Center.** Walk through a model of Key Largo's Aquarius, the world's only underwater ocean laboratory, to discover what lurks beneath the sea. Opened in January 2007, this 6,400 square-foot underwater attraction encourages visitors to venture through a variety of Florida Key habitats, from pinelands, beach dunes and mangroves to the deep sea. Touch-screen computer displays and live underwater cameras show off North America's only contiguous barrier coral reef. ✉ *35 East Quay Rd., at end of Southard St. in Truman Annex* ☎ *305/809–4750* ⊕ *www.floridakeys.noaa.gov/eco.discovery.html* 🖭 *$10* ☉ *Tues.-Sat. 9–4.*

★ ⑥ **Ernest Hemingway Home & Museum.** Guided tours of Ernest Hemingway's home are full of anecdotes about the author's life in the community and his household quarrels with wife Pauline. While living here between 1931 and 1942, Hemingway wrote about 70% of his life's work, including *For Whom the Bell Tolls*. Few of the family's belongings remain, but photographs help illustrate his life, and scores of descendants of Hemingway's cats have free reign of the property. Literary buffs should be aware that there are no curated exhibits from which to gain much insight into Hemingway's writing career. Tours begin every 10 minutes and take 25–30 minutes; then you're free to explore on your own. ⊠ *907 Whitehead St.* ☎ *305/294–1136* ⊕ *www.hemingwayhome.com* ☞ *$10* ☺ *Daily 9–5.*

④ Harry S Truman Little White House Museum. Personal glimpses are among the things that make many of the city's museums worth visiting, and this stop is no exception. For instance, in a letter to his wife during one of his visits, President Harry S Truman wrote, "Dear Bess, you should see the house. The place is all redecorated, new furniture and everything." If he visited today, he'd write something similar. There's a photographic review of visiting dignitaries and permanent audiovisual and artifact exhibits on the Florida Keys as a presidential retreat; Ulysses S. Grant, John F. Kennedy, and Jimmy Carter are among the chief executives who passed through here. Tours lasting 45 minutes begin every 15 minutes until 4:15. On the grounds of **Truman Annex,** a 103-acre former military parade grounds and barracks, the home served as a winter White House for presidents Truman, Eisenhower, and Kennedy. The two-bedroom Presidential Suite, with a veranda and sundeck, is available for a novelty overnight stay. ⊠ *111 Front St.* ☎ *305/294–9911* ⊕ *www. trumanlittlewhitehouse.com* ☞ *$11* ☺ *Daily 9–5, grounds 8–sunset; last tour at 4:30.*

⑧ Historic Seaport at Key West Bight. What used to be a funky—in some places even seedy—part of town is now an 8½-acre historic restoration project of 100 businesses, including waterfront restaurants, open-air people- and dog-friendly bars, museums, clothing stores, bait shops, docks, a marina, a wedding chapel, the Waterfront Market, the Key West Rowing Club, and dive shops. It's all linked by the 2-mi (3 km) waterfront **Harborwalk,** which runs between Front and Grinnell streets, passing big ships, schooners, sunset cruises, fishing charters, and glass-bottom boats. Additional construction continues on outlying projects.

① Key West Aquarium. Explore the fascinating underwater realm of the Keys without getting wet at this kid-friendly aquarium. Hundreds of tropical fish and sea creatures live here. A touch tank enables you to handle starfish, sea cucumbers, horseshoe and hermit crabs, even horse and queen conchs—living totems of the Conch Republic. Built in 1934 by the Works Progress Administration as the world's first open-air aquarium, most of the building has been enclosed for all-weather viewing. Guided tours include shark petting and feedings. Tickets are good for the entire day. ⊠ *1 Whitehead St.* ☎ *305/296–2051* ⊕ *www. keywestaquarium.com* ☞ *$10* ☺ *Daily 10–6; tours at 11, 1, 3, and 4:30.*

USED BOOKS

Leave any paperback novels you have finished for the crew library. You will have more room in your suitcase, and crew members will have fresh reading material.

② Key West Museum of Art & History. If you didn't get enough Hemingway at his museum, you can meet him and his "mob," a.k.a., friends, here through photographs and other visuals. But this is more about the city than the noted author. When Key West was designated a U.S. port of entry in the early 1820s, a customhouse was established. Salvaged cargoes from ships wrecked on the reefs could enter here, thus setting the stage for Key West to become the richest city in Florida. Following a $9 million restoration, the imposing redbrick-and-terra-cotta Richardsonian Romanesque–style U.S. Custom House reopened as a museum. Its main gallery displays major rotating exhibits. Smaller galleries have long-term and changing exhibits about the history of Key West, such as *Remember the Maine.* ⊠ *281 Front St.* ☎ *305/295–6616* ⊕ *www. kwahs.com* ≦ *$10* ⊘ *Daily 9–5.*

FodorśChoice ★

⑦ Lighthouse Museum. For the best view in town and a history lesson at the same time, climb the 88 steps to the top of this 92-foot lighthouse. It was built in 1847. About 15 years later, a Fresnel lens was installed at a cost of $1 million. The keeper lived in the adjacent 1887 clapboard house, which now exhibits vintage photographs, ship models, nautical charts, and lighthouse artifacts from all along the Key reefs. This site is a nearby affiliate of the Key West Museum of Art and History. ⊠ *938 Whitehead St.* ☎ *305/294–0012* ≦ *$10* ⊘ *Daily 9:30–4:30; last admission at 4:15.*

③ Mel Fisher Maritime Heritage Society Museum. The late Mel Fisher was a crusty character who battled the state of Florida for more than a decade over the remains of two riches-laden Spanish galleons that sank 40 miles off the Keys in 1622 during a hurricane. In 1985, Mel Fisher recovered the treasures from the lost ships, the *Nuestra Señora de Atocha* and the *Santa Margarita.* In this museum, see, touch, and learn about some of the artifacts, including a gold bar weighing 6.3 troy pounds and a 77.76-carat natural emerald crystal worth almost $250,000. Exhibits on the second floor rotate and might cover slave ships, including the excavated 17th-century *Henrietta Marie,* or the evolution of Florida maritime history. ⊠ *200 Greene St.* ☎ *305/294–2633* ⊕ *www.melfisher. org* ≦ *$11* ⊘ *Daily 9:30–5.*

⑨ Southernmost Point. At the foot of Whitehead Street, a huge concrete marker proclaims this spot to be the southernmost point in the continental United States. Turn left on South Street. To your right are two dwellings that both claim to be the Southernmost House. Take a right onto Duval Street, which ends at the Atlantic Ocean, and you will be at the Southernmost Beach.

Shopping

Passengers looking for T-shirts, trinkets, and other souvenirs will find them along Duval Street and around the cruise-ship piers. **Fast Buck Freddie's** (⊠ *500 Duval St.* ☎ *305/294–2007*) sells a classy, hip selection of crystal, furniture, tropical clothing, and every flamingo item imaginable. It also carries such imaginative items as a noise-activated rat in a trap and a raccoon tail in a bag. **Key West Aloe** (⊠ *540 Greene St., at Simonton St.* ☎ *305/294–5592 or 800/445–2563*) was founded in a garage in 1971; today it produces some 300 perfume, sunscreen, and skin-care products for men and women. After years downtown on Front Street, it has moved back to a new showroom at the original factory location. The **Key West Island Bookstore** (✉ *513 Fleming St.* ☎ *305/294–2904*) is the literary bookstore of the large Key West writers' community. It carries new, used, and rare titles and specializes in Hemingway, Tennessee Williams, and South Florida mystery writers. **Lucky Street Gallery** (✉ *1130 Duvall St.* ☎ *305/294–3973*) sells high-end contemporary paintings, watercolors, and a few pieces of jewelry by internationally recognized Key West–based artists.

Activities

BOAT TOURS **M/V Discovery** (✉ *Land's End Marina, 251 Margaret St., Key West 33040* ☎ *305/293–0099*) glass-bottom boats have submerged viewing rooms for 360-degree marine watching and cost $35. **Adventure Charters & Tours** (✉ *6810 Front St., 33040* ☎ *305/296–0362 or 888/817–0841* ⊕ *www.keywestadventures.com*) takes kayaks to the Great Heron National Wildlife Refuge for full-day tours; they also offer half-day tours that paddle out from Key West.

DIVING & **Captain's Corner** (✉ *Corner of Greene and Elizabeth* ☎ *305/296–8865*), SNORKELING a PADI five-star shop, has dive classes in several languages and twice-daily snorkel and dive trips to reefs and wrecks aboard the 60-foot dive boat *Sea Eagle* ($30 to $35). **Snuba of Key West** (✉ *Garrison Bight Marina, Palm Ave. between Eaton St. and N. Roosevelt Blvd.* ☎ *305/292–4616*) takes you out to the reef on a catamaran, where you listen to a 20-minute orientation, then follow your guide underwater for a one-hour tour of the coral reefs. You wear a regulator with a breathing hose that is attached to a floating air tank on the surface of the water, so you do not need to be certified. You must know how to swim. The $95 cost includes beverages.

FISHING **Key West Bait and Tackle** (✉ *241 Margaret St.* ☎ *305/292–1961*) carries live bait, frozen rigged and unrigged bait, and fishing and rigging equipment. It also has the Live Bait Lounge; unwind and sip ice-cold beer while telling tall tales after fishing. **Key West Fishing Pro Guides** (☎ *866/259–4205*) has several guides and trips ranging from flats fishing ($400 to $600) to offshore ($500 to $800) fishing.

Beaches

Key West doesn't have any great swimming beaches, but there are a few that might be worth a visit. **Fort Zachary Taylor State Historic Site** (✉ *End of Southard St., through Truman Annex*) has an uncrowded beach, which is the best in Key West. There is an adjoining picnic area with barbecue grills and shade trees. **Smathers Beach** (✉ *S. Roosevelt Blvd.*) has nearly 2 mi (3 km) of sand, restrooms, picnic areas, and volleyball courts, all of which make it popular with the spring-break crowd. Trucks along the road rent rafts, Windsurfers, and other beach "toys."

Where to Eat

$$–$$$ ✗ **Alice's Key West Restaurant.** A rather plain-Jane storefront gives way
Fodor'sChoice to a warm and cozy dining room, where chef-owner Alice Weingarten
★ works whimsical creations that are very far from plain. Color, zing, and spice are Weingarten's main ingredients. Take the tuna tartare tower:

it's spiced with a garlic-chili paste, topped with tomato ginger jam, and served between crisp wonton wafers. The Brazilian churrasco pan-seared skirt steak is served with garlicky chimichurri sauce and green chili and manchego cheese mashed potatoes. Or, try the Asian spiced wild boar baby back ribs or Cuban-style mojo marinated ostrich. It's open for breakfast and lunch, too; end your Duval Crawl here for a breakfast of eggs, fries, and toast for as little as $4. ⊠ *1114 Duval St.* ☎ *305/292–5733* ▤ *AE, D, MC, V.*

¢–$$ ✕ **Turtle Kraals.** In a city that prides itself on the battle of the bizarre, turtle races certainly are a contender for the title. They're held Monday and Friday evenings at 6 inside this restaurant and saloon named for the *kraals* (corrals) where turtles were kept from the mid-1800s until the 1970s. Today, much smaller box turtles provide the live entertainment while the menu offers an assortment of marine cuisine that includes seared jerk tuna, seafood enchiladas, and, our favorite, mango crab cakes with key lime mustard, yellow rice, black beans, and fried plantains. (If your ship leaves before race time, you can still meet the contenders during a midday visit.) ⊠ *231 Margaret St.* ☎ *305/294–2640* ▤ *MC, V.*

Nightlife

Three spots stand out for first-timers among the saloons frequented by Key West denizens. All are within easy walking distance of the cruise-ship piers. In its earliest incarnation, back in 1851, **Capt. Tony's Saloon** (⊠ *428 Greene St.* ☎ *305/294–1838*) was a morgue and icehouse, then Key West's first telegraph station. It became the original Sloppy Joe's in the mid-1930s, when Hemingway was a regular. Later, a young Jimmy Buffett sang here. Bands play nightly. The **Schooner Wharf Bar** (⊠ *202 William St.* ☎ *305/292–9520*), an open-air waterfront bar and grill in the historic seaport district, retains its funky Key West charm. There's live island music all day, plus happy hour, and special events. There's more history and good times at **Sloppy Joe's** (⊠ *201 Duval St.* ☎ *305/294–5717*), the successor to a famous 1937 speakeasy named for its founder, Captain Joe Russell. Ernest Hemingway came here to gamble and tell stories. Decorated with Hemingway memorabilia and marine flags, the bar is popular with travelers and is full and noisy all the time. Live entertainment plays daily 10 AM–2 AM.

LA ROMANA, DOMINICAN REPUBLIC

Eileen
Robinson Smith

Dominicans will extend a gracious welcome, saying, "This is your home!" and, indeed, are happy to share what they have, which is a physically beautiful island bathed by the Atlantic Ocean to the north and the Caribbean Sea to the south. Among its most precious assets are 1,000 miles of gorgeous beaches studded with coconut palms and sands ranging from pearl white to golden brown to volcanic black. The Caribbean sun kisses this exotic land (temperatures average 82°F). It's a fertile country blessed with resources, particularly cocoa, coffee, rum, tobacco, and sugar cane.

The contrasts here can be dramatic. You will most definitely see signs of wealth, for the upper strata of society lives well indeed here. However, on the country roads you'll be amazed that four people with sacks of groceries and a stalk of bananas can fit on a smoky old *motoconcho* (motor bike/taxi). Similarly, Dominicans can be fair-skinned with light eyes, or black, but mostly they are shades of brown. Poverty still prevails, though the standard of life has really come up along with the growth of North American tourism. Islanders have an affinity for all things American, and many speak English. A great Dominican dream is to go to the States and become the next Sammy Sosa, then return to be a philanthropist in his own hometown.

LA ROMANA BEST BETS

■ **Altos de Chavó.** Casa de Campo's own Tuscan hill town offers shopping and dining as well as great views. It's a worthwhile place to spend a couple of hours and perhaps have lunch.

■ **Golf.** The Teeth of the Dog is one of the Caribbean's best courses; if you are a golfer—and can get a tee time—you will never regret the expense.

■ **Kandela.** The Dominican folkloric show is a highlight if your ship stays late in port.

Essentials

CURRENCY The Dominican peso (RD$32.38 to US$1). At Casa de Campo, you can use U.S. dollars, but you may need to change some money if you explore farther afield. You will get change in pesos.

HOURS Offices and shops are open weekdays from 8 to noon and 2 to 6, Saturday from 8 to noon. About half the stores stay open all day, no longer closing for a midday siesta. Attractions are generally seen between 9 AM and 5 to 6 PM.

INTERNET Unfortunately, there is no Internet café where cruise-ship passengers can access their e-mail, either at the dock or at Casa de Campo.

TELEPHONES Telephones are available at the dock, as soon as passengers disembark, and telephone cards can be purchased there as well. Similarly, at the Marina Chavón, where a shuttle drops passengers off, you'll also find phones. Tele-cards can be bought at the supermarket. To call the U.S. or Canada from the D.R., just punch in 1 plus the area code and number. To make calls on the island, you must tap in the area code (809), plus the seven-digit number; if you are calling a Dominican cell phone, you must first punch in 1.

Coming Ashore

Ships enter the Casa de Campo International Tourist Port (Muelle Turístico Internacional Casa de Campo). A group of folkloric dancers and local musicians play merengue and greet passengers as they come down the gangway. An information booth with smiling, English-speaking staffers is there to assist cruise-ship passengers; the desk is open the entire time that the ship is in port. Most passengers explore the resort, take an excursion, and then have dinner on the ship or at the resort, and perhaps catch the bus to "Kandela," a Dominican-themed, Las Vegas–style revue performed under the stars in an amphitheater in Altos de Chavón.

It is a 15-minute walk into the town of La Romana, or you can jump into a waiting taxi. It's safe to stroll around town, but it's not particularly beautiful, quaint, or even historic; however, it is a real slice of Dominican life. Most people just board the complimentary shuttle and head for La Marina Chavón and/or Altos de Chavón, both of which are at the Casa de Campo resort. Shuttles run all day long. Since many taxi drivers do not speak English, staff members from the information kiosk will help to make taxi arrangements. Most rates are fixed and spelled out on a board: $15 to Casa de Campo's Marina Chavón, $20 to Altos de Chavón. You may be able to negotiate a somewhat lower rate if a group books a taxi for a tour. You can also rent a car at Casa de Campo (Hertz and Avis have offices near the resort reception area); rates are expensive, usually more than $70 a day. Driving into Santo Domingo can be a hair-raising experience and isn't for the faint of heart.

Shore Excursions

The following shore excursions are offered by major cruise lines in La Romana. They may not be offered by all lines, and tour names may differ as well. Times and prices are approximate.

Horseback Riding. One popular activity at the Casa de Campo resort is horseback riding from the resort's excellent equestrian center. The 90-minute ride isn't exactly backcountry riding: you're going around the manicured grounds and golf courses, but it's fun. ⏱ *2 hrs* 🖃 *$60*.

Kandela. If your ship stays late at La Romana, you may have the opportunity to see "Kandela," a splashy, Las Vegas–style Dominican cultural show, at the amphitheater in Altos de Chavón. It's usually cheaper to book this show through your ship than on your own since transportation is included. ⏱ *2 hrs* 🖃 *$31*.

Saona Adrenaline Experience. Casa de Campo's own beach is disappointing. This one isn't. After a speedboat ride down the river, you dock at Saona island for swimming at an excellent beach. Some tours stop for snorkeling in the bay on the way back. Other tours include a buffet lunch—and may cost more. ⏱ *4 hrs* 🖃 *$70*.

Santo Domingo Tour. The largest and oldest city in the Caribbean, Santo Domingo can be overwhelming, but it's historic and only 90 minutes from La Romana. The trip includes a walk around the Zona Colonial, the oldest part of the city. ⊙ *6½ hrs* 🖃 *$72.*

Exploring La Romana

Altos de Chavón is a replica of a 16th-century Mediterranean hill town with dramatic views of the Chavón River. You feel transported to centuries past as you stroll the cobblestoned streets, stopping into the quaint shops, exclusive boutiques, and art galleries located near the archaeological museum, design school, a medieval-style cathedral, and rows of restaurants, along with a French bakery and coffee bar.

Spanish civilization in the New World began in the 12-block Zona Colonial of **Santo Domingo**. Strolling its narrow streets, it's easy to imagine this old city as it was when the likes of Columbus, Cortés, and Ponce de León walked the cobblestones, pirates sailed in and out, and colonists were settling themselves. Tourist brochures tout that "history comes alive here"—a surprisingly truthful statement. A fun horse and carriage ride throughout the Zone costs $20 for an hour. The steeds are no thoroughbreds, but they clip right along, though any commentary will be in Spanish. The drivers usually hang out in front of the Sofitel Nicolas Ovando. History buffs will want to spend a day exploring the many "firsts" of our continent, which will be included in any cruise-ship excursion. Do wear comfortable shoes.

Shopping

Altos de Chavón also has many shops and art galleries, as well as restaurants. It also has the amphitheater where "Kandela" is performed most nights. Shops and galleries here are expensive, as are the restaurants. The **Casa de Campo Marina** is home to more than 60 upscale shops, galleries, and jewelers scattered among restaurants and an ice-cream parlor, a Euro-style bar, and a yacht club. It is a great place to spend a leisurely morning or afternoon of shopping and strolling, particularly if you enjoy staring at the extravagant yachts often moored here. The Jenny Polanco Boutique sells the work of a Dominican designer known for her white resort-wear for women; the shop now includes her line of contemporary jewelry and handbags. Although upscale is the operative word here, you can still buy a postcard, a pair of shorts, or a logo shirt. A supermarket sells sundries, postcards, and snacks.

Activities

Most activities available at Casa de Campo are open to cruise-ship passengers. You'll need to make reservations on the ship, particularly for golf.

FISHING Marlin and wahoo are among the fish that folks angle for here (fishing is best between January and June). **La Marina Chavon** (⊠ *Casa de Campo, Calle Barlovento 3, La Romana* ☎ *809/523–8646* ⊕ *www.marinacasadecampo.com*) is the best

CABIN OUTLETS

Most ships' cabins have only one or two electrical outlets located near the desk/vanity table (not counting the shaver-only outlet in the bathroom). A short extension cord allows you to use more than one electrical appliance at once and gives you a bit more flexibility to move around, particularly if you bring a laptop computer.

charter option near La Romana. Costs to charter a boat—with a crew, refreshments, bait, and tackle—generally range from $592 to $1,616 for a half day and from $790 to $3,191 for a full day.

GOLF *Golf* magazine has called "Teeth of the Dog" at **Casa de Campo** (✉ *La Romana* ☎ *809/523–3333* ⊕ *www.casadecampo.com.do*) the finest golf resort in the Caribbean. In 2005 it was closed for some months for a complete renovation, but it is once again luxuriant, with new tees, greens, and contoured bunkers by Pete Dye himself. Greens fees are now $232 though it drops to $145 from May through October. A second course near Altos de Chavón, "Dye Fore" ($203) hugs a cliff overlooking the ocean, as well as Río Chavón and its palm groves. A third 18-hole course called "The Links" ($145) is inland. For all courses, nonguests must reserve tee times more than a day in advance, which makes booking on the ship essential.

Beaches

Las Minitas Beach at Casa de Campo is reserved exclusively for hotel guests and villa owners. Cruise passengers must take a beach excursion or make their own arrangements for transportation to nearby beaches. In truth, all of these are better than the beach at the resort.

Catalina Island is a diminutive, picture-postcard Caribbean island off the coast of the mainland. Some cruise ships actually anchor off Catalina Island and offer excursions by tenders to it as well as to Casa de Campo. To get to the island, you'll have to take an excursion. Catalina is about a half hour away by catamaran, and most excursions offer the use of snorkeling equipment as well as a beach barbecue.

Playa Bayahibe is a beautiful stretch of beach. It is also pleasant to browse and shop in the village of Bayahibe. Shore excursions are organized by the cruise lines to the beach, which is about 30 minutes away from the cruise port by bus. You can also book your own taxi here, and the trip may be cheaper than the cost of a shore excursion if you come with a group.

Saona Island was once a pristine, idyllic isle. Now, on a busy cruise-ship day, there may be as many as 1,000 bathers there. However, the beach is beautiful. To get here, you'll have to book an excursion with your ship, often a power boat from Altos de Chavón; otherwise, you are bused to Bayahibe and board a boat there. There is usually a stop at a natural, shallow pool with a white-sand bottom, populated with starfish. The day trip usually includes a Dominican barbecue lunch.

Where to Eat

There are some casual places to eat at Marina de Chavón, but in truth the restaurants at Altos de Chavón are fairly expensive, and you'd be better off doing some shopping and then heading back to your ship for lunch. If you want to have something a little nicer at the marina, then Peperoni is the best choice.

$$–$$$ ✕ **Peperoni.** Although the name sounds as Italian as *amore,* this classy restaurant's menu is much more eclectic than Italian. It has a classy, contemporary, white-dominated decor; waiters are also dressed in white with long aprons. The classic pasta dishes, osso buco, and risottos with rock shrimp or porcinis are authentic and delectable as are such specialties as

polenta-encrusted sea bass with lentils. But you can also opt for stylishly simple charcoal-grilled steaks, burgers, pizzas, and sandwiches. ⊠ *Plaza Portafolio 16, Marina Chavón* ☎ *809/523–2228* ▭ *AE, MC, V.*

MARTINIQUE (FORT-DE-FRANCE)

Eileen
Robinson Smith

The largest of the Windward Islands, Martinique is 4,261 mi (6,817 km) from Paris, but its spirit and language are decidedly French, with more than a soupçon of West Indian spice. Tangible, edible evidence of the fact is the island's cuisine, a superb blend of French and creole. Martinique is lushly landscaped with tropical flowers. Trees bend under the weight of fruits such as mangoes, papayas, lemons, limes, and bright-red West Indian cherries. Acres of banana plantations, pineapple fields, and waving sugarcane stretch to the horizon. The towering mountains and verdant rain forest in the north lure hikers, while underwater sights and sunken treasures attract snorkelers and scuba divers. Martinique is also wonderful if your idea of exercise is turning over every 10 minutes to get an even tan and your taste in adventure runs to duty-free shopping. A popular cruise-ship excursion goes to St-Pierre, which was buried by ash when Mont Pelée erupted in 1902.

Essentials

CURRENCY   The euro (€1 to US$1.31). You will not be able to use dollars, so plan on getting some euros. You cannot cash traveler's checks or dollars at the bank, only at a bureau de change, so ATMs are your best bet if you need euros. Change Caraïbes—which has an office in Fort-de-France at 14 rue Victor Hugo and Le Bord de Mer—will still exchange both dollars and traveler's checks and usually offers fair rates.

HOURS   Banks are open weekdays from 7:30 to noon and 2:30 to 4. Post offices are generally open weekdays from 7 to 6, Saturday from 8 until noon. Stores that cater to tourists are generally open weekdays from 8:30 to 6, Saturday 8:30 to 1. Many stores in Fort-de-France close from 12:30 to 2 for lunch.

INTERNET   **Cyber Club Caraibé** (⊠ *16 rue Francois Arago, Fort-de-France* ☎ *0596/ 70–31–62*). **Internet Haut Depot** (⊠ *61 rue Victor Hugo, Fort-de-France* ☎ *0596/63–12–20*).

TELEPHONES   There are no coin-operated phone booths. Public phones now use a *télé-carte,* which you can buy at post offices, café-tabacs, hotels, and at *bureaux de change.* To call the United States from Martinique, dial 00 + 1, the area code, and the local number. To call locally, you now have to dial 0596 before the six-digit number. You can make collect calls to Canada through the Bell operator; you can get the AT&T or MCI operators from blue, special-service phones at the cruise ports and in town (try Super Sumo snack bar, on rue de la Liberté, near the library).

Coming Ashore

Most cruise ships call at the Maritime Terminal east of Fort-de-France; however, some large ships that anchor in the Baie des Flamands may tender passengers directly to the Fort-de-France waterfront. To reach the tourist information booth, which is staffed by helpful, English-speaking personnel, turn right and walk along the waterfront. Uniformed dispatchers assist in finding English-speaking taxi drivers. Ask about guided walking tours that can be arranged at the nearby open-air market.

The only practical way to get into the city from the Maritime Terminal is to take a cab, approximately €15 round-trip. Taxis are metered, and there's no extra charge for extra passengers; however, rates are fairly expensive. A journey of any distance can cost €25 or more, and traffic in Fort-de-France can be nightmarish. If you want to go to the beach, a much cheaper option is to take a ferry from Fort-de-France. *Vedettes* (ferries) operate daily between Quai d'Ensnambuc in Fort-de-France and the marina in Pointe du Bout, Anse-Mitan, and Anse-à-l'Ane. Any of the three trips takes about 15 minutes, and the ferries operate about every 30 minutes on weekdays. Renting a car in Fort-de-France is possible, but the heavy traffic can be forbidding. Rates start at €60 per day for a car with manual transmission; those with automatic transmissions are substantially more expensive and rarely available.

Shore Excursions

We consider these to be among the better shore excursions for Martinique. They may not be offered by all lines, and tour names may differ as well. Times and prices are approximate.

Island Tour with St-Pierre. Ride along the coastal road to St-Pierre, which was once the capital of Martinique. The ruined city is a museum of devastated houses, monuments, and industries destroyed by the volcanic eruption of Mt. Pelée in 1902. Some tours include the Depaz Rum Distillery. ⊘ *4 hrs* ⊠ *$76*.

Jardin de Balata. This botanical garden is one of the island's loveliest spots. A nearby church is an exact replica of Sacré-Coeur. ⊘ *3 hrs* ⊠ *$69*.

Martinique 4x4. You'll definitely hit the backroads on this trip, but you'll

> ### MARTINIQUE BEST BETS
>
> ■ **Beaches.** If you want to simply relax, the most beautiful beach is Les Salines.
>
> ■ **Shopping.** Shopping in Fort-de-France's many upscale boutiques is good, but never cheap.
>
> ■ **St-Pierre.** Like Pompeii transported to the Caribbean, Martinique's former capital was buried by ash but has been reborn.

get to see some of the wildly beautiful landscape that you'll miss if you just stick to the main highways. This tour usually includes St-Pierre and the Depaz Distillery. ⊘ *4½ hrs* ⊠ *$99*.

Exploring Martinique

Numbers in the margin correspond to points of interest on the Martinique map.

If you want to see the lush island interior and St-Pierre on your own, take the N3, which snakes through dense rain forests, north through the mountains to Le Morne Rouge, then take the coastal N2 back to Fort-de-France via St-Pierre. You can do the 40-mi (64-km) round-trip in half a day—that is if you don't get lost, can comprehend the road signs, avoid collisions in the roundabouts, drive as fast as the flow of frenetic traffic, and can ask directions in French (probably of someone on the street who only speaks a creole patois). But your best option is to hire an English-speaking driver.

☾ ❸ **Aqualand.** This U.S.-style water park is a great place for families to have a wet, happy day. ⊠ *Rte. des Pitons, Carbet* ☎ *0596/78–40–00* ⊕ *www. aqualand-martinique.fr* ⊠ *€17.50* ⊘ *Daily 10–6*.

❷ **Balata.** Built in 1923 to commemorate those who died in World War I, **Balata Church** is an exact replica of Paris's Sacré-Coeur Basilica. The **Jardin de Balata** (Balata Gardens) has thousands of varieties of tropical flowers and plants. There are shaded benches from which to take in the mountain view. ⊠ *Rte. de Balata, Balata* ☎ *0596/64–48–73* ⊠ *€7* ⊘ *Daily 9–5*.

❶ **Fort-de-France.** With its historic fort and superb location beneath the towering Pitons du Carbet on the Baie des Flamands, Martinique's capital should be a grand place. It isn't. The most pleasant districts, such as Didier, Bellevue, and Schoelcher, are on the hillside; there are some good shops with Parisian wares and lively street markets. Near the harbor is a marketplace where local crafts and souvenirs are sold.

The heart of Fort-de-France is **La Savane**, a 12½-acre park filled with trees, fountains, and benches. It's a popular gathering place and the scene of promenades, parades, and impromptu soccer matches. Along the east side are numerous snack wagons. Alas, it's no longer a desirable oasis, what with a lot of litter and other negatives often found in urban parks. A statue of Pierre Belain d'Esnambuc, leader of the island's first settlers, is unintentionally upstaged

> ### PRE-PACK
>
> Set aside a few moments every day to pack up your dirty clothes, then spend the last afternoon of your cruise doing fun things instead of packing.

by Vital Dubray's vandalized—now headless—white Carrara marble statue of the empress Joséphine, Napoléon's first wife. Across from La Savane, you can catch the ferry *La Vedette* for the beaches at Anse-Mitan and Anse-à-l'Ane and for the 20-minute run across the bay to Pointe du Bout. It's relatively cheap as well as stress-free—much safer, more pleasant, and faster than by car.

The most imposing historic site in La Savane (and in Fort-de-France) is **Fort St-Louis,** which runs along the east side of La Savane. It's open Monday through Saturday from 9 to 3, and admission is €4.

The **Bibliothèque Schoelcher** is the wildly elaborate Romanesque public library. It was named after Victor Schoelcher, who led the fight to free the slaves in the French West Indies in the 19th century. The eye-popping structure was built for the 1889 Paris Exposition, after which it was dismantled, shipped to Martinique, and reassembled piece by ornate piece. ✉ *At rue de la Liberté, runs along west side of La Savane, and rue Perrinon* ☎ *0596/70–26–67* 🖂 *Free* ☉ *Mon. 1–5:30, Tues.–Fri. 8:30–5:30, Sat. 8:30–noon.*

★ **Le Musée Régional d'Histoire et d'Ethnographie** is a learning experience that will help you better understand the history, background, and people of the island. Housed in an elaborate former residence (circa 1888) with balconies and fretwork, its displays are far-ranging. ✉ *10 bd. Général de Gaulle* ☎ *0596/72–81–87* 🖂 *€3* ☉ *Mon. and Wed.–Fri. 8:30–5, Tues. 2–5, Sat. 8:30–noon.*

Rue Victor Schoelcher runs through the center of the capital's primary shopping district, a six-block area bounded by rue de la République, rue de la Liberté, rue de Victor Severe, and rue Victor Hugo. Stores sell Paris fashions and French perfume, china, crystal, and liqueurs, as well as local handicrafts. The Romanesque **Saint-Louis Cathedral** (✉ *Rue Victor Schoelcher*) with its lovely stained-glass windows, was built in 1878, the sixth church on this site (the others were destroyed by fire, hurricane, and earthquake).

The **Parc Floral et Culturel,** in the northeastern corner of the city center, will acquaint you with the island's exotic flora. There's also an aquarium. The park contains the island's official cultural center, where there are sometimes free evening concerts. ✉ *Pl. José-Marti, Sermac* ☎ *0596/ 71–66–25* 🖂 *Grounds free; aquarium €5.60* ☉ *Park daily dawn–10 PM; aquarium daily 9–7.*

❹ **Musée Gauguin.** Martinique was a brief station in Paul Gauguin's wanderings, but a decisive moment in the evolution of his art. Disappointingly, this modest museum has no originals, only reproductions. ⊠ *Anse-Turin, Carbet* ☎ *0596/78–22–66* ⊡ *€6* ⊘ *Daily 9–5:30.*

❺ **St-Pierre.** By the turn of the 20th century St-Pierre was a flourishing city, known as the Paris of the West Indies. But on May 8, 1902, as the nearby volcano erupted, Mont Pelée split in half, belching forth a cloud of burning ash, poisonous gas, and lava that raced down the mountain at 250 mph. At 3,600°F, it instantly vaporized everything in its path; 30,000 people in St-Pierre were killed in two minutes. Only one man, a prisoner in an underground cell in the town jail, survived. Today, the city has the feel of a European seaside hill town. Stroll the main streets and check the blackboards at the sidewalk cafés before deciding where to lunch. The **Cyparis Express,** a small tourist train, will take you around to the main sights with running narrative (in French) for €10.50; English-speaking guides are available. Like stage sets for a dramatic opera, there are the ruins of the island's first church (built in 1640), the imposing theater, and toppled statues.

★ ☾ For those interested in the eruption of 1902, the **Musée Vulcanologique Frank Perret** is a must. Established in 1932, it houses photographs of the old town, documents, and a number of relics—some gruesome—excavated from the ruins, including molten glass, melted iron, and contorted clocks stopped at 8 AM. ⊠ *Rue Victor Hugo* ☎ *0596/78–15–16* ⊡ *€5* ⊘ *Daily 9–5.*

An excursion to **Depaz Distillery** is one of the island's nicest treats. There is a self-guided tour, and the tasting room sells their rums, including golden and aged rum (notably Rhum Dore) and distinctive liqueurs made from ginger and basil. ⊠ *Mont Pelée Plantation* ☎ *0596/78–13–14* ⊡ *Free* ⊘ *Mon.–Sat. 9–5.*

Shopping

French products, such as perfume, wines, liquors, designer scarves, leather goods, and crystal, are good buys in Fort-de-France. Luxury goods are discounted 20% when paid for with traveler's checks or major credit cards. Look for creole gold jewelry; white, dark, flavored, and aged rums; and handcrafted straw goods, pottery, madras fabric, and tapestries. Shops that sell luxury items are abundant around the cathedral in Fort-de-France, particularly on rue Victor Hugo, rue Moreau de Jones, rue Antoine Siger, and rue Lamartine.

The work of **Antan Lontan** (⊠ 213 rte. de Balata, Fort-de-France ☎ 0596/64–52–72) has to be seen. Sculptures, busts, statuettes, and artistic lamps portray the creole women and the story of the Martiniquaise culture. **Cadet Daniel** (⊠ 72 *rue Antoine Siger, Fort-de-France* ☎ 0596/71–41–48) sells Lalique, Limoges, and Baccarat. **Roger Albert** (⊠ 7 *rue Victor Hugo, Fort-de-France* ☎ 0596/71–71–71) carries designer crystal.

Activities

FISHING Fish cruising these waters include tuna, barracuda, dolphinfish, kingfish, bonito, and the big game—white and blue marlins. The **Centre de Peche** (⊠ *Port de Plaisance, bd. Allegre, Le Marin* ☎ 0596/76–24–20 or 0696/28–80–58), a fully loaded Davis 47-foot fishing boat, is a sportfisherman's dream. It goes out with a minimum of four anglers for €195 per person for a half day, or €390 per person for a full day, including lunch. Nonanglers can come for the ride for €95 and €190, respectively. Captain Yves speaks English fluently and is a fun guy.

GOLF   The 18-hole **Golf Country Club de la Martinique** (⊠ *Les Trois-Ilets* ☎ *0596/ 68–32–81* ⊕ *www.golfmartinique.com*) has a par-71 Robert Trent Jones course with an English-speaking pro, pro shop, bar, and restaurant. The club offers special greens fees to cruise-ship passengers (€46 for greens fees and another €46 for an electric cart). For those who don't mind walking while admiring the Caribbean view between the palm trees, club trolleys are €8. There are no caddies.

HIKING   Two-thirds of Martinique is designated as protected land. Trails, all 31 of them, are well marked and maintained. At the beginning of each, a notice is posted advising on the level of difficulty, the duration of a hike, and any interesting facts. The **Parc Naturel Régional de la Martinique** (⊠ *9 bd. Général de Gaulle, Fort-de-France* ☎ *0596/73–19–30*) organizes inexpensive guided excursions year-round. If there have been heavy rains, though, give it up. The tangle of ferns, bamboo trees, and llanai vines is dramatic, but during rainy season, the springs and waterfalls and wet, muddy trails will negate any enthusiasm.

HORSEBACK   At **Black Horse Ranch** (⊠ *Les Trois-Ilets* ☎ *0596/68–37–80*), one-hour
RIDING   trail rides (€35) go into the countryside and across waving cane fields; two hours on the trail (€40) bring riders near a river. Only western saddles are used for adults; children can ride English. Semiprivate lessons in French or English are €40 a person, less for kids if they can join a group. Some guides are English-speaking at **Ranch de Caps** (⊠ *Cap Macré, Le Marin* ☎ *0596/74–70–65 or 0696/23–18–18*), where you can take a half-day ride (western) on the wild southern beaches and across the countryside for €45. Rides go out in the morning (8:30 to noon) and afternoon (1:30 to 5) every day but Monday. If you can manage a full day in the saddle, it costs €75. A real treat is the full-moon ride. Most of the mounts are Anglo-Arabs. Riders are encouraged to help cool and wash their horses at day's end. Reserve in advance. Riders of all levels ☾ are welcome. **Ranch Jack** (⊠ *Anse-d'Arlets* ☎ *0596/68–37–69 or 0596/ 68–63–97*) has trail rides (English style) across some beautiful country for €35 an hour; half-day excursions for €50 (€58 with transfers from nearby hotels) go through the fields and forests to the beach. The lessons for kids are recommendable.

Beaches

Topless bathing is prevalent at the large resort hotels. The clean, golden sand at **Anse-Mitan** (⊠ *Les Trois-Ilets*) is lined by inexpensive waterfront hotels; there is excellent snorkeling just offshore. Chaise lounges are available for rent from hotels for about €5. **Pointe du Bout** (⊠ *Les Trois-Ilets*) has small, man-made beaches that are lined with luxury resorts. Across from the main pedestrian entrance to the marina, if you take a left— between the taxi stand and the Kalenda Hotel, then go left again, you will reach the Sofitel beach, which has especially nice facilities and options for lunch. If not crowded with hotel guests, the beach boys might rent you a chaise. Otherwise, just plop your beach towel down in the

★   sand and admire the great bay view. **Les Salines** (⊠ *Ste-Anne*), a cove of soft white sand lined with coconut palms, is about an hour from Fort-de-France. (This is doable if you cut the cost by taking a group taxi.) Les Salines is awash with families and children during holidays and on weekends, but quiet and uncrowded during the week. You can't rent chaise longues, so bring a beach towel or two (there are showers). Food vendors roam the sand.

Where to Eat

All restaurants include a 15% service charge in their prices. Leaving a little extra gives Americans a good name.

¢–$ ✕ **Linda's Café.** You will be satisfied at this classy café. You must order at the counter (it's OK to just point). Offerings are displayed in the glass case. Breakfast can be fresh-squeezed juice, gourmet coffee, and just-baked croissants. Lunch is the best possible sandwich situation. Choices abound, from fresh thyme bread with rare roast beef, to baby shrimp and avocado. Have creamy *fromage blanc* instead of mayo, and even turkey bacon. Dessert can be a perfect, dark-chocolate brownie. ⊠ *15 rue Victor Hugo, Fort-de-France* ☎ *0596/71–91–92* ▭ *MC, V* ⊗ *No dinner Sun.*

$–$$ ✕ **Chez Carole.** After spending eight years in Toulouse, Carole now cooks her island's creole specialties in the simple surroundings of the market. Tourists often pass by the loud hawkers to settle here, where they will be welcomed in English and impressed by the awards on display. Creole prix-fixe meals might include accras, fricassee of octopus and conch, chicken in coconut milk, or grilled whole fish. Accompaniments are usually lentils, red beans, yellow rice, and breadfruit. Homemade ice cream and coconut flan are among the dessert possibilities. Cruise-ship passengers love the fresh-squeezed juices (with rum, if you like) and coconut milk shakes. Dollars and traveler's checks work equally well here. ⊠ *Le Grand Marché, Rue Isambert, Fort-de-France* ☎ *0696/44–12–31* ▭ *No credit cards* ⊗ *Closed Sun. No dinner.*

MONTEGO BAY, JAMAICA

John Bigley &
Paris Permenter

Today, many explorations of MoBay are conducted from a reclining chair—frothy drink in hand—on Doctor's Cave Beach. As home of Jamaica's busiest cruise pier and the north-shore airport, Montego Bay—or MoBay—is the first taste most visitors have of the island. Travelers from around the world come and go in this bustling community, which ranks as Jamaica's second-largest city. The name Montego is derived from *manteca* ("lard" in Spanish). The Spanish first named this Bahía de Manteca, or Lard Bay. Why? The Spanish once shipped hogs from this port city. Jamaican tourism began here in 1924, when the first resort opened at Doctor's Cave Beach so that health-seekers could "take the waters." If you can pull yourself away from the water's edge and brush the sand off your toes, you can find some very interesting colonial sights in the surrounding area.

Essentials

CURRENCY   The Jamaican dollar (J$67 to US$1). Currency-exchange booths are set up on the docks at Montego Bay whenever a ship is in port; however,

Montego Bay

the U.S. dollar is accepted virtually everywhere, though change is made in Jamaican dollars.

HOURS   Normal business hours for stores are weekdays from 8:30 to 4:30, Saturday 8 to 1 with extended hours for shops in tourist areas.

INTERNET   A growing number of Internet cafés have sprung up in recent years in Montego Bay hotels and cafés. A popular option for many cruise passengers is the Internet café at **Doctor's Cave Beach** (⊠ *Montego Bay* ☎ *876/971–1050*).

TELEPHONES   Public telephones (and fax machines) are at the communications center at the Montego Bay Cruise Terminal. Travelers also find public phones in major Montego Bay malls such as the City Centre Shopping Mall. Some U.S. phone companies won't permit credit-card calls to be placed from Jamaica because they've been victims of fraud so collect calls are often the top option. GSM cell phones equipped with tri-band or world-roaming service will find coverage throughout the Montego Bay region.

Coming Ashore

Ships dock at the Montego Cruise Terminal, operated by the Port Authority of Jamaica. Located west of Montego Bay, the cruise terminal has five berths and accommodates both cruise and cargo shipping. The terminal has shops, a communications center, a Jamaica Tourist Board visitor information booth, and a taxi stand supervised by the Jamaica Tourist Board. The cruise port in Montego Bay is not within walking distance of the heart of town; however, there's one shopping center within walking distance of the docks. If you just want to visit a beach, then Doctor's Cave, a public beach, is a very good nearby alternative, and it's right in town.

From the Montego Cruise Terminal, both taxis and shuttle buses take passengers downtown. Taxi service is about US $10 each way to downtown. Expect to pay $2 per person each way by shuttle bus to the City Centre Shopping Mall or

> ## MONTEGO BAY BEST BETS
>
> ■ Doctor's Cave Beach. The public beach club right in the heart of Montego Bay is on an excellent stretch of white-sand beach and has many facilities to make a day at the beach a pleasure.
>
> ■ Dunn's River Falls. A visit to the falls is nothing but a touristy experience, and yet it's still exhilarating.
>
> ■ Martha Brae Rafting. A slow rafting trip down the river is a relaxing and enjoyable way to spend a few hours.
>
> ■ Shopping. If you just want some retail therapy, MoBay has several good shopping centers.

$3 each way to Doctor's Cave Beach. Jamaica is one place in the Caribbean where it's usually to your advantage to take an organized shore excursion offered by your ship unless you just want to do a bit of shopping in town. Taxis aren't particularly cheap, and a full-day tour for a small group will run $150 to $180 (because of road conditions and the distances in Jamaica, most tours take a full day).

If you take a private taxi, you should know that only some of Jamaica's taxis are metered; rates are per car, not per passenger. You can flag cabs on the street. All licensed and properly insured taxis display red Public Passenger (PP) license plates. Licensed minivans also bear the red PP plates. If you hire a taxi driver as a tour guide, be sure to agree on a price before the vehicle is put into gear. Because of the cost of insurance, which you must buy since most credit cards offering coverage exclude Jamaica, it's expensive to rent a car; you may also find it difficult to arrange a rental on-island. It's far easier to arrange a taxi.

Shore Excursions

We consider these to be among the better shore excursions for Montego Bay. They may not be offered by all lines, and tour names may differ as well. Times and prices are approximate.

Canopy Tour. The "tour" consists of flying from platform to platform through a forest on a zip line. It's a great experience. ☉ 4–4¼ hrs ▧ $99.

Dunn's River Falls with Lunch. Some kind of Dunn's River Falls trip is offered on all Montego Bay port calls, and it may be a combination of Dunn's River Falls with another attraction in Ocho Rios for more money. The basic (and usually cheapest) option includes a visit to the Falls and lunch at a local restaurant in Ocho Rios. ☉ 7½ hrs ▧ $79.

Montego Bay Highlights with Rose Hall. After a quick tour of town, the highlight of this trip is a visit to the supposedly haunted Rose Hall Great House. ⊘ 3½ hrs ☞ $49.

Rafting on the Martha Brae River. Pass the verdant plant life as you glide down the river on a 30-foot, two seat bamboo raft. This is decidedly still-water rafting. ⊘ 4¼ ☞ $69.

Exploring Montego Bay

Numbers in the margin correspond to points of interest on the Montego Bay map.

❶ Greenwood Great House. Although this historic home has no spooky legend to titillate, it's much better than Rose Hall at evoking life on a sugar plantation. The Barrett family, from whom the English poet Elizabeth Barrett Browning descended, once owned all the land from Rose Hall to Falmouth; they built this and several other great houses on it. (The poet's father, Edward Moulton Barrett, "the Tyrant of Wimpole Street," was born at nearby Cinnamon Hill, the estate of the late country singer Johnny Cash.) Highlights of Greenwood include oil paintings of the Barretts, china made for the family by Wedgwood, a library filled with rare books from as early as 1697, fine antique furniture, and a collection of exotic musical instruments. There's a pub on-site as well. It's 15 mi (24 km) east of Montego Bay. ⊠ *Greenwood* ☎ *876/953–1077* ⊕ *www. greenwoodgreathouse.com* ☞ *$12* ⊘ *Daily 9–6.*

❷ Martha Brae River. A gentle waterway about 25 mi (40 km) southeast of Montego Bay, it takes its name from an Arawak Indian who killed herself because she refused to reveal the whereabouts of a local gold mine to the Spanish. According to legend, she agreed to take them there and, on reaching the river, used magic to change its course, drowning herself and the greedy Spaniards with her. Her *duppy* (ghost) is said to guard the mine's entrance. Rafting on this river is a very popular activity.

❸ Rose Hall Great House. In the 1700s, Rose Hall may have been the greatest of great houses in the West Indies. Today it's popular less for its architecture than for the legend surrounding its second mistress: Annie Palmer was credited with murdering three husbands and a *busha* (plantation overseer) who was her lover. The story is told in a novel that's sold everywhere in Jamaica: *The White Witch of Rose Hall.* There's a pub on-site. The house is across the highway from the Rose Hall Resort. ⊠ *North Coast Hwy.* ☎ *876/953–9982* ☞ *$15* ⊘ *Daily 9–6.*

❹ Dunn's River Falls. A top shore excursion from Montego Bay despite the two-hour drive to get here, the falls are an eye-catching sight: 600 feet of cold, clear mountain water splashing over a series of stone steps to the warm Caribbean. The best way to enjoy the falls is to climb the slippery steps: don a swimsuit, take the hand of the person ahead of you, and trust that the chain of hands and bodies leads to an experienced guide. The leaders of the climbs are personable fellows who reel off bits of local lore while telling you where to step; you can hire a guide's service for a tip of a few dollars. After the climb, you exit through a crowded market, another reminder that this is one of Jamaica's top tourist attractions. ⊠ *Off A1, between St. Ann's and Ocho Rios* ☎ *876/974–2857* ☞ *$15* ⊘ *Daily 8:30–5.*

Fodor'sChoice
★

Shopping

Jamaican artisans express themselves in silk-screening, wood carvings, resort wear, hand-loomed fabrics, and paintings. Jamaican rum makes a great gift, as do Tia Maria (the famous coffee liqueur) and Blue Mountain coffee. Wood carvings are one of the top purchases; the finest carvings are made from the Jamaican national tree, lignum vitae, or tree of life, a dense wood that requires a talented carver to transform the hard, blond wood into dolphins, heads, or fish. Bargaining is expected with crafts vendors.

Gallery of West Indian Art (✉ *11 Fairfield Rd., Montego Bay* ☎ *876/952–4547*) is the place to find Jamaican and Haitian paintings. A corner of the gallery is devoted to hand-turned pottery (some painted) and beautifully carved and painted birds and animals.

Activities

DIVING & SNORKELING   Jamaica isn't a major dive destination, but you can find a few rich underwater regions, especially off the north coast. MoBay, known for its wall dives, has **Airport Reef** at its southwestern edge. The site is known for its coral caves, tunnels, and canyons. The first marine park in Jamaica, the **Montego Bay Marine Park,** was established to protect the natural resources of the bay; a quick look at the area and it's easy to see the treasures that lie beneath the surface. The north coast is on the edge of the Cayman Trench, so it boasts a wide array of marine life.

Scuba Jamaica (✉ *Half Moon, N. Coast Hwy., Montego Bay* ☎ *876/ 381–1113* ⊕ *www.scuba-jamaica.com*) offers serious scuba facilities for dedicated divers. This operator is a PADI and NAUI operation and also offers Nitrox diving and instruction as well as instruction in underwater photography, night diving, and open-water diving. There's a pickup service for the Montego Bay, Runaway Bay, Discovery Bay, and Ocho Rios areas.

DOLPHIN SWIM PROGRAMS   Dolphin lovers find two well-run options in both Montego Bay and Ocho Rios. **Dolphin Cove** (✉ *N. Coast Hwy., adjacent to Dunn's River Falls, Ocho Rios* ☎ *876/974–5335* ⊕ *www.dolphincovejamaica.com*) offers dolphin swims as well as lower-priced dolphin encounters for ages eight and up; dolphin touch programs for ages six and over; or simple admission to the grounds, which also includes a short nature walk. Programs cost between $39 and $179, depending on your depth of involvement with the dolphins. Advance reservations are required.

GOLF   Golfers appreciate both the beauty and the challenges offered by Jamaica's courses and some of the best are found in the Montego Bay area. Caddies are almost always mandatory throughout the island, and rates are $15 to $45. Cart rentals are available; costs are $20 to $40. Some of the best courses in the country are found near MoBay.

BINOCULARS

Binoculars are as useful indoors as they are outside. You might think they are only for bringing far-off wildlife and sights within view, but take them into museums, churches, and other buildings to examine the details of artwork, sculptures, and architectural elements.

★ **Half Moon Golf, Tennis & Beach Club** (✉ *Montego Bay* ☎ *876/953–2560*), a Robert Trent Jones–designed 18-hole course 7 mi (11 km) east of town, is the home of the Red Stripe Pro Am (greens fees are $150). In 2004 the course received an upgrade and once again draws international attention. **Ironshore** (✉ *Montego Bay* ☎ *876/953–2800*), 3 mi (5 km) east of the airport, is an 18-hole links-style course (the greens fees are $50). The **Rose Hall Resort & Country Club** (✉ *Montego Bay* ☎ *876/953–2650*) hosts several invitational tournaments (greens fees run $150 for nonguests). **Tryall Golf, Tennis & Beach Club** (✉ *North Coast Hwy., Sandy Bay* ☎ *876/ 956–5681*), 15 mi (24 km) west of Montego Bay, has an 18-hole championship course on the site of a 19th-century sugar plantation (greens fees are $125).

RIVER RAFTING Jamaica's many rivers mean a multitude of freshwater experiences, from mild to wild. Relaxing rafting trips aboard bamboo rafts poled by local boatmen are almost a symbol of Jamaica; this was the island's first tourist activity outside the beaches. Jamaicans had long used bamboo rafts to transport bananas downriver; decades ago actor and Jamaica resident Errol Flynn saw the rafts and thought they'd make a good tourist attraction. Today the slow rides are a favorite with romantic travelers and anyone looking for a quiet few hours with a trip down the **Martha Brae River,** about 25 mi (40 km) from MoBay, **River Lethe,** about 12 mi (19 km) southwest, or the **Great River,** which travels through the rain forest.

Jamaica Tours Limited (✉ *Providence Dr., Montego Bay* ☎ *876/953–3700* ⊕ *www.jamaicatoursltd.com*) conducts trips down the River Lethe, approximately 12 mi (19 km; a 50-minute trip) southwest of MoBay; the four-hour excursion costs about $54 per person, includes lunch, and takes you through unspoiled hill country. Bookings can also be made through hotel tour desks. **Martha Brae River Rafting** (✉ *Claude Clarke Ave., Montego Bay* ☎ *876/952–0889* ⊕ *www.jamaicarafting.com*) leads trips down the Martha Brae River, about 25 mi (40 km) from most hotels in MoBay. The cost is $45 per person for the 1½-hour river run.

If you're looking for a more rugged adventure, then consider a whitewater rafting trip with **Caliche Rainforest** (✉ *Montego Bay* ☎ *876/940– 1745* ⊕ *www.whitewaterraftingmontegobay.com*); you must be 14 years old for this trip. The company also offers a less strenuous rafting trip for all ages.

Beaches

Doctor's Cave Beach. Montego Bay's tourist scene has its roots right on the Hip Strip, the bustling entertainment district along Gloucester Avenue. The best beach in Jamaica outside one of the more developed resorts is also here, thanks to its plantation-style clubhouse with changing rooms, showers, gift shops, bar, grill, and even a cybercafé. Nearby, you'll find the always-popular Margaritaville. There's a fee for admission; beach chairs and umbrellas are also for rent. It's also a good spot for snorkeling, as it's within the Montego Bay Marine Park, with protected corals and marine life. More active travelers can opt for parasailing, glass-bottom boat rides, or jet skiing.

Walter Fletcher Beach. Though not as pretty as Doctor's Cave Beach—or as tidy—it's home to Aquasol Theme Park. Along with a large beach (which includes lifeguards and security), the park offers water trampolines, Jet Skis, banana boat rides, Wave Runners, glass-bottom boats, snorkeling, tennis, go-cart racing, a disco at night, a bar, and a grill. The beach is near the center of town, and there's protection from the surf on a windy day, so you can find unusually fine swimming here; the calm waters make it a good bet for children.

Where to Eat

Many restaurants add a 10% service charge to the bill. Otherwise, a tip of 10% to 20% is customary.

★ ¢–$$ ✕ **The Native.** Shaded by a large poinciana tree and overlooking Gloucester Avenue, this open-air stone terrace serves Jamaican and international dishes. To go native, start with smoked marlin, move on to the *boonoonoonoos* platter (a sampler of local dishes), and round out with coconut pie or *duckanoo* (a sweet dumpling of cornmeal, coconut, and banana wrapped in a banana leaf and steamed). Live entertainment and candlelighted tables make this a romantic choice for dinner on weekends. ✉ *29 Gloucester Ave.* ☎ *876/979–2769* ☜ *Reservations essential* ▤ *AE, MC, V.*

¢–$ ✕ **The Pork Pit.** A favorite with many MoBay locals, this no-frills eatery serves Jamaican specialties, including some fiery jerk—note that it's spiced to local tastes, not watered down for tourist palates. Many get their food to go, but you can also find picnic tables just outside. ✉ *27 Gloucester Ave.* ☎ *876/940–3008* ▤ *No credit cards.*

NASSAU, BAHAMAS

Cheryl
Blackerby

Nassau, the capital of the Bahamas, has witnessed Spanish invasions and hosted pirates, who made it their headquarters for raids along the Spanish Main. The heritage of old Nassau blends the Southern charm of British loyalists from the Carolinas, the African tribal traditions of freed slaves, and a bawdy history of blockade-running during the Civil War and rum-running in the Roaring 1920s. The sheltered harbor bustles with cruise-ship hubbub, while a block away, broad, palm-lined Bay Street is alive with commercial activity. Over it all is a subtle layer of civility and sophistication, derived from three centuries of British rule. Nassau's charm, however, is often lost in its commercialism. There's excellent shopping, but if you look past the duty-free shops, you'll also find sights of historical significance that are worth seeing.

Essentials

CURRENCY The Bahamian dollar, which trades one-to-one with the U.S. dollar, which is universally accepted. There's no need to acquire any Bahamian currency.

HOURS Banks are generally open Monday–Thursday 9:30 to 3 and Friday 9:30 to 4:30. Hours for attractions vary; most open by 9 or 10 and close by 5. Most shops are open from 10 to 6.

INTERNET You'll find Internet kiosks at Prince George Wharf.

TELEPHONES Calling locally or internationally is easy in the Bahamas. To place a local call, dial the seven-digit phone number. To call the United States, dial 1 plus the area code. Pay phones cost 25¢ per call; Bahamian and U.S. quarters are accepted, as are BATELCO phone cards. To place a call using a calling card, use your long-distance carrier's access code or dial 0 for the operator. Be aware that when placing a toll-free call from your hotel, you are charged as if for a regular long-distance call.

Coming Ashore

Cruise ships dock at one of three piers on Prince George's Wharf. Taxi drivers who meet the ships may offer you a $2 "ride into town," but the historic government buildings and duty-free shops lie just steps from the dock area. As you leave the pier, look for a tall pink tower—diagonally across from here is the tourist information office. Stop in for maps of the island and downtown Nassau. On most days you can join a one-hour walking tour ($10 per person) conducted by a well-trained guide. Tours generally start every hour on the hour from 10 AM to 4 PM; confirm the day's schedule in the office. Just outside, an ATM dispenses U.S. dollars.

As you disembark from your ship, you will find a row of taxis and air-conditioned limousines. Fares are fixed by the government by zones. The fare is $6 for trips within downtown Nassau and around Paradise Island; $9 from downtown Nassau to Paradise Island (which includes the bridge toll); $8 from Paradise Island to downtown Nassau; and $18 from Cable Beach to Paradise Island, including toll ($17 for the return trip). Fares cover two passengers; each additional passenger is $3, regardless of destination. It is customary to tip taxi drivers 15%. You can also hire a car or small van for sightseeing for $45 to $60 per hour or about $13 per person.

Beautifully painted horse-drawn carriages will take as many as four people around Nassau at a rate of $10 per adult and $5 per child for a 30-minute ride; don't hesitate to bargain. Most drivers give a comprehensive tour of the Bay Street area, including an extensive history lesson. Look for the carriages on Woodes Rogers Walk, in the center of Rawson Square.

Two people can ride around the island on a motor scooter for about $40 for a half day, $50 for a full day. Helmets and insurance for both driver and passenger are mandatory and are included in the rental price. Many hotels have scooters on the premises. You can also try Knowles,

---

NASSAU BEST BETS

- **Ardastra Gardens.** Flocks of flamingos, the country's national bird, "march" in three daily shows (you can mingle with the flamboyant pink stars afterward).

- **Shopping.** To many, shopping is one of Nassau's great delights.

- **Western Esplanade Beach.** Head to this beach (also known as Long Wharf Beach) and sit in the shade of a coconut palm while admiring a glistening white-sand beach and the mega-cruise ships coming into the harbor. (It's only a 10-minute walk from the duty-free shops on Bay Street.)

Nassau, Bahamas

300 yards
300 meters

Silver Cay

Arawak Cay

Lighthouse

Paradise Beach

Paradise Island

Cabbage Beach

TO PARADISE ISLAND
GOLF COURSE

Paradise Is. Dr.

Harbor Dr.

Casino Dr.

Paradise Beach Dr.

Paradise Lake

Casuarina Dr.

TO BEACHES

Nassau Harbour

Paradise Island Bridge

Potter's Cay

Fort Montagu

Lake Waterloo

East Bay St.

John Evans

Kemp Rd.

St. James Rd.

Sutton St.

Mackey St.

Church St.

Montrose Ave.

Mount Royal Ave.

Collins Ave.

Rosetta St.

Prince George Wharf

Union Dock

John Alfred Wharf

Woodes Rogers Walk

Frederick St.

Parliament St.

Bay St.

Dowdeswell St.

Shirley St.

Elizabeth Ave.

East St.

North St.

Sands Rd.

King St.

George St.

Cumberland Rd.

East Hill St.

Duke St.

Market St.

Blue Hill Rd.

King St.

Hospital Lane

West St.

Marlborough St.

West Hill St.

Delancy St.

Meeting St.

Nassau St.

West Bay St.

Infant View Rd.

Western Esplanade

1 Parliament Square **1**

2 Staircase ...

3 Water Tower

KEY

Beaches

Cruise Ship Terminal

Ferry

Arawak Cay .... **6** Parliament Square **1**

Ardastra Gardens   Queen's
& Conservation Centre ... **5** Staircase **2**

Fort Charlotte **4**

Fort Fincastle and the
Water Tower **3**

on West Bay Street, in the British Colonial Hilton parking lot, or check out the stands in Rawson Square. Remember to drive on the left.

The cheapest way to get to Paradise Island on your own is to take the ferry from the dock area ($3 each way).

Shore Excursions

We consider these to be among the better shore excursions for Nassau. They may not be offered by all lines, and tour names may differ as well. Times and prices are approximate.

Harbor Tour & Atlantis. After a half-hour harbor tour, your boat docks near the Atlantis Resort on Paradise Island, where you will be admitted to tour the world famous "Atlantis Dig" aquarium. Some lines also offer lunch, but these cost considerably more; most tours do not include use of the Atlantis beach or pools. ☺ 2½ hrs ▱ $56.

Nassau & Ardastra Gardens. Your tour takes in the major points of interest in Nassau, such as the Queen's Staircase and Fort Fincastle as well as Ardastra Gardens, a tropical zoo featuring pink flamingos, the national bird. ☺ 2½ hrs ▱ $49.

Sail & Snorkel. You sail, usually on a large catamaran, to a snorkeling spot, where the boat anchors while you swim among the fishies. Refreshments are provided. ☺ 3½ hrs ▱ $49.

Stingray Snorkel & Beach Break. You're taken to Blackbeard's Cay, where you'll get to snorkel among stingrays. Food and beverages are sold on-site. Snorkeling equipment is provided. ☺ 3 hrs ▱ $49.

Exploring Nassau

Numbers in the margin correspond to points of interest on the Nassau map.

Nassau's sheltered harbor bustles with cruise-ship hubbub, while a block away, broad, palm-lined Bay Street is alive with commercial activity. Shops angle for tourist dollars with fine imported goods at duty-free prices, yet you will find a handful of stores overflowing with authentic Bahamian crafts, foods, and other delights. Most of Nassau's historic sites are centered around downtown.

With its thoroughly revitalized downtown—the revamped British Colonial Hilton leads the way—Nassau is recapturing some of its glamour. Nevertheless, modern influence is apparent: fancy restaurants, suave clubs, and trendy coffeehouses have popped up everywhere. This trend comes partly in response to the burgeoning upper-crust crowds that now supplement the spring-breakers and cruise passengers who have traditionally flocked to Nassau.

Today the seedy air of the town's not-so-distant past is almost unrecognizable. Petty crime is no greater than in other towns of this size, and the streets not only look cleaner but feel safer. You can still find a wild club or a rowdy bar, but you can also sip cappuccino while viewing contemporary Bahamian art or dine by candlelight beneath prints of old Nassau, serenaded by soft, island-inspired calypso music.

❻ **Arawak Cay.** For a literal taste of Bahamian culture throughout the island chain, take the slightly long walk west on Bay Street to this cluster of eateries and shops. You can buy crafts and food, especially squeaky-fresh conch salad, often made before your very eyes. An ice-cold Kalik beer makes the perfect foil. ✉ *W. Bay St.* 🎫 *Free* 🕐 *Daily.*

🌙 ❺ **Ardastra Gardens & Conservation Centre.** Marching flamingos? These national birds of the Bahamas give a parading performance at Ardastra daily at 10:30, 2, and 4. The zoo, with more than 5 acres of tropical greenery and flowering shrubs, also has an aviary of rare tropical birds, native Bahamian creatures such as rock iguanas, and a global collection of small animals. ✉ *Chippingham Rd., south of W. Bay St.* 🎫 *242/323–5806* ⊕ *www.ardastra.com* 🎫 *$12* 🕐 *Daily 9–5.*

★ ❹ **Fort Charlotte.** Built in the late 18th century, this imposing fort comes complete with a waterless moat, drawbridge, ramparts, and dungeons. Lord Dunmore, who built it, named the massive structure in honor of George III's wife. At the time, some called it Dunmore's Folly because of the staggering expense of its construction. It cost eight times more than was originally planned. (Dunmore's superiors in London were less than ecstatic with the high costs, but he managed to survive unscathed.) Ironically, no shots were ever fired in battle from the fort. It is about 1 mi (1½ km) west of central Nassau. ✉ *W. Bay St. at Chippingham Rd.* 🎫 *Free* 🕐 *Local guides conduct tours daily 8–4.*

❸ **Fort Fincastle.** Shaped like a paddle-wheel steamer and perched near the top of the **Queen's Staircase,** Fort Fincastle—named for Royal Governor Lord Dunmore (Viscount Fincastle)—was completed in 1793 to serve as a lookout post for marauders trying to sneak into the harbor. It served as a lighthouse in the early 19th century. The fort's 126-foot-tall **water tower,** which is more than 200 feet above sea level, is the island's highest point but has been closed for some time for renovations. ✉ *Top of Elizabeth Ave. hill, south of Shirley St., Nassau* 🕐 *Daily 8–5.*

❶ **Parliament Square.** Nassau is the seat of the national government. The Bahamian Parliament comprises two houses—a 16-member Senate (Upper House) and a 40-member House of Assembly (Lower House)— and a ministerial cabinet headed by a prime minister. Parliament Square's pink, colonnaded government buildings were constructed in the early 1800s by Loyalists who came to the Bahamas from North Carolina. The square is dominated by a statue of a slim young Queen Victoria that was erected on her birthday, May 24, in 1905. In the immediate area are a half dozen magistrates' courts (open to the public; obtain a pass at the door to view a session). Behind the House of Assembly is the **Supreme Court.** Its four-times-a-year opening ceremonies (held the first weeks of January, April, July, and October) recall the wigs and mace-bearing pageantry of the Houses of Parliament in London. The Royal Bahamas Police Force Band is usually on hand for the event. ✉ *Bay St., Nassau* 🎫 *242/322–7500 for information on Supreme Court ceremonies* 🎫 *Free* 🕐 *Weekdays 10–4.*

❷ **Queen's Staircase.** These 65 steps are thought to have been carved out of a solid limestone cliff by slaves in the 1790s. The staircase was later named to honor Queen Victoria's 65-year reign. Recent innovations include a waterfall cascading from the top, and an ad hoc straw market along the narrow road that leads to the site. ⊠ *Top of Elizabeth Ave. hill, south of Shirley St.*

Shopping

Duty-free shopping is a major pastime in Nassau, and there are plenty of bargains to be found. Most of the stores selling duty-free items are clustered along an eight-block stretch of Bay Street in Old Nassau and on a few downtown side streets. Most stores are open Monday through Saturday from 9 to 5 and accept credit cards.

On Bay Street at Market Street, the **Straw Market** has convened for hundreds of years. After a disastrous fire in 2001, it relocated to a nearby concrete structure. Its counterpart on Paradise Island, **BahamaCraft Centre,** is set up in a collection of colorful kiosks. The straw markets carry inexpensive straw and carved items, plus T-shirts and other souvenir apparel and jewelry.

Doongalik Studios Gallery (⊠ *18 Village Rd., Paradise Island* ☎ *242/394–1886*) showcases Bahamian fine art, crafts, and culture in an old-Bahamian setting with a focus on the islands' annual Junkanoo festival.

Activities

FISHING   The waters here are generally smooth and alive with many species of game fish, which is one of the reasons why the Bahamas has more than 20 fishing tournaments open to visitors every year. A favorite spot just west of Nassau is the Tongue of the Ocean, so called because it looks like that part of the body when viewed from the air. The channel stretches for 100 mi. For boat rentals, parties of two to six will pay $300 or so for a half day, $600 for a full day.

Born Free Charters (☎ *242/393–4144* ⊕ *www.bornfreefishing.com/*) has three boats and guarantees a catch on full-day charters—if you don't get a fish, you don't pay. **Brown's Charters** (☎ *242/324–2061*) specializes in 24-hour shark fishing trips, as well as reef and deep-sea fishing. **Chubasco Charters** (☎ *242/324–3474* ⊕ *www.chubascocharters.com*) has four boats for sportfishing and shark fishing charters.

GOLF   **Cable Beach Golf Club** (⊠ *Cable Beach* ☎ *800/214–4281* ⊕ *www. radisson-cablebeach.com*), at 7,040 yards and with a par of 72, is the oldest golf course in the Bahamas. The links are owned by the Radisson Cable Beach Casino & Golf Resort. **Ocean Club Golf Course** (⊠ *Paradise Island Dr., Paradise Island* ☎ *242/363–6682, 800/321–3000 in the U.S.* ⊕ *www.oneandonlyresorts.com*) was designed by Tom Weiskopf. The par-72 championship course is surrounded by the ocean on three sides, which means that winds can get stiff. Tee times can be reserved 60 days in advance.

Beaches

New Providence is blessed with stretches of white sand studded with palm and sea grape trees. Some of the beaches are small and crescent-shaped; others stretch for miles. On the north side of the island lies Paradise Island's showpiece, **Cabbage Beach,** which is popular with locals and tourists and is the home of most of the island's resorts. The beach rims the north coast from the Atlantis lagoon to Snorkeler's Cove. At the north end you can rent Jet Skis and nonmotorized pedal boats and go parasailing. **Cable Beach** is on New Providence's north shore, about 3 mi (5 km) west of downtown Nassau. Resorts line much of this beautiful, broad swath of white sand, but there is public access. Jet-skiers and beach vendors abound, so don't expect quiet isolation. Just west of Cable Beach is a rambling pink house on the Rock Point promontory, where much of the 1965 James Bond movie *Thunderball* was filmed. Downtown, the **Western Esplanade** sweeps westward from the British Colonial Hotel on Bay Street (a 10-minute walk from the cruise-ship pier). It's just across the street from shops and restaurants, and it has restrooms, a snack bar, and changing facilities. **Paradise Beach** stretches for more than 1 mi (1½ km) on the western end of Paradise Island.

Where to Eat

$–$$ ✕ **Athena Café.** A mainstay since 1960, this Greek restaurant provides a break from the Nassau culinary routine. Sit on the second floor among Grecian statuary, or on the balcony overlooking the action below. Enjoy souvlaki, moussaka, and spanakopita, among other specialties, along with Greek beer in a relaxed and friendly atmosphere. Gregarious owner Peter Mousis and his family serve tasty fare at moderate prices, including breakfast seven days a week. ⊠ *Bay St. at Charlotte St.* ☎ *242/322–8833* ▭ *AE, D, MC, V* ☺ *No dinner Sun.*

$–$$ ✕ **Portofino.** Nassau's movers and shakers meet here for breakfast, lunch, and dinner. In the British Colonial Hilton Nassau, Portofino offers homemade Italian pasta dishes and pizza as well as Bahamian favorites such as pan-seared snapper with mango sauce, conch chowder, and guava duff. The lavish lunch buffet far surpasses the usual hotel fare. For breakfast, don't miss the Bahamian johnnycakes. Ask for a window seat so you can see the cruise ships come and go in the harbor. After dinner, you can walk to the hotel's private beach for a lovely view of the harbor and Paradise Island. ⊠ *No. 1 W. Bay St., Nassau* ☎ *242/ 322–3301* ▭ *AE, MC, V.*

Nightlife

Some ships stay late into the night or until the next day so that passengers can enjoy Nassau's nightlife. You'll find nonstop entertainment nightly along Cable Beach and on Paradise Island. All the larger hotels offer lounges with island combos for listening or dancing and restaurants with soft guitar or piano music.

CASINOS At 50,000 square feet (100,000 if you include the dining and drinking areas), the **Atlantis Casino** (⊠ *Atlantis Resort, Paradise Island* ☎ *242/ 363–3000* ⊕ *www.atlantis.com*) is the Caribbean's largest gambling hall. Ringed with restaurants, it offers more than 1,000 slot machines, baccarat, blackjack, roulette, craps tables, and such local specialties as Caribbean stud poker. There's a high-limit table area, additional games available at most of the eateries within its walls, and a spectacularly open and airy design. Tables are open from 10 AM to 4 AM daily; slots, 24 hours daily. At the **Crystal Palace Casino** (✉ *Nassau Marriott Resort, Cable Beach* ☎ 242/327–6200), slots, craps, baccarat, blackjack, roulette, Big Six, and face-up 21 are among the games in the 35,000-square-foot space. There's a Sports Book facility for sports betting, equipped with big-screen TVs, which air ongoing sporting events. Both VIPs and low-limit bettors have their own areas. Casino gaming lessons are available for beginners. Tables and slots are open 24 hours daily.

NIGHTCLUBS   **Club Waterloo** (✉ *E. Bay St., Nassau* ☎ 242/393–7324) claims to be Nassau's largest indoor-outdoor nightclub, with five bars and nonstop dancing Monday through Saturday until 4 AM (with bands on weekends). Try the spring-break-special Waterloo Hurricane, a mixture of rums and punches.

NEVIS (CHARLESTOWN)

Jordan Simon   In 1493, when Columbus spied a cloud-crowned volcanic isle during his second voyage to the New World, he named it Nieves—the Spanish word for "snows"—because it reminded him of the peaks of the Pyrenees. Nevis rises from the water in an almost perfect cone, the tip of its 3,232-foot central mountain hidden by clouds. Even less developed than sister island St. Kitts—just 2 mi (3 km) away at their closest point, Nevis is known for its long beaches with white and black sand, its lush greenery, the charming if slightly dilapidated Georgian capital of Charlestown, and its restored sugar plantations that now house charming inns. Even on a day trip Nevis feels relaxed and quietly upscale. You might run into celebrities at the Four Seasons or lunching at the beach bars on Pinney's, the showcase strand. Yet Nevisians (not to mention the significant expat American and British presence) never put on airs, offering warm hospitality to all visitors.

Essentials

CURRENCY   The Eastern Caribbean dollar (EC$$2.70 to US$1). U.S. dollars, major credit cards, and traveler's checks are readily accepted, although large U.S. bills may be difficult to change in small shops—and you'll receive change in the local currency.

HOURS   Most stores remain open Monday through Saturday from 9 to 4. Some attractions close early on Saturday.

INTERNET   **Downtown Cybercafe** (✉ *Main St., Charlestown* ☎ 869/469–1999).

TELEPHONES   Phone cards, which you can buy in denominations of $5, $10, and $20, are handy for making local phone calls, calling other islands, and accessing U.S. direct lines. To make a local call, dial the seven-digit number. To call Nevis from the United States, dial the area code 869, then access code 465, 466, 468, or 469 and the local four-digit number.

Coming Ashore

Cruise ships dock in Charlestown harbor; all but the smallest ships bring passengers in by tender to the central downtown ferry dock. The pier leads smack onto Main Street, with shops and restaurants steps away.

Taxi drivers often greet tenders, and there's also a stand a block away. Fares are fairly expensive, but a three-hour driving tour of Nevis costs about $60 for up to four people. Several restored great-house plantation inns are known for their lunches; your driver can provide information and arrange drop-off and pickup. Before setting off in a taxi, be sure to clarify whether the rate quoted is in E.C. or U.S. dollars.

If your ship docks in St. Kitts, Nevis is a 30- to 45-minute ferry ride from Basseterre. You can tour Charlestown, the capital, in a half hour or so, but you'll need three to four hours to explore the entire island. Most cruise ships arrive in port at around 8 AM, and the ferry schedule (figure $18 round-trip) can be irregular, so many passengers sign up for a cruise line–run shore excursion. If you travel independently, confirm departure times with the tourist office to be sure you'll make it back to your ship on time.

Shore Excursions

We consider these to be among the better shore excursions for Nevis. They may not be offered by all lines, and tour names may differ as well. Times and prices are approximate.

Beach & Trail Horseback Riding. The horseback ride takes you on trails through small villages as well as down to the beach. ⊙ 2 ½ hrs ⊠ $109.

Hiking Herbert Heights. This hiking trip goes from Rawlins Plantation up to Herbert Heights. Some of the trips go by donkey. ⊙ 3 hrs ⊠ $59.

Exploring Nevis

Numbers in the margin correspond to points of interest on the Nevis map.

❷ **Bath Springs.** The Caribbean's first hotel, the Bath Hotel was so popular in the 19th century that visitors, including such dignitaries as Samuel Taylor Coleridge and Prince William Henry, traveled two months by ship to "take the waters" in the property's hot thermal springs. It suffered extensive hurricane and probably earthquake damage over the years and languished in disrepair until recently. Local volunteers have cleaned up the spring and built a stone pool and steps to enter the waters; now, residents and visitors enjoy the springs, which range from 104°F to 108°F, though signs still caution that you bathe at your own risk. Follow Main Street south from Charlestown. ⊠ *Charlestown outskirts.*

★ ❹ **Botanical Gardens of Nevis.** In addition to terraced gardens and arbors, this remarkable 7.8-acre site in the glowering shadow of Mt. Nevis has natural lagoons, streams, and waterfalls, superlative bronze mermaids, egrets and herons, and extravagant fountains. You can find a proper rose garden, sections devoted to orchids and bromeliads, cacti, and

NEVIS BEST BETS

■ **Hiking.** Even if you don't want to tackle Mount Nevis, getting out in the countryside on foot is one of the best ways to experience this small island.

■ **Horseback Riding.** For those who would rather someone (or something) else do the walking for them, the views from horseback are just as good as those from closer to the ground.

flowering trees and shrubs—even a bamboo garden. A splendid re-creation of a plantation-style great house contains a tearoom with sweeping sea views and a souvenir shop. ☒ *Montpelier Estate* ☎ *869/469–3509* ▨ *$9* ☉ *Mon.–Sat. 9–4:30.*

★ ❶ **Charlestown.** About 1,200 of Nevis's 10,000 inhabitants live in the capital. The town faces the Caribbean, about 12½ mi (20 km) south of Basseterre on St. Kitts. It's easy to imagine how tiny Charlestown, founded in 1660, must have looked in its heyday. The weathered buildings still have their fanciful galleries, elaborate gingerbread fretwork, wooden shutters, and hanging plants. The stonework building with the clock tower (1825, but mostly rebuilt after a devastating 1873 fire) houses the courthouse and the second-floor **library** (a cool respite on sultry days). The little park next to the library is Memorial Square, dedicated to the fallen of World Wars I and II. Down the street from the square, archaeologists have discovered the remains of a Jewish cemetery and synagogue (Nevis reputedly had the Caribbean's second-oldest congregation), but there's little to see. The **Alexander Hamilton Birthplace,** which contains the Museum of Nevis History, is on the waterfront, covered in bougainvillea and hibiscus. This Georgian-style house is a reconstruction; the original had been built in 1680 and is thought to have been destroyed during an earthquake in the mid-19th century. Hamilton was born here in 1755 and moved to St. Croix when he was about 12. A few years later, at 17, he moved to the American colonies to continue his education; he became Secretary of the Treasury to George Washington and died in a duel with political rival Aaron Burr. The Nevis House of Assembly occupies the second floor of this building, and the museum downstairs contains Hamilton memorabilia, documents pertaining to the island's history, and displays on island geology, politics, architecture, culture, and cuisine. The gift shop is a wonderful source for historic maps, crafts, and books on Nevis. ⊠ *Low St., Charlestown* ☎ *869/ 469–5786* ⊕ *www.nevis-nhcs.org* ⊠ *$5 ($7 includes admission to Nelson Museum)* ⊙ *Weekdays 9–4, Sat. 9–noon.*

❸ Nelson Museum. This collection merits a visit for its memorabilia of Lord Horatio Nelson, including letters, documents, paintings, and even furniture from his flagship. Historical archives of the Nevis Historical and Conservation Society are housed here and are available for public viewing. Nelson was based in Antigua but on military patrol came to Nevis, where he met and eventually married Frances Nisbet, who lived on a 64-acre plantation here. Half the space is devoted to often provocative displays on island life, from leading families to vernacular architecture to the adaptation of traditional African customs, from cuisine to Carnival. ⊠ *Bath Rd., outside Charlestown* ☎ *869/469–0408* ⊕ *www.nevis-nhcs.org* ⊠ *$5 ($7 includes admission to Museum of Nevis History)* ⊙ *Weekdays 9–4, Sat. 9–noon.*

Shopping

Nevis is certainly not the place for a shopping spree, but there are some wonderful surprises, notably the island's stamps, fragrant honey, and batik and hand-embroidered clothing. Other than a few hotel boutiques and isolated galleries, virtually all shopping is concentrated on or just off Main Street in Charlestown. The lovely old stonework and wood floors of the waterfront Cotton Ginnery Complex make an appropriate setting for shops of local artisans.

★ Cheryl "Cherrianne" Liburd's **Bocane Ceramics** (⊠ *Main St., Stoney Grove* ☎ *869/469–5437*) stocks beautifully designed and glazed local pottery, such as platters painted with marine life, pineapple tea sets, and coffee tables topped with mosaic depictions of chattel houses. **The Craft-House** (⊠ *Pinney's Rd., Charlestown* ☎ *869/469–5505*) is a marvelous source for local specialties from vetiver mats to leather moccasins; there's a smaller branch in the Cotton Ginnery. **Island Fever** (⊠ *Main St., Charlestown* ☎ *869/469–0867*) has become the island's classiest boutique, with an excellent selection of everything from bathing suits and dresses to straw bags and jewelry. The **Nevis Handicraft Co-op Society** (⊠ *Main St., Charlestown* ☎ *869/469–1746*), next to the tourist office, offers works by local artisans (clothing, ceramic ware, woven goods) and locally produced honey, hot sauces, and jellies (try the guava and soursop).

Activities

GOLF Duffers doff their hats to the beautiful, impeccably maintained Robert
FodorsChoice Trent Jones, Jr.–designed 18-hole, par-72, 6,766-yard championship
★ **Four Seasons Golf Course** (⊠ *Four Seasons Resort Nevis, Pinney's Beach* ☎ *869/469–1111*): the virtual botanical gardens surrounding the fair-

ways almost qualify as a hazard in themselves. The signature hole is the 15th, a 660-yard monster that encompasses a deep ravine; other holes include bridges, steep drops, rolling pitches, extremely tight and unforgiving fairways, sugarmill ruins, and fierce doglegs. Attentive attendants canvas the course with beverage buggies, handing out chilled, peppermint-scented towels. Greens fees are $120 per person for 9 holes, $195 for 18.

HIKING   The center of the island is Nevis Peak—also known as Mount Nevis— which soars 3,232 feet and is flanked by Hurricane Hill on the north and Saddle Hill on the south. If you plan to scale Nevis Peak, a day-long affair, it's highly recommended that you go with a guide. Your hotel can arrange it (and a picnic lunch) for you. The **Upper Round Road Trail** is a 9-mi (14½-km) road constructed in the late 1600s and cleared and restored by the Nevis Historical and Conservation Society. It connects the Golden Rock Hotel, on the east side of the island, with Nisbet Plantation Beach Club, on the northern tip. The trail encompasses numerous vegetation zones, including pristine rain forest, and impressive plantation ruins. The original cobblestones, walls, and ruins are still evident in many places.

Herbert Heights Village Experience (☎ *869/469–2856* ⊕ *www. herbertheights.com*) is run by the Herbert family, who have fashioned their own unique activities. They lead four-hour nature hikes up to panoramic Herbert Heights, where you drink in fresh local juices and the views of Montserrat; the powerful telescope makes you feel as if you're staring right into that island's simmering volcano. The price is $15; for $35 you can ride one of their donkeys. **Sunrise Tours** (☎ *869/469–2758* ⊕ *www.nevisnaturetours.com*), run by Lynell and Earla Liburd, offers a range of hiking tours, but their most popular is Devil's Copper, a rock configuration full of ghostly legends. Local people gave it its name because at one time the water was hot—a volcanic thermal stream. The area features pristine waterfalls and splendid bird-watching. Hikes range from $20 to $40 per person, and you receive a certificate of

★   achievement. **Top to Bottom** (☎ *869/469–9080* ⊕ *www.walknevis.com*), run by Jim and Nikki Johnston, offers ecorambles (slow tours) and hikes that emphasize Nevis's volcanic and horticultural heritage (including pointing out folkloric herbal and "murderous" medicines). Three-hour rambles or hikes are $20 per person (snacks and juice included); it's $35 for more strenuous climbs (two offered) up Mount Nevis.

HORSEBACK   **Nevis Equestrian Centre** (✉ *Cotton Ground, Pinney's Beach* ☎ *869/* RIDING   *469–8118*) arranges leisurely beach rides, more demanding trail rides ($55–$80), and lessons from caring, careful owners Erika and John.

WINDSURFING   Waters are generally calm and northeasterly winds steady yet gentle, making Nevis an excellent spot for beginners and intermediates. **Windsurf-**
★   **ing Nevis** (✉ *Oualie Beach* ☎ *869/469–9682* ⊕ *www.windsurfingnevis. com*) offers top-notch instructors (Winston Crooke is one of the best in the islands) and equipment for $25 per half hour. Groups are kept small (eight maximum), and the equipment is state-of-the-art from Mistral North and Tushingham.

Beaches

All beaches are free to the public (the plantation inns cordon off "private" areas on Pinney's Beach for guests), but there are no changing facilities, so wear a swimsuit under your clothes. **Oualie Beach,** south of Mosquito Bay and north of Cades and Jones bays, is a beige-sand beach where the folks at Oualie Beach Hotel can mix you a drink and fix you up with water-sports equipment. **Pinney's Beach,** the island's showpiece, has almost 4 mi (6½ km) of soft, golden sand on the calm Caribbean. The Four Seasons Resort is here, as are the private cabanas and pavilions of several mountain inns and casual beach bars.

★

Where to Eat

$–$$$ ✕ **Sunshine's.** Everything about this beach shack is larger than life, including the Rasta man Llewelyn "Sunshine" Caines himself. Flags and license plates from around the world complement the international patrons (including an occasional movie star), who wander over from the adjacent Four Seasons. Picnic tables are splashed with bright sunrise-to-sunset colors; even the palm trees are painted. Fishermen cruise up with their catch—you might savor lobster rolls or snapper creole. Don't miss the lethal house specialty, Killer Bee rum punch. As Sunshine boasts, "One and you're stung, two you're stunned, three it's a knockout." ⊠ *Pinney's Beach* ☎ *869/469–1089* ⊟ *No credit cards.*

$–$$$ ✕ **Unella's.** It's nothing fancy here—just tables on a second-floor porch overlooking Charlestown's waterfront. Stop for exceptional lobster (more expensive than the rest of the menu), curried lamb, island-style spareribs, and steamed conch, all served with local vegetables, rice, and peas. Unella opens shop around 9 AM, when locals and boaters appear eager for their breakfast, and stays open all day as island ladies stop by in curlers, and cops and cabbies flirt shyly with the waitresses. ⊠ *Waterfront, Charlestown* ☎ *869/469–5574* ⊟ *No credit cards.*

OCHO RIOS, JAMAICA

John Bigley & Paris Permenter

About two hours east of Montego Bay lies Ocho Rios (often just "Ochi"), a lush destination that's favored by honeymooners for its tropical beauty. Often called the garden center of Jamaica, this community is perfumed by flowering hibiscus, bird of paradise, bougainvillea, and other tropical blooms year-round. Ocho Rios is a popular cruise port and the destination where you'll find one of the island's most recognizable attractions: the stair-step Dunn's River Falls, which invites travelers to climb in daisy-chain fashion, hand-in-hand behind a surefooted guide. This spectacular waterfall is actually a series of falls that cascades from the mountains to the sea. That combination of hills, rivers and sea also means many activities in the area from seaside horseback rides to mountain biking and lazy river rafting.

Essentials

CURRENCY   The Jamaican dollar (J$67 to US$1). Currency-exchange booths are set up on the docks at Ocho Rios whenever a ship is in port. The U.S. dollar is accepted virtually everywhere; at some places, change is made in Jamaican dollars. Prices given are in U.S. dollars unless otherwise indicated.

HOURS   Normal business hours for stores are weekdays from 8:30 to 4:30, Saturday 8 to 1, with extended hours for shops in tourist areas.

INTERNET   A growing number of facilities offer Internet service; expect to pay about US$2 for 20 minutes. At the Taj Mahal Centre, **Jerkin £ Taj Internet Bar and Grill** (✉ *Ocho Rios* ☎ *876/974–7438*) offers numerous terminals for staying in touch by e-mail while traveling.

TELEPHONES   Public telephones are located at the communications center at the Ocho Rios Cruise Pier. Travelers also find public phones in major Ocho Rios malls. Some U.S. phone companies won't permit credit-card calls to be placed from Jamaica because they've been victims of fraud so collect calls are often the top option. GSM cell phones equipped with tri-band or world-roaming service will find coverage throughout the Ocho Rios region.

Coming Ashore

Most cruise ships dock at this port on Jamaica's north coast, near Dunn's River Falls. Less than 1 mi (2 km) from the Ocho Rios pier are the Taj Mahal Duty-Free Shopping Center and the Ocean Village Shopping Center. Getting anywhere else in Ocho Rios will require a taxi; expect to pay $10 for a taxi ride downtown. The pier, which includes a cruise terminal with the basic services and transportation, is also within easy walking distance of Turtle Beach.

Licensed taxis are available at the pier; expect to pay about $35 per hour for a guided taxi tour. Jamaica is one place in the Caribbean where it's usually to your advantage to take an organized shore excursion offered by your ship unless you just want to go to the beach or do a bit of shopping in town. Car rental isn't recommended in Jamaica due to high prices, bad roads, and aggressive drivers.

Shore Excursions

We consider these to be among the better shore excursions for Ocho Rios. They may not be offered by all lines, and tour names may differ as well. Times and prices are approximate.

ATV Tour. You'll drive your own ATV around the hills outside Ocho Rios. ◷ *3½ hrs* ⊡ *$89.*

Beach Horseback Riding. After riding your horse along a beach, you'll then ride it bareback into the surf for a swim. ◷ *4 hrs* ⊡ *$89.*

Canopy Tour. The "tour" consists of flying from platform to platform through a forest on a zip line. It's a great experience. ◷ *4–4¼ hrs* ⊡ *$99.*

> ## OCHO RIOS BEST BETS
>
> ■ **Chukka Cove.** Any of the great adventure tours here is sure to please, though you'll need to book them through your ship.
>
> ■ **Dunn's River Falls.** A visit to the falls is nothing but a touristy experience, and yet it's still exhilarating.
>
> ■ **Reggae Xplosion.** Reggae fans should check out this museum of the island sound that's right in Ocho Rios in one of the town's largest shopping centers.

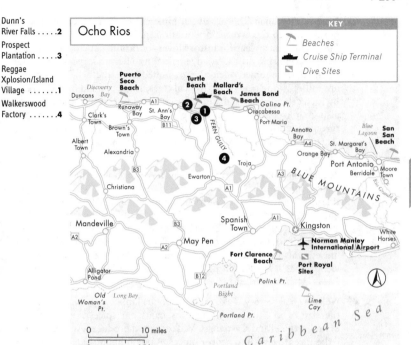

Ocho Rios

KEY

Beaches

Cruise Ship Terminal

Dive Sites

Green Grotto Caves & Dunn's River Falls. Some kind of Dunn's River Falls trip is offered on all Ocho Rios port calls, and it may be a combination of Dunn's River Falls with another attraction for more money. The basic (and usually cheapest) option combines the Green Grotto Caves with nearby Dunn's River Falls. ⏱ *4½ hrs* ⚓ *$59.*

Rafting on the Martha Brae River. Pass the verdant plant life as you glide down the river on a 30-foot, two-seat bamboo raft. This is decidedly still-water rafting. ⏱ *6 hrs* ⚓ *$58.*

Exploring Ocho Rios

Numbers in the margin correspond to points of interest on the Ocho Rios map.

❷ **Dunn's River Falls.** The falls are an eye-catching sight: 600 feet of cold, clear mountain water splashing over a series of stone steps to the warm Caribbean. The best way to enjoy the falls is to climb the slippery steps: don a swimsuit, take the hand of the person ahead of you, and trust that the chain of hands and bodies leads to an experienced guide. The leaders of the climbs are personable fellows who reel off bits of local lore while telling you where to step; you can hire a guide's service for a tip of a few dollars. After the climb, you exit through a crowded market, another reminder that this is one of Jamaica's top tourist attractions. ⊠ *Off A1, between St. Ann's and Ocho Rios* ☎*876/974–2857* ⚓*$10* ⏱ *Daily 8:30–5.*

❸ Prospect Plantation. To learn about Jamaica's former agricultural economy, a trip to this working plantation, just west of town, is a must. But it's not just a place for history lovers or farming aficionados; everyone seems to enjoy the views over the White River Gorge and the tour by jitney (a canopied open-air cart pulled by a tractor). The grounds are full of exotic fruits and tropical trees, some planted over the years by such celebrities as Winston Churchill and Charlie Chaplin. You can also go horseback riding on the plantation's 900 acres or play miniature golf, grab a drink in the bar, or buy souvenirs in the gift shop. ⊠ *Hwy. A1, west of Ocho Rios* ☎ *876/994–1058* ≊ *$29* ⊙ *Daily 8–5; tours Mon.–Sat. 10:30, 2, and 3:30.*

★ **❶ Reggae Xplosion.** In the open-air **Island Village** shopping and entertainment center, which is owned by Island Records tycoon Chris Blackwell, this attraction traces the history of Jamaican music. Ska, mento, dancehall, reggae, and more are featured in a series of exhibits spanning two stories. Special sections highlight the careers of some of Jamaica's best-known talents, including Bob Marley, Peter Tosh, and Bunny Wailer. The museum also includes an extensive gift shop with recordings and collectibles. ⊠ *N. Coast Hwy., Island Village* ☎ *876/675–8895* ⊕ *www. islandjamaica.com* ≊ *$10* ⊙ *Mon.–Sat. 9–5.*

★ **❹ Walkerswood Factory.** To learn more about Jamaican cuisine (as well as the island's bountiful supply of herbs, fruits, and spices), visit the source of many sauces and seasonings. Walkerswood produces everything from jerk sauces to jams and pepper sauces. A one-hour guided tour provides a look at herb gardens, a visit to a re-created hut to learn more about historic countryside life, a jerk marinade demonstration, and samples of Walkswood products. The site includes a gift shop and snack bar featuring local dishes. ⊠ *About 6 mi (10 km) south of Ocho Rios on A3 in Walkerswood, St. Ann* ☎ *876/917–2318* ⊕ *www.walkerswood.com* ≊ *$15* ⊙ *Mon.–Sat. 9–4.*

Shopping

Resort wear, jewelry, Jamaican rum, and Blue Mountain coffee are all popular offerings throughout Ocho Rios stores, while the crafts market is filled with wood carvings and paintings. The crafts market is located steps from the cruise-ship dock but, before launching into a shopping expedition, consider your tolerance for pandemonium and price haggling. If you're looking to spend money, head for Pineapple Place, Ocean Village, the Taj Mahal, Coconut Grove, and Island Plaza. Some cruise lines run shore excursions that focus on shopping. A fun mall that also serves as an entertainment center is **Island Village.** Located near the cruise port, this mall is home to shops selling Jamaican handicrafts, duty-free goods and clothing, a Margaritaville restaurant, a Jamaican music museum, and a small beach area with a water trampoline.

> **BINOCULARS**
>
> Binoculars are as useful indoors as they are outside. You might think they are only for bringing far-off wildlife and sights within view, but take them into museums, churches, and other buildings to examine the details of artwork, sculptures, and architectural elements.

Harmony Hall (✉ *Hwy. A1, Ocho Rios* ☎ *876/975–4222*), an eight-minute drive east of the main part of town, is a restored great house, where Annabella Proudlock sells her unique wooden boxes (their covers are decorated with reproductions of Jamaican paintings). Also on sale—and magnificently displayed—are larger reproductions of paintings, lithographs, and signed prints of Jamaican scenes and hand-carved wooden combs. In addition, Harmony Hall is well-known for its shows by local artists.

Activities

DOLPHIN SWIM PROGRAMS **Dolphin Cove** (✉ *N. Coast Hwy., adjacent to Dunn's River Falls, Ocho Rios* ☎ *876/974–5335* ⊕ *www.dolphincovejamaica.com*) offers dolphin swims as well as lower-priced dolphin encounters for ages eight and up; dolphin touch programs for ages six and over; or simple admission to the grounds, which also includes a short nature walk. Programs cost between $39 and $179, depending on your depth of involvement with the dolphins. Advance reservations are required.

GOLF Although not as well-known as a golf capital as Montego Bay, the Ocho Rios area is home to several excellent courses. Caddies are almost always mandatory throughout the island, and rates are $15 to $45. Cart rentals are available.

The Runaway Bay golf course is found at **Breezes Runaway Bay** (✉ *N. Coast Hwy., Runaway Bay* ☎ *876/973–7319*). This 18-hole course has hosted many championship events (greens fees are $80 for nonguests; guests play for free) and is also home to an extensive golf academy. The golf course at **Sandals Golf & Country Club** (✉ *Ocho Rios* ☎ *876/975–0119*) is 700 feet above sea level (greens fees for 18 holes are $100, or $70 for 9 holes for nonguests; complimentary greens fees for guests).

HORSEBACK RIDING Ocho Rios has excellent horseback riding, but the best of the operations is **Chukka Cove Adventure Tours** (✉ *Llandovery, St. Ann's Bay* ☎ *876/972–2506* ⊕ *www.chukkacaribbean.com*), which is adjacent to the polo field, just west of town. The trainers here originally exercised the polo ponies by taking them for therapeutic rides in the sea; soon there were requests from visitors to ride the horses in the water. The company now offers a three-hour beach ride that ends with a bareback swim on the horses in the sea from a private beach. It's a highlight of many trips to Jamaica. Rather than be part of a guided group ride, you can opt to rent a horse by the hour at **Prospect Plantation** (✉ *Ocho Rios* ☎ *876/994–1058*), which offers horseback riding for $48 per hour, but advance reservations are required.

MOUNTAIN BIKING Ocho Rios's hilly terrain makes the region a fun challenge for mountain bikers. **Blue Mountain Bicycle Tours** (✉ *121 Main St., Ocho Rios* ☎ *876/974–7075* ⊕ *www.bmtoursja.com*) takes travelers on guided rides in the spectacular Blue Mountains. The excursion, an all-day outing, starts high and glides downhill, so all levels of riders can enjoy the tour. The trip ends with a dip in a waterfall; the package price includes transportation from Ocho Rios, brunch, lunch, and all equipment. From its location outside of Montego Bay, **Chukka Caribbean Adventures** (✉ *Sandy Bay, Hanover* ☎ *876/972–2506* ⊕ *www.chukkacaribbean.com*) offers both biking and ATV tours. There's a minimum age of 16 on the ATV tours. The noisy ATVs jostle and splash their way along trails on a 10-mi (16-km) ride through the hills before returning so visitors can take a dip in the sea. From its Ocho Rios location, **Chukka Caribbean Adventures** (✉ *Llandovery, St. Ann's Bay* ☎ *876/972–2506* ⊕ *www.chukkacaribbean.com*) offers a 3½-hour bike tour through St. Ann and the village of Mount Zion with several stops and even snorkeling at the end. There is also an ATV tour. There's a minimum age of 6 for bikes, 16 for ATVs.

RIVER RAFTING   Jamaica's many rivers mean a multitude of freshwater experiences, from mild to wild. Bamboo rafting is almost a symbol of Jamaica, and in the Ocho Rios area, relaxing floats are offered on the **White River.** For white-water buffs, **Chukka Caribbean Adventures** offers white-water tubing on the White River, a soft adventure that doesn't require any previous rafting experience. Rafters travel in a convoy along the river and through some gentle rapids. ✉ *Ocho Rios* ☎ *876/972–2506* ⊕ *www.chukkacaribbean.com.*

Beaches

★ **Dunn's River Falls Beach,** at the foot of the falls, is usually crowded. Although tiny—especially considering the crowds—it's got a great view, as well as a beach bar and grill. Look up from the sands for a spectacular view of the cascading water, whose roar drowns out the sea as you approach. ✉ *Rte. A1, between St. Ann's and Ocho Rios.*

East of Ocho Rios in the village of Oracabessa is **James Bond Beach,** which is popular because of the reggae performances that take place on its bandstand. There's a $5 admission fee. **Turtle Beach,** stretching behind the Sunset Jamaica Grande, is the busiest beach in Ocho Rios (where the islanders come to swim). Though much more convenient for cruise-ship passengers, it's not nearly as pretty as James Bond Beach. There's also a small beach at the foot.

Where to Eat

Many restaurants add a 10% service charge to the bill. Otherwise, a tip of 10% to 20% is customary.

$$–$$$ ✕ **Evita's Italian Restaurant.** Just about every celebrity who has visited Ocho
Fodor'sChoice   Rios has dined at this hilltop restaurant, and Evita has the pictures to
★   prove it. Guests feel like stars themselves, with attentive waitstaff helping to guide them through a list of about 30 kinds of pasta, ranging from lasagna Rastafari (vegetarian) and fiery jerk spaghetti to *rotelle colombo* (crabmeat with white sauce and noodles). Kids under 12 eat for half price, and light eaters will appreciate half portions. The restaurant offers free transportation from area hotels. ✉ *Mantalent Inn, Eden Bower Rd.* ☎ *876/974–2333* ▭ *AE, D, MC, V.*

¢–$ ✕ **Scotchie's Too.** The new Ocho Rios branch of the longtime Montego
Fodor'sChoice   Bay favorite has already been lauded by international chefs for its ex-
★   cellent jerk. The open-air eatery offers plates of jerk chicken, sausage, fish, pork, and ribs, all accompanied by festival, bammy, and some fire-breathing hot sauce. Be sure to step over to the kitchen to watch the preparation of the jerk over the pits. ✉ *North Coast Hwy., Drax Hall* ☎ *876/794–9457* ▭ *AE, D, MC, V.*

PROGRESO, MEXICO

Michele Joyce   The waterfront town closest to Mérida, Progreso is not particularly historic. It's also not terribly picturesque; still, it provokes a certain sentimental fondness for those who know it well. On weekdays during most of the year, the beaches are deserted, but when school is out (Easter week, July, and August) and on summer weekends it's bustling with families from Mérida. Progreso's charm—or lack of charm—seems to hinge on the weather. When the sun is shining, the water looks translucent green and feels bathtub-warm, and the fine sand makes for lovely long walks. When the wind blows during one of Yucatán's winter *nortes,* the water churns with whitecaps and looks gray and unappealing. Whether the weather is good or bad, however, everyone ends up eventually at one of the restaurants lining the main street, Calle 19. Across the street from the oceanfront malecón, these all serve up cold beer, seafood cocktails, and freshly grilled fish. Most cruise passengers head immediately for Mérida or one of the nearby archaeological sites.

Essentials

CURRENCY   The Mexican peso (MX$11.13 to US$1). U.S. dollars and credit cards are accepted by everyone at the port. There is no advantage to paying in dollars, but there may be an advantage to paying in cash. Ten pesos are worth a little bit less than 1 dollar.

HOURS   Many shops close between 1 and 4. Banks are generally open weekdays 9 to 5, and offices are usually open weekdays 9 to 2 and 4 to 7.

INTERNET   The cruise terminal isn't terribly close to Progreso's downtown area, but if you take a bus or taxi into town, you'll easily find an Internet café with pretty cheap service. If you take an excursion to Mérida, you'll find that Internet cafés there are ubiquitous, particularly the main square and Calles 61 and 63; most charge $1 to $3 per hour.

TELEPHONES   Most pay phones accept prepaid Ladatel cards, sold in 30-, 50-, or 100-peso denominations. To use the card, insert it in the pay phone's slot, dial 001 (for calls to the U.S.) or 01 (for calls within Mexico), followed by the area code and number. Credit is deleted from the card as you use it, and the balance is displayed on the small screen on the phone.

Coming Ashore

The pier in Progreso is long, and cruise ships dock at its end, so passengers are shuttled to the foot of the pier, where the Progreso Cruise Terminal offers visitors their first stop. The terminal houses small restaurants and shops selling locally produced crafts. These are some of the best shops in sleepy Progreso (a much wider selection is available in nearby Mérida). The beach lies just east of the pier and can easily be reached on foot. If you want to enjoy the sun and a peaceful afternoon, a drink at one of the small palapa-roof restaurants that line the beach is a good option.

If you are looking to explore, there are plenty of taxis around the pier. A trip around town should not cost more than $5, but ask the taxi driver to quote you a price. If you want to see more of Progreso, a cab can

Mérida

Calle 55
Calle 57
Calle 59
Calle 61
Calle 63
Calle 65
Calle 58
Calle 56
Calle 62
Calle 64
Calle 66
Calle 68

4

1

3

2

5 6

Parque Zoologico
El Centenario

100 yards
100 meters

Northwest Yucatan

Golfo de México

San Felipe Parque Nacional

Punta Baz

Sisal

Celestún

Parque Natural Ria Celestún

Progreso

Telchac Puerto

Santa Clara

Dzilam de Bravo

Dzilam González

Temax

Motul

281

261

Mérida

Umán

Maxcanú

Muna

281

180

Tixkokob

Kantunil

Mama

Mayapán

18

Uxmal **8**

Kabah

Sayil

Labná

261

184

Oxcutzcab

Tzucacab

Dzitás

Pisté

Chichén Itzá **7**

176

180

80

YUCATAN

CAMPECHE

0   4 miles
0   4 kilometers

Casa de Montejo **2**
Catedral de
San Ildefonso **3**
Chichén Itzá **7**
Palacio Cantón **5**
Paseo Montejo **6**
Teatro Peón
Contreras **4**
Uxmal **8**
Zócalo **1**

also take you to the local sightseeing tour bus, a bright blue, open-air, double-decker bus that travels through town and only costs $2. A taxi ride from Progreso to Mérida runs about $22, and most drivers charge around $12 per hour to show you around. If you plan on renting the cab for a good part of the day, talk about the number of hours and the cost with the driver before you take off. It's difficult to rent a car, so most people just band together in a taxi.

Shore Excursions

We consider these to be among the better shore excursions for Progreso. They may not be offered by all lines, and tour names may differ as well. Times and prices are approximate.

Caves & Cavern Snorkeling. This unique trip gives you the opportunity to snorkel in the clear waters of an underground river. ⊗ *7 hrs* ⌦ *$84.*
Chichén Itzá. While you could probably do the trip on your own by rental car, it's easier to jump on a ship-sponsored bus for the 2-hour trip and tour that includes a box lunch. ⊗ *7 hrs* ⌦ *$89.*
Progreso Beach Break. If ruins aren't your thing, a day pass for a resort on a lovely white-sand beach may be. Since good beaches are in short supply here, it's better to bite the bullet and go to this resort for an all-inclusive beach day. ⊗ *4 hrs* ⌦ *$79.*
Uxmal. Another major Maya archaeological site is easily reached by ship-sponsored excursion. ⊗ *7 hrs* ⌦ *$89.*

Exploring Mérida

Numbers in the margin correspond to points of interest on the Mérida map.

Just south of Progreso (about 20 or 30 minutes by taxi), Mérida, the cultural and intellectual hub of the Yucatán, offers a great deal to explore. Mérida is rich in art, history, and tradition. Most streets are numbered, not named, and most run one-way. North-south streets have even numbers, which descend from west to east; east-west streets have odd numbers, which ascend from north to south. One of the best ways to see the city is to hire a *calesa,* a horse-drawn carriage. They congregate on the main square or at the Palacio Cantón, near the anthropology museum; expect to pay at least $13 per hour.

❷ **Casa de Montejo.** This stately palace sits on the south side of the plaza, on Calle 63. Francisco de Montejo—father and son—conquered the peninsula and founded Mérida in 1542; they built their "casa" 10 years later. In the late 1970s, it was restored by banker Agustín Legorreta and converted to a branch of the Banamex bank. Built in the French style, it represents the city's finest—

PROGRESO BEST BETS

Chichén Itzá. Difficult to reach from Cancún and most other Yucatán ports, the famous Maya city is an easy day trip from Progreso.
Mérida. This delightful, though busy, town is where you should head immediately upon landing if you aren't interested in the region's archaeological sites.
Uxmal. One of the most beautiful Maya cities is reachable on a day trip from Progreso. If you've seen Chichén Itzá, go here.

and oldest—example of colonial plateresque architecture, which typically has elaborate ornamentation. A bas-relief on the doorway—the facade is all that remains of the original house—depicts Francisco de Montejo the younger, his wife, and daughter as well as Spanish soldiers standing on the heads of the vanquished Maya. Even if you have no banking to do, step into the building weekdays between 9 and 5, Saturday 9 to 1, to glimpse the leafy inner patio.

❸ Catedral de San Ildefonso. Begun in 1561, St. Ildefonso is the oldest cathedral on the continent. It took several hundred Maya laborers, working with stones from the pyramids of the ravaged Maya city, 36 years to complete it. Designed in the somber Renaissance style by an architect who had worked on the Escorial in Madrid, its facade is stark and unadorned, with gunnery slits instead of windows, and faintly Moorish spires. Inside, the black Cristo de las Ampollas (Christ of the Blisters)—at 7 meters tall, perhaps the tallest Christ in Mexico—occupies a side chapel to the left of the main altar. The statue is a replica of the original, which was destroyed during the revolution; this is also when the gold that typically decorated Mexican cathedrals was carried off. According to one of many legends, the Christ figure burned all night yet appeared the next morning unscathed—except that it was covered with the blisters for which it is named. You can hear the pipe organ play at 11 AM Sunday Mass. ⊠ *Calles 60 and 61, Centro* ☎ *No phone* ☉ *Daily 7–11:30 and 4:30–8.*

❺ Palacio Cantón. The most compelling of the mansions on **Paseo Montejo,** the stately palacio was built as the residence for a general between 1909 and 1911. Designed by Enrique Deserti, who also did the blueprints for the Teatro Peón Contreras, the building has a grandiose air that seems more characteristic of a mausoleum than a home: there's marble everywhere, as well as Doric and Ionic columns and other Italianate Beaux Arts flourishes. The building also houses the air-conditioned **Museo de Antropología e Historia,** which gives a good introduction to ancient Maya culture. Temporary exhibits sometimes brighten the standard collection. ⊠ *Paseo Montejo 485, at Calle 43, Paseo Montejo* ☎ *999/923–0469* ☞ *$3* ☉ *Tues.–Sat. 8–8, Sun. 8–2.*

❻ Paseo Montejo. North of downtown, this 10-block-long street was *the* place to reside in the late 19th century, when wealthy plantation owners sought to outdo each other with the opulence of their elegant mansions. Inside, the owners typically displayed imported Carrara marble and antiques, opting for the decorative styles popular in New Orleans, Cuba, and Paris rather than the style in Mexico City. (At the time there was more traffic by sea via the Gulf of Mexico and the Caribbean than there was overland across the lawless interior.) The broad boulevard, lined with tamarind and laurel trees, has lost much of its former panache; some of the once-stunning mansions have fallen into disrepair. Others, however, are being restored as part of a citywide, privately funded beautification program, and it's still a great place to wander, or to see by horse-drawn carriage.

❹ Teatro Peón Contreras. This 1908 Italianate theater was built along the same lines as grand turn-of-the-20th-century European theaters and opera houses. In the early 1980s the marble staircase, dome, and frescoes were restored. Today, in addition to performing arts, the theater also houses the **Centro de Información Turística** (Tourist Information Center), which provides maps, brochures, and details about attractions in the city and state. The theater's most popular attraction, however, is the café/bar spilling out into the street facing Parque de la Madre. It's crowded every night with people enjoying the balladeers singing romantic and politically inspired songs. ✉ *Calle 60 between Calles 57 and 59, Centro* ☎ *999/924–9290 Tourist Information Center, 999/923—7344 and 999/924–9290 theater* ☉ *Theater daily 7 AM–1 AM; Tourist Information Center daily 8 AM–8 PM.*

❶ **Zócalo.** Mérida's main square is in the oldest part of town—the Centro Histórico. It is a good spot from which to begin a tour of the city, to watch music or dance performances, or to chill in the shade of a laurel tree when the day gets too hot. Cafés along this route are perfect places from which to watch the parade of people as well as folk dancers and singers. Calle 60 between Parque Santa Lucía and the main square gets especially lively; restaurants here set out tables in the streets, which quickly fill with patrons enjoying the free hip-hop, tango, salsa, or jazz performances. ✉ *Bordered by Calles 60, 62, 61, and 63.*

Farther Afield

❼ **Chichén Itzá.** One of the most dramatically beautiful of the ancient Maya cities, Chichén Itzá was discovered by Europeans in the mid-1800s, and much here remains a mystery. Experts have little information about who the Itzás might have been and the reason that they abandoned the city around 1224 is also unknown. ✉ *Approximately 120 km (75 mi) east of Mérida on Carretera 180* 🏛 *Site, museum, and sound-and-light show $9.50; parking $2; use of video camera $3 (keep this receipt if visiting other archaeological sites on the same day)* ☉ *Daily 8–5; sound-and-light show just after 5 pm (at 8 pm in Spanish with translations for $2.50)* ⊕ *www.inah.gob.mx.*

❽ **Uxmal.** If Chichén Itzá is the most expansive Mayan ruin in Yucatán, Uxmal is arguably the most elegant. The architecture here reflects the Late Classical renaissance of the 7th to the 9th century and is contemporary with that of Palenque and Tikal. ✉ *78 km (48 mi) south of Mérida on Carretera 261* 🏛 *Site, museum, and sound-and-light show $9.50; parking $1; use of video camera $3 (keep this receipt if visiting other archaeological sites on the same day)* ☉ *Daily 8–5; sound-and-light show just after dusk (at 7 or 8 pm depending on the time of year)* ⊕ *www.inah.gob.mx.*

Shopping

In Progreso, there is also a small downtown area that is a better place to walk than to shop, between Calle 80 and Calle 31, with small restaurants that serve simple Mexican fare (like *tortas* and *tacos*), small shops with everyday goods for locals, banks, and supermarkets.

Just south of Progreso, Mérida offers more places to shop, including colorful Mexican markets selling local goods. The **Mercado Municipal** (✉ *Calles 56 and 67, Centro*) has lots of things you won't need, but which are fascinating to look at: songbirds in cane cages, mountains of mysterious fruits and vegetables, dippers made of hollow gourds (the same way they've been made here for a thousand years). There are also lots of crafts for sale, including hammocks, sturdy leather *huaraches,* and piñatas in every imaginable shape and color. Sunday brings an array of wares into Mérida; starting at 9 AM, the Handicrafts Bazaar, or **Bazar de Artesanías** (⊠ *At main square, Centro*), sells lots of *huipiles* (traditional, white embroidered dresses) as well as hats and costume jewelry. As its name implies, popular art, or handicrafts, are sold at the **Bazar de Artes Populares** (⊠ *Parque Santa Lucía, at Calles 60 and 55, Centro*) beginning at 9 AM on Sunday. If you're interested in handicrafts, **Bazar García Rejón** (⊠ *Calles 65 and 62, Centro*) has rows of indoor stalls that sell items like leather goods, palm hats, and handmade guitars.

The **Mercado de Artesanís Garcí Rejón** (⊠ *Calles 60 and 65*) sells some quality items, and the shopping experience here can be less of a hassle than at the municipal market. You'll find reasonable prices on palm-fiber hats, hammocks, leather sandals, jewelry, and locally made liqueurs; persistent but polite bargaining may get you even better deals.

Activities

Progreso is not so much about lovely beaches, but you can easily walk to the town beach from the cruise-ship pier. Aside from archaeological sites, the main activity in the region is bird-watching, especially watching the many flamingos that nest in the region.

BIRD-WATCHING One of the most spectacular area sports and activities is bird-watching, which you can enjoy at the **Parque Natural Ri` Lagartos,** about 2½ hours from Progreso by car. The real spectacle these days is the birds; more than 350 species nest and feed in the area, including flocks of flamingos, snowy and red egrets, white ibis, great white herons, cormorants, pelicans, and peregrine falcons. The easiest way to book a trip is through the Núñez family at the Isla Contoy restaurant, where you can also eat a delicious meal of fresh seafood. Call ahead to reserve an English- or Italian-speaking guide through their organization, Ría Lagartos Expeditions. This boat trip will take you through the mangrove forests to the flamingo feeding grounds (where, as an added bonus, you can paint your face or body with supposedly therapeutic green mud). A 2½-hour tour, which accommodates five or six people, costs $60; the 3½-hour tour costs $75 (both per boat, not per person). Other tour options are available. ⊠ *Calle 19 No. 134, at Calle 14* 🕾 *986/862–0000* ⊕ *www. riolagartos.com* ▭ *No credit cards.*

Where to Eat

$ ✕ **Flamingos.** This restaurant facing Progreso's long cement promenade is a cut above its neighbors. Service is professional and attentive, and soon after arriving you'll get at least one free appetizer—maybe black beans with corn tortillas, or a plate of shredded shark meat stewed with tomatoes. The creamy cilantro soup is a little too cheesy (literally, not figuratively), but the large fish fillets are perfectly breaded and lightly fried. Breakfast is served after 7 AM. There's a full bar, and although there's no air-conditioning, large, glassless windows let in the ocean breeze. ⊠ *Calle 19 No. 144-D, at Calle 72, Progreso* ☎ *969/935–2122* ▤ *MC, V.*

$ ✕ **La Via Olimpo.** Lingering over coffee is a great way to relax at this great Internet café. In the air-conditioned dining room, you can feast on poc chuc (slices of pork marinated in sour-orange juice and spices), turkey sandwiches, or burgers and fries. Crepes are also popular, and there are lots of salads and juices. ⊠ *Calle 62 No. 502, between Calles 63 and 61, Mérida* ☎ *999/923–4843* ▤ *MC, V.*

PUERTO LIMÓN, COSTA RICA   4

Jeff Van Fleet   Christopher Columbus became Costa Rica's first tourist when he landed on this stretch of coast in 1502 during his fourth and final voyage to the New World. Expecting to find vast mineral wealth, he named the region "Costa Rica" (rich coast). Imagine the Spaniards' surprise eventually to find there was none. Save for a brief skirmish some six decades ago, the country *did* prove itself rich in a long tradition of peace and democracy. No other country in Latin America can make that claim. Costa Rica is also abundantly rich in natural beauty, managing to pack beaches, volcanoes, rain forests, and diverse animal life into an area the size of Vermont and New Hampshire combined. It has successfully parlayed those qualities into its role as one of the world's great ecotourism destinations. A day visit is short, but time enough for a quick sample.

Essentials

CURRENCY   The colón (₡529 to US$1). Most businesses in port gladly accept U.S. dollars.

HOURS   Stores and businesses open weekdays from 8 AM to 6 PM, with a two-hour break at midday. Places close at noon or 2 PM on Saturday, and little is open on Sunday. Most tourist-oriented businesses remain open when cruise ships are in port.

INTERNET   A bank of Internet computers is yours to use at the cruise terminal. In town, log on at **Internet Cinco Estrellas** (⊠ *50 m north of Terminal de Cruceros* ☎ *758–5752*).

TELEPHONES   Telephone numbers have seven digits. Merely dial the number. There are no area codes. You'll find ample phones for use in the cruise terminal. Public phones accept locally purchased calling cards.

Coming Ashore

Ships dock at Limón's spacious, spiffy Terminal de Cruceros (cruise terminal), one block south of the city's downtown. You'll find telephones, Internet computers, a crafts market, tourist information and tour operators' desks inside the terminal, as well as a small army of manicurists who do a brisk business. Step outside and walk straight ahead one block to reach Limón's downtown.

A fleet of red taxis waits on the street in front of the terminal. Drivers are happy to help you put together a do-it-yourself tour. Most charge

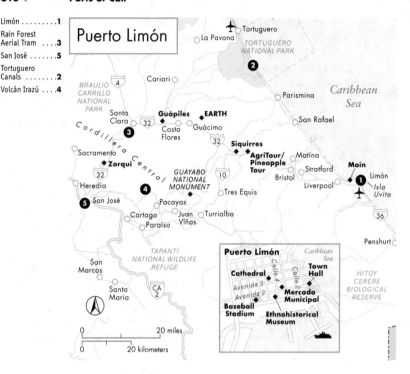

$75 to $100 per carload for a day of touring. There is no place to rent a car here, but you're better off leaving the driving to someone else. Cruise lines offer dozens of shore excursions in Costa Rica, and if you want to go any farther afield than Limón or the coast south, we suggest you take an organized tour. The country looks disarmingly small on a map—it is—but hills give rise to mountains the farther inland you go, and road conditions range from "okay" to "abysmal." Distances are short as the toucan flies, but travel times are longer than you'd expect.

Shore Excursions

We consider these to be among the better shore excursions for Puerto Limón. They may not be offered by all lines, and tour names may differ as well. Times and prices are approximate.

Flower Farm Tour. One of the world's largest ornamental plant farms operates a couple of hours inland from the coast. That diffenbachia sitting near your picture window back home might have come from here. Tours conclude with your chance to arrange a take-away tropical flower bouquet. ⏱ 5 hrs 🏷 $59.

Ride the Jungle Train. Passenger rail service once connected San José to Limón, but, alas, no longer. You can recapture some of that romantic era on a restored train that rumbles on tracks that still serve the region's banana plantations, and stop to see how the country's favorite yellow fruit is harvested, processed, and packaged. ⊙ *3¼ hrs* 🖂 *$69.*

Sloth Sanctuary. This quintessential animal-lover's shore excursion is arguably what Costa Rica is all about. Kindhearted owners Luis and Judy Arroyo operate Aviarios del Caribe, a sloth rescue center an hour south of Limón. (Your entry fee supports their work.) Follow the tour with a hike and canoe ride through the estuary on the grounds. ⊙ *5 hrs* 🖂 *$84.*

Tortuguero Canals Tour. The best (and only) way to see the canals is aboard a boat. It's easier to take a ship-sponsored shore excursion than to do it on your own. ⊙ *4 ½ hrs* 🖂 *$59.*

Exploring Limón
Numbers in the margin correspond to points of interest on the Puerto Limón map.

❶ **Limón.** "Sultry and sweltering" describes this port community of 90,000. The country's most ethnically diverse city mixes the Latino flavor of the rest of Costa Rica with Afro-Caribbean and Asian populations, descendants of laborers brought to do construction and farming in the 19th century. As in most of the rest of Costa Rica, you'll see no street signs here. Locals use a charmingly archaic system of designating addresses: The place you're looking for may be "100 meters south and 75 meters west of some landmark," where "100 meters" equals one city block, regardless of actual distance. Just north and east of the cruise terminal lies the city's palm-lined central park, **Parque Vargas,** with a promenade facing the ocean. Nine or so Hoffman's two-toed sloths live in its trees; ask a passerby to point them out, as spotting them requires a trained eye.

❸ **Rain Forest Aerial Tram.** This 4-square-km (2½-square-mi) preserve houses a privately owned and operated engineering marvel: a series of gondolas strung together in a modified ski-lift pulley system. (To lessen the impact on the jungle, the support pylons were lowered into place by helicopter.) The tram gives you a way of seeing the rain-forest canopy and its spectacular array of epiphyte plant life and birds from just above, a feat you could otherwise accomplish only by climbing the trees yourself. Though purists might complain that it treats the rain forest like an amusement park, it's an entertaining way to learn the value and beauty of rain-forest ecology. ⊠ *Braulio Carrillo National Park, 120 km (76 mi) west of Limón* ☎ *257–5961* ⊕ *www.rfat.com* 🖂 *$55* ⊙ *Mon. 9–4, Tues.–Sun. 6:30–4.*

❺ **San José.** Costa Rica's sprawling, congested capital sits in the middle of the country about three hours in-

PUERTO LIMÓN BEST BETS

■ The Rain Forest Tram. This attraction takes you up into the canopy of the rain forest to see it from a unique angle.

■ Tortuguero Canals. Whether you go on a ship-sponsored tour or arrange it on your own, you see a wild part of Costa Rica that isn't reachable by anything but boat.

■ Zip-Line Tours. If you have never done one of these thrilling tours, flying from tree to tree, Costa Rica is the original place to do it.

land from the coast. Despite the distance, San José figures as a shore excursion—a long one to be sure—on most ships' itineraries. (The vertical distance is substantial too; the capital sits on a plateau just under a mile above sea level. You'll appreciate a jacket here after so many days at sea level.) Although the city dates from the mid-18th century, little from the colonial era remains. The **Teatro Nacional** (National Theater) is easily the most enchanting building in Costa Rica, and San José's must-see sight. Coffee barons constructed the Italianate sandstone building, modeling it on a composite of European opera houses, and inaugurating it in 1897. ⊠ *Plaza de la Cultura* ☏ *221–1329* ⊕ *www.teatronacional. go.cr* ⊡ *$5* ⊙ *Mon.–Sat. 9–4.*

The **Museo Nacional** is housed in a whitewashed fortress dating from 1870 that now serves as the country's National Museum. Notice the bullet holes: this former army headquarters saw fierce fighting during a brief 1948 civil war. But it was also here that the government abolished the country's military in 1949. ⊠ *C. 17, between Avdas. Central and 2* ☏ *257–1433* ⊕ *www.museocostarica.go.cr* ⊡ *$4* ⊙ *Tues.–Sat. 8:30–4:30, Sun. 9–4:30.*

The northeastern San José suburb of **Moravia** is chock-full of souvenir stores lining a couple of blocks behind the city's church. ⊠ *160 km (100 mi) west of Limón.*

❷ Tortuguero Canals. The largely forested region north of Limón is one of those Costa Rican anomalies: roadless and remote, it's nevertheless one of the country's most-visited places. A system of inland canals runs parallel to the shoreline providing safer access to the region than a dangerous journey for smaller vessels up the sea coast. Some compare the densely layered greenery highlighted by brilliantly colored flowers, whose impact is doubled by the jungle's reflection in the mirror-smooth canal surfaces, to the Amazon. That might be stretching it, but there's still an Indiana Jones mystique to the journey up here, especially when you get off the main canals and into the narrower lagoons. Your guide will point out the abundant wildlife: sloths hang in the trees; howler monkeys let out their plaintive calls; egrets soar above the river surface; and crocodiles laze on the banks. ⊠ *North of Limón.*

❹ Volcán Irazú. Five active volcanoes loom over Costa Rica's territory (as well as many inactive ones). Irazú clocks in at the highest at about 3,700 meters (11,000 feet) and the farthest east and most accessible from Limón, though still a three-hour drive. The volcano last erupted in 1965, but gases and steam have billowed from fumaroles on its northwestern slope ever since. You can go right up to the top, although cloudy days—there are many—can obscure the view. ⊠ *140 km (84 mi) southwest of Limón* ⊡ *$7* ⊙ *Daily 8–3:30.*

Shopping

The cruise-ship terminal contains an orderly maze of souvenir stalls. Vendors are friendly, and there's no pressure to buy. Many shops populate the restored port building across the street. Here's the place to stock up on some of Costa Rica's signature products, most notably the country's pride and joy, its coffee. **Caribbean Banana** (⊠ *50 m north Terminal de*

Cruceros, west side of Parque Vargas ☎ *No phone*) Spelling is not its forte, but this shop stands out from the others in the cruise-terminal area with a terrific selection of wood carvings.

Activities

WHITEWATER RAFTING You can experience some of the world's premier white-water rafting in Costa Rica. The Río Reventazón in the eastern part of the country offers a few Class II–III sectors if you've never rafted before. **Ríos Tropicales** (⊠ *Siquirres, 72 km (44 mi) west of Limón* ☎ *233–6455* ⊕ *www.riostropicales.com*), one of Costa Rica's long-established outfitters, leads excursions on the Reventazón River from its operations center about an hour from Limón.

ZIP-LINE TOURS Costa Rica gave birth to the so-called canopy tour, a system of zip lines that transports you from platform to platform in the rain forest treetops courtesy of a very secure harness. Though billed as a way to get up close with nature, your Tarzan-like yells will probably scare any wildlife away. Think of it more as an outdoor amusement-park ride. **Original Canopy Tour** (⊠ *Veragua de Liverpool, 15 km (9 mi) west of Limón* ☎ *291–4465* ⊕ *www.canopytour.com*) opened only in 2006, but these folks are a branch of the oldest canopy-tour operator in the country.

Beaches

The dark-sand beaches on this sector of the coast are pleasant enough, but won't dazzle you if you've made previous stops at Caribbean islands with their white-sand strands. Nicer beaches than Limón's Playa Bonita lie farther south along the coast and can be reached by taxi or organized shore excursion. Strong undertows make for ideal surfing conditions on these shores, but risky swimming. Exercise caution.

Playa Bonita. The name of Limón's own strand translates as "pretty beach," but it's your typical urban beach, a bit on the cluttered side. ⊠ *2 km (1 mi) north of Limón.*

Playa Blanca. One of the coast's only white-sand beaches lies within the boundaries of Cahuita National Park right at the southern entrance of the pleasant little town of Cahuita. The park's rain forest extends right to the edge of the beach, and the waters here offer good snorkeling. ⊠ *44 km (26 mi) southeast of Limón Cahuita.*

Playa Cocles. The region's most popular strand of sand lies just outside Puerto Viejo de Talamanca, one of Costa Rica's archetypal beach towns, with its attendant cafés and bars and all-around good times to be had. ⊠ *63 km (38 mi) southeast of Limón, Puerto Viejo de Talamanca.*

Where to Eat

$–$$ ✕ **Brisas del Caribe.** You'll undoubtedly run across a few of your fellow passengers here at this old standby fronting the north side of the park. The food is good and filling. Seafood and surprisingly decent hamburgers, a real rarity in Costa Rica, are the fare here. ⊠ *North side of Parque Vargas* ☎ *758–0138* ▤ *AE, DC, MC, V* ☾ *Breakfast served.*

$–$$ ✕ **Hotel Park.** Take refuge from the sweltering midday heat in the air-conditioned restaurant of Limón's pastel-and-pink, mid-range business-class hotel. Decent pastas, seafood, and desserts are on the menu, and the pleasant ocean view is tossed in for free. ⊠ *Avda. 3, between Cs. 2 and 3* ☎ *798–0555* ⊟ *AE, DC, MC, V.*

ROATÁN, HONDURAS

Jeff Van Fleet

You'll swear you hear Jimmy Buffett singing as you step off the ship onto Roatán. The flavor is decidedly Margaritaville, but with all there is to do on this island off the north coast of Honduras, you'll never waste away here. Roatán is the largest and most important of the Bay Islands, though at a mere 65 km (40 mi) from tip to tip, and no more than five km (three mi) at its widest, "large" is relative here. As happened elsewhere on Central America's Caribbean coast, the British got here first—the Bay Islands didn't become part of Honduras until the mid-1800s—and left an indelible imprint in the form of place names such as Coxen Hole, French Harbour, and West End, and of course, their language, albeit a Caribbean-accented English. The eyes of underwater enthusiasts mist over at the mention of Roatán, one of the world's premier diving destinations, but plenty of topside activity will keep you busy too.

CURRENCY   The Honduran leimpira (L18.9 to US$1). You'll find an ATM at Banco BAC in the town of Coxen Hole, where cruise ships arrive. Credit cards are widely accepted, although merchants frequently add a surcharge to offset the high processing fees they are charged by card companies.

HOURS   Stores and businesses are open from 8 to 6. Many close for a couple of hours over lunch, as well as all day on Sunday, although those catering to the tourist trade make a point to stay open when cruise ships are in port.

INTERNET   Check your e-mail at **Hondusoft Internet** (⊠ *Main St. Coxen Hole*), just a couple of blocks from the cruise terminal.

TELEPHONES   Phone numbers in Honduras have seven digits. There are no area codes, so just dial the number. You'll find public phones at the cruise terminal, as well as around populated areas on the island.

Coming Ashore

Ships dock at the Terminal de Cruceros (cruise terminal) in the village of Coxen Hole, the island's administrative center. You'll find telephones, Internet computers, and stands with tour information inside the terminal, as well as a flea market of crafts vendors just outside the gate. At this writing, a public

---

ROATÁN BEST BETS

- **Diving.** Roatán is one of the world's great diving destinations. If you're certified, suit up. There's snorkeling too.

- **Explore Garífuna Culture.** You'd never know it wandering West End, but the island has an original culture that predated the arrival of tourism, and which still dominates Roatán's eastern side.

- **Copán.** It will have to be done on a very expensive, ship-sponsored tour, but Copán is one of the best Maya sites in the Caribbean.

concession has been granted to Royal Caribbean to construct and operate a new $16 million cruise terminal nearby. The current terminal dates only from 2001, but traffic here has outpaced its capacity. The new terminal, which will be open to all cruise lines, is expected to open in 2009.

A fleet of white taxis waits outside the gate, and here is your contact with one of the few negatives about Roatán. Drivers use a two-tier fare system, one for locals, and another, much higher "gringo" level. The $15 you'll be charged for the few miles to West End bears no resemblance to what a resident pays. Negotiate if you feel up to it. The local public-transport system consists of blue minivans that leave from Main Street in Coxen Hole to various points on the island until 6 PM. A journey to even the farthest reaches of the island does not exceed $1. Look for the cadre of tourist police if you need help with anything. They wear yellow shirts and dark-green trousers and are evident on cruise days. You certainly can rent a car here, but the island's compact size makes it unnecessary. Taxis will happily take you anywhere; expect to pay $40 to $80 for a day's private tour.

Shore Excursions

We consider these to be among the better shore excursions for Roatán. They may not be offered by all lines, and tour names may differ as well. Times and prices are approximate.

Diving Excursion. For certified divers who don't want to make their own arrangements, a ship-sponsored diving excursion is the best route. This two-tank boat-dive excursion will explore some of the island's best reefs. ⊙ 4½ hrs ⊠ $125.

Discover Roatán. A tour by boat and land will explore some of the island's interesting coves and includes a trip to visit the Garéfuna on the east end. ⊙ 4 hrs ⊠ $54.

Eco-Hike with Beach. After climbing Carombola Mountain, you visit the botanical gardens there and then head down to Las Palmas for a beach break. ⊙ 4½ hrs ⊠ $76.

Shipwreck Snorkel & Beach. For non-divers, a guided snorkeling trip will allow you to see something of the island's great reefs, as well as an interesting shipwreck. ⊙ 4½ hrs ⊠ $52.

Exploring Roatán

Numbers in the margin correspond to points of interest on the Roatán map.

④ Carambola Botanical Gardens. One of the country's premier gardens contains an extensive orchid collection, and is home to many different varieties of tropical plants. Take a self-guided tour. The trails and plants are well marked. The complex also serves as a breeding area for iguanas. ⊠ *Across from Anthony's Key Resort, Sandy Bay* ☎ 445–3117 ⊠ $5 ⊙ *Daily 7–5.*

⑦ Copán. The magnificent Maya city of Copán easily wins the "Honduras' Most Famous Sight" title, and this mainland destination is included on a few ships' shore-excursion itineraries. A cadre of colorful parrots greets you at the gate to one of the most breathtaking archae-

Roatán Island

Caribbean Sea

Bahía de Honduras

ological sites in Central America. Down a tree-lined path you'll find a series of beautifully reconstructed temples. The intricate carvings on the stone structures, especially along the Hieroglyphic Stairway, are remarkably well preserved. Here you can marvel at the artistry of a city that many have called the "Paris of Central America."

The area open to the public covers only a small part of the city's ceremonial center. Copán once extended for nearly 2 km (1¼ mi) along the river, making it as large as many Maya archaeological sites in Guatemala. It's also just as old—more than 3,000 years ago there was an Olmec settlement on this site. Because new structures were usually built on top of existing ones, the great temples that are visible today were built during the reigns of the city's last few rulers. Nearby stands the little town of Copán Ruinas, chock full of pleasant cafés and shops. ⊠ *1½ km (1 mi) east of Copán Ruinas* ☎ *No phone* 🎫 *$10* ⊙ *Daily 8–4.*

❷ Roatán Butterfly Garden. Hundreds of butterflies fluttering around you, all species native to Honduras. More than 20 colorful varieties are found here at any given time. Outside the screened-in butterfly house you will find a variety of tropical trees, including cashews, hogplums, and breadfruit. ⊠ *West side, Sandy Bay* ☎ *445–1096* ⊕ *www. roatanbutterfly.com* 🎫 *$5* ⊙ *Sun.–Fri. 9–5.*

3 **Roatán Institute for Marine Sciences.** Roatán's answer to Florida's Sea World is famous for its dolphin shows, always a crowd pleaser as the animals leap through hoops and balance balls on their noses, but don't ignore the informative bilingual exhibits about the geology and marine life of the Bay Islands. ⊠ *Anthony Key Resort, Sandy Bay* ☎ *445–1327* ⊡ *$5* ⊙ *Daily 8–5; dolphin shows Thurs.–Tues. 10 AM and 4 PM.*

5 **Sherman Arch's Iguana Farm.** Somebody has to love iguanas, and bless longtime resident Sherman Arch for doing so. He has opened his farm to some 2,700 of four species found on the island, and the animals roam freely here. (Feeding time is around noon.) Your visit is a chance to learn about iguanas, and your admission goes to the conservation of an animal that was slowly being lost to hunters on the island. ⊠ *French Harbour turnoff, French Key* ☎ *445–1498* ⊡ *$5* ⊙ *Daily 8–4.*

1 **West End.** At the far western tip of the island lies one of the world's quintessential beach towns, and tourism central for Roatán. The town pulses but at half-pace—most of its streets are still unpaved—and is an enjoyable place to stroll and take in the shops and bars. ⊠ *West End.*

6 **Yubu.** The intermarriage of African slaves with European and indigenous peoples on Honduras' Caribbean coast gave rise to the region's distinctive Garífuna culture, which holds sway on the less-traveled east side of the island. Yubu is part museum, part theater, part store, and an opportunity to learn about a side of Roatán just 20 miles—but a world away—from the tourism hubbub of West End. ⊠ *Punta Gorda just before you enter town* ☎ *No phone* ⊡ *$5* ⊙ *Tues.–Fri. 9–3.*

Shopping

Crafts vendors set up shop outside the cruise-terminal gates, and a small selection of souvenir shops are scattered around the center of Coxen Hole, a short walk from the docks. Few of the souvenirs for sale here—or anywhere else on the island for that matter—were actually made in Roatán; most come from mainland Honduras. Standout shop **Yaba Ding Ding** (⊠ *Main St., Coxen Hole* ☎ *445–1683*) takes its name from a Garífuna expression that loosely translates as "artifact." The shop, just a short stroll from the cruise terminal, deals in quality reproductions of indigenous artifacts, most of which were made in the mainland highlands near Copán. You'll also find a good selection of quality T-shirts here, far more distinctive than the standard, ubiquitous LIFE'S A BEACH ones.

Activities

DIVING & SNORKELING   Most of the activity on Roatán centers on scuba diving and snorkeling, as well as the newest sensation, snuba, a cross between the two, whereby your mask is connected to an air tube above. Warm water, great visibility, and thousands of colorful fish make the island a popular destination. Add to this a good chance of seeing a whale shark, and you'll realize why so many people head here each year. Dive sites cluster off the island's western and southern coasts. Competition among the dive shops is fierce in West End, so check out a few. When shopping around, ask about the condition of the diving equipment, and the safety equipment on the dive boat. **Native Sons** (⊠ *Half Moon Bay, West End*

☎ 445–1335 ⊕ *www.nativesonsroatan.com*) is one of the most popular dive shops in town. It's run by a native of Roatán who really knows the area. In business for more than a decade, **West End Divers** (✉ *Half Moon Bay, West End* ☎ 445–1531 ⊕ *www.westendivers.com*) has a pair of dive boats. The company is committed to protecting the fragile marine ecology.

Beaches

You almost can't go wrong with any of Roatán's white-sand beaches. Even those adjacent to populated areas manage to stay clean and uncluttered, thanks to efforts of residents. Water is rougher for swimming on the less-protected north side of the island.

Half Moon Bay. Roatán's most popular beach is also one of its prettiest. Coconut palms and foliage come up to the crescent-shape shoreline. The beach lies just outside the tourist-friendly West End. Crystal-clear waters offer abundant visibility for snorkeling. ✉ *North side, West End.*

Tabyana Beach. Locals refer to this lovely beach simply as **"West Bay,"** but the travel brochures name it after its prominent Tabyana Beach Resort. It's a de rigueur listing on every shore-excursions list, and the resort sets aside its facilities for its cruise passengers as a private beach. The complex also offers zip-line tours, which take you through the treetops courtesy of a series of cables and a very secure harness. ✉ *West Bay.*

Where to Eat

$$ ✕ **¿Qué Tal? Café.** A good spot for a quick and simple meal, this friendly little café serves up salads, sandwiches, and other light fare. Located opposite the main road into Coxen Hole, it also offers Internet access. It's only open until 4 PM, however. ✉ *Thicket Rd., Coxen Hole* ☎ 445–1007 ▭ *No credit cards* ⊗ *No dinner.*

$$–$$$ ✕ **Rudy's.** By far the best place in West End for breakfast, this café opens at 6:30 AM. Divers crowd into the little garden to devour the excellent banana pancakes. For lunch try one of the fruit smoothies. ✉ *West End* ☎ *No phone* ▭ *No credit cards* ⊗ *No dinner.*

SAMANÁ, DOMINICAN REPUBLIC

Eileen
Robinson Smith

Samaná, the name of both a peninsula in the Dominican Republic as well as the largest town on Samaná Bay, is one of the least known regions of the country, but the new international airport that opened in late 2006 may change that perception quickly. Much development is planned, so a visit now will be to a place that is not yet geared to a great deal of mainstream, mass tourism. But with the use of the port by some mega-ships, that too is changing quickly. Samaná is one of the Dominican Republic's newest cruise-ship destinations, with one of the island's greatest varieties of shore excursions. You can explore caves and see an amazing waterfall. And since many humpback whales come here each year to mate and give birth, it's a top whale-watching destination from January through March. While some cruise lines still use Cayo Levantado as a private-island type of experience, for other lines it is just one of several options.

Essentials

CURRENCY   The Dominican peso (RD$32.50 to US$1). Get local currency if you are touring on your own, but most places accept U.S. dollars, though any change will be in pesos. Banks and *cambios* (currency exchange offices) are common.

HOURS   Stores and attractions are typically open from 10 to 6. Many places close from noon to 2 for a lunch/siesta break, but when a ship is in port, you may find more businesses open.

INTERNET   You'll find several convenient Internet cafés in town. The price of going online ranges between RD$30 and RD$80 per hour, inexpensive to be sure. However, don't be surprised if you go and are told that the computers: *"No sirve, porque no hay electricidad."* Translation: this is still a developing destination, and often half the day is spent without electricity. Although most hotels and restaurants have generators, usually these shops do not. **Centro Llamada Edwards** (⊠ *4 Francisco Rosario Sanchez, Samaná* ☎ *809/538–2476*) has 5 computers and charges only RD$30 an hour to connect. **Deleon Communications** (⊠ *13 Maria Trinidad Sanchez, Samaná, across from the landmark Palacio Justicia* ☎ *809/538–3538*) has six computers and four phone booths.

TELEPHONES   You can call a U.S. or Canadian number easily; just dial 1 plus the area code and number. **Centro de Communicationes Verizon** (⊠ *8 Francisco Rosario Sanchez, Samaná* ☎ *809/538–2901* ✉ *Maria Trinidad Sanchez, Samaná, next door to Pharmacia Gisella*) is a good place to make phone calls. Only cash is taken, preferably pesos. At the first location, there are public computers for checking your e-mails; at the second, you won't be able to go online, but it is closer to the pier.

Coming Ashore

Cruise ships anchor at a point that is equidistant between the town of Samaná and Cayo Levantado, an island at the mouth of Samaná Bay with a great beach and facilities to receive 1,500 cruise-ship passengers. Tenders will take you to one of three docks, located on the Malecón, referred to as the Samaná Bay Piers. The farthest is a five-minute walk from the town center. The Verizon office is just before the public market.

Renting a car, although possible, isn't a good option. Driving in the D.R. can be a hectic and even harrowing experience; if you are only in port one day, don't risk it. Yes, taxis are expensive, but so are rental cars. You'll do better if you combine your resources with friends from the ship and share a taxi to do some independent exploring. Negotiate prices, and settle before getting in the taxi. To give you an idea of what to

> ### SAMANÁ BEST BETS
>
> ■ **Cayo Levantado.** This resort island in the bay does put on an excellent show for day-trippers.
>
> ■ **Los Haitises National Park.** The caves filled with Taïno drawings and the pristine mangrove forests make this a top ecotourism destination in the region.
>
> ■ **Whale-watching.** In season, this is the top activity in the Samaná Peninsula.

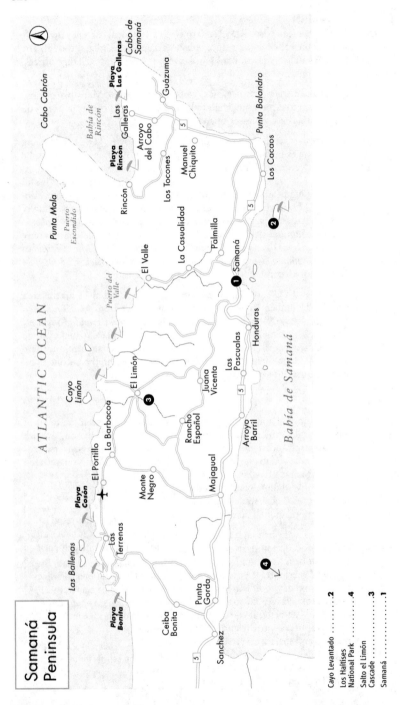

Samaná Peninsula

expect, a minivan that can take eight people will normally charge $90 for the round-trip to Las Terranas, including a two-hour wait while you explore or enjoy the beach. Similarly, you'll pay $80 to travel to Las Galleras or Playa Rincón. Many of the drivers speak some English. Within Samaná, rickshaws are far less costly and are also fun. Called *motoconchos de carretas,* they are not unlike larger versions of the Thai tuk-tuk, but can hold up to six people. The least you will pay is RD$10. They're fine to get around town, but don't even think about going the distance with them.

If you decide to rent a car, consider using **Javier Inversiones Rent-a-Car** (⊠ *7 Francisco Rosario Sanchez, Samaná* ☎ *809/249–5937*), which can put you in a Jeep or even a Toyota Camry, although there is not a large inventory of automatics. You can expect to pay at least $50 a day—more for an automatic—but that does include insurance.

Shore Excursions

We consider these to be among the better shore excursions for Samaná. They may not be offered by all lines, and tour names may differ as well. Times and prices are approximate.

ATV Tours. ATVs go inland, halfway to the town of Sanchez, where there are incredible mountain views. The route follows a meandering jungle river. Normally, there is a stop at a coconut plantation to watch the processing, and to have a tasting. Then it's off to Playa El Valle, a golden beach, for a swim and even a siesta, after what is quite a bumpy ride. More expensive tours may include lunch. ⏱ *3½–6 hrs.* 🎫 *$65–$109.*
Cave and Mangrove Exploration. Guided tours are the only way to explore the caves and mangrove forests of Los Haitises (pronounced Hi *tee* sis). The boat docks to allow passengers to walk quietly around a mangrove swamp and visit various cavern systems. Some trips also hike to the village of Crystal in the rain forest, where you can bathe in a crystal-clear, freshwater lagoon. ⏱ *3 hrs.* 🎫 *$70–$79.*
Jeep Safaris. These four-wheel-drive vehicles follow the same course as the ATVs. Along the way you will stop at a typical Dominican country home, see beautiful beaches, rock formations, and rivers that emanate from caves. Some guides take you on a 15-minute walk to witness a stunning waterfall. ⏱ *4½ hrs.* 🎫 *$64–$70.*
Salto El Limón Cascade. The best way to do this trip is on horseback, and that makes it a very worthwhile excursion. The waterfall itself is beautiful, and you will have the opportunity to swim in the clear pool. ⏱ *4½ hrs.* 🎫 *$65.*

Exploring Samaná Peninsula

Numbers in the margin correspond to points of interest on the Samaná map.

② **Cayo Levantado.** Residents of Samaná call Cayo Levantado their *pasa dia en la playa* (the place to pass the day on the beach). Today, the small island in Samaná Bay has been improved to receive up to 1,500 cruiseship passengers per day, with dining facilities, bars, restrooms, and lounge chairs on the beautiful beach. The company that runs cruise-ship services on the island has even applied for the coveted "Blue Flag" that designates a beach as clean and unpolluted. Independent restaurants and vendors also ply their wares. This isn't the most tranquil island, but you can quite happily spend the day here if you don't want to go into the town of Samaná. The new Grand Bahia Principe Cayo Levantado, an upscale, all-inclusive resort opened in December 2006 and claims the eastern two-thirds of the island for its private use. Day-use of the island will either be included in your cruise fare or will be treated as a regular shore excursion, for which the lines usually charge $40 to $60. ⊠ *Samaná Bay* ☎ *809/538-2579* ✉ *Donations appreciated* ⊙ *Daily dawn–dusk.*

❹ **Los Haitises National Park.** A guided tour is the only way to explore Los Haitises' (pronounced Hi *tee* sis), which is across Samaná Bay from the peninsula. The park is famous for its Karst limestone formations, caves, and grottoes filled with pictographs and petroglyphs left by the indigenous Taïno before the discovery of the Americas. Mangrove forests shelter many coastal bird species, including Louisiana night herons and the magnificent American frigate birds, making this a bird-watchers' delight as well. Typical trips cruise the coastline dotted with small islands and spectacular cliff faces, finally docking to allow passengers to walk quietly around a mangrove swamp and visit the various caves. Some trips allow you to hike to the village of Crystal in the rain forest, where you can swim in a crystal-clear, freshwater lagoon.

❸ **Salto el Limón Cascade.** Provided that you are fit, an adventurous guided trip to this spectacular waterfall is a delight. The journey is usually done mostly on horseback but includes walking down rocky, sometimes muddy trails. The well-mannered horses take you across rivers and up mountains to El Limón, where you'll find the waterfall amid luxuriant vegetation. Some snacks and drinks are usually included in the guided trip. ⊠ *El Limón.*

❶ **Samaná.** The official name of the city is Santa Barbara de Samaná; alas, that saint's name is falling into disuse, and you'll more often hear simply "Samaná" these days. An authentic port town, not just a touristic zone, it has a typical *malecón* (seaside promenade) with gazebos and park benches, ideal for strolling and watching the boats in the harbor. The main road that borders this green zone, Avenida Malecón, is lined with restaurants, shops, and small businesses. A small but bustling town, Samaná is filled with friendly residents, skilled local craftsmen selling their wares, and many outdoor cafés.

The **Whale Museum & Nature Center** is dedicated to the mighty mammals of the sea, and you will learn everything you have ever wanted to know about whales here. Samaná has one of the largest marine mammal sanctuaries in the world and is a center for whale-watching in the migration season. The C.E.B.S.E (Center for Conservation and Ecodevelopment of Samaná Bay and its Environment) manages this facility. ⊠ *Tiro Blanco* ☎ *809/538-2042* ⊕ *samana.org.do* ✉ *RD $50* ⊙ *Daily 8–12 and 2–5.*

The historic **Dominican Evangelical Church** is the oldest original building left in Samaná. It actually came across the ocean from England in

1881 in a hundred pieces and was reassembled here, serving the spiritual needs of African-American freedmen who emigrated here from Philadelphia, Pennsylvania in 1824. ✉ *Calle Chaseurox, in front of the Catholic church* ☎ *809/538–2579* 🖃 *Donations appreciated* ⊙ *Daily dawn–dusk.*

Shopping

Rum, coffee, and cigars are popular local products. You may also find good coconut handicrafts, including coconut-shell candles. Whale-oriented gift items are particularly popular. Most of the souvenir shops are on Samaná's Malecón or in the market plaza; you will find more on the major downtown streets in town, all within easy walking distance of the tender piers. A shopping mall called **Plublito Carabeño Plaza** (✉ *20 Francisco Rosario Sanchez*) is near the piers; it has a bevy of shops and food outlets (including American fast-food).

Activities

At this writing, only one excursion company, Bahia Cruise Services, is licensed to offer services to ships, so some of the tours in the region may be available only on ship-sponsored excursions. But there are some independent companies in the area.

DIVING & SNORKELING In 1979, three atolls disappeared following a seaquake off of Las Terrenas, providing an opportunity for truly memorable dives. **Aqua Center** (✉ *Viva Wyndham Samaná Resort, Las Terrenas* ☎ *809/240—5050 ext. 2217* ⊕ *www.aqua-center.com*) offers one close dive at Las Ballenas (i.e., "the Whales"), a cluster of four little islands for $43 for certified divers only. You can also sign up for a resort dive for $85, but you will only be allowed to go down to 40 feet. Trips can be tailored around your cruise ship's schedule. Also, there are four dive masters here who offer PADI, PIRA, and SSI instruction that can count toward certification. In addition to transportation time, allow 2 hours to do a dive, with 45 minutes underwater. The center also offers snorkeling trips aboard a 35-foot catamaran to Playa Jackson, a tranquil virgin beach. This 3½-hour trip costs $25 per person. A longer trip includes lunch, but you must reserve in advance.

WHALE WATCHING Humpback whales come to Samaná Bay to mate and give birth each year, from approximately January 15 through March 30. Samaná Bay is considered one of the top 10 destinations in the world to watch whales. **Victoria Marine/ Whale Samaná** (✉ *Across the street from the cement town dock, beside the park Samaná* ☎ *809/538–2494*) is owned by Kim Beddall, a Canadian who is incredibly knowledgeable about whales and Samaná at large, having lived here for 20-some years. Her operation is the region's best. Kim herself does almost all the English-speaking trips. The $50 price does not include the RD$100 Marine Mammal Sanctuary entrance fee. Kim welcomes cruise passengers but requires advance reservations. You must be able to arrive onshore by 9 AM for the morning trip and by 1:30 PM for the afternoon trip.

Beaches

There are no recommendable beaches in Samaná itself. You will have to travel to one of the beautiful ones elsewhere on the peninsula, another reason why the Cayo Levantado excursion is very popular on most ships.

Playa Bonito. Las Terrenas, about an hour away from Samaná, is a bohemian enclave favored by the French. It has become commercialized and can have a frenetic energy, but its beaches are legendary. On Playa Bonito you can bounce between the golden beach (BYO towel—no chaises) and one of the hotels directly across the rough road, where you can have lunch. Hotel Acaya is one of these hotels and has an open-air restaurant. Just yards away, at Hotel Bahia Las Bellenas, is Paco's, which specializes in fresh seafood. ⊠ *Las Terrenas.*

Playa Cosón. The closest good beach to Samaná is some 15 minutes away from the town of Las Terranas, and about an hour from Samaná. You can buy a day pass for a reasonable price (about $35) at the resort Viva Wyndham Samaná, which is smack on Bahia Cosón. ⊠ *Bahia Cosón, Las Terrenas.*

Playa Las Galleras. The beach within this tiny coastal town, a 30-minute drive northeast from the port, is lovely, long, and uncluttered. The sand is white, and the Atlantic waters are generally calm. It has been designated a "Blue Flag" beach, which means that it is crystal clean with no pollution, though there are several hotels here. Generally, cruisers gravitate toward Casa Marina Bay Resort, and many cruise lines sell day passes for that all-inclusive resort. This is a good snorkeling spot, too. ⊠ *Las Galleras.*

Playa Rincón. This beautiful, white-sand beach is considered one of the top beaches in the Caribbean. It is relatively undeveloped, and at the far-right end is a sheltered area, where you can snorkel. At the other end, cliffs segue way into the turquoise water of Caño Frio, an ice-cold river that runs down from the mountains and forms a splash pool, ideal for rinsing off the salt water. There are no facilities per se, but local ladies will sell you the freshest lobster and fish in coconut sauce with rice, and other creole dishes as well as cold drinks. ⊠ *Turn right at the tiny town of El Rincón.*

Where to Eat

$–$$ ✕ **Le France.** From your first glance, you can tell that this corner restaurant has a charismatic appeal. With a red-tile roof and just one white wall, it has a massive mirror that reflects the tranquil bay view and the busy pedestrian traffic. It could be called a coconut palace, what with all the decorations. The food is not easy to categorize; expect a *comida international* that is French-accented, with seafood a major element. You can get off easy by ordering crêpes or pasta, or you can splurge on grilled shrimp. For starters, consider the original gazpacho with lambi (conch). This is one time you might want to chance beef tartare; loyal followers come all the way from Santo Domingo for it. ⊠ *6 Ave. de la Marina* ☎ *809/538–2257* ▭ *No credit cards* ⊘ *Closed Mon.*

$–$$$ ✕ **La Mata Rosada.** A popular pick of local expats and foodies, this spot will guarantee you a water view and some flavorful food, be it the sea and country salad (conch, potatoes, greens, and bacon) or the "gourmet" plate (a mix of grilled lobster and other shellfish). There is even a daily plat du jour for a song. Ceviche, a specialty of this port town, is made with dorado (mahimahi) here and is speckled with capers, tomatoes, and even mushrooms. Whether you go local or international, order the creole shrimp or a substantial salad, and you should leave satisfied. ⊠ *5 Avenida Malecon* ☎ *809/538–2388* ▤ *AE, MC, V* ☉ *Closed Tues. June–Nov.*

ST. BARTHÉLEMY (GUSTAVIA)

Elise Meyer

Hilly St. Barthélemy, popularly known as St. Barth (or St. Barts) is just 8 square mi (21 square km), but the island has at least 20 good beaches. What draws visitors is its sophisticated but unstudied approach to relaxation: the finest food, excellent wine, high-end shopping, and lack of large-scale commercial development. A favorite among upscale cruiseship passengers, who also appreciate the shopping opportunities and fine dining, St. Barths isn't really equipped for mega-ship visits, which is why most ships calling here are from smaller premium lines. This is one place where you don't need to take the ship's shore excursions to have a good time. Just hail a cab or rent a car and go to one of the many wonderful beaches, where you will find some of the best lunchtime restaurants, or wander around Gustavia, shopping and eating. It's the best way to relax on this most relaxing of islands.

Essentials

CURRENCY The euro (€1 to US$1.31); however, U.S. dollars are accepted in almost all shops and in many restaurants. Credit cards are widely accepted.

HOURS Stores are usually open from 8:30 to noon and 2 to 5 on weekdays (some stay open until 7), and 8:30 to noon on Saturdays. Many stores are closed Wednesday afternoon.

INTERNET Check your e-mail at the **Centre Alizes** (⊠ *Rue de la République, Gustavia*).

TELEPHONES Public telephones accept *télécartes,* prepaid calling cards that you can buy at the gas station next to the airport and at post offices in Lorient, St-Jean, and Gustavia. Making an international call using a télécarte is the best way to go.

Coming Ashore

Even medium-size ships must anchor in Gustavia Harbor and bring passengers ashore on tenders. The tiny harbor area is right in Gustavia, which is easily explored on foot. Taxis, which meet all cruise ships, can be expensive. Technically, there's a flat rate for rides up to five minutes long. Each additional three minutes is an additional amount. In reality, however, cabbies usually name a fixed rate—and will not budge. Fares are 50% higher on Sundays and holidays. St. Barths is one port where it's really worth it to arrange a car rental for a full-day exploration of the island, including the island's out-of-the-way beaches. But be aware that during high season there is often a three-day minimum, so this may not be possible except through your ship (and then you'll pay premium rates indeed). Most car-rental firms operate at the airport; expect to pay about €50 a day, which is cheaper than what you'll get if you go with one of the ship's car rentals. The new St. Barth Shuttle service can be convenient and much less expensive than a taxi if you are just one or two people, but it still doesn't completely negate the need for a car.

Shore Excursions

Catamaran Snorkel Tour. Superb coral reefs are only a short sail from Gustavia Harbor, where you board your catamaran at the pier and head for your snorkel site. Equipment and instructions are provided and refreshments are served during the sail back to the pier. ☉ *3 hrs* ▭ *$149.*

Independent Exploration. One of the best—and most popular—ways to explore St. Barths is by rental car, so you can stop at your favorite beaches and take your time on the twisting roads. But you must be able to drive a manual transmission. ☉ *5½ hrs* ▭ *$129–$149.*

Island Tour. Your tour encompasses the highlights on a round-the-island trip by minibus. ☉ *1¼ hrs* ▭ *$49.*

Exploring St. Barths

With a little practice, negotiating St. Barths' narrow, steep roads soon becomes fun. Free maps are everywhere, roads are well marked, and painted signs will point you where you want to be. Take along a towel, sandals, and a bottle of water, and you will surely find a beach upon which to linger.

Numbers in the margin correspond to points of interest on the St. Barthélemy map.

2 **Corossol.** The island's French-provincial origins are most evident in this two-street fishing village with a little rocky beach. Older local women weave lantana straw into handbags, baskets, hats, and delicate strings of birds. Ingenu Magras's **Inter Oceans Museum** has more than 9,000 seashells and an intriguing collection of sand samples from around the world. You can buy souvenir shells. ⊠ *Corossol* ☎ *0590/27–62–97* ⊠ *€3* ☉ *Tues.–Sun. 9–12:30 and 2–5.*

1 **Gustavia.** You can easily explore all of Gustavia during a two-hour stroll. Street signs in both French and Swedish illustrate the island's history. Most shops close from noon to 2, so plan lunch accordingly. A good spot to park your car is rue de la République, where catamarans, yachts, and sailboats are moored. The **tourist office** (☎ *0590/27–87–27*) on the pier can provide maps and a wealth of information. It's open Monday from 8:30 to 12:30, Tuesday through Friday from 8 to noon and 2 to 5, and Saturday from 9 to noon. On the far side of the harbor known as La Pointe is the charming **Municipal Museum,** where you can find watercolors, portraits, photographs, and historic documents detailing the island's history as well as displays of the island's flowers, plants, and marine life. ☎ *599/29–71–55* ⊠ *€2* ☉ *Mon., Tues., Thurs., and Fri. 8:30–12:30 and 2:30–6, Sat. 9–12:30.*

4 **Lorient.** Site of the first French settlement, Lorient is one of the island's two parishes; a restored church, a school, and a post office mark the spot. Note the gaily decorated graves in the cemetery. One of St. Barths' secrets is **Le Manoir** (☎ *0590/27–79–27*), a 1610 Norman manor, now a guesthouse, which was painstakingly shipped from France and reconstructed in Lorient in 1984. Look for the entrance by the Ligne St. Barths building.

3 **St-Jean.** The half-mile-long crescent of sand at St-Jean is the island's most popular beach. Windsurfers skim along the water here, catching the strong trade winds. A popular activity is watching and photographing the hair-raising airplane landings. You'll also find some of the best shopping on the island here, as well as several restaurants.

Shopping

St. Barths is a duty-free port, and with its sophisticated crowd of visitors, shopping in the island's 200-plus boutiques is a definite delight. In Gustavia, boutiques line the three major shopping streets. The **Quai du République,** nicknamed "Rue du Couturier," which is right on the harbor, rivals New York's

ST. BARTHS BEST BETS

■ **Soaking up the Atmosphere.** It's the French Riviera transported to the Caribbean. Simply enjoy.

■ **Beautiful Beaches.** Pick any of the lovely, uncrowded beaches and spread out for a day in the sun.

■ **French Food.** St. Barths has some of the best restaurants in the Caribbean. This is the best place to splurge on a leisurely French lunch.

■ **Shopping.** The Caribbean's best selection of high fashion is not cheap but it is unparalleled.

Madison Avenue, or Paris's Avenue Montaigne for high-end "designer" retail. These shops often carry items that are not available in the U.S. Shops are also clustered in **La Savane Commercial Center** (across from the airport), **La Villa Créole** (in St-Jean), and **Espace Neptune** (on the road to Lorient). It's worth working your way from one end to the other at these shopping complexes—just to see or, perhaps, be seen. Boutiques in all three areas carry the latest in French and Italian sportswear and some haute couture. You probably are not going to find any bargains as long as the euro remains high, but you might be able to snag that *pochette* that is sold out stateside, and in any case, you'll have a lot of fun hunting around.

Look for Fabienne Miot's unusual gold jewelry at **L'Atelier de Fabienne** (⊠ *Rue de la République, Gustavia* ☎ *0590/27–63–31*). Fans of Longchamp handbags and leather goods will find a good selection at about 20% off stateside prices at **Elysée Caraïbes** (⊠ *Le Carré d'Or, Gustavia* ☎ *0590/52–00–94*). The **Hermès** (⊠ *Rue de la République, Gustavia* ☎ *0590/27–66–15*) store in St. Barths is an independently owned franchise, and prices are slightly below those in the States. Don't miss **Lolita Jaca** (⊠ *Le Carré d'Or, Gustavia* ☎ *0590/27–59–98*) for trendy, tailored sportswear. **Sindbad** (⊠ *Carré d'Or, Gustavia* ☎ *0590/27–52–29*) is a tiny shop with funky, unique couture fashion jewelry by Gaz Bijou of St. Tropez, crystal collars for your pampered pooch, chunky ebony pendants on silk cord, Nomination bracelets, and other reasonably priced, up-to-the-minute styles. **Pati de Saint Barth** (⊠ *Passage de la Crémaillière, Gustavia* ☎ *0590/29–78–04*) is the largest of the three shops that stock the chic, locally made T-shirts that have practically become the logo of St. Barths. The newest styles have hand-done graffiti-style lettering. **Stéphane & Bernard** (⊠ *Rue de la République, Gustavia* ☎ *0590/27–69–13*) stocks a well-edited, large selection of superstar French fashion designers, including Rykiel, Tarlazzi, Kenzo, Feraud, and Mugler.

In Lorient, don't miss the superb skin-care products made on-site from local tropical plants by **Ligne de St. Barths** (⊠ *Rte. de Saline, Lorient* ☎ *0590/27–82–63*).

Black Swan (⊠ *Le Carré d'Or, Gustavia* ☎ *0590/27–65–16* ⊠ *La Villa Créole, St-Jean*) has an unparalleled selection of bathing suits. The wide range of styles and sizes is appreciated. Local works of art, including paintings, are sold in the bright **Made in St-Barth La Boutique** (⊠ *La Villa Créole, St-Jean* ☎ *0590/27–56–57*). **SUD SUD.ETC.Plage** (⊠ *Galerie du Commerce, St-Jean* ☎ *0590/27–98–75*) stocks everything for the beach: inflatables, mats, bags, and beachy shell jewelry.

Activities

BEACHES   There are many *anses* (coves) and nearly 20 *plages* (beaches) scattered around the island, each with a distinctive personality and each open to the general public. Even in season you can find a nearly empty beach. Topless sunbathing is common, but nudism is technically forbidden—although both Saline and Gouverneur are de facto nude beaches. Because **Anse du Gouverneur** is so secluded, nude sunbathing is popular here; the beach is truly beautiful, with blissful swimming and views of St. Kitts, Saba, and St. Eustatius. Like a mini Côte d'Azur—beachside bistros, bungalow hotels, bronzed bodies, windsurfing, and lots of day-trippers— the reef-protected strip along **Baie de St-Jean** is divided by Eden Rock promontory, and there's good snorkeling west of the rock. The shallow, reef-protected beach at **Anse de Grand Cul de Sac** is especially nice for small children, fly fishermen, and windsurfers; it has excellent lunch spots and lots of pelicans. The big salt ponds of Grande Saline are no longer in use, and the place looks a little desolate. Don't be put off—by all means, climb the short hillock behind the ponds for a surprise. Secluded, with a sandy ocean bottom, **Anse de Grande Saline** is just about everyone's favorite beach and a great place for swimmers. In spite of the prohibition, young and old alike go nude. It can get windy here, so go on a calm day.

4

BOATING St. Barths is a popular yachting and sailing center, thanks to its location midway between Antigua and St. Thomas. Gustavia's harbor, 13 to 16 feet deep, has mooring and docking facilities for 40 yachts. There are also good anchorages available at Public, Corossol, and Colombier. Day sails are popular activities and will take you to snorkeling spots that aren't reachable by land. **Marine Service** (⊠ *Gustavia* ☎ *0590/27–70–34* ⊕ *www.st-barths.com/marine.service*) offers full-day outings, either on a 42- or 46-foot catamaran, to the uninhabited Île Fourchue for swimming, snorkeling, cocktails, and lunch. The cost is $100 per person; an unskippered motor rental runs about $260 a day.

DIVING & You can arrange scuba excursions to several local sites. Depending on
SNORKELING the weather conditions, you may dive at Pain de Sucre, Coco Island, or even nearby Saba. There's also an underwater shipwreck to explore, plus sharks, rays, sea tortoises, coral, and the usual varieties of color fish. The waters on the island's leeward side are the calmest. If you're not a certified diver, there's an accessible shallow reef right off the beach at Anse de Cayes if you want to do snorkeling from the beach. **Plongée Caraïbe** (☎ *0590/27–55–94*) is recommended for its up-to-the-minute equipment and dive boat. Marine Service operates the only five-star, PADI-certified diving center on the island, called **West Indies Dive** (☎ *0590/27–70–34* ⊕ *www.westindiesdive.com*). Scuba trips, packages, resort dives, night dives, and certifications start at $90, including gear.

WINDSURFING Windsurfing fever has definitely caught on in St. Barths. Gentle, constant trade winds make conditions ideal on some beaches, such as Anse de Grand Cul de Sac or Baie de St-Jean. You can rent boards for about €20 an hour at water-sports centers on the beaches. Lessons are offered for about $40 an hour at **Eden Rock Sea Sport Club** (⊠ *Eden Rock Hotel, Baie de St-Jean* ☎ *0590/27–74–77*), which also rents boards. **Wind Wave Power** (⊠ *St. Barth Beach Hotel, Grand Cul de Sac* ☎ *0590/27–82–57*) offers an extensive, six-hour training course. For €60, you can have a one-hour introductory lesson, along with the use of the Windsurfer for as long as you can stand up.

Where to Eat
Check restaurant bills carefully. A service charge is always added by law, but you should leave the server 5% to 10% extra in cash. It is generally advisable to charge restaurant meals on a credit card, as the issuer will offer a better exchange rate than the restaurant.

$$–$$$　✕ **Le Repaire.** This friendly brasserie overlooks Gustavia's harbor and is a popular spot from its early-morning opening at 7 AM to its late-night closing at midnight. The menu ranges from cheeseburgers, which are served only at lunch along with the island's best fries, to simply grilled fish and meat. The composed salads always please. Wonderful ice-cream sundaes round out the menu. ✉ *Quai de la République, Gustavia* ☎ *0590/27–72–48* ▭ *MC, V.*

★ **$$$–$$$$**　✕ **Le Tamarin.** A leisurely lunch here en route to Grand Saline beach is a St. Barths *must*. Delicious French and creole cuisine is served at this sophisticated open-air restaurant. Get to know the parrot, or relax in a hammock after the house-special carpaccios of salmon, tuna, and beef. The lemon tart deserves its excellent reputation. ✉ *Salines* ☎ *0590/27–72–12* ▭ *AE, MC, V* ☉ *Open erratically May–Nov. Call to confirm.*

ST. JOHN, U.S. VIRGIN ISLANDS

Lynda Lohr

St. John's heart is Virgin Islands National Park, a treasure that takes up a full two-thirds of St. John's 20 square mi (53 square km). The park helps keep the island's interior in its pristine and undisturbed state, but if you go at midday, you'll probably have to share your stretch of beach with others, particularly at Trunk Bay. The island is booming, and while it can get a tad crowded at the ever-popular Trunk Bay Beach during the busy winter season, you won't find traffic jams or pollution. It's easy to escape from the fray, however: just head off on a hike. St. John doesn't have a grand agrarian past like her sister island, St. Croix, but if you're hiking in the dry season, you can probably stumble upon the stone ruins of old plantations. The less adventuresome can visit the repaired ruins at the park's Annaberg Plantation and Caneel Bay resort. Of the three U.S. Virgin Islands, St. John, which has 5,000 residents, has the strongest sense of community, which is primarily rooted in a desire to protect the island's natural beauty.

Essentials

CURRENCY　The U.S. dollar is the official currency of the U.S. Virgin Islands; you'll find a few ATMs in Cruz Bay.

HOURS　Bank hours are generally Monday through Thursday 9 to 3 and Friday 9 to 5; a handful open Saturday 9 to noon. On St. John, store hours run from 9 or 10 to 5 or 6. Wharfside Village and Mongoose Junction shops in Cruz Bay are often open into the evening.

INTERNET　**Keep Me Posted** (✉ *Cocoloba shopping center, Rte. 107, Coral Bay, St. John* ☎ *340/775–1727*). **Surf da Web** (✉ *St. John Marketplace, 2nd floor, Cruz Bay, St. John* ☎ *340/693–9152* ⊕ *www.surfdaweb.com*).

TELEPHONES　Both GSM and Sprint phones work in most of St. John (take care that you're not roaming on the Tortola cell network on the island's north coast, though). It's as easy to call home from St. John as from any city in the United States. On St. John, public phones are in front of the post office, east of the tender landing, and at the ferry dock.

Coming Ashore

While smaller ships drop anchor at St. John, most people taking a cruise aboard a larger ship visit St. Thomas's sister island on a shore excursion or on an independent day trip from St. Thomas. If you prefer to not take a tour, ferries leave St. Thomas from the Charlotte Amalie waterfront and Red Hook. You'll have to take a taxi to reach the ferry dock.

If you're aboard a smaller ship that calls in St. John, your ship may simply pause outside Cruz Bay Harbor to drop you off or drop anchor if it's spending the day. You'll be tendered to shore at the main town of Cruz Bay. The shopping district starts just across the street from the tender landing. You'll find an eclectic collection of shops, cozy restaurants, and places where you can just sit and take it all in. The island has few sights to see. Your best bet is to take a tour of the Virgin Islands National Park. (If your ship doesn't offer such a tour, arrange one with one of the taxi drivers who will meet your tender.) The drive takes you past luscious beaches to a restored sugar plantation. With only a single day in port, you're better off just using the island's shared taxi vans rather than renting a car, but if you want to do some independent exploring, you can rent a car in Cruz Bay.

> ### ST. JOHN BEST BETS
>
> ■ **Hiking in the National Park.** Most of the island has been preserved, and the hiking trails that crisscross the terrain are easy enough for beginners and offer breathtaking scenery.
>
> ■ **Snorkeling Cruises.** There are almost countless islands within easy reach, many with very good snorkeling possibilities.
>
> ■ **Trunk Bay Beach.** St. John's national park beach is beautiful and has an underwater snorkeling trail.

Shore Excursions

We consider these to be among the better shore excursions for St. John. They may not be offered by all lines, and tour names may differ as well. Times and prices are approximate.

Annaberg Plantation and Island Tour. This tour takes you around the island by safari bus and includes a stop at the ruins of the Annaberg Plantation as well as some beach time at Trunk Bay. ☉ 4½ hrs 🖼 $34–$49.

Catamaran Sailing Trip. With many small islets within easy reach, St. John is an ideal place to do a half-day sailing trip. These trips always include time for snorkeling. ☉ 3½ hrs 🖼 $49–$59.

SNUBA. If you choose snuba in St. John, you'll do your shallow-water diving at beautiful Trunk Bay near the National Park Service's snorkeling trail. ☉ 2½ hrs 🖼 $75–$84.

Exploring St. John

★ ❹ **Annaberg Plantation.** In the 18th century, sugar plantations dotted the steep hills of this island. Slaves and free Danes and Dutchmen toiled to harvest the cane that was used to create sugar, molasses, and rum for export. Built in the 1780s, the partially restored plantation at Leinster Bay was once an important sugar mill. Although there are no official visiting hours, the National Park Service has regular tours, and some well-informed taxi drivers will show you around. Occasionally you may see a living-history demonstration—someone making johnnycake or weaving baskets. For information on tours and cultural events, contact the St. John National Park Service Visitors Center. ⊠ *Leinster Bay Rd., Annaberg* ☎ *340/776–6201* ⊕ *www.nps.gov/viis* ☒ *Free* ☼ *Daily sunrise–sunset.*

★ ❸ **Bordeaux Mountain.** St. John's highest peak rises to 1,277 feet. Route 10 passes near enough to the top to offer breathtaking views. Don't stray into the road here—cars whiz by at a good clip along this section. Instead, drive nearly to the end of the dirt road that heads off next to the restaurant and gift shop for spectacular views at Picture Point and the trailhead of the hike downhill to Lameshur. Get a trail map from the park service before you start. ⊠ *Rte. 10.*

❶ **Cruz Bay.** St. John's main town may be compact (it consists of only several blocks), but it's definitely a hub: the ferries from St. Thomas and the BVI pull in here, and it's where you can get a taxi or rent a car to travel around the island. There are plenty of shops in which to browse, a number of watering holes where you can stop for a breather, many restaurants, and a grassy square with benches where you can sit back and take everything in. Look for the current edition of the handy, amusing "St. John Map" featuring Max the Mongoose. To pick up a useful guide to St. John's hiking trails, see various large maps of the island, and find out about current park service programs, including guided walks and cultural demonstrations, stop by the **V. I. National Park Visitors Center** (⊠ *Near the baseball field, Cruz Bay* ☎ *340/776–6201* ⊕ *www.nps. gov/viis*). It's open daily from 8 to 4:30.

★ ❷ **Reef Bay Trail.** Although this is one of the most interesting hikes on St. John, unless you're a rugged individualist who wants a physical challenge (and that describes a lot of people who stay on St. John), you can probably get the most out of the trip if you join a hike led by a park service ranger who can identify the trees and plants on the hike down, fill you in on the history of the Reef Bay Plantation, and tell you about the petroglyphs on the rocks at the bottom of the trail. A side trail takes you to the plantation's great house, a gutted but mostly intact structure that maintains vestiges of its former beauty. Take the safari bus from the park's visitor center. A boat takes you from the beach at Reef Bay back to the visitor center, saving you the uphill climb. ⊠ *Rte. 10, Reef Bay* ☎ *340/776–6201 Ext. 238 reservations* ⊕ *www.nps.gov/viis* 🎫 *Free, safari bus $6, return boat trip to Cruz Bay $15* ☉ *Tours at 9:30 AM, days change seasonally.*

Shopping

In St. John, the small shopping district runs from Wharfside Village near the ferry landing to Mongoose Junction, just up the street from the cruise-ship dock and tender landing, with lots of shops tucked in between. The owner of **Bamboula** (⊠ *Mongoose Junction, N. Shore Rd., Cruz Bay* ☎ *340/693–8699*), Jo Sterling, travels the Caribbean and beyond to find unusual housewares, art, rugs, bedspreads, accessories, shoes, and men's and women's clothes for this multicultural boutique. If you want to look like you stepped out of the pages of the resort-wear spread in an upscale travel magazine, try **Bougainvillea Boutique** (⊠ *Mongoose Junction, N. Shore Rd., Cruz Bay* ☎ *340/693–7190*). Owner Susan Stair carries chic men's and women's clothes, straw hats, leather handbags, and fine gifts. Owner Radha Speer of **Caravan Gallery** (⊠ *Mongoose Junction, N. Shore Rd., Cruz Bay* ☎ *340/779–4566*) travels the world to find much of the unusual jewelry she sells here. And the more you look, the more you see—folk art, tribal art, and masks cover the walls and tables, making this a great place to browse.

Pink Papaya (⊠ *Lemon Tree Mall, King St., Cruz Bay* ☎ *340/693–8535*) is the home of longtime Virgin Islands resident M. L. Etre's well-known artwork, plus a huge collection of one-of-a-kind gifts, including bright tablecloths, unusual trays, dinnerware, and unique tropical jewelry. **St. John Editions** (⊠ *N. Shore Rd., Cruz Bay* ☎ *340/693–8444*) has nifty cotton dresses that go from beach to dinner with a change of shoes and accessories. Owner Molly Soper also carries attractive straw hats and inexpensive jewelry.

Activities

DIVING &   **Cruz Bay Watersports** (☎ *340/776–6234* ⊕ *www.divestjohn.com*) has two
SNORKELING   locations: in Cruz Bay at the Lumberyard Shopping Complex and at the

Westin St. John Resort. Owners Marcus and Patty Johnston offer regular reef, wreck, and night dives and USVI and BVI snorkel tours. The company holds both PADI five-star facility and NAUI Dream Resort status. **Low Key Watersports** (☎ *340/693–8999 or 800/835–7718* ⊕ *www.divelowkey.com*), at Wharfside Village, offers one- and two-tank dives and specialty courses. It's certified as a PADI five-star training facility.

FISHING   Well-kept charter boats—approved by the U.S. Coast Guard—head out to the north and south drops or troll along the inshore reefs, depending on the season and what's biting. The captains usually provide bait, drinks, and lunch, but you need to bring your own hat and sunscreen. Fishing charters run between $550 and $750 per half day for the boat. **Gone Ketchin'** (☎ *340/714–1175* ⊕ *www.goneketchin.com*), in St. John, arranges trips with old salt Captain Grizz.

HIKING   Although it's fun to go hiking with a Virgin Islands National Park guide, don't be afraid to head out on your own. To find a hike that suits your ability, stop by the park's visitor center in Cruz Bay and pick up the free trail guide; it details points of interest, dangers, trail lengths, and estimated hiking times. Although the park staff recommends long pants to protect against thorns and insects, most people hike in shorts because it can get very hot. Wear sturdy shoes or hiking boots even if you're hiking to the beach. Don't forget to bring water and insect re-
Fodor'sChoice   pellent. The **Virgin Islands National Park** (⊠ *1300 Cruz Bay Creek, St.*
★   *John* ☎ *340/776–6201* ⊕ *www.nps.gov/viis*) maintains more than 20 trails on the north and south shores and offers guided hikes along popular routes. A full-day trip to Reef Bay is a must; it's an easy hike through lush and dry forest, past the ruins of an old plantation, and to a sugar factory adjacent to the beach. It can be a bit arduous for young kids, however. Take the $6 safari bus from the park's visitor center to the trailhead, where you can meet a ranger who'll serve as your guide. The park provides a boat ride back to Cruz Bay for $15 to save you the walk back up the mountain. The schedule changes from season to season; call for times and reservations, which are essential.

Beaches

Long, sandy **Cinnamon Bay** (⊠ *North Shore Rd., Rte. 20, about 4 mi (6 km) east of Cruz Bay*) faces beautiful cays and abuts the national park campground. Facilities are open to the public and include cool showers, toilets, a commissary, and a restaurant. You can rent water-sports equipment here. There's excellent snorkeling off the point to the right; look for the big angelfish and large schools of purple triggerfish. Afternoons on Cinnamon Bay can be windy, so arrive early to beat the gusts. **Hawksnest Beach** (⊠ *North Shore Rd., Rte. 20, about 2 mi (3 km) east of Cruz Bay*) is the closet beach to Cruz Bay, so it's often crowded. Sea grape trees line this narrow beach, and there are restrooms, cooking grills, and a cov-
Fodor'sChoice   ered shed for picnicking. **Trunk Bay** (⊠ *North Shore Rd., Rte. 20, about*
★   *2½ mi (4 km) east of Cruz Bay*), St. John's most-photographed beach, is also the preferred spot for beginning snorkelers because of its underwater trail, but if you're looking for seclusion, don't come here because it's the island's busiest. Crowded or not, this stunning beach is still beautiful. There are changing rooms, a snack bar, picnic tables, a gift shop,

phones, lockers, and snorkeling-equipment rentals. You have to pay an entrance fee of $4 if you don't have a National Park Pass.

Where to Eat

🍴 **$–$$** ✕ **Uncle Joe's Barbecue.** Juicy ribs and tasty chicken legs dripping with the house barbecue sauce make for one of St. John's best dining deals. An ear of corn, rice, and a generous scoop of macaroni salad or coleslaw round out the plate. This casual spot crowds the edge of a busy sidewalk in the heart of Cruz Bay. Even though there are a few open-air tables for dining "in," the ambience is more than a tad on the pedestrian side, so takeout is a better bet. ⊠ *North Shore Rd., across from post office* ☎ *340/693–8806* ▤ *No credit cards.*

$ ✕ **Sun Dog Cafe.** There's an unusual assortment of dishes at this charming alfresco restaurant, which you'll find tucked into a courtyard in the upper reaches of the Mongoose Junction shopping center. Kudos to the white pizza with artichoke hearts, roasted garlic, mozzarella cheese, and capers. The Jamaican jerk chicken sub and the black-bean quesadilla are also good choices. ⊠ *Mongoose Junction, North Shore Rd.* ☎ *340/ 693–8340* ▤ *AE, MC, V* ☯ *No dinner.*

ST. KITTS (BASSETERRE)

Jordan Simon

Mountainous St. Kitts, the first English settlement in the Leeward Islands, crams some stunning scenery into its 65 square mi (168 square km). Vast, brilliant green fields of sugarcane (the former cash crop, now slowly being replanted) run to the shore. The fertile, lush island has some fascinating natural and historical attractions: a rain forest replete with waterfalls, thick vines, and secret trails; a central mountain range, dominated by the 3,792-foot Mt. Liamuiga, whose crater has long been dormant; and Brimstone Hill, known in the 17th century as the Gibraltar of the West Indies. St. Kitts and Nevis, along with Anguilla, achieved self-government as an Associated State of Great Britain in 1967. In 1983, St. Kitts & Nevis became an independent nation. English with a strong West Indian lilt is spoken here. People are friendly but shy; always ask before you take photographs. Also, be sure to wear wraps or shorts over beach attire when you're in public places.

CURRENCY Eastern Caribbean (E.C.) dollar (EC$2.70 to US$1). U.S. dollars are accepted practically everywhere, but you'll usually get change in E.C. currency.

HOURS Hours vary somewhat for banks but are typically Monday through Thursday from 8 to 2 and Friday from 8 to 4. There are numerous ATMs. Post offices are open Monday and Tuesday from 8 to 4, Wednesday through Friday from 8 to 3:30, and occasionally Saturday from 8 to noon. Although shops used to close for lunch from noon to 1, more and more establishments are remaining open Monday through Saturday from 8 to 4.

INTERNET **Leyton's Sun Surf Internet Cafe** (⊠ *TDC Mall, Fort St., Basseterre, St. Kitts* ☎ *869/465–5925*).

TELEPHONES Phone cards, which you can buy in denominations of $5, $10, and $20, are handy for making local phone calls, calling other islands, and accessing U.S. direct lines. To make a local call, dial the seven-digit number. To call St. Kitts from the United States, dial the area code 869, then access code 465, 466, 468, or 469 and the local four-digit number.

Coming Ashore

Cruise ships calling at St. Kitts dock at Port Zante, which is a deep-water port directly in Basseterre, the capital of St. Kitts. The cruise-ship terminal is right in the downtown area, two minutes' walk from sights and shops. Taxi rates on St. Kitts are fixed and should be posted right at the dock. If you'd like to go to Nevis, several daily ferries (30 to 45 minutes, $8 one-way) can take you to Charlestown in Nevis; the byzantine schedule is subject to change, so double-check times.

> ### ST. KITTS BEST BETS
>
> ■ **Brimstone Hill Fortress.** This UN World Heritage Site has some of the best views on St. Kitts.
>
> ■ **Nevis.** If your ship doesn't stop there, a trip to St. Kitts's beautiful sister island of Nevis is a worthwhile way to spend your day.
>
> ■ **Romney Manor.** This partially restored manor house is a treat, and it's made better by the chance to view the wares of excellent Caribelle Batik.

Taxi rates on St. Kitts are fairly expensive, and you may have to pay $32 for a ride to Brimstone Hill (for one to four passengers). A four-hour tour of St. Kitts is about $70. It's often cheaper to arrange an island tour with one of the local companies than to hire a taxi driver to take your group around. Several restored great-house plantations are known for their lunches; your driver can provide information and arrange drop-off and pickup. Before setting off in a cab, be sure to clarify whether the rate quoted is in E.C. or U.S. dollars.

Shore Excursions

We consider these to be among the better shore excursions for St. Kitts. They may not be offered by all lines, and tour names may differ as well. Times and prices are approximate.

Brimstone Hill Fortress & Gardens. You will visit Brimstone Hill, a 300-year-old fortress and World Heritage Site before going to Romney Gardens, where you can browse through the wares of Caribelle Batik Studio. Your tour ends after a drive through Basseterre. ☉ *3 hrs* ▭ *$54.*

Nevis Catamaran Getaway. Sail from St. Kitts to the island of Nevis for a day of snorkeling and a beach barbecue at Pinneys Beach. Some tours also include a bus trip to Alexander Hamilton Museum and the Botanical Garden, but these will cost more. ☉ *7 hrs* ▭ *$109.*

Sea Kayaking & Snorkeling. After kayaking in White House Bay, you have the opportunity to snorkel in Friars Bay. ☉ *3 hrs* ▭ *$89.*

St. Kitts Scenic Railway. After a bus trip to the rail station, you board a double-decker, narrow-gauge railway car for a trip partway around the island. Each passenger gets a comfortable downstairs air-conditioned seat fronting vaulted picture windows and an upstairs open-air observation spot. The conductor's running discourse embraces not only the history of sugar cultivation but the railway's construction, island folklore, island geography, even other agricultural mainstays from papayas and pineapples to pigs. Refreshments are provided. ☉ *3½ hrs* ▭ *$109.*

Exploring St. Kitts

Numbers in the margin correspond to points of interest on the St. Kitts map.

❶ Basseterre. On the south coast, St. Kitts's walkable capital is graced with tall palms, and although many of the buildings appear run-down, there are interesting shops, excellent art galleries, and some beautifully maintained houses. Duty-free shops and boutiques line the streets and courtyards radiating from the octagonal Circus, built in the style of London's famous Piccadilly Circus. There are lovely gardens on the site of a former slave market at **Independence Square** (✉ *Off Bank St.*). The square is surrounded on three sides by 18th-century Georgian buildings. **St. George's Anglican Church** (✉ *Cayon St.*) is a handsome stone building with a crenellated tower originally built by the French in 1670 and called Notre-Dame. The British burned it down in 1706 and rebuilt it four years later, naming it after the patron saint of England. Since then it has suffered a fire, an earthquake, and hurricanes, and was once again rebuilt in 1869. In the restored former Treasury Building, the **National Museum** (✉ *Bay Rd., Basseterre* ☎ *869/465–5584*) presents an eclectic collection reflecting the history and culture of the island—as a collaboration of the St. Christopher Heritage Society and the island government. Admission is $1, and it's open Tuesday through Friday from 9–1 and 2–5 (only from 9:30–2 Monday and Saturday).

★ ❹ **Brimstone Hill.** The well-restored 38-acre fortress, a UNESCO World Heritage Site, is well worth a trip, particularly if military history and/or spectacular views interest you. After routing the French in 1690, the English erected a battery here, and by 1736 the fortress held 49 guns,

> **CAUTION**
>
> Pack a small flashlight just in case there's an emergency. You don't want to be stumbling around in the dark.

earning it the moniker "Gibraltar of the West Indies." A hurricane severely damaged the fortress in 1834, and in 1852 it was evacuated and dismantled. The citadel has been partially reconstructed and its guns remounted. A seven-minute orientation film recounts the fort's history and restoration. An on-site museum is mildly interesting, but it's the views that are astounding. Nature trails snake through the tangle of surrounding hardwood forest and savanna (a fine spot to catch the green vervet monkeys—inexplicably brought by the French and now outnumbering the residents—skittering about). ⊠ *Main Rd., Brimstone Hill* ☎ *869/465–2609* ⊕ *www.brimstonehillfortress.org* ☜ *$8* ⊙ *Daily 9:30–5:30.*

★ ❸ **Romney Manor.** The ruins of this partially restored house and surrounding cottages that duplicate the old chattel-house style are set in 6 acres of gardens, with exotic flowers, an old bell tower, and an enormous, gnarled, 350-year-old *samaan* tree (sometimes called a rain tree). Inside, at **Caribelle Batik,** you can watch artisans hand-printing fabrics. Look for signs indicating a turnoff for Romney Manor near Old Road.

❷ **St. Kitts Scenic Railway.** The old narrow-gauge train that had transported sugarcane circles the island in just under four hours. Each passenger gets a comfortable, downstairs air-conditioned seat fronting vaulted picture windows and an upstairs open-air observation spot. The conductor's running discourse embraces not only the history of sugar cultivation but the railway's construction, local folklore, island geography, and even other agricultural mainstays from papayas to pigs. You can drink in complimentary tropical beverages (including luscious guava daiquiris) along with the sweeping rain-forest and ocean vistas. There's a break at the halfway point (La Vallee), where cruise-ship passengers on ship-sponsored tours disembark. By then, the trip may seem slow as molasses, but it's certainly uniquely Caribbean. ⊠ *Needsmust* ☎ *869/465–7263* ⊕ *www.StKittsScenicRailway.com* ☜ *$89* ⊙ *June–Sept., departures Mon. at 1 PM and Wed. at 9:30 AM; Oct.–May, departures vary according to cruise-ship schedules.*

Shopping

St. Kitts has limited shopping, but there are a few duty-free shops with good deals on jewelry, perfume, china, and crystal. Don't forget to pick up some CSR, a "new cane spirit drink" that's distilled from fresh sugarcane right on St. Kitts or Brinley Gold's luscious flavored rums. Most shopping plazas are in downtown Basseterre—try the **Shoreline Plaza,** next to the Treasury Building; the **Pelican Mall,** across the street from Port Zante (which has a tourism office); and **Port Zante,** which has about 25 shops of its own.

Caribelle Batik (⊠ *Romney Manor, Old Road* ☏ *869/465–6253*) sells batik wraps, kimonos, caftans, T-shirts, dresses, wall hangings, and the like. **Kate Design** (⊠ *Bank St., Basseterre* ☏ *869/465–5265*) showcases the highly individual style of Kate Spencer, whose original paintings, serigraphs, note cards, and other pieces that she regularly introduces, are also available from her studio on the Rawlins Plantation grounds. **The Potter's House** (⊠ *Camps Estate Great House, Camps Estate* ☏ *869/465–5947*) is the atelier-home of Carla Astaphan, whose beautifully glazed ceramics and masks celebrate the Afro-Caribbean heritage. **Spencer Cameron Art Gallery** (⊠ *10 N. Independence Sq., Basseterre* ☏ *869/465–1617*) has historical reproductions of Caribbean island charts and prints, in addition to owner Rosey Cameron's popular Carnevale clown prints and a wide selection of exceptional artwork by Caribbean artists. They will mail anywhere.

Activities

DIVING & SNORKELING

St. Kitts has more than a dozen excellent dive sites. The surrounding waters feature shoals, hot vents, shallows, canyons, steep walls, and caverns at depths from 40 to nearly 200 feet, with hundreds of wrecks. **Dive St. Kitts** (⊠ *Frigate Bay, 2 mi [3 km] east of Basseterre* ☏ *869/465–1189* ⊕ *www.divestkitts.com*), a PADI–NAUI facility, offers competitive prices; friendly, laid-back dive masters; and an international clientele. The Bird Rock location features superb beach diving: common sightings 20 feet to 30 feet out include octopi, nurse sharks, manta, spotted eagle rays, and sea horses. Shore dives are unlimited when you book packages. Kenneth Samuel of **Kenneth's Dive Center** (⊠ *Bay Rd., Newtown* ☏ *869/465–2670* ⊕ *www.kennethsdivecenter.com*) takes small groups of divers with C cards to nearby reefs. Rates average $40 for single-tank dives, $75 for double-tank dives; add $10 to $15 for equipment. After 25 years' experience, former fisherman Samuel is considered an old pro and strives to keep groups small and prices reasonable. Austin Macleod, a PADI-certified dive master–instructor and owner of **Pro-Divers** (⊠ *Ocean Terrace Inn, Basseterre* ☏ *869/466–3483* ⊕ *www.prodiversstkitts.com*), offers resort and certification courses. His prices for an open-water certification course and dive package prices are the lowest on the island. He also takes groups to snorkeling sites accessible only by boat.

GOLF

The **Royal St. Kitts Golf Club** (⊠ *St. Kitts Marriott Resort, Frigate Bay* ☏ *869/466–2700* ⊕ *www.royalstkittsgolfclub.com*) is an 18-hole, par-71 links-style championship course that underwent a complete redesign by Thomas McBroom to maximize Caribbean and Atlantic views and increase the challenge. Greens fees are $135 for Marriott guests in high season, $175 for nonguests. The development includes practice bunkers, putting green, and a short-game chipping area.

HIKING

Trails in the central mountains of St. Kitts vary from easy to don't-try-it-by-yourself. Monkey Hill and

> **STORAGE**
>
> Take along a hanging shoe organizer for the closet to extend storage space for small items and to keep shoes off the floor. An over-the-door, pocket-style shoe organizer can be hung on the bathroom door. Slip bathroom necessities in the pockets so they are handy and out of the way.

Verchild's Peak aren't difficult, although the Verchild's climb will take the better part of a day. Don't attempt Mt. Liamuiga without a guide. Tour rates range from $35 for a rain-forest walk to $65 for a volcano expedition. Earl of **Duke of Earl's Adventures** (☎ 869/465–1899) is as entertaining as his nickname suggests—and his prices are slightly cheaper. He genuinely loves his island and conveys that enthusiasm, encouraging hikers to swing on vines or sample unusual-looking fruits during his rain-forest trip. He also conducts a thorough volcano tour to the crater's rim. Greg Pereira of **Greg's Safaris** (☎ 869/465–4121 ⊕ *www.gregssafaris. com*), whose family has lived on St. Kitts since the early 19th century, takes groups on half-day trips into the rain forest and on full-day hikes up the volcano and through the grounds of a private 18th-century great house. The rain-forest trips include visits to sacred Carib sites, abandoned sugar mills, and an excursion down a 100-foot coastal canyon containing a wealth of Amerindian petroglyphs. The Off the Beaten Track Plantation Tour provides a thorough explanation of the role sugar and rum played in the Caribbean economy and colonial wars. He and his staff relate fascinating historical, folkloric, and botanical information. Oliver Spencer of **Off the Beaten Path** (☎ 869/465–6314) leads rain-forest treks to the ruins of an abandoned coffee plantation taken over by spreading banyan trees, explaining folklore and flora, including herbal remedies, along the way.

HORSEBACK　Wild North Frigate Bay and desolate Conaree Beach are great for rid-
RIDING　ing, as is the rain forest. Guides from **Trinity Stables** (☎ 869/465–3226) offer beach rides ($40) and trips into the rain forest ($50). The latter is intriguing as guides discuss plants' medicinal properties along the way (such as sugarcane to stanch bleeding) and pick oranges right off a tree to squeeze fresh juice. Otherwise, the staffers are cordial but shy, and this isn't a place for beginners' instruction.

Beaches

The powdery white-sand beaches of St. Kitts, free and open to the public (even those occupied by hotels), are in the Frigate Bay area or on the lower peninsula. **Banana Bay,** one of the island's loveliest beaches, stretches over 1 mi (1½ km) at the southeastern tip of the island, with majestic views of Nevis. **Cockleshell Bay,** Banana Bay's twin beach, is another eyebrow of glittering sand backed by lush vegetation and reachable on foot. Locals consider the Caribbean (southern) side of **Friar's Bay** the island's finest beach. Unfortunately, the upcoming Marine World development has co-opted nearly half the strand. Still, several hopping, happening bars, including Shipwreck and Sunset Grill serve terrific, inexpensive local food and cheap, frosty drinks. You can haggle with fishermen here to take you snorkeling off the eastern point. The waters on the Atlantic (northern) side are rougher, but the beach has a wild, desolate beauty. On the Caribbean side of **Frigate Bay** you'll find talcum powder–fine sand and several lively thatched beach boîtes, while the 4-mi-wide (6½-km-wide) Atlantic side—regrettably dominated by the leviathan Marriott—is a favorite with horseback riders.

Where to Eat

Restaurants occasionally add a 10% service charge to your bill; if this information isn't printed on the menu, ask about it. When there's no service charge, a tip of 15% is appropriate.

★ $$–$$$ ╳ **Turtle Beach Bar & Grill.** Treats at this popular daytime watering hole at the south end of S.E. Peninsula Road include honey-mustard ribs, coconut-shrimp salad, grilled lobster (a best-buy special Friday nights), decadent bread pudding with rum sauce, and an array of tempting tropical libations. Business cards and pennants from around the world plaster the bar; the room is decorated with a variety of nautical accoutrements. You can snorkel here, spot hawksbill turtles, feed the tame monkeys that boldly belly up to the bar (they adore green bananas and peaches), serve Wilbur the pig a beer, laze in a palm-shaded hammock, or rent a kayak or snorkel gear. Locals come Sunday afternoons for dancing to live bands and for fun but fiercely contested volleyball. ✉ *S.E. Peninsula Rd., Turtle Beach* ☎ *869/469–9086* ▤ *AE, D, MC, V* ⊙ *No dinner Mon.–Thurs.*

$–$$$ ╳ **Ballahoo.** This second-floor terrace restaurant creates an appropriately tropical ambience with decor featuring whirring ceiling fans, potted palms, and colorful island prints, and lilting calypso and reggae on the sound system. Specialties include chili shrimp, conch simmered in garlic butter, Madras beef curry, and a toasted rum-and-banana sandwich topped with ice cream. Go at lunchtime, when you can watch the bustle of the Circus, and specials such as rotis bursting with curried chicken or vegetables slash prices nearly in half. Grab fresh local juices (tamarind, guava) if you can. Though the service is lackadaisical bordering on rude, the food is at least plentiful, the daiquiris killer, and the people-watching delightful. ✉ *Fort St., Basseterre* ☎ *869/465–4197* ▤ *AE, MC, V* ⊙ *Closed Sun.*

ST. LUCIA (CASTRIES)

Jane Zarem

Magnificent St. Lucia—with towering mountains, dense rain forest, fertile green valleys, and acres of banana plantations—lies in the middle of the Windward Islands. Nicknamed "the Helen of the West Indies" because of its natural beauty, St. Lucia is distinguished from its neighbors by its unusual geological landmarks, the Pitons—the twin peaks on the southwest coast that soar nearly ½ mi (1 km) above the ocean floor and have become a symbol of this island. Nearby, outside the former French colonial capital of Soufrière, is a "drive-in" volcano, neighboring sulfur springs that have rejuvenated bathers for nearly three centuries, and one of the most beautiful botanical gardens in the Caribbean. A century and a half of battles between the French and English resulted in St. Lucia's changing hands 14 times before 1814, when England established possession. In 1979 the island became an independent state within the British Commonwealth of Nations. The official language is English, although most people also speak a French-creole patois.

Essentials

CURRENCY Eastern Caribbean (E.C.) dollar (EC$2.70 to US$1). U.S. dollars are generally accepted, but change is given in E.C. dollars.

HOURS   Banks are open Monday through Thursday from 8 to 3, Friday 8 to 5;
a few branches in Rodney Bay are also open Saturday from 9 to noon.
Post offices are open weekdays from 8:30 to 4:30. Most stores are open
weekdays from 8:30 to 12:30 and 1:30 to 4:30, Saturday from 8 to 12:30.

INTERNET   There are several Internet cafés in the Rodney Bay Marina. **Cyber Connections** (✉ *Rodney Bay Marina, Gros Islet* ☎ *758/450–9309*). **Destination
St. Lucia (DSL) Ltd.** (✉ *Rodney Bay Marina, Gros Islet* ☎ *758/452–8531*).

TELEPHONES   You can make direct-dial overseas and interisland calls from St. Lucia,
and the connections are excellent. You can charge an overseas call to a
major credit card with no surcharge by dialing 811. Phone cards can be
purchased at many retail outlets.

Coming Ashore

Most cruise ships dock at the capital city of Castries, on the island's northwest coast. Either of two docking areas is used: Pointe Seraphine, a port
of entry and duty-free shopping complex, or Port Castries, a commercial wharf across the harbor. Ferry service connects the two piers.
Smaller vessels occasionally call at Soufrière, on the island's southwest
coast. Ships calling at Soufrière must usually anchor offshore and bring
passengers ashore via tender. Tourist information booths are located at
Pointe Seraphine in Castries and along the waterfront on Bay Street in
Soufrière. Downtown Castries is within walking distance of the pier, and
the produce market and adjacent crafts and vendors' markets are the
main attractions. Soufrière is a sleepy West Indian town, but it's worth
a short walk around the central square to view the French colonial architecture; most of the island's best sights are near Soufrière. Taxis are
available at the docks in Castries. Although they are unmetered, the standard fares are posted at the entrance to Pointe Seraphine. Taxi drivers
are well informed and can give you a full tour—often an excellent one—
thanks to government-sponsored
training programs. From the Castries
area, full-day island tours cost about
$140 for up to four people; sightsee-
ing trips to Soufrière, around $120.
If you plan your own day, expect to
pay the driver at least $20 per hour
plus a 10% tip. Whatever your destination, negotiate the price with
the driver before you depart—and
be sure that you both understand
whether the rate is in E.C. or U.S.
dollars.

Shore Excursions

We consider these to be among the
better shore excursions for St. Lucia.
They may not be offered by all lines,
and tour names may differ as well.
Times and prices are approximate.

ST. LUCIA BEST BETS

■ **The Pitons.** You have to see St.
Lucia's famous twin peaks, and
the most pleasant way to get
down here from Castries is by
boat.

■ **The Rain Forest.** Whatever activity you might be interested in,
do it. St. Lucia's lush rain forest
is one of the best natural environments in the Caribbean.

■ **Pigeon Island.** This national
park is both historic and a great
natural environment good for
kayaking.

Gros Piton Climb. While very strenuous, you get a unique view from the top of Gros Piton, making this trip quite worthwhile for the physically fit. ⏱ *7 hrs* 🚌 *$129.*

Pigeon Island Sea Kayaking. This is a good kayaking adventure for the novice. You paddle from Rodney Bay to Pigeon Island, tour the island itself, and spend some time at the beach. The return is by bus. ⏱ *3 hrs* 🚌 *$62.*

Rain-forest Hike. St. Lucia has a well-protected rain forest, and this hike will take you into the forest along the Canaries River. There's a refreshment stop on the way back to Castries. ⏱ *5½ hrs* 🚌 *$52.*

Soufrière Coastal Cruise. The best tours travel down to Soufrière by catamaran and then put guests on buses that stop to visit the volcano, Diamond Botanical Gardens, and lunch at Morne Coubaril. Then you sail back. ⏱ *7½ hrs* 🚌 *$84.*

Exploring St. Lucia

Numbers in the margin correspond to points of interest on the St. Lucia map.

❸ Castries. The capital, a busy commercial city of about 65,000 people, wraps around a sheltered bay. Morne Fortune rises sharply to the south of town, creating a dramatic green backdrop. The charm of Castries lies almost entirely in its liveliness, since most of the colonial buildings were destroyed by four fires that occurred between 1796 and 1948. Freighters (exporting bananas, coconut, cocoa, mace, nutmeg, and citrus fruits) and cruise ships come and go daily, making Castries Harbour one of the Caribbean's busiest ports.

Derek Walcott Square, a green oasis bordered by Brazil, Laborie, Micoud, and Bourbon streets, honors the hometown poet who won the 1992 Nobel prize for literature. Buildings from the 19th century can be seen on Brazil Street, the square's southern border. On the Laborie Street side, a huge, 400-year-old samaan tree shades a good portion of the square.

Directly across Laborie Street is the Roman Catholic **Cathedral of the Immaculate Conception,** which was built in 1897.

At the corner of Jeremie and Peynier streets, spreading beyond its brilliant orange roof, is the **Castries Market.** Full of excitement and bustle, the market is open every day except Sunday. It's liveliest on Saturday morning, when farmers bring their fresh produce and spices to town, as they have for more than a century. Next door to the produce market is the Craft Market, where you can buy pottery, wood carvings, and handwoven straw articles.

Across Peynier Street from the Craft Market, at the **Vendor's Arcade,** there are still more handicrafts and souvenirs.

☺ ❺ Diamond Botanical Gardens & Waterfall. Water bubbling to the surface from underground sulfur springs streams downhill in rivulets to become Diamond Waterfall, deep within these splendid botanical gardens. For a small price, you can soak in one of the curative mineral baths. ✉ *Soufrière Estate, Soufrière* ☎ *758/452–4759 or 758/454–7565*

$2.75, *outside bath $2.50, private bath $3.75* ☉ *Mon.–Sat. 10–5, Sun. 10–3.*

❼ Fond Doux Estate. This plantation just outside Soufrière was one of the earliest French estates established by land grant (1745 and 1763); its 135 hilly acres still produce cocoa, citrus, bananas, coconut, and vegetables; the restored plantation house (built in 1864) is still in use. A tour can include lunch; souvenirs are sold at the boutique. ✉ *Chateaubelair, Soufrière* ☎ *758/459–7545* ⊕ *www.fonddouxestate.com* $6, *buffet lunch $14* ☉ *Daily 9–4.*

☾ ❽ La Soufrière Drive-In Volcano. As you approach, your nose will pick up the strong scent of the sulfur springs. You actually drive up within a few hundred feet of the gurgling, steaming mass, then follow a guide around a fault in the substratum rock on foot. ✉ *Bay St., Soufrière* ☎ *758/459–5500* $1.25 ☉ *Daily 9–5.*

☾ ❶ Pigeon Island. This former hideout for pirate Jambe de Bois (Wooden Leg) is now a national landmark. You can swim or snorkel at two small beaches, look at ruins that date from 18th century French and English battles, or take in a multimedia display about the island's ecological and historical significance. ✉ *Pigeon Island, St. Lucia National Trust, Rodney Bay* ☎ *758/452–5005* ⊕ *www.slunatrust.org* $4 ☉ *Daily 9–5.*

❻ The Pitons. These two unusual mountains, which rise precipitously from the cobalt blue Caribbean Sea just south of Soufrière, have become the symbol of St. Lucia. Covered with thick tropical vegetation, the massive outcroppings were formed by lava from a volcanic eruption 30 to 40 million years ago. They are not identical twins since—confusingly—2,619-foot Petit Piton is taller than 2,461-foot Gros Piton, though Gros Piton is, as the word translates, broader. You can also climb Gros Piton. ☎ *758/450–2231, 758/450–2078 for St. Lucia Forest & Lands Department, 758/459–9748 for Pitons Tour Guide Association* Guide services $45 ☉ *Daily by appointment only.*

❷ Rodney Bay. This man-made lagoon is home to the Rodney Bay Marina, where you can arrange yacht charters and sightseeing day trips. The Rodney Bay Ferry makes hourly crossings between the marina and the shopping complex, as well as daily excursions to Pigeon Island.

❹ Soufrière. The wharf is the center of activity in this sleepy town, the oldest in St. Lucia and the former French colonial capital. It's located 1½ hours from Castries by car, 45 minutes by boat. The **Soufrière Tourist Information Centre** (✉ *Bay St., Soufrière* ☎ *758/459–7200*) provides information about area attractions. Note that outside some of the popular attractions in and around Soufrière, souvenir vendors can be persistent. Be polite but firm if you're not interested in their wares.

> **BAG IT**
>
> A mesh laundry bag or a "pop-up" mesh clothes hamper are two fairly light items that pack flat in your suitcase. The bag can hang from the closet, but either will keep your closet neat, allow damp clothing to dry out, and help you tote dirty clothes to the self-service laundry room so you can avoid high cleaning charges.

4

Shopping

The island's best-known products are artwork and wood carvings; clothing and household articles made from batik and silk-screen fabrics, designed and printed in island workshops; and clay pottery. You can also take home straw hats and baskets and locally grown cocoa, coffee, and spices. The only duty-free shopping is at **Pointe Seraphine** or **La Place Carenage,** on opposite sides of the harbor. You must show your passport and cabin key card to get duty-free prices. You'll want to experience the **Castries Market** and scour the adjacent **Vendor's Arcade** and **Craft Market** for handicrafts and souvenirs at bargain prices.

Artsibit Gallery (⊠ *Brazil and Mongiraud Sts., Castries* 🕿 *758/452–7865*) exhibits and sells moderately priced pieces by St. Lucian painters and sculptors. **Bagshaw Studios** (⊠ *La Toc Rd., La Toc Bay, Castries* 🕿 *758/452–2139 or 758/451–9249*) sells clothing and table linens in colorful tropical patterns using Stanley Bagshaw's original designs. The fabrics are silk-screened by hand in the adjacent workroom. At **Caribelle Batik** (⊠ *La Toc Rd., Morne Fortune, Castries* 🕿 *758/452–3785*), craftspeople demonstrate the art of batik and silk-screen printing. Meanwhile, seamstresses create clothing and wall hangings, which you can purchase in the shop. **Eudovic Art Studio** (⊠ *Morne Fortune, Castries* 🕿 *758/452–2747*) is a workshop and studio where you can buy trays, masks, and figures sculpted from local mahogany, red cedar, and eucalyptus wood. **Noah's Arkade** (⊠ *Jeremie St., Castries* 🕿 *758/452–2523* ⊠ *Pointe Seraphine, Castries* 🕿 *758/452–7488*) has hammocks, wood carvings, straw mats, T-shirts, books, and other regional goods.

Activities

DIVING   The coral reefs at Anse Cochon and Anse Chastanet, on the southwest coast, are popular beach-entry dive sites. In the north, Pigeon Island is the most convenient site. **Buddies** (⊠ *Rodney Bay Marina, Rodney Bay* 🕿 *758/452–8406*) offers wall, wreck, reef, and deep dives; open-water certification with advanced and specialty courses are taught by PADI-certified instructors. **Dive Fair Helen** (⊠ *Vigie Marina, Castries* 🕿 *758/451–7716 or 888/855–2206 in the U.S. and Canada* ⊕ *www.divefairhelen. com*) is a PADI center that offers half- and full-day excursions to wreck, wall, and marine reserve areas, as well as night dives. **Scuba St. Lucia** (⊠ *Anse Chastanet, Soufrière* 🕿 *758/459–7755* ⊕ *www.scubastlucia. com*) is a PADI five-star training facility. Daily beach and boat dives and certification courses are offered; underwater photography and snorkeling equipment are available. Day trips from the Castries port area include round-trip speedboat transportation.

FISHING   Among the deep-sea creatures you can find in St. Lucia's waters are dolphin (also called dorado or mahimahi), barracuda, mackerel, wahoo, kingfish, sailfish, and white or blue marlin. Sportfishing is generally done on a catch-and-release basis. Neither spearfishing nor collecting live fish in coastal waters is permitted. Half- or full-day deep-sea fishing excursions can be arranged at either Vigie Cove or Rodney Bay Marina. A half day of fishing on a scheduled trip runs about $75 to $80 per person. Beginners are welcome. **Captain Mike's** (⊠ *Vigie Cove* 🕿 *758/452–1216 or 758/452–7044* ⊕ *www.captmikes.com*) has a fleet of Bertram power boats (31- to 38-feet) that accommodate as many as eight passengers; tackle and cold drinks are supplied. **Mako Watersports** (✉ *Rodney Bay Marina, Rodney Bay* ☎ *758/452–0412*) takes fishing enthusiasts out on the well-equipped six-passenger *Annie Baby.*

GOLF   **St. Lucia Golf & Country Club** (✉ *Cap Estate* ☎ *758/452–8523* ⊕ *www.stluciagolf.com*), the island's only public course, is at the island's northern tip and offers panoramic views of both the Atlantic and Caribbean. It's an 18-hole championship course (6,829 yards, par 71). The clubhouse has a bar and a pro shop where you can rent clubs and shoes and arrange lessons. Greens fees are $70 for 9 holes or $95 for 18 holes; carts are required and included; club and shoe rentals are available. Reservations are essential. Complimentary transportation from your cruise ship is provided for parties of three or more people.

HORSEBACK   Creole horses, an indigenous breed, are fairly small, fast, sturdy, and even-
RIDING   tempered animals suitable for beginners. Established stables can accommodate all skill levels and offer countryside trail rides, beach rides with picnic lunches, plantation tours, carriage rides, and lengthy treks. Prices run about $40 for one hour, $50 for two hours, and $70 for a three-hour beach ride and barbecue. Transportation is usually provided between the stables and nearby hotels. People sometimes appear on beaches with their steeds and offer 30-minute rides for $10; ride at your own risk. **Country Saddles** (✉ *Marquis Estate, Babonneau* ☎ *758/450–5467*), 45 minutes east of Castries, guides beginners and advanced riders through banana plantations, forest trails, and along the Atlantic coast. **International Riding Stables** (✉ *Beauséjour Estate, Gros Islet* ☎ *758/452–8139 or 758/450–8665*) offers either English- or western-style riding. Their beach-picnic ride includes time for a swim—with or without your horse. **Trim's National Riding Stable** (✉ *Cas-en-Bas, Gros Islet* ☎ *758/452–8273 or 758/450–9971*), the island's oldest establishment, offers four riding sessions per day, plus beach tours, trail rides, and carriage tours to Pigeon Island.

Beaches

All of St. Lucia's beaches are open to the public, but Pigeon Point, Reduit, and Vigie beaches are particularly accessible to cruise-ship passengers. At **Pigeon Point,** a small beach within Pigeon Island National Historic Park, a restaurant serves snacks and drinks, but this is also a perfect spot for picnicking. It's about a 30-minute taxi ride ($20) from Pointe Seraphine. **Reduit Beach,** a long stretch of golden sand, is next to Rodney Bay. The Rex St. Lucian Hotel, which faces the beach, has a water-sports center. Many feel that Reduit (pronounced red-*wee*) is the island's finest beach. **Vigie Beach,** a 2-mi (3-km) strand in Castries, is not far from the port. It runs parallel to the George F. L. Charles Airport runway and continues on to become Malabar Beach, the beachfront for the Rendezvous resort.

Where to Eat

An 8% government tax is applicable to your bill, and most restaurants add a 10% service charge in lieu of tip.

★ **$$** ✕ **Jacques Waterside Dining.** Chef-owner Jacky Rioux creates magical dishes in his open-air garden restaurant (known for years as Froggie Jack's) overlooking Vigie Cove. The cooking style is decidedly French, as is Rioux, but fresh produce and local spices create a fusion cuisine that's memorable at lunch or dinner. You might start with a bowl of creamy tomato-basil or pumpkin soup, a grilled portobello mushroom, or octopus and conch in curried coconut sauce. Main courses include fresh seafood, such as oven-baked kingfish with a white wine and sweet pepper sauce, or breast of chicken stuffed with smoked salmon in a citrus butter sauce. The wine list is also impressive. ⊠ *Vigie Marina, Castries* ☎ *758/458-1900* ⚶ *Reservations essential* ▤ *AE, MC, V* ⊘ *Closed Sun.*

$–$$ ✕ **Lifeline Restaurant at the Hummingbird.** Cajou, the chef at this cheerful restaurant-bar in the Hummingbird Beach Resort, specializes in French creole cuisine, starting with fresh seafood or chicken seasoned with local herbs and accompanied by a medley of vegetables just picked from the Hummingbird's garden. Sandwiches and salads are also available. If you stop for lunch, be sure to visit the batik studio and art gallery of proprietor Joan Alexander and her son, adjacent to the dining room. ⊠ *Hummingbird Beach Resort, Anse Chastanet Rd., Soufrière* ☎ *758/459-7232* ▤ *AE, D, MC, V.*

ST. MARTIN/ST. MAARTEN (PHILLIPSBURG)

Roberta
Sotonoff

St. Martin/St. Maarten: one tiny island, just 37 square mi (59 square km), with two different accents, and ruled by two sovereign nations. Here French and Dutch have lived side by side for hundreds of years, and when you cross from one country to the next there are no border patrols, no customs. In fact, the only indication that you have crossed a border at all is a small sign and a change in road surface. St. Martin/St. Maarten epitomizes tourist islands in the sun, where services are well developed but there's still some Caribbean flavor. The Dutch side is ideal for people who like plenty to do. The French side has a more genteel ambience, more fashionable shopping, and a Continental flair. The combination makes an almost ideal port. On the negative side, the island has been completely developed. It can be fun to shop, and you'll find an occasional bargain, but many goods are cheaper in the United States.

Essentials

CURRENCY Legal tender on the Dutch side is the Netherlands Antilles florin (guilder), written NAf; on the French side, the official currency is the euro (€1.31 to US$1). There's little need to exchange money. Prices are usually quoted in both NAf and U.S. dollars on the Dutch side and euros on the French side, but dollars are accepted all over the island.

HOURS Banks on the Dutch side are open Monday through Friday from 8:30 to 3:30. French banks are open weekdays from 8:30 to 12:30 and 2:30 to 4; they are usually closed on Wednesday afternoons and afternoons preceding holidays. Shops on the Dutch side are generally open Monday through Saturday from 9 to noon and 2 to 6; on the French side, Monday through Saturday from 9 to 1 and 3 to 7. Increasingly, shops on both sides remain open during lunch. Some of the larger shops are open on Sunday and holidays when cruise ships are in port.

INTERNET There is Wi-Fi service on the boardwalk behind Front Street if you have your own laptop. **Cyber Link** (✉ *53 Front St., Phillipsburg*).

TELEPHONES To phone from the Dutch side to the French, you first must dial (00–590–590) for local numbers, or (00–590–690) for cell phones, then the six-digit local number. To call from the French side to the Dutch, dial 00–599 then the seven-digit local number. Remember that a call from one side to the other is an international call.

At the Landsradio in Philipsburg, there are facilities for overseas calls and a USADirect phone, where you're directly in touch with an operator who will accept collect or credit-card calls. To call direct with an AT&T credit card or operator, dial 001–800/872–2881. On the French side, AT&T can be accessed by calling 080–099–00–11. If you need to use public phones, go to the special desk at Marigot's post office and buy a *télécarte*. There's a public phone at the tourist office in Marigot where you can make credit-card calls: the operator takes your card number (any major card) and assigns you a PIN (Personal Identification Number), which you then use to charge calls to your card.

Coming Ashore

Most cruise ships drop anchor off the Dutch capital of Philipsburg or dock in the marina at the southern tip of the Philipsburg harbor. If your ship anchors, tenders will ferry you to the town pier in the middle of town, where taxis await passengers. If your ship docks at the marina, downtown is a 15-minute taxi ride away. The walk is not recommended. The island is small, and most spots aren't more than a 30-minute drive from Marigot or Phillipsburg.

Doing your own thing will be much less expensive here than a ship-sponsored tour, and since rental cars are cheap (starting at $25 per day for a local car rental), you can easily strike out as soon as your ship docks. This is the best thing to do if you just want to see the island and spend a little time at a beach. Taxis are government-regulated and fairly costly, so they aren't really an option if you want to do much exploring. Authorized taxis display stickers of the St. Maarten Taxi Association. Taxis are also available at Marigot. You may be able to negotiate a favorable deal with a taxi driver for a 2- to 3-hour island tour for as little as $40 plus $15 for each additional person.

> ## ST. MAARTEN BEST BETS
>
> - **The 12-metre Challenge.** This mock America's Cup race is considered by many to be the best shore excursion in the whole Caribbean.
>
> - **Loterie Farm.** On the slopes of Pic du Paradis, this is an amazing eco-friendly preserve with fun activities and even food.
>
> - **Shopping.** Phillipsburg's Front Street is chockablock with stores of every strip, but hit those in Marigot for more French fashions.

Shore Excursions

We consider these to be among the better shore excursions for St. Martin/St. Maarten. They may not be offered by all lines, and tour names may differ as well. Times and prices are approximate.

America's Cup 12-Metre Challenge. This yacht race uses actual sailing ships used in the America's Cup. Anyone can help the crew grind winches, trim sails, and punch the stopwatch, or you can just sit back and watch everyone else work. The St. Maarten Challenge imitates an abbreviated America's Cup route. It's difficult to book this trip if you don't do it with your ship. ⊙ 3 hrs 🖭 $99.

Beach Sojourn. A short bus ride takes you from the pier on the Dutch side of St. Martin to Orient Beach on the island's French side. Often referred to as the French Riviera of the Caribbean, it's a lively beach where you will find restaurants, bars, lounge chairs, and umbrellas. Drinks are included; some ships offer lunch as well, but these trips cost more. ⊙ 3 hrs 🖭 $44.

Hidden Forest Adventure Tour. You're taken to Loterie Farm, on the hills of Pic du Paradis to explore this small private reserve. This tour includes lunch. ⊙ 3½ hrs 🖭 $94.

Marigot and the Butterfly Farm. Explore the upscale boutiques, duty-free shops and bistros of Marigot, stroll its waterfront, then visit the Butterfly Farm. At any given time in the terrariumlike sphere, as many as 600 butterflies (40 different species) flutter inside its garden. ⊙ 3½ hrs 🖭 $39.

Exploring St. Martin/St. Maarten

Numbers in the margin correspond to points of interest on the St. Martin/St. Maarten map.

❹ **Butterfly Farm.** Visitors enter a serene, tropical environment when they walk through the terrariumlike Butterfly Sphere. At any given time, as many as 600 butterflies, representing some 40 species, flutter inside the garden under a tented net. ⊠ *Rte. de Le Galion, Quartier d'Orléans* ☎ *590/87–31–21* ⊕ *www.thebutterflyfarm.com* ✑ *$12* ☉ *Daily 9–3.*

❻ **French Cul de Sac.** North of Orient Bay Beach, the French colonial mansion of St. Martin's mayor is nestled in the hills. The area is peaceful and good for hiking. From the beach here, shuttle boats make the five-minute trip to Ilet Pinel, an uninhabited island that's fine for picnicking, sunning, and swimming.

❼ **Grand Case.** The island's culinary hot spot is in the heart of the French side on a beach at the foot of green hills and pastures. Though it has only a 1-mi-long (1½-km-long) main street, it's known as the restaurant capital of the Caribbean. Grand Case Beach Club is at the end of this road.

❷ **Guana Bay Point.** On the rugged, windswept east coast about 10 minutes north of Philipsburg, Guana Bay Point offers isolated, untended beaches and a spectacular view of St. Barths.

❽ **Marigot.** This town's southern European flavor is most in evidence at its beautiful harborfront, with its shopping stalls, open-air cafés, and fresh-food vendors. From here, you can catch the ferry for Anguilla or St. Barths. Though not much remains of the structure itself, **Le Fort Louis,** completed by the French in 1789, commands a sweeping view of Marigot, its harbor, and the English island of Anguilla, which alone makes it worth the climb. ⊠ *Marigot.*

❸ **Orléans.** The island's oldest settlement, also known as the French Quarter, has classic, vibrantly painted West Indian–style homes with elaborate gingerbread fretwork.

❶ **Philipsburg.** The capital of Dutch St. Maarten stretches about 1 mi (1½ km) along an isthmus between Great Bay and the Salt Pond and has five parallel streets. Most of the village's dozens of shops and restaurants are on Front Street, narrow and cobblestoned, closest to Great Bay. Because of its numerous duty-free shops and several casinos, it's generally congested when cruise ships are in port. Little lanes called *steegjes* connect Front Street with Back Street, which has fewer shops and considerably less congestion.

Wathey Square (pronounced watty) is in the heart of the village. Directly across from the square are the town hall and the courthouse, in the striking white building with the cupola. The structure was built in 1793 and has served as the commander's home, a fire station, a jail, and a post office. The streets surrounding the square are lined with hotels, duty-free shops, fine restaurants, and cafés. The **Captain Hodge Pier,** just off the square, is a good spot to view Great Bay and the beach that stretches alongside. The **Sint Maarten Museum** hosts rotating cultural exhibits and a permanent historical display called Forts of St. Maarten–St. Martin. The artifacts range from Arawak pottery shards to objects salvaged from the wreck of the HMS *Proselyte*. ⊠ *7 Front St., Philipsburg* ☎ *599/542–4917* ☜ *Free* ☉ *Weekdays 10–4, Sat. 10–2.*

❺ Pic du Paradis. From Friar's Bay Beach, a bumpy, tree-canopied road leads inland to this peak. At 1,492 feet, it's the island's highest point. There are two observation areas. From them, the tropical forest unfolds below and the vistas are breathtaking. The road is quite isolated, so it's best to travel in groups. It's also quite steep and not in particularly good shape, becoming a single lane as you near the summit; if you don't have a four-wheel-drive vehicle, you will not make it. Parking at the top is iffy, and it's best if you turn around before you park. It may not be so easy later. Near the bottom of Pic du Paradis is **Loterie Farm,** a peaceful 150-acre private nature preserve opened to the public in 1999 by American expat B. J. Welch. Designed to preserve island habitats, Loterie Farm offers a rare glimpse of Caribbean forest and mountain land. Welch has renovated an old farmhouse and welcomes visitors for horseback riding, hiking, mountain biking, ecotours, or less strenuous activities, such as meditation and yoga. Raves accompany lunch and dinner fare at the Hidden Forest Café since chef Julie Purkis took over the kitchen. The restaurant is open Tuesday through Sunday. The Loterie Farm's newest attraction, the **Fly Zone,** allows Tarzan wannabes to soar over the forest canopy via a series of ropes, cables, and suspended bridges. ⊠ *Rte. de Pic du Paradis* ☎ *590/87–86–16 or 590/57–28–55* ⊕ *www.loteriefarm. com* ☜ *$5, 1½-hr tour $25, 4-hr tour $45* ☉ *Daily sunrise–sunset.*

Shopping

It's true that the island sparkles with its myriad outdoor activities—diving, snorkeling, sailing, swimming, and sunning—but shopaholics are drawn to sparkle within the jewelry stores. The huge array of such stores is almost unrivaled in the Caribbean. In addition, duty-free shops offer substantial savings—about 15% to 30% below U.S. and Canadian prices—on cameras, watches, liquor, cigars, and designer clothing. It's no wonder that each year 500 cruise ships make Philipsburg a port of call. As is the case on many of the port stops, it is just common sense to keep a close watch on your valuables.

Philipsburg's **Front Street** has reinvented itself. Now it's mall-like, with redbrick walks and streets, palm trees lining the sleek boutiques, jewelry stores, souvenir shops, outdoor restaurants, and the old reliables—including McDonald's and Burger King. Here and there a school or a church appears to remind visitors there's more to the island than shopping. On Back Street is the **Philipsburg Market Place,** an open-air market where you can haggle for bargains on items such as handicrafts, souvenirs, and cover-ups. **Old Street,** near the end of Front Street, has stores, boutiques, and open-air

> **TIP**
>
> Germicidal hand cleaner is a must-have for adventure excursions or where water might be at a premium. Bring a small bottle you can carry along with you.

cafés offering French crêpes, rich chocolates, and island mementos. You can find an outlet mall amid the more upscale shops at the **Maho** shopping plaza. The **Plaza del Lago** at the Simpson Bay Yacht Club complex has an excellent choice of restaurants as well as shops.

On the French side, wrought-iron balconies, colorful awnings, and gingerbread trim decorate Marigot's smart shops, tiny boutiques, and bistros in the **Marina Royale** complex and on the main streets, **rue de la Liberté** and **rue de la République.** Also in Marigot is the pricey **West Indies Mall** and the **Plaza Caraïbes,** which houses designer shops like Hermès and Ralph Lauren.

Activities

DIVING & SNORKELING Although St. Maarten is not known as a dive destination, the water temperature here is rarely below 70°F, and visibility is usually excellent, averaging about 100 feet (30 m). For snorkelers, the area around Orient Bay, Caye Verte (Green Key), Ilet Pinel, and Flat Island is especially lovely and is officially classified, and protected, as a regional underwater nature reserve. You can take a half-day snorkeling trip for around $25. On the Dutch side, **Dive Safaris** (⊠ *Bobby's Marina, Yrausquin Blvd., Philipsburg* ☎ *599/544–9001* ⊕ *www.thescubashop.net*) is a full-service outfit for divers. SSI- (Scuba Schools International) and PADI-certified dive centers include **Ocean Explorers Dive Shop** (⊠ *113 Welfare Rd., Simpson Bay* ☎ *599/544–5252* ⊕ *www.stmaartendiving.com*).

On the French side, **Blue Ocean** (⊠ Sandy Ground Rd., Baie Nettlé ☎ 590/87–89–73) is a PADI-certified dive center that also offers regularly scheduled snorkeling trips. Arrange equipment rentals and snorkeling trips through **Kontiki Watersports** (⊠ *Northern beach entrance, Baie Orientale* ☎ 590/87–46–89).

FISHING You can angle for yellowtail snapper, grouper, marlin, tuna, and wahoo on deep-sea excursions. Costs range from $150 per person for a half day to $250 for a full day. Prices usually include bait and tackle, instruction for novices, and refreshments. Ask about licensing and insurance. **Big Sailfish Too** (⊠ *Anse Marcel* ☎ *690/27–40–90*) is your best bet on the French side of the island. **Lee's Deepsea Fishing** (⊠ *Welfare Rd. 82, Simpson Bay* ☎ *599/544–4233 or 599/544–4234* ⊕ *www.leesfish.com*) organizes excursions, and when you return, Lee's Roadside Grill will cook your tuna, wahoo, or whatever else you catch and keep. **Rudy's Deep Sea Fishing** (⊠ *14 Airport Rd., Simpson Bay* ☎ *599/545–2177 or 599/522–7120* ⊕ *www.rudysdeepseafishing.com*) has been around for years and is one of the more experienced sport-angling outfits.

GOLF St. Maarten is not a golf destination. Although **Mullet Bay Golf Course** (⊠ *Airport Rd., north of the airport* ☎ *599/545–2801*), on the Dutch side, is an 18-hole course, it's the island's *only* one. Though lately it has been better tended, it's still not in the best of shape and many feel not worth the cost.

Beaches

The island's 10 mi (16 km) of beaches are all open to cruise-ship passengers. You can rent chairs and umbrellas at most of the beaches, primarily from beachside restaurants. The best beaches are on the French side. Topless bathing is common on the French side. If you take a cab to a remote beach, be sure to arrange a specific time for the driver to return for you. Don't leave valuables unattended on the beach or in a rental car, even in the trunk.

★ The nice, well-maintained beach at **Baie des Friars** is at the end of a poorly maintained dirt road. On a small, picturesque cove between Marigot and Grand Case, it attracts a casual crowd of locals and has a couple of good beachside restaurants. Getting to secluded **Baie Longue**, a 1-mi-long (1½-km-long) curve of white sand on the island's westernmost tip, requires a bumpy, 10-minute, we-must-be-lost drive off the main road, with just one small, unmarked entry down to the water. Though the beach is gravelly in places, this is a good place for snorkeling and swimming, but beware of a strong undertow when the waters are rough. If you want privacy, visit this isolated spot. There are no facilities or vendors.

Fodor'sChoice
★
By far the most beautiful beach on the island, 1-mi-long (1½-km-long) **Baie Orientale** has something for everyone, with its clean white sand, clear blue water, and an assortment of beach bars serving Mexican, Caribbean, American, and even kosher fare. There are plenty of places to rent equipment for water activities. The conservative north end is more family-oriented while the liberal south end is clothing-optional and eventually becomes a full-scale nude beach. A protected nature reserve, kid-friendly **Ilet Pinel** is a five-minute ferry ride from French Cul de Sac ($5 per person round-trip). The water is clear and shallow, and the shore is sheltered. If you like snorkeling, don your gear and swim along both sides of the coasts of this pencil-shape speck in the ocean. Food is available at the isle's two restaurants.

Where to Eat

Restaurants on the French side often figure a service charge into the menu prices. On the Dutch side, most restaurants add 10% to 15% to the bill. You can, if so moved by exceptional service, leave a tip.

$$-$$$ ✕ **Claude Mini-Club.** This brightly decorated upstairs restaurant, with a sweeping view of Marigot Harbor, has served traditional creole and French cuisine since 1969. The chairs and madras tablecloths are a mélange of sun yellow and orange. The whole place is built (tree-house-style) around the trunks of coconut trees. It's the place to be on Wednesday and Saturday nights, when the dinner buffet (40€) includes conch or onion soup, baked ham, blackened goose meat, lobster, roast beef, and all the trimmings. Fresh snapper is one of the specialties on the à la carte menu. There's live music nightly. ⊠ *Front de Mer, Marigot* ☎ *590/87–50–69* ▤ *AE, MC, V* ☉ *No lunch Sun.*

¢-$ ✕ **Kangaroo Court Café.** This little restaurant is renowned for its great coffee, but the gourmet burgers, pizza, salads, fruit frappés, and one of the island's largest selection of wines by the glass are not too shabby either. The funky patio area in the former childhood home of well-known islander Norman Wathey, is a pleasant place to enjoy your repast. Ruins from an old salt storage area, a small waterfall, and a huge ficus tree are the main decor. Almond trees shade it so well that nets are installed to keep nuts and leaves from hitting diners. ⊠ *6 Henrick St., Philipsburg* ☎ *599/542–7557 or 599/542–1644* ▤ *AE, D, MC, V* ☉ *No dinner.*

ST. THOMAS, U.S. VIRGIN ISLANDS

Carol
Bareuther

St. Thomas is the busiest cruise port of call in the world. Up to eight giant ships may visit in a single day. Don't expect an exotic island experience: one of the three U.S. Virgin Islands (with St. Croix and St. John), St. Thomas is as American as any place on the mainland, complete with McDonald's and HBO. The positive side of all this development is that there are more tours here than anywhere else in the Caribbean, and every year the excursions get better. Of course, shopping is the big draw in Charlotte Amalie, but experienced travelers remember the days of "real" bargains. Today, so many passengers fill the stores that it's a seller's market. On some days, there are so many cruise passengers on St. Thomas that you must book a ship-sponsored shore excursion if you want to do more than just take a taxi to the beach or stroll around Charlotte Amalie.

Essentials

CURRENCY The U.S. dollar is the official currency of U.S. Virgin Islands, and ATMs are plentiful.

HOURS Bank hours are generally Monday through Thursday 9 to 3 and Friday 9 to 5; a handful open Saturday 9 to noon. Stores on Main Street in Charlotte Amalie are open weekdays and Saturday 9 to 5. The hours of the shops in the Havensight Mall (next to the cruise-ships dock) are the same, though occasionally some stay open until 9 on Friday, depending on how many cruise ships are at the dock. You may also find some shops open on Sunday.

INTERNET **Beans, Bytes & Websites** (⊠ *Royal Dane Mall, behind Tavern on the Waterfront, Charlotte Amalie, St. Thomas* ☎ *340/775–5262* ⊕ *www. usvi.net/cybercafe*). **Cyber Zone** (⊠ *Port of $ale, Charlotte Amalie, St. Thomas* ☎ *340/714–7743*).

TELEPHONES Both GSM and Sprint phones work in St. Thomas. It's as easy to call home from St. Thomas and St. John as from any city in the United States. On St. Thomas, public phones are easily found, and AT&T has a telecommunications center across from the Havensight Mall and on the Waterfront in Charlotte Amalie across from Emancipation Gardens.

Coming Ashore

Depending on how many ships are in port, cruise ships drop anchor in the harbor at Charlotte Amalie and tender passengers directly to the waterfront duty-free shops, dock at the Havensight Mall at the eastern end of the crescent-shaped bay, or dock at Crown Bay Marina a few miles west of town.

The distance from Havensight to the duty-free shops is 1½ mi (3 km), which can be walked in less than half an hour; a taxi ride there costs $6 per person ($5 for each additional person). Tourist information offices are at the Havensight Mall (across from Building No. 1) for docking passengers and downtown near Fort Christian (at the eastern end of the waterfront shopping area) for those coming ashore by tender. Both offices distribute free maps. From Crown Bay, it's also a half-hour walk or a $5 per person cab ride ($4 for each additional person). Taxi drivers on St. Thomas do not typically do island tours, but there are myriad tour operators who will. You can rent a car in St. Thomas, but with all the tour options, it's often easier and cheaper to take an organized excursion or just hop in a cab.

Shore Excursions

We consider these to be among the better shore excursions for St. Thomas. They may not be offered by all lines, and tour names may differ as well. Times and prices are approximate.

Helmet Dive. This is a unique diving opportunity for non-divers at Coral World Marine Park in St. Thomas, using helmets that provide oxygen as you walk along the bottom of

---

ST. THOMAS BEST BETS

- **Coral World Marine Park.** This aquarium attraction is a great bet for families, and it's on one of the best snorkeling beaches.

- **Magen's Bay Beach.** St. Thomas has one of the most picture-postcard perfect beaches you'll ever see. It's great for swimming.

- **St. John.** It's easy to hop on the ferry to St. John for a day of hiking, then relax for an hour or two on the beach afterward.

- **Shopping.** Charlotte Amalie is one of the best places in the Caribbean to shop.

---

the sea. Afterward, you can also visit the aquarium. ☉ *3 hrs* 🖃 *$89–$99.*
Kayaking & Snorkeling Tour. Paddle your kayak through a marine sanctuary as your guide narrates both the above- and underwater scenery. ☉ *3½ hrs* 🖃 *$72–$89.*
Turtle Cove Sail & Snorkel. Sail aboard a private yacht with a small group to Turtle Cove on St. Thomas's own Buck Island for snorkeling and swimming to view a sunken ship, tropical fish, and coral. ☉ *3½ hrs* 🖃 *$59.*
St. John Eco Hike. After a ferry ride to St. John, you hike approximately 1¼ mi (3 km) to Linde Point and then to Honeymoon Beach for a swim. Continue on to Caneel Bay to visit some ruins before returning to the ferry landing by safari van. ☉ *4½ hrs* 🖃 *$54–$58.*
St. John Island Tour. Either your ship tenders you to St. John before docking in St. Thomas or you are transferred to the St. Thomas ferry dock in for the ride to St. John. On St. John, an open-air safari bus winds through the national park to a beach for snorkeling, swimming, and sunbathing. (If you have the option, you might avoid the often-crowded beach at Trunk Bay.) ☉ *4½ hrs* 🖃 *$46.*
Water Island Bike Trip. After riding a mountain bike around Water Island, which is just off the western end of St. Thomas, you stop for a refreshing swim at a beautiful sandy beach. ☉ *3½ hrs* 🖃 *$79.*

Exploring St. Thomas

Numbers in the margin correspond to points of interest on the St. Thomas map.

① Charlotte Amalie. St. Thomas's major burg is a hilly shopping town. There are also plenty of interesting historic sights—so take the time to see at least a few.

Emancipation Garden was built to honor the freeing of slaves in 1848; a bronze bust of a freed slave blowing a symbolic conch shell commem-

St. Thomas

KEY

🚢 Ferry

⚓ Cruise Ship Terminal

orates the 150th anniversary of this event. A bust of Denmark's King Christian and a scaled-down model of the U.S. Liberty Bell show the island's Danish-American ties. ⊠ *Between Tolbod Gade and Fort Christian.*

Fort Christian, St. Thomas's oldest standing structure, was built between 1672 and 1680 and now has U.S. National Landmark status. The clock tower was added in the 19th century. This remarkable building has, over time, been used as a jail, governor's residence, town hall, courthouse, and church. Closed for major structural renovations since 2005, the building is scheduled to reopen in 2007. ⊠ *Waterfront Hwy., east of shopping district* ☎ *340/776–4566.*

Frederick Lutheran Church has a massive mahogany altar, and its pewsóeach with its own door were once rented to families of the congregation. ⊠ *Norre Gade* ☎ *340/776–1315* ☉ *Mon.–Sat. 9–4.*

Built in 1867, **Government House** houses the offices for the governor of the Virgin Islands. Inside, the staircases are of native mahogany, as are the plaques hand lettered in gold with the names of the governors appointed and, since 1970, elected. ⊠ *Government Hill* ☎ *340/774–0294* ▭ *Free* ☉ *Weekdays 8–5.*

The pastoral-looking lime-green exterior of the **Legislature Building,** seat of U.S. Virgin Islands elected representatives, conceals the vociferous political wrangling of the Virgin Islands Senate going on inside. You're welcome to sit in on sessions in the upstairs chambers. ⊠ *Waterfront Hwy., across from Fort Christian* ☎ *340/774–0880* ☉ *Daily 8–5.*

❻ Coral World Ocean Park. Coral World has an offshore underwater observatory that houses the Predator Tank, one of the world's largest coral-reef tanks, and an aquarium with more than 20 portholes providing close-ups of Caribbean sea life. *Sea Trekkin'* lets you tour the reef outside the park at a depth of 15 feet, thanks to specialized high-tech headgear and a continuous air supply that's based on the surface. A guide leads the ½-hour tour and the narration is piped through a specialized microphone inside each trekker's helmet; the minimum age to participate is eight years. The park also has several outdoor pools where you can touch starfish, pet a baby shark, feed stingrays, and view endangered sea turtles. In addition there's a mangrove lagoon and a nature trail full of lush tropical flora. Daily feedings and talks take place at most every exhibit. ⊠ *Coki Point, north of Rte. 38, Estate Frydendal* ⌂ *6450 Estate Smith Bay, St. Thomas 00802* ☎ *340/775–1555* ⊕ *www.coralworldvi.com* ▭ *$18, Sea Trek $68, Shark Encounter $43* ☉ *Daily 9–5.*

☾ ❸ Drake's Seat. Sir Francis Drake was supposed to have kept watch over his fleet and looked for enemy ships from this particularly good vantage point. The panorama is especially breathtaking (and romantic) at dusk. ⊠ *Rte. 40, Estate Zufriedenheit.*

☾ ❹ Mountain Top. Stop at Mountain Top for a banana daiquiri and spectacular views from the observation deck more than 1,500 feet above sea level. Kids will like talking to the parrots and hearing them answer back. ⊠ *Head north off Rte. 33, look for signs* ⊕ *www.greathouse-mountaintop.com.*

★ ⚫ ❷ **Paradise Point Tramway.** Fly skyward in a gondola to Paradise Point, an overlook with breathtaking views of Charlotte Amalie and the harbor. There are several shops, a bar, restaurant, and a wedding gazebo; kids enjoy the tropical bird show held daily at 10:30 AM, 1:30 PM, and 3:30 PM. A ¼-mi (½-km) hiking trail leads to spectacular views of St. Croix to the south. Wear sturdy shoes; the trail is steep and rocky. ✉ *Rte. 30, across from Havensight Mall, Charlotte Amalie* ☎ *340/774–9809* ⊕ *www.paradisepointtramway.com* 🎫 *$16* ⊙ *Thurs.–Tues. 9–5, Wed. 9–9.*

❺ **Tillett Gardens.** East of Charlotte Amalie, Tillett Gardens is an oasis of artistic endeavor across from the Tutu Park Shopping Mall. You can watch artisans produce silk-screen fabrics, pottery, candles, watercolors, jewelry, and other handicrafts. ✉ *Rte. 38.*

Shopping

The prime shopping area in **Charlotte Amalie** is between Post Office and Market squares; it consists of three parallel streets that run east–west (Waterfront Highway, Main Street, and Back Street) and the alleyways that connect them. Particularly attractive are the historic **A. H. Riise Alley, Royal Dane Mall, Palm Passage,** and pastel-painted **International Plaza**—quaint alleys between Main Street and the Waterfront. **Vendors Plaza,** on the waterfront side of Emancipation Gardens in Charlotte Amalie, is a central location for vendors selling handmade earrings, necklaces, and bracelets; straw baskets and handbags; T-shirts; fabrics; African artifacts; and local fruits. Look for the many brightly colored umbrellas.

At the Crown Bay cruise-ship pier, the **Crown Bay Center,** off the Harwood Highway in Sub Base about ½ mi (¾ km) has quite a few shops.

Havensight Mall, next to the cruise-ship dock, may not be as charming as downtown Charlotte Amalie, but it does have more than 60 shops. It also has an excellent bookstore, a bank, a pharmacy, a gourmet grocery, and smaller branches of many downtown stores. The shops at **Port of $ale,** adjoining Havensight Mall (its buildings are pink instead of brown), sell discount goods. Next door to Port of $ale is the **Yacht Haven Grande** complex, with many upscale shops.

Shopping maps are available at the tourist offices and often from your ship's shore-excursion desk. Remember that you must pack any alcohol in your checked bags. **A. H. Riise Liquors** (✉ *37 Main St., at Riise's Alley, Charlotte Amalie* ☎ *340/776–2303* ✉ *Havensight Mall, Bldg. I, Rte. 30, Charlotte Amalie* ☎ *340/776–7713*) offers a large selection of tobacco and liquor. The wine selection is large at warehouse-style **Al Cohen's Discount Liquor** (✉ *Rte. 30 across from Havensight Mall, Charlotte Amalie* ☎ *340/774–3690*).

Caribbean Marketplace (✉ *Havensight Mall, Rte. 30, Charlotte Amalie* ☎ *340/776–5400*) is a great place to buy handicrafts from the Caribbean and elsewhere. **Down Island Traders** (✉ *Waterfront Hwy. at Post Office Alley, Charlotte Amalie* ☎ *340/776–4641*) carries hand-painted calabash bowls; finely printed Caribbean note cards; jams, jellies, spices, hot sauces, and herbs; teas made of lemongrass, passion fruit, and mango; coffee from Jamaica; and handicrafts from throughout the Caribbean.

Little Switzerland (⊠ *5 Dronningens Gade, across from Emancipation Garden, Charlotte Amalie* ☎ *340/776–2010* ⊠ *3B Main St., Charlotte Amalie* ☎ *340/776–2010* ⊠ *Havensight Mall, Bldg. II, Rte. 30, Charlotte Amalie* ☎ *340/776–2198*) is a good source for china, crystal, and jewelry. **Local Color** (⊠ *Royal Dane Mall, at Waterfront, Charlotte Amalie* ☎ *340/774–2280*) carries casual and island clothing. More than 40 local artists—including schoolchildren, senior citizens, and people with disabilities—create the handcrafted items for sale at **Native Arts & Crafts Cooperative** (⊠ *Tolbod Gade, across from Emancipation Garden and next to visitor center, Charlotte Amalie* ☎ *340/777–1153*).

Activities

DIVING & SNORKELING

Chris Sawyer Diving Center (☎ *340/775–7320 or 877/929–3483* ⊕ *www.sawyerdive.vi*) is a PADI five-star outfit that specializes in dives to the 310-foot-long *Rhone,* in the British Virgin Islands. Hotel-dive packages are offered through the Wyndham Sugar Bay Beach Club & Resort. **Snuba of St. Thomas** (⊠ *Rte. 388, at Coki Point, Estate Smith Bay* ☎ *340/693–8063* ⊕ *www.visnuba.com*) offers something for nondivers, a cross between snorkeling and scuba diving: a 20-foot air hose connects you to the surface. The cost is $68. Children must be eight or older to participate.

FISHING

Fishing here is synonymous with blue marlin angling. If you're not into marlin fishing, try hooking sailfish in the winter, dolphinfish come spring, and wahoo in the fall. To really find the trip that will best suit you, walk down the docks at either American Yacht Harbor or Sapphire Beach Marina in the late afternoon and chat with the captains and crews. The **Charter Boat Center** (⊠ *6300 Red Hook Plaza, Red Hook* ☎ *340/775–7990* ⊕ *www.charterboat.vi*) is a major source for sportfishing charters, both marlin and inshore. For inshore trips, **Peanut Gallery Charters** (⊠ *Crown Bay Marina, Rte. 304, Estate Contant* ☎ *340/775–5274* ⊕ *www.fishingstthomas.com*) offers trips on its 18-foot *Dauntless* or 28-foot custom sportfishing catamaran.

GOLF

The **Mahogany Run Golf Course** (⊠ *Rte. 42, Estate Lovenlund* ☎ *340/777–6006 or 800/253–7103* ⊕ *www.mahoganyrungolf.com*) attracts golfers for its spectacular view of the British Virgin Islands and the challenging 3-hole Devil's Triangle. At this Tom and George Fazio–designed par-70, 18-hole course, there's a fully stocked pro shop, snack bar, and open-air clubhouse. Greens and half-cart fees for 18 holes are $150. The course is open daily, and there are frequently informal weekend tournaments. It's the only course on St. Thomas.

Beaches

FodorsChoice

All beaches in the USVI are public, but occasionally you'll need to stroll through a resort to reach the sand. **Coki Beach** (⊠ *Rte. 388, next to Coral World Marine Park*), next to Coral World (turn north off Route 38), is the island's best snorkeling spot. Colorful beachside shops rent watersports equipment. Some also sell snack foods, cold drinks, and even fish food (dry dog food).

Fodor'sChoice ★ On Route 35, **Magens Bay** (⊠ *Rte. 35, at end of road on north side of island*) is usually lively because of its spectacular crescent of white sand, more than ½ mi (¾ km) long, and its calm waters, which are protected by two peninsulas. It's often listed among the world's most beautiful beaches. (If you arrive between 8 AM and 5 PM, you have to pay an entrance fee of $3 per person, $1 per vehicle, and 25¢ per child under age 12.) The bottom is flat and sandy, so this is a place for sunning and swimming rather than snorkeling. There's also a bar, snack bar, and bathhouses with toilets and saltwater showers. Close to Charlotte Amalie

★ and fronting the Marriott Frenchman's Reef Hotel, pretty **Morning Star Beach** (⊠ *Rte. 315, 2 mi (3 km) southeast of Charlotte Amalie, past Havensight Mall and cruise-ship dock*) is where many young locals bodysurf or play volleyball. Snorkeling is good near the rocks when the current doesn't affect visibility. There's a fine view of St. John and other islands

★ from **Sapphire Beach** (⊠ *Rte. 38, Sapphire Bay*). The snorkeling is excellent at the reef to the right, or east, near Pettyklip Point. The constant breeze makes this a great spot for windsurfing. The condo resort at **Secret Harbor** (⊠ *Rte. 32, Red Hook*) doesn't detract from the attractiveness of the cove-like beach. Not only is this East End spot pretty, but it also has superb snorkeling—head out to the left, near the rocks.

Where to Eat

Some restaurants add a 10% to 15% service charge. If not, leave a 15% tip.

$$ ✕ **Cuzzin's Caribbean Restaurant & Bar.** The top picks in this restaurant in a 19th-century livery stage are Virgin Islands staples. For lunch, order tender slivers of conch stewed in a rich onion butter sauce, savory braised oxtail, or curried chicken. At dinner, the island-style mutton, served in a thick gravy and seasoned with locally grown herbs, offers a tasty treat that's deliciously different. Side dishes include peas and rice, boiled green bananas, fried plantains, and potato stuffing. ⊠ *7 Wimmelskafts Gade, also called Back St.* ☎ *340/777–4711* ▭ *AE, MC, V.*

$–$$ ✕ **Gladys' Cafe.** Even if the local specialties—conch in butter sauce, salt
Fodor'sChoice ★ fish and dumplings, hearty red bean soup—didn't make this a recommended café, it would be worth coming for Gladys's smile. While you're here, pick up a $5 or $10 bottle of her special hot sauce. There are mustard-, oil and vinegar-, and tomato-based versions; the last is the hottest. ⊠ *Waterfront, at Royal Dane Mall* ⌂ *28 Dronningens Gade, Charlotte Amalie, St. Thomas 00802* ☎ *340/774–6604* ▭ *AE* ☽ *No dinner.*

ST. VINCENT (KINGSTOWN)

Jane Zarem You won't find glitzy resorts or flashy discos on St. Vincent. Rather, you'll be fascinated by picturesque villages, secluded beaches, and fine sailing waters. St. Vincent is the largest and northernmost island in the Grenadines archipelago; Kingstown, the capital city of St. Vincent & the Grenadines, is the government and business center and major port. Except for one barren area on the island's northeast coast—remnants of the 1979 eruption of La Soufrière, one of the last active volcanoes in the Caribbean—the countryside is mountainous, lush, and green. St. Vincent's mountains and forests thwarted European settlement for many years. As colonization advanced elsewhere in the Caribbean, in fact, the island became a refuge for Carib Indians—descendants of whom still live in northeastern St. Vincent. After years of fighting and back-and-forth territorial claims, British troops prevailed by overpowering the French and banishing Carib warriors to Central America. Independent since 1979, St. Vincent & the Grenadines remains a member of the British Commonwealth.

Essentials

CURRENCY Eastern Caribbean (E.C.) dollar (EC$2.70 to US$1). U.S. dollars are generally accepted, but change is given in E.C. dollars.

HOURS Banks are open Monday through Thursday from 8 to 1 or 3, Friday until 3 or 5. The General Post Office, on Halifax Street in Kingstown, is open weekdays from 8:30 to 3, Saturday from 8:30 to 11:30. Shops and businesses in Kingstown are open weekdays from 8 to 4; some close for lunch from noon to 1. Saturday hours are from 8 to noon.

INTERNET **E@gles Internet Cafe** (⊠ *Halifax St., opposite the General Post Office, Kingstown, St. Vincent*) offers high-speed computers and broadband Internet access for as little as $2 per hour.

TELEPHONES Pay phones are readily available and best operated with the prepaid phone cards that are sold at many stores and can be used on many Caribbean islands. Telephone services are available at the cruise-ship terminal in Kingstown, St. Vincent. For an international operator, dial 115; to charge your call to a credit card, call 117.

Coming Ashore

The cruise-ship terminal at Kingstown, St. Vincent's capital city, accommodates two cruise ships; additional vessels anchor outside the harbor and bring passengers to the jetty by launch. The facility has about two dozen shops that sell duty-free items and handicrafts. There's a communications center, post office, tourist information desk, restaurant, and food court.

Buses and taxis are available at the wharf. Taxi drivers are well equipped to take you on an island tour; expect to pay $25 per hour for up to four passengers. The ferry to Bequia (one hour each way) is at the adjacent pier. Renting a car for just one day isn't advisable, since car rentals are expensive (at least $55 per day) and require a $20 temporary driving permit on top of that. It's almost always more financially favorable to take a tour, though you don't have to limit yourself to those offered by your ship.

Shore Excursions

We consider these to be among the better shore excursions for St. Lucia. They may not be offered by all lines, and tour names may differ as well. Times and prices are approximate. Ships that dock in St. Vincent often include some shore excursions to Bequia. In that case, they will include a one-hour ferry ride, each way, between St. Vincent and Bequia.

Bequia by Catamaran. This day-long sailing trip takes you to Bequia and Petit Nevis with time to stroll, shop, and swim. The trip includes a beach picnic at Princess Margaret Beach. It's expensive but worthwhile. ⊘ *7 hrs* ⌸ *$149*.

Scenic Island Tour. It's hard to appreciate how beautiful St. Vincent is unless you get out and do some exploring. This tour takes you to Fort Charlotte, the Botanical Garden, and the Mesopotamia Valley. ☉ *3 hrs* 🎫 *$52.*

Hiking the Vermont Nature Trail. This hike takes you about a mile through the rain forest and includes a refreshment stop. ☉ *4 hrs* 🎫 *$52.*

St. Vincent Garden Tour. This tour includes both the Montreal Estate and the St. Vincent Botanical Garden, which has breadfruit trees brought by Captain Bligh of the *Bounty.* ☉ *4 hrs* 🎫 *$56.*

Exploring St. Vincent
Numbers in the margin correspond to points of interest on the St. Vincent map.

★ ☕ ❷ **Botanical Garden.** A few minutes north of downtown by taxi is the oldest botanical garden in the Western Hemisphere, founded in 1765. Captain Bligh—of *Bounty* fame—brought the first breadfruit tree to this island for landowners to propagate. The prolific bounty of the breadfruit tree was used to feed the slaves. You can see a direct descendant of this original tree among the specimen mahogany, rubber, teak, and other tropical trees and shrubs in the 20 acres of gardens. Two dozen rare St. Vincent parrots live in the small aviary. Guides explain all the medicinal and ornamental trees and shrubs; they also appreciate a tip at the end of the tour. ✉ *Off Leeward Hwy., Montrose* ☎ *784/457–1003* 🎫 *$3* ☉ *Daily 6–6.*

★ ❺ **Falls of Baleine.** The falls are impossible to reach by car, so book an escorted, all-day boat trip from Villa Beach or the Lagoon Marina. The boat ride along the coast offers scenic island views. When you arrive, you have to wade through shallow water to get to the beach. Then local guides help you make the easy five-minute trek to the 60-foot falls and the rock-enclosed freshwater pool the falls create—plan to take a dip.

★ ☕ ❸ **Fort Charlotte.** Started by the French in 1786 and completed by the British in 1806, the fort was named for King George III's wife. It sits on Berkshire Hill, a dramatic promontory 636 feet above sea level, with a stunning view of Kingstown and the Grenadines. Interestingly, cannons face inward—the fear of attack by native peoples was far greater than any threat approaching from the sea, though, truth be told, the fort saw no action. Nowadays the fort serves as a signal station for ships; its ancient cells house paintings, by Lindsay Prescott, depicting early island history.

❶ **Kingstown.** The capital city of St. Vincent & the Grenadines is on the island's southwestern coast.

ST. VINCENT BEST BETS

■ **Ferry to Bequia.** You can easily get to laid-back Bequia on a one-hour ferry trip for better beaches than you'll find on St. Vincent.

■ **Hiking.** Whether you hike in the rain forest or do the more difficult climb of La Soufrière, it's worth exploring some of the island's rugged terrain.

■ **Tobago Cays.** These uninhabited islands are the top destination in the southern Grenadines for snorkeling, and it's reachable on a day-long excursion from St. Vincent.

St. Vincent

KEY

- Beaches
- Cruise Ship Terminal
- Dive Sites
- Ferry

St. Vincent Passage

Porter Pt.
Baleine Bay
Fancy
Commantawana Bay
Owia
Espagnol Pl.
Owia Salt Pond
Sandy Bay

5

6
Crater Lake

Larikai Bay

Caribbean Sea

Overland Village

Richmond

Richmond Peak

Georgetown

ATLANTIC OCEAN

Petit Bordel Bay
Chateaubelair Bay
Dark Head
Chateaubelair
Troumaka

Grand Bonum

Colonarie River

Colonarie

Cumberland Bay

4

Barrouallie

Peter's Hope

Sans Souci

Colonarie Bay

Leeward Hwy.

Layou

Mt. St. Andrew

Greiggs

Biabou

Buccament Bay

Questelle's Bay

2

7 Mesopotamia
Grant's Bay

Yambou River

Argyle Beach

Anchor Reef,
New Guinea Reef,
The Forest

3 **1**

Kingstown Bay

E. T. Joshua Airport

Indian Bay

Villa Beach

Young Island

Villa

Calliaqua

Vigie Hwy.

Argyle

Stubbs Bay

Calliaqua Bay

Milligan Cay

St. Vincent

Bequia

The Grenadines

0   2 miles

0   2 km

TO BEQUIA

The town of 13,500 residents wraps around Kingstown Bay; a ring of green hills and ridges, studded with homes, forms a backdrop for the city. This is very much a working city, with a busy harbor and few concessions to tourists. Kingstown Harbour is the only deepwater port on the island.

What few gift shops there are can be found on and around **Bay Street,** near the harbor. Upper Bay Street, which stretches along the bayfront, bustles with daytime activity—workers going about their business and housewives doing their shopping. Many of Kingstown's downtown buildings are built of stone or brick brought to the island in the holds of 18th-century ships as ballast (and replaced with sugar and spices for the return trip to Europe). The Georgian-style stone arches and second-floor overhangs on former warehouses create shelter from midday sun and the brief, cooling showers common to the tropics.

Grenadines Wharf, at the south end of Bay Street, is busy with schooners loading supplies and ferries loading people bound for the Grenadines. The **Cruise Ship Complex,** south of the commercial wharf, has a mall with a dozen or more shops, plus restaurants, a post office, communications facilities, and a taxi–minibus stand.

An almost infinite selection of produce fills the **Kingstown Produce Market,** a three-story building that takes up a whole city block on Upper Bay, Hillsboro, and Bedford streets in the center of town. It's noisy, colorful, and open Monday through Saturday—but the busiest times (and the best times to go) are Friday and Saturday mornings. In the courtyard, vendors sell local arts and crafts. On the upper floors, merchants sell clothing, household items, gifts, and other products.

Little Tokyo, so called because funding for the project was a gift from Japan, is a waterfront shopping area with a bustling indoor fish market and dozens of stalls where you can buy inexpensive homemade meals, drinks, ice cream, bread and cookies, clothing, and trinkets, and even get a haircut.

St. George's Cathedral, on Grenville Street, is a pristine, creamy-yellow Anglican church built in 1820. The dignified Georgian architecture includes simple wooden pews, an ornate chandelier, and beautiful stained-glass windows; one was a gift from Queen Victoria, who actually commissioned it for London's St. Paul's Cathedral in honor of her first grandson. When the artist created an angel with a red robe, she was horrified and sent it abroad. The markers in the cathedral's graveyard recount the history of the island. Across the street is **St. Mary's Cathedral of the Assumption** (Roman Catholic), built in stages beginning in 1823. The strangely appealing design is a blend of Moorish, Georgian, and Romanesque styles applied to black brick. Nearby, freed slaves built the **Kingstown Methodist Church** in 1841. The exterior is brick, simply decorated with quoins (solid blocks that form the corners), and the roof is held together by metal straps, bolts, and wooden pins. **Scots Kirk** (1839–80) was built by and for Scottish settlers but became a Seventh-Day Adventist church in 1952.

6 La Soufrière. The volcano, which last erupted in 1979, is 4,000 feet high and so huge in area that it covers virtually the entire northern third of the island. The eastern trail to the rim of the crater, a two-hour ascent, begins at Rabacca Dry River.

7 Montreal Gardens. Welsh-born landscape designer Timothy Vaughn renovated 7½ acres of neglected commercial flower beds and a falling-down plantation house into a stunning, yet informal, garden spot. Anthuriums, ginger lilies, birds-of-paradise, and other tropical flowers are planted in raised beds; tree ferns create a canopy of shade along the walkways. The gardens are in the shadow of majestic Grand Bonhomme mountain, deep in the beautiful Mesopotamia Valley, about 12 mi (19 km) from Kingstown. ⊠ *Montreal St., Mesopotamia* ☎ *784/458–1198* ☜ *$3* ⊘ *Dec.–Aug., weekdays 9–4.*

4 Wallilabou Bay. *The Pirates of the Caribbean* left their mark at Wallilabou (pronounced wally-la-*boo*), a location used for filming the recent movies. Many of the buildings and docks built as stage sets remain, giving the pretty bay an intriguingly historic appearance. You can sunbathe, swim, picnic, or buy your lunch at Wallilabou Anchorage. This is a favorite stop for day-trippers returning from the Falls of Baleine and boaters anchoring for the evening. Nearby there's a river with a small waterfall where you can take a freshwater plunge.

Shopping

The 12 blocks that hug the waterfront in **downtown Kingstown** comprise St. Vincent's main shopping district. Among the shops that sell goods to fulfill household needs are a few that sell local crafts, gifts, and souvenirs. Bargaining is neither expected nor appreciated. The **Cruise Ship Complex,** on the waterfront in Kingstown, has a collection of a dozen or so boutiques, shops, and restaurants that cater primarily to cruise-ship passengers but welcome all shoppers. St. Vincent is not a major duty-free shopping port, but you will find a few duty-free shops.

At **FranPaul's Selections** (⊠ *2nd fl., Bonadie's Plaza, Bay St., Kingstown* ☎ *784/456–2662*), Francelia St. John fashions dresses, pants, and shirts from colorful fabrics she selects in Trinidad. The emphasis is on African, Afro-Caribbean, and casual wear. **Nzimbu Browne** (⊠ *McKie's Hill, Kingstown* ☎ *784/457–1677*) creates original art from dried banana leaves, carefully selecting and snipping bits and arranging them on pieces of wood to depict local scenes. He often sets up shop on Bay Street, near the Cobblestone Inn. **St. Vincent Craftsmen's Centre** (⊠ *Frenches St., Kingstown* ☎ *784/457–2516*), three blocks from the wharf, sells locally made grass floor mats, place mats, and other straw articles, as well as batik cloth, handmade West Indian dolls, hand-painted calabashes, and framed artwork. The large grass mats can be rolled and folded for easy transport home. No credit cards are accepted.

Activities

DIVING & SNORKELING Novices and advanced divers alike will be impressed by the marine life in the waters surrounding St. Vincent & the Grenadines—brilliant sponges, huge deepwater coral trees, and shallow reefs teeming with colorful fish. The best dive spots on St. Vincent are in the small bays along the coast between Kingstown and Layou; many are within 20 yards of shore and only 20 feet to 30 feet down.

Anchor Reef has excellent visibility for viewing a deep-black coral garden, schools of squid, sea horses, and maybe a small octopus. **The Forest,** a shallow dive, is still dramatic, with soft corals in pastel colors and schools of small fish. **New Guinea Reef** slopes to 90 feet (28 m) and can't be matched for its quantity of corals and sponges. The pristine waters surrounding the **Tobago Cays,** in the Southern Grenadines, will give you a world-class diving experience.

Fantasea Tours (⊠ *Villa Beach, St. Vincent* ☎ *784/457–5555* ⊕ *www. fantaseatours.com*) will take you on a 38-foot power cruiser to the Falls of Baleine, Bequia, and Mustique, or on a snorkeling trip to the Tobago Cays. **Dive St. Vincent** (⊠ *Young Island Dock, Villa Beach* ☎ *784/457–4714 or 784/547–4928* ⊕ *www.divestvincent.com*) is where NAUI- and PADI-certified instructor Bill Tewes and his staff offer beginner and certification courses and dive trips to the St. Vincent coast and the southern Grenadines.

FISHING From Villa Beach or Indian Bay on St. Vincent, you can go on a full-day fishing trip or boat ride around the Grenadines for about $120–$140 per person, including all equipment and lunch. **Crystal Blue Charters** (⊠ *Indian Bay* ☎ 784/457–4532 🖷 784/456–2232) offers sportfishing charters on a 34-foot pirogue for amateur and serious fishermen.

Beaches

St. Vincent's origin is volcanic, so its beaches range in color from golden-brown to black. Swimming is recommended only in the lagoons and bays along the leeward coast. By contrast, beaches on the Bequia and the rest of the Grenadines have pure white sand, palm trees, and crystal-clear aquamarine water; some are even within walking distance of the jetty. **Buccament Bay** is good for swimming. This tiny black-sand beach is 20 minutes north of Kingstown. South of Kingstown, **Indian Bay** has golden sand but is slightly rocky; it's a good place for snorkeling. **Questelle's Bay** (pronounced keet-*ells*), north of Kingstown and next to Campden Park, has a black-sand beach.

Where to Eat

A 7% government tax is applicable to your bill, and most restaurants add a 10% service charge in lieu of tip. If they do not, leave an appropriate tip; otherwise, anything additional is expected only for special service.

$$–$$$ ✕ **Lime Restaurant & Pub.** Named for the *pursuit* of liming (relaxing), this sprawling waterfront restaurant also has mostly green decor. An extensive all-day menu caters to beachgoers and boaters who drop by for a roti and a bottle of Hairoun—or burgers, curries, sandwiches, gourmet pizzas, pastas, soups, and salads. Dinner choices include fresh seafood, volcano chicken (with a creole sauce that's as spicy as lava is hot), curried goat, and pepper steak. Casual and congenial by day, it's candlelit and romantic at night—enhanced by the twinkling lights of anchored boats and the soft sound of waves quietly breaking against

the seawall. ✉ *Young Island Channel, Villa Harbour* ☎ *784/458–4227* ▭ *AE, D, DC, MC, V.*

$–$$ ✕ **Basil's Bar & Restaurant.** It's not just the air-conditioning that makes this restaurant cool. Downstairs at the Cobblestone Inn is owned by Basil Charles, whose Basil's Beach Bar on Mustique is a hangout for the vacationing rich and famous. This is the Kingstown power-lunch venue. Local businesspeople gather for the daily buffet or a full menu of salads, sandwiches, barbecued chicken, or fresh seafood platters. Dinner entrées of pasta, local seafood, and chicken (try it poached in fresh ginger and coconut milk) are served at candlelit tables. There's a Chinese buffet on Friday, and takeout is available that night only. ✉ *Cobblestone Inn, Upper Bay St., Kingstown* ☎ *784/457–2713* ▭ *AE, MC, V.*

SAN JUAN, PUERTO RICO

Mark Sullivan | Although Puerto Rico is a commonwealth of the United States, few cities in the Caribbean are as steeped in Spanish tradition as San Juan. Within a seven-square-block area in Old San Juan are restored 16th-century buildings, museums, art galleries, bookstores, and 200-year-old houses with balustraded balconies overlooking narrow, cobblestone streets. In contrast, San Juan's sophisticated Condado and Isla Verde areas have glittering hotels, fancy boutiques, casinos, and discos. Out in the countryside is the 28,000-acre El Yunque rain forest, with more than 240 species of trees growing at least 100 feet high. You can stretch your sea legs on dramatic mountain ranges, numerous trails, vast caves, coffee plantations, old sugar mills, and hundreds of beaches. No wonder San Juan is one of the busiest ports of call in the Caribbean. Like any other big city, San Juan has its share of crime, so guard your wallet or purse, and avoid walking in the area between Old San Juan and the Condado.

CURRENCY | The U.S. dollar is the official currency of Puerto Rico.

HOURS | Street shops are open Monday through Saturday from 9 to 6. Banks are generally open weekdays from 8 to 4 or 9 to 5; a few branches are open Saturday from 9 to noon or 1.

INTERNET | You can check your e-mail at **CyberNet Café** (✉ *1128 Av. Ashford, Condado*). **Diner's Restaurant** (✉ *357 Calle San Francisco, Old San Juan*) has Internet service.

TELEPHONES | Calling the United States from Puerto Rico is the same as calling within the U.S. You can use the long-distance telephone service office in the cruise-ship terminal, or you can use your calling card by dialing the toll-free access number of your long-distance provider from any pay phone. You'll find a phone center by the Paseo de la Princesa.

Coming Ashore

Cruise ships dock within a couple of blocks of Old San Juan. The Paseo de la Princesa, a tree-lined promenade beneath the city wall, is a nice place for a stroll—you can admire the local crafts and stop at the refreshment kiosks. A tourist information booth is in the cruise-terminal area. Major sights in the Old San Juan area are mere blocks from the piers, but be aware that the streets are narrow and steeply inclined in places.

It's particularly easy to get to Cataño and the Bacardí Rum Plant on your own; take the ferry (50¢) that leaves from the cruise piers every half hour and then a taxi from the other side. Taxis, which line up to meet ships, are the best option if you want to explore the city itself. White taxis labeled TAXI TURISTICO charge set fares of $6 to $16. Metered cabs authorized by the Public Service Commission charge an initial $1; after that, it's about 10¢ for each additional $\frac{1}{13}$ mi. If you take a metered taxi, insist that the meter be turned on, and pay only what is shown, plus a tip of 10% to 15%. You can negotiate with taxi drivers for specific trips, and you can hire a taxi for as little as $25 per hour for sightseeing tours.

Shore Excursions

Don't waste your money on an expensive guided walking tour of Old San Juan; the area is easily accessible, though some streets are steep and covered with uneven cobblestones. Free tourist trolleys will take you to all the top sights in Old San Juan from a stop across from Pier 4. If you want to see more of the island but don't want to drive, then you may want to consider a shore excursion, though almost all trips can be booked with local tour operators. The following are good choices in San Juan. They may not be offered by all cruise lines. Times and prices are approximate.

ATV Tour of El Yunque. This ATV tour goes around the El Yunque foothills. It's a very popular tour. ⊙ *4 hrs* 🖼 *$109.*

Bio-lumniscent Bay Kayaking Trip. Laguna Grande in Fajardo has a good bioluminscent bay. Kayaking, which will bring you closer to the water, is the best way to do the trip. ⊙ *5½ hrs* 🖼 *$69.*

El Yunque Rain Forest Hike. A 45-minute bus ride delivers you to the Caribbean National Forest, where you will be taken on a guided 2-hour hike. ⊙ *5½ hrs* 🖼 *$49.*

Horseback Riding. It's also possible to ride Paso Fino horses in the El Yunque foothills. ⊙ *4 hrs* 🖼 *$89.*

Exploring San Juan

Numbers in the margin correspond to points of interest on the Old San Juan map.

Old San Juan, the original city founded in 1521, contains authentic and carefully preserved examples of 16th- and 17th-century Spanish-colonial architecture. Graceful wrought-iron balconies decorated with lush hanging plants extend over narrow, cobblestone streets. Seventeenth-century walls still partially enclose the old city. Designated a U.S. National Historic Zone in 1950, it is packed with shops, open-air cafés, private homes, tree-shaded squares, monuments, plaques, pigeons, people, and traffic jams. It's faster to walk than to take a cab. If your feet fail you in Old San Juan, climb aboard the free open-air trolleys that rumble through the narrow streets. Take one from the docks or board anywhere along the route.

❽ Alcaldía. San Juan's city hall was built between 1604 and 1789. In 1841 extensive alterations were made so that it would resemble the city hall in Madrid. Renovations have refreshed the facade of the building and some interior rooms, but the architecture remains true to its colonial style. ✉ *153 Calle San Francisco, Plaza de Armas, Old San Juan* ☎ *787/724–7171* 🖅 *Free* ☉ *Weekdays 8–4.*

❹ **Casa Blanca.** The original structure on this site was a frame house built in 1521 as a home for Ponce de León. But he died in Cuba, never having lived in the home, which was virtually destroyed by a hurricane in 1523. Afterward, his son-in-law had the present masonry home built. His descendants occupied the house for 250 years. A museum devoted to archaeology is on the second floor. The surrounding garden, cooled by fountains, is a tranquil spot for a restorative pause. ✉ *1 Calle San Sebastián, Old San Juan* ☎ *787/725–1454* ⊕ *www.icp.gobierno.pr* 🖅 *$2* ☉ *Tues.–Sat. 8:30–4:20.*

❺ **Catedral de San Juan.** The Catholic shrine of Puerto Rico had humble beginnings in the early 1520s as a thatch-top, wooden structure. Hurricane winds tore off the thatch and destroyed the church. It was reconstructed in 1540, when it was given a graceful circular staircase and vaulted Gothic ceilings. Most of the work on the present cathedral, however, was done in the 19th century. The remains of Ponce de León are in a marble tomb near the transept. ✉ *151 Calle Cristo, Old San Juan* ☎ *787/722–0861* ⊕ *www.catedralsanjuan.com* 🖅 *$1 donation suggested* ☉ *Mon.–Sat. 8–5, Sun. 8–2:30.*

❸ **Convento de los Dominicos.** Built by Dominican friars in 1523, this convent often served as a shelter during Carib Indian attacks and, more recently, as headquarters for the Antilles command of the U.S. Army. Now home to some offices of the Institute of Puerto Rican Culture, the beautifully restored building contains religious manuscripts, artifacts, and art. The institute also maintains a book and music shop on the premises. Classical concerts are held here occasionally. ✉ *98 Calle Norzagaray, Old San Juan* ☎ *787/721–6866* 🖅 *Free* ☉ *Mon.–Sat. 9–5.*

❻ **La Fortaleza.** Sitting on a hill overlooking the harbor, La Fortaleza was built as a fortress in 1533. Not a very good fortress, mind you. It was attacked numerous times and taken twice, by the British in 1598 and by the Dutch in 1625. When the city's other fortifications were finished, La Fortaleza was transformed into a palace. Guided tours of the extensive gardens and the circular dungeon are conducted on the hour in English, on the half hour in Spanish; both include a short video presentation. ✉ *Calle Recinto Oeste, Old San Juan* ☎ *787/721–7000 Ext. 2211* ⊕ *www.fortaleza.gobierno.pr* 🖅 *Free* ☉ *Weekdays 9–3:30.*

9 **Fuerte San Cristóbal.** This 18th-century fortress guarded the city from land attacks. Even larger than El Morro, San Cristóbal was known in its heyday as the Gibraltar of the West Indies. ⊠ *Calle Norzagaray, Old San Juan* ☎ *787/729–6960* ⊕ *www.nps.gov/saju* 🎫 *$3; $5 includes admission to El Morro* ⊙ *Daily 9–5.*

1 **Fuerte San Felipe del Morro.** On a rocky promontory at the Old City's northwestern tip is El Morro, which was built by the Spaniards between 1540 and 1783. Rising 140 feet above the sea, the fort boasts six massive levels. It's a labyrinth of dungeons, barracks, towers, and tunnels. Its museum traces the history of the fortress. Tours and a video show are available in English. ⊠ *Calle Norzagaray, Old San Juan* ☎ *787/729–6960* ⊕ *www.nps.gov/saju* 🎫 *$3; $5 includes admission to Fuerte San Cristóbal* ⊙ *Daily 9–5.*

2 **Museo de las Américas.** On the second floor of the imposing former military barracks, Cuartel de Ballajá, the Museum's permanent exhibit, "Las Artes Populares en las Américas," focusing on the popular and folk art of Latin America, contains religious figures, musical instruments, basketwork, costumes, and farming and other implements. ⊠ *Calle Norzagaray and Calle del Morro, Old San Juan* ☎ *787/724–5052* ⊕ *www.museolasamericas.org* 🎫 *Free* ⊙ *Tues.–Sun. 10–4.*

❼ Plaza de Armas. This is the original main square of Old San Juan. The plaza, bordered by Calles San Francisco, Fortaleza, San José, and Cruz, has a lovely fountain with 19th-century statues representing the four seasons.

In **Puerta de Tierra,** ½ mi (1 km) east of the pier, is **El Capitolio,** Puerto Rico's white-marble capitol, dating from the 1920s. Another ½ mi (1 km) east, at the tip of Puerta de Tierra, tiny **Fort San Jerónimo** perches over the Atlantic like an afterthought. Added to San Juan's fortifications in the late 18th century, the structure barely survived the British attack of 1797.

Santurce, the district between Miramar on the west and the Laguna San José on the east, is a busy mixture of shops, markets, and offices. A Georgian-style structure, once a public school, is home of the **Museo Contemporáneo del Arte de Puerto Rico** (*Museum of Contemporary Puerto Rican Art;* ⊠ *Av. Ponce de León at Av. R. H. Todd, Santurce* ☏ *787/ 977–4030* ⊕ *www.museocontemporaneopr.org*). Closed Monday; free. The former San Juan Municipal Hospital is now the **Museo de Arte de Puerto Rico** (*Museum of Puerto Rican Art;* ⊠ *299 Av. José De Diego, Santurce* ☏ *787/977–6277* ⊕ *www.mapr.org*), which displays a permanent collection of Puerto Rican art and changing exhibits. Closed Monday; $6 admission.

Casa Bacardí Visitor Center. Exiled from Cuba, the Bacardí family built a small distillery here in the 1950s. Today it's one of the world's largest, with the capacity to produce 100,000 gallons of spirits a day and 221 million cases a year. You can hop on a little tram to take a 45-minute tour of the bottling plant, distillery, and museum. Yes, you'll be offered a free sample. If you don't want to drive, you can reach the factory by taking the ferry from Pier 2 for 50¢ each way and then a public car from the ferry pier to the factory for about $2 or $3 per person. ⊠ *Rte. 888, Km 2.6, Cataño* ☏ *787/788–1500 or 787/788–8400* ⊕ *www. casabacardi.org* ☑ *Free* ☉ *Mon.–Sat. 8:30–5:30, Sun. 10–5. Tours every 15–30 min.*

Shopping

San Juan is not a duty-free port, so you won't find bargains on electronics and perfumes. However, shopping for native crafts can be fun. Popular souvenirs and gifts include *santos* (small, hand-carved figures of saints or religious scenes), hand-rolled cigars, handmade lace, and carnival masks. Look for vendors selling crafts from kiosks at the **Artesanía Puertorriqueña** (⊠ *Plaza Dársenas, Old San Juan, San Juan* ☏ *787/ 722–1709*) in the tourism company's La Casita near Pier 1. Several vendors also set up shop to sell articles such as belts, handbags, and toys along Calle San Justo in front of Plaza Dársenas. **Artefacto** (⊠ *99 Calle Cristo* ☏ *787/386–6164*) is the cleverest shop in San Juan. At first the items on display look like traditional crafts, but look again and you notice that everything is a little offbeat. A little wooden shrine, for example, might be sheltering an image of Marilyn Monroe. At the **Convento de los Dominicos** (⊠ *98 Calle Norzagaray, Old San Juan, San Juan* ☏ *787/721–6866*)—the Dominican Convent on the north side of the old city that houses the offices of the Instituto de Cultura Puertor-riqueña—you can find baskets, masks, the famous *cuatro* guitars, san-tos, and reproductions of Taíno artifacts.

Activities

GOLF Though there are no courses in San Juan proper, it's possible to do a golf outing to one of Puerto Rico's stellar courses as a day trip. The Robert Trent Jones–designed courses at the **Hyatt Dorado Beach Resort & Country Club** (✉ *Rte. 693, Km 10.8, Dorado* ☎ *787/796–1234 or 800/233–1234*) got a face-lift in 2005. Six new holes and six redesigned holes mean that the Pineapple and the Sugar Cane courses feel completely differ-ent. With El Yunque as a backdrop, the two 18-hole courses at the **Westin Río Mar Beach Golf Resort & Spa** (✉ *6000 Río Mar Blvd., Río Grande* ☎ *787/888–6000*) are inspirational. The River Course was designed by Greg Norman, the Ocean course by George and Tom Fazio.

Beaches

By law, all of Puerto Rico's beaches are open to the public. The **Balneario de Carolina** is so close to the airport that the leaves rustle when planes take off. The long stretch of sand, which runs parallel to Avenida Los Gobernadores, is shaded by palms and almond trees. **Playa del Condado** is overshadowed by an unbroken string of hotels and apartment buildings. Beach bars, water-sports outfitters, and chair-rental places abound. The stretch of sand near Calle Vendig is especially popular with the gay community.

Where to Eat

Tips of 15% to 20% are expected, and appreciated, by restaurant wait-staff if a service charge is not included in the bill.

$$$–$$$$ ✕ **Aguaviva.** The name means "jellyfish," which explains why this ultra-cool, ultramodern place has lighting fixtures shaped like that sea crea-ture. Elegantly groomed oysters and clams float on cracked ice along the raw bar. The extensive menu is alive with inventive ceviches, some with tomato or roasted red peppers and olives, and fresh takes on clas-sics like paella. For something more filling, try dorado served with a shrimp salsa, or tuna accompanied by seafood enchiladas. ✉ *364 Calle La Fortaleza, Old San Juan* ☎ *787/722–0665* ✍ *Reservations not accepted* ▭ *AE, D, MC, V.*

$–$$ ✕ **La Fonda del Jibarito.** Sanjuaneros have favored this casual, family-run restaurant for years. The conch ceviche and chicken fricassee are among the specialties on the menu of comida criollo dishes. The back porch is filled with plants, and the dining room is filled with fanciful depictions of life on the street outside. ✉ *280 Calle Sol, Old San Juan* ☎ *787/725–8375* ✍ *Reservations not accepted* ▭ *AE, MC, V.*

Nightlife

Almost every ship stays in San Juan late or even overnight to give pas-sengers an opportunity to revel in the nightlife—the most sophisticated in the Caribbean.

CASINOS By law, all casinos are in hotels. The atmosphere is refined, and many patrons dress to the nines, but informal attire (no shorts or tank tops) is usually fine. Casinos set their own hours, which change seasonally, but generally operate from noon to 4 AM, although the casino in the Condado Plaza Hotel & Casino is open 24 hours. Other hotels with casinos include the Inter-Continental San Juan Resort & Casino, the Ritz-Carlton San Juan Hotel, Spa & Casino, and the Sheraton Old San Juan Hotel & Casino.

BARS & DANCE CLUBS
A wildly popular hole-in-the-wall, **El Batey** (⊠ *101 Calle Cristo, Old San Juan* ☎ *787/725–1787*) won't win any prizes for its decor. Grab a marker to add your own message to the graffiti-covered walls, or add your business card to the hundreds that cover the lighting fixtures. The ceiling may leak, but the jukebox has the best selection of oldies in town. Join locals in a game of pool. **Candela** (⊠ *110 San Sebastián, Old San Juan* ☎ *787/977–4305*), a lounge–art gallery housed in a historic building, hosts some of the most innovative local DJs on the island and often invites star spinners from New York or London. This is the island's best showcase for experimental dance music. The festive, late-night haunt is open Tuesday through Saturday from 8 PM onward, and the conversation can be as stimulating as the dance floor. At **Liquid** (⊠ *Water Club, 2 Calle Tartak, Isla Verde* ☎ *787/725–4664 or 787/725–4675*), the lobby lounge of San Juan's chicest boutique hotel, glass walls are filled with undulating water, and the fashionable patrons drink wild cocktails to pounding music. With a large dance and stage area and smokin' Afro-Cuban bands, **Rumba** (⊠ *152 Calle San Sebastián, Old San Juan, San Juan* ☎ *787/725–4407*) is one of the best parties in town. Popular with gay men and lesbians, **Starz** (⊠ *365 Av. de Diego, at Av. Ponce de León, Santurce* ☎ *787/721–8645*) is a cavernous club with dancing on Friday and Saturday nights, as well as a popular after-the-beach party on Sunday evening.

SANTO DOMINGO, DOMINICAN REPUBLIC

Eileen
Robinson Smith
Spanish civilization in the New World began in Santo Domingo's 12-block Zona Colonial (Colonial Zone). As you stroll its narrow streets, it's easy to imagine this old city as it was when the likes of Columbus, Cortés, and Ponce de León walked the cobblestones, when pirates sailed in and out of the harbor, and when colonists first started building the New World's largest city. Tourist brochures tout that "history comes alive here"—a surprisingly truthful statement. However, many tourists bypass the large, sprawling, and noisy city; it's their loss. The Dominican Republic's seaside capital—despite such detractions as poverty and sprawl, not to mention a population of some 2 million people—has some of the country's best hotels, restaurants, and nightlife (not to mention great casinos). Many of these are right on or near the Malecón and within the historic Zona Colonial area, which is separated from the rest of the city by Parque Independencia. If your ship calls or even embarks here, you'll be treated to a vibrant cultural center unlike any other in the Caribbean.

Essentials

CURRENCY
The Dominican peso (RD$32.38 to US$1). Independent merchants willingly accept U.S. dollars, but you may need to change some money. Cam-

bios (money exchange offices) are common, but you'll get the best rates at either a bank or a casino. Banco Popular has ATMS in the Zona Colonial, but you will be able to get only pesos.

HOURS Offices and shops are open weekdays from 8 to noon and 2 to 6, Saturday from 8 to noon. About half the stores stay open all day, no longer closing for a midday siesta. Attractions are generally seen between 9 AM and 5 to 6 PM

INTERNET In the Colonial Zone, a convenient place to check your e-mail is **Verizon Comunicaciones** (✉ *256 Calle Conde, Zona Colonial* ☎ *809/221–4249*). You will have to pay cash—pesos or dollars. Look "up," and you will see many Internet cafés on The Conde, usually with second-floor locations.

TELEPHONES From the D.R., you need only dial 1 plus the area code and number to call the U.S. To make a local call, you must now dial 809 plus the seven-digit number. Phone cards, which are sold at gift shops and grocery stores, can give you considerable savings on your calls home. If you have a tri-band GSM phone, it should work on the island. Verizon calling centers, like **Verizon Comunicaciones** (✉ *256 Calle Conde, Zona Colonial* ☎ *809/221–4249*) have equally good rates to the States and Canada, now about 35¢ U.S. a minute. Know you need to pay in cash.

Coming Ashore

Santo Domingo has two cruise-ship terminals. The Port of Don Diego is on the Ozuma River, facing the Don Diego Highway, and across the street are steps that lead up to the main pedestrian shopping street of the Zona Colonia, Calle Conde. Diagonally across the river from Don Diego is the Sans Souci Dock, on avenida Francisco Alberto Caaman; from Sans Souci, you will need to jump into a waiting taxi ($5). Should you want to go to The Malecón or shop in the modern city, $20 an hour is the going rate. Don't rent a car; it's expensive, and traffic and parking are both difficult.

The new Don Diego terminal is a lovely yellow and white building, with faux gas lights and artistic mosaic work with an ocean theme on the facade; unfortunately, it has few passenger facilities except for three ATMs. When a ship is in, vendors set up colorful tables to sell their wares: cigars; larimar and amber jewelry, and handicrafts. The Ministry of Tourism has a table with an English-speaking staffer to answer questions and to assist passengers with taxi negotiations. No formal tours are offered here, although some passengers do partake of the tours offered on board their ship. The remodeling of the Sans Souci Dock is a work in progress, which is slated for completion in November 2007.

You can easily tour the Zona Colonial on your own; you can get a free walking-tour map and (usually) brochures in English at the Secretaria de Estado de Turismo office at Parque Colón, where you may be approached by freelance, English-speaking guides. They'll work enthusiastically for $20 an hour for four people. Do wear comfortable shoes.

AIRPORT
TRANSFERS If you are embarking in Santo Domingo, you should fly into **Las Américas International Airport** (SDQ ✉ *Santo Domingo* ☎ *809/549–0450*), about 24 km (15 mi) east of downtown. Transportation into the city is strictly by taxi; figure on $35 for a taxi to or from hotels on the Malecón or in the Zona Colonial. You'll be greeted by a melee of hawking taxi drivers and their English-speaking solicitors (who expect to be tipped, as do the freelance porters who will undoubtedly scoop up your luggage). If you are spending the night in Santo Domingo before a cruise, you can probably arrange a driver through your hotel, so you'll be met with someone holding a sign with your name (it's worth the extra

> ## SANTO DOMINGO BEST BETS
>
> - **Dining.** Some of the D.R.'s best restaurants can be found in the capital. Take advantage of them if you have any extra time to spend here.
> - **Shopping.** The country's best shopping scene can be found in Santo Domingo, and Calle Conde is the main shopping street of Zona Colonial.
> - **Zona Colonial.** Santo Domingo's colonial zone is a World Heritage Site and a great place to shop and stroll.

$10 or so to avoid the hassle). If you're going straight to your cruise ship, consider taking the cruise line's prearranged transfer. When you disembark from your ship, expect long lines at check-in, and be sure to give yourself a full two hours for check-in and security.

Shore Excursions

All-inclusive Beach Trip. If you don't want to see the historic parts of Santo Domingo, then this is probably your best alternative, though you'll find better and cheaper options on other islands. You'll get free food and drink and the option to lie about and do nothing. ⊙ *5 hrs* ▭ *$89.*

Santo Domingo Walking Tour. The best way to see the Zona Colonial is on foot, and if you don't feel comfortable doing it on your own, this is your best option. ⊙ *3½ hrs* ▭ *$45.*

Santo Domingo Sightseeing. If you want to do a bus tour of the city, the better option is one that includes a tour of the botanical gardens as well as the other main sights. ⊙ *3¼ hrs* ▭ *$39.*

Exploring Santo Domingo

Numbers in the margin correspond to points of interest on the Santo Domingo map.

History buffs will want to spend a day exploring the many "firsts" of our continent. A horse and carriage ride throughout the Colonial Zone costs $20 an hour. The steeds are no thoroughbreds, but they clip right along, though any commentary will be in Spanish. You can also negotiate to use them as a taxi, say down to the Malecón. The drivers hang out in front of the Sofitel Nicolas Ovando hotel.

❶ **Alcazar de Colón.** The 22-room castle of Don Diego Colón, built in 1517, has 40-inch-thick coral-limestone walls. The Renaissance-style structure, with its balustrade and double row of arches, is furnished in a style to which the viceroy of the island would have been accustomed. ✉ *Plaza de*

España, off Calle Emiliano Tejera at foot of Calle Las Damas, Zona Colonial ☎ *809/687–5361* 🎟 *RD$20* ⊘ *Mon. and Wed.–Fri. 9–5, Sat. 9–4, Sun. 9–1.*

❸ **Calle Las Damas.** The Street of the Ladies was named after the elegant ladies of the court who, in the Spanish tradition, promenaded in the evening. Here you can see a sundial dating from 1753 and the Casa de los Jesuitas, which houses a fine research library for colonial history as well as the Institute for Hispanic Culture; admission is free, and it's open weekdays from 8 to 4:30.

❹ **Catedral Santa María la Menor.** The coral-limestone facade of the first cathedral in the New World (1540) towers over the south side of the Parque Colón. Spanish workmen began building the cathedral in 1514, but left to search for gold in Mexico. The church, with its altar of hammered silver, is composed of architectural elements from the late Gothic style. ⊠ *Calle Arzobispo Meriño, Zona Colonial* ☎ *809/689–1920* 🎟 *Free* ⊘ *Mon.–Sat. 9–4; Sun. Masses begin at 6 AM.*

❺ **El Malecón.** Avenida George Washington, better known as the Malecón, runs along the Caribbean and has tall palms, cafés, hotels, and sea breezes.

❷ **Parque Colón.** The huge statue of Christopher Columbus in the park named after him dates from 1887 and is the work of sculptor Ernesto Gilbert.

Like all the parks in The Zone, this one has been restored. ⊠ *El Conde at Arzobispo Meriño, Zona Colonial.*

Beaches

If you are just in port for a day, you'll have a better time if you skip the beach and spend some time in the Zona Colonial and on The Malecón. The closest good beach to Santo Domingo is **Boca Chica** (⊠ *Autopista Las Americas, 21 mi (34 km) east of Santo Domingo Boca Chica*), which is popular mainly with Dominicans and Europeans, but is one of the better places to go to the beach. Hang out at one of the popular restaurants, like El Pelicano.

Shopping

Exquisitely hand-wrapped cigars continue to be the hottest commodity coming out of the D.R. Only reputable cigar shops sell the real thing. Dominican rum and coffee are also good buys. *Mamajuana,* an herbal liqueur, is said to be the Dominican answer to Viagra. Look also for the delicate, faceless ceramic figurines that symbolize Dominican culture. Though locally crafted products are often very affordable, expect to pay for designer jewelry made of amber and larimar, an indigenous semiprecious stone the color of the Caribbean. Amber, a fossilization of resin from a prehistoric pine tree, often encasing ancient animal and plant life, from leaves to spiders to tiny lizards, is mined extensively. (Beware of fakes, which are especially prevalent in street stalls.)

One of the main shopping streets in the Zone is **Calle El Conde,** a pedestrian thoroughfare. The dull and dusty stores with dated merchandise are giving way to some hip, new shops. However, many of the offerings are still of a caliber and cost that the Dominicans can afford. The **Malecón Center** is the newest complex and is adjacent to the nearly new Hilton Santo Domingo. It will house 170 shops, boutiques, and services plus several movie theaters, when completely occupied. In the tower above are luxury apartments and Sammy Sosa, in one of the penthouses. **Plaza Central,** between Avenidas Winston Churchill and 27 de Febrero, is where you can find many top international boutiques and a Jenny Polanco shop (an upscale Dominican designer who has incredible white outfits, artistic jewelry, and purses).

Ambar Tres (⊠ *La Atarazana 3, Zona Colonial* ☎ 809/688–0474) carries a wide selection of amber jewelry. **Cigar King** (⊠ *Calle Conde 208, Baguero Bldg., Zona Colonial* ☎ 809/686–4987) keeps Dominican and Cuban cigars in a temperature-controlled cedar room. **L'Ile Au Tresor** (⊠ *Arzobispo Merino #352, Esq. Calle Mercedes (across from Sofitel Frances), Zona Colonial* ☎ 809/685–3983) may have a "pirates of the Caribbean" theme, but it is fun and has some of the most attractive and creative designer pieces in native larimar, amber, and even conch. **Plaza Toledo Bettye's Galeria** (⊠ *Isabel la Católica 163, Zona Colonial* ☎ 809/688–7649) sells a fascinating array of artwork, including Haitian voodoo banners, metal sculptures, even souvenirs, chandeliers, and estate jewelry.

Where to Eat

★ **$–$$$**   ✕ **Café Bellini.** This café has always had a panache far and above its counterparts, for the Italian owners also have the adjacent furniture design center. The moderne, wicker-weave barrel chairs, and the contemporary art and light fixtures, are all achingly hip. Previously, the domineering Italian chef would send out what he wanted you to eat and the cost was celestial. The present chef is right on and the prices are democratic. The menu is the same at lunch and dinner and your first glance should be at the daily specials, where a main course, like the trio of raviolis made with spinach, beet, and pumpkin prices out at about $10. If local king crab is on the menu, order it. It's served in its crimson shell with a fresh tomato-basil sauce over spaghetti. Service is laudable and it's friendly and fun here; you can even choose the CDs, say a Tony Bennett. ✉ *Arzobispo Merino, corner of Padre Bellini, Zona Colonial* ☎ *809/686–3387* ⌕ *Reservations essential* ▭ *AE, MC, V.*

★ **$–$$$**   ✕ **La Residence.** This fine-dining enclave has always had the setting—Spanish colonial architecture, with pillars and archways overlooking a courtyard—and an esoteric lunch-dinner menu with high prices that did not always deliver. Now it has a seasoned French chef (and manager) serving classic yet innovative cuisine with many moderately priced choices. The daily Menu del Chef has a main course for less than $10. It could be brochettes of spit-roasted duck, chicken with poivre sauce, and vegetable risotto. You could start with a salad of panfried young squid for about $5 and go bonkers over the $3 dark- and white-chocolate terrine. Veer from the daily specials menu and it's certainly more pricey but fair; even the grilled fillet and braised oxtail with foie gras sauce and wild mushrooms is reasonable. ✉ *In Sofitel Nicolas de Ovando, Calle Las Damas, Zona Colonial* ☎ *809/685–9955* ▭ *AE, MC, V.*

Where to Stay

Since Santo Domingo is the home port for at least one cruise ship, we've recommended some places to stay in case you choose to spend the night here before you sail. When looking for a good price at a Santo Domingo hotel, go online first when checking rates, as the Internet deals can be a fraction of the rack rates. Last-minute price breaks are another possibility.

★ **$$$–$$$$**   ▦ **Sofitel Nicolas Ovando.** This luxury hotel, sculpted from the residence of the first Governor of the Americas, is the best thing to happen in the Zone since Diego Columbus's palace was finished in 1517. Colonial rooms have canopied king-size beds, tall ceilings, original stone window benches, and shutters. Some prefer the sunny (smaller) rooms in the contemporary annex; with the river views, these are smart examples of French minimalist style. The pool is shaded by trees and tropical plantings, and swimmers leave the sun for a fitness break in the gym. The bar is a social scene, particularly when the music man plays at cocktail hour, which includes complimentary hors d'oeuvres. The breakfast spread is lavish. ✉ *Calle Las Damas, Zona Colonial* ☎ *809/*

685–9955 or 800/763–4835 🖷 *809/685–9302* ⊕ *www.sofitel.com* ➲ *100 rooms, 4 suites* ☐ *In-room: safe, refrigerator. In-hotel: restaurant, room service, bars, pool, gym, concierge, laundry service, public Internet, public Wi-Fi, parking (no fee), some pets allowed* ☰ *AE, MC, V* ❀ *BP.*

★ **$–$$** ⊡ **The Hilton Santo Domingo.** This has become *the* address on the Malecón for businesspeople, convention attendees, and leisure travelers. The five luxurious executive floors are wired for business, each with three phones, Internet ports, actual corner offices with imposing desks and ergonomic leather chairs, and DSL lines. Creature comforts are satisfied with the plush duvets, rain showers, and surround sound in the bathrooms, oversize flat-screen TVs, and sea views. Service might just be the best in the country, and rates are surprisingly moderate, particularly with online packages that include a lavish and healthy buffet breakfast. ⊠ *Av. George Washington 500, Zona Colonial* ☎ *809/685–0000* 🖷 *809/685–0202* ⊕ *www.hiltoncaribbean.com* ➲ *228 rooms, 32 suites* ☐ *In-room: safe, refrigerator, Ethernet. In-hotel: 2 restaurants, bars, pool, gym, spa, concierge, executive floor, public Internet, public Wi-Fi* ☰ *AE, D, MC, V* ❀ *EP.*

SANTO TOMÁS DE CASTILLA, GUATEMALA

Jeff Van Fleet

Guatemala's short Caribbean shoreline doesn't generate the buzz of that of neighboring Belize and Mexico. The coast weighs in at a scant 123 km (74 mi), and this mostly highland country, which wears its indigenous culture on its sleeve, has historically looked inland rather than to the sea. You'll be drawn inland, too, with a variety of shore excursions. This is the land of the Maya, after all. But there's plenty to keep you occupied here in the lowlands. Tourist brochures tout the Caribbean coast as "The Other Guatemala." The predominantly indigenous and Spanish cultures of the highlands give way to an Afro-Caribbean tradition that listens more closely to the rhythms of far-off Jamaica rather than taking its cue from Guatemala City. Think of it as mixing a little reggae with your salsa.

Essentials

CURRENCY
The Guatemalan quetzal, named for the brightly plumed bird that is the symbol of the country (Q7.67 to US$1). Take care of any banking matters in the cruise terminal in Santo Tomás de Castilla. You'll find ATMs in Puerto Barrios and Livingston but nowhere else in this region.

HOURS
Businesses generally are open from 8 to 6, with many closing for a couple of hours over lunch.

INTERNET
The Terminal de Cruceros in Santo Tomás de Castilla has Internet computers for your use, the easiest option if you're a day visitor.

TELEPHONES
Guatemalan phone numbers have eight digits. There are no city or area codes. Simply dial the number for any in-country call. Most towns have offices of Telgua, the national telephone company, where you can place both national and international calls. Avoid the ubiquitous public phones with signs promising FREE CALLS TO THE USA. The number back home being called gets socked with a hefty bill.

Coming Ashore

Cruise ships dock at the modern, spacious Terminal de Cruceros, where you'll find a bank, post office, money exchange, telephones, Internet access, a lively crafts market, and an office of INGUAT, Guatemala's national tourist office. A marimba band serenades you with its clinking xylophonelike music; a Caribbean ensemble dances for you (and may even pull you in to take part.)

Taxis, both vehicular and water, take you to various destinations in the area. Plan on paying $2 to Santo Tomás de Castilla proper, and $5 to Puerto Barrios. Boats transport cruise visitors to Livingston, charging about $5 for the 20-minute trip. The Amantique Bay Resort provides water taxis from port to resort for $8 per person. Vehicular taxis charge $15 per head to travel by land to the resort.

Shore Excursions

We consider these to be among the better shore excursions for Santo Tomás. They may not be offered by all lines, and tour names may differ as well. Times and prices are approximate.

Río Dulce Tour. Spanish explorers and pirates all made their way upriver on the Río Dulce—the construction of a 16th-century fort stopped the latter from getting too far—and your journey through the heavily forested canyon will be no less intriguing and exciting. Tours often include a stop in Livingston. ☉ *4 hrs* 🚢 *$89.*

Quiriguá Archaeological Ruins. Other Maya ruins in the region are bigger and more spectacular, but those of the sixth-century AD city of Quiriguá offer you no less a fascinating experience, on a smaller and more manageable scale. The added bonus? Quiriguá lies close to the coast, making it a doable half-day excursion. ☉ *4½ hrs* 🚢 *$89.*

Banana Plantation Tour. Neighboring Honduras was the original "banana republic," but the name once applied to Guatemala too. The Caribbean is still banana country, and Chiquita is still one of the region's main employers. A visit to its plantation at nearby Omagua lets you see the processing from cultivation to packing and shipping of the country's second most famous crop. (Coffee is the first.) ☉ *4 hrs* 🚢 *$49.*

Exploring Santo Tomás de Castilla

Numbers in the margin correspond to points of interest on the Santo Tomás map.

❸ **Amatique Bay.** "Bahía de Amatique" denotes the large bay that washes the Caribbean coast of Guatemala and southern Belize, but for most travelers the name is inexorably linked with the Amatique Bay Resort & Marina, part of the Clarion chain, and the region's only five-star hotel. The 61-room resort opens itself up for day visitors, and many cruise passengers stop by for a drink, a meal, or an entire day of swimming, watersliding, kayaking, horseback riding, or bicycling. ✉ *10 km (6 mi) north of Santo Tomás* ☎ *7948–1800, 2421–3333 in Guatemala City* ⊕ *www. amatiquebay.net.*

❼ **Copán.** The famous Maya ruins of Copán lie just across the border from this region in neighboring Honduras, but are accessible enough from Santo Tomás to be an excursion on many itineraries. Bring your passport since this entails an international border crossing. For a description of the ruins and what you will experience there, see ⇨ *Copán Ruins in Roatán, Honduras* ✉ *50 km (30 mi) south of Quiriguá* ☎ *No phone* 🚢 *$10* ☉ *Daily 8–4.*

❹ **Livingston.** Visitors compare Livingston with Puerto Barrios across the bay, and the former wins hands down, for its sultry, seductive Caribbean flavor. Wood houses, some on stilts, congregate in this old fishing town, once an important railroad hub, but today inaccessible by land from the outside world. Livingston proudly trumpets its Garífuna heritage, a culture unique to Central America's eastern coast and descended from the intermarriage of African slaves with Caribbean in-digenous peoples. Music and dance traditions and a Caribbean-accented English remain, even if old-timers lament the creeping outside influ-ences, namely Spanish, rap, and reggae. ⊠ *25 km (15 mi) by water north-west of Santo Tomás.*

② **Puerto Barrios.** Puerto Barrios maintains the atmosphere of an old ba-nana town, humid and a tad down at the heels, perhaps longing for bet-ter days. Santo Tomás has replaced it as the country's largest port, and you'll likely zip through the Caribbean coast's biggest city on your way to somewhere else, but the cathedral and municipal market are worth a look if you find yourself here. Water taxis depart the municipal docks for Livingston, across the bay, from where you start your trip up the Río Dulce. ⊠ *5 km (3 mi) north of Santo Tomás de Castilla.*

④ **Quiriguá.** Construction began on the Guatemalan lowlands' most im-portant Maya ruins about AD 500. Its hieroglyphics tell its story: Quiriguá served at the time as a satellite state under the control of Copán, about 50 km (30 mi) away in present-day Honduras. By the height of its power in the seventh century, Quiriguá had overpowered Copán, but just as quickly, fell back into submissive status. Quiriguá's ruins still today live in the shadow of their more well-known neighbor across the bor-der, and of the Tikal ruins in the northern part of Guatemala, but a visit here is rewarding for the carvings of *stelae,* the ornate sculptures de-picting the city's rulers, and the largest such works in Central America. (Quiriguá's stelae stand 10 meters (33 feet) tall, dwarfing those of Copán.) Ease of access from the Caribbean coast makes Quiriguá well worth a visit too. ⊠ *90 km (54 mi) southwest of Santo Tomás* ☎ *No phone* 🎟 *$4* ☉ *Daily 8–4.*

⑤ **Río Dulce.** The natural crown jewel of this region is the 13,000-hectare (32,000-acre) national park that protects the river leading inland from Livingston to Lago de Izabal, Guatemala's largest lake. Pelicans, herons, egrets, and terns nest and fly along the Río Dulce, which cuts through a heavily forested limestone canyon. Excursions often approach the park by land, but we recommend making the trip upriver from Livingston to immerse yourself in the entire Indiana Jones experience. ⊠ *South-west of Livingston.*

The **Castillo de San Felipe de Lara** (☎ *No phone* ☉ *Daily 8–5* 🎟 *$1*) looms inland over the river's entrance to Lake Izabal near the town of Fronteras. Spanish colonists constructed the fortress in 1595 to guard the inland waterway from incursions by Dutch and English pirates. A 1999 earthquake in this region destroyed the river pier as well as dam-aging portions of the fort. If you wish to visit, rather than simply see the fort from the water, you need to approach the park overland rather than upriver.

A short launch from Fronteras takes you to **Hacienda Tijax** (☎ *7902–0859*), an old rubber plantation, now reforestation project, which offers hiking and kayaking, and a chance to view the cultivation of orchids and spices.

❶ **Santo Tomás de Castilla.** Belgian immigrants settled Santo Tomás in the 19th century, but little remains of their heritage today, save for the preponderance of French and Flemish names in the local cemetery. Most visitors move on. Santo Tomás has experienced a small renaissance as the country's most important port, receiving growing numbers of cruise and cargo ships, and serving as the headquarters of the Guatemalan navy.

❽ **Tikal.** The high point of any trip to Guatemala is a visit to Tikal, Central America's most impressive indigenous ruins. There's nothing quite like the sight of the towering temples, ringed on all sides by miles of virgin forest, but you need a lot of *quetzales* to get here—tour operators charge about $500 for a day trip from Santo Tomás. The cruise lines that do offer Tikal on their itineraries transport you via plane from the airstrip outside Santo Tomás to the small airport in Santa Elena near the ruins.

Although the region was home to Maya communities as early as 600 BC, Tikal itself wasn't established until sometime around 200 BC. By AD 500 it's estimated that the city had a population of close to 100,000. For almost 1,000 years Tikal remained engulfed by the jungle. The conquistadors who came here searching for gold and silver must have passed right by the overgrown ruins, mistaking them for rocky hills. Excavation began in earnest in the mid-1800s. Today, after more than 150 years of digging, researchers say that Tikal includes some 3,000 buildings. Countless more are still covered by the jungle. The ancient city's center is filled with awe-inspiring temples and acropolises. **Temple I,** known as the Temple of the Great Jaguar, is in the dramatic **Great Plaza.** It was built around AD 700 by Ah-Cacao. His tomb was discovered beneath the Temple of the Great Jaguar, and the theory is that his queen is buried beneath **Temple II,** called the Temple of the Masks. The **North Acropolis** is a mind-boggling conglomeration of temples built over layers of previous construction. Be sure to see the stone mask of the rain god at Temple 33.

If you climb to the top of one of the pyramids, you'll see the roofs of others rising above the rain forest's canopy. **Temple V** is now open to the public, and **Temple IV,** the tallest-known structure built by the Maya, offers an unforgettable view from the top. At the park headquarters, two good archaeological museums display Mayan artifacts. ⊠ *Parque Nacional Tikal* ☎ *No phone* 🕮 *$7* ☯ *Daily 6–6.*

Shopping

The rest of Guatemala overflows with indegnous crafts and art, but the famous market towns of the highlands are nowhere to be found in the Caribbean region. Quite honestly, your best bet for shopping is the Terminal de Cruceros at Santo Tomás de Castilla, and you'll have plenty of opportunity to buy before you board your ship. What you'll find here comes from the Guatemala's highlands—the Caribbean has never developed a strong artisan tradition—with a good selection of fabrics, weavings, woodwork, and basketry to choose from. Markets in Puerto Barrios and Livingston, the only real urban areas you'll encounter in this region, are more geared to the workaday needs of its residents rather than visitors.

Activities

BEACHES &
WATER SPORTS
A beach culture has just never developed in this region of Guatemala the way it has in neighboring Belize and Mexico. The only real beach in the region is found within the confines of the **Amantique Bay Resort & Marina.** (✉ *5 km (3 mi) north of Puerto Barrios*), which is the only place here that has a resort feel to it. Day visitors partake of swimming, waterslides, and kayaking. The resort's launch will bring you over from the cruise-ship terminal in Santo Tomás.

HIKING &
KAYAKING
Hacienda Tijax (✉ *Las Fronteras* ☎ *7902–0859*), inland, near the point where the Río Dulce meets Lake Izabal provides kayaking and hiking for day visitors.

Where to Eat

$–$$$$ ✕ **Amatique Bay Resort & Marina.** Most cruise visitors pass through the Amatique Bay Resort to drink or dine, and you have three options to choose from at this complex: diners line up for the Caribbean-style buffet at Puerto Chico; Mango's provides a romantic place to take in the sunset—the resort sits on the eastern side of Amantique Bay, so, yes, the sunsets are fabulous; and El Berrinche offers a formal dining experience unmatched by any other place in the region (and by few other places in Guatemala). Seafood reigns at all the restaurants. ✉ *5 km (3 mi) north of Puerto Barrios* ☎ *7948–1800* 🞸 *AE, DC, MC, V.*

TORTOLA, BRITISH VIRGIN ISLANDS

Lynda Lohr
Once a sleepy backwater, Tortola is definitely busy these days, particularly when several cruise ships tie up at the Road Town dock. Passengers crowd the streets and shops, and open-air jitneys filled with cruise-ship passengers create bottlenecks on the island's byways. That said, most folks visit Tortola to relax on its deserted sands or linger over lunch at one of its many delightful restaurants. Beaches are never more than a few miles away, and the steep green hills that form Tortola's spine are fanned by gentle trade winds. The neighboring islands glimmer like emeralds in a sea of sapphire. Tortola doesn't have many historic sights, but it does have abundant natural beauty. Beware of the roads, which are extraordinarily steep and twisting, making driving demanding. The best beaches are on the north shore.

Essentials

CURRENCY
The U.S. dollar is the official currency. Some places accept cash only, but major credit cards are widely accepted. You'll find ATMs in Road Town.

HOURS
Banking hours are usually Monday through Thursday from 9 to 2:30 and Friday from 9 to 2:30 and 4:30 to 6. Post offices are open weekdays from 9 to 5 and Saturday from 9 to noon. Stores are generally open Monday through Saturday from 9 to 5. Some may be open on Sunday.

INTERNET
Trellis Bay Cybercafé (✉ *Trellis Bay, Tortola* ☎ *284/495–2447*).

TELEPHONES To call anywhere in the BVI once you've arrived, dial all seven digits. A local call from a pay phone costs 25¢, but such phones are sometimes on the blink. An alternative is a Caribbean phone card, available in $5, $10, and $20 denominations. They're sold at most major hotels and many stores and can be used to call within the BVI, as well as all over the Caribbean, and to access USADirect from special phone-card phones. If you're coming ashore at the cruise-ship dock, you'll find pay phones right on the dock. If a tender drops you right in Road Town at the ferry dock, phones are located in the terminal.

Cingular has service in nearby St. John, USVI, so it's possible to get service from there in some spots in Road Town and along the waterfront highway that leads to the West End. You may not have to pay international roaming charges on some U.S. cell phone plans if you can connect with this network.

Coming Ashore

Large cruise ships usually anchor in Road Town Harbor and bring passengers ashore by tender. Small ships can sometimes tie up at Wickham's Cay dock. Either way, it's a short stroll to Road Town. If your ship isn't going to Virgin Gorda, you can make the 12-mi (19-km) trip by ferry from the dock in Road Town in about 30 minutes for about $27 round-trip, but you'll still have to take a taxi to get to The Baths for swimming and snorkeling, so it's not necessarily a bad deal to go on your ship's shore excursion.

There are taxi stands at Wickham's Cay and in Road Town. Taxis are unmetered, and there are minimums for travel throughout the island, so it's usually cheaper to travel in groups. Negotiate to get the best fares, as there is no set fee schedule. If you are in the islands for just a day, it's usually more cost-effective to share a taxi with a small group than to rent a car, since you'd have to pay an agency at Wickham's Cay or in Road Town $10 for a temporary license and car-rental charges of at least $50 a day. You must be at least age 25 to rent a car.

Shore Excursions

We consider these to be among the better shore excursions for Tortola. They may not be offered by all lines, and tour names may differ as well. Times and prices are approximate.

Sage Mountain National Park Hike and Snorkel. The first stop on this excursion is the highest peak in the Virgin Islands, where you do a 1-mi (1½-km) hike through the rain forest to get to the best view. Then it's to a white-sand beach (usually Cane Garden Bay) for some swimming and snorkeling. ☺ 3½ hrs 🖃 $35.

TORTOLA BEST BETS

- **The *Rhone*.** For certified divers, this is one of the best wreck dives in the Caribbean.

- **Sage Mountain.** The highest peak in the Virgin Islands has breathtaking views and is a great hiking destination.

- **Sailing Trips.** Because of its proximity to small islets and good snorkeling sights, Tortola is the sailing capital of the Caribbean.

Tortola

KEY

🚢 Ferry

🚢 Cruise Ship Terminal

Dolphin
Discovery **5**
Fort Burt **4**
J.R. O'Neal
Botanic
Gardens **2**

Old Government House
Museum **3**
Road Town **1**
Sage Mountain
National Park **6**

Sailing Excursion. Embark on a sailing yacht in Road Town harbor, Tortola, and sail past some of the smaller surrounding islands with stops to swim and snorkel. Full-day trips, which are usually considerably more expensive, include lunch. ⊙ *4 hrs* ✉ *$54.*

Scuba Diving the Wreck of the *Rhone*. If you are a certified diver, this trip explores one of the best wreck dives in the Caribbean region. No kids under 12. ⊙ *5½ hrs* ✉ *$142.*

Virgin Gorda Highlights & the Baths. From Tortola, you take a regularly scheduled ferry for the 40-minute cruise to Virgin Gorda, where you see the island sights and stop at the famous Baths and later for snorkeling at Savannah Bay, where most cruise lines provide snorkeling equipment. ⊙ *5½ hrs* ✉ *$59 (sometimes less if your cruise ship anchors off Spanish Town).*

Exploring Tortola
Numbers in the margin correspond to points of interest on the Tortola map.

🐚 ❺ **Dolphin Discovery.** Get up close and personal with dolphins as they swim in a spacious seaside pen. There are two different programs that provide a varying range of experiences. In the Royal Swim, dolphins tow participants around the pen. The less expensive Encounter allows you to touch the dolphins. ⊠ *Prospect Reef Resort, Road Town* ☎ *284/494–7675* ⊕ *www.dolphindiscovery.com* ✉ *Royal Swim $139, Encounter $79* ⊙ *Daily, by appointment only.*

❹ **Fort Burt.** The most intact historic ruin on Tortola was built by the Dutch in the early 17th century to safeguard Road Harbour. It sits on a hill at the western edge of Road Town and is now the site of a small hotel and restaurant. The foundations and magazine remain, and the structure offers a commanding view of the harbor. ⊠ *Waterfront Dr., Road Town* ☎ *No phone* ✉ *Free* ⊙ *Daily dawn–dusk.*

❷ **J. R. O'Neal Botanic Gardens.** Take a walk through this 4-acre showcase of lush plant life. There are sections devoted to prickly cacti and succulents, hothouses for ferns and orchids, gardens of medicinal herbs, and plants and trees indigenous to the seashore. From the Tourist Board office in Road Town, cross Waterfront Drive and walk one block over to Main Street and turn right. Keep walking until you see the high school. The gardens are on your left. ⊠ *Botanic Station, Road Town* ☎ *284/494–3904* ✉ *$3* ⊙ *Mon.–Sat. 9–4:30.*

❸ **Old Government House Museum.** The seat of government until 1987, this gracious building now displays a nice collection of items from Tortola's past. The rooms are filled with period furniture, hand-painted china, books signed by Queen Elizabeth II on her 1966 and 1977 visits, and numerous items reflecting Tortola's seafaring legacy. ⊠ *Waterfront Dr., Road Town* ☎ *284/494–3701* ✉ *Free* ⊙ *Weekdays 8:30–4:30.*

❶ **Road Town.** The laid-back capital of the BVI looks out over Road Town Harbour. It takes only an hour or so to stroll down Main Street and along the waterfront, checking out the traditional West Indian build-

ings, painted in pastel colors and
sporting high-pitched, corrugated-tin
roofs; bright shutters; and delicate
fretwork trim. For hotel and sightseeing brochures and the latest information on everything from taxi
rates to ferry-boat schedules, visit the
BVI Tourist Board office. Or just
choose a seat on one of the benches

CAUTION	
If you pick an outside cabin, check to make sure your view of the sea is not obstructed by a lifeboat. The ship's deck plan will help you figure it out.	

in Sir Olva Georges Square, on Waterfront Drive, and watch the people come and go from the ferry dock and customs office across the street.

❻ Sage Mountain National Park. At 1,716 feet, Sage Mountain is the highest peak in the BVI. From the parking area, a trail leads you in a loop
not only to the peak itself (and extraordinary views) but also to a small
rain forest, sometimes shrouded in mist. Most of the forest was cut down
over the centuries to clear land for sugarcane, cotton, and other crops;
to create pastureland; or to simply utilize the stands of timber. In 1964
this park was established to preserve what remained. Up here you can
see mahogany trees, white cedars, mountain guavas, elephant-ear vines,
mamey trees, and giant bullet woods, to say nothing of such birds as
mountain doves and thrushes. Take a taxi from Road Town or drive up
Joe's Hill Road and make a left onto Ridge Road toward Chalwell and
Doty villages. The road dead-ends at the park. ⊠ *Ridge Rd., Sage
Mountain* ☎ *284/494–3904* ⊕ *www.bvinationalparkstrust.org* ⊠ *$3*
☉ *Daily dawn–dusk.*

Shopping

Many shops and boutiques are clustered along and just off Road Town's
Main Street. You can shop in Road Town's **Wickham's Cay I** area adjacent to the marina, where cruise ships tender their passengers in. Don't
be put off by an informal shop entrance; some of the best finds in the
BVI lie behind shabby doors.

The **BVI Post Office** (⊠ *Main St., Road Town* ☎ *284/494–3701*) is a phi-
latelist's dream. It has a worldwide reputation for exquisite stamps in
all sorts of designs. Although the stamps carry U.S. monetary designa-
tions, they can be used for postage only in the BVI. The **Gallery** (⊠ *102
Main St., Road Town* ☎ *284/494–6680*) carries art by owner Lisa Gray
and paintings by other Tortola artists. **Pusser's Company Store** (⊠ *Main
St. at Waterfront Rd., Road Town* ☎ *284/494–2467* ⊠ *Soper's Hole
Marina, West End* ☎ *284/495–4599*) sells nautical memorabilia, ship
models, and marine paintings. There's also an entire line of clothing for
both men and women, handsome decorator bottles of Pusser's rum, and
gift items bearing the Pusser's logo. **Samarkand** (⊠ *Main St., Road
Town* ☎ *284/494–6415*) crafts charming gold-and-silver pendants, earrings, bracelets, and pins, many with island themes like seashells, lizards,
pelicans, and palm trees. There are also reproduction Spanish pieces of
eight (old Spanish coins worth eight reals) that were found on sunken
galleons. **Sunny Caribbee** (⊠ *Main St., Road Town* ☎ *284/494–2178*),
in a brightly painted West Indian house, packages its own herbs, teas,
coffees, vinegars, hot sauces, soaps, skin and suntan lotions, and exotic

concoctions—Arawak Love Potion and Island Hangover Cure, for example. There are also Caribbean books and art and hand-painted decorative accessories.

Activities

DIVING & SNORKELING   Clear waters and numerous reefs afford some wonderful opportunities for underwater exploration. In 1867 the RMS *Rhone*, a 310-foot-long royal mail steamer, split in two when it sank in a devastating hurricane. It's so well preserved that it was used in the movie *The Deep*. You can see the crow's nest and bowsprit, the cargo hold in the bow, and the engine and enormous propeller shaft in the stern. Every dive outfit in the BVI runs superlative scuba and snorkel tours here. Rates start at around $60 for a one-tank dive and $85 for a two-tank dive. **Blue Waters Divers** (✉ *Nanny Cay* ☎ 284/494–2847 ✉ *Soper's Hole, West End* ☎284/495–1200 ⊕*www.bluewaterdiversbvi. com*) teaches resort, open-water, rescue, and advanced diving courses, and also makes daily dive trips. If you're chartering a sailboat, the company's boat will meet your boat at Peter, Salt, or Cooper Island for a rendezvous dive. Rates include all equipment as well as instruction. Make arrangements two days in advance. **Dive Tortola** (✉ *Prospect Reef* ☎ 284/ 494–9200 ⊕ *www.divetortola.com*) offers beginner and advanced diving courses and daily dive trips. Trainers teach open-water, rescue, advanced diving, and resort courses. Dive Tortola also offers a rendezvous diving option for folks on charter sailboats.

FISHING   Most of the boats that take you deep-sea fishing for bluefish, wahoo, swordfish, and shark leave from nearby St. Thomas, but local anglers like to fish the shallower water for bonefish. A half day of bone fishing runs about $480, a full day around $850. Call **Caribbean Fly Fishing** (✉ Nanny Cay ☎ 284/494–4797 ⊕ www.caribflyfishing.com).

SAILING   The BVI are among the world's most popular sailing destinations. They're close together and surrounded by calm waters, so it's fairly easy to sail from one anchorage to the next. **Aristocat Charters** (✉ *West End* ☎ 284/ 499–1249 ⊕*www.aristocatcharters.com*) sets sail daily to the Indians and Peter Island aboard a 48-foot catamaran. **White Squall II** (✉ *Village Cay Marina, Road Town* ☎ 284/494–2564 ⊕*www.whitesquall2.com*) takes you on regularly scheduled day sails to the Baths at Virgin Gorda, Jost Van Dyke, or the Caves at Norman Island on an 80-foot schooner.

Beaches

Tortola's north side has several perfect palm-fringed white-sand beaches that curl around turquoise bays and coves. Nearly all are accessible by car (preferably one with four-wheel drive), albeit down bumpy roads that corkscrew precipitously. Facilities run the gamut from absolutely none to a number of beachside bars and restaurants as well as places to rent water-sports equipment. The water at **Brewers Bay** is good for snorkeling, and you can find a campground with showers and bathrooms and beach bar tucked in the foliage right behind the beach. An old sugar mill and ruins of a rum distillery are just north of the beach

> **CAUTION**
>
> Check the balance of your shipboard account before the end of your cruise. You'll avoid a long line at the Purser's Desk that last morning after the final bill arrives.

along the road. The beach is easy to find, but the paved roads leading down the hill to it can be a bit daunting. You can get there from either Brewers Bay Road East or Brewers Bay Road West. Enticing **Cane Garden Bay** has exceptionally calm, crystalline waters and a silky stretch of sand except when storms at sea turn the water murky. Snorkeling is good along the edges. Casual guesthouses, restaurants, bars, and even shops are just steps off the beach in the growing village of the same name. It's a laid-back, even somewhat funky, place to put down your beach towel. Water-sports shops rent equipment. It's the closest beach to Road Town—one steep uphill and downhill drive—and one of the BVI's best-known anchorages; it's where cruise ships usually send their passengers. Have your camera ready for snapping the breathtaking approach to the 1-mi (2-km) stretch of white sand at **Long Bay West.** Although Long Bay Resort sprawls along part of it, the entire beach is open to the public. The water isn't as calm here as at Cane Garden or Brewers Bay, but it's still swimmable. Rent water-sports equipment and enjoy the beachfront restaurant at the resort. Turn left at Zion Hill Road, then travel about a ½ mi (1 km).

Where to Eat

🕒 **$–$$** ✕ **Pusser's Road Town Pub.** Almost everyone who visits Tortola stops here at least once to have a bite to eat and to sample the famous Pusser's Rum Painkiller (fruit juices and rum). The nonthreatening menu includes cheesy pizza, shepherd's pie, fish-and-chips, and hamburgers. Dine inside in air-conditioned comfort or outside on the veranda, which looks out on the harbor. ⊠ *Waterfront Dr.* 🕾 *284/494–3897* ▤ *AE, D, MC, V.*

★ **¢–$$** ✕ **Capriccio di Mare.** The owners of the well-known Brandywine Bay restaurant also run this authentic Italian outdoor café. Stop by for an espresso, fresh pastry, a bowl of perfectly cooked penne, or a crispy tomato and mozzarella pizza. Drink specialties include a mango Bellini, an adaptation of the famous cocktail served at Harry's Bar in Venice. ⊠ *Waterfront Dr.* 🕾 *284/494–5369* ⌕ *Reservations not accepted* ▤ *MC, V* ☉ *Closed Sun.*

TRINIDAD (PORT OF SPAIN)

Vernon O'Reilly Ramesar

Trinidad, the big sister in the twin island republic of Trinidad & Tobago, is the most southerly in the Caribbean and a melting pot of African, Indian, European, and South American cultures, which happily exist together. But it's not a typical Caribbean island since it is a major energy producer and relies very little on tourism for income. But Trinidadians do know how to party, and the island's population is always celebrating or preparing for some sort of festival, the biggest of which is, undoubtedly Carnival, which takes over much of Port of Spain every year for two days of bacchanalian excess. Those expecting pristine white beaches may find the island disappointing, but lovers of the rain forest and wildlife will find paradise.

Essentials

CURRENCY The Trinidad & Tobago dollar (TT$6.20 to $1US). Most places catering to tourists will accept U.S. currency, but the exchange rate may vary wildly from place to place.

HOURS   Most shops are open weekdays from 8 to 4:30, Saturday from 8 to noon; malls stay open later during the week, often until at least 6 or 7 PM, and operate all day Saturday.

INTERNET   **Computer Planet Ltd.** (✉ *Corner of Ariapita Ave. and Luis St., Port of Spain, Trinidad* ☎ *868/622–6888*).

TELEPHONES   Pay phones are located in the cruise terminal. To make an international call from a pay phone, you must first purchase a prepaid "companion" card, which is readily available from most convenience stores, then simply follow the instructions on the card. Cards are available in various denominations. Phones and calling cards are also available from the main phone company, TSTT, which has an office on Independence Square about a 10-minute walk from the port.

Coming Ashore

Port of Spain is a bustling and sprawling metropolis with seemingly endless traffic jams. The capital of the twin-island republic is a work in progress, with government investing billions of dollars into upgrading the port area and many other areas of the city. The scale of this project means that the port will be a construction zone for some time to come, but the result is expected to be a mile-long facility designed to offer a range of facilities and services to visitors.

Because of the driving habits of Trinidadians and the often confusing road signs and narrow roads, it is not advisable to rent a car. Taxis flock to the port whenever a cruise ship arrives. Authorized taxis always have a license plate starting with the letter "H" (for "hire"). Though rates are technically fixed, it is never a bad idea to negotiate with the driver.

Shore Excursions

We consider these to be among the better shore excursions for Trinidad. They may not be offered by all lines, and tour names may differ as well. Times and prices are approximate.

Port of Spain Tour. Explore the vibrant capital city full of architectural surprises ranging from the huge red parliament building to a replica of a Scottish castle. Visit the botanical gardens, and then enjoy a cultural show. ⏱ *3½ hrs* 🎫 *$45.*

Maracas Bay. The drive to this peach-sand beach is as breathtaking as the beach itself, heading straight through the rain forest of Trinidad's Northern range of mountains with the ocean below on one side and lush greenery on the other. The descent allows for some magnificent aerial shots of the beach. Once at the beach there is ample time for sunning and swimming ⏱ *4 hrs* 🎫 *$40.*

Exploring Trinidad

Numbers in the margin correspond to points of interest on the Trinidad map.

🌀 ❷   **Caroni Bird Sanctuary.** This large swamp with mazelike waterways is bordered by mangrove trees, some plumed with huge termite nests. If you're lucky, you may see lazy caimans idling in the water and large snakes hanging from branches on the banks taking in the sun. In the middle of the sanctuary are several islets that are home to Trinidad's national bird, the

scarlet ibis. ✢ ½ *hr from Port of Spain; take Churchill Roosevelt Hwy.*
east to Uriah Butler south; turn right and in about 2 min, after passing
Caroni River Bridge, follow sign for sanctuary ✉ *Free* ☉ *Daily dawn–dusk.*

❸ Chaguaramas Military History & Aerospace Museum. On the former U.S.
military base, this is a must-see for history buffs. The exhibits are in a
large hangarlike shed without air-conditioning, so dress appropriately.
Exhibits cover everything from Amerindian history to the Cold War, but
the emphasis is on the two World Wars. There's a decidedly charming
and homemade feel to the place; in fact, most exhibits were made by
the curator and founder, Commander Gaylord Kelshall of the T&T Coast
Guard. The museum is set a bit off the main road but is easily spotted
by the turquoise BWIA L1011 jet parked out front (Trinidad & Tobago's
former national airline). ✉ *Western Main Rd., Chaguaramas* ☎ *868/*
634-4391 ✉ *TT$20* ☉ *Mon.–Sat. 9–5.*

☙❹ Dattatreya Yoga Centre. This impressive temple site was constructed by
artisans brought in from India. It is well worth a visit to admire the intricate architectural details of the main temple, learn about Trinidad Hin-
duism, and marvel at the towering 85-foot statue of the god Hanuman.
This is a religious site, so appropriate clothing is required (no shorts),
and shoes must be left outside the temple door. The temple is half an
hour from Port of Spain; take Churchill Roosevelt Highway east to Uriah

Butler south; turn right until the Chase Village flyover; follow the signs south to Waterloo; then follow signs to the temple. ✉ *Datta Dr. at Orangefield Rd., Carapichaima* ☎ *868/673–5328* 🖬 *Free* ⊘ *Daily dawn–dusk, services daily.*

❶ **Port of Spain.** Most organized tours begin at the port. If you're planning to explore on foot, which will take two to four hours, start early in the day; by midday the port area can be as hot and packed as Calcutta. It's

best to end your tour on a bench in the Queen's Park Savannah, sipping a cool coconut water bought from one of the vendors operating out of flatbed trucks. For about 50¢ he'll lop the top off a green coconut with a deft swing of the machete and, when you've finished drinking, lop again, making a bowl and spoon of coconut shell for you to eat the young pulp. As in most cities, take extra care at night; women should not walk alone.

The town's main dock, **King's Wharf,** entertains a steady parade of cruise and cargo ships, a reminder that the city started from this strategic harbor. When hurricanes threaten other islands, it's not unusual to see as many as five large cruise ships taking advantage of the safety of the harbor. It's on Wrightson Road, the main street along the water on the southwest side of town. The National Government has embarked on a massive development plan, which means that most of the wharf area is an active construction zone. The plan is to turn the area into a vibrant and attractive commercial and tourism zone, but it's likely to be a work in progress for several years.

Across Wrightson Road and a few minutes' walk from the south side of King's Wharf, the busy **Independence Square** has been the focus of the downtown area's major gentrification. On its south side the cruise-ship complex, full of duty-free shops, forms an enclave of international anonymity with the Crowne Plaza Trinidad. On the eastern end of the square is the Cathedral of the Immaculate Conception; it was by the sea when it was built in 1832, but subsequent landfill around the port gave it an inland location.

Frederick Street, Port of Spain's main shopping drag, starting north from the midpoint of Independence Square, is a market street of scents and sounds—perfumed oils sold by sidewalk vendors and music tapes being played from vending carts—and crowded shops. Although it may be tempting to purchase CDs from these street vendors, they are selling pirated material and doing so robs local artists of their livelihood.

At Prince and Frederick streets, **Woodford Square** has served as the site of political meetings, speeches, public protests, and occasional violence. It's dominated by the magnificent Red House, a Renaissance-style building that takes up an entire city block. Trinidad's House of Parliament takes its name from a paint job done in anticipation of Queen Victoria's Diamond Jubilee in 1897. The original Red House was burned to the ground in a 1903 riot, and the present structure was built four years later. The chambers are open to the public.

If the downtown port area is the pulse of Port of Spain, the great green expanse of **Queen's Park Savannah,** roughly bounded by Maraval Road, Queen's Park West, Charlotte Street, and Saddle Road, is the city's soul. You can walk straight north on Frederick Street and get there within 20 minutes. Its 2-mi (3-km) circumference is a popular jogger's track. The northern end of the Savannah is devoted to plants. A rock garden, known as the Hollows, and a fishpond add to the rusticity. In the middle of the Savannah you will find a small graveyard where members of the Peschier family—who originally owned the land—are buried. While the perimeter of the Savannah is busy and safe, you shouldn't walk across the park, as there have been occasional reports of muggings.

A series of astonishing buildings constructed in several 19th-century styles—known collectively as the **Magnificent Seven**—flanks the western side of the Savannah. Notable are Killarney, patterned (loosely) after Balmoral Castle in Scotland; Whitehall, constructed in the style of a Venetian palace; Roomor, a flamboyantly baroque colonial house with a preponderance of towers, pinnacles, and wrought-iron trim; and the Queen's Royal College, in German Renaissance style, with a prominent tower clock that chimes on the hour. Sadly, several of these fine buildings have fallen into advanced decay.

Head over to the southeast corner of the Savannah to see the **National Museum & Art Gallery,** especially its Carnival exhibitions, the Amerindian collection and historical re-creations, and the fine 19th-century paintings of Trinidadian artist Cazabon. ⊠ *117 Upper Frederick St., Port of Spain* ☎ *868/623–5941* 🖾 *Free* ✆ *Tues.–Sat. 10–6.*

The cultivated expanse of parkland north of the Savannah is the site of the president's and prime minister's official residences and also the **Emperor Valley Zoo & Botanical Gardens.** A meticulous lattice of walkways and local flora, the parkland was first laid out in 1820 for Governor Ralph Woodford. In the midst of the serene wonderland is the 8-acre zoo, which exhibits mostly birds and animals of the region—from the brilliantly plumed scarlet ibis to slithering anacondas and pythons; you can also see (and hear) the wild parrots that breed in the surrounding foliage. The zoo draws a quarter of a million visitors a year. The admission prices are a steal, and tours are free. ⊠ *Botanical Gardens, Port of Spain* ☎ *868/622–3530 or 868/622–5343* 🖾 *Zoo TT$4, gardens free* ✆ *Daily 9:30–5:30.*

Shopping

Trinidad offers the choice of shopping in the hectic downtown core of Port of Spain, where the prices are generally cheaper, or in any of a number of air-conditioned malls, where the atmosphere is calmer and the prices are higher. Local calypso and steel-band music CDs are a popular choice as is rum produced on the island. For painted plates, ceramics, aromatic candles, wind chimes, and carved wood pieces and instruments, check out **Cockey** (⊠ *Long Circular Mall, Long Circular Rd., St. James, Port of Spain* ☎ *868/628–6546).* **Just CDs and Accessories** (⊠*Long Circular Mall, Long Circular Rd., St. James, Port of Spain* ☎*868/ 622–7516)* has a good selection of popular local musicians as well as other music genres. A fine designer shop, **Meiling** (⊠ *Kapok Hotel, Maraval, Port of Spain* ☎ *868/627–6975),* sells classically detailed Caribbean resort clothing. **Radical** (⊠ *The Falls at West Mall, Western Main Rd., Westmoorings* ☎ *868/632–5800* ⊠ *Long Circular Mall, Long Circular Rd., St. James, Port of Spain* ☎ *868/628–5693* ⊠ *Excellent City Centre, Independence Square, Port of Spain* ☎ *868/627–6110),* which carries T-shirts and original men's and women's clothing, is something like the Gap of the Caribbean. **Poui Boutique** (⊠ *Ellerslie Plaza, Long Circular Rd., Maraval, Port of Spain* ☎ *868/622–5597)* has stylish handmade batik articles, Ajoupa ware (an attractive, local terra-cotta pottery), and many other gift items. The miniature ceramic houses and local scenes are astoundingly realistic, and are all handcrafted by owners Rory and Bunty O'Connor. The design duo of Barbara Jardine and Rachel Ross creates the Alchemy jewelry line. Their handmade works of art with sterling silver, 18K gold, and precious and semiprecious stones are for sale at **Precious Little** (⊠ *5 Pole Carew St., Woodbrook* ☎ *868/ 622–7655).*

Activities

GOLF The best course in Trinidad is the 18-hole course at **St. Andrew's Golf Club** (⊠ *Moka, Saddle Rd., Maraval, Port of Spain* ☎ *868/629–2314),* just outside Port of Spain. Greens fees are approximately $45 for 9 holes. The most convenient tee times are available on weekdays.

Beaches

★ **Maracas Bay** (⊠ *North Coast Rd.*), a long stretch of sand with a cove and a fishing village at one end, is *the* local favorite, so it can get crowded on weekends. Lifeguards will guide you away from strong currents. Parking sites are ample, and there are snack bars and restrooms. Try a shark-and-bake ($2, to which you can add any of dozens of toppings, such as tamarind sauce and coleslaw) at one of the beach huts or in the nearby car park (Richard's is by far the most popular). Take the North Coast Road from Maraval (it intersects with Long Circular Road right next to KFC Maraval) over the Northern Range; the beach is about 7 mi (11 km) from Maraval.

Where to Eat

$–$$$ ✕ **The Verandah.** Owner and hostess Phyllis Vieira has been hosting
Fodor'sChoice diners since the 1980s and prides herself on her "free-style Caribbean"
★ menu, which is one of the best-kept secrets on the island. But the reasonable prices and consistently excellent cuisine make this a secret we can no longer keep. The open veranda, interior, and courtyard of this beautiful gingerbread-style colonial house provide a suitable setting for the menu, which changes weekly and is brought to you on a blackboard by the attentive, white-garbed staff. ⊠ *10 Rust St., St. Clair, Port of Spain*

☎ 868/622–6287 ⚓ *Reservations essential* ▭ *No credit cards* ⊘ *Closed Sun. No dinner Mon.–Wed. and Fri.*

🕙 **$–$$** ✕ **Veni Mangé.** The best lunches in town are served in this traditional
Fodor'sChoice West Indian house. Credit Allyson Hennessy—a Cordon Bleu–trained
★ chef and local television celebrity—and her friendly, flamboyant sister and partner, Rosemary (Roses) Hezekiah. Despite Allyson's training, home cooking is the order of the day here. The creative creole menu changes regularly, but there's always an unusual and delicious vegetarian entrée. Veni's version of Trinidad's national dish, callaloo, is considered one of the best on the island. The *chip chip* (a small local clam) cocktail is deliciously piquant and is a restaurant rarity. ⊠ *67A Ariapita Ave., Woodbrook, Port of Spain* ☎ *868/624–4597* ⚓ *Reservations essential* ▭ *AE, MC, V* ⊘ *Closed weekends. No dinner Mon., Tues., or Thurs.*

VIRGIN GORDA, BRITISH VIRGIN ISLANDS

Lynda Lohr

Virgin Gorda, or "Fat Virgin," received its name from Christopher Columbus. The explorer envisioned the island as a pregnant woman in a languid recline with Gorda Peak being her big belly and the boulders of the Baths her toes. Different in topography from Tortola, with its arid landscape covered with scrub brush and cactus, Virgin Gorda has a slower pace of life, too. Goats and cattle own the right-of-way, and the unpretentious friendliness of the people is winning. The top sight (and beach for that matter) is The Baths, which draws scores of cruise-ship passengers and day-trippers to its giant boulders and grottoes that form a perfect snorkeling environment. While ships used to stop only in Tortola, saving Virgin Gorda for shore excursions, smaller ships are coming increasingly to Virgin Gorda directly.

Essentials

CURRENCY The U.S. dollar is the official currency here. Some places accept cash only, but major credit cards are widely accepted. First Caribbean International, which has an ATM, isn't far from the ferry dock in Spanish Town.

HOURS Banking hours are usually Monday through Thursday from 9 to 2:30 and Friday from 9 to 2:30 and 4:30 to 6. Post offices are open weekdays from 9 to 5 and Saturday from 9 to noon. Stores are generally open Monday through Saturday from 9 to 5. Some may be open on Sunday.

INTERNET At this writing, there are no Internet cafés on Virgin Gorda.

TELEPHONES To call anywhere in the BVI once you've arrived, dial all seven digits. A local call from a pay phone costs 25¢, but such phones are sometimes

---

VIRGIN GORDA BEST BETS

■ The *Rhone*. For certified divers, this is one of the best wreck dives in the Caribbean.

■ Sage Mountain. The highest peak in the Virgin Islands has breathtaking views and is a great hiking destination.

■ Sailing Trips. Because of its proximity to small islets and good snorkeling sights, Tortola is the sailing capital of the Caribbean.

on the blink. An alternative is a Caribbean phone card, available in $5, $10, and $20 denominations. They're sold at most major hotels and many stores and can be used to call within the BVI, as well as all over the Caribbean, and to access USADirect from special phone-card phones. If you're coming ashore at the cruise-ship dock, you'll find pay phones right on the dock. If a tender drops you right in Road Town at the ferry dock, phones are located in the terminal.

You'll find pay phones in Spanish Town at the public dock, Virgin Gorda Yacht Harbor, and the Post Office, all located near spots where cruise-ship tenders land. If Leverick Bay is your destination, you'll find pay phones in the marina. Passengers coming ashore in North Sound will find pay phones at the Gun Creek public dock.

Coming Ashore

Ships often dock off Spanish Town, Leverick Bay, or in North Sound and tender passengers to the ferry dock. A few taxis will be available at Leverick Bay and at Gun Creek in North Sound—you can set up an island tour for about $45 for two people—but Leverick Bay and North Sound are far away from The Baths, the island's must-see beach, so a shore excursion is often the best choice. If you are tendered to Spanish Town, then it's possible to take a shuttle taxi to The Baths for as little as $4 per person each way. If you are on Virgin Gorda for just a day, it's usually more cost-effective to share a taxi with a small group than to rent a car, since you'd have to pay an agency $10 for a temporary license and car-rental charges of at least $50 a day. You must be at least age 25 to rent a car.

Shore Excursions

We consider these to be among the better shore excursions for Virgin Gorda. They may not be offered by all lines, and tour names may differ as well. Times and prices are approximate.

Anegada. After a short flight, you'll get a tour of the only coral atoll in the British Virgin Islands ☉ 5½ hrs 🖃 $280.

Island Tour. You'll see all the island's sights on this tour, including Gorda Peak and The Baths. ☉ 2½ hrs 🖃 $63.

Snorkeling Trip. With many sights within easy reach, a snorkeling excursion is a worthwhile tour here. ☉ 2 hrs 🖃 $49.

Exploring Virgin Gorda

There are few roads on Virgin Gorda, and most byways don't follow the scalloped shoreline. The main route sticks resolutely to the center of the island, linking The Baths at the tip of the southern extremity with Gun Creek and Leverick Bay at North Sound and providing exhilarating views. The craggy coast, scissored with grottoes and fringed by palms and boulders, has a primitive beauty. If you drive, you can hit all the sights in one day. Stop to climb Gorda Peak, in the island's center.

Numbers in the margin correspond to points of interest on the British Virgin Islands map.

② The Baths. At Virgin Gorda's most celebrated sight, giant boulders are scattered about the beach and in the water. Some are almost as large as houses and form remarkable grottoes. Climb between these rocks to swim

FodorśChoice
★

in the many pools. If it's privacy you crave, follow the shore northward to quieter bays—Spring Bay, the Crawl, Little Trunk, and Valley Trunk—or head south to Devil's Bay. ⊠ *Off Tower Rd., The Baths* ☎ *284/494–3904* ⊕ *www.bvinationalparktrust.org* ⊠ *$3* ⊙ *Daily dawn–dusk.*

❸ **Copper Mine Point.** Here stand a tall, stone shaft silhouetted against the sky and a small stone structure that overlooks the sea. These are the ruins of a copper mine established 400 years ago and worked first by the Spanish, then by the English, until the early 20th century. In April 2003 this historic site became the 20th park under the BVI National Parks Trust jurisdiction. ⊠ *Copper Mine Rd.* ☎ *No phone* ⊕ *www. bvinationalparktrust.org* ⊠ *Free.*

❶ **Spanish Town.** Virgin Gorda's peaceful main settlement, on the island's southern wing, is so tiny that it barely qualifies as a town at all. Also known as The Valley, Spanish Town has a marina, some shops, and a couple of car-rental agencies. Just north of town is the ferry slip. At the Virgin Gorda Yacht Harbour you can stroll along the dock and do a little shopping.

❹ **Virgin Gorda Peak National Park.** There are two trails at this 265-acre park, which contains the island's highest point, at 1,359 feet. Small signs on North Sound Road mark both entrances. It's about a 15-minute hike from either entrance up to a small clearing, where you can climb a ladder to the platform of a wooden observation tower and a spectacular 360-degree view. ⊠ *North Sound Rd., Gorda Peak* ☎ *No phone* ⊕ *www.bvinationalparktrust.org* ⊠ *Free.*

Shopping

Most boutiques are within hotel complexes—one of the best is at Little Dix Bay. There is a respectable and diverse scattering of shops in the bustling yacht harbor complex in Spanish Town.

Thee Artistic Gallery (⊠ *Virgin Gorda Yacht Harbour, Spanish Town* ☎ *284/495–5104*) has Caribbean-made jewelry, 14-karat-gold nautical charms, maps, collectible coins, crystal, and Christmas tree ornaments with tropical themes. **Margo's Boutique** (⊠ *Virgin Gorda Yacht Harbour, Spanish Town* ☎ *284/495–5237*) is the place to buy handmade silver, pearl, and shell jewelry. **Next Wave** (⊠ *Virgin Gorda Yacht Harbour, Spanish Town* ☎ *284/495–5623*) sells T-shirts, canvas tote bags, and locally made jewelry.

Activities

DIVING & SNORKELING There are some terrific snorkel and dive sites off Virgin Gorda, including areas around The Baths, North Sound, and The Dogs. The **Bitter End Yacht Club** (⊠ *North Sound* ☎ *284/494–2746* ⊕ *www.beyc.com*) offers two snorkeling trips a day. **Dive BVI** (⊠ *Virgin Gorda Yacht Harbour, Spanish Town* ☎ *284/495–5513 or 800/848–7078* ⊠ *Leverick Bay Resort and Marina, Leverick Bay* ☎ *284/495–7328* ⊕ *www. divebvi.com*) offers expert instruction, certification, and day trips. **Sunchaser Scuba** (⊠ *Bitter End Yacht Club, North Sound* ☎ *284/495–9638 or 800/932–4286* ⊕ *www.sunchaserscuba.com*) offers resort, advanced, and rescue courses.

FISHING The sportfishing here is so good that anglers come from all over the world. **Charter Virgin Gorda** (⊠ *Leverick Bay, North Sound* ☎ *284/495–7421* ⊕ *www.chartervirgingorda.com*) offers a choice of trips aboard its 46-foot Hatteras, the *Mahoe Bay,* for full-day marlin hunting. Plan to spend $800 to $1,200.

> **CAUTION**
>
> If you pick an outside cabin, check to make sure your view of the sea is not obstructed by a lifeboat. The ship's deck plan will help you figure it out.

SAILING The BVI waters are calm, and terrific places to learn to sail. The **Bitter End Sailing & Windsurfing School** (⊠ *Bitter End Yacht Club, North Sound* ☎ *284/494–2746* ⊕ *www.beyc.com*) offers classroom, dockside, and on-the-water lessons for sailors of all levels. Private lessons are $60 per hour. If you just want to sit back, relax, and let the captain take the helm, choose a sailing or power yacht from **Double "D" Charters** (⊠ *Virgin Gorda Yacht Harbour, Spanish Town* ☎ *284/499–2479* ⊕ *www.doubledbvi. com*). Rates are $60 for a half-day trip and $95 for a full-day island-hopping excursion. Private full-day cruises or sails for up to eight people run $950. If you'd rather rent a Sunfish or Hobie Wave, check out **Leverick Bay Watersports** (⊠ *Leverick Bay, North Sound* ☎ *284/495–7376* ⊕ *www.watersportsbvi.com*).

Beaches

The best beaches are easily reached by water, although they're also accessible on foot, usually after a moderately strenuous 10- to 15-minute hike. Anybody going to Virgin Gorda should experience swimming or snorkeling among its unique boulder formations, which can be visited at several beaches along Lee Road. The most popular of these spots is The Baths, but there are several others nearby that are easily reached. **The Baths** is usually crowded midday with day-trippers. Public bathrooms and a handful of bars and shops are close to the water and at the start of the path that leads to the beach. Beach lockers are available to keep belongings safe. Admission is $3. **Savannah Bay** is a wonderfully private beach close to Spanish Town. It may not always be completely deserted, but it's a long stretch of soft, white sand. There are no facilities. **Spring Bay Beach,** just off Tower Road, gets much less traffic than the nearby Baths and has the similarly large, imposing boulders that create interesting grottos for swimming. The snorkeling is excellent, and the grounds include swings and picnic tables.

Where to Eat

$$ ✕ **The Bath & Turtle.** You can sit back and relax at this informal tavern with a friendly staff—although the noise from the television can sometimes be a bit much. Well-stuffed sandwiches, homemade pizzas, pasta dishes, and daily specials like conch soup round out the casual menu. Live musicians perform Wednesday night. ⊠ *Virgin Gorda Yacht Harbour, Spanish Town* ☎ *284/495–5239* 🖬 *AE, MC, V.*

¢ ✕ **Mad Dog's.** Piña coladas are *the* thing at this breezy bar just outside the entrance to the Baths. The menu includes great triple-decker sandwiches and hot dogs. ⊠ *The Valley* ☎ *284/495–5830* 🖬 *No credit cards* ☉ *No dinner.*

INDEX

NOTES

NOTES

NOTES